Melody

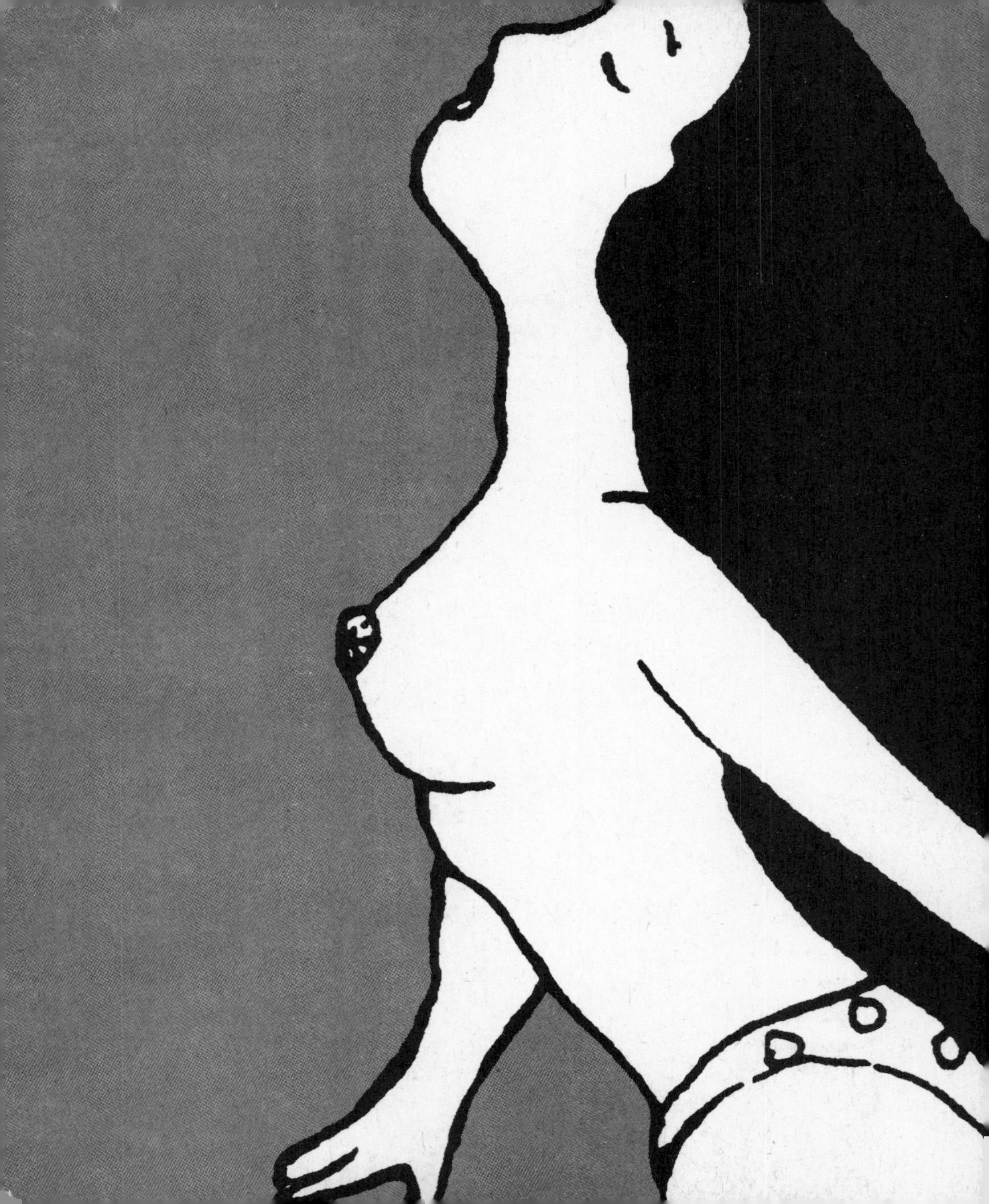

Melody
Story of a Nude Dancer

Sylvie Rancourt

Translation by Helge Dascher

Drawn & Quarterly

A Cartoonist Who Knew What She Was Doing

Introduction by CHRIS WARE

For years during visits to Chicago's Quimby's Bookstore in the mid-1990s,
I kept passing by a perfectly compact and apparently handbound book of simple
black-and-white picture-stories titled *Melody*, by a Sylvie Rancourt (it was signed
within), which for its striking visual simplicity and iconic clarity was unlike
anything I'd seen before in comics. I kept picking it up, fascinated by how
seemingly honest and direct the simple, almost childlike drawings were; the
word "naive" kept coming to mind — but also "life," and "reality." Save for Justin
Green's *Binky Brown*, Art Spiegelman's *Maus*, and Harvey Pekar's *American
Splendor*, at that time there were few comics that tried to capture, let alone
acknowledge, the existence, rhythms, and complexities of actual daily human
life. But for me, there were three caveats to *Melody*, as I first found it: one, it was
expensive (fifty dollars, if I remember correctly); two, it was in French, which I
couldn't read; and three, it was about a stripper and full of sex. Not that there
was anything wrong with this last part; I had plenty of underground comics, but
this book seemed somehow different; it had a decidedly intimate quality to it, a
weird-yet-familiar human confidentiality that reminded one of Aline Kominsky-
Crumb's and Phoebe Gloeckner's work, but not exactly. Frankly, it was a quality
that, paired with the unreadable French, left me unable to determine if it was
just, well, fictional pornography. (If it was intended to be pornography, it was
pretty bad pornography; I could at least tell that much.) The more I looked at
it, however, the more I admired the grounded, elementary drawings, the more I
was fascinated by the repeating little guileless faces. I finally spent enough time
leafing through it that I'd noted a couple of curiously elegant, almost Matisse-
like drawings, plain caricatures of people that felt very specific despite their simplicity, and, especially, a structural feature that made it almost certainly apparent
it couldn't just be smut: carefully repeated page compositions between chapters

that linked specific events and moments. It seemed this was a cartoonist who knew what she was doing, and I bought it.

Had I lived in Montreal, Quebec, in the 1980s, however, I would've almost certainly heard of Ms. Rancourt and her work. Though perhaps not strictly "famous," she was noticed and noted for her decidedly unusual professional life as both an erotic dancer and cartoonist. Born and raised in Abitibi, a rural region of Quebec roughly 370 miles from the city of Montreal where she moved in 1980 to become a strip-club performer at the suggestion of her boyfriend — and, it should be noted, without any prior "experience," if there is such a thing — having an interest in and facility for drawing ("the only subject in which I was good at school"),[i] after a few years Rancourt decided to start drawing an autobiographical comic strip about this unusual night job. Titled *Mélody*, she photocopied them as small stapled French language booklets, selling the first five hundred copies "table to table"[ii] in the bars where she worked. Seeking greater distribution, she visited the largest Quebec magazine distributor and followed their advice to produce a more "professional" version of her work, with the aid of Canadian cartoonist Jacques Boivin, creating a magazine-sized periodical with colour covers that were printed offset; Boivin drew the covers and Jean-Pierre Thibodeau handled the lettering for the first few issues, which Boivin took over thereafter. Rather incredibly, the magazine was then accepted by this distributor and appeared in general newsstands across Quebec, bringing to the non-strip-club-going public what *bande-dessinée* historian and writer Patrick Gaumer has called the "first autobiographical Canadian comic." Operating under this more professional approach, Rancourt produced six issues at an apparently steady rate, but newsstand returns stored in her home encouraged the foundations and floors to "crack with the weight...I woke up in the night and I could hear the creaking. I could not go back to sleep, so I decided to stop."[iii]

At around the same time, Boivin offered to create a small-edition English-language version "because I knew there were people who would appreciate its value, not just view it as an amateurish curiosity."[iv] Boivin sent this translated version of Rancourt's work to various American comics publishers, including Fantagraphics, Eclipse, *RAW*, and Kitchen Sink, but receiving only a favourable

i   *Zoo* magazine, interview with Sylvie Rancourt, 2013.

ii   Bernard Joubert, preface to Ego comme X edition, 2013 (afterword in present book).

iii Interview, *Zoo* magazine, 2013.

iv Letter to the author, 2014.

response from the latter, which eventuated an expanded ten-issue series under the same title, written by Rancourt and drawn by Boivin (which I now realize I'd casually seen but somehow had not connected with this original work). The visibility of Rancourt's original drawing translated into English indeed brought her comics not only new readers, such as Aline Kominsky-Crumb, but also new commercial viability back in her home country, a Quebec publisher reissuing Rancourt's seven homemade comics in a limited edition signed hardcover, advertised and promoted by Denis Kitchen (and apparently the book I found years later in Chicago).

Even though I couldn't read it, I was captivated by Rancourt's straightforward, simple drawing approach (I won't call it a "style"; it's how she sees and remembers life) and I think at some point I may have even referred to the work as "pure" comics, which I guess more or less still gets at the core of her visual-linguistic achievement, if I may invent terms. Even today, there are few cartoonists whose work resembles Rancourt's in appearance or tone (Ben Jones comes to mind, maybe Marjane Satrapi, and to a certain degree the felt-tone of earlier manga artist Seiichi Hayashi). To an uptight artist such as myself, there are so many things that seem "wrong" in it: thick black lines on elements that apparently don't matter, thin lines around characters who should be emphasized, balloons in non-synchronous placement. It contradicted what I thought I knew about what made comics "good," forcing me just to read and to start to feel the blank power that runs through it — to say nothing of basically proving that good cartooning is not about good drawing but about something else entirely. See the beautiful composition of Melody getting into the tub on page 16, then see that same pose and composition repeat on page 80, transformed from being just a nice drawing to a present perfect moment, and then even to a musical note. Rancourt repeats the same introduction with variations at the beginning of each chapter and ends each chapter with the same shrinking panels, each instance again acting almost as musical phrases, restated and recapitulated.

But this is just the formal stuff. Finally getting to read the story after all these years was an eye-opening and heartening experience because the book is even smarter, more interesting, and more sophisticated than I'd ever guessed. Since this is an introduction, I won't spoil things by analyzing or giving away the story, but the life into which Melody/Sylvie falls with her seemingly irrepressible layabout/criminal boyfriend, "Nick" (all names have been changed), feels very real, raw, and experienced; there is nothing false, titillating, or intentionally sordid anywhere in this book, which is really something of an achievement, given its subject and the traditional ease that comics has for being false, titillating, and intentionally sordid (see: pretty much every superhero comic ever published). There are also no moral resolutions, no messages, no comeuppances. People do dumb things, nice things, generous things, and deeply wrong things, just like in real life. The urge that one feels for Melody to just dump Nick builds and builds, and then — anyway, you'll see. There's even a sort of surprising sympathy for men-in-general running through Rancourt's writing, from her repeated annoying forgiveness of Nick to her amusing imaginings of the thoughts of the regulars in the club. (Though I was tempted to read her book as a simplistic indictment of my gender, of whom I'm no fan myself, she has said, "I'm not a feminist, I love men. It's not...being a feminist to look at reality as it is."[v] As a reader, it is generous dispensation for Rancourt to allow us into her musings while she pursues her trade. (And, even more meta-amusingly, while also probably observing the patrons reading the comics she'd just passed out to them: "There was not one client who didn't buy a copy and find it interesting...They would even read it from cover to cover in the bar instead of watching the stage shows. And that's when I thought, Damn! It must be good!")[vi]

The apparent childishness of Rancourt's drawings is a quality that extends throughout the story in both its tone and in its text, and it is no affectation or posture; without it, in fact, the book would lose its strength. Though the situations in the book are frequently tawdry, horrible, and even cruel, the effect overall is one of detached innocence, embodied first by Melody's almost Krazy Kat-esque approach to life and then, beyond that, to the man-children who surround her in a co-dependency that is aesthetically dismantled cleanly and clearly. The experience is like watching children play "house" (or, well, "strip club"). Without this cognitive disconnect of Rancourt's charming, innocent, and empathetic writing and drawing, the story could easily begin to approach the "pornography" that *Family Circle* claimed it was.[vii] But it doesn't, and it isn't. In our post-*Boogie Nights*, post-pay-per-view, post-internet world where even the *New York Times* reports on the sex industry, there is little in this book now to immediately shock one, apart from how emotionally direct and simple it is. I believe Rancourt's approach was

---

v   Interview with Sylvie Rancourt by Yves Alix, *La Criée*, 1986.

vi   Rick Trembles, 2000 interview with Sylvie Rancourt and Jacques Boivin by Mia Dee, snubdom.com, May 31, 2001 (originally published in sex workers' magazine *ConStellation*).

vii Trembles, 2001.

wholly intentional; she said herself that she wanted to tell her story "without making something dramatic, and without morals."[viii] The many dancing scenes remind me of the bar scenes in Bresson's *Mouchette*, where the director seemingly asked the actors to move as little and as artificially as possible. Similarly, frequently whenever any of Rancourt's characters say something painful or hurtful, they do it smilingly, and at the "camera"; the filmmaker Yasujiro Ozu employs the same approach. With this warm distance — not unlike the "tenderness" critic Jacques Samson has termed Rancourt's disposition toward her customers — she passes the reader a gift: the ability to experience and see a venal adult life through the forgiving, blameless, and easily-wounded eyes of a child.

Rancourt was ahead of her time. Not only was she willing to write sympathetically and unironically about something many people didn't even want to think about thirty years ago, she also had ambitions of setting up a public agency for her coworkers to offer health care, addiction counseling, child care, etc.,[ix] ideas that have gained acceptance only in the past decade as the internet has made the sex "industry" more irrepressibly prevalent and non-invisible. Rancourt, however, long ago gave up the employment that begat this book, yet has never entirely given up comics (witness a recent mini-comic drawn in reaction to the *Charlie Hebdo* events in Paris), living with her second husband in rural Quebec on a farm, occasionally making paintings, raising her younger child, and still mothering her older children, some of whom now have children of their own. Though she originally intended to create a work outside the sphere of moral judgement, she apparently does not exempt herself from such judgement now, considering herself once a "lost girl, now recovered, who assumes the consequences of her actions."[x] The consequences of some of her actions are, thankfully, that she's made one of the great, monumental early works of memoir in comics form, one that shows reality, and especially her reality, "as it is."

---

viii Interview, *La Criée*, 1986.
ix Interview, *La Criée*, 1986.
x Interview, *Zoo* magazine, 2013.

CHRIS WARE is the author of Jimmy Corrigan: The Smartest Kid on Earth and Building Stories, which was deemed a Top Ten Fiction Book of 2012 by the New York Times and Time magazine. A contributor to the New Yorker, his work has been exhibited at the MOCA Los Angeles, the MCA Chicago, and the Whitney Museum of American Art.

Melody Gets
Started

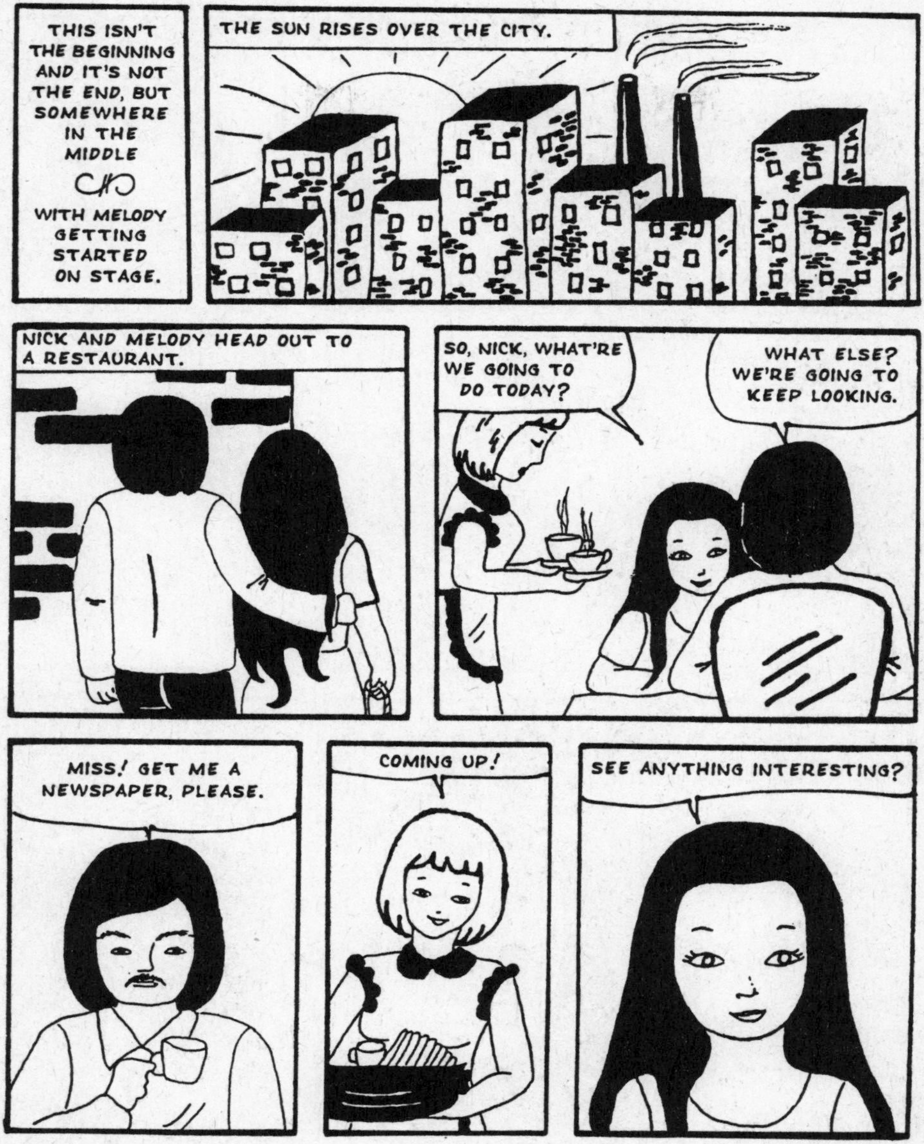
THIS ISN'T THE BEGINNING AND IT'S NOT THE END, BUT SOMEWHERE IN THE MIDDLE
WITH MELODY GETTING STARTED ON STAGE.
THE SUN RISES OVER THE CITY.
NICK AND MELODY HEAD OUT TO A RESTAURANT.
SO, NICK, WHAT'RE WE GOING TO DO TODAY?
WHAT ELSE? WE'RE GOING TO KEEP LOOKING.
MISS! GET ME A NEWSPAPER, PLEASE.
COMING UP!
SEE ANYTHING INTERESTING?

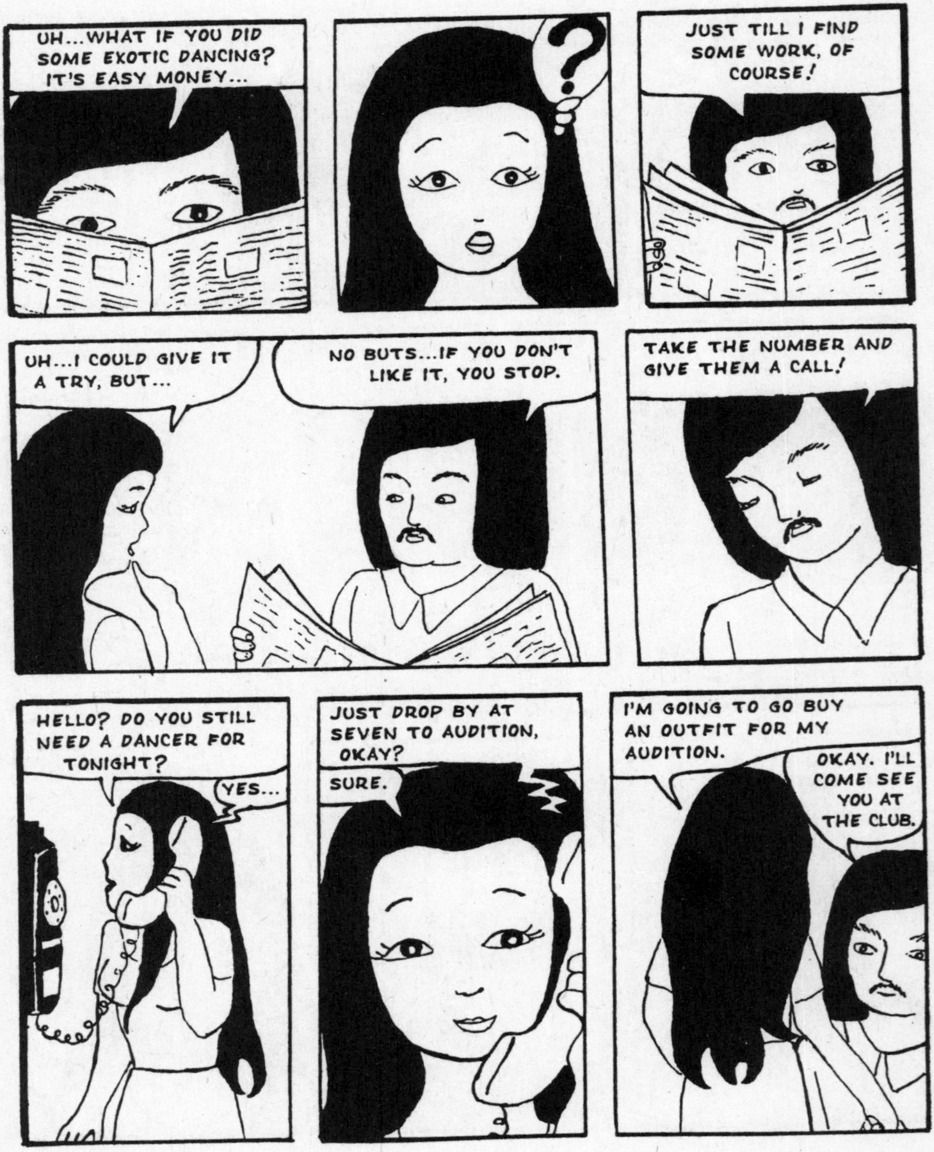
UH...WHAT IF YOU DID SOME EXOTIC DANCING? IT'S EASY MONEY...
?
JUST TILL I FIND SOME WORK, OF COURSE!
UH...I COULD GIVE IT A TRY, BUT...
NO BUTS...IF YOU DON'T LIKE IT, YOU STOP.
TAKE THE NUMBER AND GIVE THEM A CALL!
HELLO? DO YOU STILL NEED A DANCER FOR TONIGHT?
YES...
JUST DROP BY AT SEVEN TO AUDITION, OKAY?
SURE.
I'M GOING TO GO BUY AN OUTFIT FOR MY AUDITION.
OKAY. I'LL COME SEE YOU AT THE CLUB.

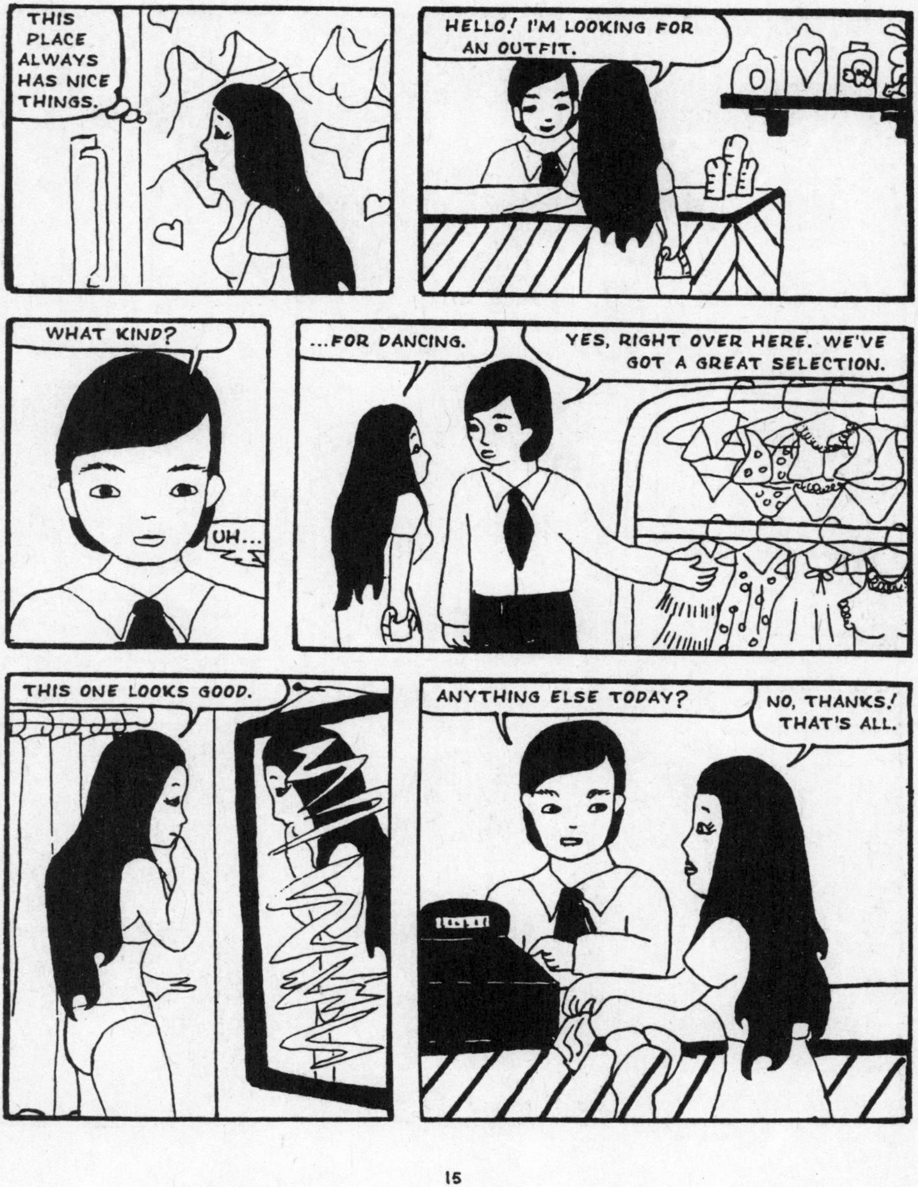
THIS PLACE ALWAYS HAS NICE THINGS.
HELLO! I'M LOOKING FOR AN OUTFIT.
WHAT KIND?
UH...
...FOR DANCING.
YES, RIGHT OVER HERE. WE'VE GOT A GREAT SELECTION.
THIS ONE LOOKS GOOD.
ANYTHING ELSE TODAY?
NO, THANKS! THAT'S ALL.

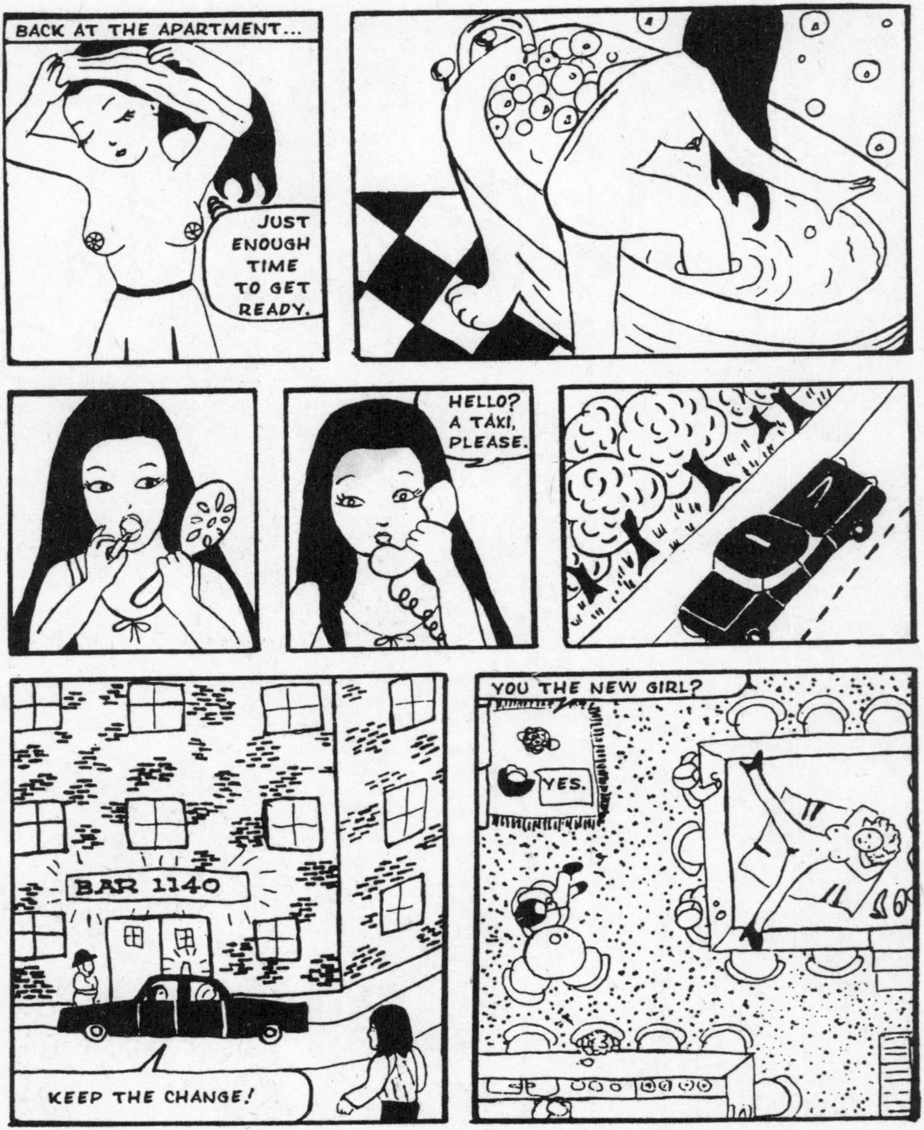
BACK AT THE APARTMENT...
JUST ENOUGH TIME TO GET READY.
HELLO? A TAXI, PLEASE.
BAR 1140
KEEP THE CHANGE!
YOU THE NEW GIRL?
YES.

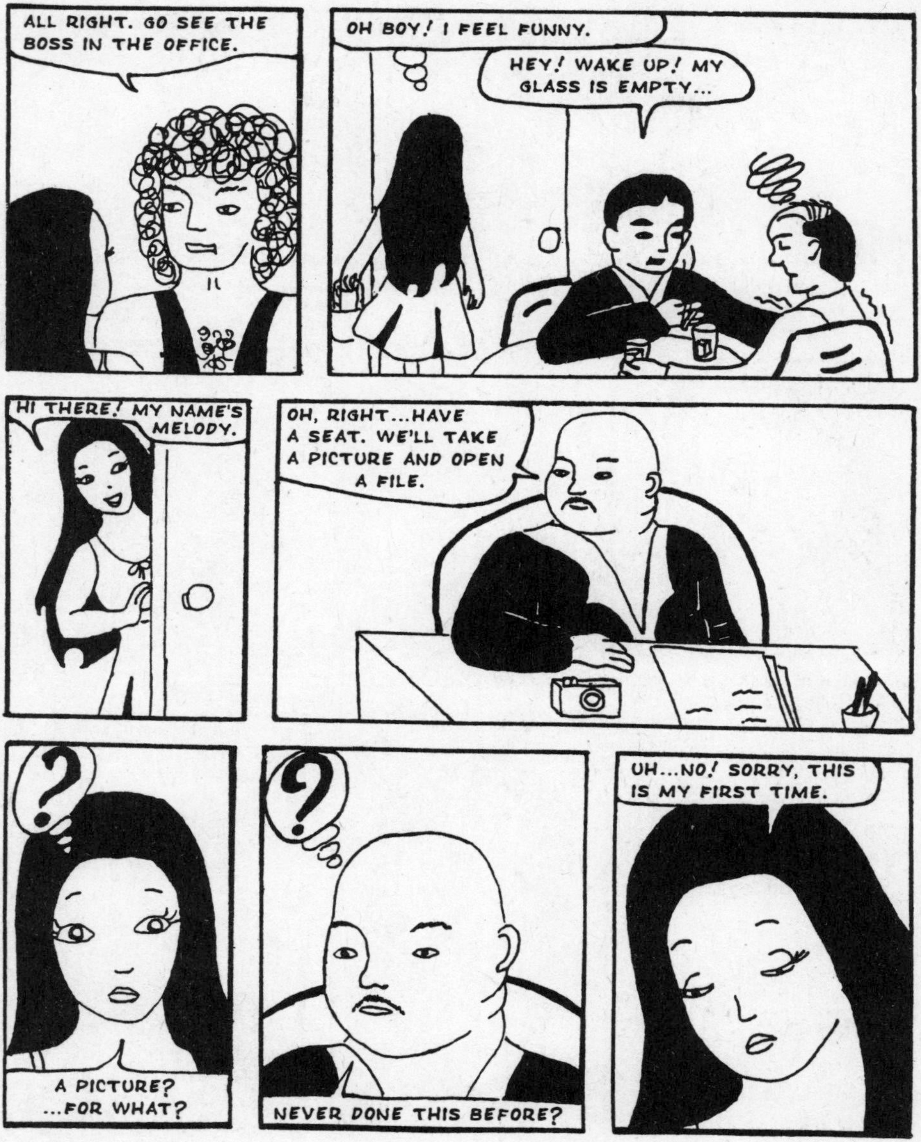
ALL RIGHT. GO SEE THE BOSS IN THE OFFICE.
OH BOY! I FEEL FUNNY.
HEY! WAKE UP! MY GLASS IS EMPTY...
HI THERE! MY NAME'S MELODY.
OH, RIGHT...HAVE A SEAT. WE'LL TAKE A PICTURE AND OPEN A FILE.
A PICTURE? ...FOR WHAT?
NEVER DONE THIS BEFORE?
UH...NO! SORRY, THIS IS MY FIRST TIME.

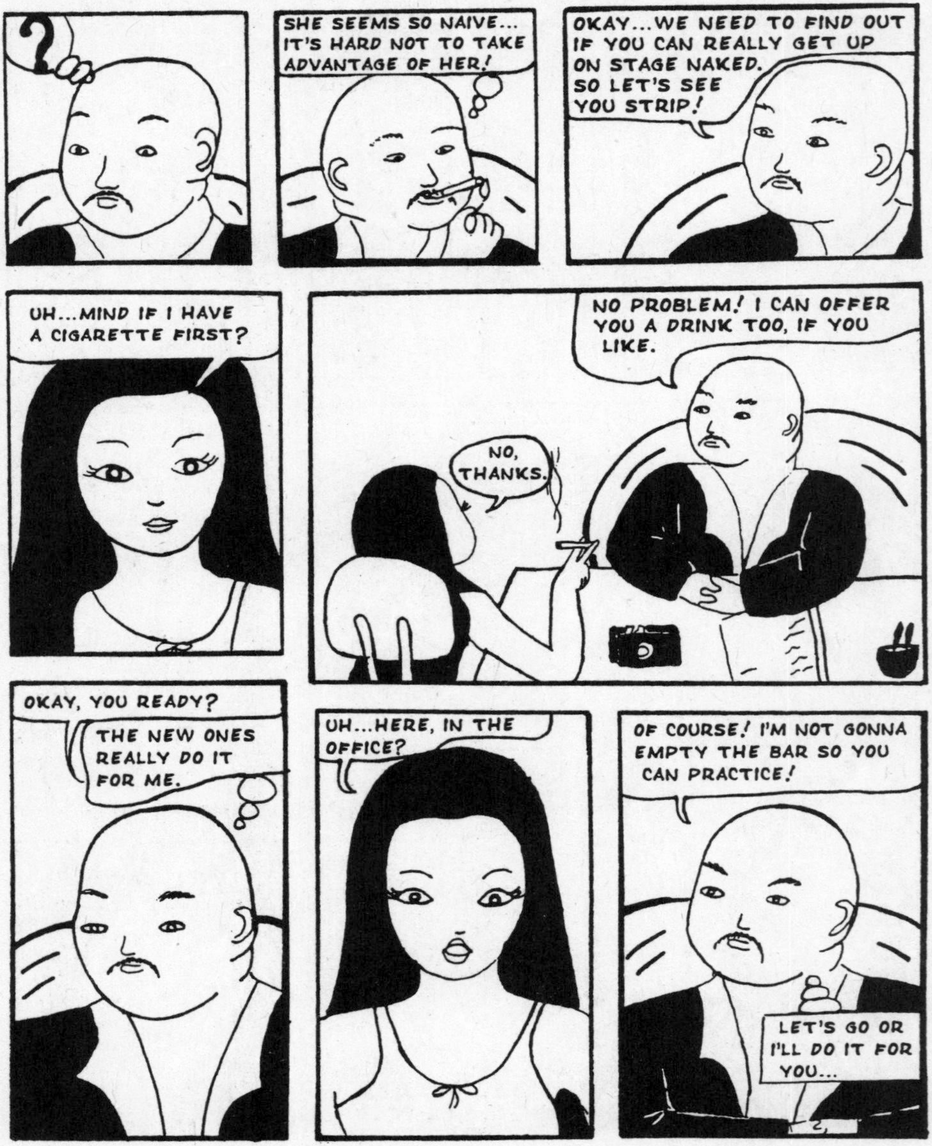
?
SHE SEEMS SO NAIVE... IT'S HARD NOT TO TAKE ADVANTAGE OF HER!
OKAY...WE NEED TO FIND OUT IF YOU CAN REALLY GET UP ON STAGE NAKED. SO LET'S SEE YOU STRIP!
UH...MIND IF I HAVE A CIGARETTE FIRST?
NO PROBLEM! I CAN OFFER YOU A DRINK TOO, IF YOU LIKE.
NO, THANKS.
OKAY, YOU READY?
THE NEW ONES REALLY DO IT FOR ME.
UH...HERE, IN THE OFFICE?
OF COURSE! I'M NOT GONNA EMPTY THE BAR SO YOU CAN PRACTICE!
LET'S GO OR I'LL DO IT FOR YOU...

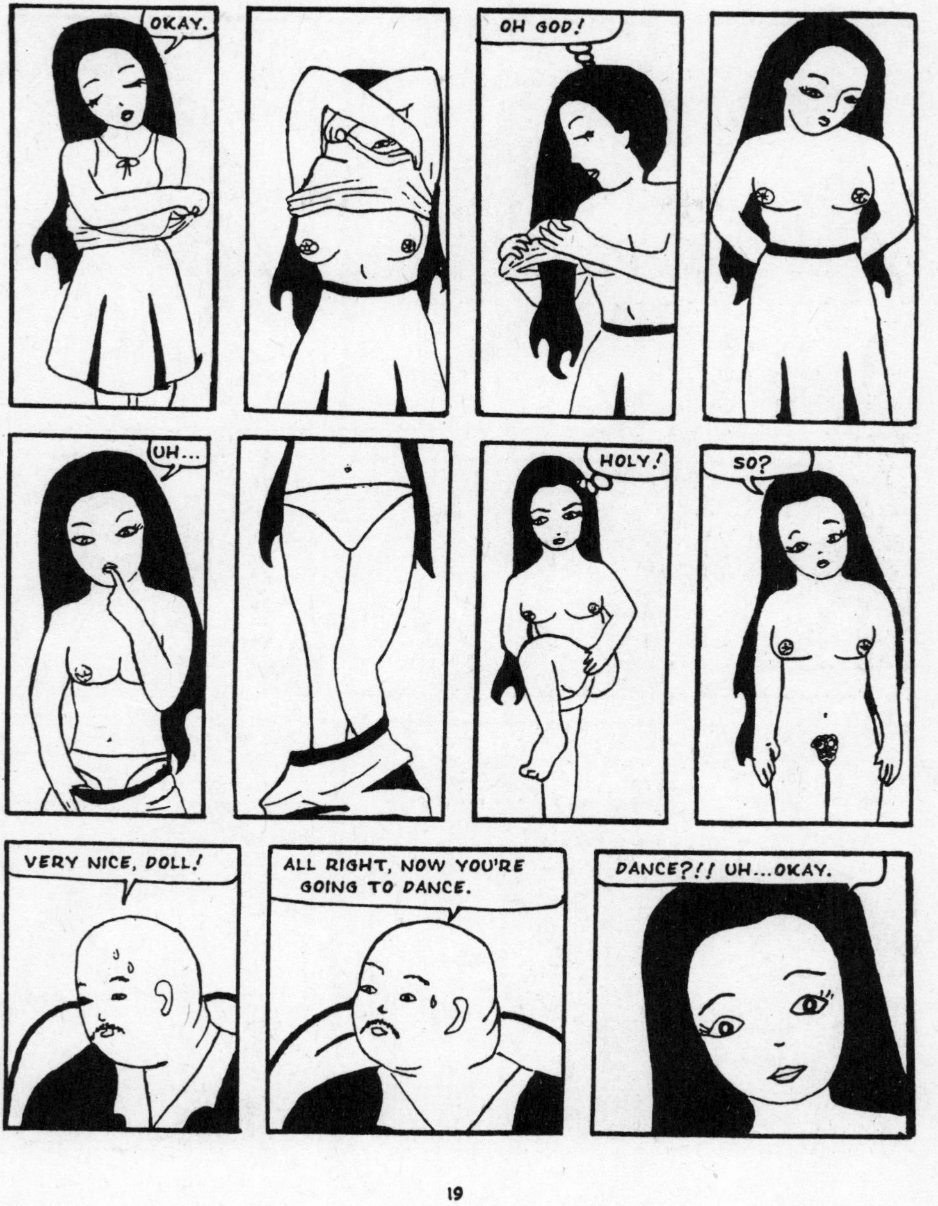
OKAY.
OH GOD!
UH...
HOLY!
SO?
VERY NICE, DOLL!
ALL RIGHT, NOW YOU'RE GOING TO DANCE.
DANCE?!! UH...OKAY.

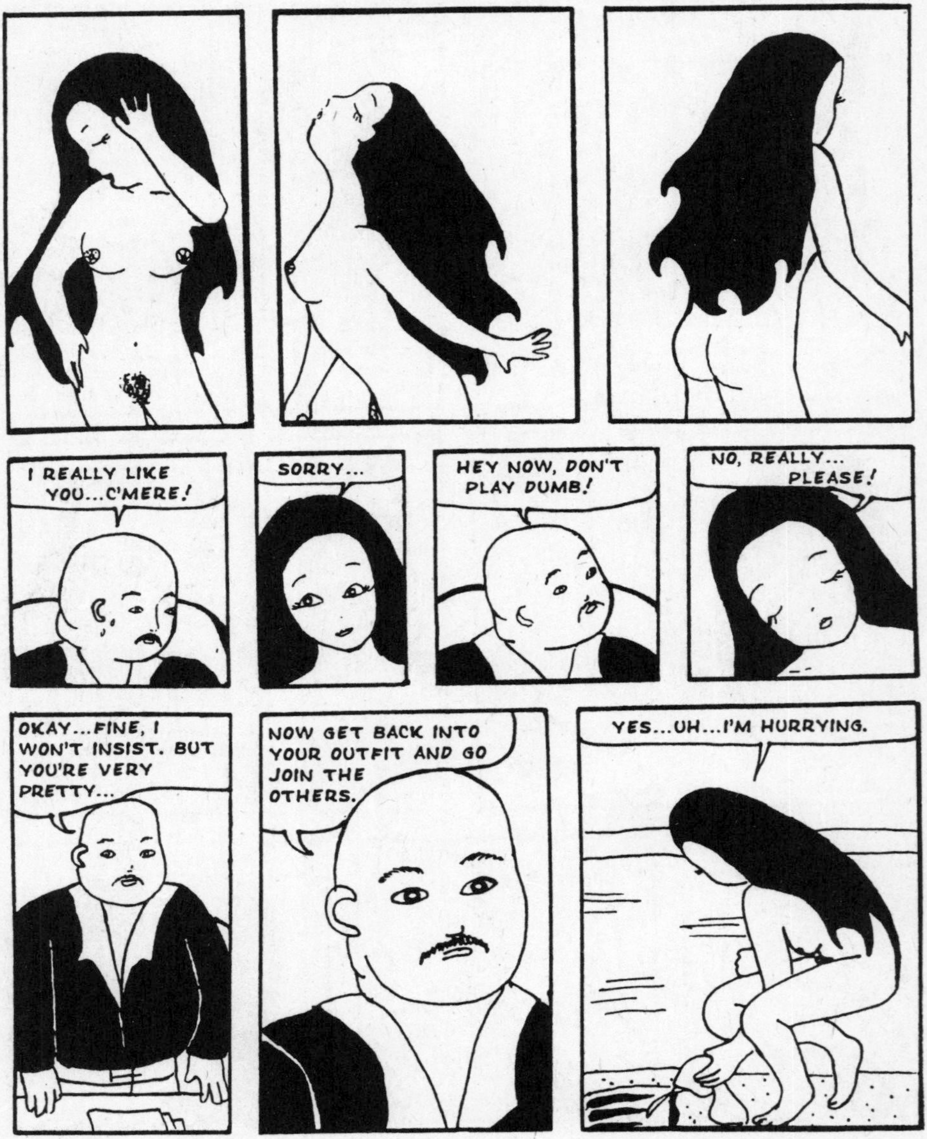
I REALLY LIKE YOU...C'MERE!
SORRY...
HEY NOW, DON'T PLAY DUMB!
NO, REALLY... PLEASE!
OKAY...FINE, I WON'T INSIST. BUT YOU'RE VERY PRETTY...
NOW GET BACK INTO YOUR OUTFIT AND GO JOIN THE OTHERS.
YES...UH...I'M HURRYING.

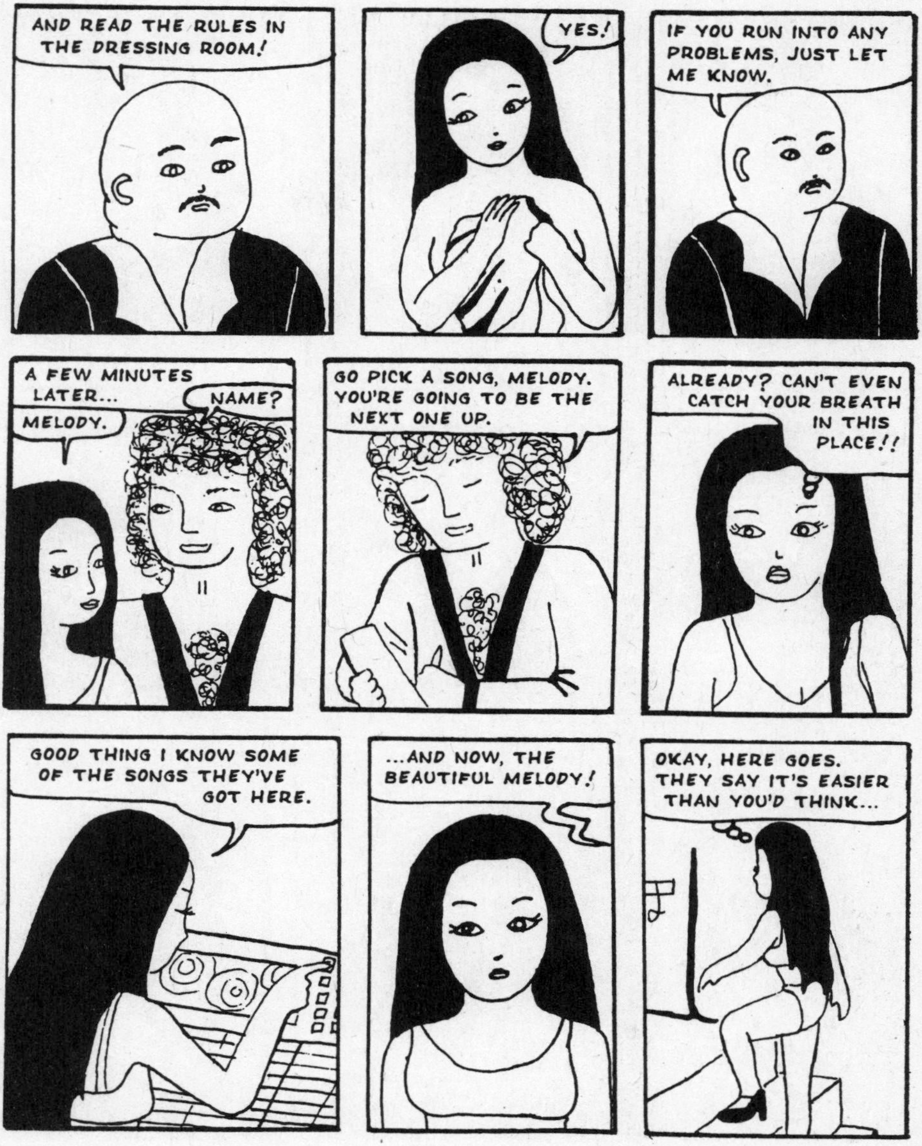

AND READ THE RULES IN THE DRESSING ROOM!
YES!
IF YOU RUN INTO ANY PROBLEMS, JUST LET ME KNOW.
A FEW MINUTES LATER...
NAME?
MELODY.
GO PICK A SONG, MELODY. YOU'RE GOING TO BE THE NEXT ONE UP.
ALREADY? CAN'T EVEN CATCH YOUR BREATH IN THIS PLACE!!
GOOD THING I KNOW SOME OF THE SONGS THEY'VE GOT HERE.
...AND NOW, THE BEAUTIFUL MELODY!
OKAY, HERE GOES. THEY SAY IT'S EASIER THAN YOU'D THINK...

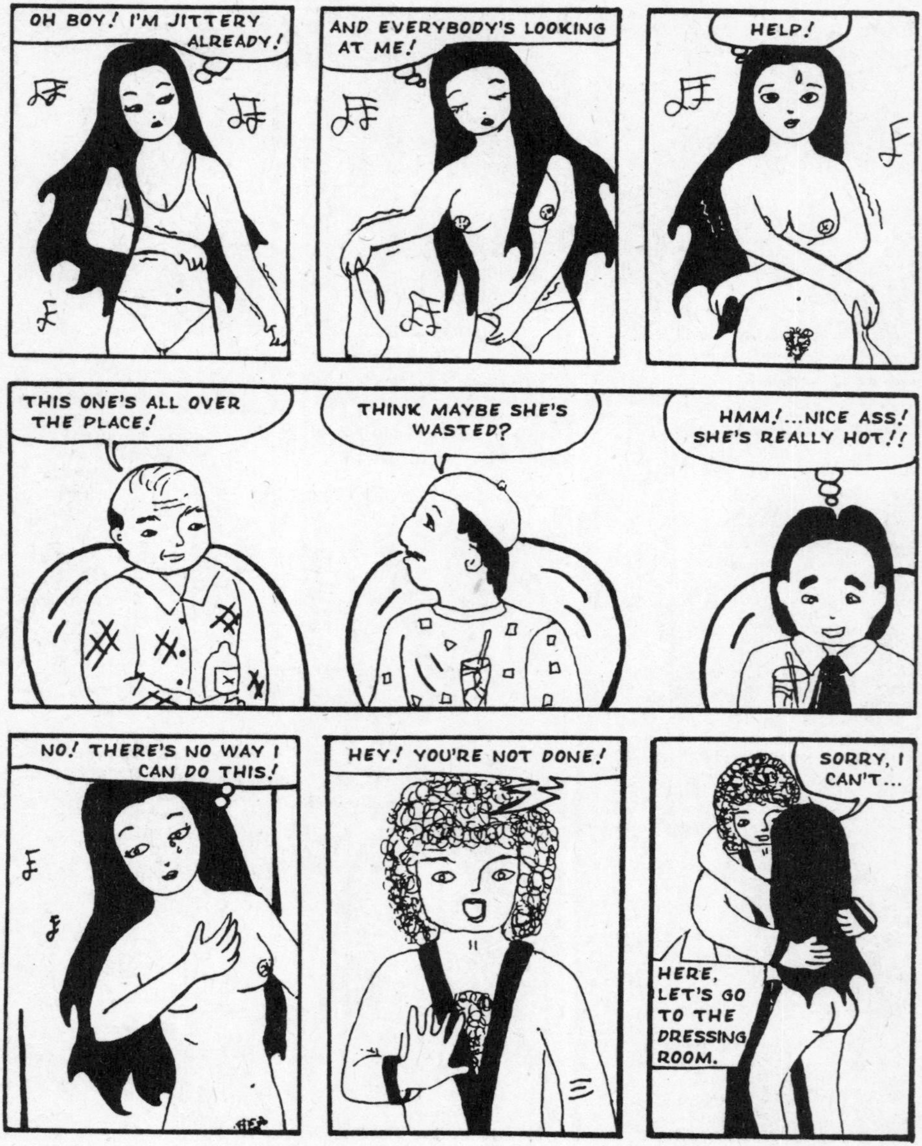
OH BOY! I'M JITTERY ALREADY!
AND EVERYBODY'S LOOKING AT ME!
HELP!
THIS ONE'S ALL OVER THE PLACE!
THINK MAYBE SHE'S WASTED?
HMM!...NICE ASS! SHE'S REALLY HOT!!
NO! THERE'S NO WAY I CAN DO THIS!
HEY! YOU'RE NOT DONE!
SORRY, I CAN'T...
HERE, LET'S GO TO THE DRESSING ROOM.

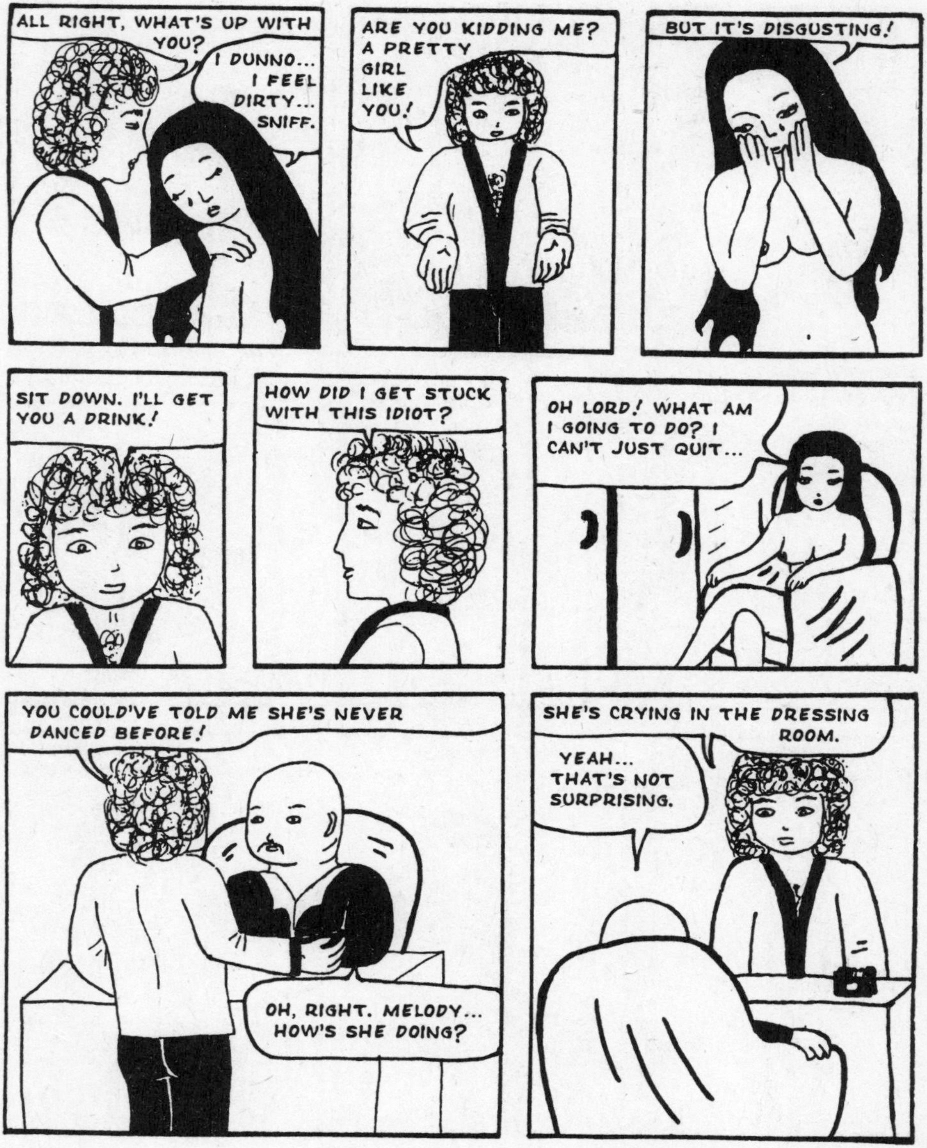
ALL RIGHT, WHAT'S UP WITH YOU?
I DUNNO... I FEEL DIRTY... SNIFF.
ARE YOU KIDDING ME? A PRETTY GIRL LIKE YOU!
BUT IT'S DISGUSTING!
SIT DOWN. I'LL GET YOU A DRINK!
HOW DID I GET STUCK WITH THIS IDIOT?
OH LORD! WHAT AM I GOING TO DO? I CAN'T JUST QUIT...
YOU COULD'VE TOLD ME SHE'S NEVER DANCED BEFORE!
OH, RIGHT. MELODY... HOW'S SHE DOING?
SHE'S CRYING IN THE DRESSING ROOM.
YEAH... THAT'S NOT SURPRISING.

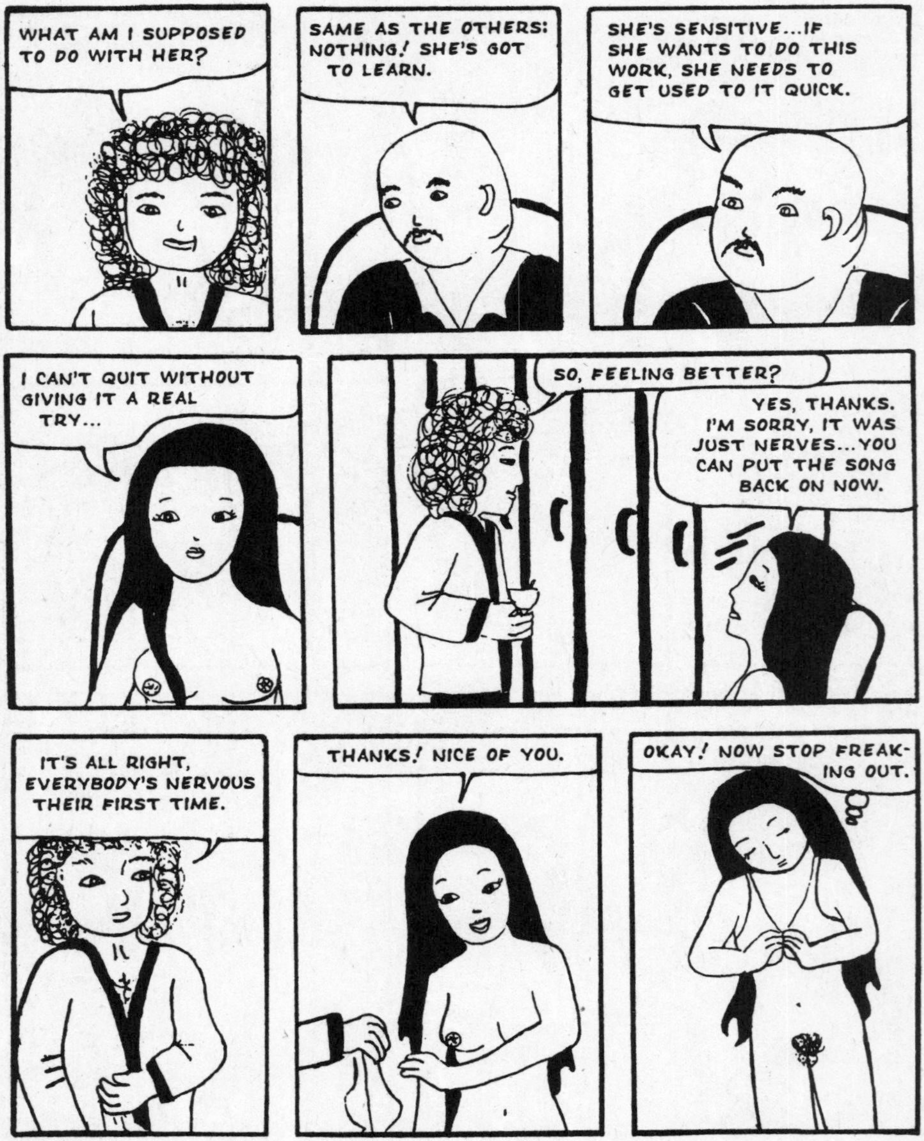
WHAT AM I SUPPOSED TO DO WITH HER?
SAME AS THE OTHERS: NOTHING! SHE'S GOT TO LEARN.
SHE'S SENSITIVE...IF SHE WANTS TO DO THIS WORK, SHE NEEDS TO GET USED TO IT QUICK.
I CAN'T QUIT WITHOUT GIVING IT A REAL TRY...
SO, FEELING BETTER?
YES, THANKS. I'M SORRY, IT WAS JUST NERVES...YOU CAN PUT THE SONG BACK ON NOW.
IT'S ALL RIGHT, EVERYBODY'S NERVOUS THEIR FIRST TIME.
THANKS! NICE OF YOU.
OKAY! NOW STOP FREAKING OUT.

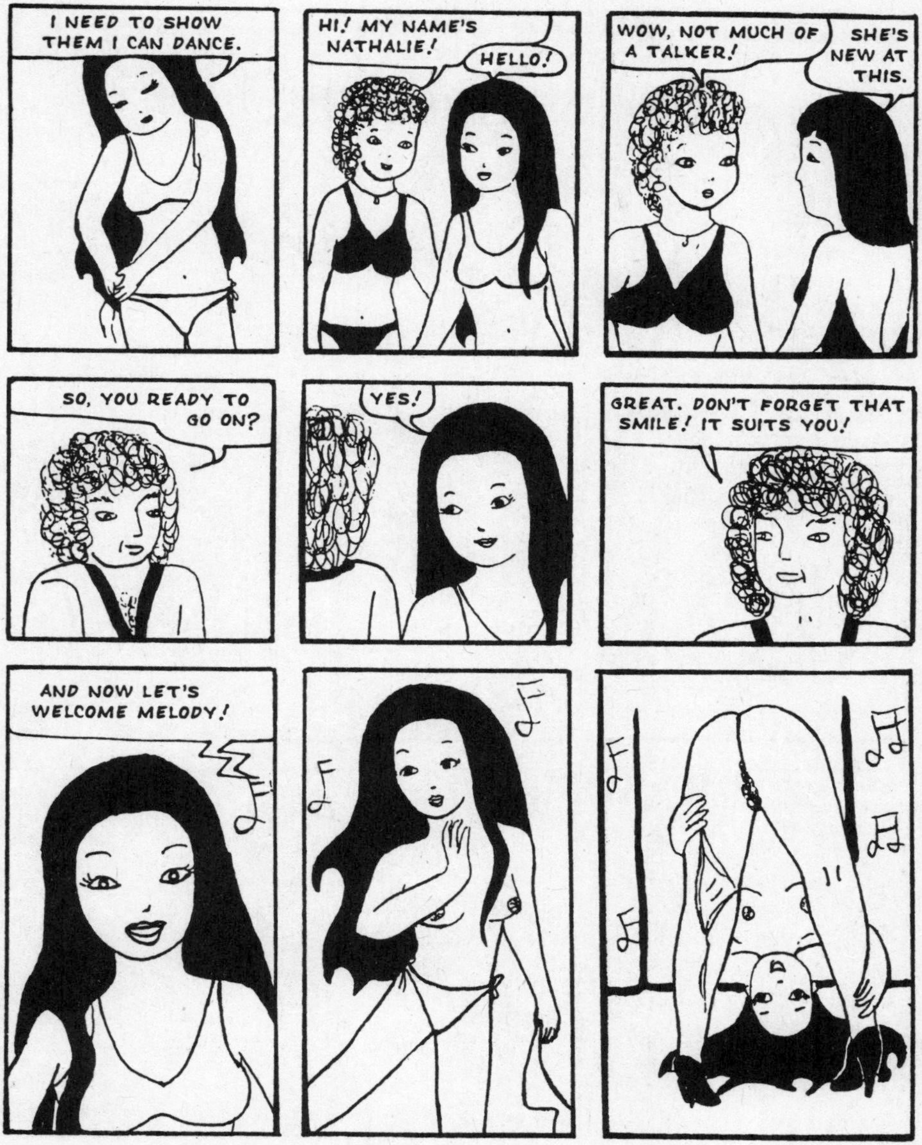
I NEED TO SHOW THEM I CAN DANCE.
HI! MY NAME'S NATHALIE!
HELLO!
WOW, NOT MUCH OF A TALKER!
SHE'S NEW AT THIS.
SO, YOU READY TO GO ON?
YES!
GREAT. DON'T FORGET THAT SMILE! IT SUITS YOU!
AND NOW LET'S WELCOME MELODY!

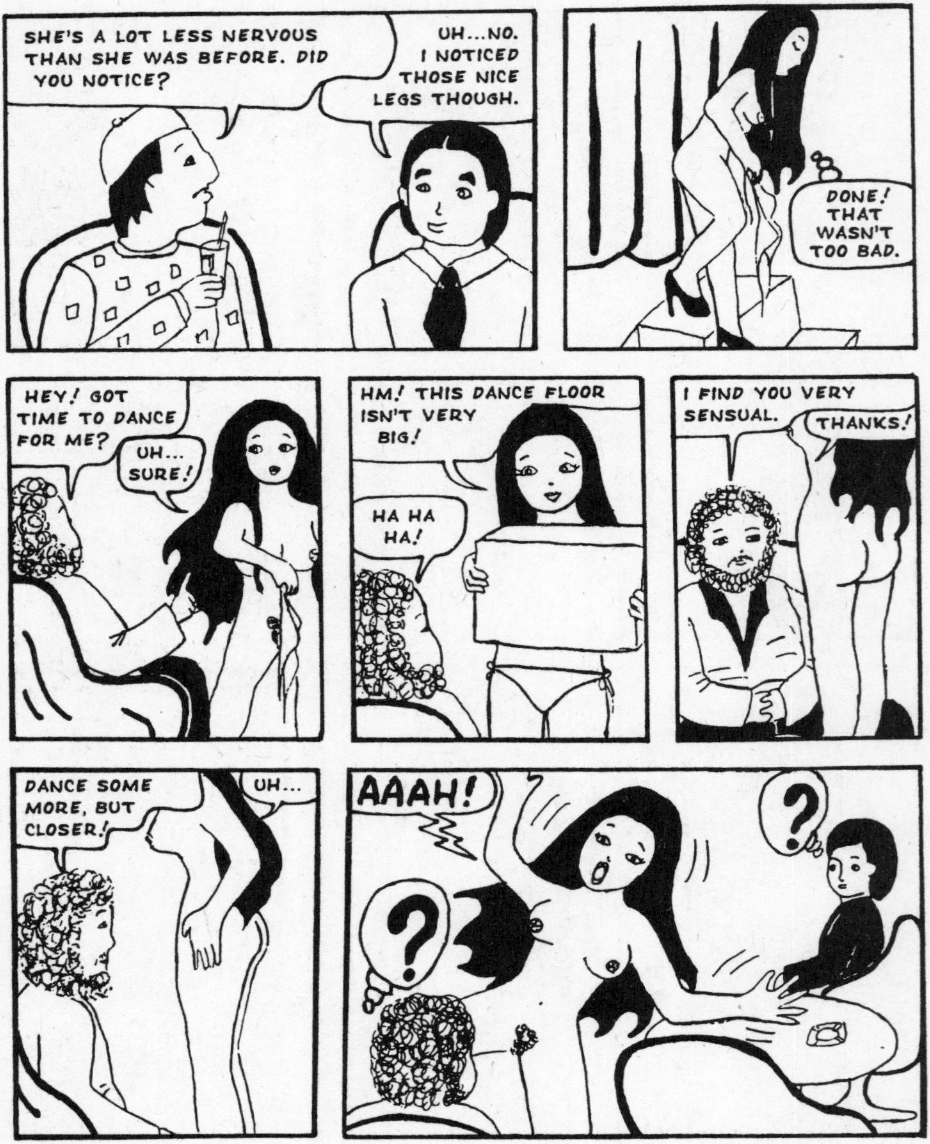
SHE'S A LOT LESS NERVOUS THAN SHE WAS BEFORE. DID YOU NOTICE?
UH...NO. I NOTICED THOSE NICE LEGS THOUGH.
DONE! THAT WASN'T TOO BAD.
HEY! GOT TIME TO DANCE FOR ME?
UH... SURE!
HM! THIS DANCE FLOOR ISN'T VERY BIG!
HA HA HA!
I FIND YOU VERY SENSUAL.
THANKS!
DANCE SOME MORE, BUT CLOSER!
UH...
AAAH!
?
?

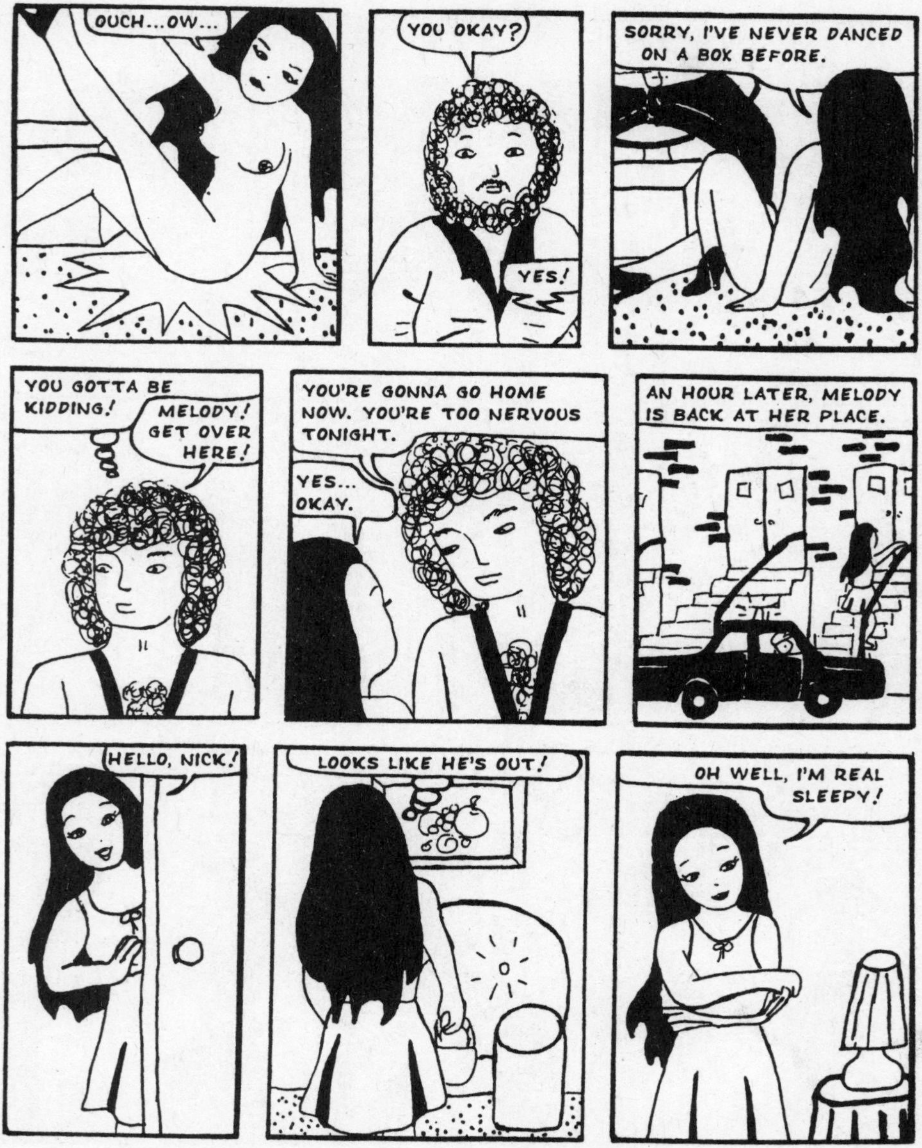
OUCH...OW...
YOU OKAY?
YES!
SORRY, I'VE NEVER DANCED ON A BOX BEFORE.
YOU GOTTA BE KIDDING!
MELODY! GET OVER HERE!
YOU'RE GONNA GO HOME NOW. YOU'RE TOO NERVOUS TONIGHT.
YES... OKAY.
AN HOUR LATER, MELODY IS BACK AT HER PLACE.
HELLO, NICK!
LOOKS LIKE HE'S OUT!
OH WELL, I'M REAL SLEEPY!

ZZ...ZZ...

POOR BABY! MUST'VE BEEN TIRED. SHE'S OUT COLD.

NEXT DAY, AT THE RESTAURANT...

SO, DID YOU DROP BY THE BAR LAST NIGHT?

YES, BUT YOU WERE GONE.

NICK, THERE'S SOMETHING I NEED TO TELL YOU.

WHAT?

UH...WELL, THE BOSS ASKED ME TO HAVE SEX WITH HIM. I DON'T KNOW WHAT TO THINK.

YOU SLEPT WITH THE BOSS?

UH...NO. HE DIDN'T INSIST. BUT WHAT DO I DO IF HE ASKS AGAIN?

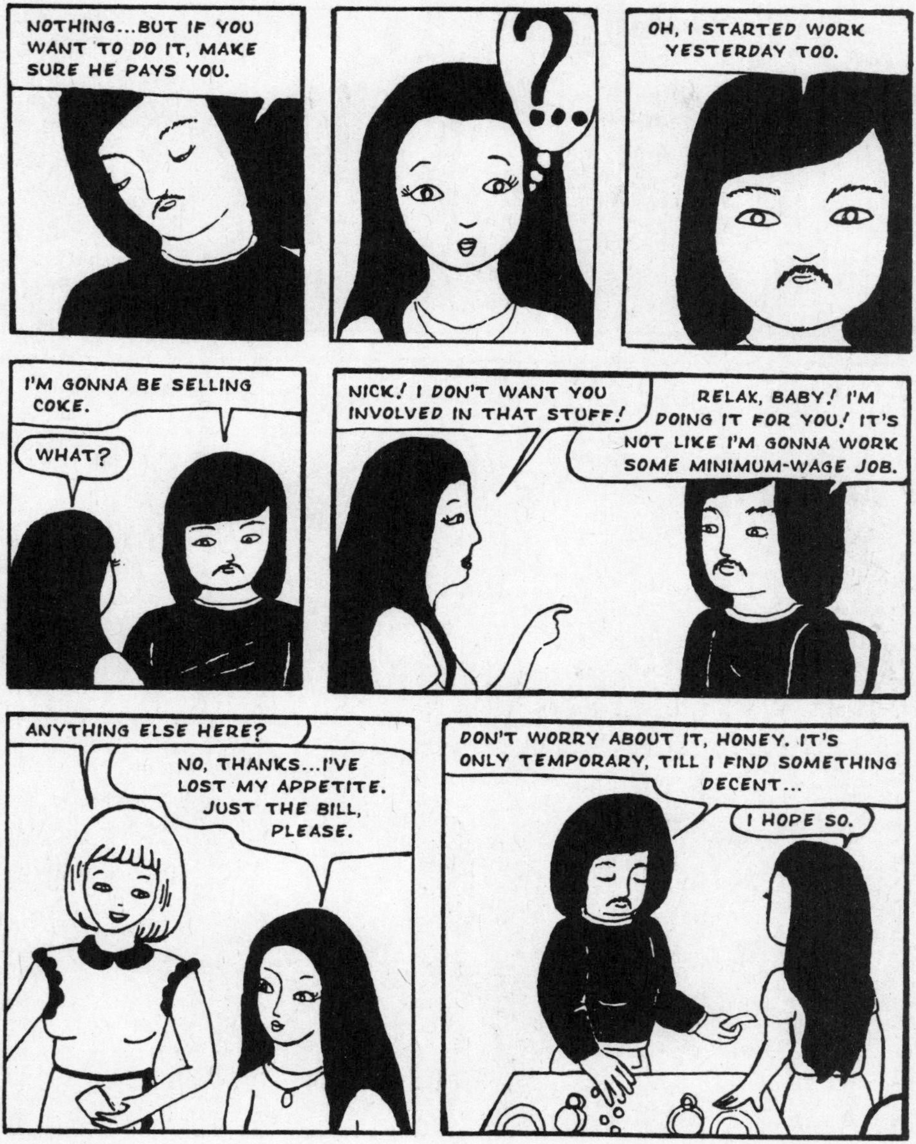
NOTHING...BUT IF YOU WANT TO DO IT, MAKE SURE HE PAYS YOU.
?...
OH, I STARTED WORK YESTERDAY TOO.
I'M GONNA BE SELLING COKE.
WHAT?
NICK! I DON'T WANT YOU INVOLVED IN THAT STUFF!
RELAX, BABY! I'M DOING IT FOR YOU! IT'S NOT LIKE I'M GONNA WORK SOME MINIMUM-WAGE JOB.
ANYTHING ELSE HERE?
NO, THANKS...I'VE LOST MY APPETITE. JUST THE BILL, PLEASE.
DON'T WORRY ABOUT IT, HONEY. IT'S ONLY TEMPORARY, TILL I FIND SOMETHING DECENT...
I HOPE SO.

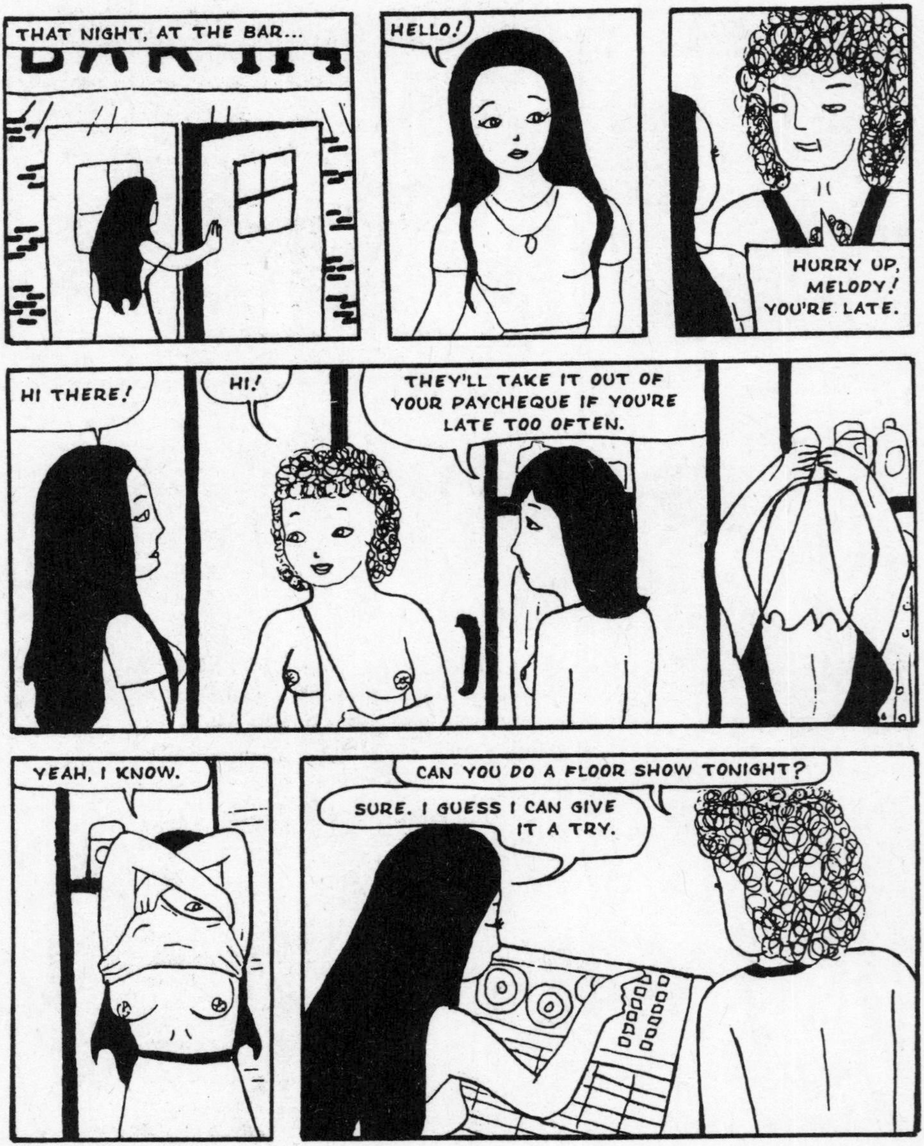
THAT NIGHT, AT THE BAR...
HELLO!
HURRY UP, MELODY! YOU'RE LATE.
HI THERE!
HI!
THEY'LL TAKE IT OUT OF YOUR PAYCHEQUE IF YOU'RE LATE TOO OFTEN.
YEAH, I KNOW.
CAN YOU DO A FLOOR SHOW TONIGHT?
SURE. I GUESS I CAN GIVE IT A TRY.

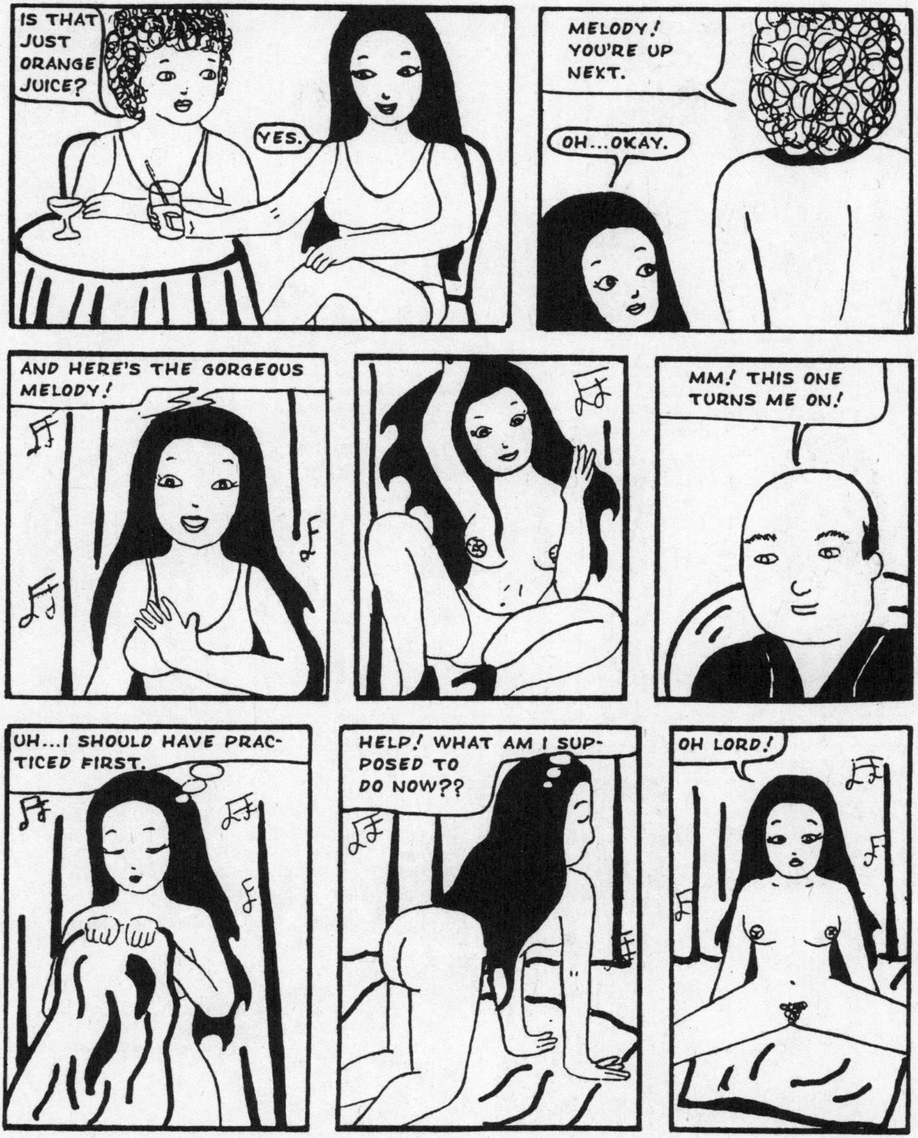
IS THAT JUST ORANGE JUICE?
YES.
MELODY! YOU'RE UP NEXT.
OH...OKAY.
AND HERE'S THE GORGEOUS MELODY!
MM! THIS ONE TURNS ME ON!
UH...I SHOULD HAVE PRACTICED FIRST.
HELP! WHAT AM I SUPPOSED TO DO NOW??
OH LORD!

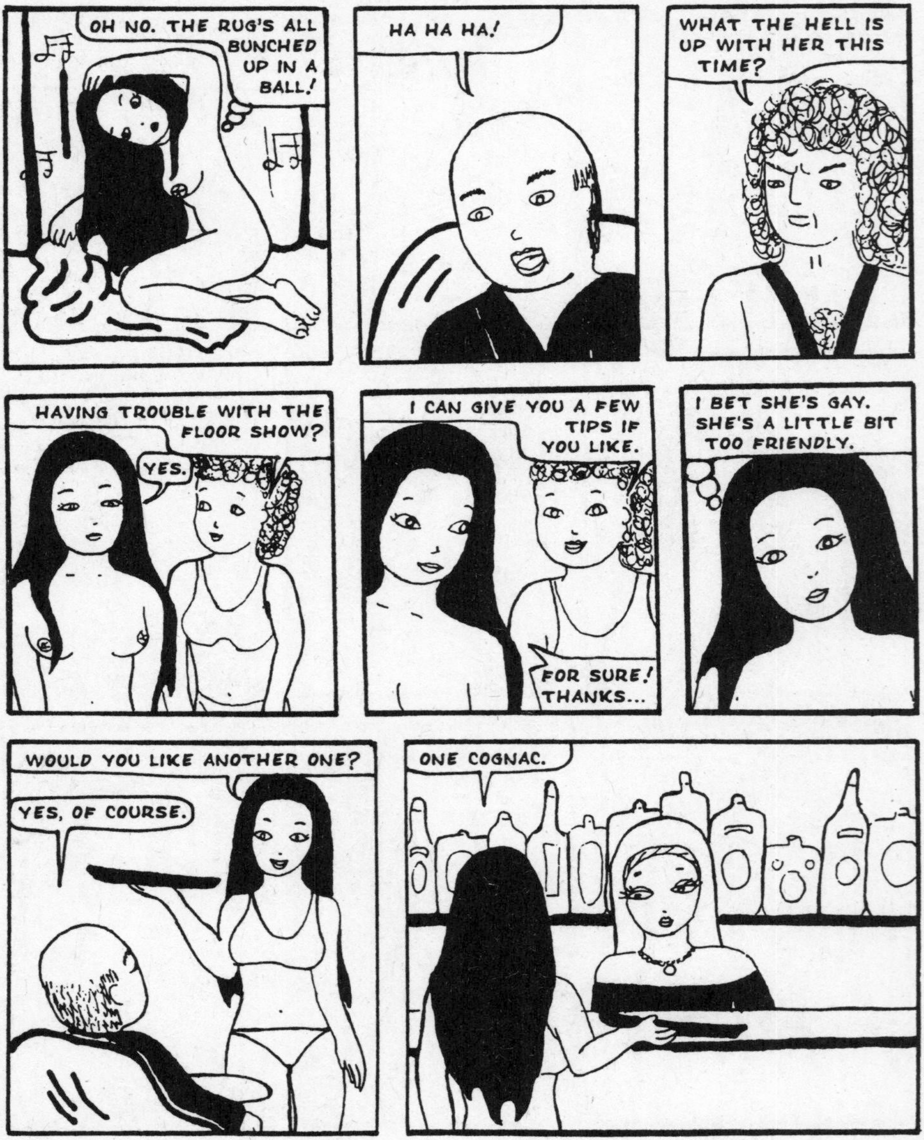
OH NO. THE RUG'S ALL BUNCHED UP IN A BALL!
HA HA HA!
WHAT THE HELL IS UP WITH HER THIS TIME?
HAVING TROUBLE WITH THE FLOOR SHOW?
YES.
I CAN GIVE YOU A FEW TIPS IF YOU LIKE.
FOR SURE! THANKS...
I BET SHE'S GAY. SHE'S A LITTLE BIT TOO FRIENDLY.
WOULD YOU LIKE ANOTHER ONE?
YES, OF COURSE.
ONE COGNAC.

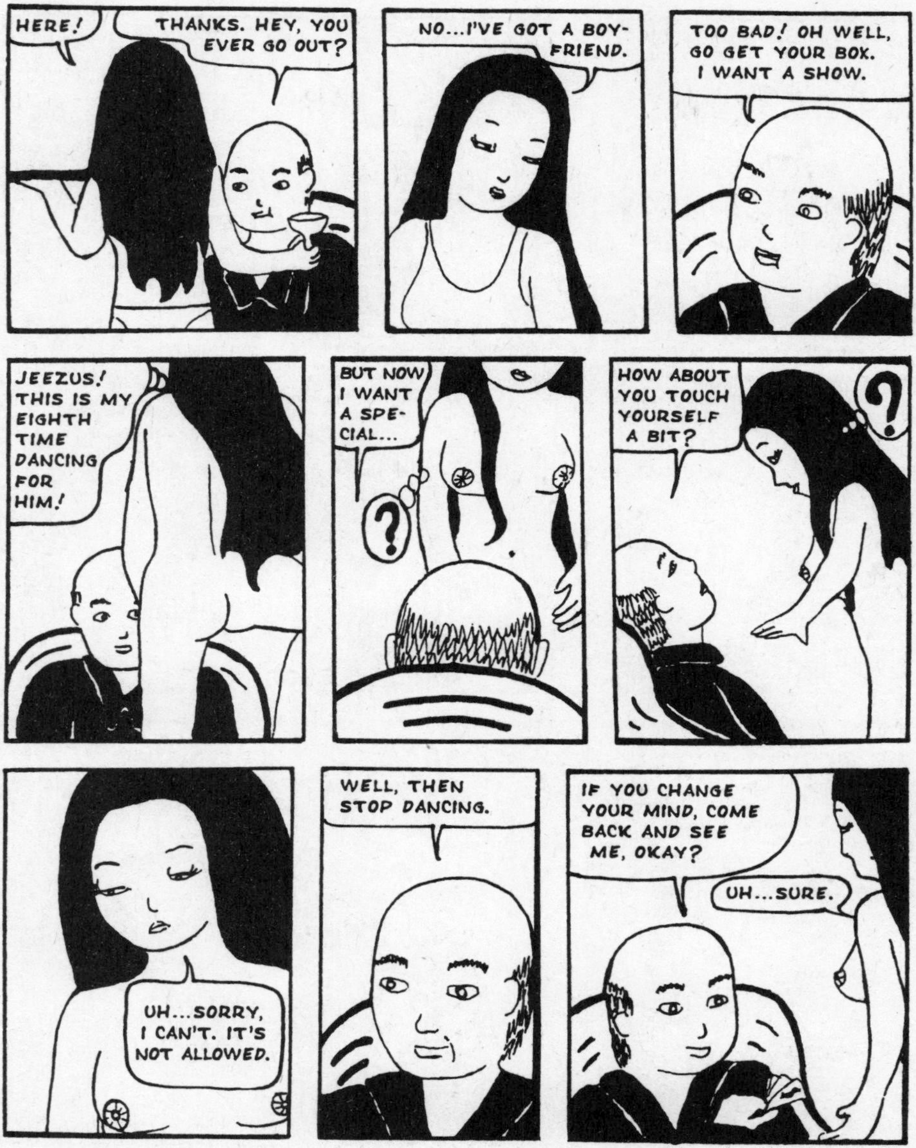
HERE!
THANKS. HEY, YOU EVER GO OUT?
NO...I'VE GOT A BOY-FRIEND.
TOO BAD! OH WELL, GO GET YOUR BOX. I WANT A SHOW.
JEEZUS! THIS IS MY EIGHTH TIME DANCING FOR HIM!
BUT NOW I WANT A SPE-CIAL...
?
HOW ABOUT YOU TOUCH YOURSELF A BIT?
?
UH...SORRY, I CAN'T. IT'S NOT ALLOWED.
WELL, THEN STOP DANCING.
IF YOU CHANGE YOUR MIND, COME BACK AND SEE ME, OKAY?
UH...SURE.

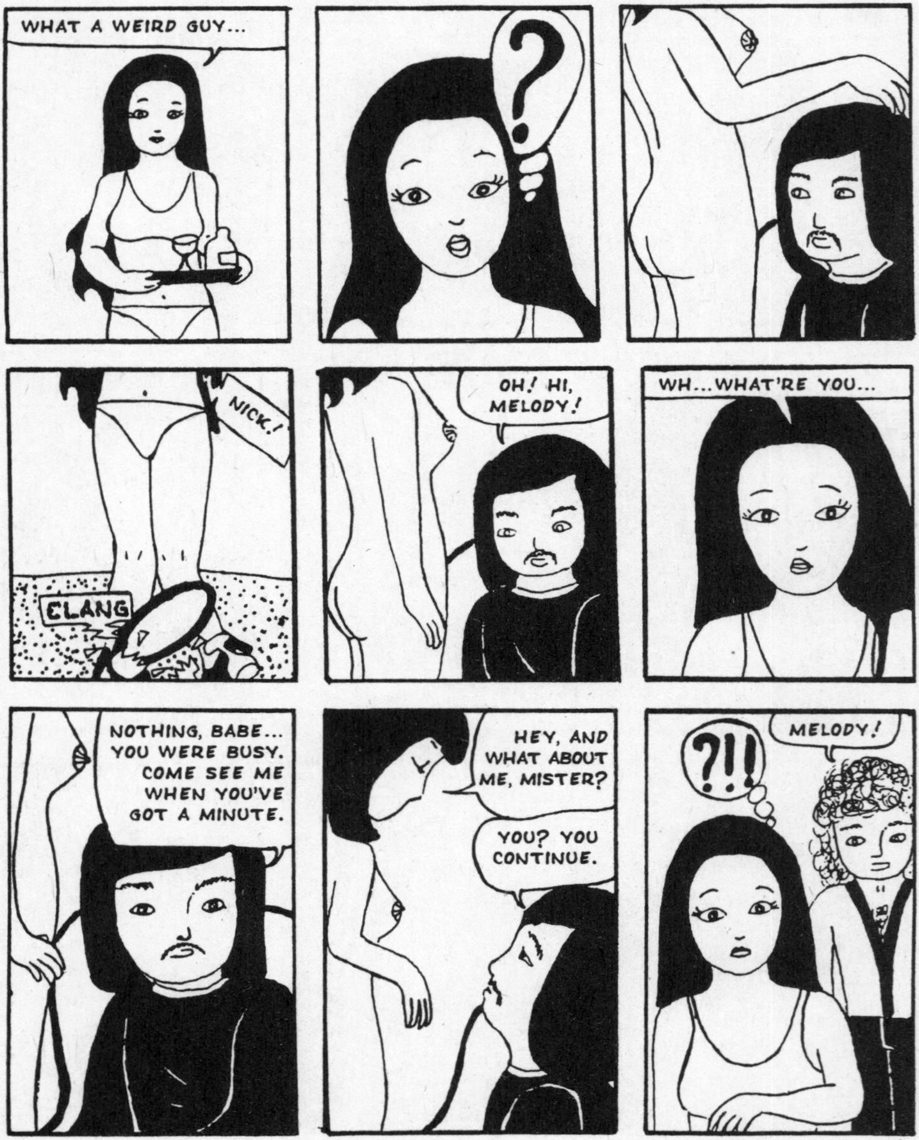
WHAT A WEIRD GUY...
?
NICK!
CLANG
OH! HI, MELODY!
WH...WHAT'RE YOU...
NOTHING, BABE... YOU WERE BUSY. COME SEE ME WHEN YOU'VE GOT A MINUTE.
HEY, AND WHAT ABOUT ME, MISTER?
YOU? YOU CONTINUE.
?!!
MELODY!

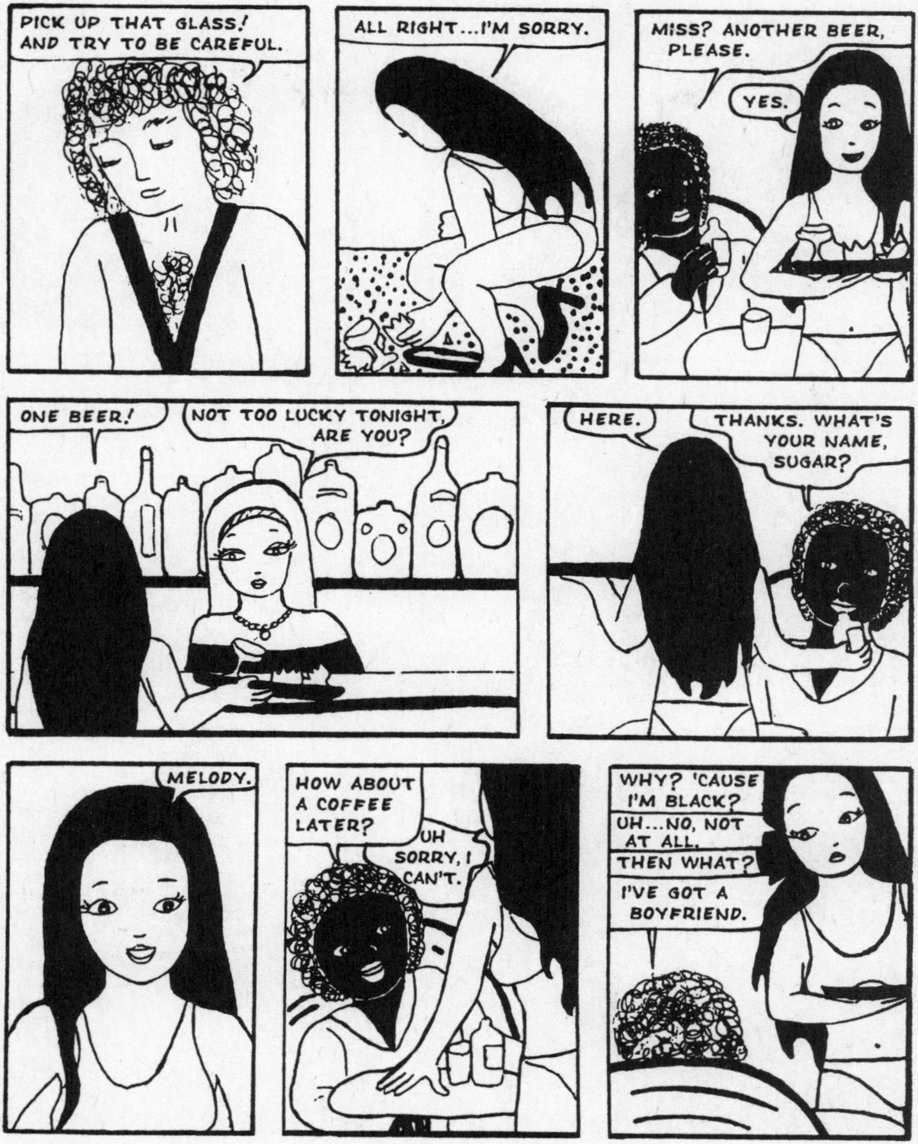
PICK UP THAT GLASS! AND TRY TO BE CAREFUL.
ALL RIGHT...I'M SORRY.
MISS? ANOTHER BEER, PLEASE.
YES.
ONE BEER!
NOT TOO LUCKY TONIGHT, ARE YOU?
HERE.
THANKS. WHAT'S YOUR NAME, SUGAR?
MELODY.
HOW ABOUT A COFFEE LATER?
UH SORRY, I CAN'T.
WHY? 'CAUSE I'M BLACK?
UH...NO, NOT AT ALL.
THEN WHAT?
I'VE GOT A BOYFRIEND.

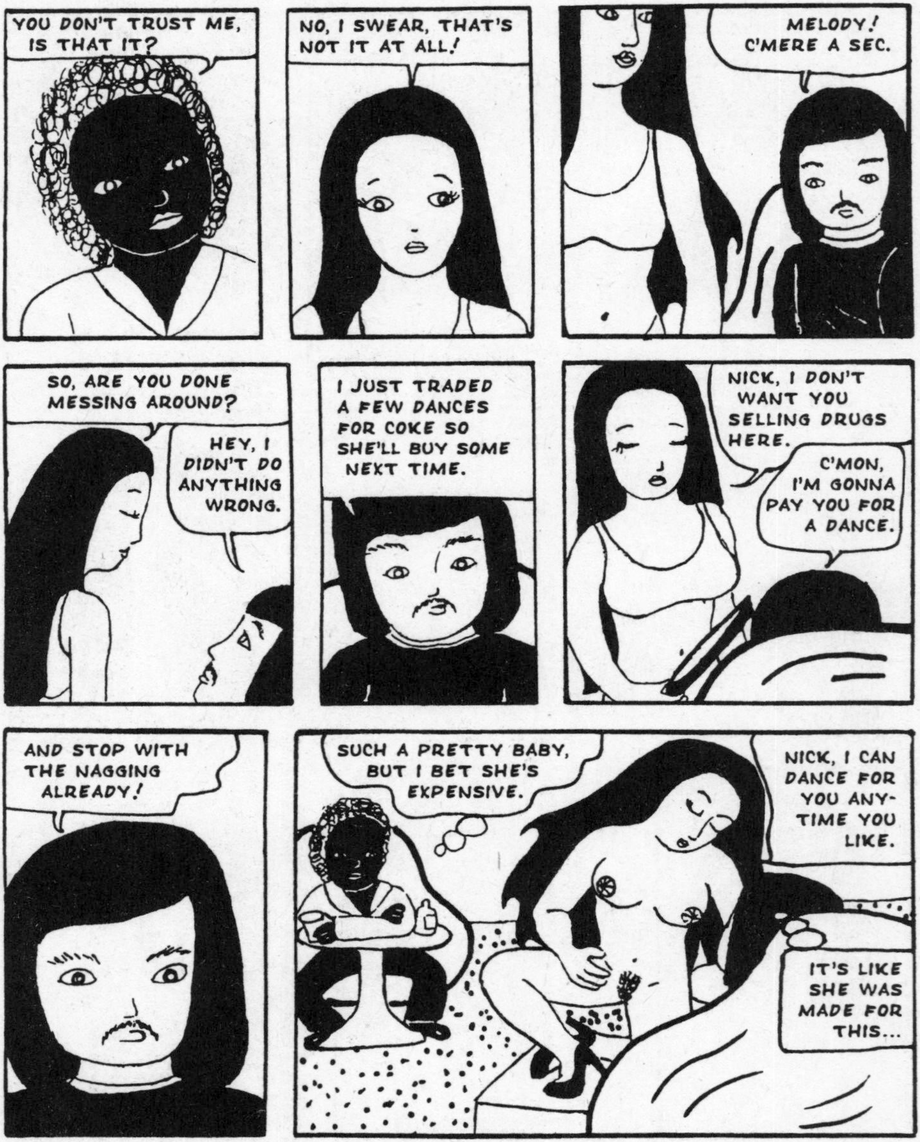
YOU DON'T TRUST ME, IS THAT IT?
NO, I SWEAR, THAT'S NOT IT AT ALL!
MELODY! C'MERE A SEC.
SO, ARE YOU DONE MESSING AROUND?
HEY, I DIDN'T DO ANYTHING WRONG.
I JUST TRADED A FEW DANCES FOR COKE SO SHE'LL BUY SOME NEXT TIME.
NICK, I DON'T WANT YOU SELLING DRUGS HERE.
C'MON, I'M GONNA PAY YOU FOR A DANCE.
AND STOP WITH THE NAGGING ALREADY!
SUCH A PRETTY BABY, BUT I BET SHE'S EXPENSIVE.
NICK, I CAN DANCE FOR YOU ANY-TIME YOU LIKE.
IT'S LIKE SHE WAS MADE FOR THIS...

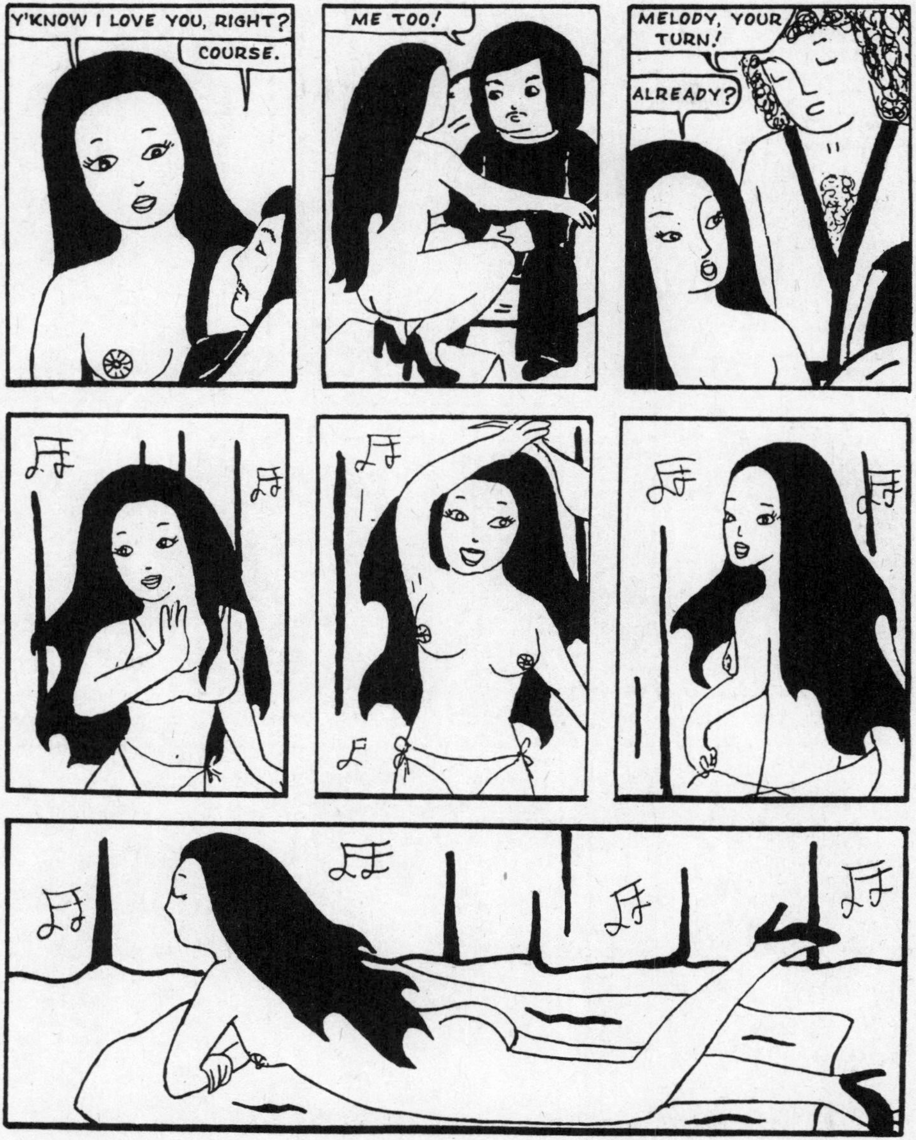

Y'KNOW I LOVE YOU, RIGHT?
COURSE.
ME TOO!
MELODY, YOUR TURN!
ALREADY?

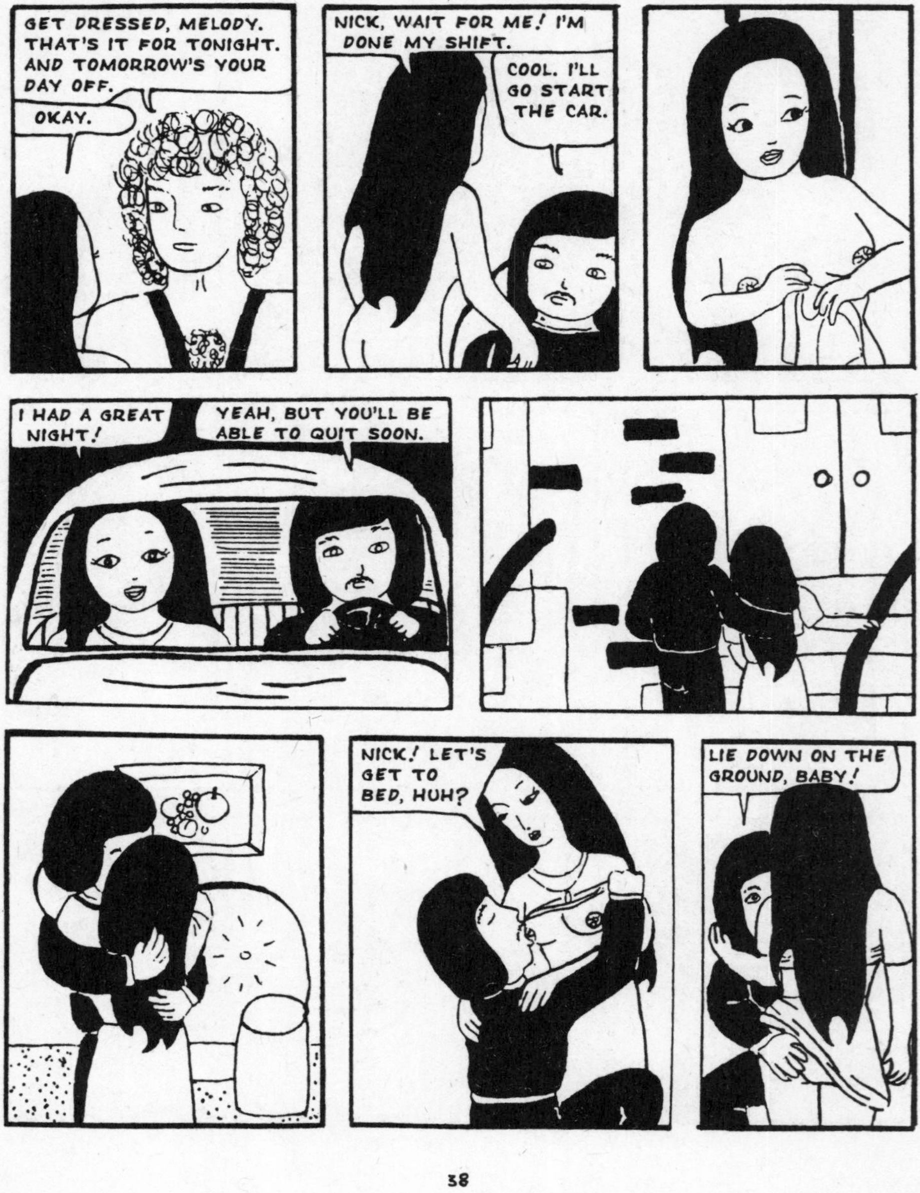
GET DRESSED, MELODY. THAT'S IT FOR TONIGHT. AND TOMORROW'S YOUR DAY OFF.
OKAY.
NICK, WAIT FOR ME! I'M DONE MY SHIFT.
COOL. I'LL GO START THE CAR.
I HAD A GREAT NIGHT!
YEAH, BUT YOU'LL BE ABLE TO QUIT SOON.
NICK! LET'S GET TO BED, HUH?
LIE DOWN ON THE GROUND, BABY!

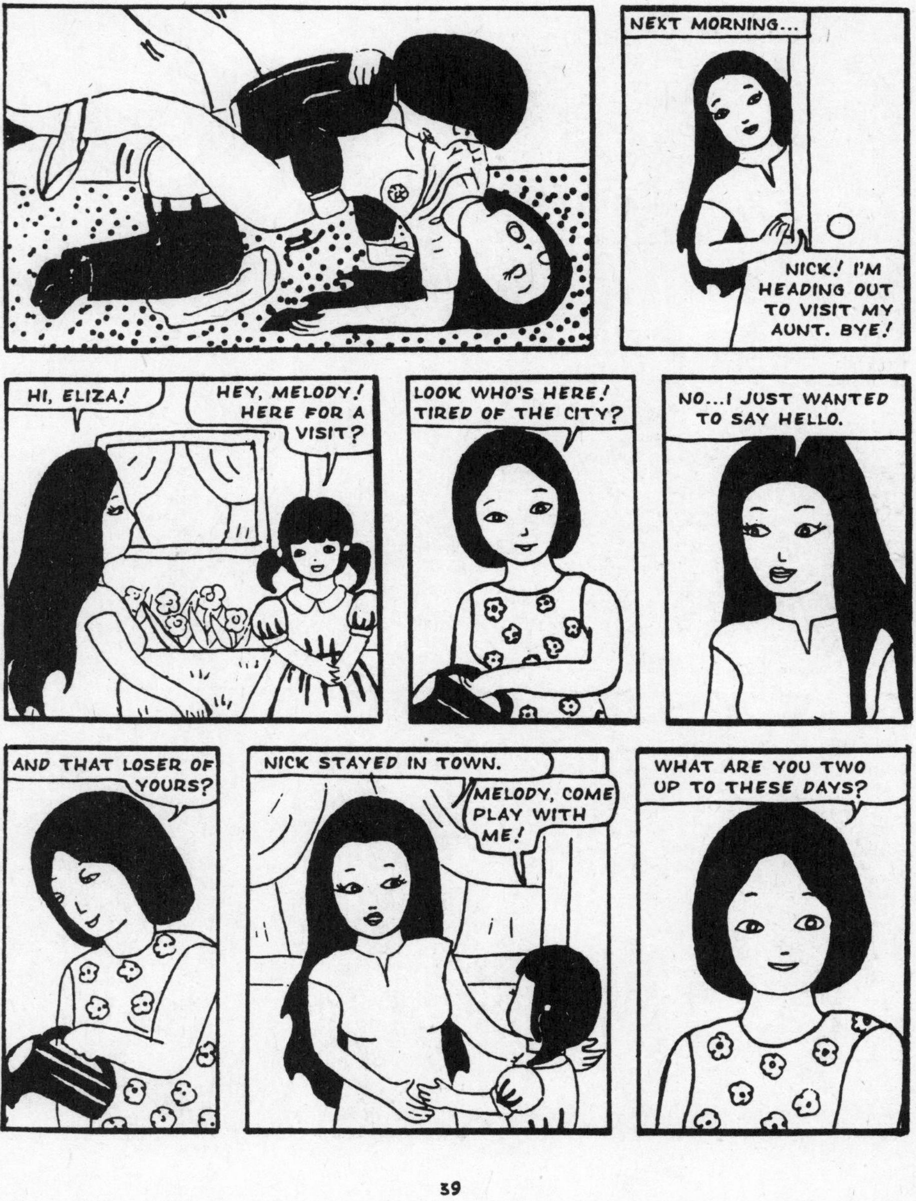

NEXT MORNING...
NICK! I'M HEADING OUT TO VISIT MY AUNT. BYE!
HI, ELIZA!
HEY, MELODY! HERE FOR A VISIT?
LOOK WHO'S HERE! TIRED OF THE CITY?
NO...I JUST WANTED TO SAY HELLO.
AND THAT LOSER OF YOURS?
NICK STAYED IN TOWN.
MELODY, COME PLAY WITH ME!
WHAT ARE YOU TWO UP TO THESE DAYS?

NICK, NOTHING. BUT I'M DANCING.
HA HA HA!
?
MELODY, I RAISED YOU BETTER THAN THAT. IT'S NICK, ISN'T IT?
COURSE NOT...
HA HA! HIGHER, MELODY!
IF MY MOM WERE STILL ALIVE, MAYBE THINGS WOULD BE DIFFERENT.
COME ON! THAT'S NOT FAIR, MELODY. YOU NEVER LIKED SCHOOL...AND YOU'VE ALWAYS DONE WHATEVER YOU WANTED. YOU CAN'T BLAME IT ON ANYBODY ELSE!
OKAY, FINE...I DIDN'T COME HERE TO ARGUE.
ALL RIGHT. PLEASE JUST BE CAREFUL, MELODY!

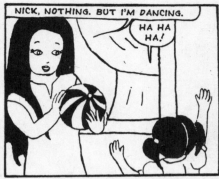

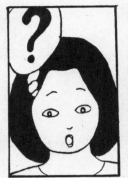

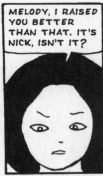

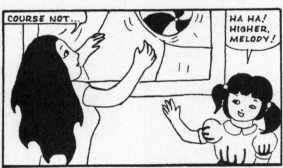

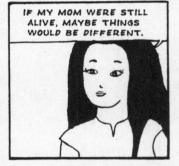

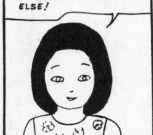

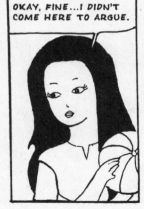

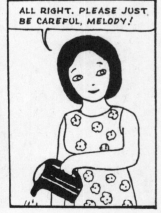

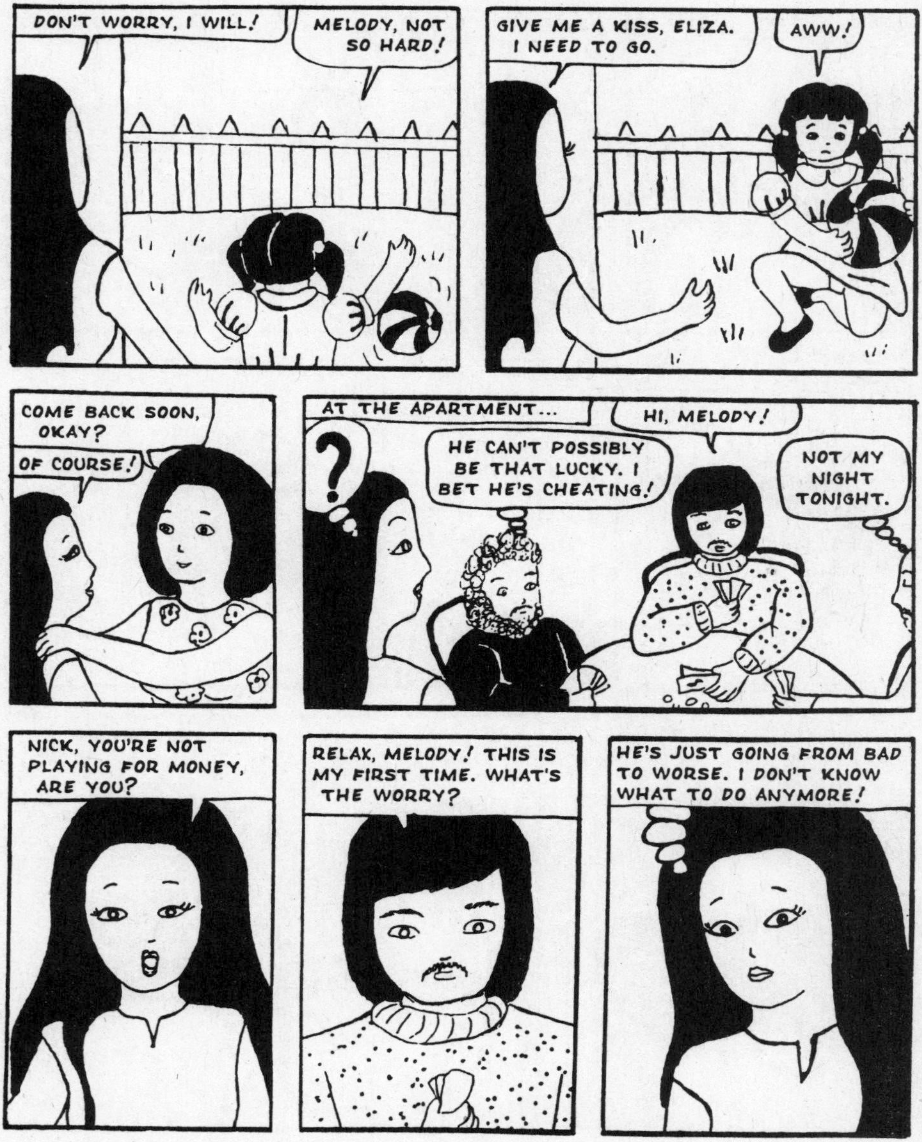
DON'T WORRY, I WILL!
MELODY, NOT SO HARD!
GIVE ME A KISS, ELIZA. I NEED TO GO.
AWW!
COME BACK SOON, OKAY?
OF COURSE!
AT THE APARTMENT...
HI, MELODY!
?
HE CAN'T POSSIBLY BE THAT LUCKY. I BET HE'S CHEATING!
NOT MY NIGHT TONIGHT.
NICK, YOU'RE NOT PLAYING FOR MONEY, ARE YOU?
RELAX, MELODY! THIS IS MY FIRST TIME. WHAT'S THE WORRY?
HE'S JUST GOING FROM BAD TO WORSE. I DON'T KNOW WHAT TO DO ANYMORE!

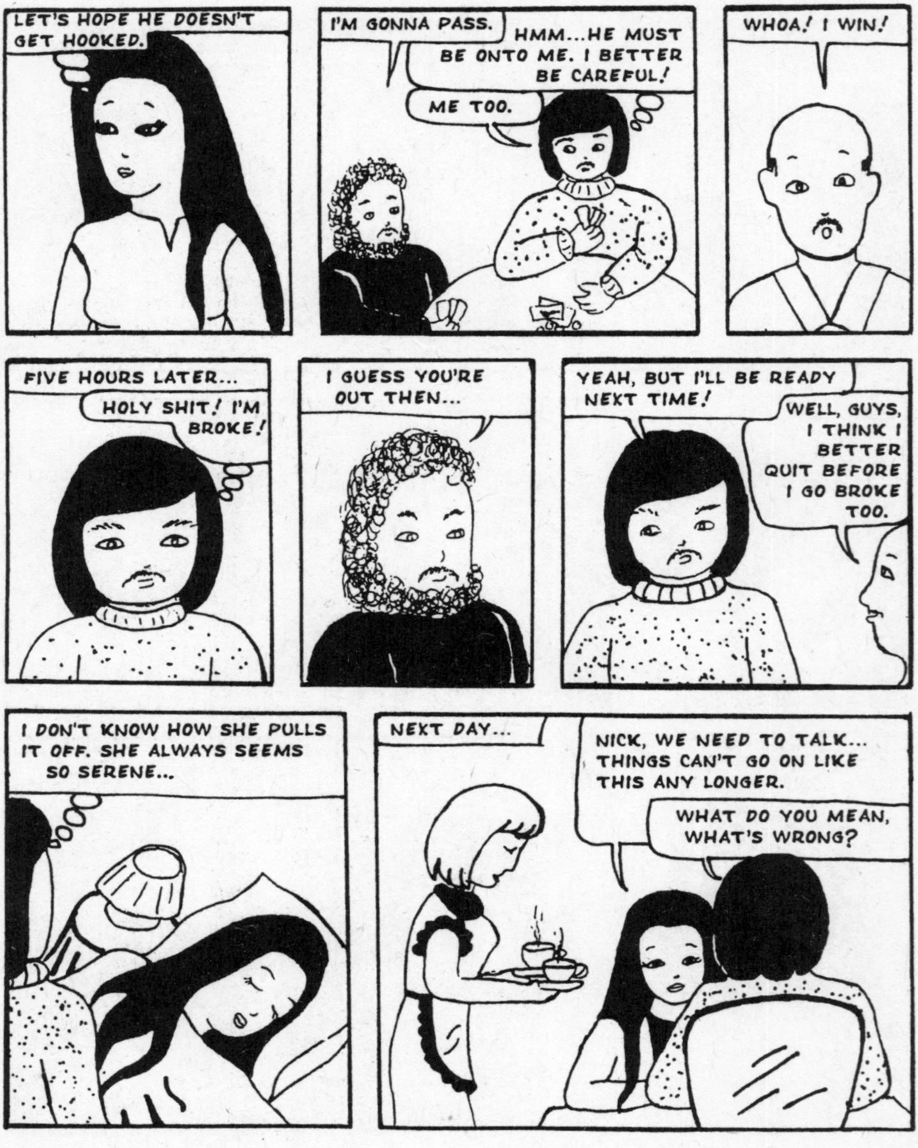
LET'S HOPE HE DOESN'T GET HOOKED.
I'M GONNA PASS.
HMM...HE MUST BE ONTO ME. I BETTER BE CAREFUL!
ME TOO.
WHOA! I WIN!
FIVE HOURS LATER...
HOLY SHIT! I'M BROKE!
I GUESS YOU'RE OUT THEN...
YEAH, BUT I'LL BE READY NEXT TIME!
WELL, GUYS, I THINK I BETTER QUIT BEFORE I GO BROKE TOO.
I DON'T KNOW HOW SHE PULLS IT OFF. SHE ALWAYS SEEMS SO SERENE...
NEXT DAY...
NICK, WE NEED TO TALK... THINGS CAN'T GO ON LIKE THIS ANY LONGER.
WHAT DO YOU MEAN, WHAT'S WRONG?

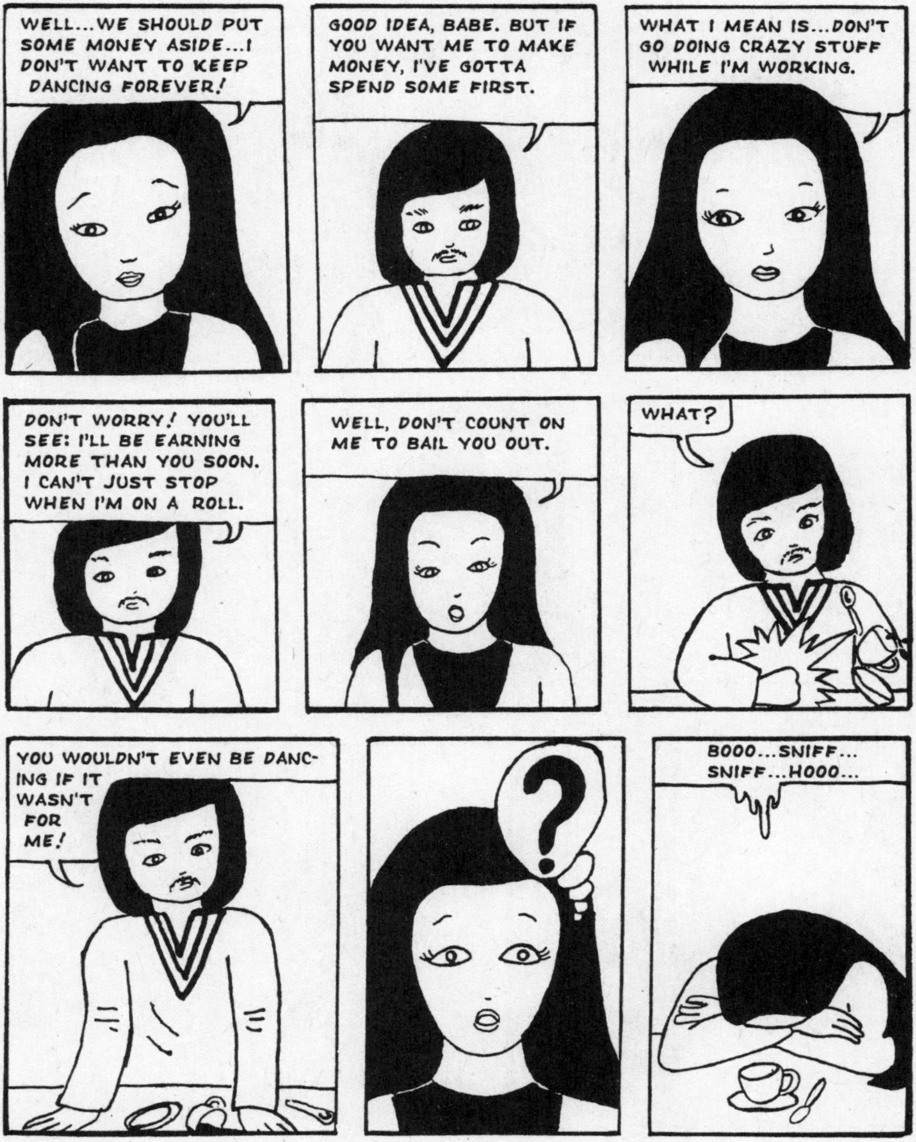
WELL...WE SHOULD PUT SOME MONEY ASIDE...I DON'T WANT TO KEEP DANCING FOREVER!
GOOD IDEA, BABE. BUT IF YOU WANT ME TO MAKE MONEY, I'VE GOTTA SPEND SOME FIRST.
WHAT I MEAN IS...DON'T GO DOING CRAZY STUFF WHILE I'M WORKING.
DON'T WORRY! YOU'LL SEE: I'LL BE EARNING MORE THAN YOU SOON. I CAN'T JUST STOP WHEN I'M ON A ROLL.
WELL, DON'T COUNT ON ME TO BAIL YOU OUT.
WHAT?
YOU WOULDN'T EVEN BE DANCING IF IT WASN'T FOR ME!
?
BOOO...SNIFF... SNIFF...HOOO...

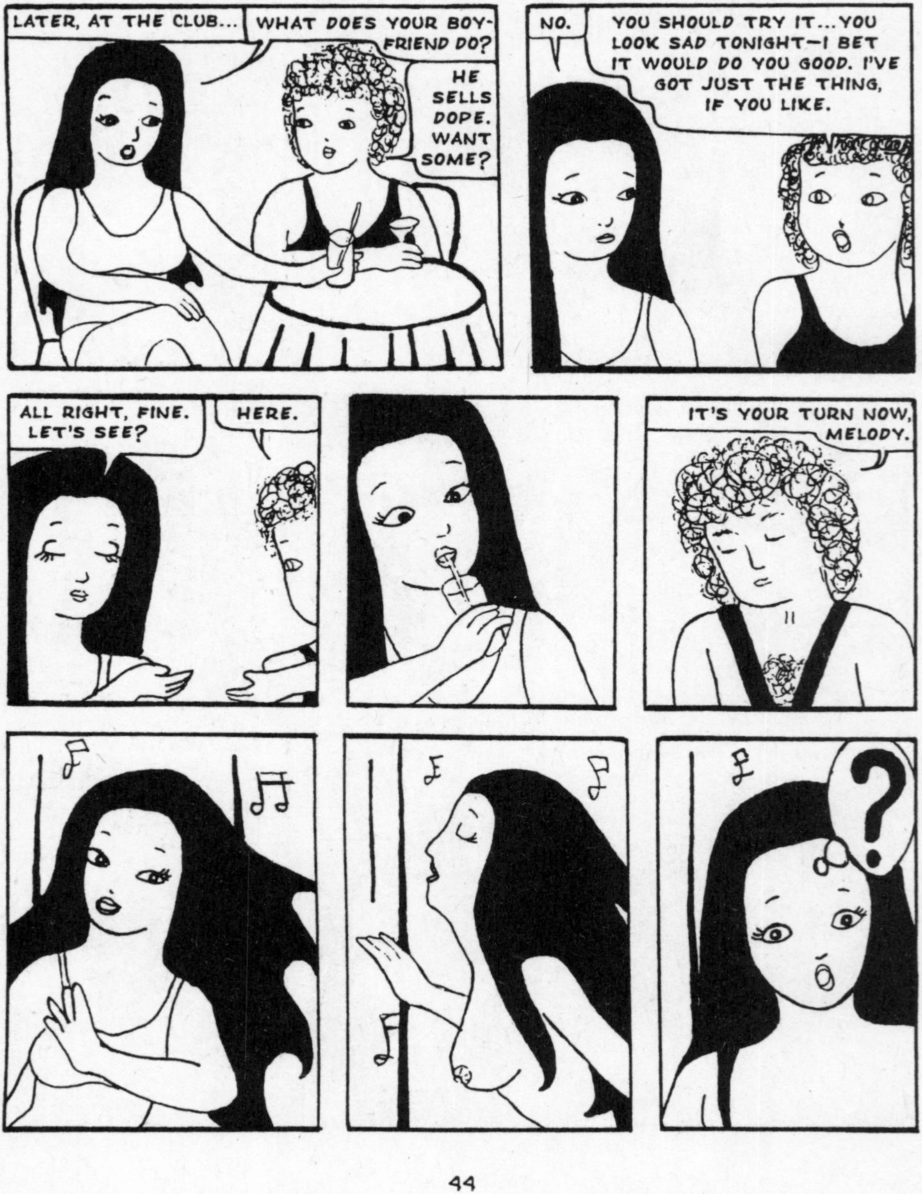
LATER, AT THE CLUB...
WHAT DOES YOUR BOY-FRIEND DO?
HE SELLS DOPE. WANT SOME?
NO.
YOU SHOULD TRY IT...YOU LOOK SAD TONIGHT—I BET IT WOULD DO YOU GOOD. I'VE GOT JUST THE THING, IF YOU LIKE.
ALL RIGHT, FINE. LET'S SEE?
HERE.
IT'S YOUR TURN NOW, MELODY.
?

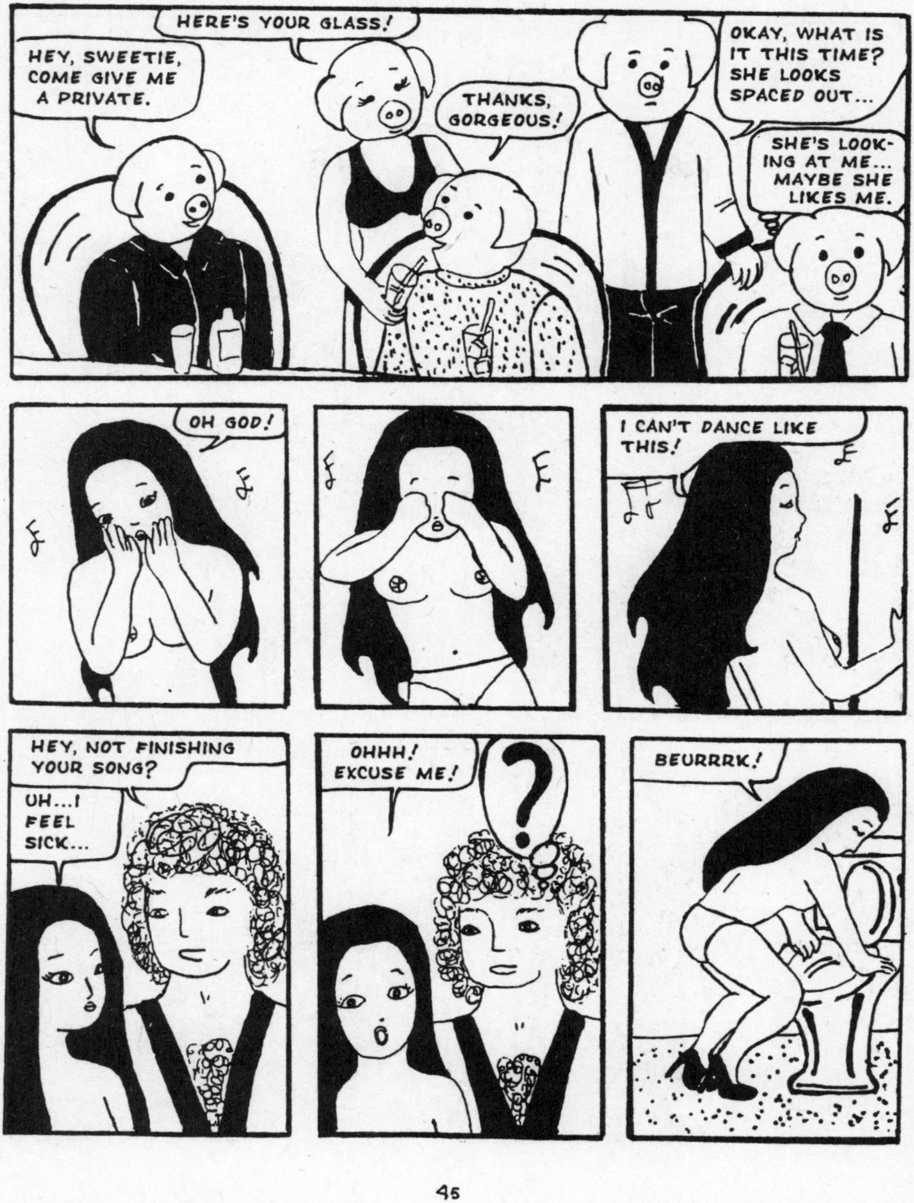
HEY, SWEETIE, COME GIVE ME A PRIVATE.
HERE'S YOUR GLASS!
THANKS, GORGEOUS!
OKAY, WHAT IS IT THIS TIME? SHE LOOKS SPACED OUT...
SHE'S LOOKING AT ME... MAYBE SHE LIKES ME.
OH GOD!
I CAN'T DANCE LIKE THIS!
HEY, NOT FINISHING YOUR SONG?
UH...I FEEL SICK...
OHHH! EXCUSE ME!
?
BEURRRK!

BETTER NOW?
NO, NOT REALLY!
OKAY, GO REST UP A BIT IN THE DRESSING ROOM.
TWO HOURS LATER...
YOU SEEN MELODY?
NO!
I HAVEN'T SEEN HER IN A WHILE...
I WONDER WHAT SHE'S UP TO NOW?
?
ZZZ...ZZZ...

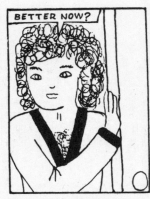

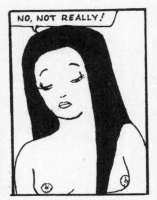

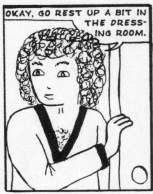

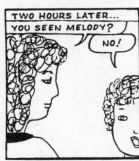

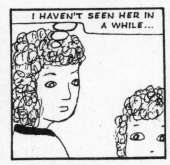

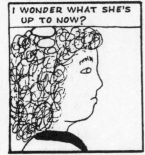

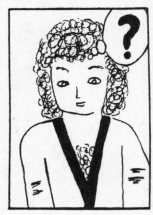

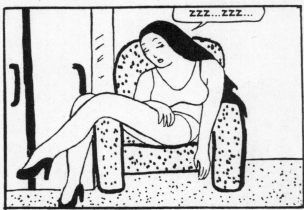

MELODY!
HM...
OOH!
GET YOURSELF BACK OUT THERE!
DARN!
MELODY AND LOUISELLE, C'MERE!
YOU TWO ARE GOING TO DO A NUMBER TOGETHER!
?
?
GOT ANY IDEAS?
NOT REALLY...I'VE NEVER DONE A DOUBLE BEFORE!

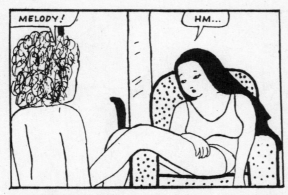

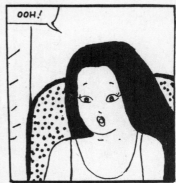

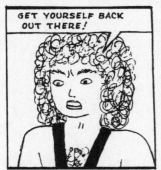

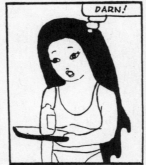

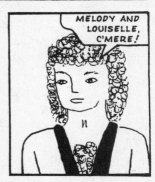

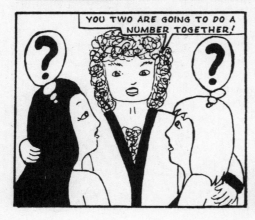

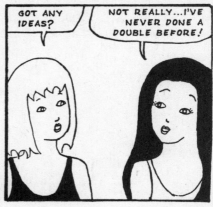

DOUBLE TREAT TONIGHT, GENTLEMEN!
MMM...I'D GIVE ANYTHING TO SEE THAT IN MY LIVING ROOM!
TWO HOT CHICKS TOGETHER! TALK ABOUT A TURN-ON!
YES...VERY INTERESTING!

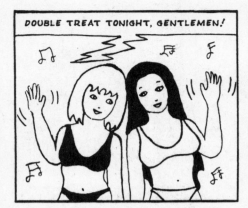

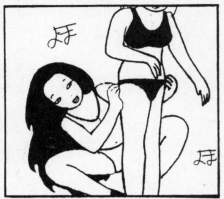

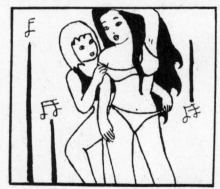

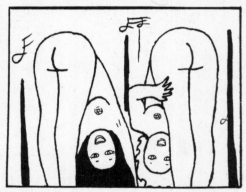

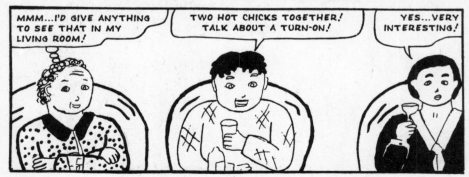

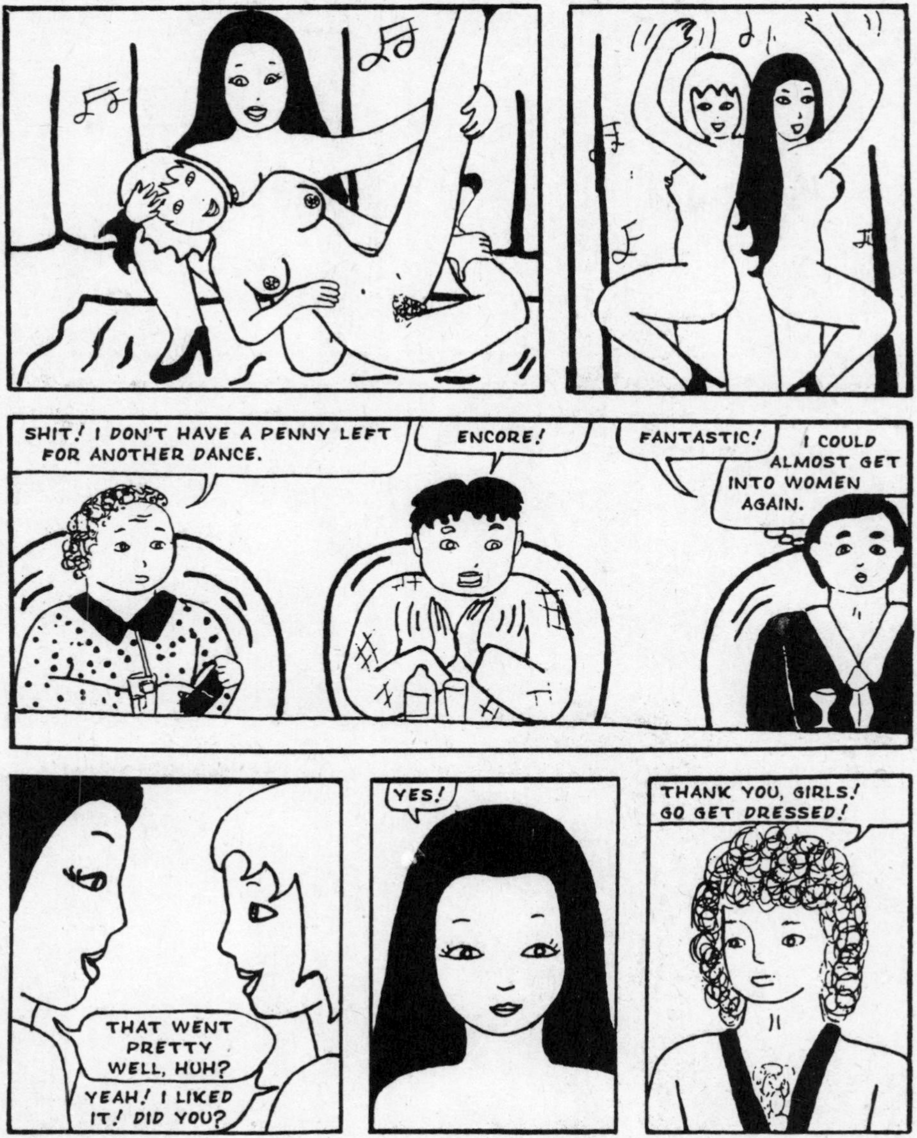

SHIT! I DON'T HAVE A PENNY LEFT FOR ANOTHER DANCE.
ENCORE!
FANTASTIC!
I COULD ALMOST GET INTO WOMEN AGAIN.
THAT WENT PRETTY WELL, HUH?
YEAH! I LIKED IT! DID YOU?
YES!
THANK YOU, GIRLS! GO GET DRESSED!

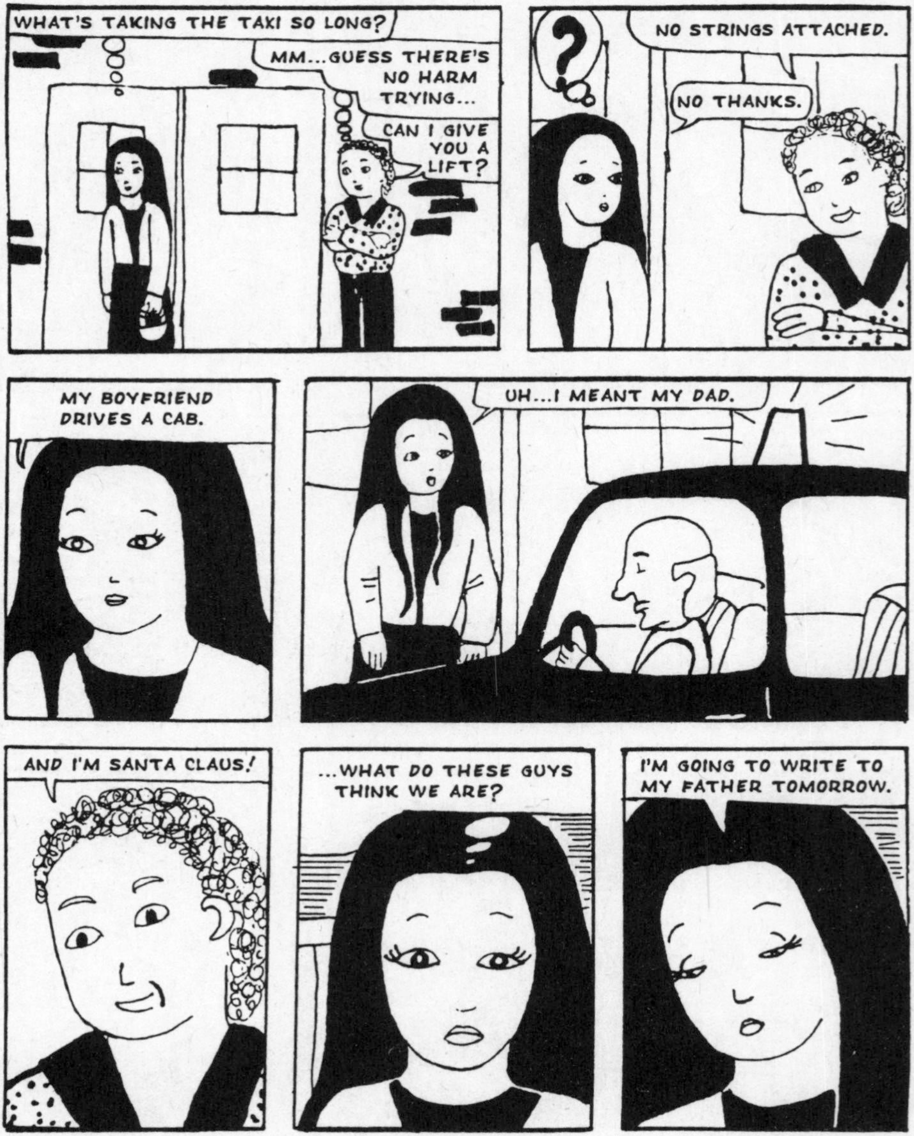

WHAT'S TAKING THE TAXI SO LONG?
MM...GUESS THERE'S NO HARM TRYING...
CAN I GIVE YOU A LIFT?
?
NO STRINGS ATTACHED.
NO THANKS.
MY BOYFRIEND DRIVES A CAB.
UH...I MEANT MY DAD.
AND I'M SANTA CLAUS!
...WHAT DO THESE GUYS THINK WE ARE?
I'M GOING TO WRITE TO MY FATHER TOMORROW.

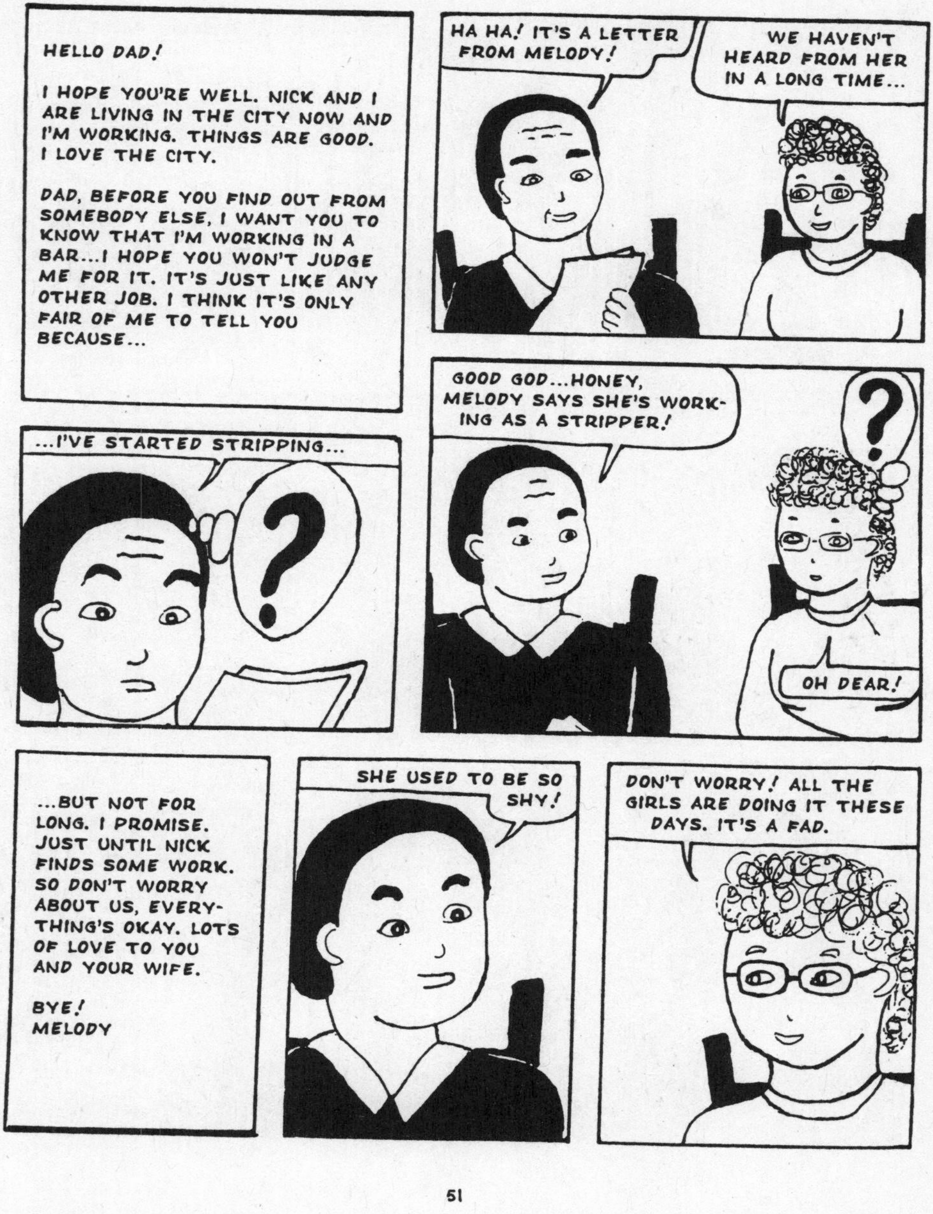
HELLO DAD!
I HOPE YOU'RE WELL. NICK AND I ARE LIVING IN THE CITY NOW AND I'M WORKING. THINGS ARE GOOD. I LOVE THE CITY.
DAD, BEFORE YOU FIND OUT FROM SOMEBODY ELSE, I WANT YOU TO KNOW THAT I'M WORKING IN A BAR...I HOPE YOU WON'T JUDGE ME FOR IT. IT'S JUST LIKE ANY OTHER JOB. I THINK IT'S ONLY FAIR OF ME TO TELL YOU BECAUSE...
HA HA! IT'S A LETTER FROM MELODY!
WE HAVEN'T HEARD FROM HER IN A LONG TIME...
...I'VE STARTED STRIPPING...
?
GOOD GOD...HONEY, MELODY SAYS SHE'S WORKING AS A STRIPPER!
?
OH DEAR!
...BUT NOT FOR LONG. I PROMISE. JUST UNTIL NICK FINDS SOME WORK. SO DON'T WORRY ABOUT US, EVERYTHING'S OKAY. LOTS OF LOVE TO YOU AND YOUR WIFE.
BYE!
MELODY
SHE USED TO BE SO SHY!
DON'T WORRY! ALL THE GIRLS ARE DOING IT THESE DAYS. IT'S A FAD.

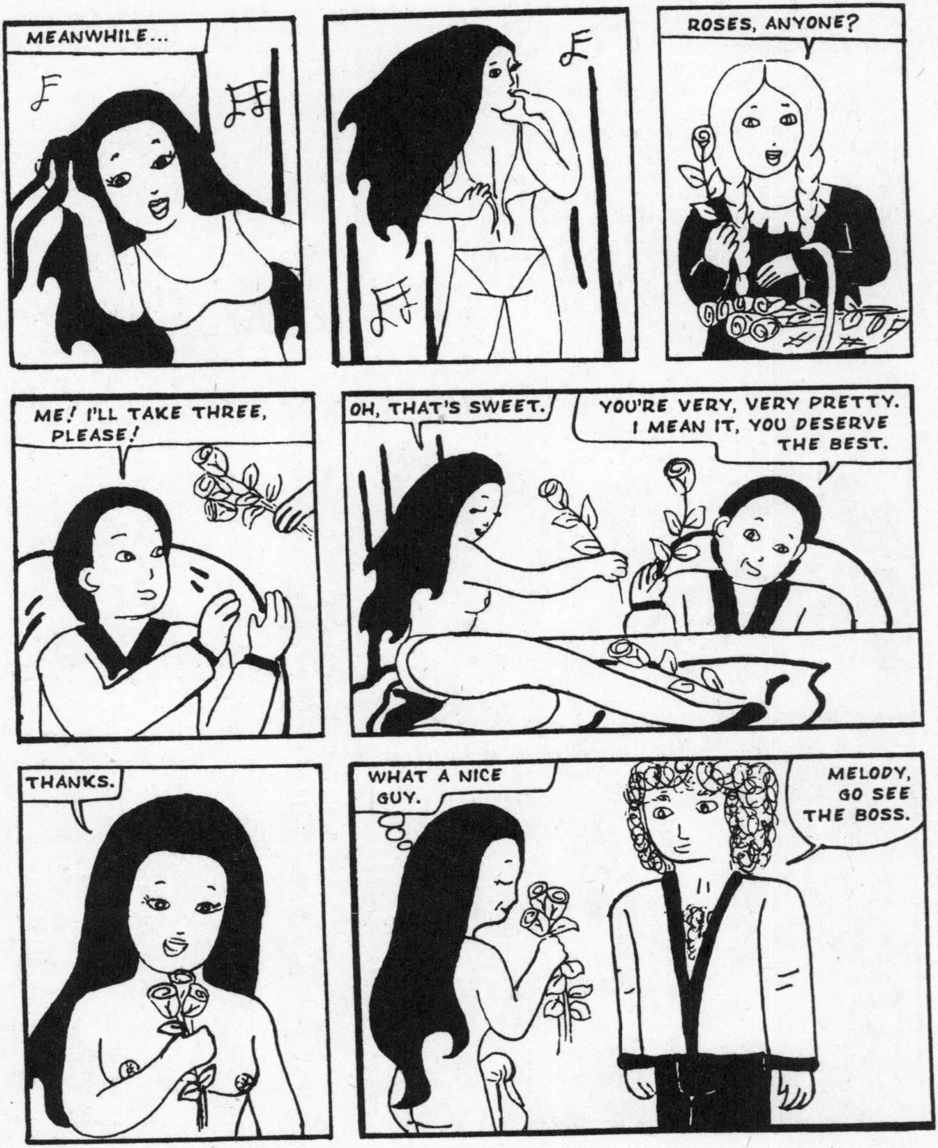

MEANWHILE...
ROSES, ANYONE?
ME! I'LL TAKE THREE, PLEASE!
OH, THAT'S SWEET.
YOU'RE VERY, VERY PRETTY. I MEAN IT, YOU DESERVE THE BEST.
THANKS.
WHAT A NICE GUY.
MELODY, GO SEE THE BOSS.

WHAT'S HE WANT FROM ME?

HOW ARE YOU?

GOOD.

I'VE GOT YOUR PAY-CHEQUE FOR YOU.

OH, OKAY!

THINK YOU'D LIKE TO STAY ON HERE?

UH...THAT DEPENDS...

LISTEN...YOU DON'T NEED TO WORRY BECAUSE OF LAST TIME.

ALL RIGHT, I'LL STAY.

EXCELLENT. YOU'RE DOING GREAT FOR A BEGINNER.

GOODNIGHT! SEE YOU TOMORROW!

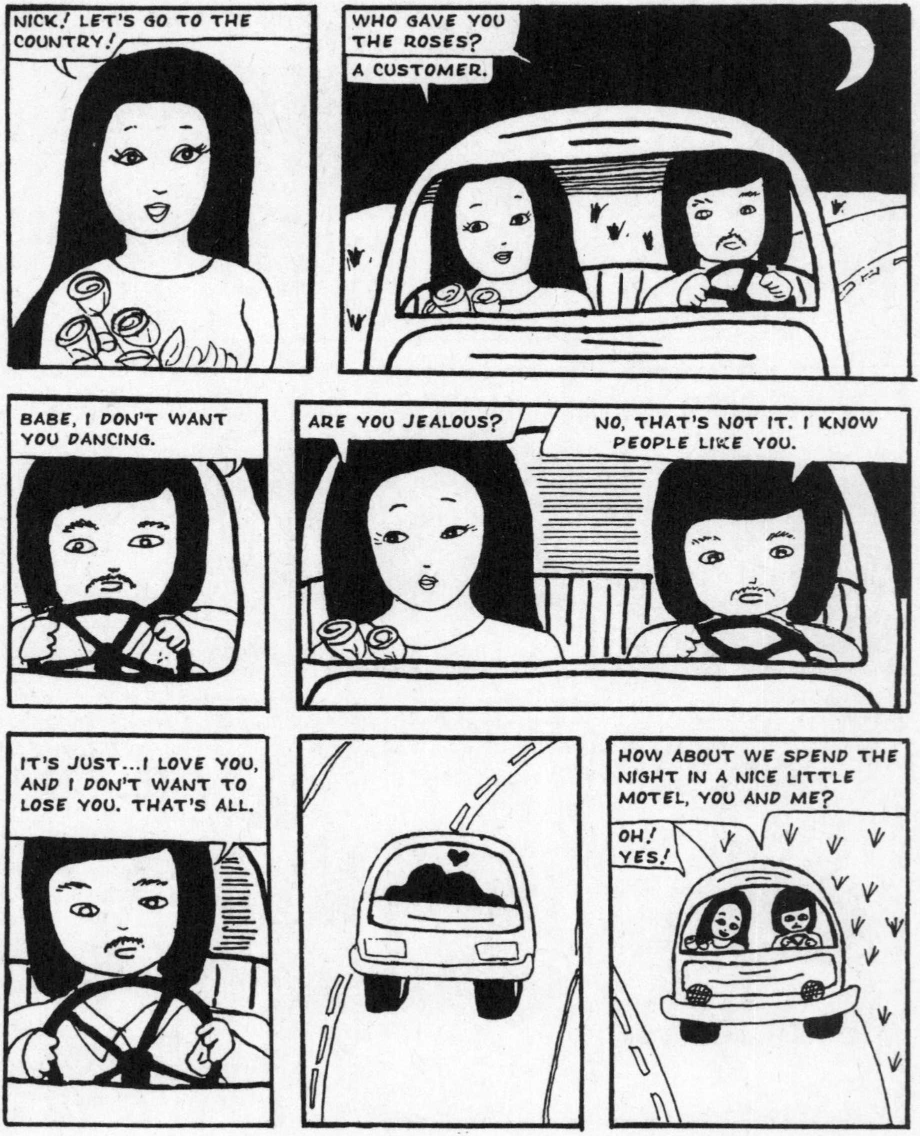
NICK! LET'S GO TO THE COUNTRY!
WHO GAVE YOU THE ROSES?
A CUSTOMER.
BABE, I DON'T WANT YOU DANCING.
ARE YOU JEALOUS?
NO, THAT'S NOT IT. I KNOW PEOPLE LIKE YOU.
IT'S JUST...I LOVE YOU, AND I DON'T WANT TO LOSE YOU. THAT'S ALL.
HOW ABOUT WE SPEND THE NIGHT IN A NICE LITTLE MOTEL, YOU AND ME?
OH! YES!

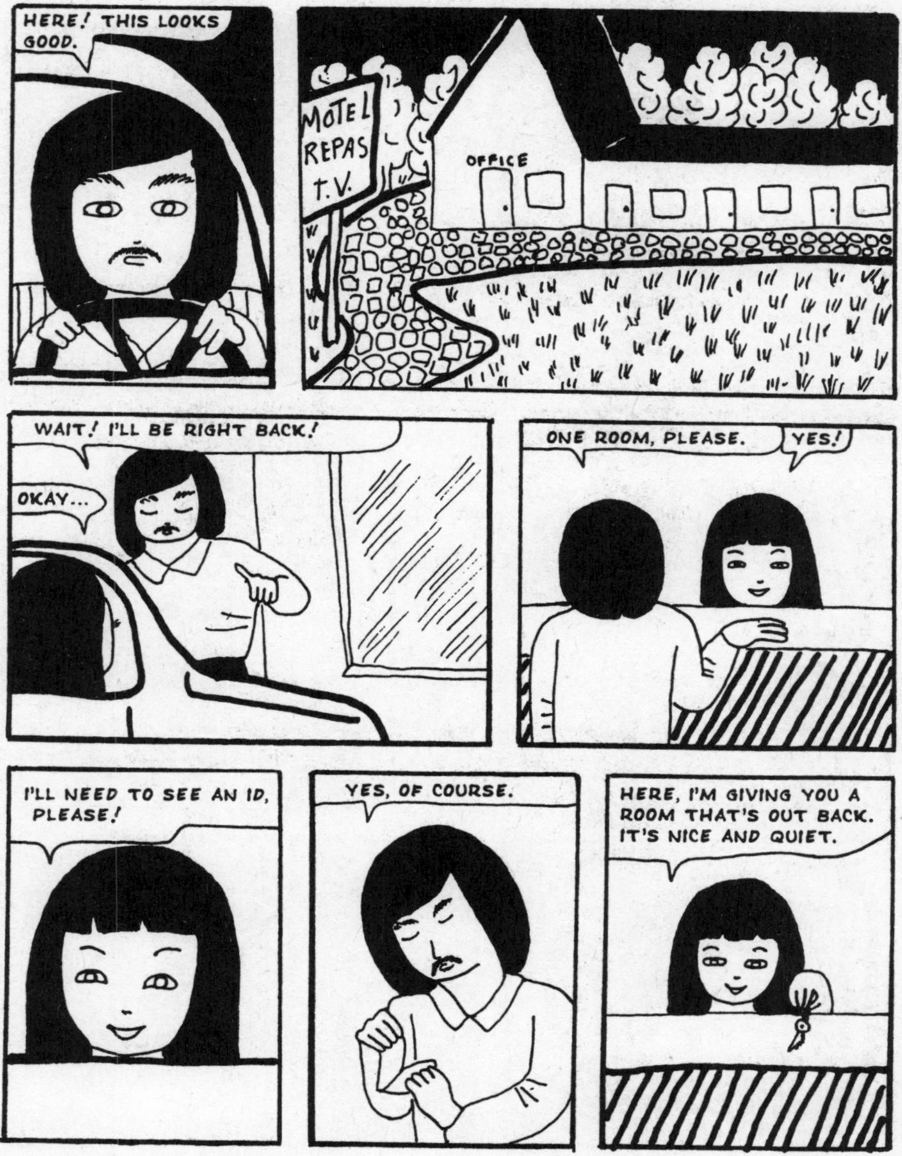
HERE! THIS LOOKS GOOD.
MOTEL
REPAS
T.V.
OFFICE
WAIT! I'LL BE RIGHT BACK!
OKAY...
ONE ROOM, PLEASE.
YES!
I'LL NEED TO SEE AN ID, PLEASE!
YES, OF COURSE.
HERE, I'M GIVING YOU A ROOM THAT'S OUT BACK. IT'S NICE AND QUIET.

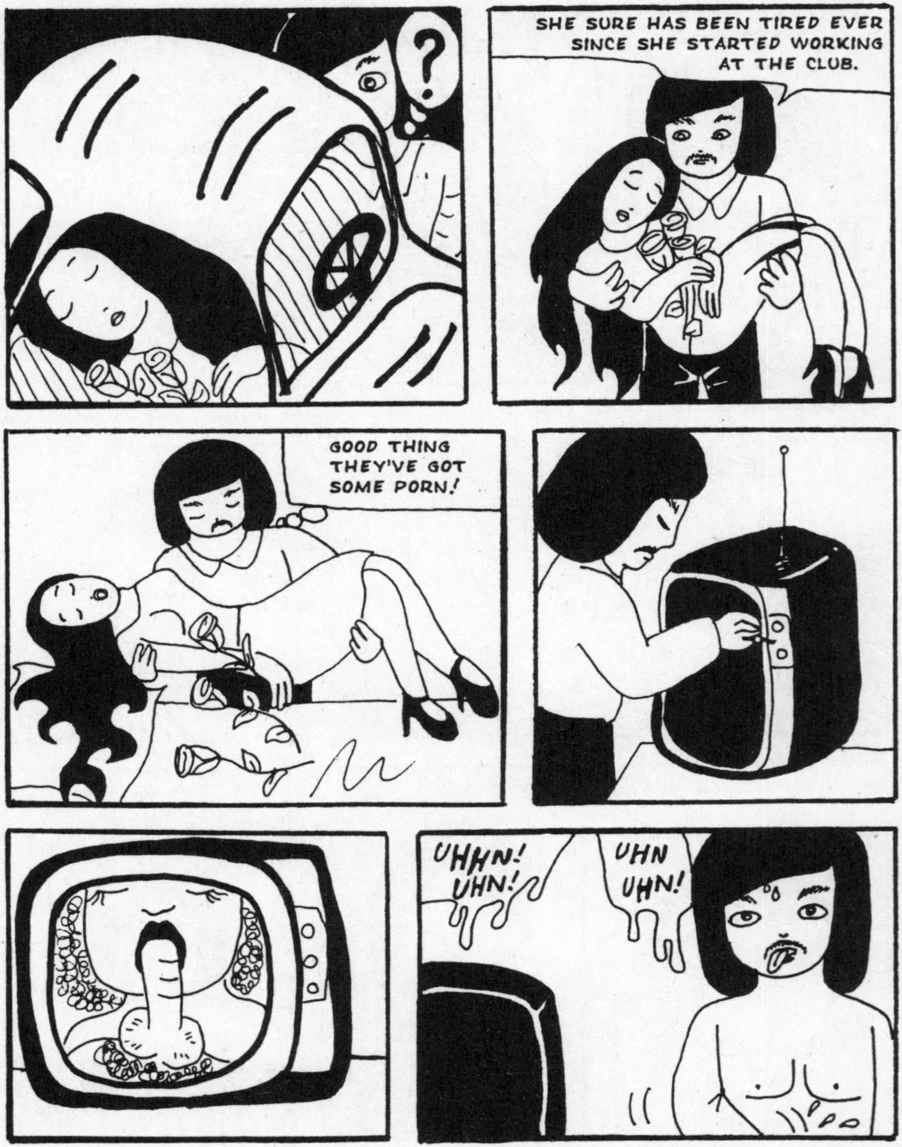
SHE SURE HAS BEEN TIRED EVER SINCE SHE STARTED WORKING AT THE CLUB.
GOOD THING THEY'VE GOT SOME PORN!
UHHN! UHN!
UHN UHN!

THE END
?
THE END?
HEY! I'M NOT DONE YET!

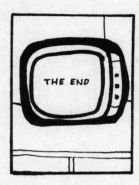

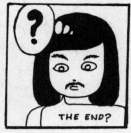

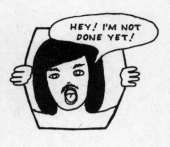

Melody and
Her Dolls

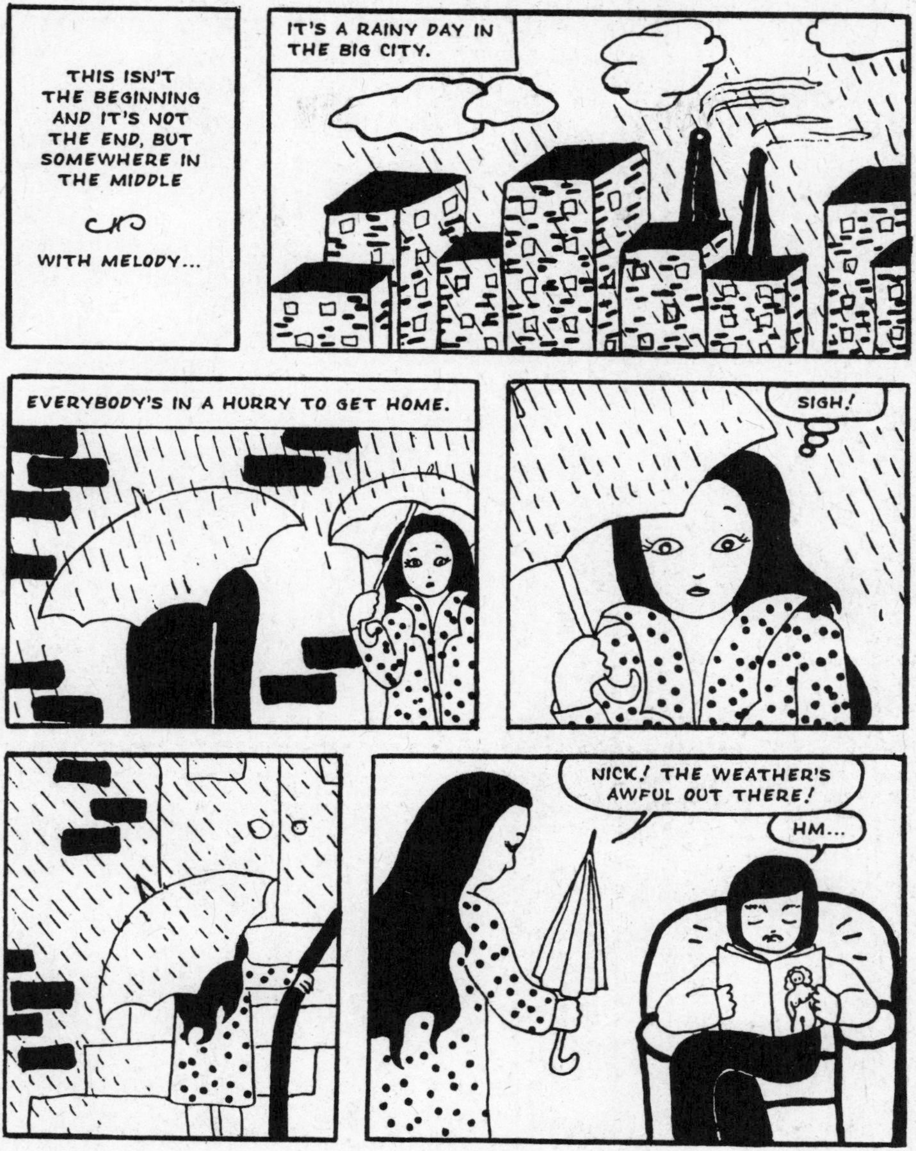
THIS ISN'T THE BEGINNING AND IT'S NOT THE END, BUT SOMEWHERE IN THE MIDDLE
WITH MELODY...
IT'S A RAINY DAY IN THE BIG CITY.
EVERYBODY'S IN A HURRY TO GET HOME.
SIGH!
NICK! THE WEATHER'S AWFUL OUT THERE!
HM...

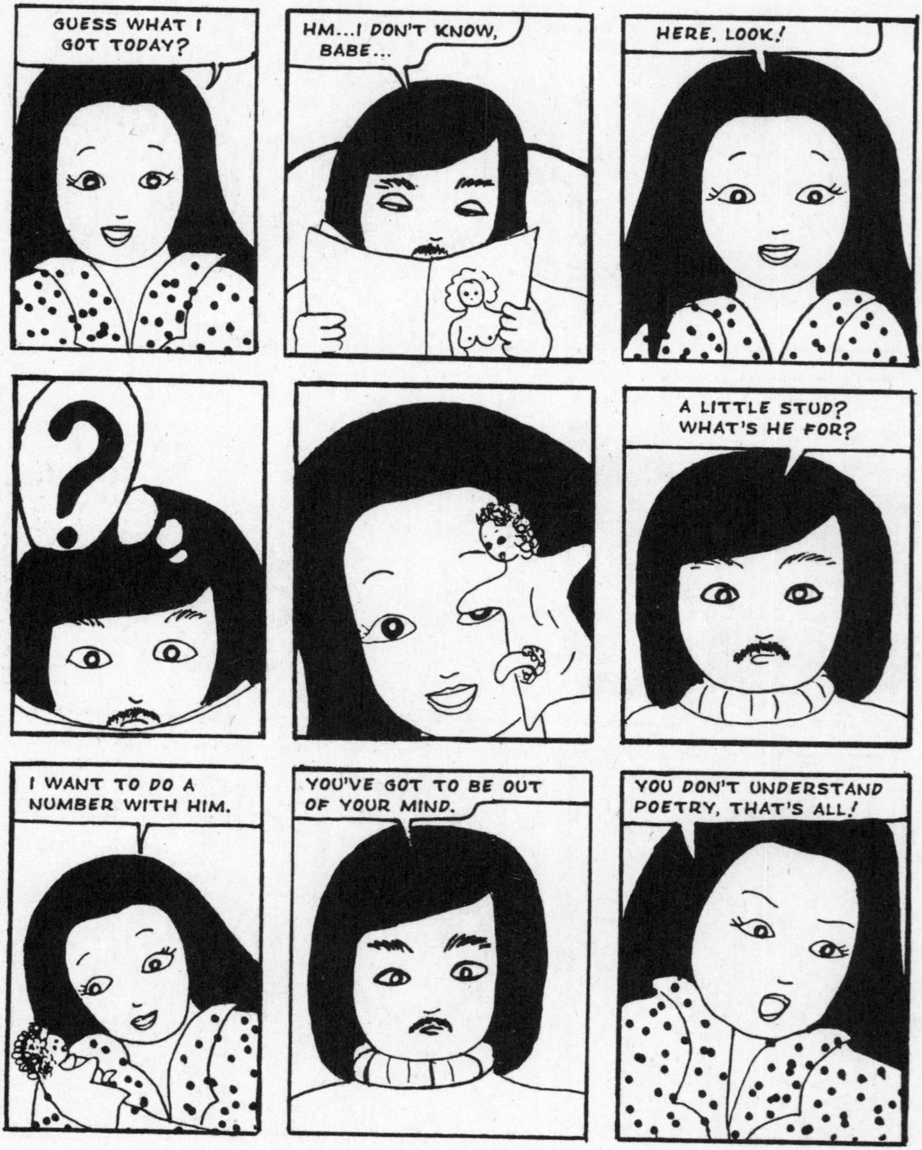
GUESS WHAT I GOT TODAY?
HM...I DON'T KNOW, BABE...
HERE, LOOK!
A LITTLE STUD? WHAT'S HE FOR?
I WANT TO DO A NUMBER WITH HIM.
YOU'VE GOT TO BE OUT OF YOUR MIND.
YOU DON'T UNDERSTAND POETRY, THAT'S ALL!

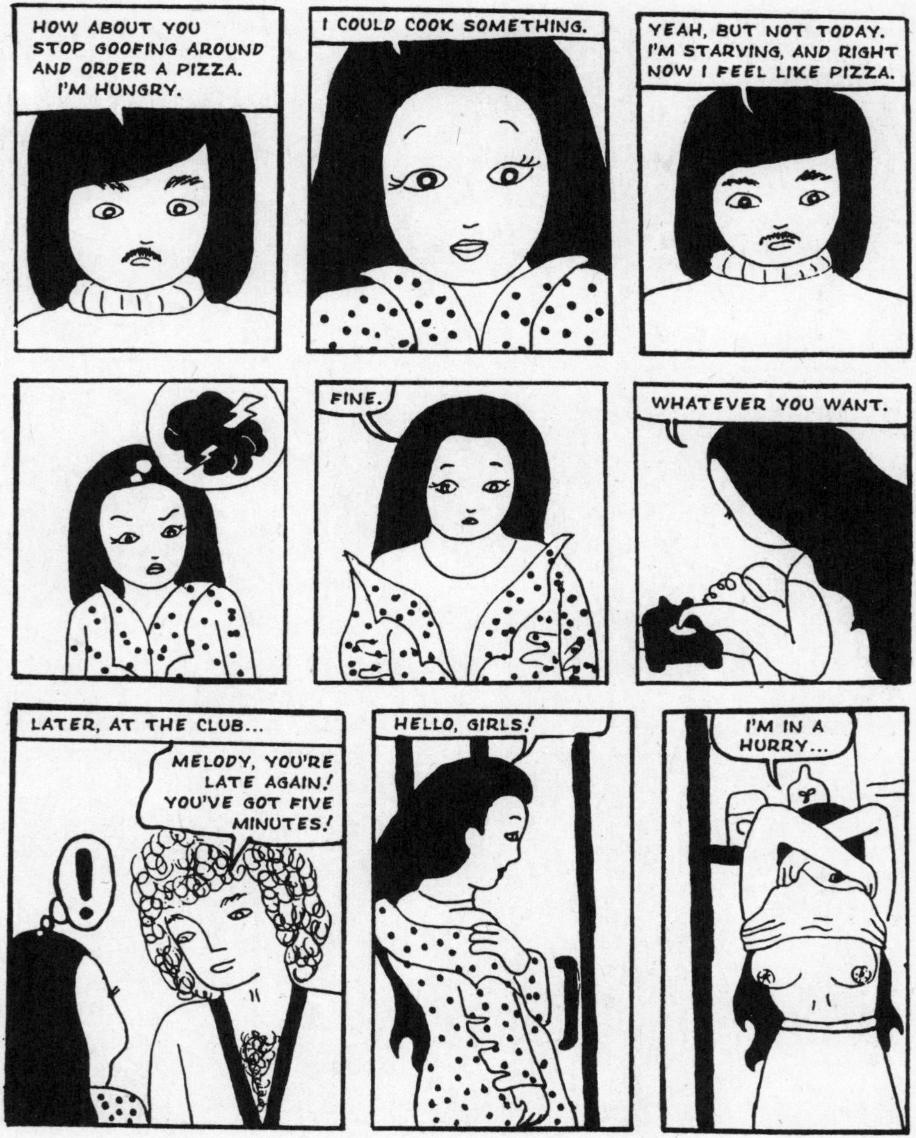
HOW ABOUT YOU STOP GOOFING AROUND AND ORDER A PIZZA. I'M HUNGRY.
I COULD COOK SOMETHING.
YEAH, BUT NOT TODAY. I'M STARVING, AND RIGHT NOW I FEEL LIKE PIZZA.
FINE.
WHATEVER YOU WANT.
LATER, AT THE CLUB...
MELODY, YOU'RE LATE AGAIN! YOU'VE GOT FIVE MINUTES!
!
HELLO, GIRLS!
I'M IN A HURRY...

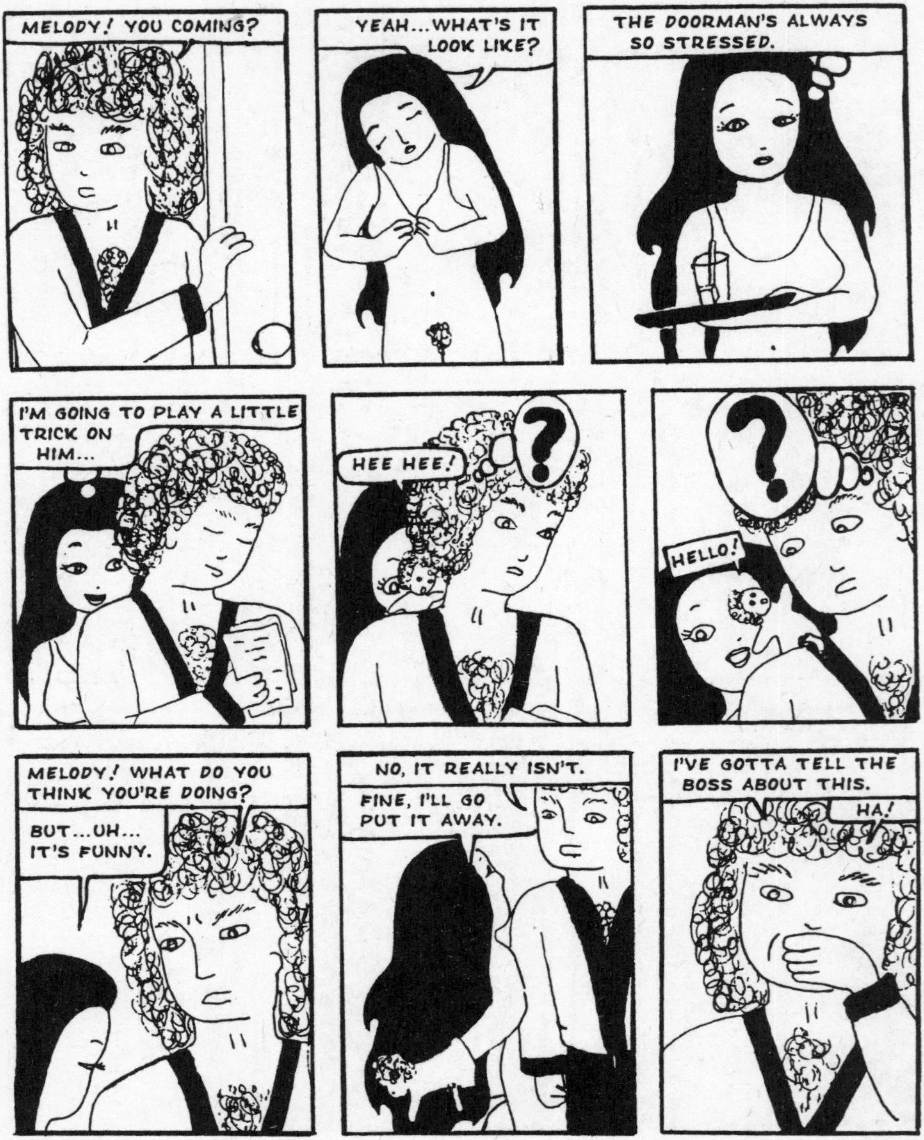
MELODY! YOU COMING?
YEAH...WHAT'S IT LOOK LIKE?
THE DOORMAN'S ALWAYS SO STRESSED.
I'M GOING TO PLAY A LITTLE TRICK ON HIM...
HEE HEE!
?
?
HELLO!
MELODY! WHAT DO YOU THINK YOU'RE DOING?
BUT...UH... IT'S FUNNY.
NO, IT REALLY ISN'T.
FINE, I'LL GO PUT IT AWAY.
I'VE GOTTA TELL THE BOSS ABOUT THIS.
HA!

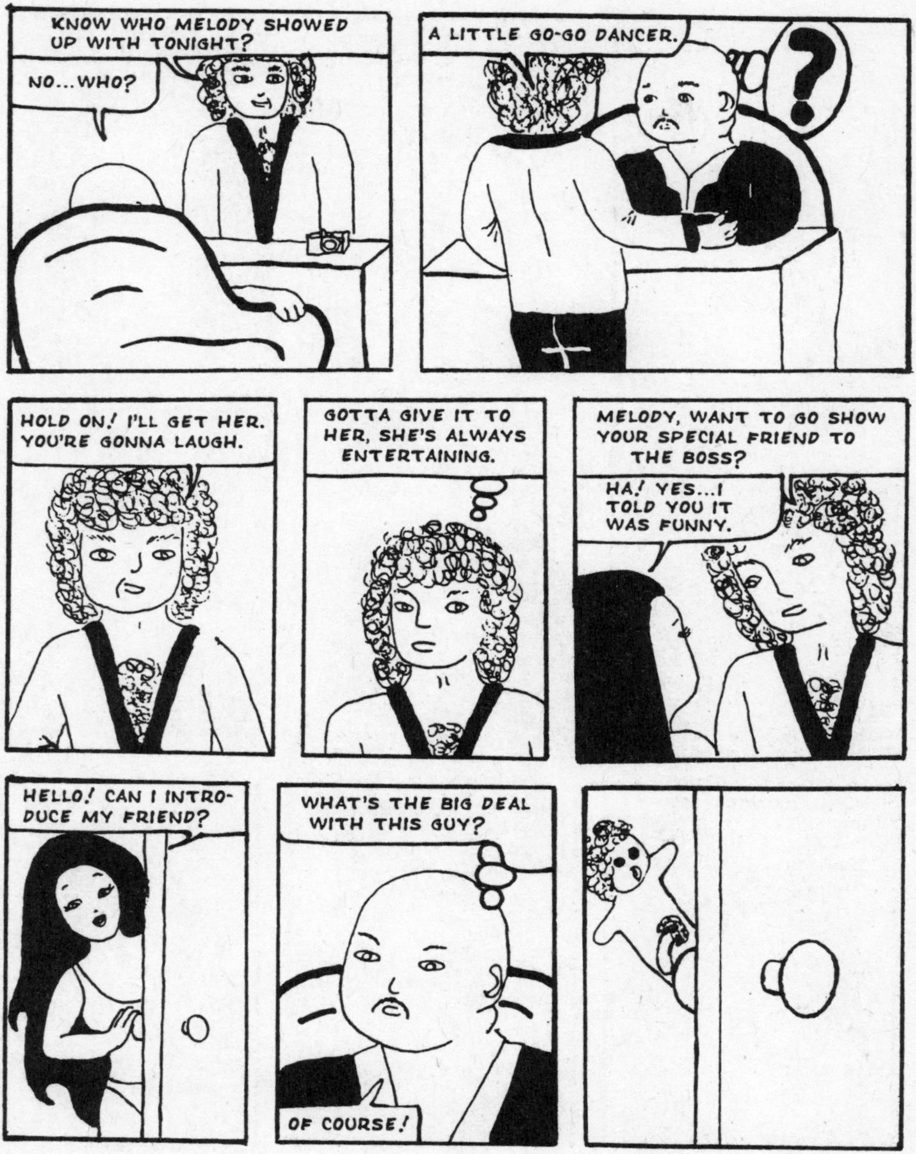
KNOW WHO MELODY SHOWED UP WITH TONIGHT?
NO...WHO?
A LITTLE GO-GO DANCER.
?
HOLD ON! I'LL GET HER. YOU'RE GONNA LAUGH.
GOTTA GIVE IT TO HER, SHE'S ALWAYS ENTERTAINING.
MELODY, WANT TO GO SHOW YOUR SPECIAL FRIEND TO THE BOSS?
HA! YES...I TOLD YOU IT WAS FUNNY.
HELLO! CAN I INTRODUCE MY FRIEND?
WHAT'S THE BIG DEAL WITH THIS GUY?
OF COURSE!

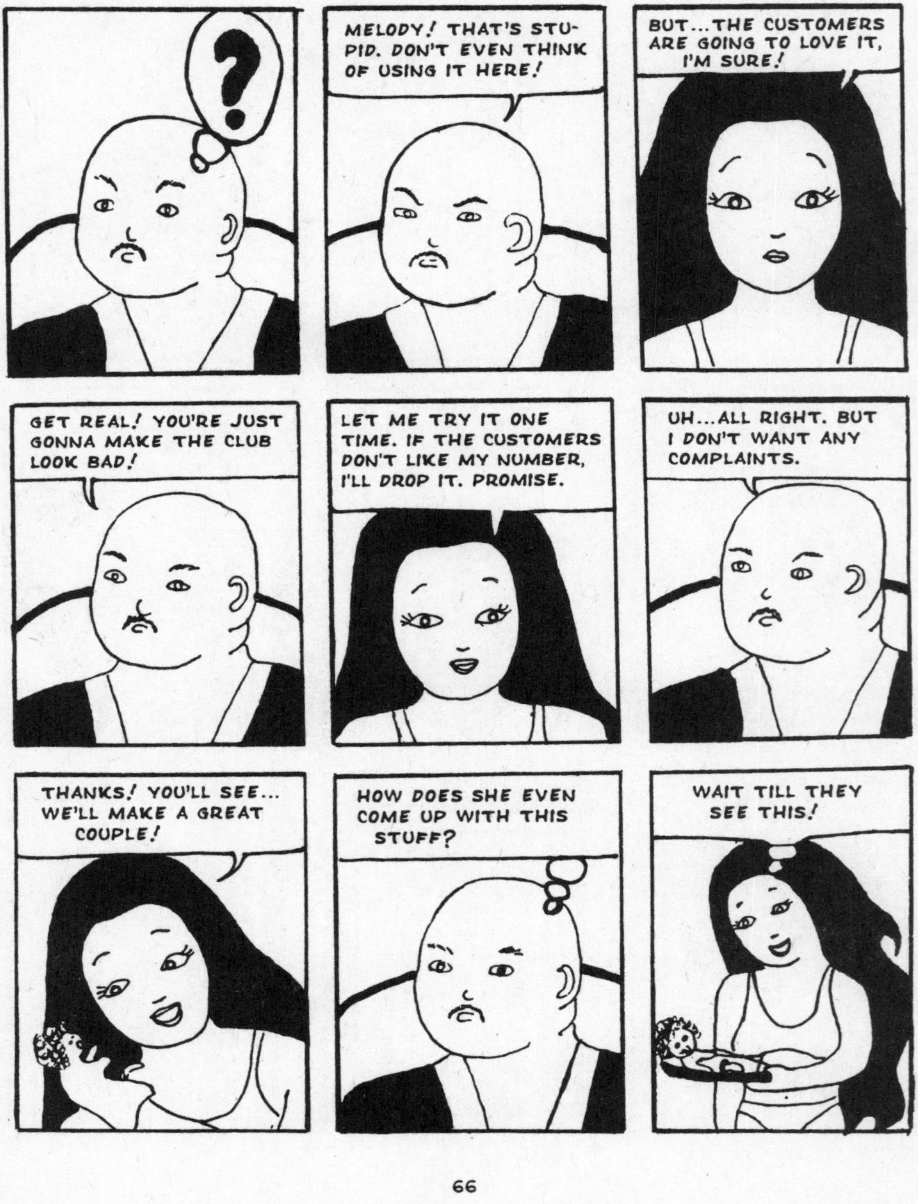
?
MELODY! THAT'S STUPID. DON'T EVEN THINK OF USING IT HERE!
BUT... THE CUSTOMERS ARE GOING TO LOVE IT, I'M SURE!
GET REAL! YOU'RE JUST GONNA MAKE THE CLUB LOOK BAD!
LET ME TRY IT ONE TIME. IF THE CUSTOMERS DON'T LIKE MY NUMBER, I'LL DROP IT. PROMISE.
UH... ALL RIGHT. BUT I DON'T WANT ANY COMPLAINTS.
THANKS! YOU'LL SEE... WE'LL MAKE A GREAT COUPLE!
HOW DOES SHE EVEN COME UP WITH THIS STUFF?
WAIT TILL THEY SEE THIS!

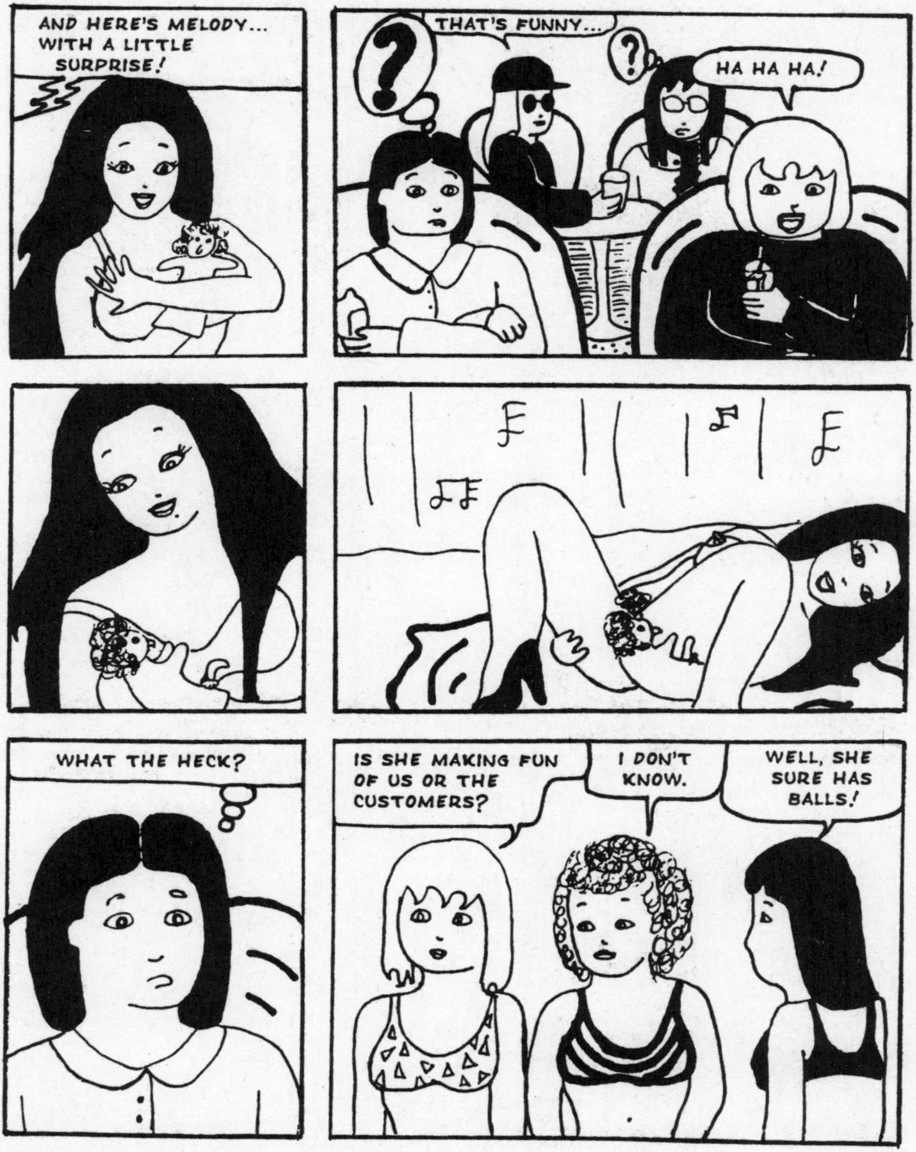
AND HERE'S MELODY... WITH A LITTLE SURPRISE!
THAT'S FUNNY...
HA HA HA!
WHAT THE HECK?
IS SHE MAKING FUN OF US OR THE CUSTOMERS?
I DON'T KNOW.
WELL, SHE SURE HAS BALLS!

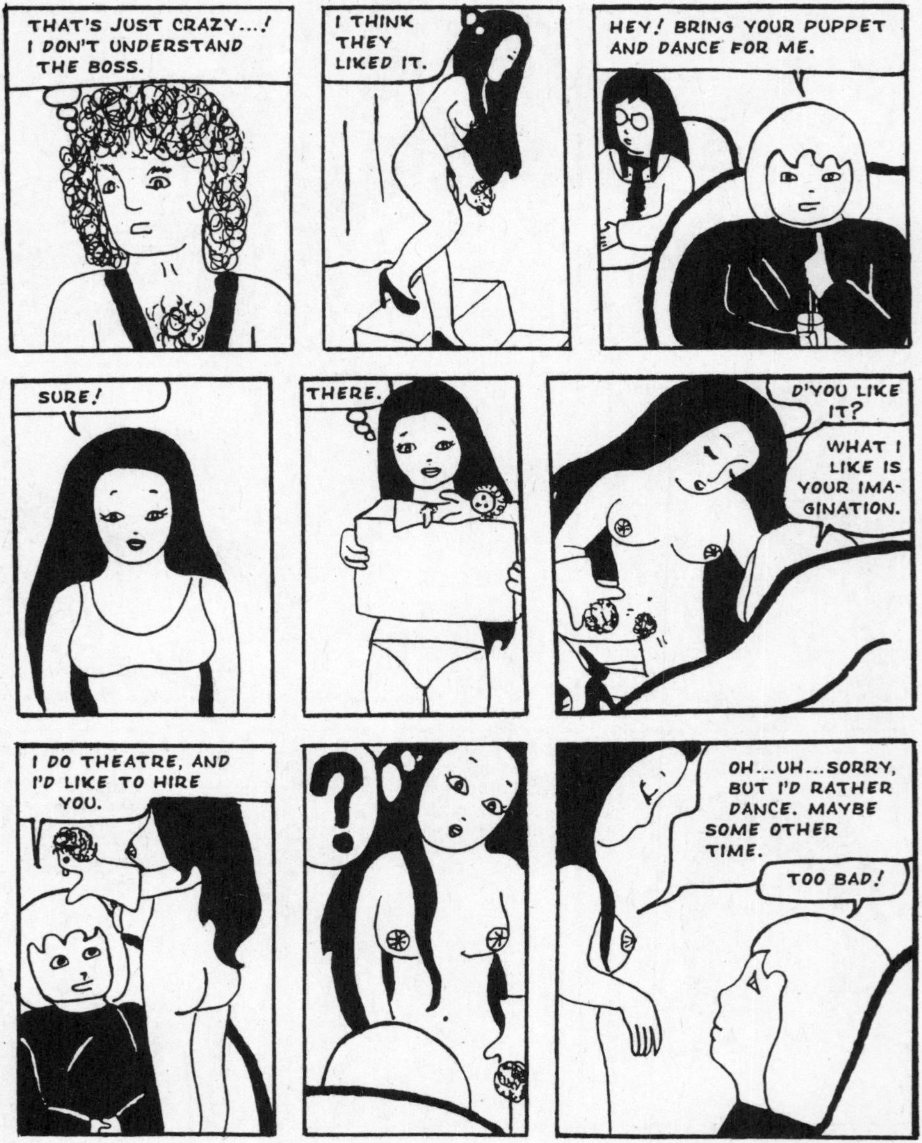

THAT'S JUST CRAZY...! I DON'T UNDERSTAND THE BOSS.
I THINK THEY LIKED IT.
HEY! BRING YOUR PUPPET AND DANCE FOR ME.
SURE!
THERE.
D'YOU LIKE IT?
WHAT I LIKE IS YOUR IMAGINATION.
I DO THEATRE, AND I'D LIKE TO HIRE YOU.
?
OH...UH...SORRY, BUT I'D RATHER DANCE. MAYBE SOME OTHER TIME.
TOO BAD!

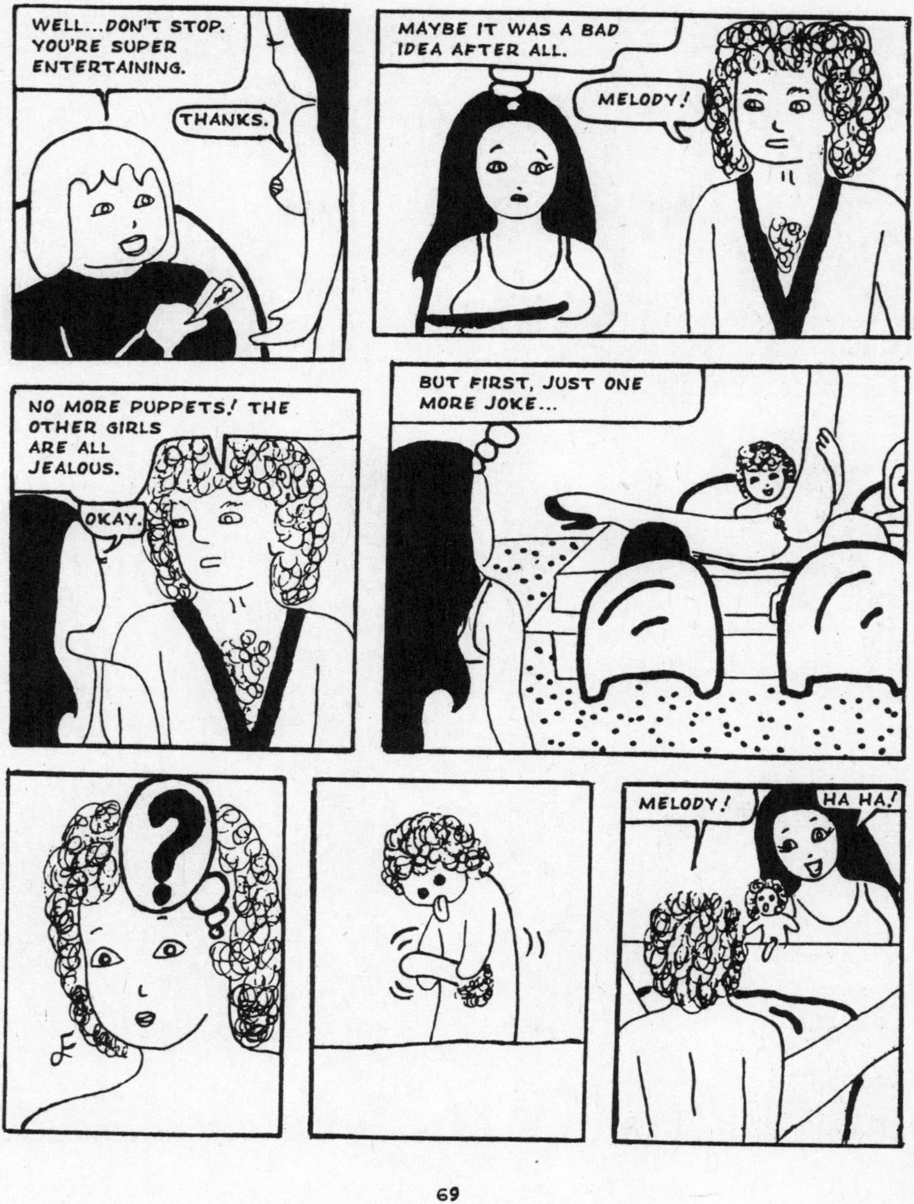
WELL...DON'T STOP. YOU'RE SUPER ENTERTAINING.
THANKS.
MAYBE IT WAS A BAD IDEA AFTER ALL.
MELODY!
NO MORE PUPPETS! THE OTHER GIRLS ARE ALL JEALOUS.
OKAY.
BUT FIRST, JUST ONE MORE JOKE...
?
MELODY!
HA HA!

MELODY! YOU'RE OUT OF LINE. I'M CONFISCATING THIS.

AFTER HER SHIFT, MELODY GOES BACK HOME...

NICK!

MUST BE ASLEEP.

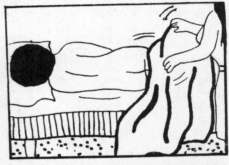

MELODY! WHAT'RE YOU DOING?

NOTHING...I JUST WANTED TO SEE HOW HANDSOME YOU ARE!

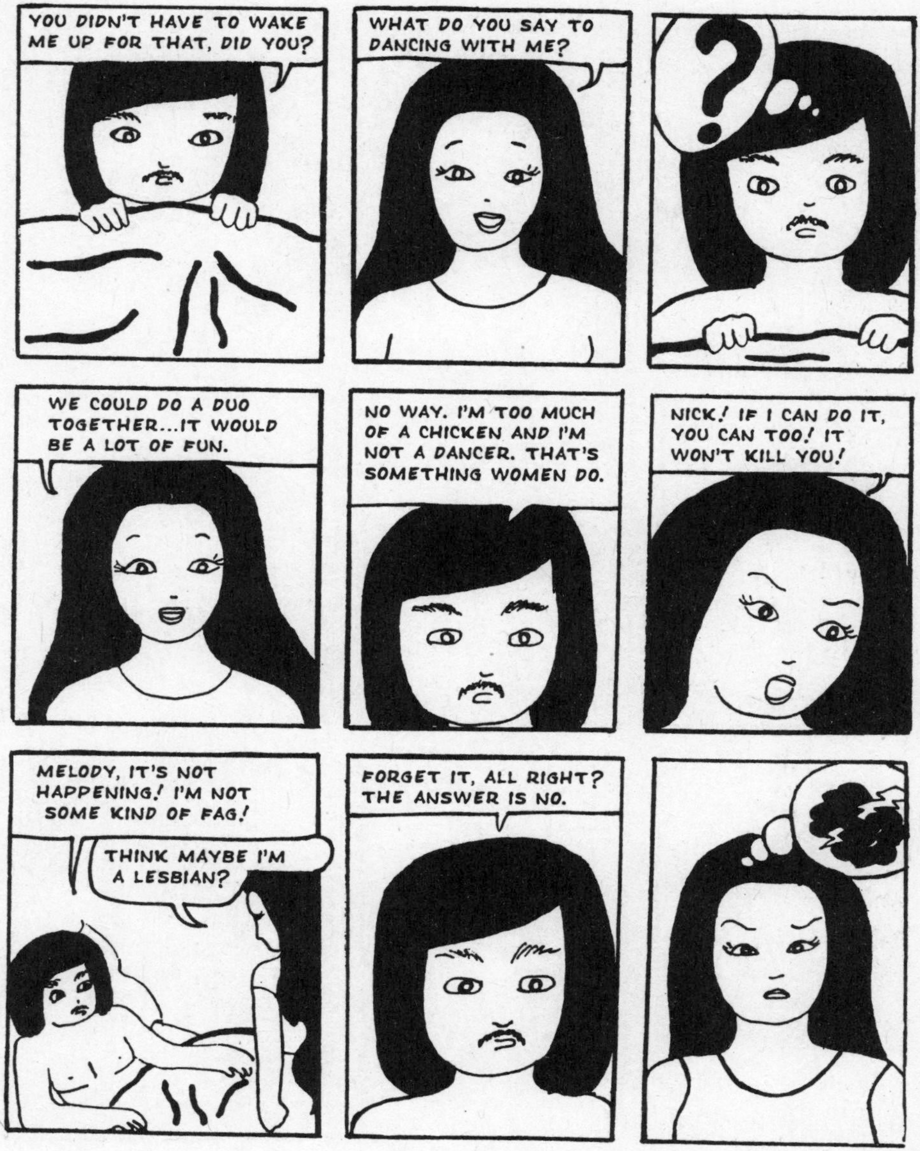
YOU DIDN'T HAVE TO WAKE ME UP FOR THAT, DID YOU?
WHAT DO YOU SAY TO DANCING WITH ME?
?
WE COULD DO A DUO TOGETHER...IT WOULD BE A LOT OF FUN.
NO WAY. I'M TOO MUCH OF A CHICKEN AND I'M NOT A DANCER. THAT'S SOMETHING WOMEN DO.
NICK! IF I CAN DO IT, YOU CAN TOO! IT WON'T KILL YOU!
MELODY, IT'S NOT HAPPENING! I'M NOT SOME KIND OF FAG!
THINK MAYBE I'M A LESBIAN?
FORGET IT, ALL RIGHT? THE ANSWER IS NO.

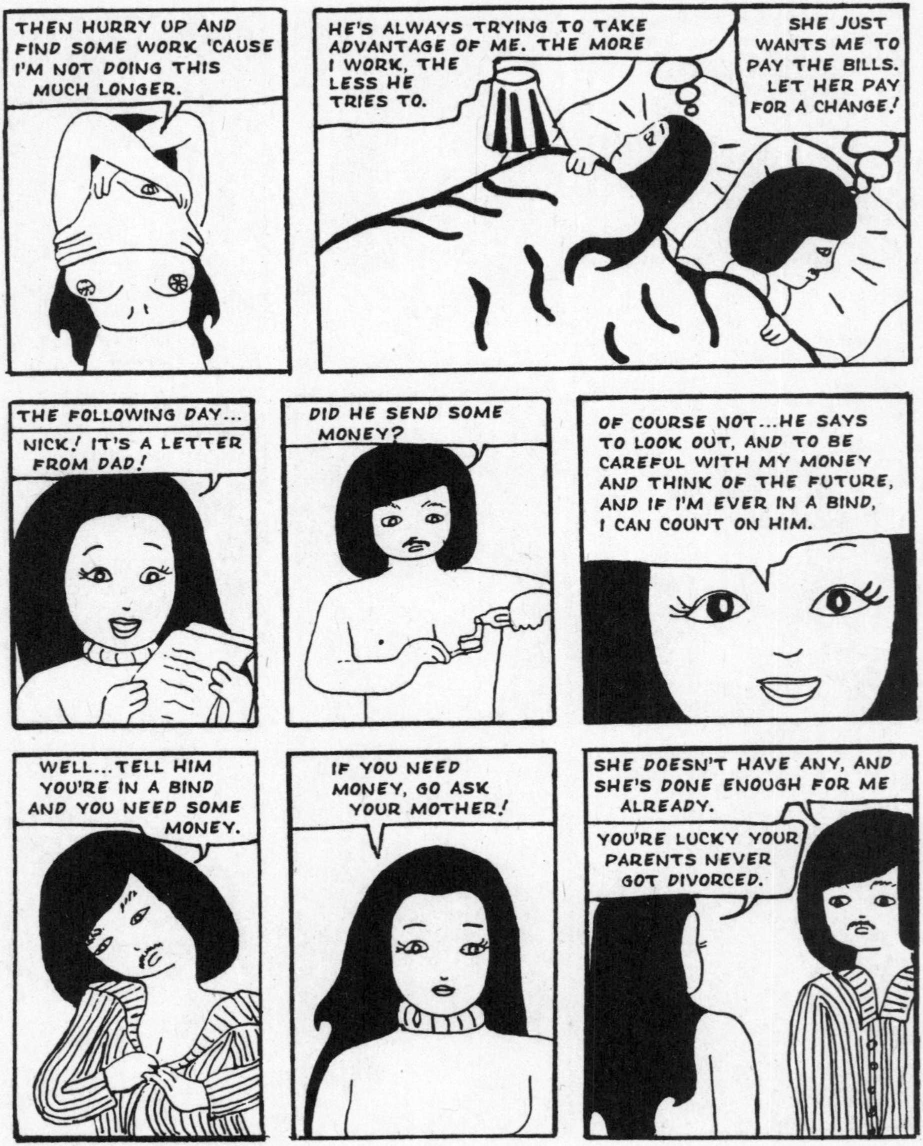
THEN HURRY UP AND FIND SOME WORK 'CAUSE I'M NOT DOING THIS MUCH LONGER.
HE'S ALWAYS TRYING TO TAKE ADVANTAGE OF ME. THE MORE I WORK, THE LESS HE TRIES TO.
SHE JUST WANTS ME TO PAY THE BILLS. LET HER PAY FOR A CHANGE!
THE FOLLOWING DAY...
NICK! IT'S A LETTER FROM DAD!
DID HE SEND SOME MONEY?
OF COURSE NOT...HE SAYS TO LOOK OUT, AND TO BE CAREFUL WITH MY MONEY AND THINK OF THE FUTURE, AND IF I'M EVER IN A BIND, I CAN COUNT ON HIM.
WELL...TELL HIM YOU'RE IN A BIND AND YOU NEED SOME MONEY.
IF YOU NEED MONEY, GO ASK YOUR MOTHER!
SHE DOESN'T HAVE ANY, AND SHE'S DONE ENOUGH FOR ME ALREADY.
YOU'RE LUCKY YOUR PARENTS NEVER GOT DIVORCED.

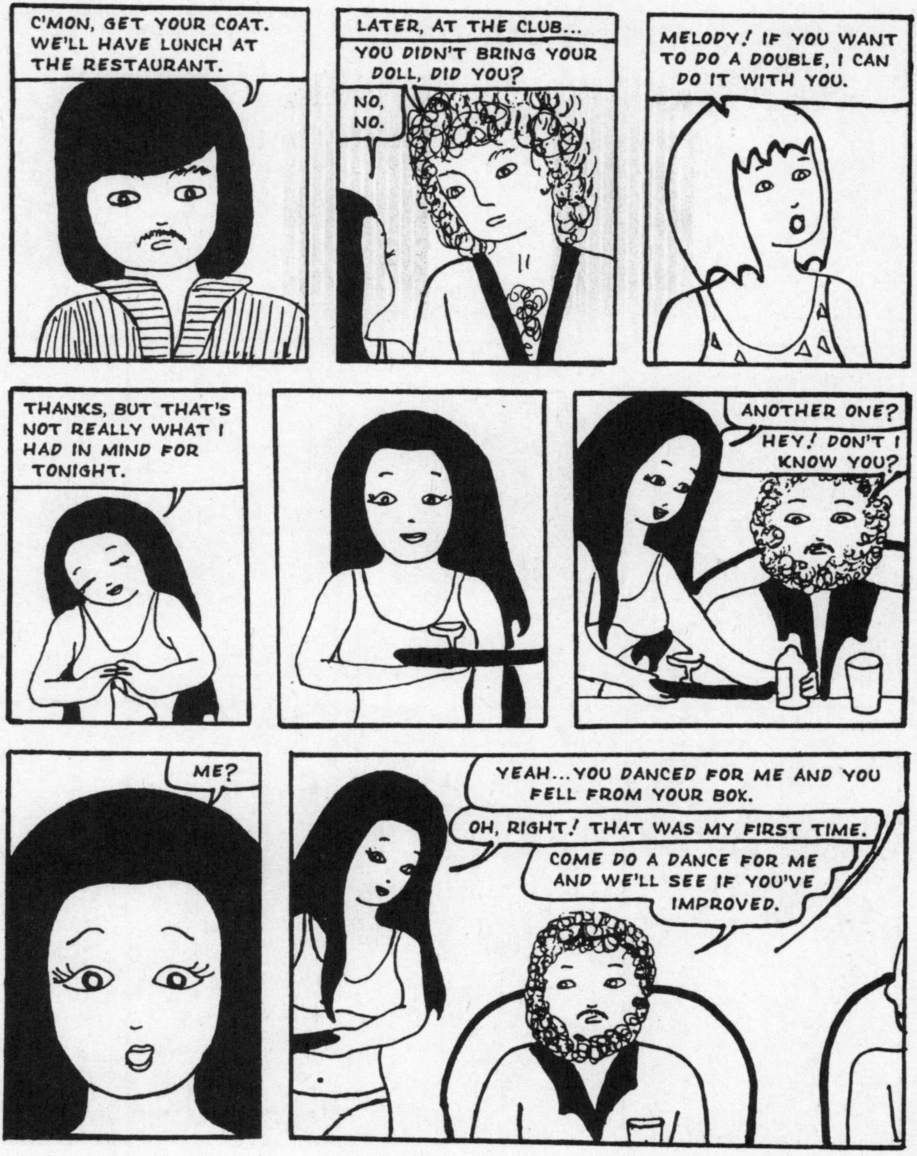
C'MON, GET YOUR COAT. WE'LL HAVE LUNCH AT THE RESTAURANT.
LATER, AT THE CLUB...
YOU DIDN'T BRING YOUR DOLL, DID YOU?
NO, NO.
MELODY! IF YOU WANT TO DO A DOUBLE, I CAN DO IT WITH YOU.
THANKS, BUT THAT'S NOT REALLY WHAT I HAD IN MIND FOR TONIGHT.
ANOTHER ONE?
HEY! DON'T I KNOW YOU?
ME?
YEAH...YOU DANCED FOR ME AND YOU FELL FROM YOUR BOX.
OH, RIGHT! THAT WAS MY FIRST TIME.
COME DO A DANCE FOR ME AND WE'LL SEE IF YOU'VE IMPROVED.

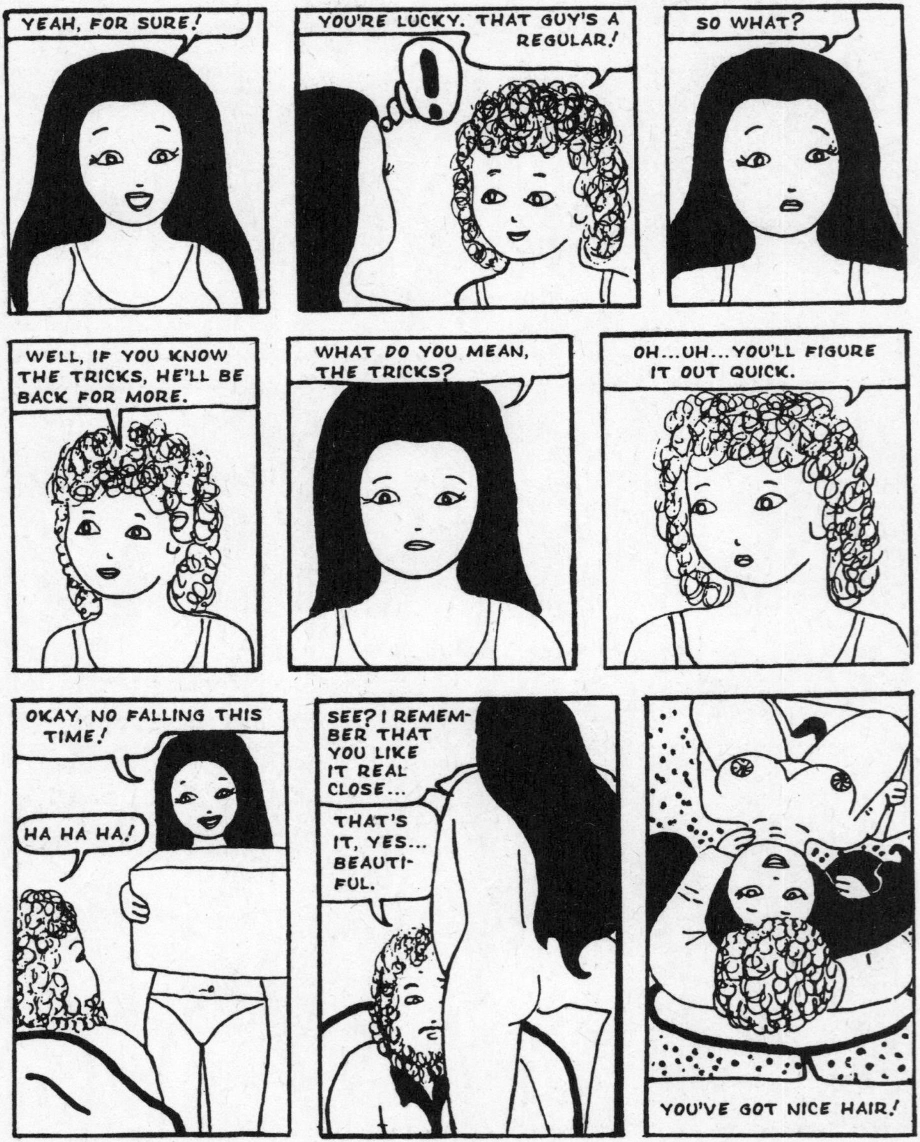

YEAH, FOR SURE!
YOU'RE LUCKY. THAT GUY'S A REGULAR!
!
SO WHAT?
WELL, IF YOU KNOW THE TRICKS, HE'LL BE BACK FOR MORE.
WHAT DO YOU MEAN, THE TRICKS?
OH...UH...YOU'LL FIGURE IT OUT QUICK.
OKAY, NO FALLING THIS TIME!
HA HA HA!
SEE? I REMEMBER THAT YOU LIKE IT REAL CLOSE...
THAT'S IT, YES... BEAUTIFUL.
YOU'VE GOT NICE HAIR!

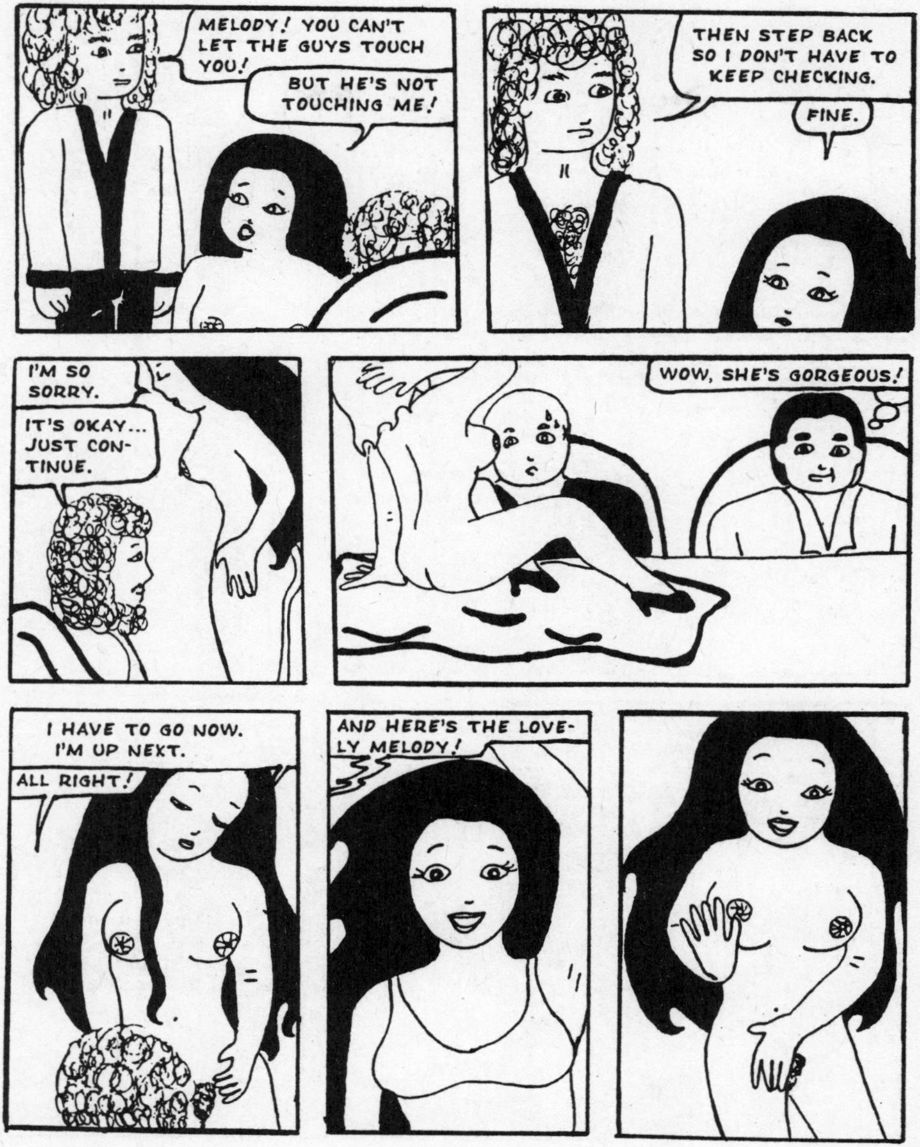
MELODY! YOU CAN'T LET THE GUYS TOUCH YOU!
BUT HE'S NOT TOUCHING ME!
THEN STEP BACK SO I DON'T HAVE TO KEEP CHECKING.
FINE.
I'M SO SORRY.
IT'S OKAY... JUST CONTINUE.
WOW, SHE'S GORGEOUS!
I HAVE TO GO NOW. I'M UP NEXT.
ALL RIGHT!
AND HERE'S THE LOVELY MELODY!

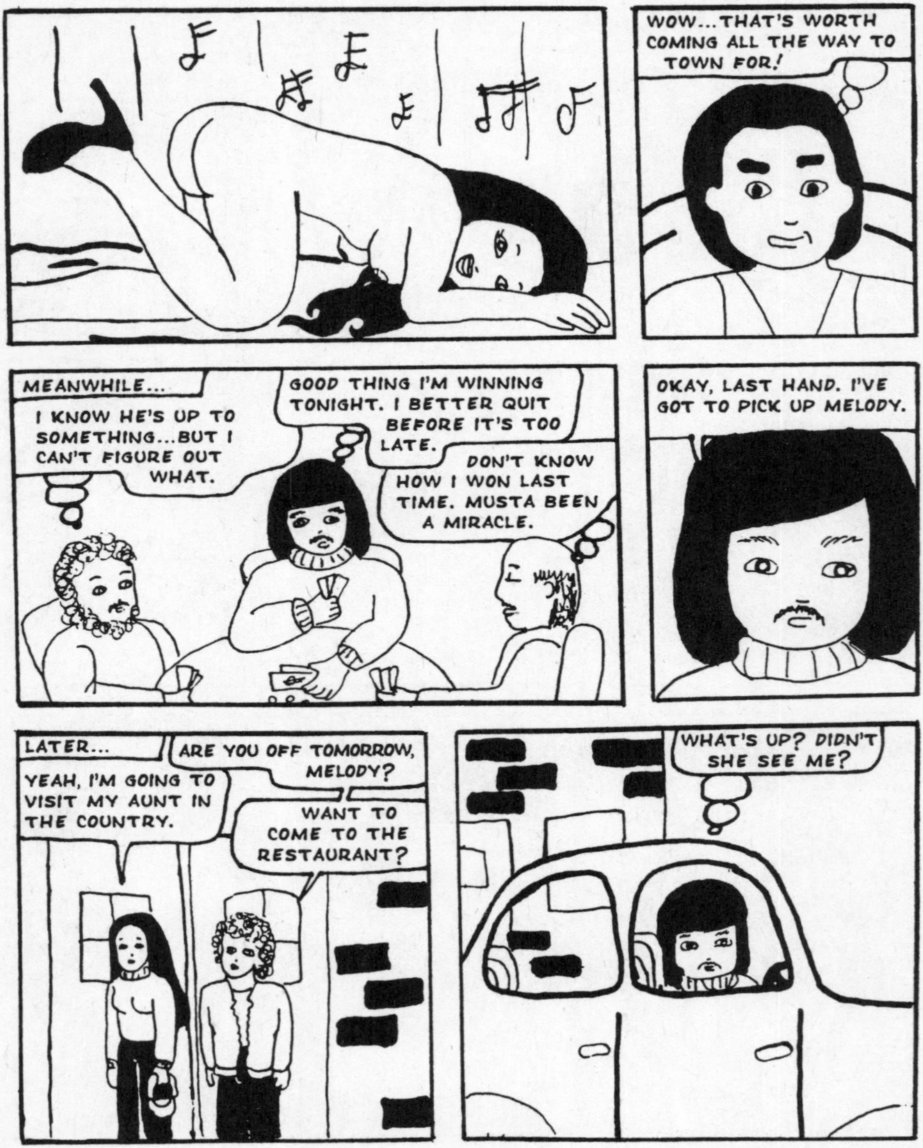
WOW...THAT'S WORTH COMING ALL THE WAY TO TOWN FOR!
MEANWHILE...
I KNOW HE'S UP TO SOMETHING...BUT I CAN'T FIGURE OUT WHAT.
GOOD THING I'M WINNING TONIGHT. I BETTER QUIT BEFORE IT'S TOO LATE.
DON'T KNOW HOW I WON LAST TIME. MUSTA BEEN A MIRACLE.
OKAY, LAST HAND. I'VE GOT TO PICK UP MELODY.
LATER...
ARE YOU OFF TOMORROW, MELODY?
YEAH, I'M GOING TO VISIT MY AUNT IN THE COUNTRY.
WANT TO COME TO THE RESTAURANT?
WHAT'S UP? DIDN'T SHE SEE ME?

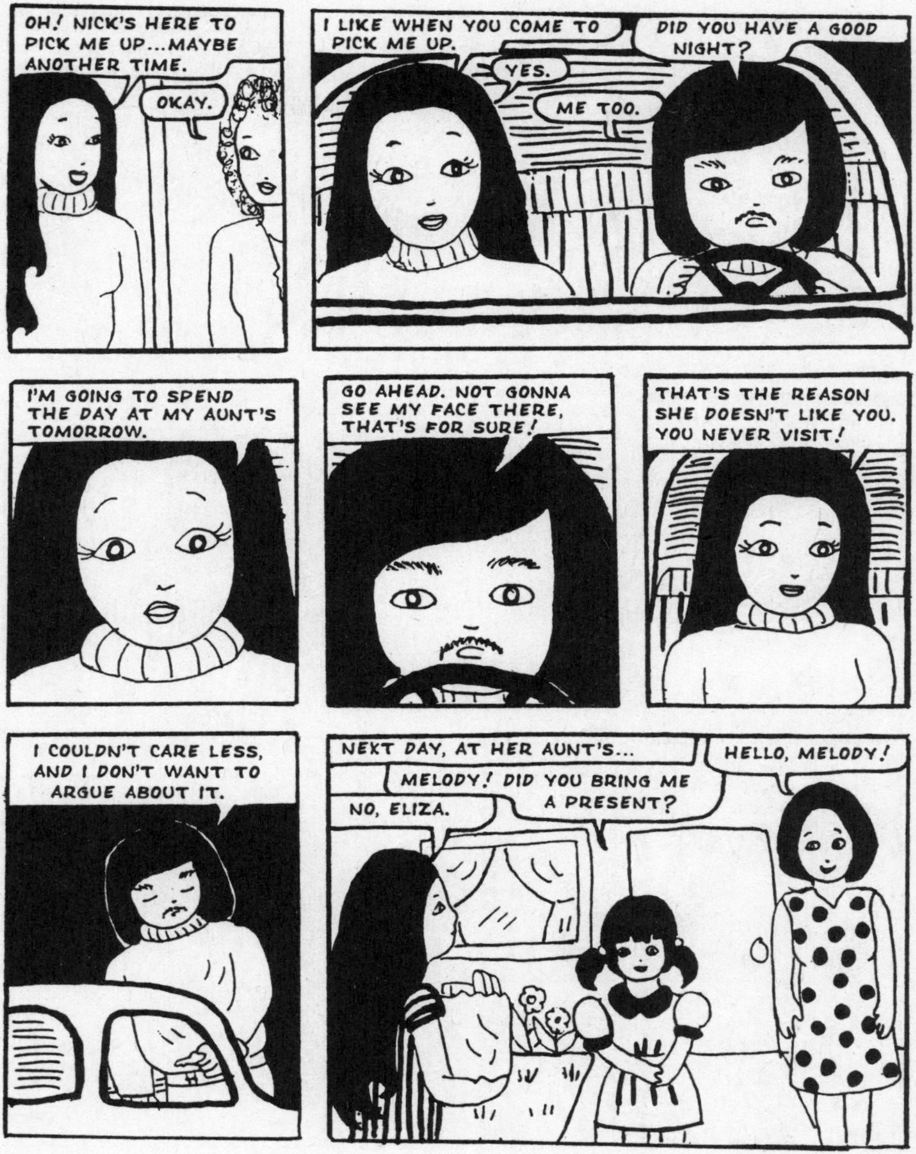
OH! NICK'S HERE TO PICK ME UP...MAYBE ANOTHER TIME.
OKAY.
I LIKE WHEN YOU COME TO PICK ME UP.
DID YOU HAVE A GOOD NIGHT?
YES.
ME TOO.
I'M GOING TO SPEND THE DAY AT MY AUNT'S TOMORROW.
GO AHEAD. NOT GONNA SEE MY FACE THERE, THAT'S FOR SURE!
THAT'S THE REASON SHE DOESN'T LIKE YOU. YOU NEVER VISIT!
I COULDN'T CARE LESS, AND I DON'T WANT TO ARGUE ABOUT IT.
NEXT DAY, AT HER AUNT'S...
HELLO, MELODY!
MELODY! DID YOU BRING ME A PRESENT?
NO, ELIZA.

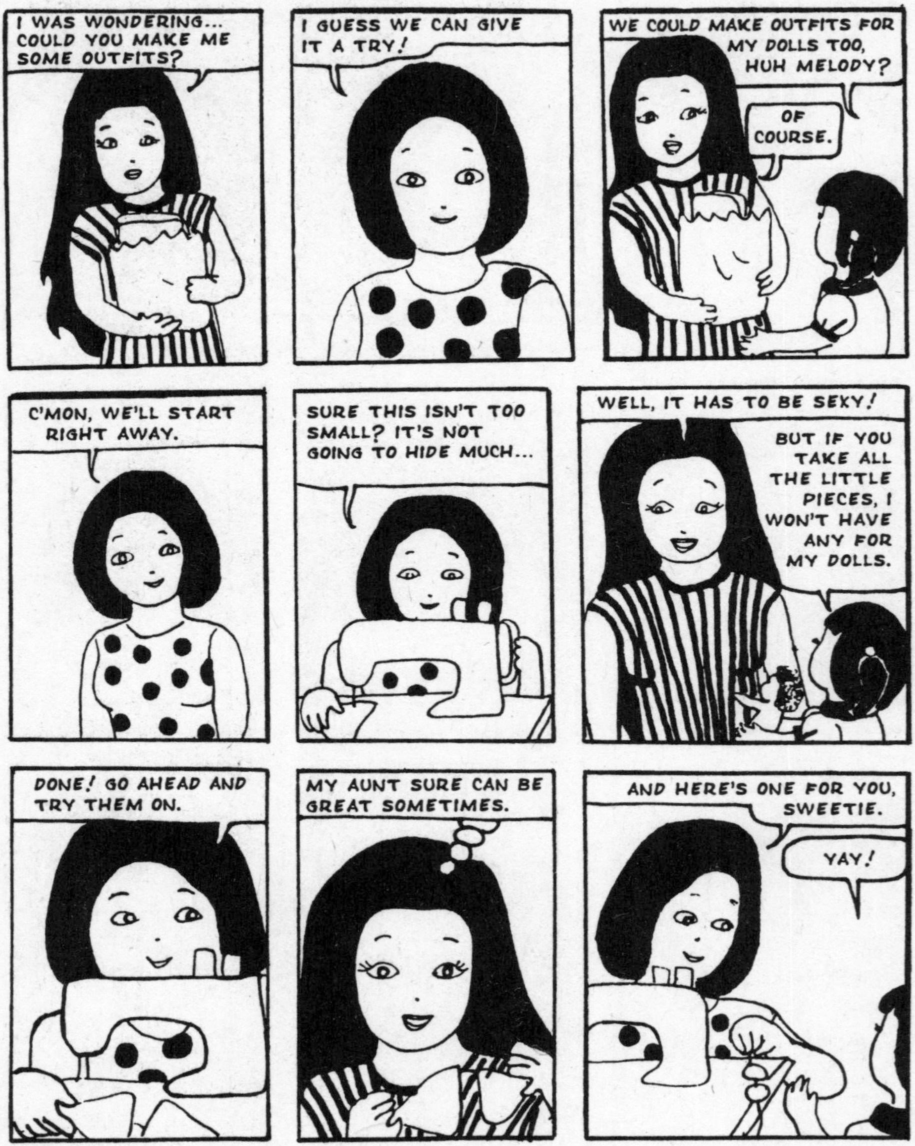
I WAS WONDERING... COULD YOU MAKE ME SOME OUTFITS?
I GUESS WE CAN GIVE IT A TRY!
WE COULD MAKE OUTFITS FOR MY DOLLS TOO, HUH MELODY?
OF COURSE.
C'MON, WE'LL START RIGHT AWAY.
SURE THIS ISN'T TOO SMALL? IT'S NOT GOING TO HIDE MUCH...
WELL, IT HAS TO BE SEXY!
BUT IF YOU TAKE ALL THE LITTLE PIECES, I WON'T HAVE ANY FOR MY DOLLS.
DONE! GO AHEAD AND TRY THEM ON.
MY AUNT SURE CAN BE GREAT SOMETIMES.
AND HERE'S ONE FOR YOU, SWEETIE.
YAY!

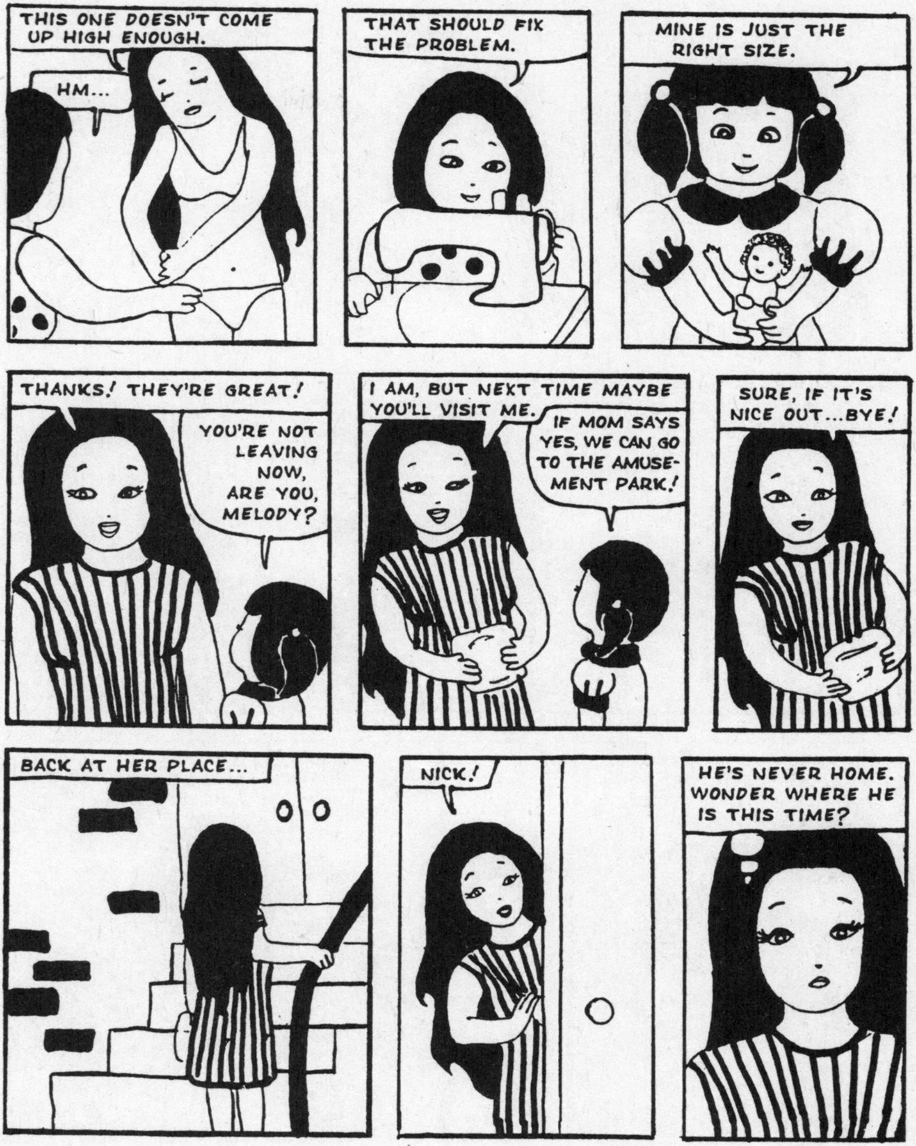
THIS ONE DOESN'T COME UP HIGH ENOUGH.
HM...
THAT SHOULD FIX THE PROBLEM.
MINE IS JUST THE RIGHT SIZE.
THANKS! THEY'RE GREAT!
YOU'RE NOT LEAVING NOW, ARE YOU, MELODY?
I AM, BUT NEXT TIME MAYBE YOU'LL VISIT ME.
IF MOM SAYS YES, WE CAN GO TO THE AMUSEMENT PARK!
SURE, IF IT'S NICE OUT...BYE!
BACK AT HER PLACE...
NICK!
HE'S NEVER HOME. WONDER WHERE HE IS THIS TIME?

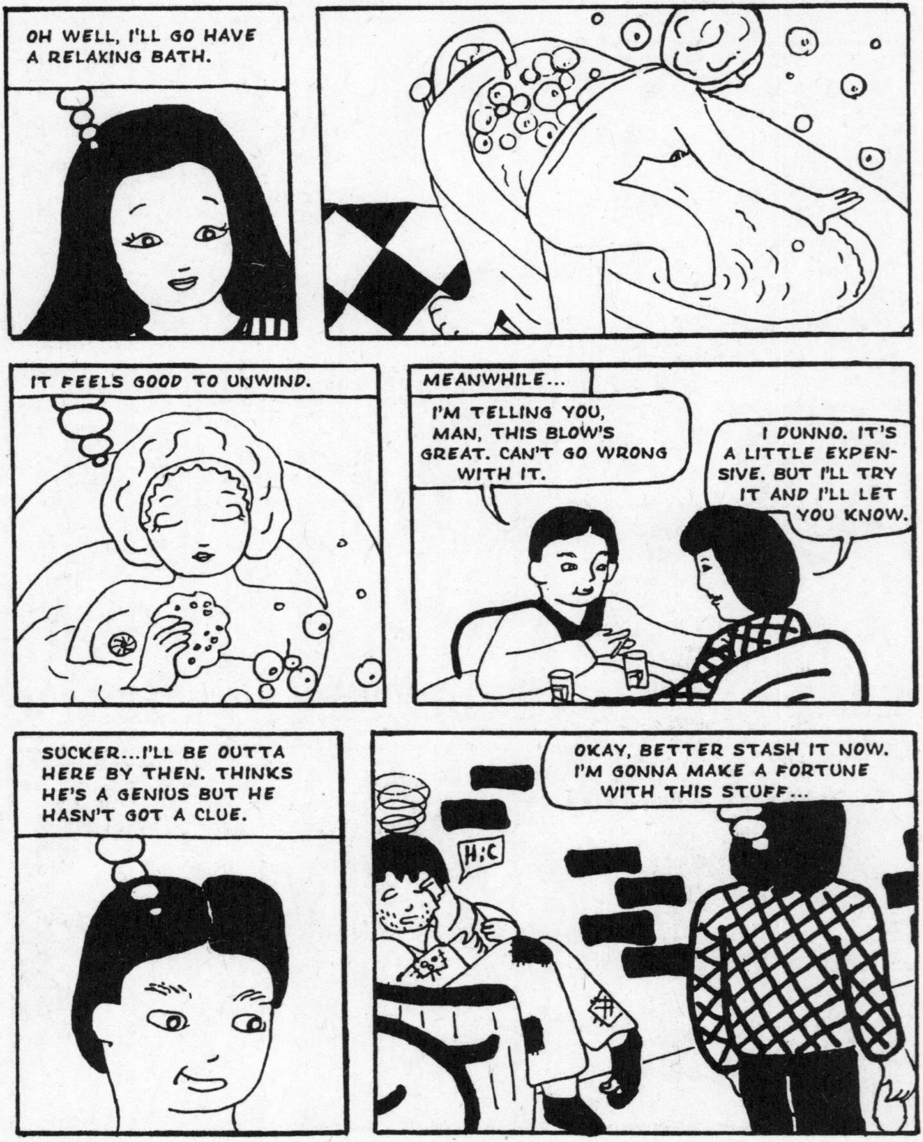
OH WELL, I'LL GO HAVE A RELAXING BATH.
IT FEELS GOOD TO UNWIND.
MEANWHILE...
I'M TELLING YOU, MAN, THIS BLOW'S GREAT. CAN'T GO WRONG WITH IT.
I DUNNO. IT'S A LITTLE EXPENSIVE. BUT I'LL TRY IT AND I'LL LET YOU KNOW.
SUCKER...I'LL BE OUTTA HERE BY THEN. THINKS HE'S A GENIUS BUT HE HASN'T GOT A CLUE.
OKAY, BETTER STASH IT NOW. I'M GONNA MAKE A FORTUNE WITH THIS STUFF...
HIC

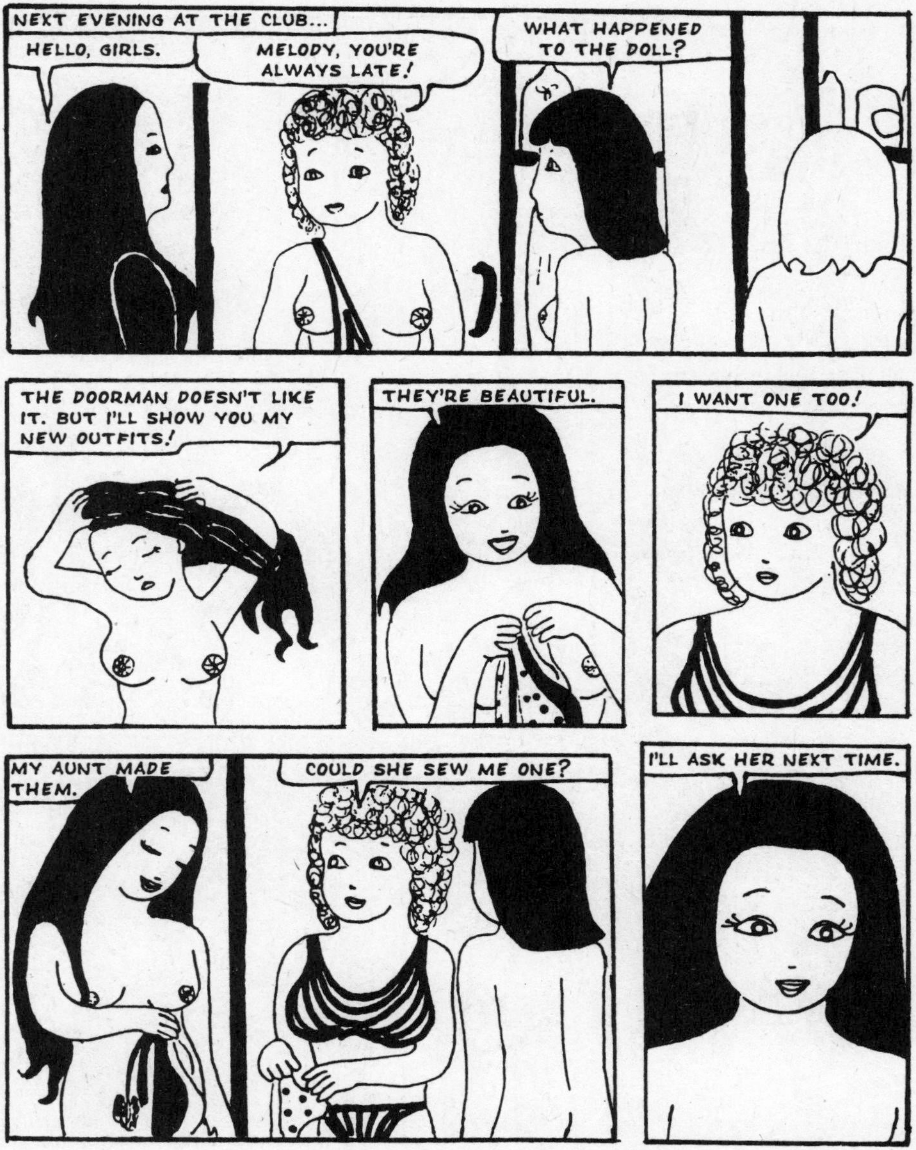
NEXT EVENING AT THE CLUB...
HELLO, GIRLS.
MELODY, YOU'RE ALWAYS LATE!
WHAT HAPPENED TO THE DOLL?
THE DOORMAN DOESN'T LIKE IT. BUT I'LL SHOW YOU MY NEW OUTFITS!
THEY'RE BEAUTIFUL.
I WANT ONE TOO!
MY AUNT MADE THEM.
COULD SHE SEW ME ONE?
I'LL ASK HER NEXT TIME.

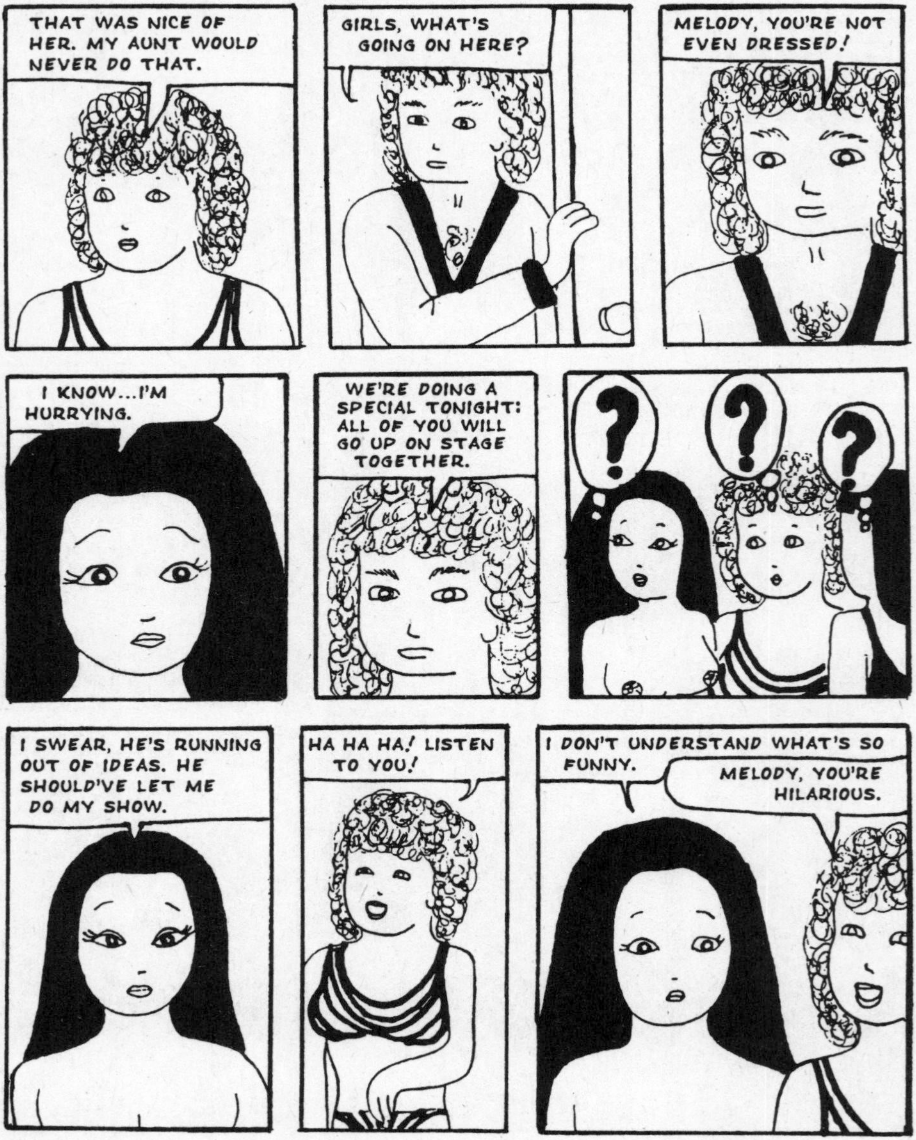

THAT WAS NICE OF HER. MY AUNT WOULD NEVER DO THAT.
GIRLS, WHAT'S GOING ON HERE?
MELODY, YOU'RE NOT EVEN DRESSED!
I KNOW...I'M HURRYING.
WE'RE DOING A SPECIAL TONIGHT: ALL OF YOU WILL GO UP ON STAGE TOGETHER.
?
?
?
I SWEAR, HE'S RUNNING OUT OF IDEAS. HE SHOULD'VE LET ME DO MY SHOW.
HA HA HA! LISTEN TO YOU!
I DON'T UNDERSTAND WHAT'S SO FUNNY.
MELODY, YOU'RE HILARIOUS.

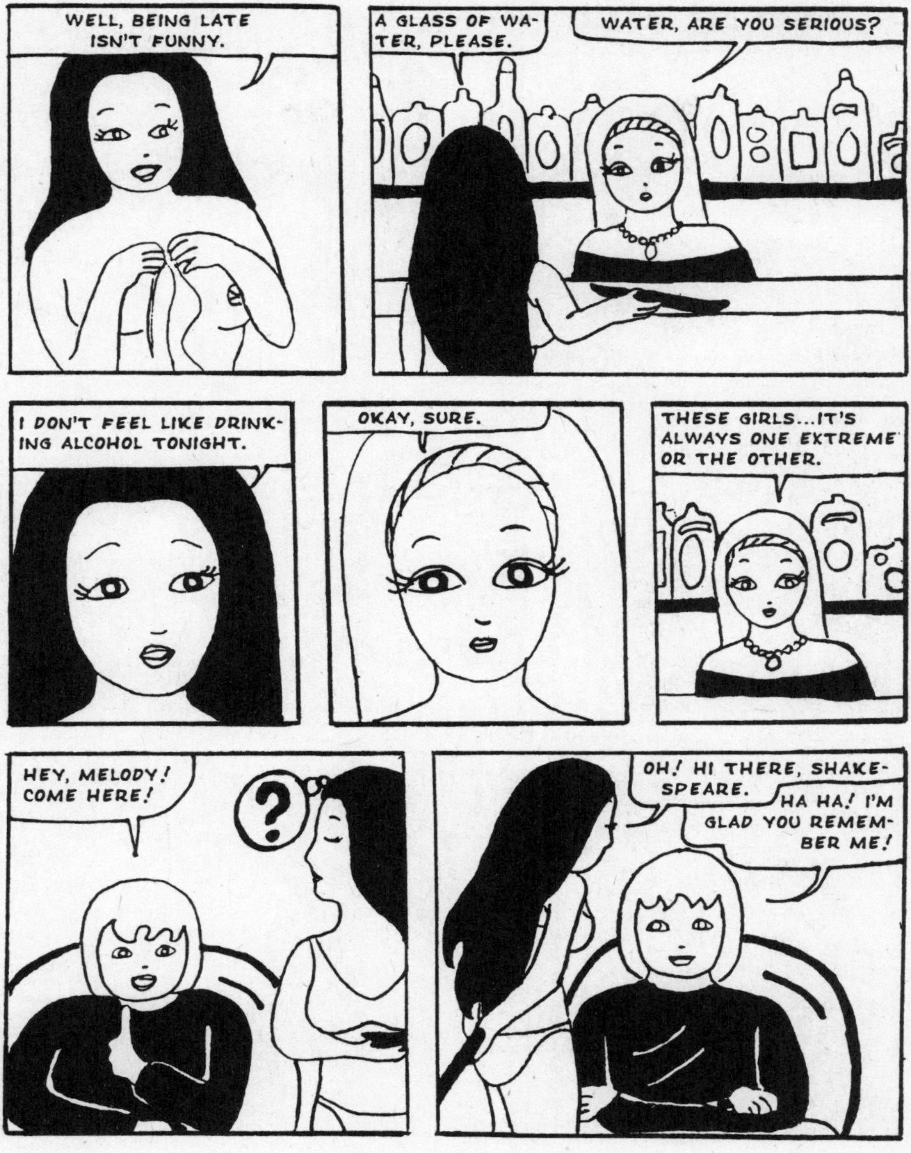
WELL, BEING LATE ISN'T FUNNY.
A GLASS OF WATER, PLEASE.
WATER, ARE YOU SERIOUS?
I DON'T FEEL LIKE DRINKING ALCOHOL TONIGHT.
OKAY, SURE.
THESE GIRLS...IT'S ALWAYS ONE EXTREME OR THE OTHER.
HEY, MELODY! COME HERE!
?
OH! HI THERE, SHAKESPEARE.
HA HA! I'M GLAD YOU REMEMBER ME!

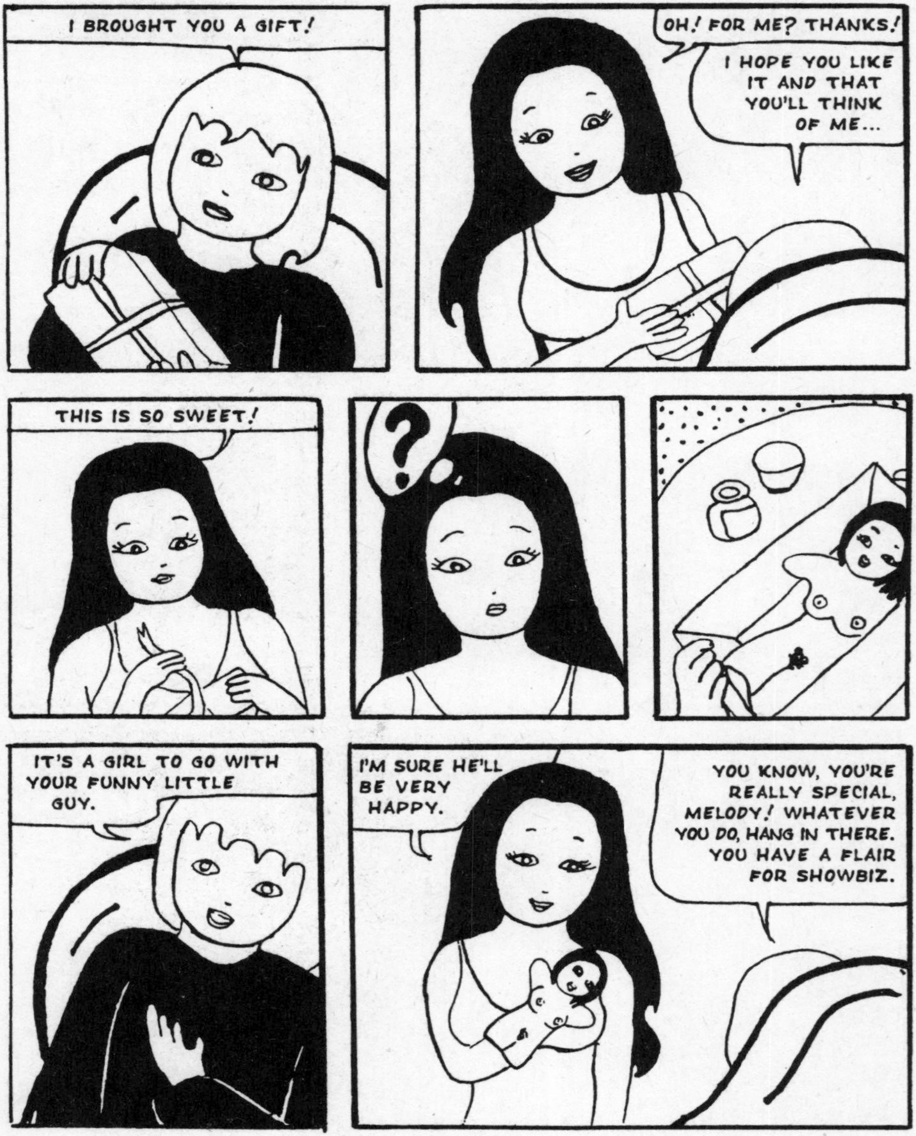
I BROUGHT YOU A GIFT!
OH! FOR ME? THANKS!
I HOPE YOU LIKE IT AND THAT YOU'LL THINK OF ME...
THIS IS SO SWEET!
?
IT'S A GIRL TO GO WITH YOUR FUNNY LITTLE GUY.
I'M SURE HE'LL BE VERY HAPPY.
YOU KNOW, YOU'RE REALLY SPECIAL, MELODY! WHATEVER YOU DO, HANG IN THERE. YOU HAVE A FLAIR FOR SHOWBIZ.

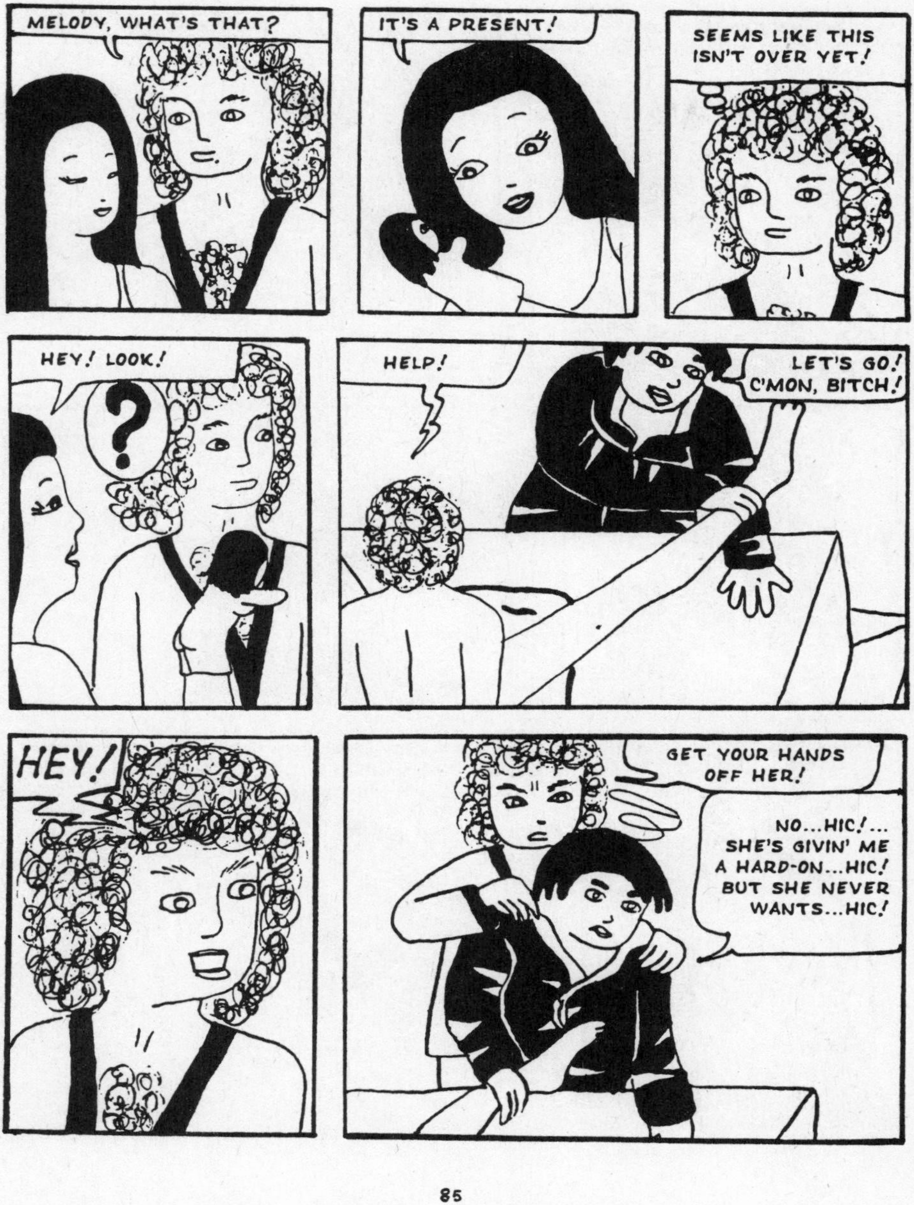
MELODY, WHAT'S THAT?
IT'S A PRESENT!
SEEMS LIKE THIS ISN'T OVER YET!
HEY! LOOK!
?
HELP!
LET'S GO! C'MON, BITCH!
HEY!
GET YOUR HANDS OFF HER!
NO...HIC!... SHE'S GIVIN' ME A HARD-ON...HIC! BUT SHE NEVER WANTS...HIC!

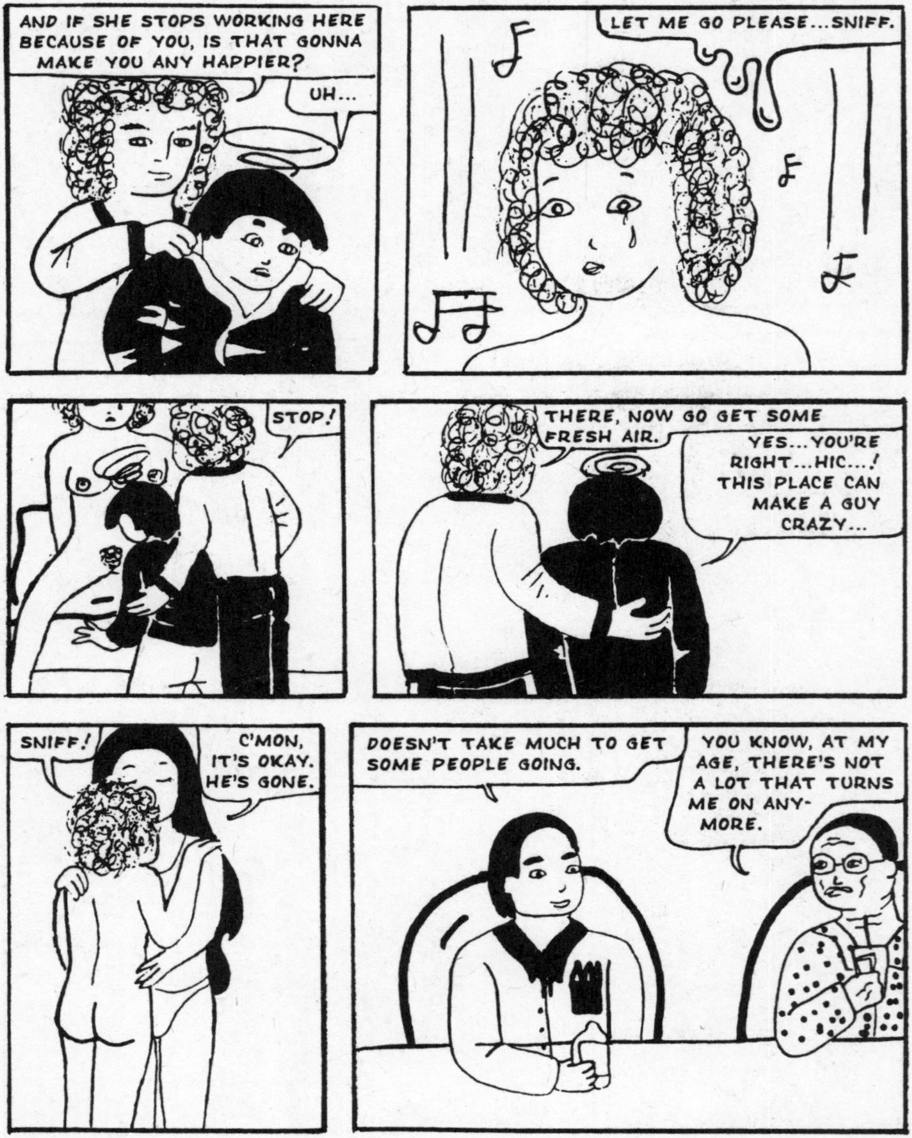
AND IF SHE STOPS WORKING HERE BECAUSE OF YOU, IS THAT GONNA MAKE YOU ANY HAPPIER?
UH...
LET ME GO PLEASE...SNIFF.
STOP!
THERE, NOW GO GET SOME FRESH AIR.
YES...YOU'RE RIGHT...HIC...! THIS PLACE CAN MAKE A GUY CRAZY...
SNIFF!
C'MON, IT'S OKAY. HE'S GONE.
DOESN'T TAKE MUCH TO GET SOME PEOPLE GOING.
YOU KNOW, AT MY AGE, THERE'S NOT A LOT THAT TURNS ME ON ANY-MORE.

ALL RIGHT, GIRLS! ENOUGH WITH THE STANDING AROUND. I WANT TO SEE ALL OF YOU ON STAGE!

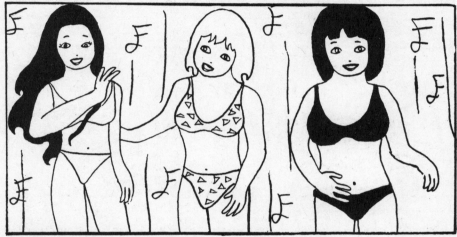

YOU CAN GO TAKE A BREAK.

THANKS.

IT'S NICE WHEN THEY MIX IT UP, HUH?

YEAH, 'CEPT YOU DON'T KNOW WHERE TO LOOK.

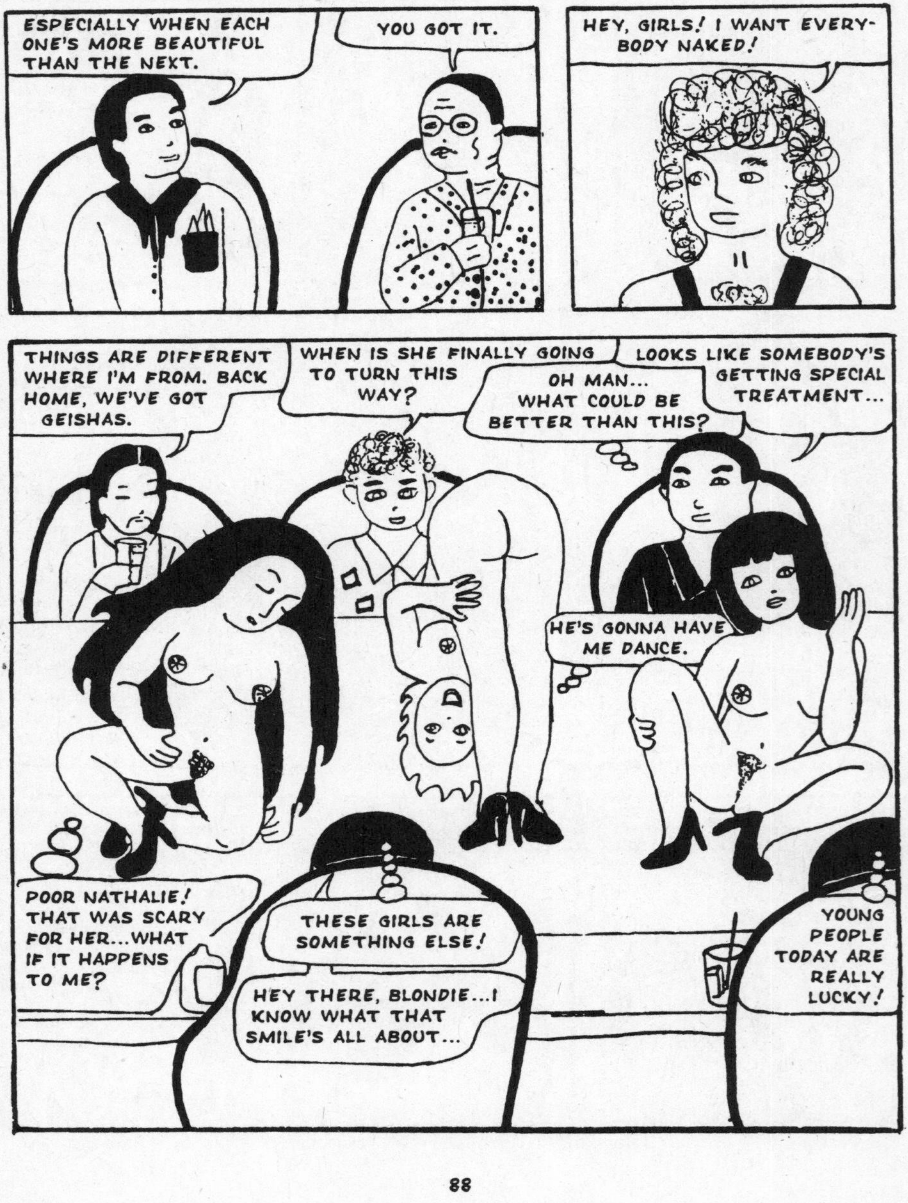
ESPECIALLY WHEN EACH ONE'S MORE BEAUTIFUL THAN THE NEXT.
YOU GOT IT.
HEY, GIRLS! I WANT EVERY-BODY NAKED!
THINGS ARE DIFFERENT WHERE I'M FROM. BACK HOME, WE'VE GOT GEISHAS.
WHEN IS SHE FINALLY GOING TO TURN THIS WAY?
OH MAN... WHAT COULD BE BETTER THAN THIS?
LOOKS LIKE SOMEBODY'S GETTING SPECIAL TREATMENT...
HE'S GONNA HAVE ME DANCE.
POOR NATHALIE! THAT WAS SCARY FOR HER...WHAT IF IT HAPPENS TO ME?
THESE GIRLS ARE SOMETHING ELSE!
HEY THERE, BLONDIE...I KNOW WHAT THAT SMILE'S ALL ABOUT...
YOUNG PEOPLE TODAY ARE REALLY LUCKY!

I'M JUST IN TIME! THERE'S A SHOW.
YES?
YOU HER BOYFRIEND?
I'LL HAVE A BEER. GO AHEAD AND PUT IT ON MELODY'S TAB.
YES. IF I'M NOT HERE, I'LL BE IN THE JOHN.
MAYBE I'LL FIND A BUYER.
LOOKING FOR GOOD COKE? I'VE GOT SOME.
NO THANKS, I DON'T DO THAT SHIT.
?
I KNOW SOMEBODY WHO'S NOT GONNA BE HAPPY ABOUT THIS.
SOME JERK OUT THERE WANTS TO GET IN ON OUR BUSINESS.
OH YEAH? WELL, BUY SOME OF HIS STUFF AND WE'LL SEE HOW IT IS.
?

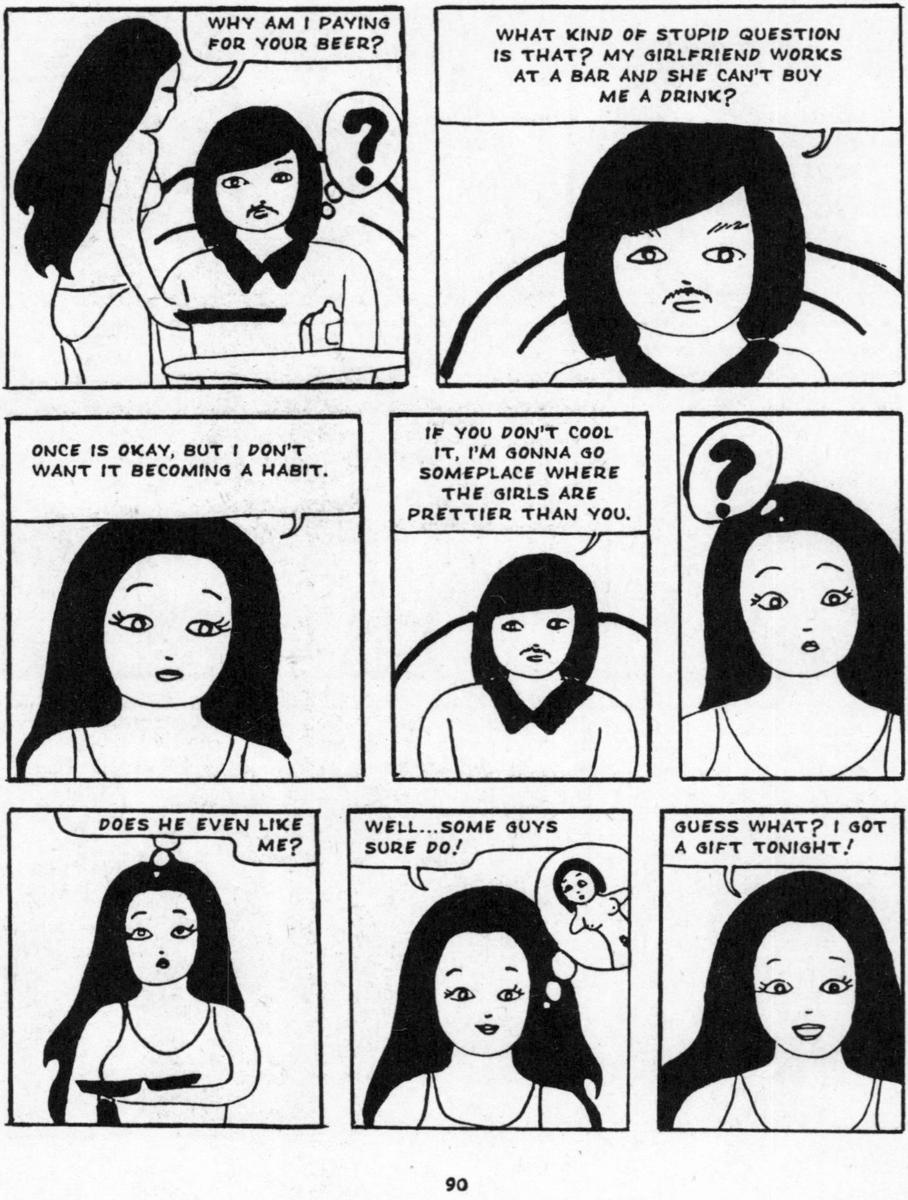
WHY AM I PAYING FOR YOUR BEER?
WHAT KIND OF STUPID QUESTION IS THAT? MY GIRLFRIEND WORKS AT A BAR AND SHE CAN'T BUY ME A DRINK?
ONCE IS OKAY, BUT I DON'T WANT IT BECOMING A HABIT.
IF YOU DON'T COOL IT, I'M GONNA GO SOMEPLACE WHERE THE GIRLS ARE PRETTIER THAN YOU.
DOES HE EVEN LIKE ME?
WELL...SOME GUYS SURE DO!
GUESS WHAT? I GOT A GIFT TONIGHT!

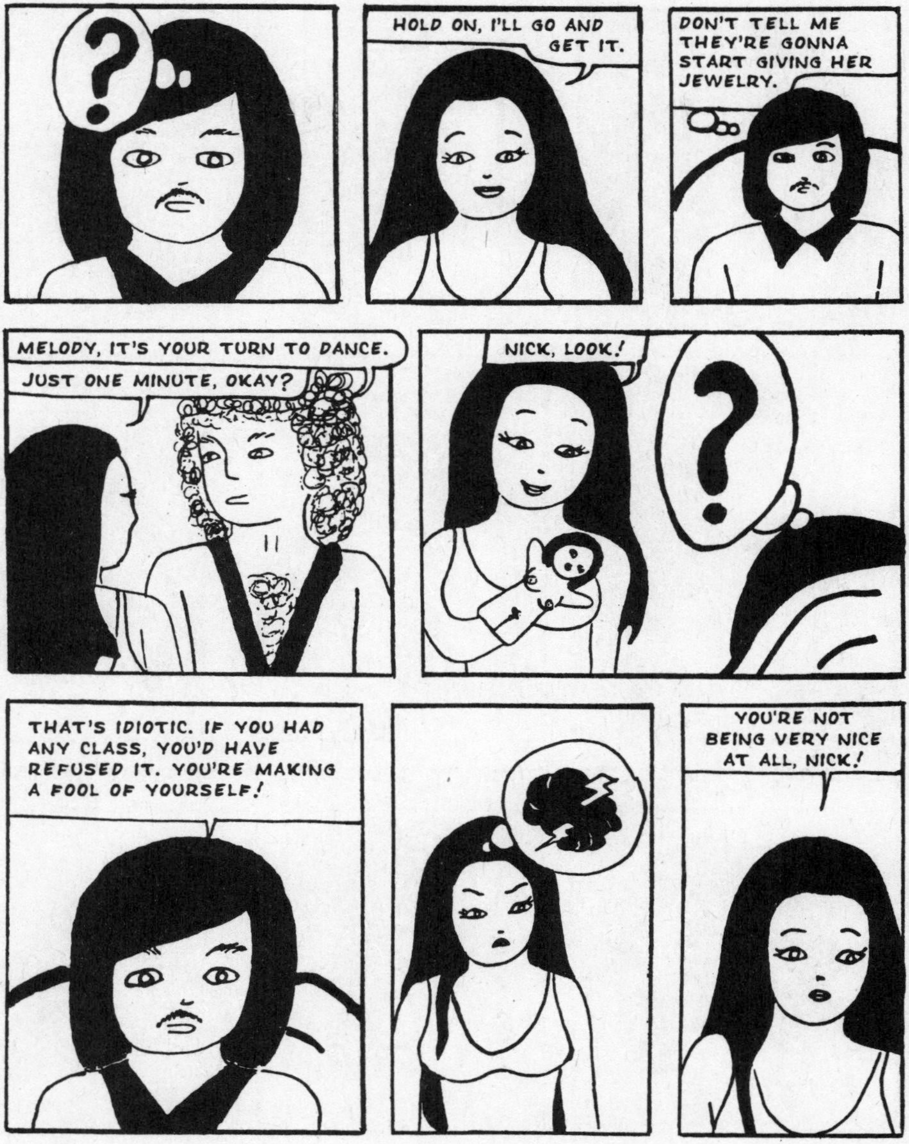
HOLD ON, I'LL GO AND GET IT.
DON'T TELL ME THEY'RE GONNA START GIVING HER JEWELRY.
MELODY, IT'S YOUR TURN TO DANCE.
JUST ONE MINUTE, OKAY?
NICK, LOOK!
THAT'S IDIOTIC. IF YOU HAD ANY CLASS, YOU'D HAVE REFUSED IT. YOU'RE MAKING A FOOL OF YOURSELF!
YOU'RE NOT BEING VERY NICE AT ALL, NICK!

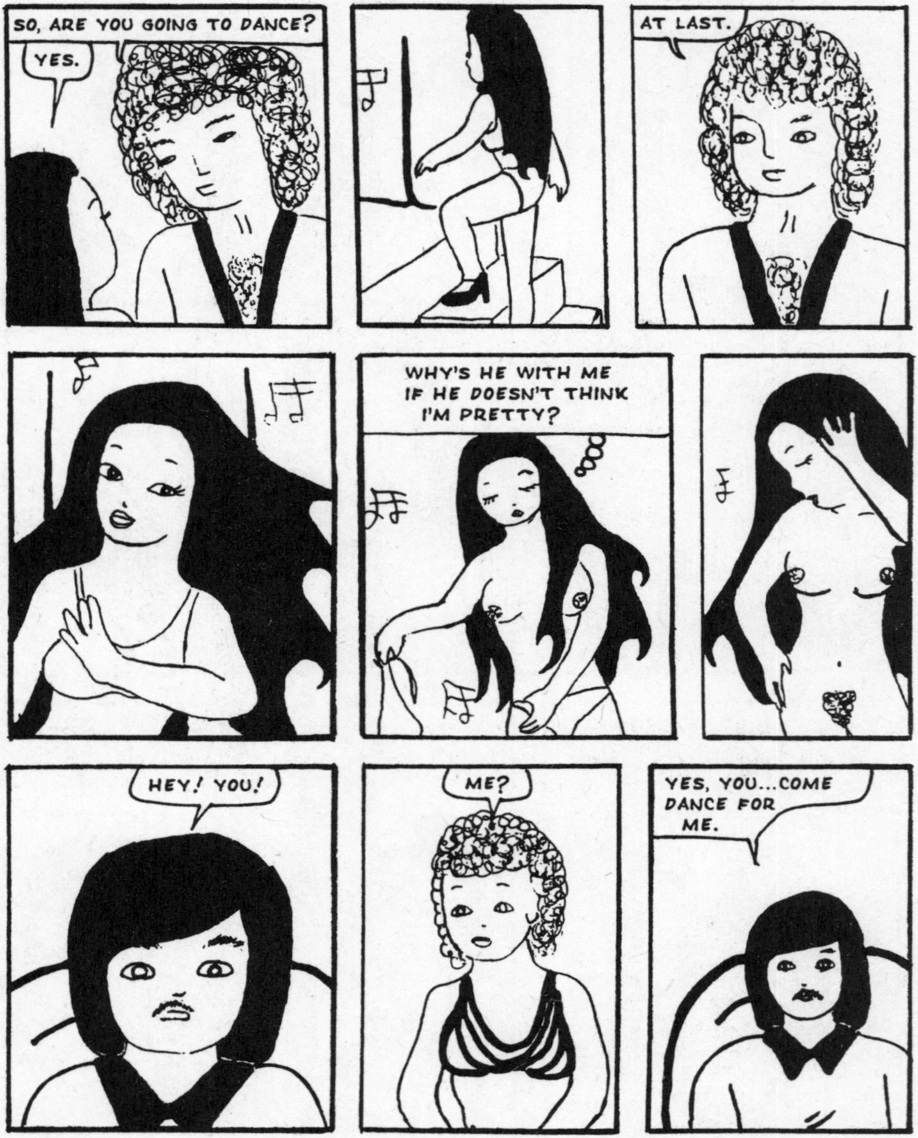
SO, ARE YOU GOING TO DANCE?
YES.
AT LAST.
WHY'S HE WITH ME IF HE DOESN'T THINK I'M PRETTY?
HEY! YOU!
ME?
YES, YOU...COME DANCE FOR ME.

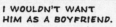
 I WOULDN'T WANT HIM AS A BOYFRIEND.

 WHAT ABOUT ME?

 MELODY!

 YES?

WHAT'S UP WITH YOU TODAY? IS SOMETHING ON YOUR MIND?

 WHY DO YOU ASK?

 YOU DON'T SEEM LIKE YOUR USUAL SELF.

 YOU'RE ALL OVER THE PLACE. YOU'RE NOT TAKING CARE OF BUSINESS, SERVING THE CUSTOMERS, OR CLEANING THE TABLES...

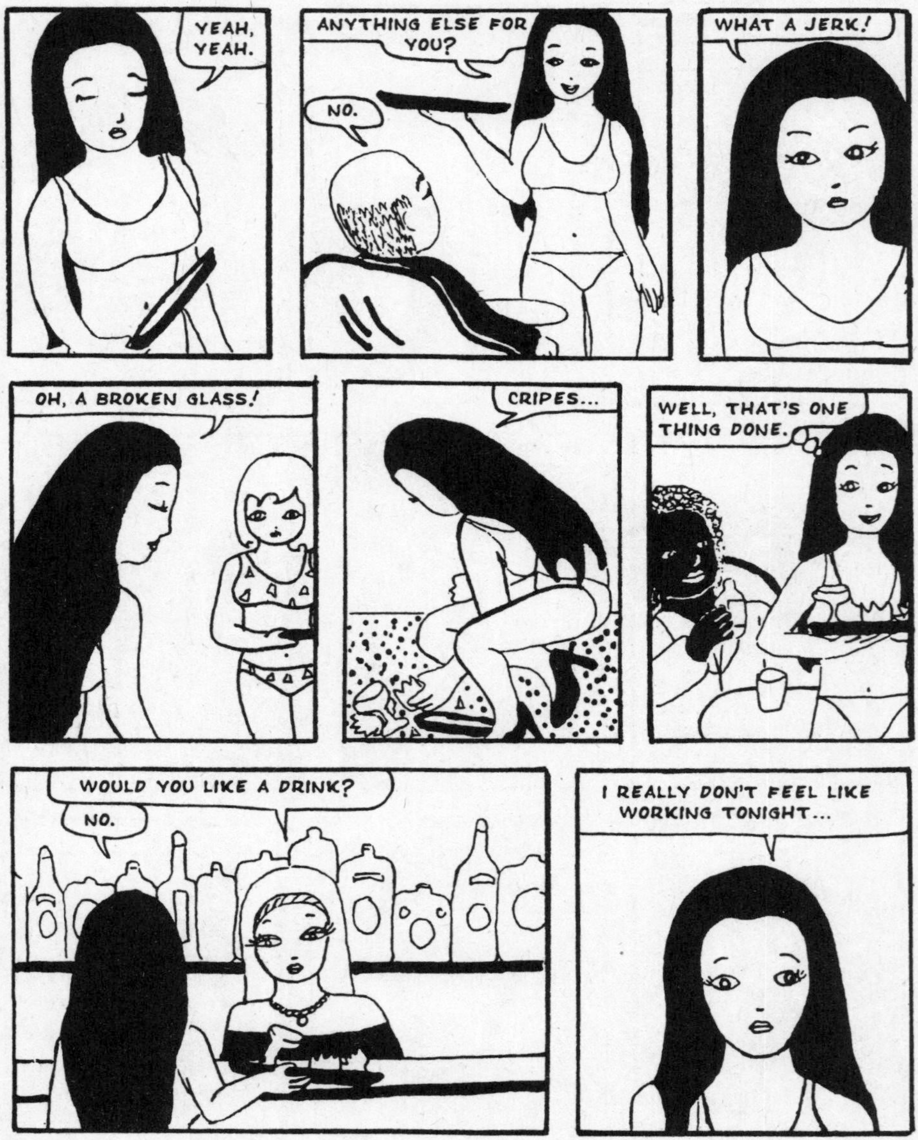
YEAH, YEAH.
ANYTHING ELSE FOR YOU?
NO.
WHAT A JERK!
OH, A BROKEN GLASS!
CRIPES...
WELL, THAT'S ONE THING DONE.
WOULD YOU LIKE A DRINK?
NO.
I REALLY DON'T FEEL LIKE WORKING TONIGHT...

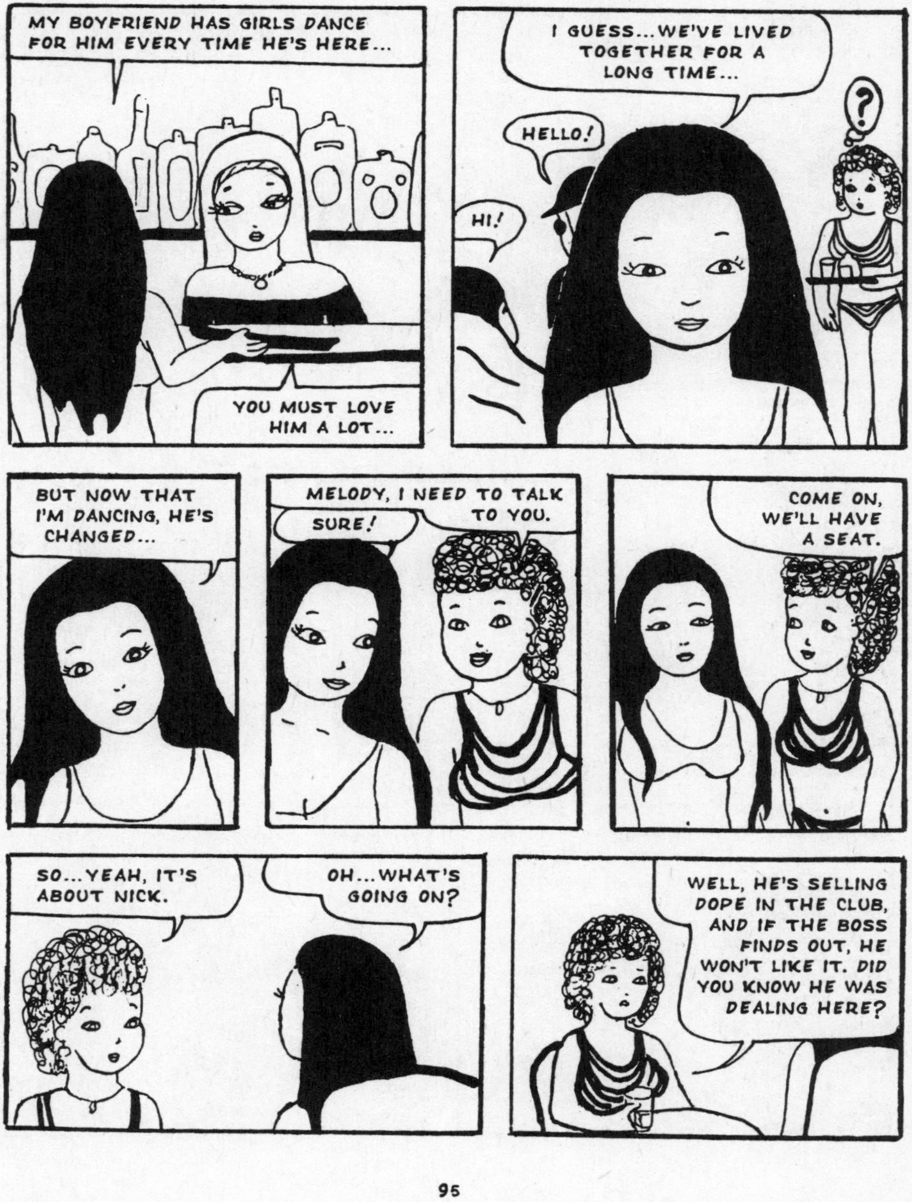
MY BOYFRIEND HAS GIRLS DANCE FOR HIM EVERY TIME HE'S HERE...
YOU MUST LOVE HIM A LOT...
I GUESS...WE'VE LIVED TOGETHER FOR A LONG TIME...
HELLO!
HI!
?
BUT NOW THAT I'M DANCING, HE'S CHANGED...
MELODY, I NEED TO TALK TO YOU.
SURE!
COME ON, WE'LL HAVE A SEAT.
SO...YEAH, IT'S ABOUT NICK.
OH...WHAT'S GOING ON?
WELL, HE'S SELLING DOPE IN THE CLUB, AND IF THE BOSS FINDS OUT, HE WON'T LIKE IT. DID YOU KNOW HE WAS DEALING HERE?

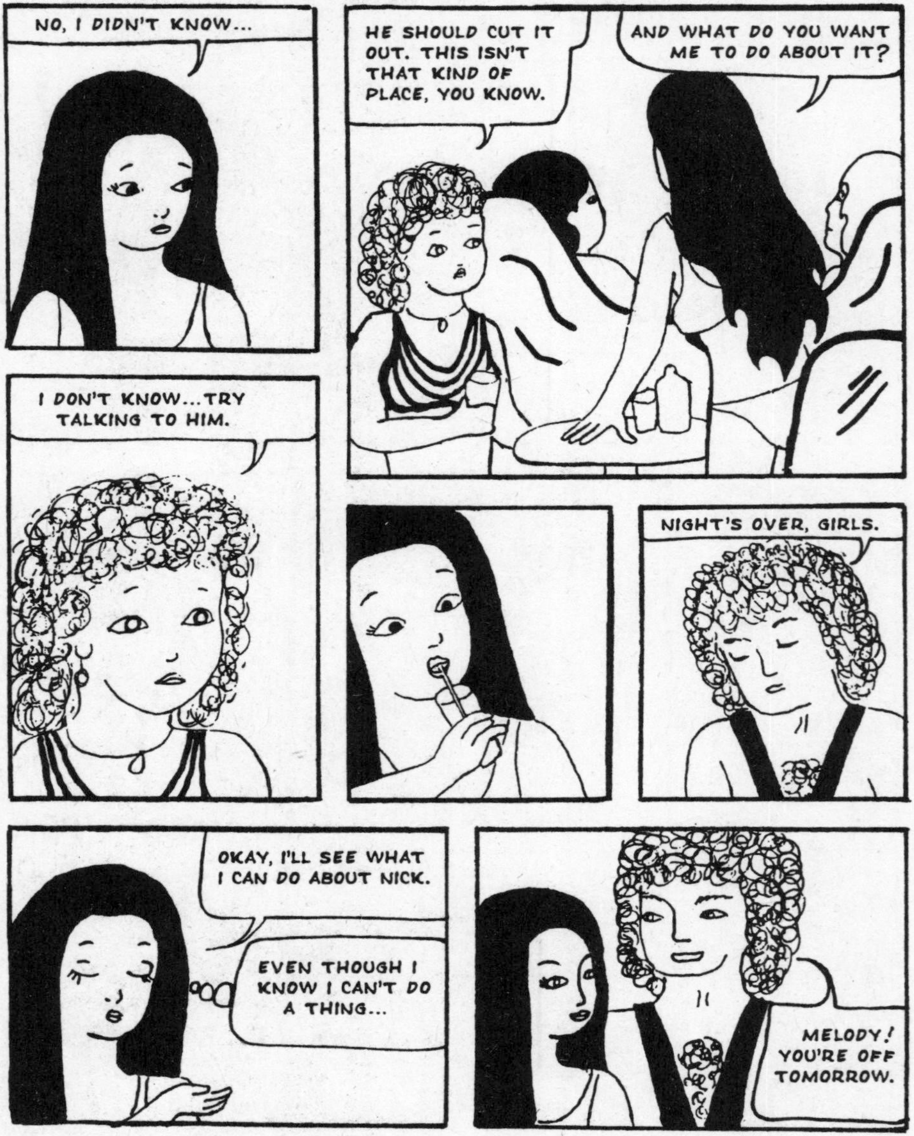
NO, I DIDN'T KNOW...
HE SHOULD CUT IT OUT. THIS ISN'T THAT KIND OF PLACE, YOU KNOW.
AND WHAT DO YOU WANT ME TO DO ABOUT IT?
I DON'T KNOW...TRY TALKING TO HIM.
NIGHT'S OVER, GIRLS.
OKAY, I'LL SEE WHAT I CAN DO ABOUT NICK.
EVEN THOUGH I KNOW I CAN'T DO A THING...
MELODY! YOU'RE OFF TOMORROW.

NICK, MIND STARTING THE CAR?

I'LL FINISH MY BEER AND GO.

GREAT. I'LL HURRY.

HAVE YOU ASKED YOUR AUNT ABOUT THE OUTFITS?

NO, NOT YET...

HERE!

OH! THANKS!

A FEW MOMENTS LATER...

NICK, I DON'T WANT YOU SELLING AT THE CLUB.

WHY NOT?

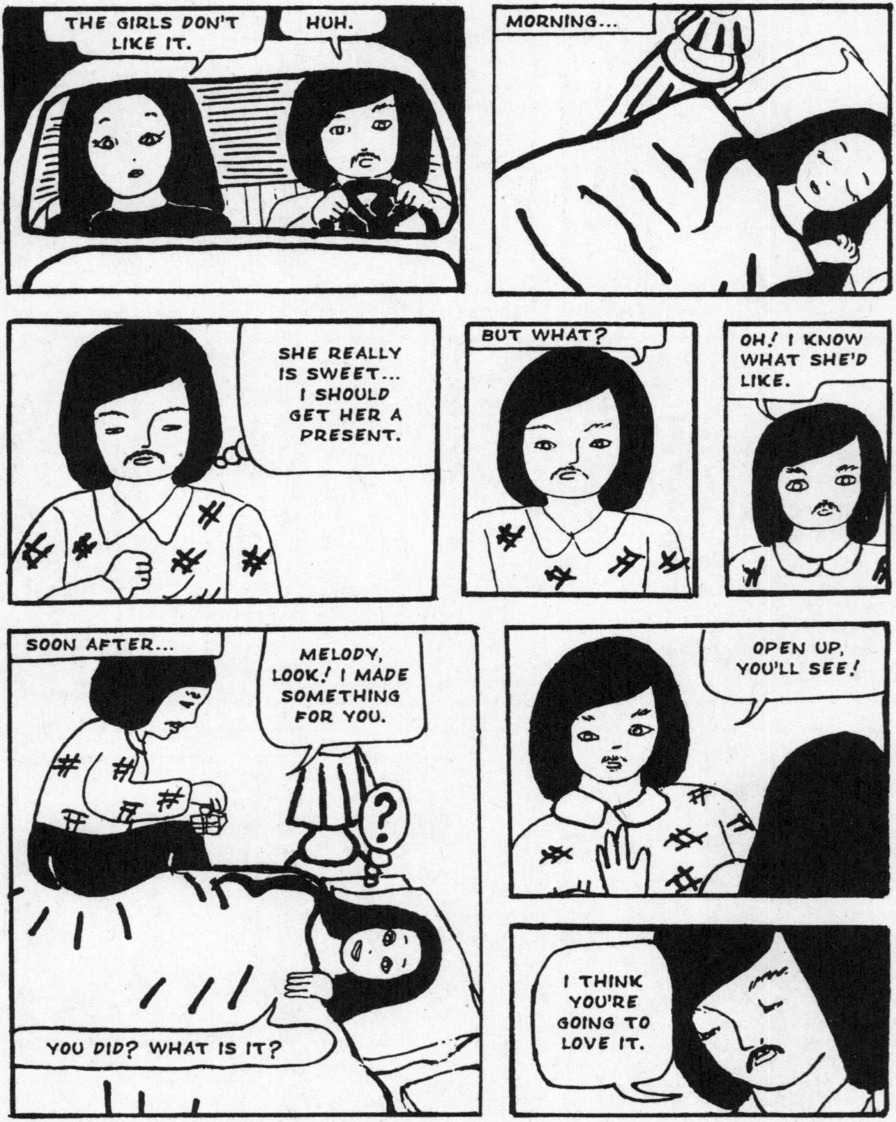
THE GIRLS DON'T LIKE IT.
HUH.
MORNING...
SHE REALLY IS SWEET... I SHOULD GET HER A PRESENT.
BUT WHAT?
OH! I KNOW WHAT SHE'D LIKE.
SOON AFTER...
MELODY, LOOK! I MADE SOMETHING FOR YOU.
?
YOU DID? WHAT IS IT?
OPEN UP, YOU'LL SEE!
I THINK YOU'RE GOING TO LOVE IT.

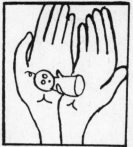

WHAT'S THIS FOR?

YOUR TWO LITTLE PUPPETS HAD A BABY!

UH...I SEE... THAT'S NICE OF YOU.

IT GOES ON YOUR FINGER, LIKE THIS.

THAT'S STUPID!

STUPID! IF A CUSTOMER GAVE IT TO YOU, YOU'D BE THRILLED!

NO I WOULDN'T!

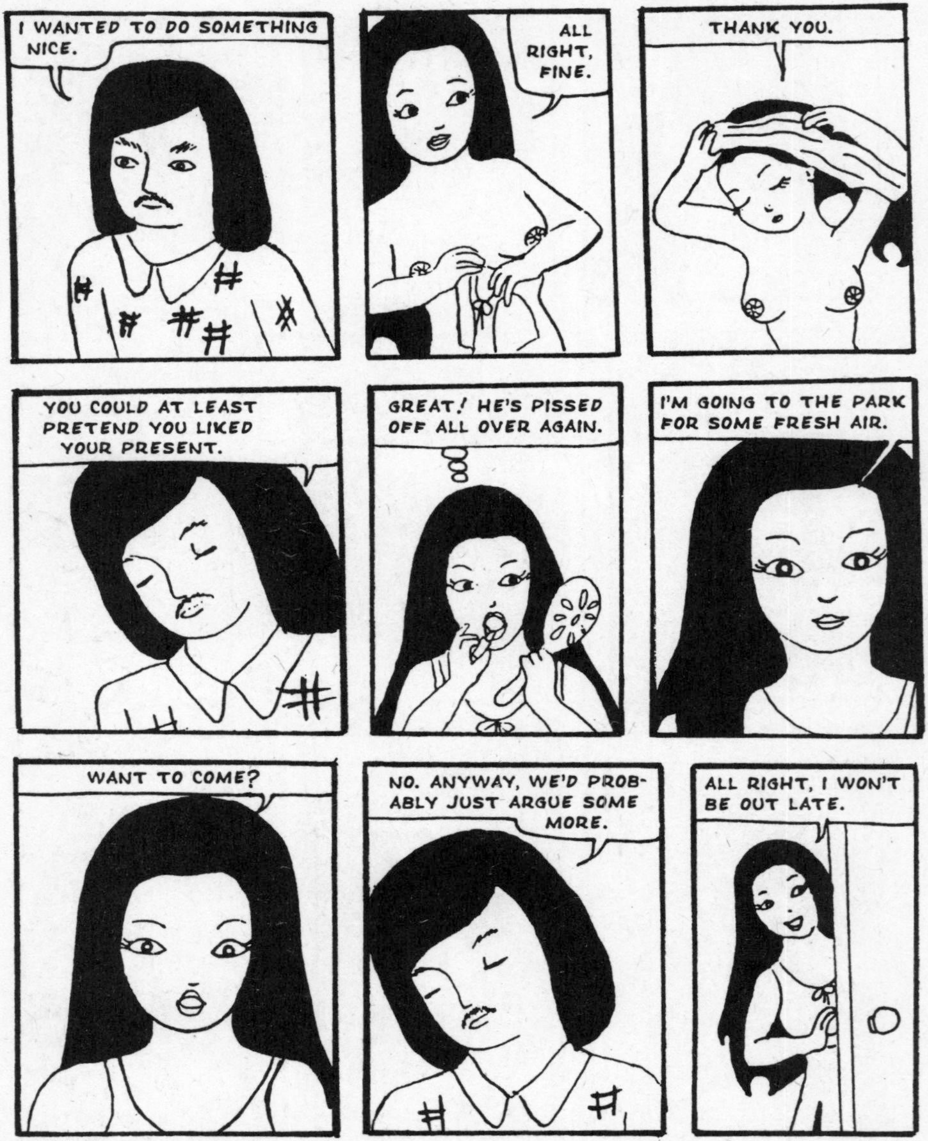
I WANTED TO DO SOMETHING NICE.
ALL RIGHT, FINE.
THANK YOU.
YOU COULD AT LEAST PRETEND YOU LIKED YOUR PRESENT.
GREAT! HE'S PISSED OFF ALL OVER AGAIN.
I'M GOING TO THE PARK FOR SOME FRESH AIR.
WANT TO COME?
NO. ANYWAY, WE'D PROB-ABLY JUST ARGUE SOME MORE.
ALL RIGHT, I WON'T BE OUT LATE.

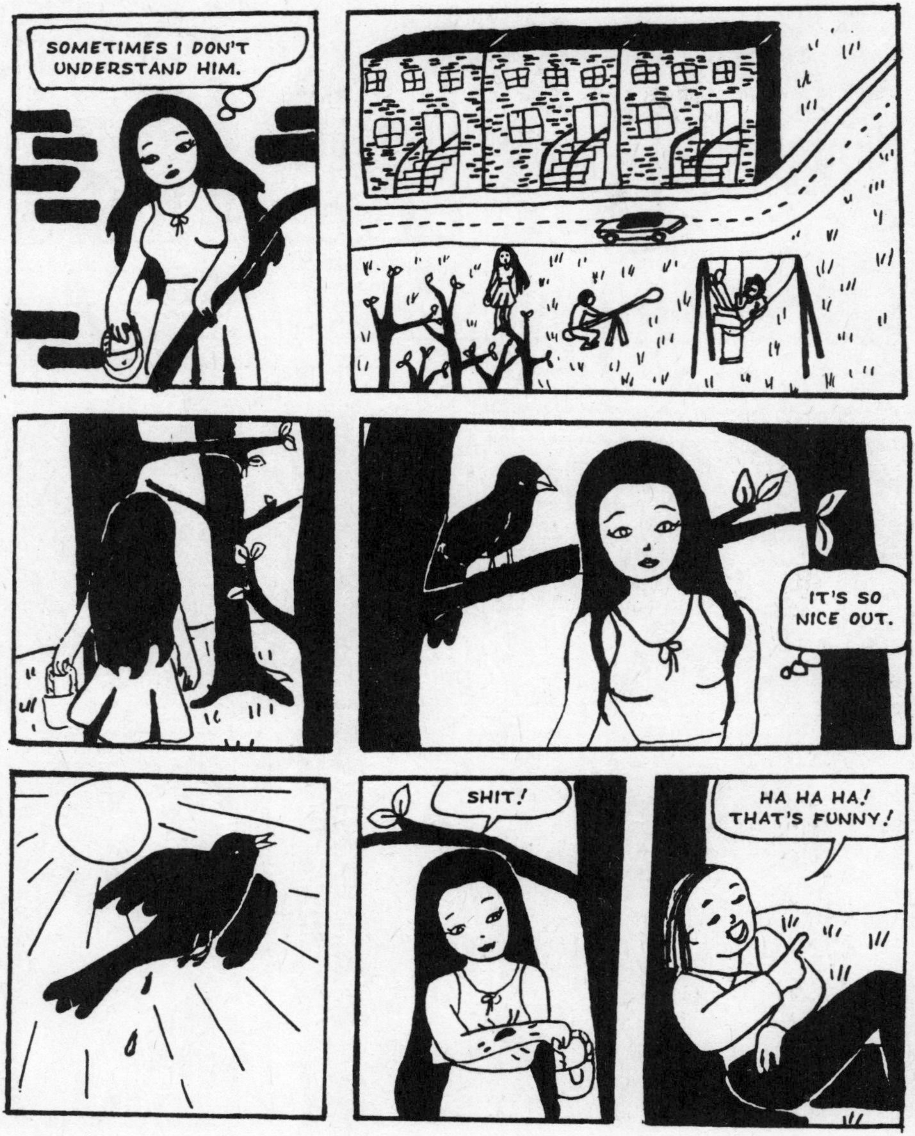
SOMETIMES I DON'T UNDERSTAND HIM.
IT'S SO NICE OUT.
SHIT!
HA HA HA! THAT'S FUNNY!

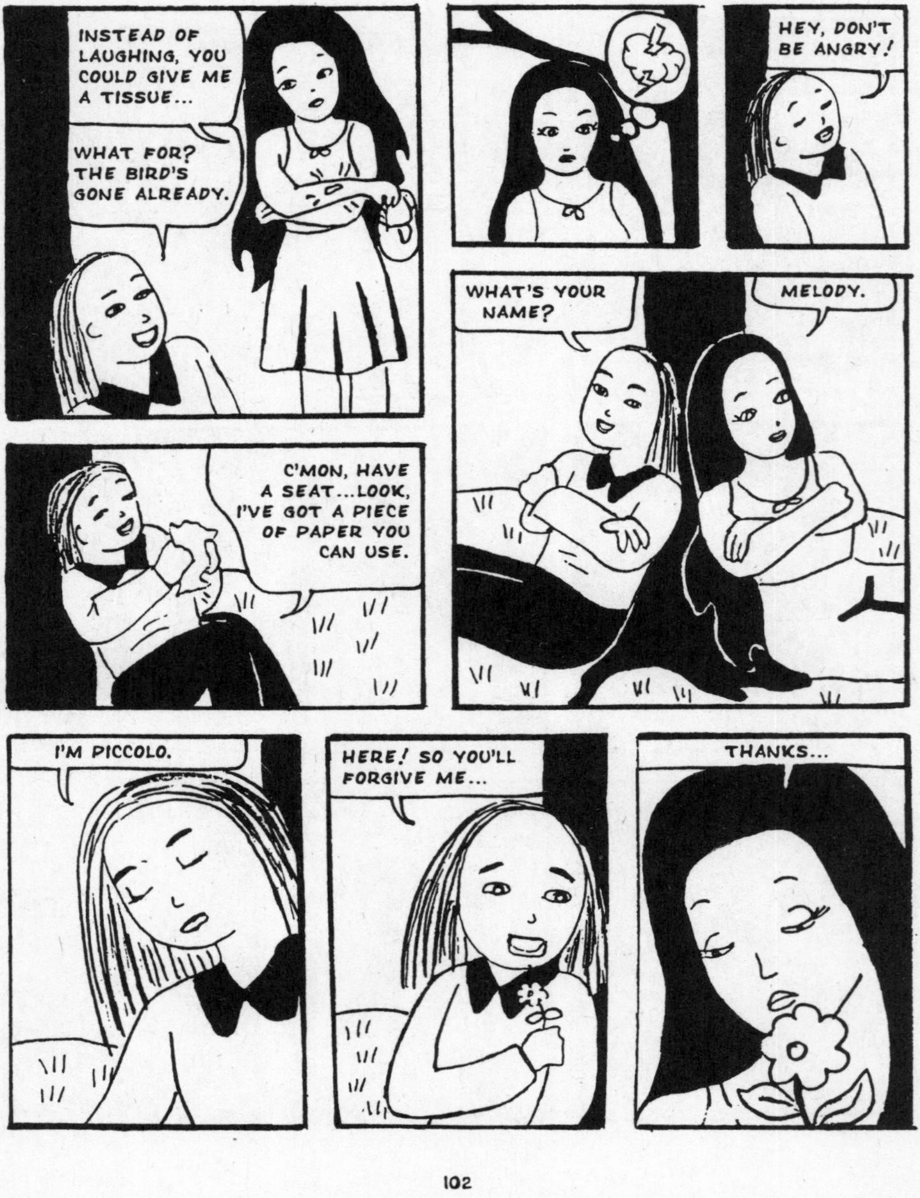
INSTEAD OF LAUGHING, YOU COULD GIVE ME A TISSUE...
WHAT FOR? THE BIRD'S GONE ALREADY.
HEY, DON'T BE ANGRY!
C'MON, HAVE A SEAT...LOOK, I'VE GOT A PIECE OF PAPER YOU CAN USE.
WHAT'S YOUR NAME?
MELODY.
I'M PICCOLO.
HERE! SO YOU'LL FORGIVE ME...
THANKS...

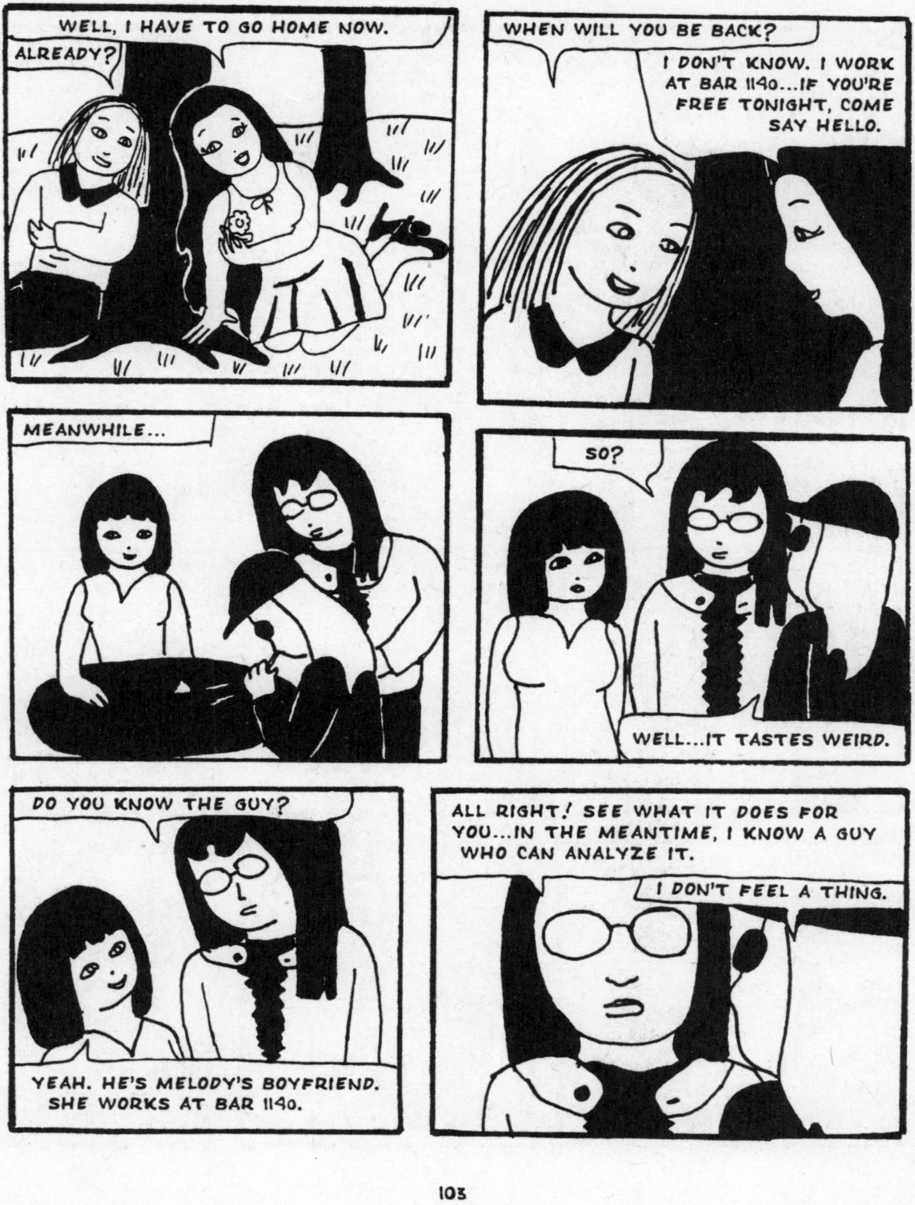
WELL, I HAVE TO GO HOME NOW.
ALREADY?
WHEN WILL YOU BE BACK?
I DON'T KNOW. I WORK AT BAR 1140...IF YOU'RE FREE TONIGHT, COME SAY HELLO.
MEANWHILE...
SO?
WELL...IT TASTES WEIRD.
DO YOU KNOW THE GUY?
YEAH. HE'S MELODY'S BOYFRIEND. SHE WORKS AT BAR 1140.
ALL RIGHT! SEE WHAT IT DOES FOR YOU...IN THE MEANTIME, I KNOW A GUY WHO CAN ANALYZE IT.
I DON'T FEEL A THING.

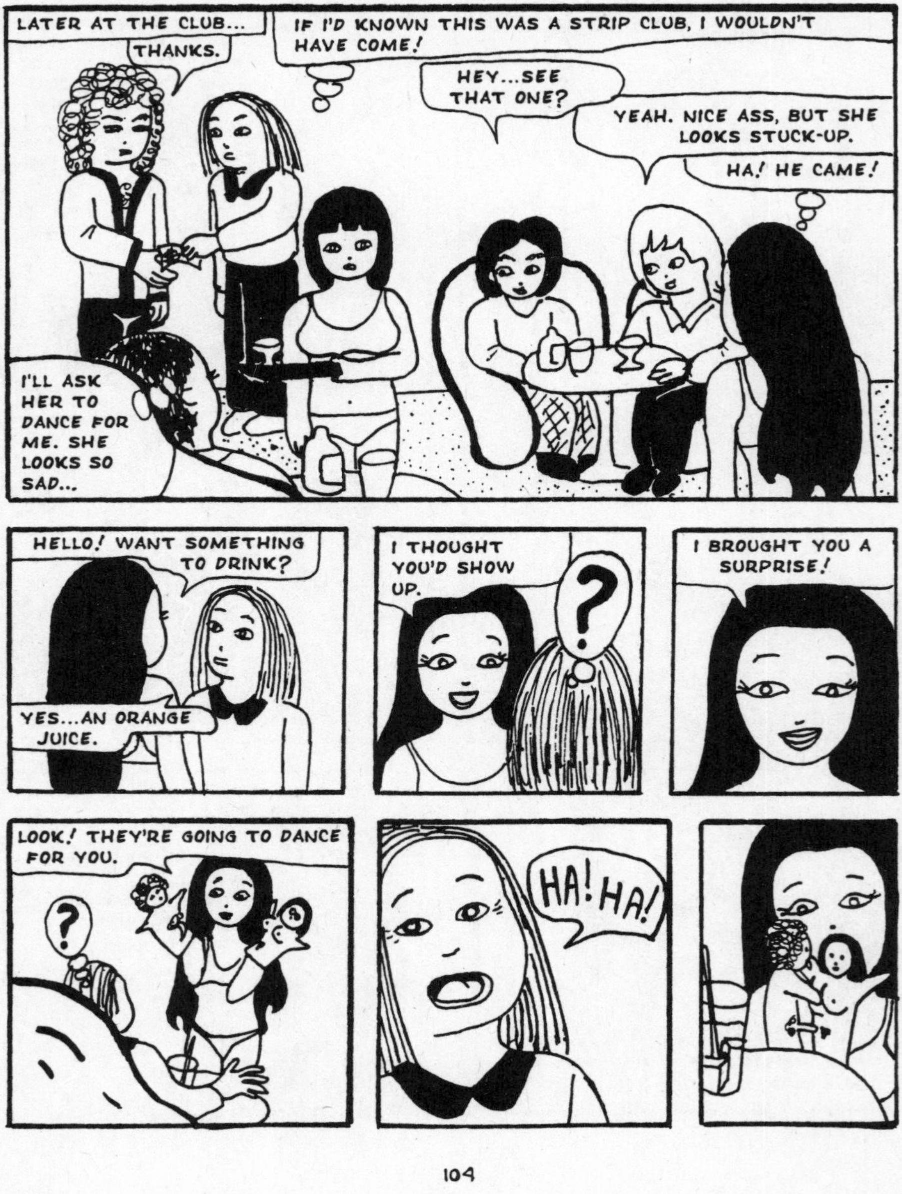
LATER AT THE CLUB...
THANKS.
IF I'D KNOWN THIS WAS A STRIP CLUB, I WOULDN'T HAVE COME!
HEY...SEE THAT ONE?
YEAH. NICE ASS, BUT SHE LOOKS STUCK-UP.
HA! HE CAME!
I'LL ASK HER TO DANCE FOR ME. SHE LOOKS SO SAD...
HELLO! WANT SOMETHING TO DRINK?
YES...AN ORANGE JUICE.
I THOUGHT YOU'D SHOW UP.
?
I BROUGHT YOU A SURPRISE!
LOOK! THEY'RE GOING TO DANCE FOR YOU.
?
HA! HA!

YOU KNOW, MELODY, I'M REALLY GLAD I CAME... YOU'RE VERY SPECIAL.
QUICK! BEFORE IT'S OVER...
OH YES... DON'T STOP!
OH NO!
WAIT!

Melody and
the Police

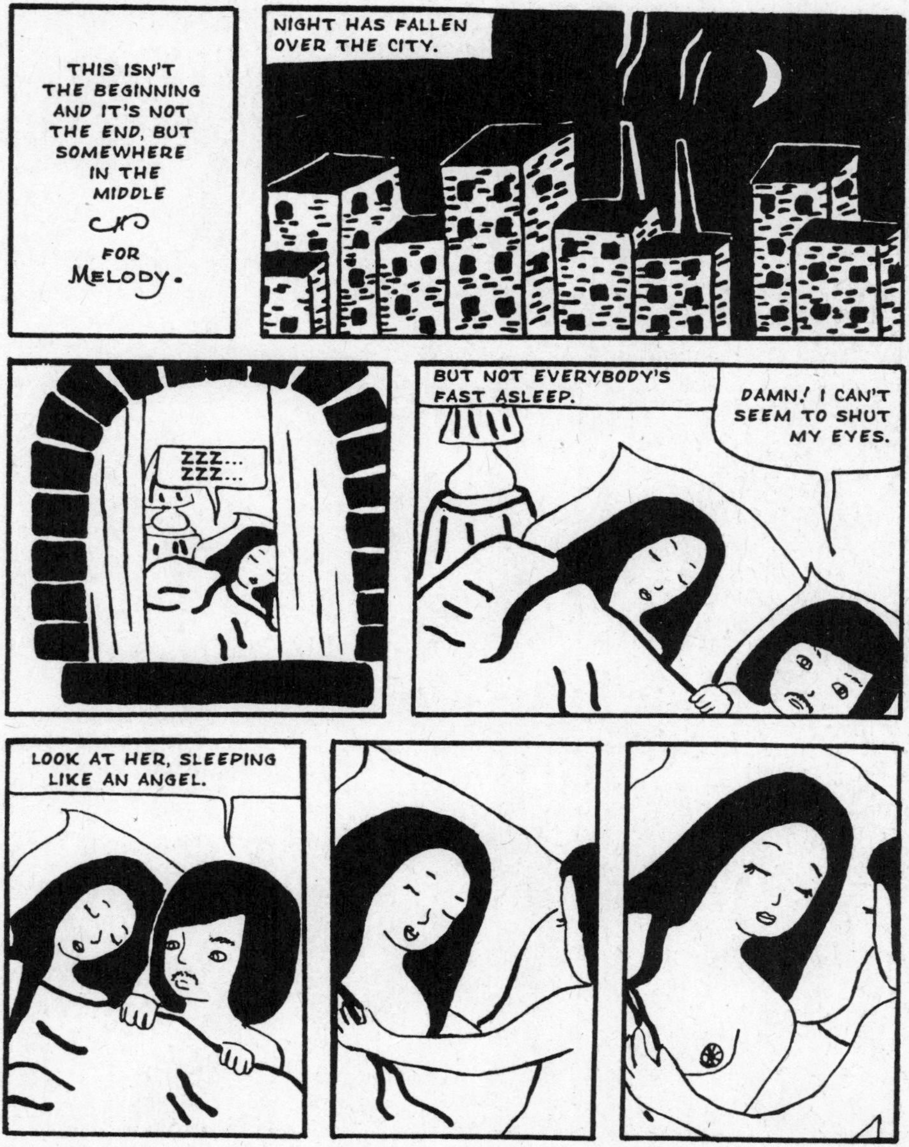
THIS ISN'T THE BEGINNING AND IT'S NOT THE END, BUT SOMEWHERE IN THE MIDDLE
FOR MELODY.
NIGHT HAS FALLEN OVER THE CITY.
ZZZ... ZZZ...
BUT NOT EVERYBODY'S FAST ASLEEP.
DAMN! I CAN'T SEEM TO SHUT MY EYES.
LOOK AT HER, SLEEPING LIKE AN ANGEL.

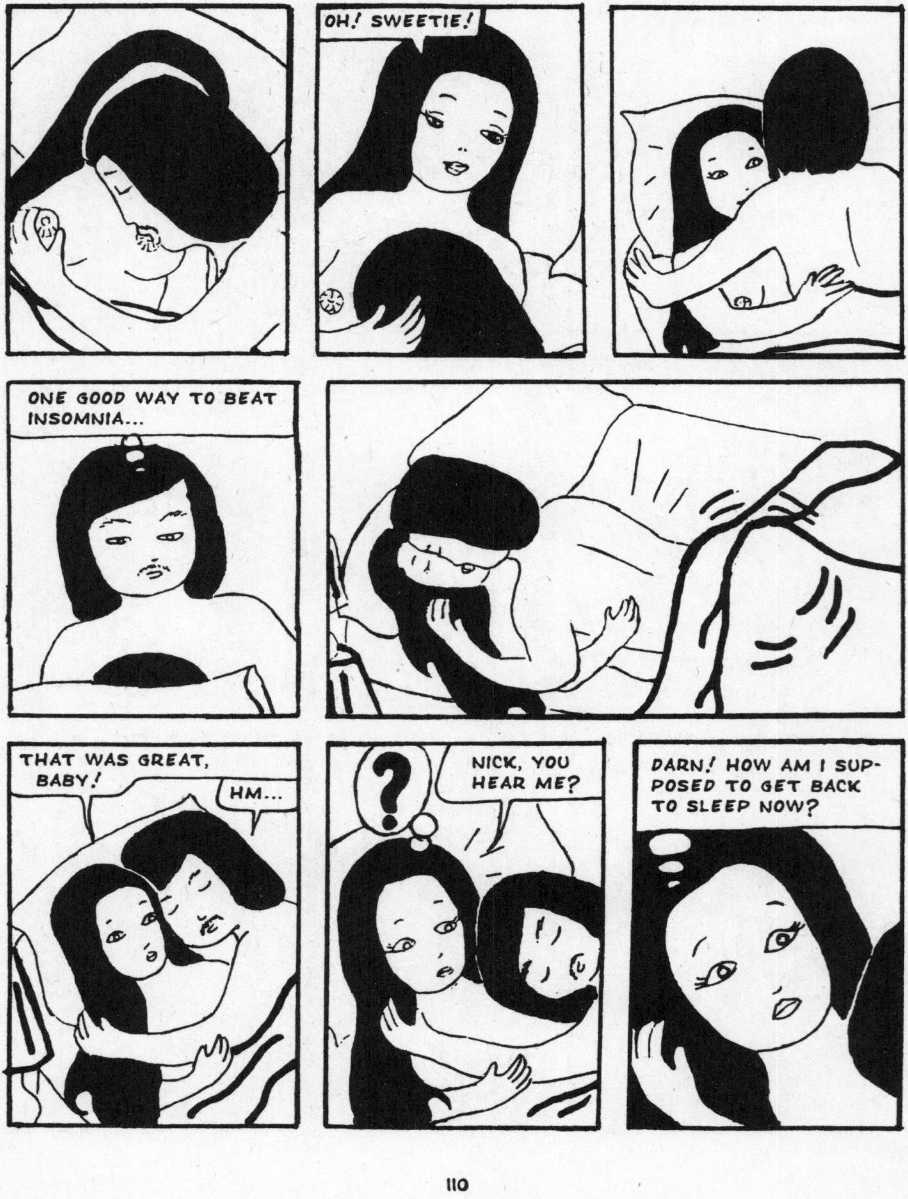
OH! SWEETIE!
ONE GOOD WAY TO BEAT INSOMNIA...
THAT WAS GREAT, BABY!
HM...
?
NICK, YOU HEAR ME?
DARN! HOW AM I SUPPOSED TO GET BACK TO SLEEP NOW?

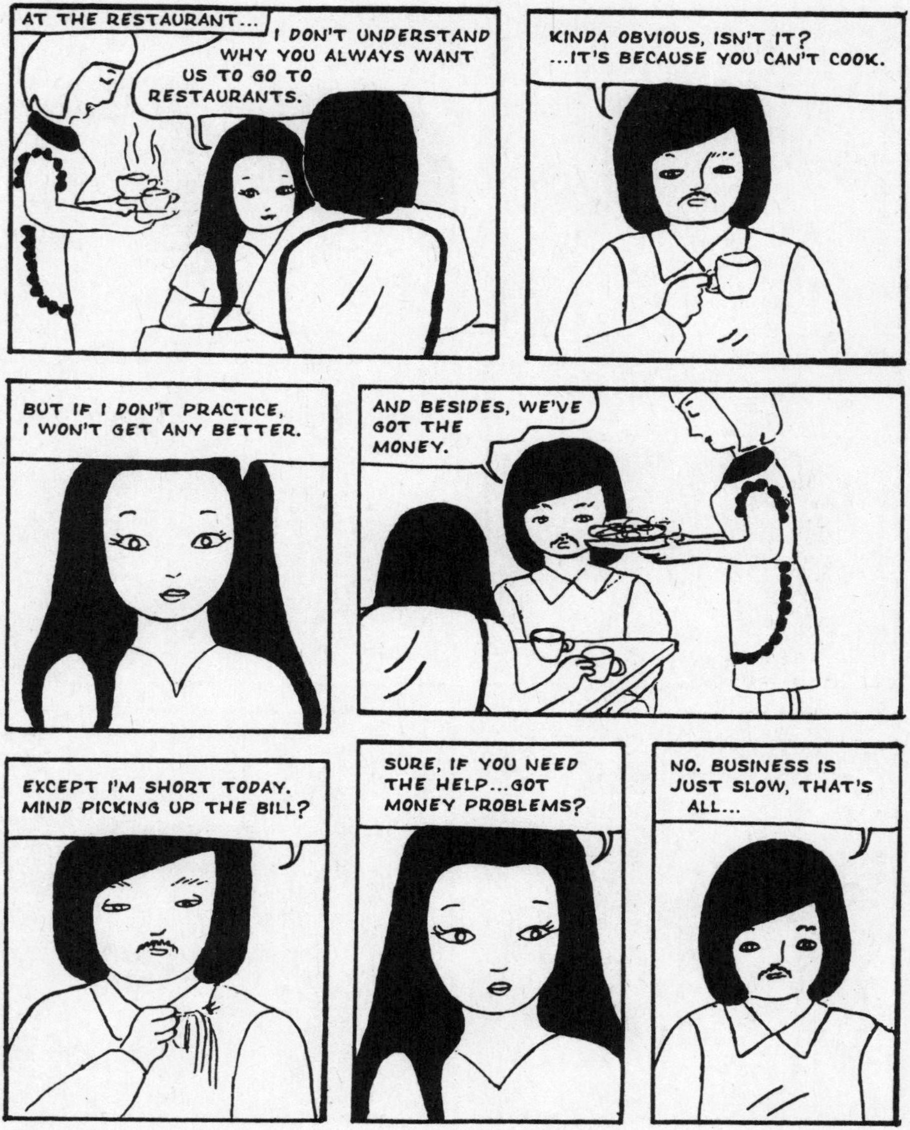
AT THE RESTAURANT...
I DON'T UNDERSTAND WHY YOU ALWAYS WANT US TO GO TO RESTAURANTS.
KINDA OBVIOUS, ISN'T IT? ...IT'S BECAUSE YOU CAN'T COOK.
BUT IF I DON'T PRACTICE, I WON'T GET ANY BETTER.
AND BESIDES, WE'VE GOT THE MONEY.
EXCEPT I'M SHORT TODAY. MIND PICKING UP THE BILL?
SURE, IF YOU NEED THE HELP...GOT MONEY PROBLEMS?
NO. BUSINESS IS JUST SLOW, THAT'S ALL...

YOU KNOW I DON'T LIKE YOU SELLING DOPE.
I DON'T LIKE YOU DANCING, BUT YOU DON'T SEE ME COMPLAINING.
ALL RIGHT, LET'S NOT ARGUE ABOUT THIS.
I'M GOING SHOPPING.
DON'T FORGET TO PAY THE BILL ON YOUR WAY OUT.
THIS BETTER NOT BECOME A HABIT...
I'LL GO DO THE GROCERIES.
JUST WAIT! I'LL SHOW HIM I CAN COOK!

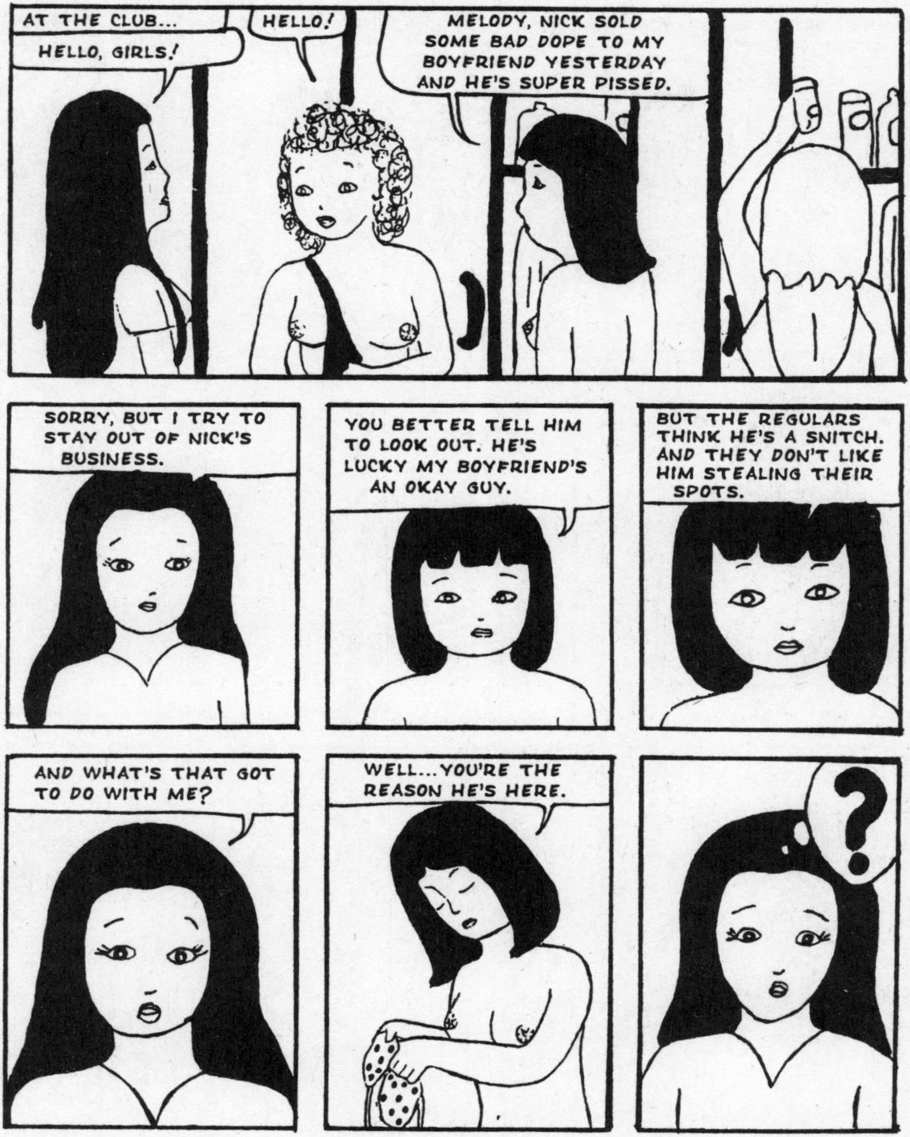
AT THE CLUB...
HELLO, GIRLS!
HELLO!
MELODY, NICK SOLD SOME BAD DOPE TO MY BOYFRIEND YESTERDAY AND HE'S SUPER PISSED.
SORRY, BUT I TRY TO STAY OUT OF NICK'S BUSINESS.
YOU BETTER TELL HIM TO LOOK OUT. HE'S LUCKY MY BOYFRIEND'S AN OKAY GUY.
BUT THE REGULARS THINK HE'S A SNITCH. AND THEY DON'T LIKE HIM STEALING THEIR SPOTS.
AND WHAT'S THAT GOT TO DO WITH ME?
WELL... YOU'RE THE REASON HE'S HERE.
?

HEY, GIRLS, YOU PLANNING ON COMING OUT?
UH...
OF COURSE, ONE SEC!
RELAX! YOU DON'T ALWAYS HAVE TO FREAK OUT.
MELODY, YOU WAITIN' FOR ME TO UNDRESS YOU?
NO, NO. COMING!
HERE GOES, ANOTHER SHIFT.
SO...HOW LONG HAVE YOU GIRLS BEEN DANCING?
ABOUT SEVEN YEARS NOW.
A MONTH, AND I DON'T LIKE IT.

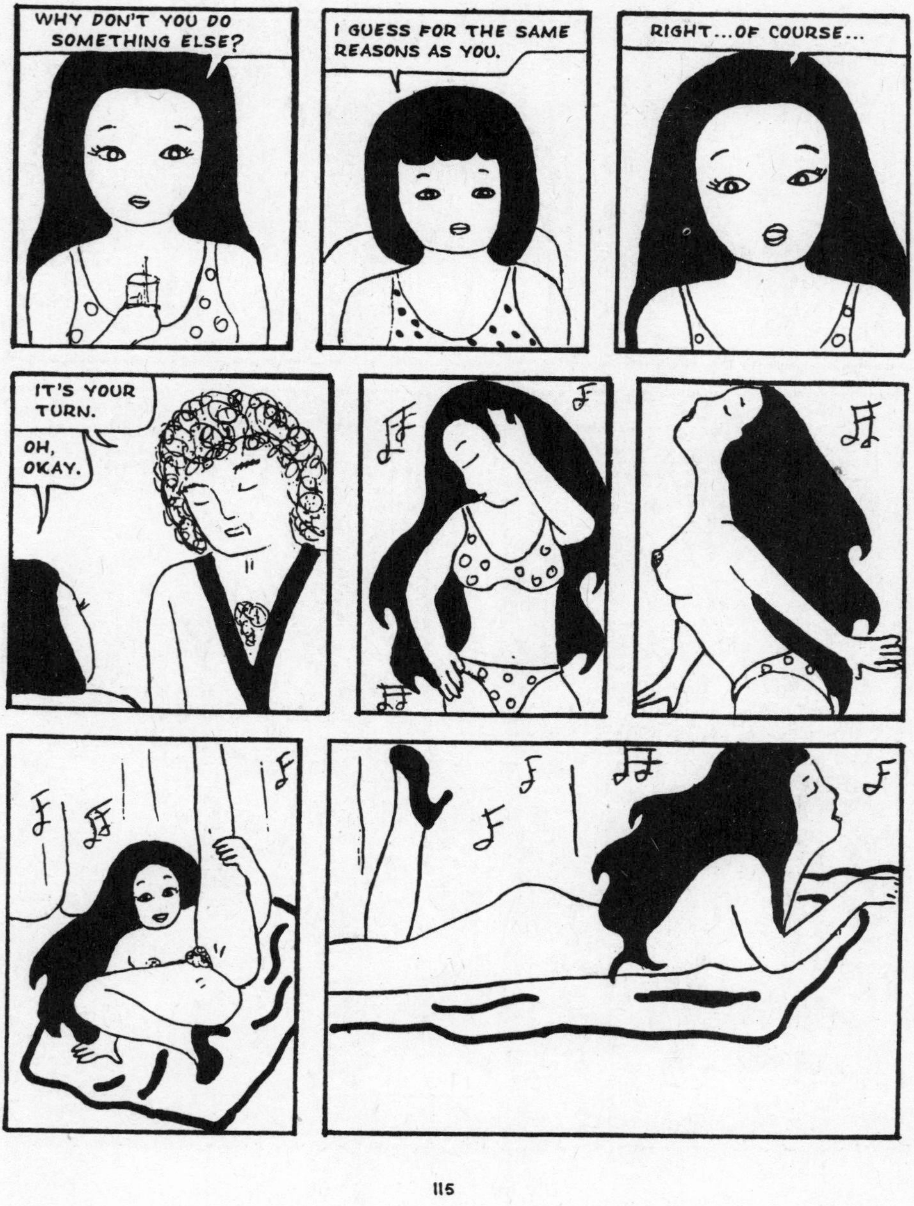
WHY DON'T YOU DO SOMETHING ELSE?
I GUESS FOR THE SAME REASONS AS YOU.
RIGHT...OF COURSE...
IT'S YOUR TURN.
OH, OKAY.

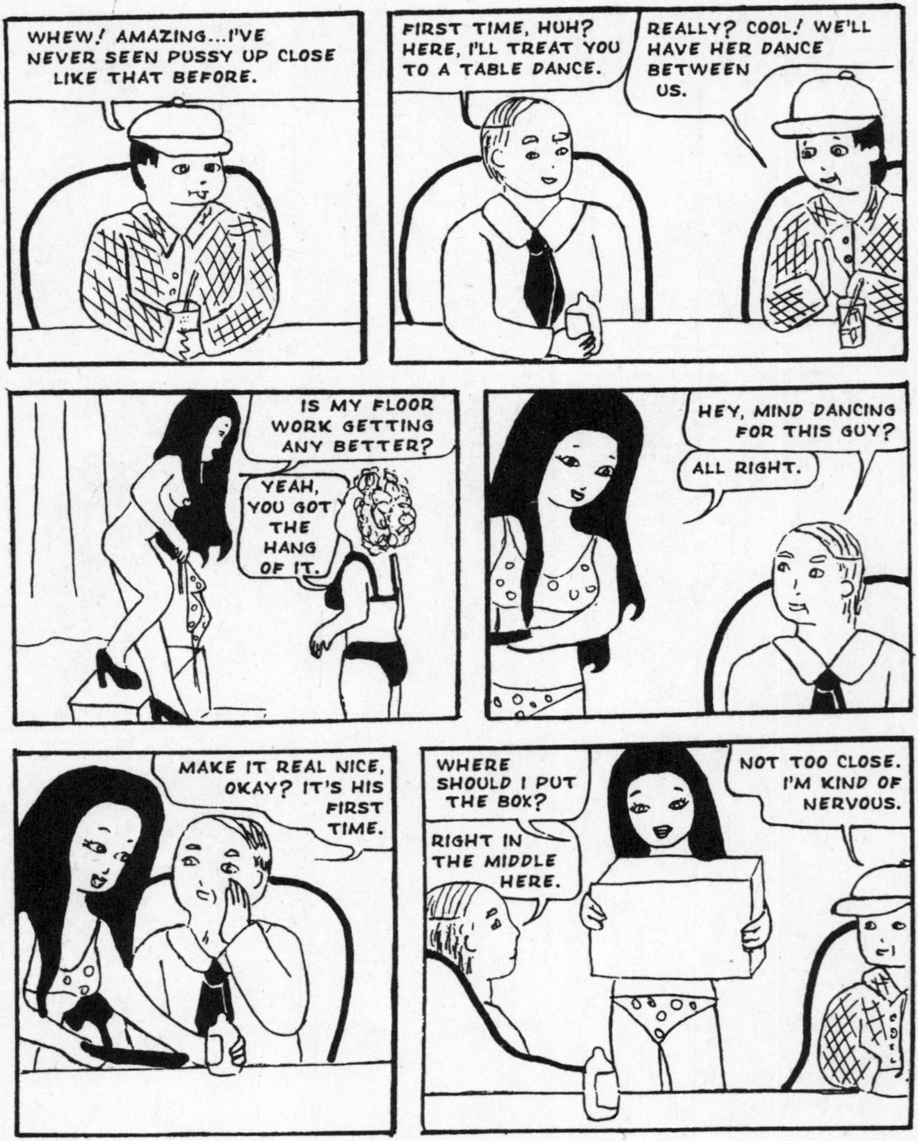
WHEW! AMAZING...I'VE NEVER SEEN PUSSY UP CLOSE LIKE THAT BEFORE.
FIRST TIME, HUH? HERE, I'LL TREAT YOU TO A TABLE DANCE.
REALLY? COOL! WE'LL HAVE HER DANCE BETWEEN US.
IS MY FLOOR WORK GETTING ANY BETTER?
YEAH, YOU GOT THE HANG OF IT.
HEY, MIND DANCING FOR THIS GUY?
ALL RIGHT.
MAKE IT REAL NICE, OKAY? IT'S HIS FIRST TIME.
WHERE SHOULD I PUT THE BOX?
RIGHT IN THE MIDDLE HERE.
NOT TOO CLOSE. I'M KIND OF NERVOUS.

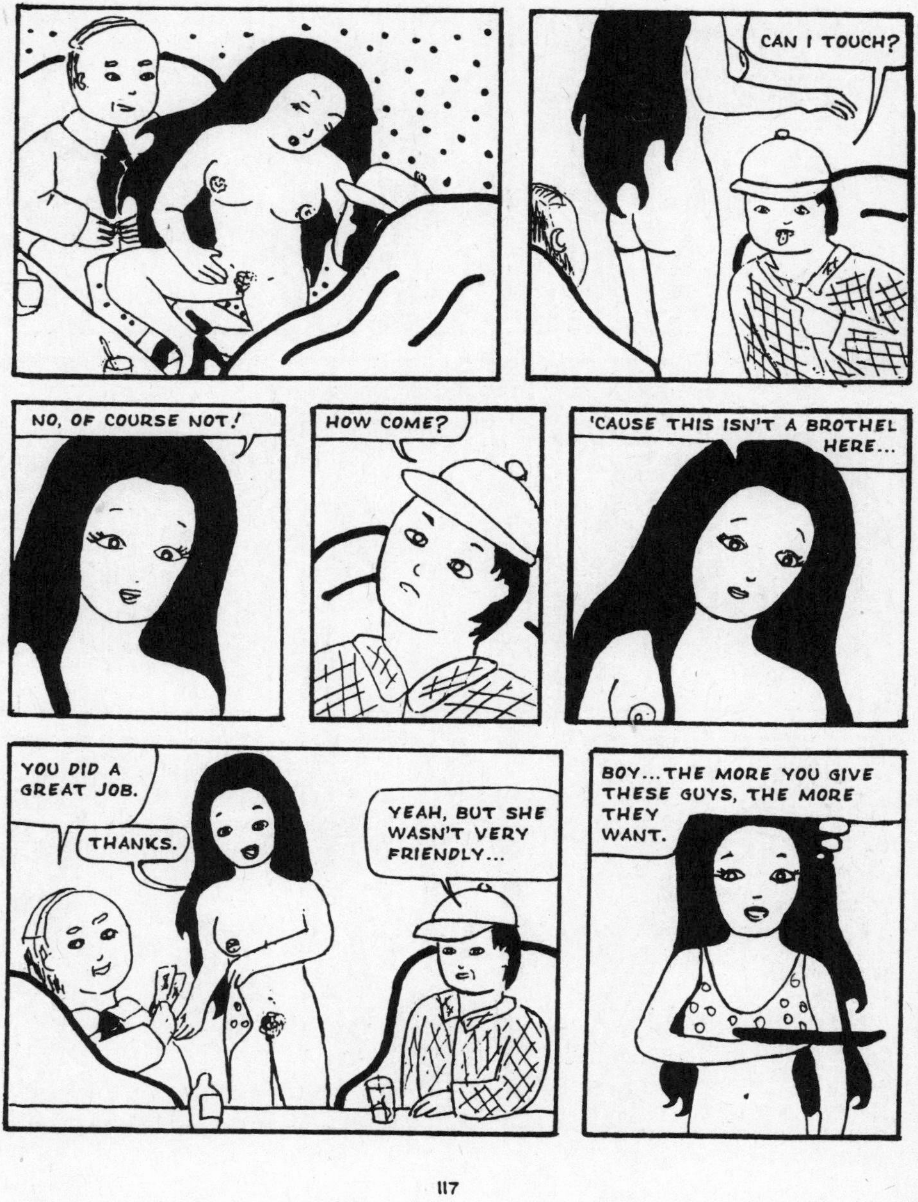
CAN I TOUCH?
NO, OF COURSE NOT!
HOW COME?
'CAUSE THIS ISN'T A BROTHEL HERE...
YOU DID A GREAT JOB.
THANKS.
YEAH, BUT SHE WASN'T VERY FRIENDLY...
BOY... THE MORE YOU GIVE THESE GUYS, THE MORE THEY WANT.

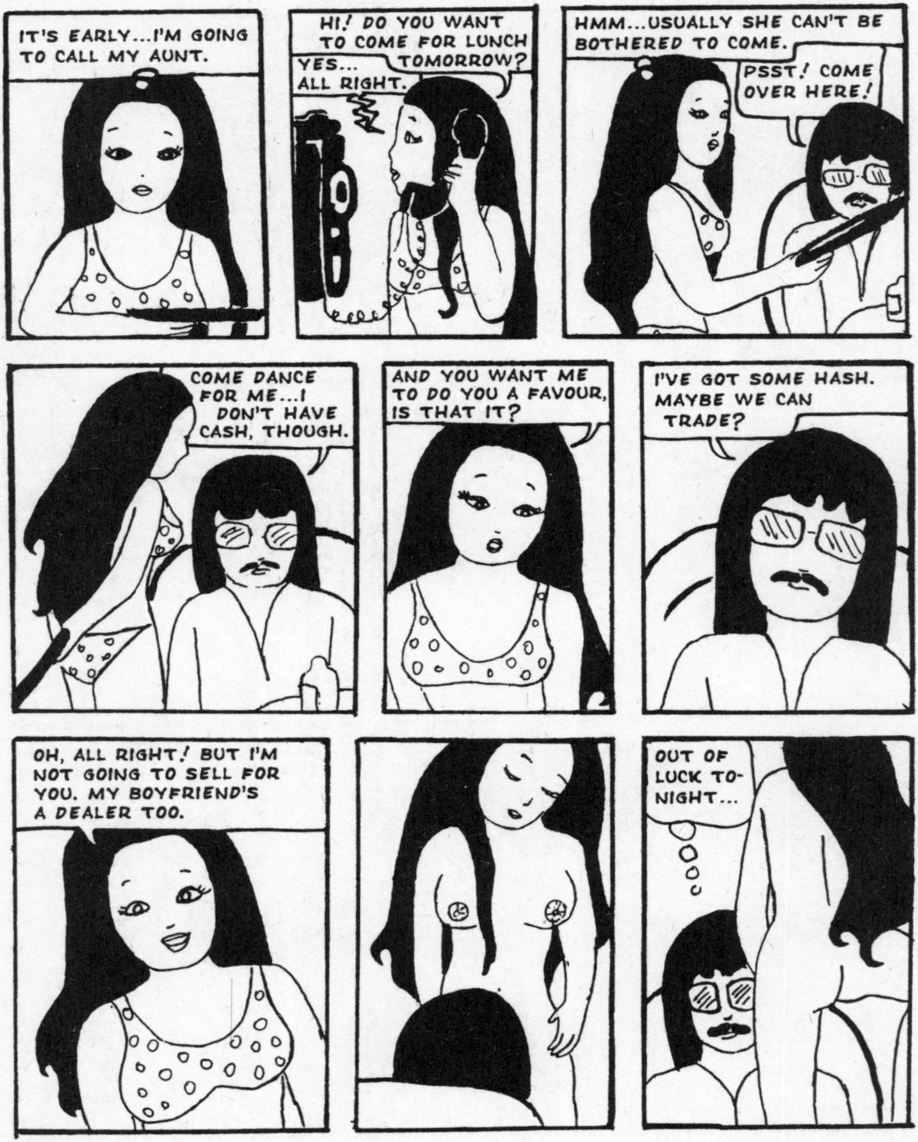
IT'S EARLY...I'M GOING TO CALL MY AUNT.
HI! DO YOU WANT TO COME FOR LUNCH TOMORROW?
YES... ALL RIGHT.
HMM...USUALLY SHE CAN'T BE BOTHERED TO COME.
PSST! COME OVER HERE!
COME DANCE FOR ME...I DON'T HAVE CASH, THOUGH.
AND YOU WANT ME TO DO YOU A FAVOUR, IS THAT IT?
I'VE GOT SOME HASH. MAYBE WE CAN TRADE?
OH, ALL RIGHT! BUT I'M NOT GOING TO SELL FOR YOU. MY BOYFRIEND'S A DEALER TOO.
OUT OF LUCK TO-NIGHT...

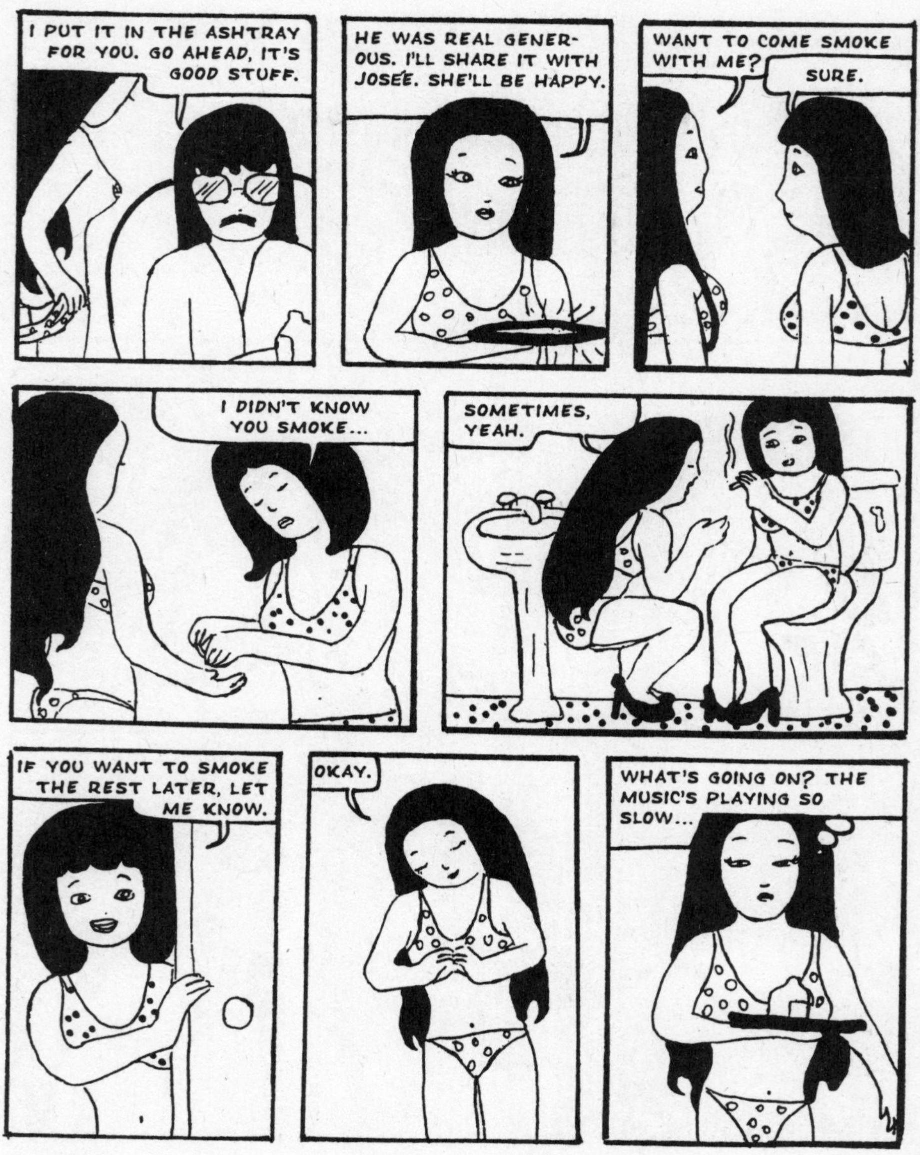
I PUT IT IN THE ASHTRAY FOR YOU. GO AHEAD, IT'S GOOD STUFF.
HE WAS REAL GENER-OUS. I'LL SHARE IT WITH JOSÉE. SHE'LL BE HAPPY.
WANT TO COME SMOKE WITH ME?
SURE.
I DIDN'T KNOW YOU SMOKE...
SOMETIMES, YEAH.
IF YOU WANT TO SMOKE THE REST LATER, LET ME KNOW.
OKAY.
WHAT'S GOING ON? THE MUSIC'S PLAYING SO SLOW...

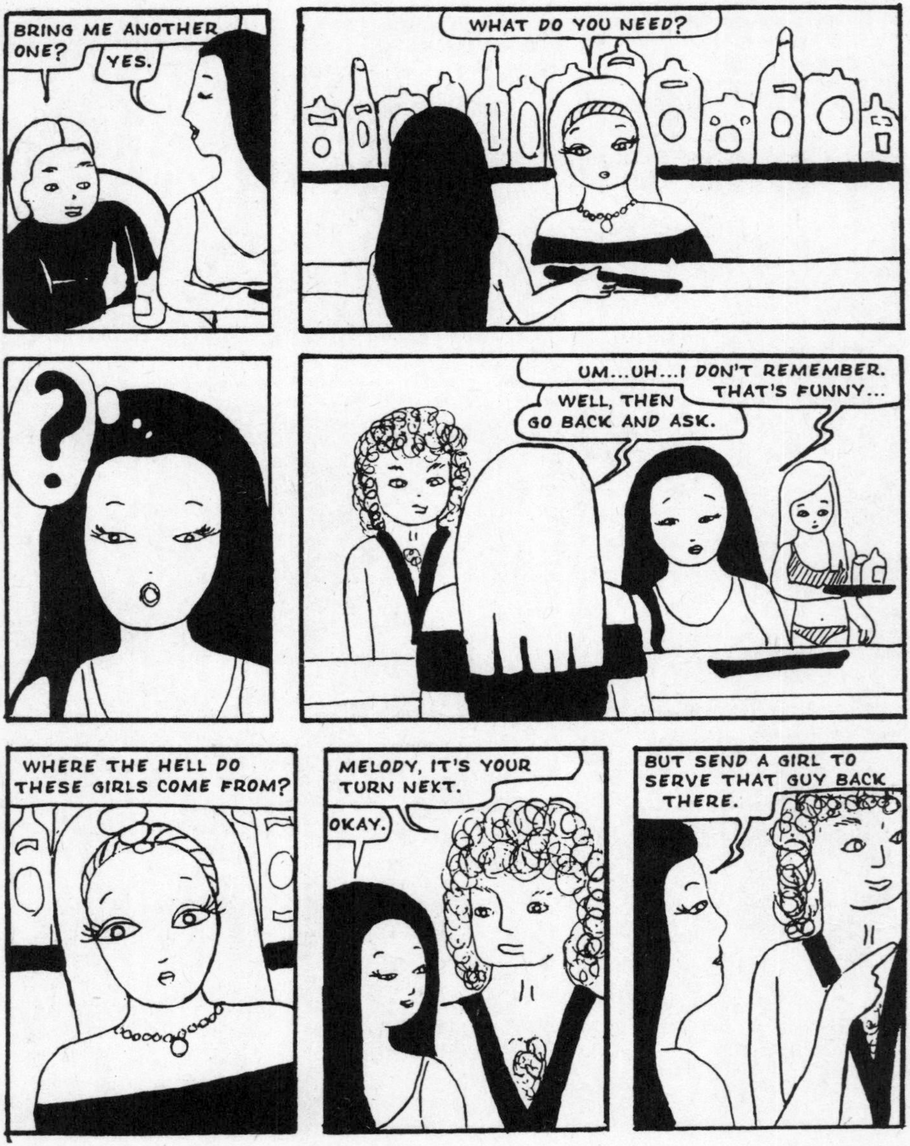
BRING ME ANOTHER ONE?
YES.
WHAT DO YOU NEED?
UM...UH...I DON'T REMEMBER. THAT'S FUNNY...
WELL, THEN GO BACK AND ASK.
WHERE THE HELL DO THESE GIRLS COME FROM?
MELODY, IT'S YOUR TURN NEXT.
OKAY.
BUT SEND A GIRL TO SERVE THAT GUY BACK THERE.

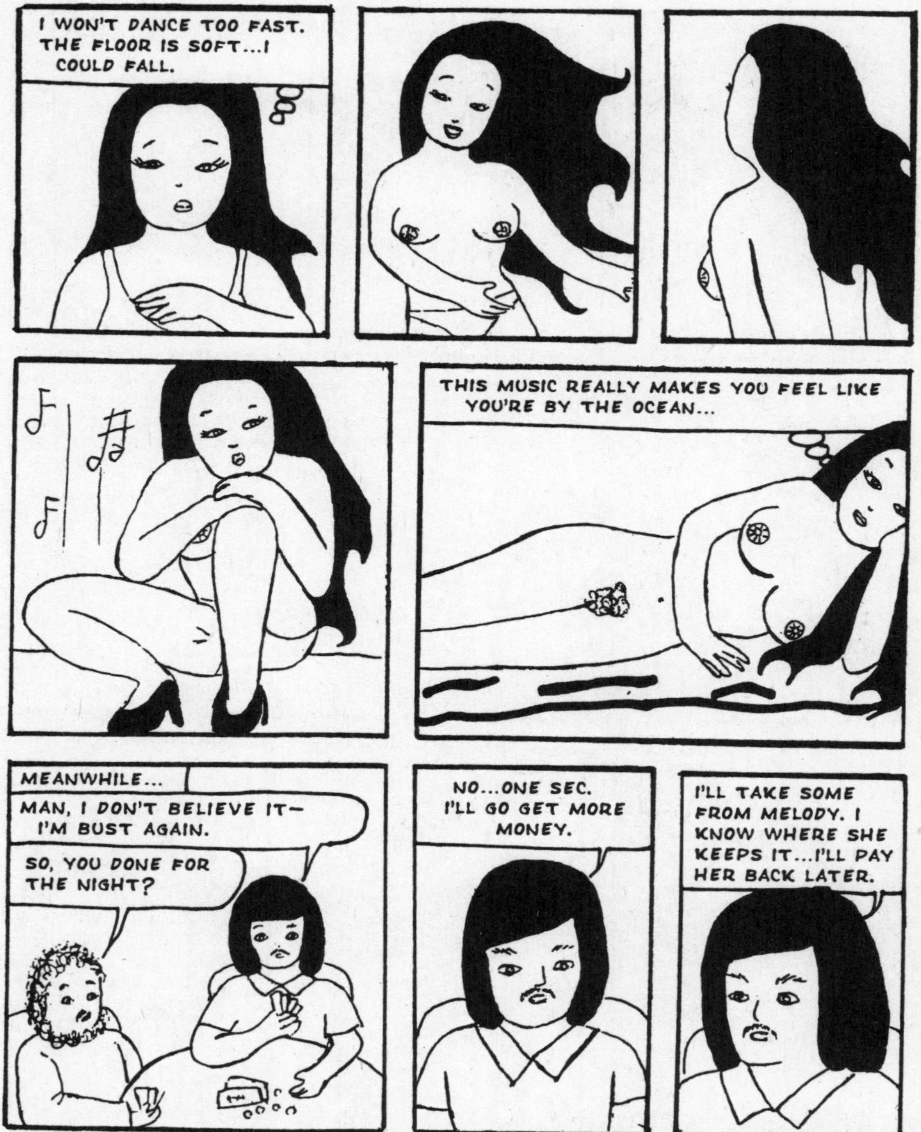
I WON'T DANCE TOO FAST. THE FLOOR IS SOFT...I COULD FALL.
THIS MUSIC REALLY MAKES YOU FEEL LIKE YOU'RE BY THE OCEAN...
MEANWHILE...
MAN, I DON'T BELIEVE IT— I'M BUST AGAIN.
SO, YOU DONE FOR THE NIGHT?
NO...ONE SEC. I'LL GO GET MORE MONEY.
I'LL TAKE SOME FROM MELODY. I KNOW WHERE SHE KEEPS IT...I'LL PAY HER BACK LATER.

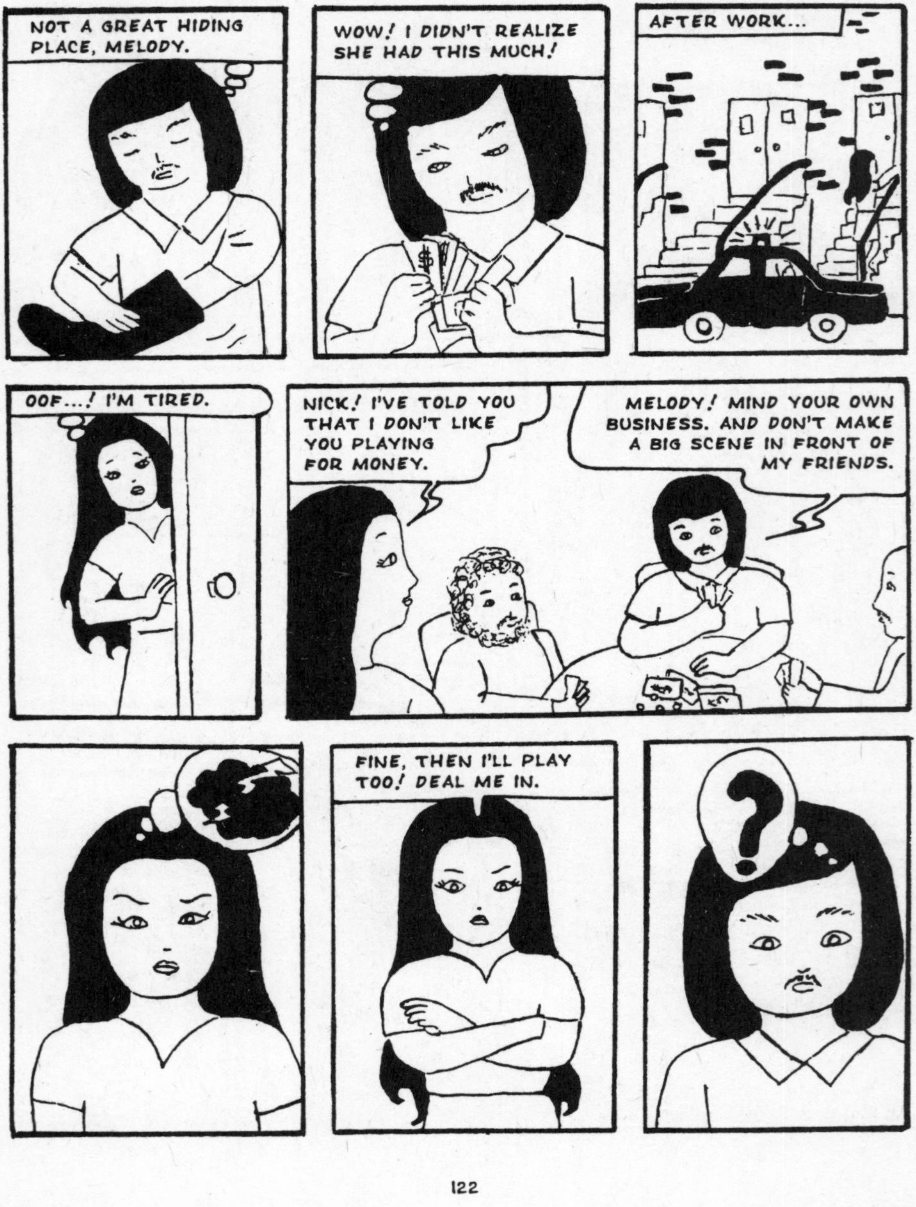
NOT A GREAT HIDING PLACE, MELODY.
WOW! I DIDN'T REALIZE SHE HAD THIS MUCH!
AFTER WORK...
OOF...! I'M TIRED.
NICK! I'VE TOLD YOU THAT I DON'T LIKE YOU PLAYING FOR MONEY.
MELODY! MIND YOUR OWN BUSINESS. AND DON'T MAKE A BIG SCENE IN FRONT OF MY FRIENDS.
FINE, THEN I'LL PLAY TOO! DEAL ME IN.

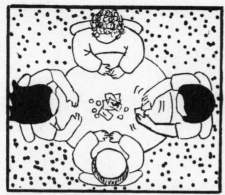

A FEW HOURS LATER...

SHE'S LUCKY...LOOKS LIKE SHE'S GONNA BE THE BIG WINNER TONIGHT.

LAST HAND AND THEN IT'S BEDTIME.

NEXT MORNING...

KNOCK! KNOCK! KNOCK!

YOU LOOK SURPRISED. FORGOT ABOUT US, HUH?

HI, MELODY.

NO, BUT I JUST WENT TO BED. I WORK NIGHTS...COME IN.

FINE. GO GET DRESSED. I'LL MAKE BREAKFAST.

GOOD GRIEF! THIS IS GONNA BE A ROUGH DAY!
?
HA! MELODY WRAPPED SOME CHOCOLATE IN LITTLE PIECES OF PAPER.
NICK'S NOT HUNGRY?
NO...AND HE'S NOT READY TO GET UP YET.
MELODY, I THINK YOU'RE OVERDOING IT. MAYBE YOU SHOULD QUIT YOUR JOB.
YEAH, AND I WANT YOU TO COME PLAY BALL WITH ME.
FOR SURE, ELIZA. I'LL HAVE SOME TIME OFF REALLY SOON.
I'LL *DO* THE DISHES AND THEN WE'LL BE ON OUR WAY.

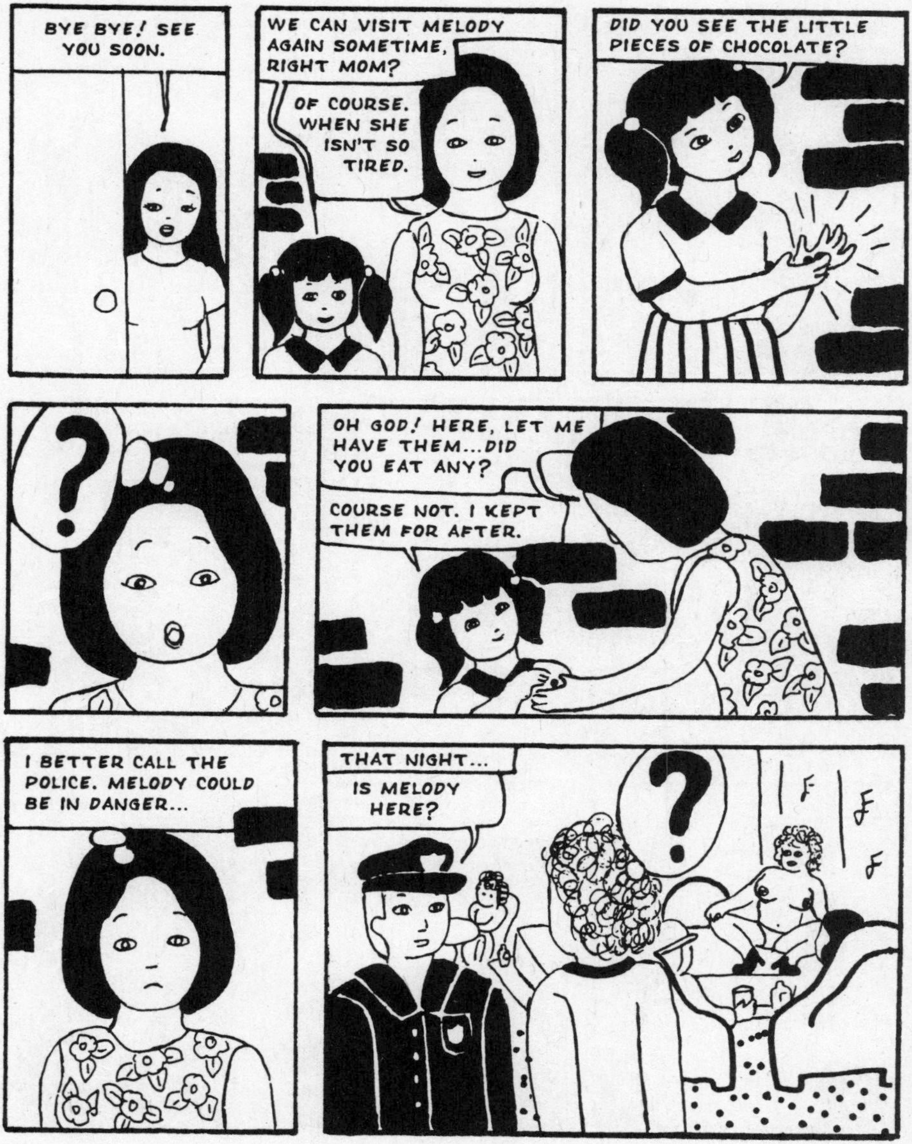
BYE BYE! SEE YOU SOON.
WE CAN VISIT MELODY AGAIN SOMETIME, RIGHT MOM?
OF COURSE. WHEN SHE ISN'T SO TIRED.
DID YOU SEE THE LITTLE PIECES OF CHOCOLATE?
?
OH GOD! HERE, LET ME HAVE THEM...DID YOU EAT ANY?
COURSE NOT. I KEPT THEM FOR AFTER.
I BETTER CALL THE POLICE. MELODY COULD BE IN DANGER...
THAT NIGHT...
IS MELODY HERE?
?

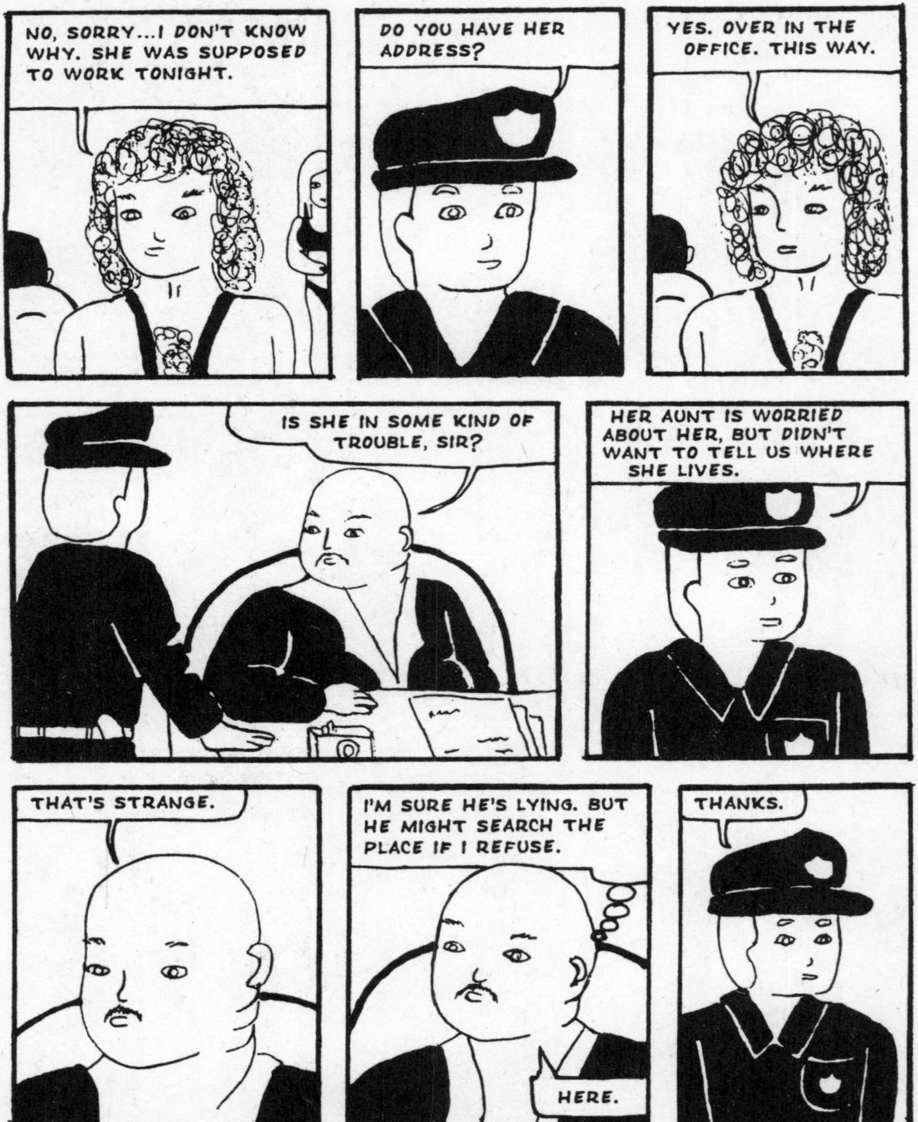
NO, SORRY...I DON'T KNOW WHY. SHE WAS SUPPOSED TO WORK TONIGHT.
DO YOU HAVE HER ADDRESS?
YES. OVER IN THE OFFICE. THIS WAY.
IS SHE IN SOME KIND OF TROUBLE, SIR?
HER AUNT IS WORRIED ABOUT HER, BUT DIDN'T WANT TO TELL US WHERE SHE LIVES.
THAT'S STRANGE.
I'M SURE HE'S LYING. BUT HE MIGHT SEARCH THE PLACE IF I REFUSE.
HERE.
THANKS.

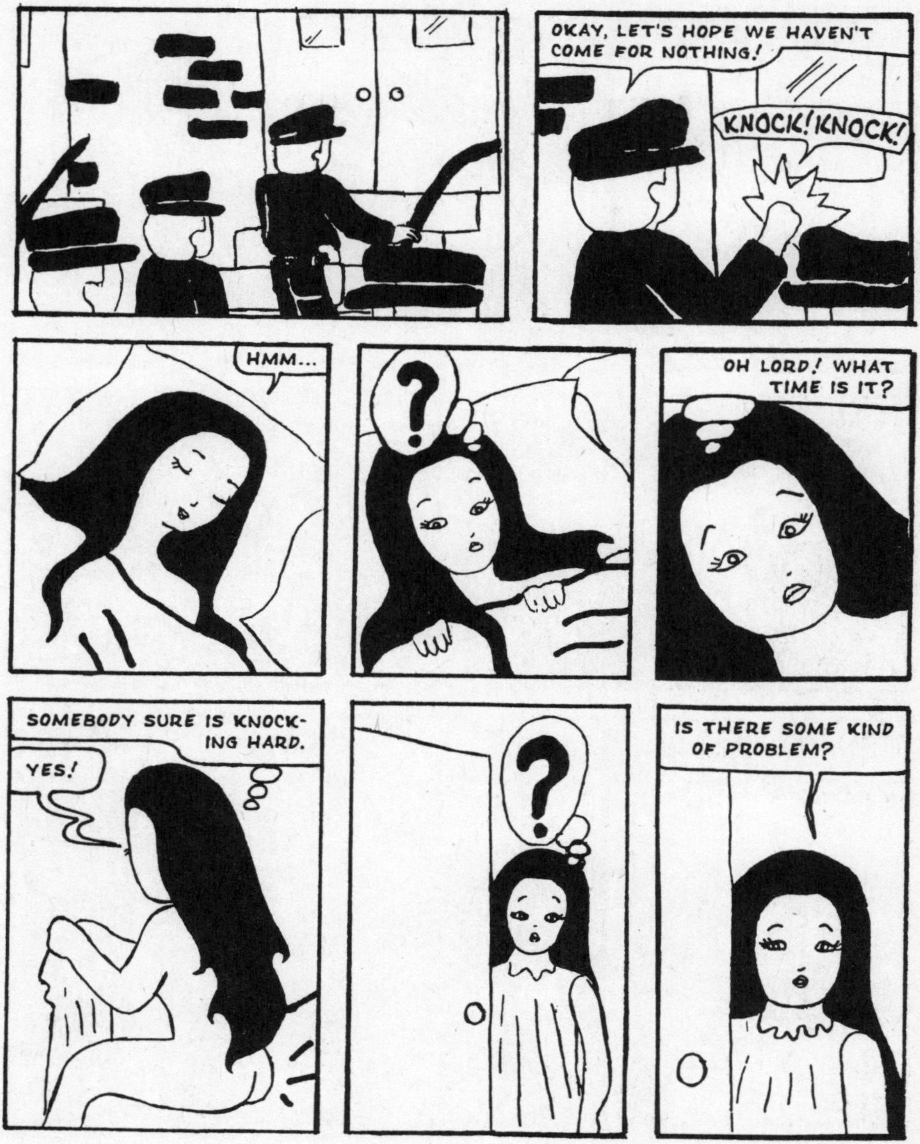
OKAY, LET'S HOPE WE HAVEN'T COME FOR NOTHING!
KNOCK! KNOCK!
HMM...
?
OH LORD! WHAT TIME IS IT?
SOMEBODY SURE IS KNOCK-ING HARD.
YES!
?
IS THERE SOME KIND OF PROBLEM?

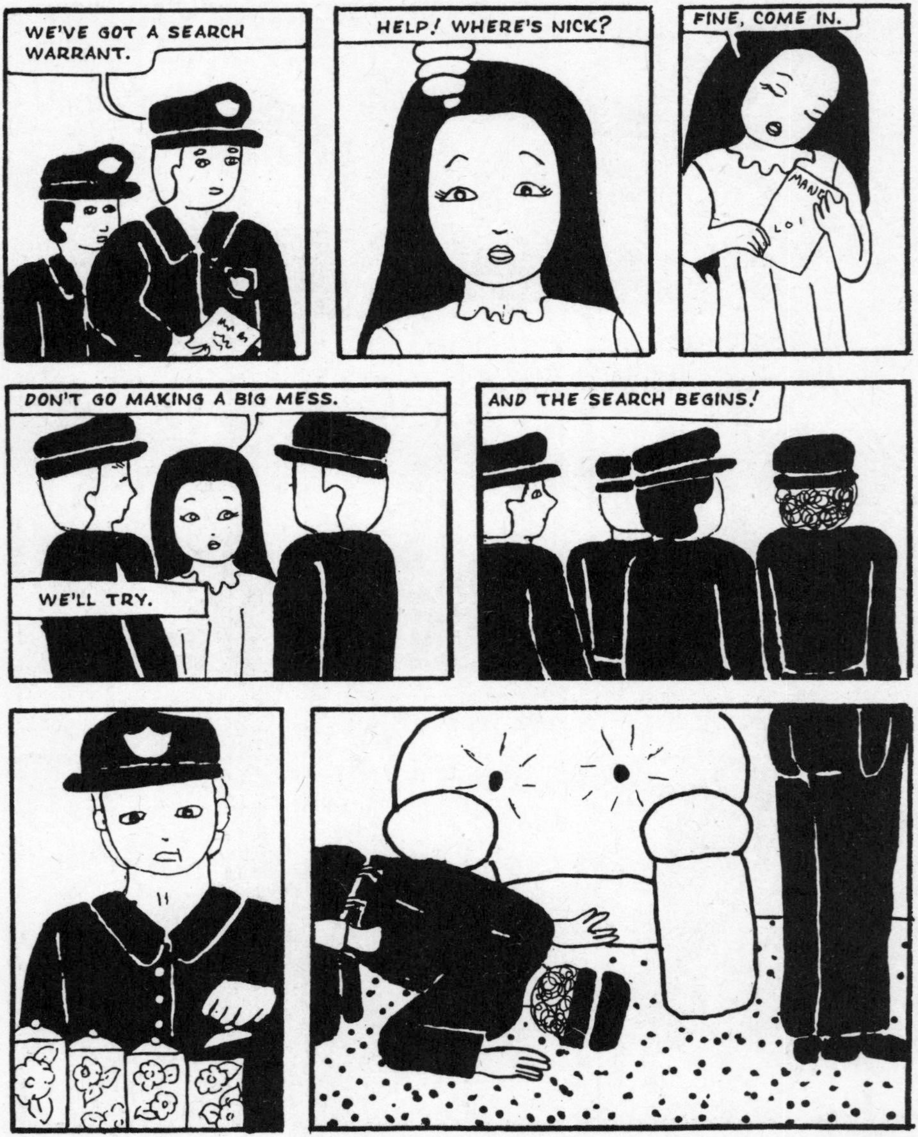
WE'VE GOT A SEARCH WARRANT.
HELP! WHERE'S NICK?
FINE, COME IN.
DON'T GO MAKING A BIG MESS.
WE'LL TRY.
AND THE SEARCH BEGINS!

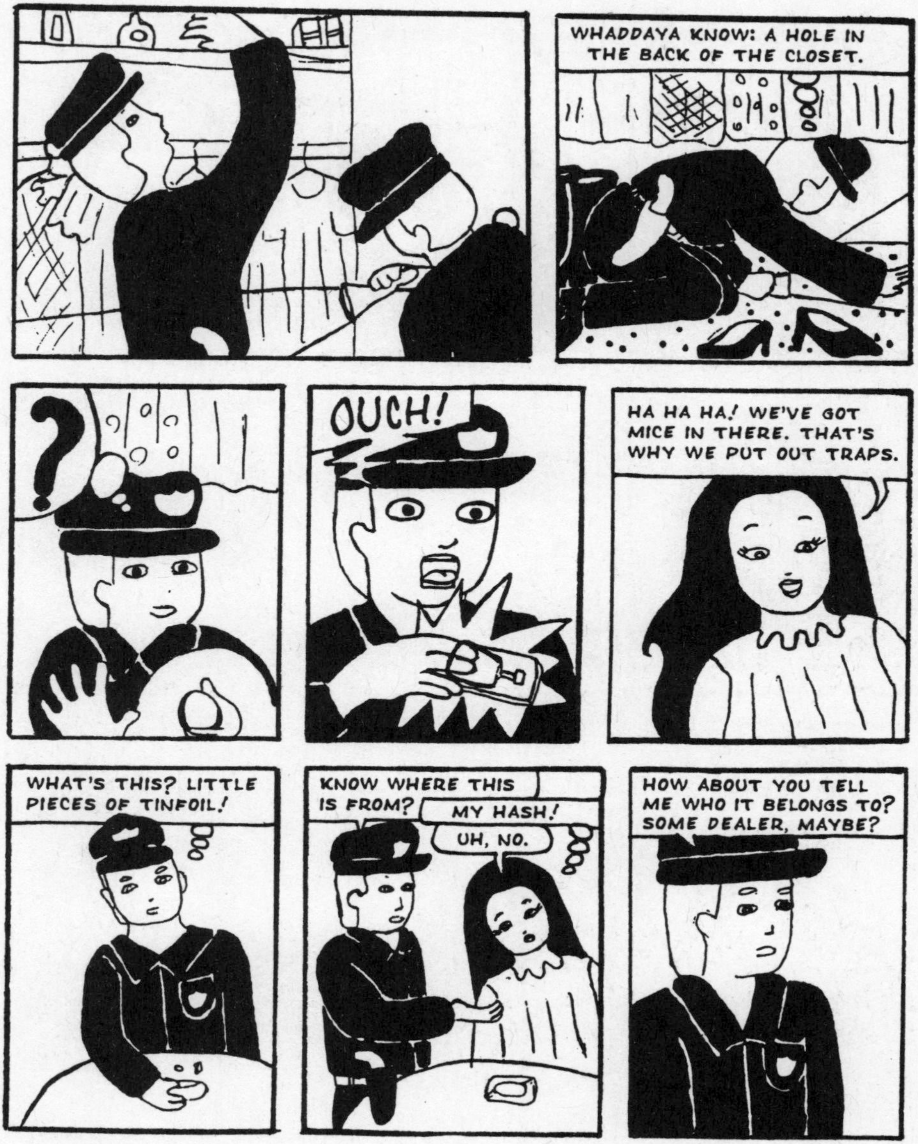
WHADDAYA KNOW: A HOLE IN THE BACK OF THE CLOSET.
OUCH!
HA HA HA! WE'VE GOT MICE IN THERE. THAT'S WHY WE PUT OUT TRAPS.
WHAT'S THIS? LITTLE PIECES OF TINFOIL!
KNOW WHERE THIS IS FROM?
MY HASH!
UH, NO.
HOW ABOUT YOU TELL ME WHO IT BELONGS TO? SOME DEALER, MAYBE?

I SWEAR I DON'T KNOW... A CUSTOMER GAVE IT TO ME FOR A FEW DANCES.

ANYWAY, YOU CAN'T ARREST ME FOR A COUPLE OF SCRAPS OF TINFOIL...

DON'T NEED 'EM. WE GOT THE CONTENTS AT THE STATION, AND THE PROOF HERE.

WE'RE JUST GOING TO ASK YOU TO NOT LEAVE THE CITY. YOU'LL GET A COURT SUMMONS SOON.

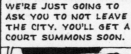

I GUESS I'VE GOT NO CHOICE.

MEANWHILE...

I NEED TO HEAD HOME. IT'S GETTING LATE.

OKAY IF I GIVE YOU SOME COKE INSTEAD OF CASH?

YOU BET!

I WONDER WHY SHE DIDN'T SHOW UP TONIGHT?
SHE'S ALWAYS SO DAMN UNPREDICTABLE.
WHATEVER SHE'S UP TO, SHE BETTER NOT QUIT WORKING AT THE CLUB.
?
NICK! AT LAST!
BOO HOO! SNIFF!
HEY, BABE, WHAT THE HELL IS GOING ON?
OH, NICK!
THE POLICE WERE HERE. THEY WANT TO THROW ME IN JAIL BECAUSE OF SOME TINFOIL...! SNIFF... AND NOW I'M A PRISONER IN THE CITY...OH, NICK...
OKAY...RELAX, THEY'RE GONE.
OH MY GOD!
?

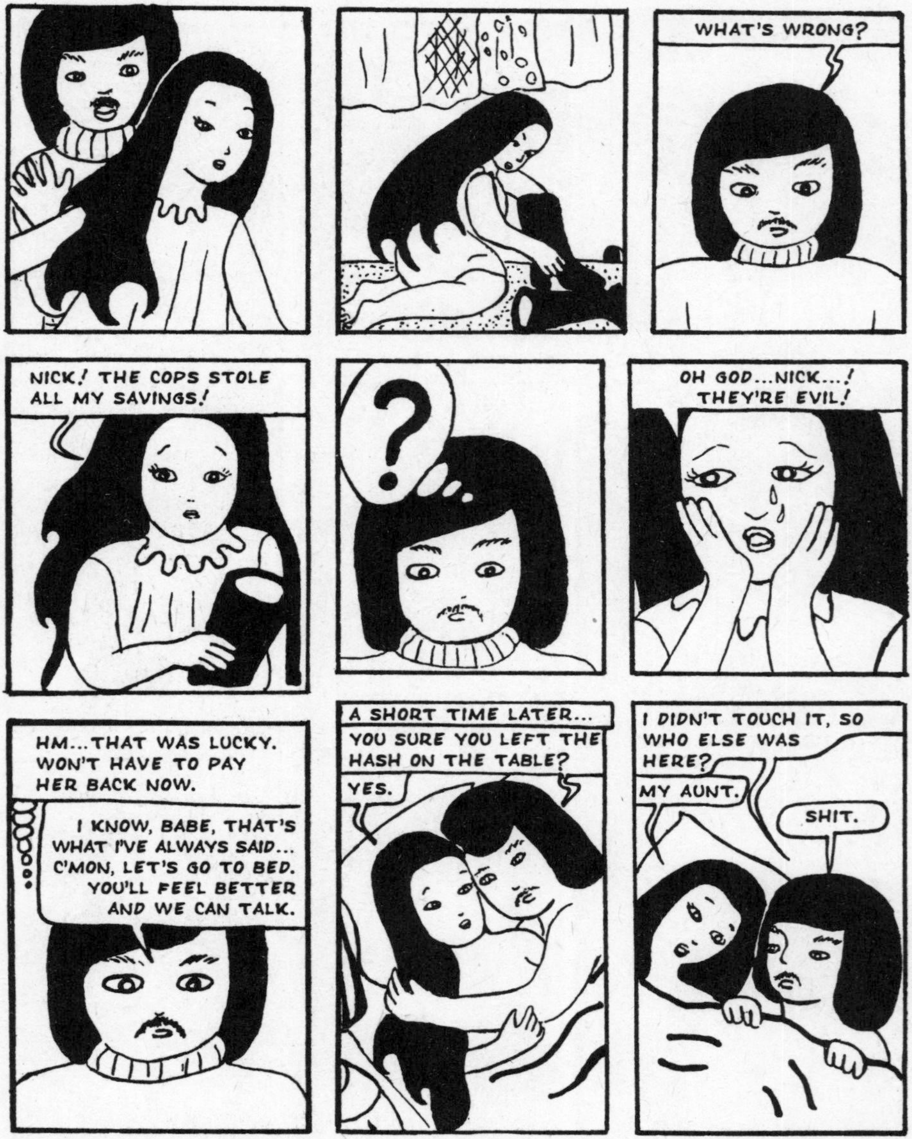
WHAT'S WRONG?
NICK! THE COPS STOLE ALL MY SAVINGS!
?
OH GOD...NICK...! THEY'RE EVIL!
HM...THAT WAS LUCKY. WON'T HAVE TO PAY HER BACK NOW.
I KNOW, BABE, THAT'S WHAT I'VE ALWAYS SAID... C'MON, LET'S GO TO BED. YOU'LL FEEL BETTER AND WE CAN TALK.
A SHORT TIME LATER...
YOU SURE YOU LEFT THE HASH ON THE TABLE?
YES.
I DIDN'T TOUCH IT, SO WHO ELSE WAS HERE?
MY AUNT.
SHIT.

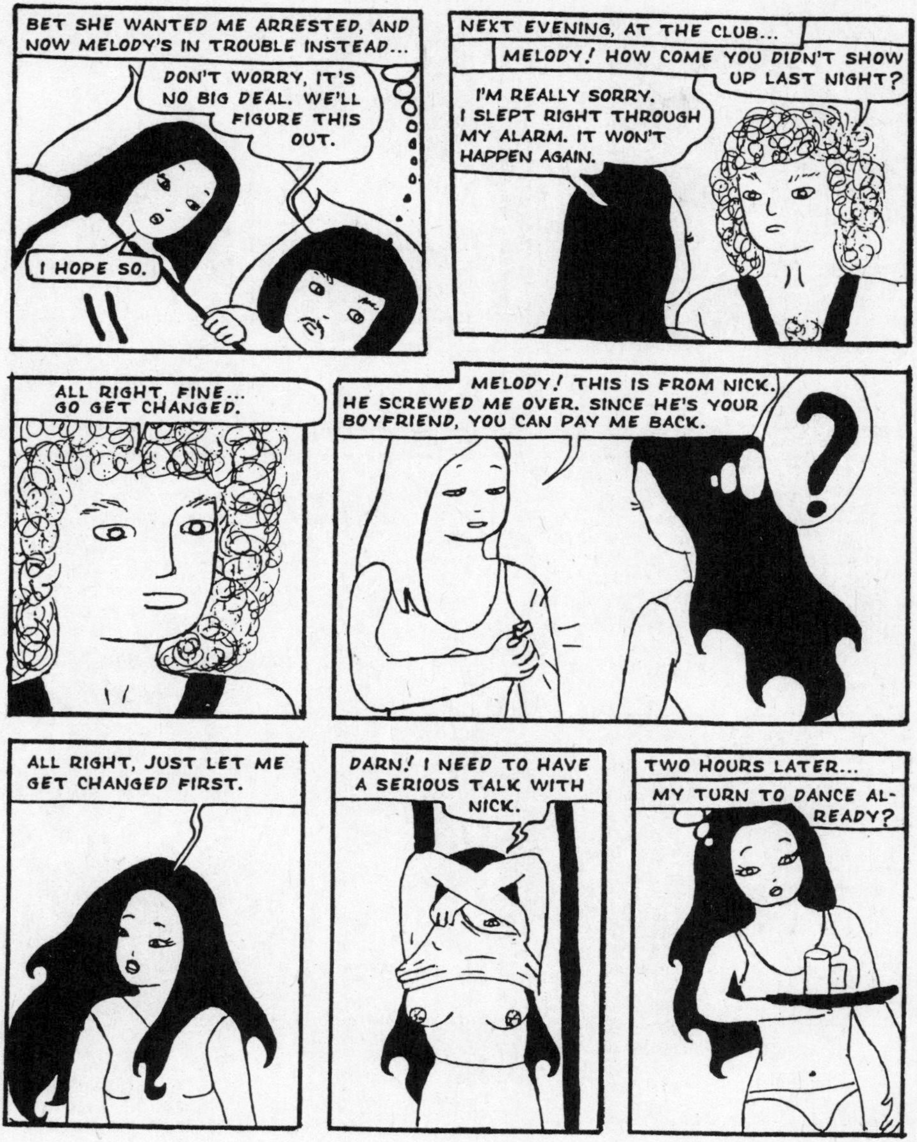

BET SHE WANTED ME ARRESTED, AND NOW MELODY'S IN TROUBLE INSTEAD...
DON'T WORRY, IT'S NO BIG DEAL. WE'LL FIGURE THIS OUT.
I HOPE SO.
NEXT EVENING, AT THE CLUB...
MELODY! HOW COME YOU DIDN'T SHOW UP LAST NIGHT?
I'M REALLY SORRY. I SLEPT RIGHT THROUGH MY ALARM. IT WON'T HAPPEN AGAIN.
ALL RIGHT, FINE... GO GET CHANGED.
MELODY! THIS IS FROM NICK. HE SCREWED ME OVER. SINCE HE'S YOUR BOYFRIEND, YOU CAN PAY ME BACK.
?
ALL RIGHT, JUST LET ME GET CHANGED FIRST.
DARN! I NEED TO HAVE A SERIOUS TALK WITH NICK.
TWO HOURS LATER...
MY TURN TO DANCE ALREADY?

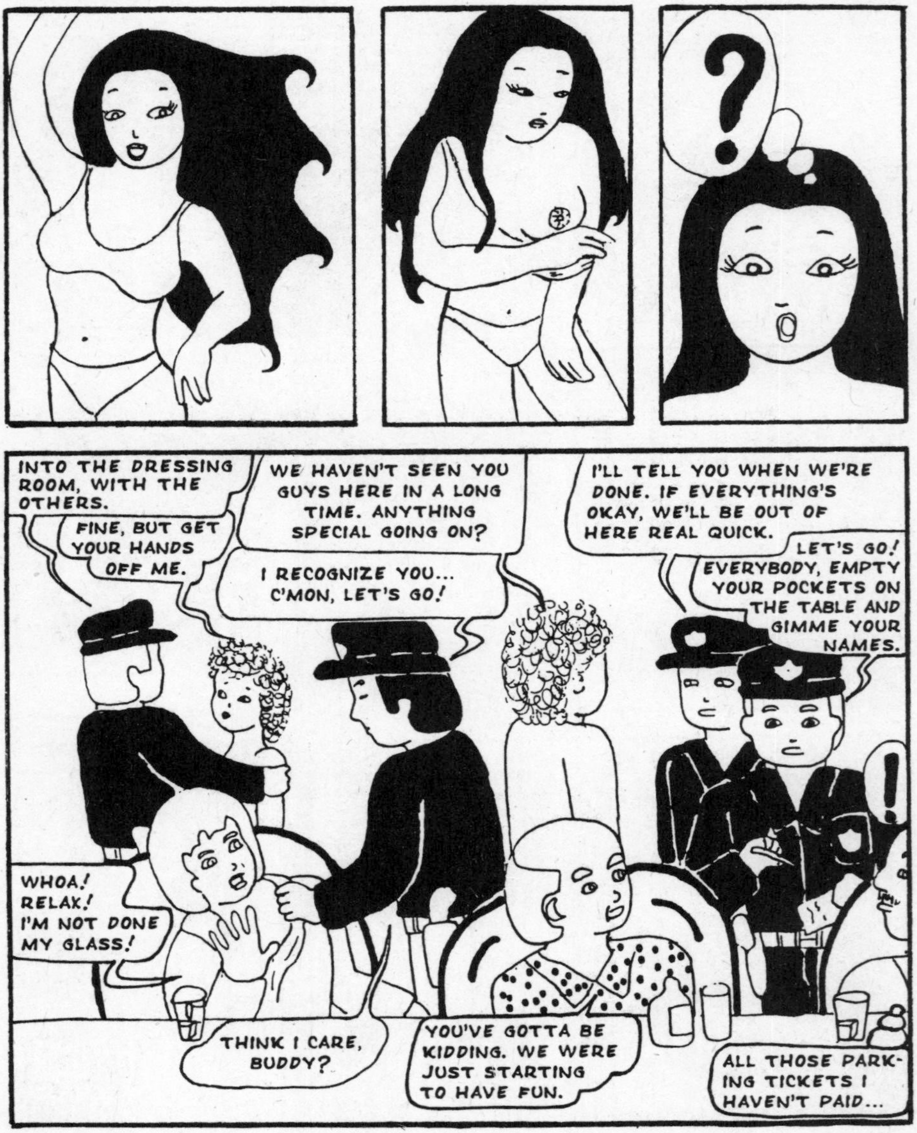
?
INTO THE DRESSING ROOM, WITH THE OTHERS.
FINE, BUT GET YOUR HANDS OFF ME.
WE HAVEN'T SEEN YOU GUYS HERE IN A LONG TIME. ANYTHING SPECIAL GOING ON?
I RECOGNIZE YOU... C'MON, LET'S GO!
I'LL TELL YOU WHEN WE'RE DONE. IF EVERYTHING'S OKAY, WE'LL BE OUT OF HERE REAL QUICK.
LET'S GO! EVERYBODY, EMPTY YOUR POCKETS ON THE TABLE AND GIMME YOUR NAMES.
!
WHOA! RELAX! I'M NOT DONE MY GLASS!
THINK I CARE, BUDDY?
YOU'VE GOTTA BE KIDDING. WE WERE JUST STARTING TO HAVE FUN.
ALL THOSE PARKING TICKETS I HAVEN'T PAID...

YOU'LL HAVE FUN AFTER.
FINE, I'VE GOT NOTHING TO HIDE.
HE'S GONNA TAKE ME ALONG FOR SURE.
I WONDER WHAT THEY'RE LOOKING FOR IN MY CLUB?
YOUR TURN TO EMPTY YOUR POCKETS.
?
FINE.
AND HERE I'VE GOT ALL THESE GIRLS WITH FAKE IDS.
YEAH, PLUS THEY'RE UNDERAGE.
HEY, I KNOW YOUR FACE. YOUR MOTHER'S LOOKING FOR YOU.
DAMN!
I'VE NEVER SEEN AN ACTUAL POLICE RAID BEFORE!
?

HEY, YOU! GET DOWN FROM THERE AND GO TO THE DRESSING ROOM!
YES, OF COURSE.
UH OH...
OPEN YOUR LOCKER.
POOR MELODY.
OKAY.
INTERESTING...C'MON, INTO THE VAN.
OH NO!
ONE MORE...
HA! THERE'S STILL SOME ROOM.
WHAT'VE I GOT MYSELF INTO THIS TIME?!

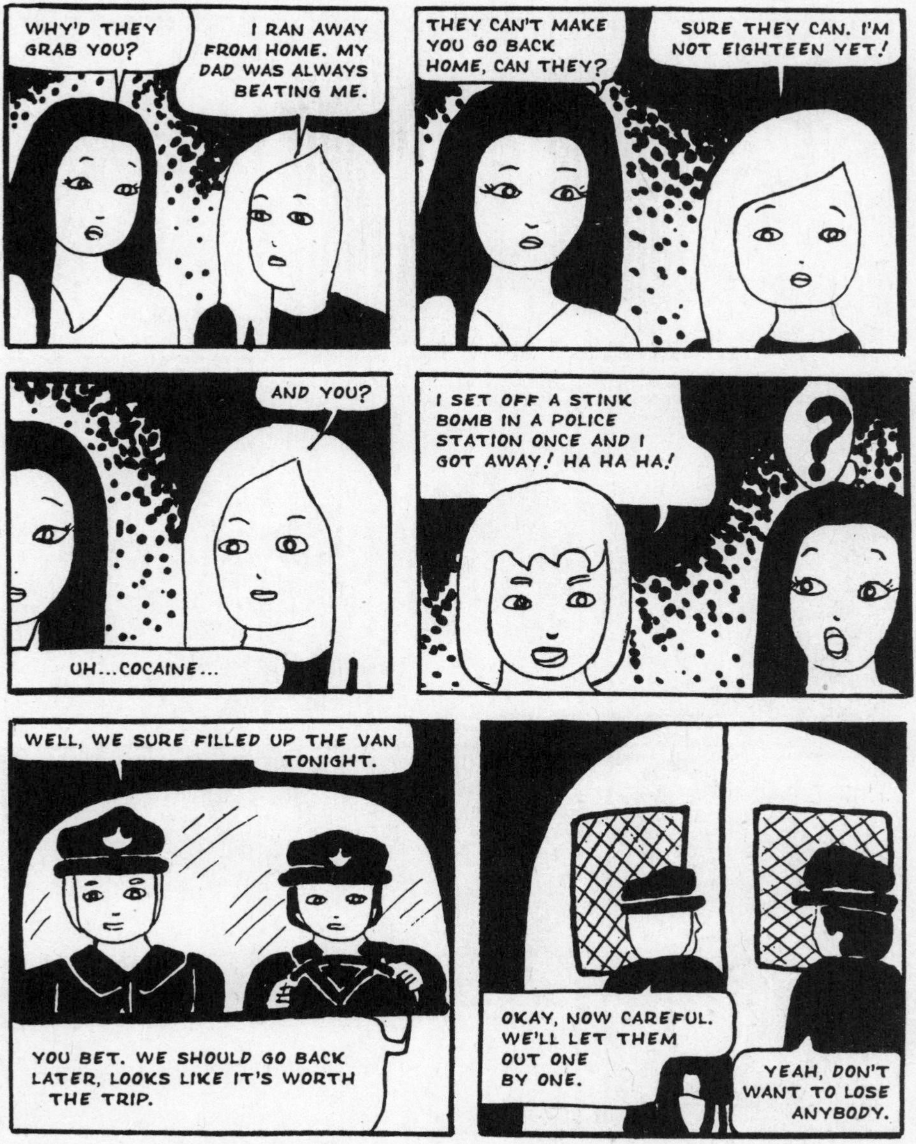
WHY'D THEY GRAB YOU?
I RAN AWAY FROM HOME. MY DAD WAS ALWAYS BEATING ME.
THEY CAN'T MAKE YOU GO BACK HOME, CAN THEY?
SURE THEY CAN. I'M NOT EIGHTEEN YET!
AND YOU?
UH...COCAINE...
I SET OFF A STINK BOMB IN A POLICE STATION ONCE AND I GOT AWAY! HA HA HA!
?
WELL, WE SURE FILLED UP THE VAN TONIGHT.
YOU BET. WE SHOULD GO BACK LATER, LOOKS LIKE IT'S WORTH THE TRIP.
OKAY, NOW CAREFUL. WE'LL LET THEM OUT ONE BY ONE.
YEAH, DON'T WANT TO LOSE ANYBODY.

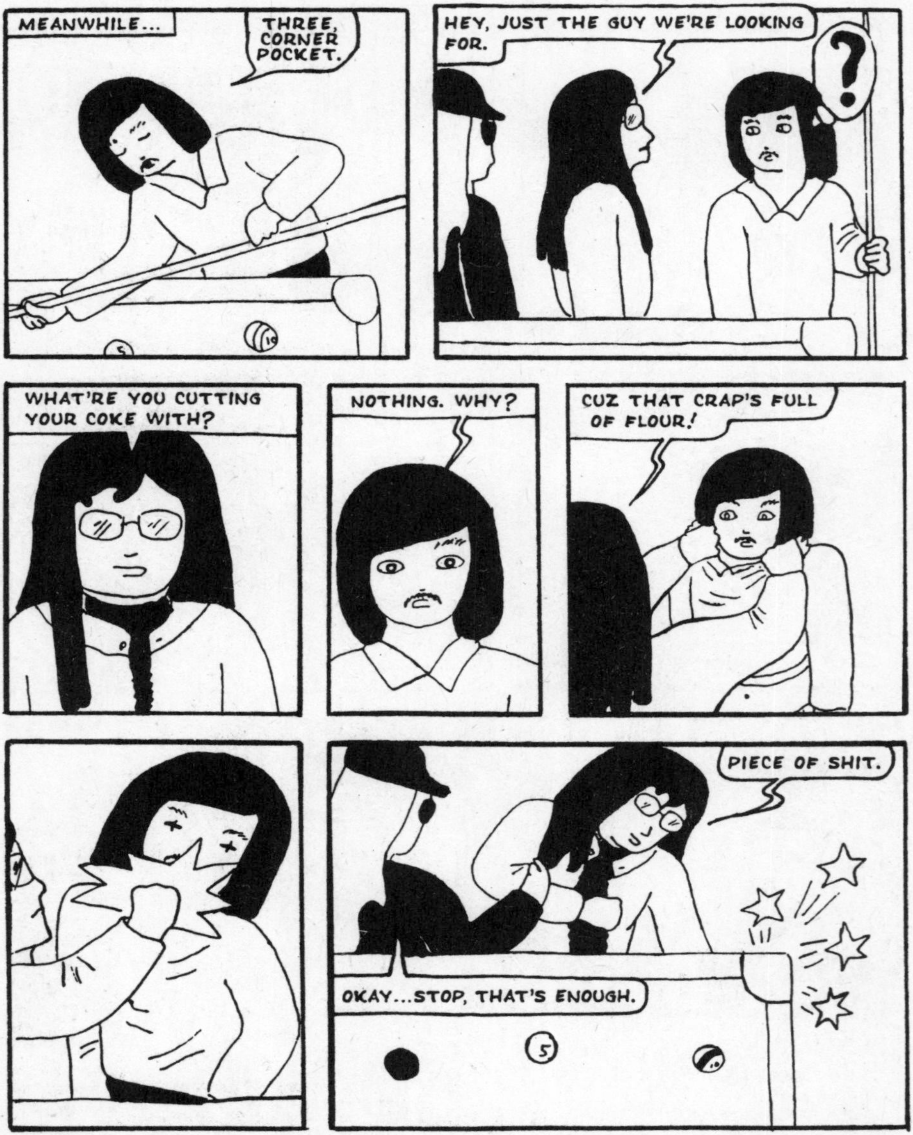
MEANWHILE...
THREE, CORNER POCKET.
HEY, JUST THE GUY WE'RE LOOKING FOR.
?
WHAT'RE YOU CUTTING YOUR COKE WITH?
NOTHING. WHY?
CUZ THAT CRAP'S FULL OF FLOUR!
PIECE OF SHIT.
OKAY...STOP, THAT'S ENOUGH.

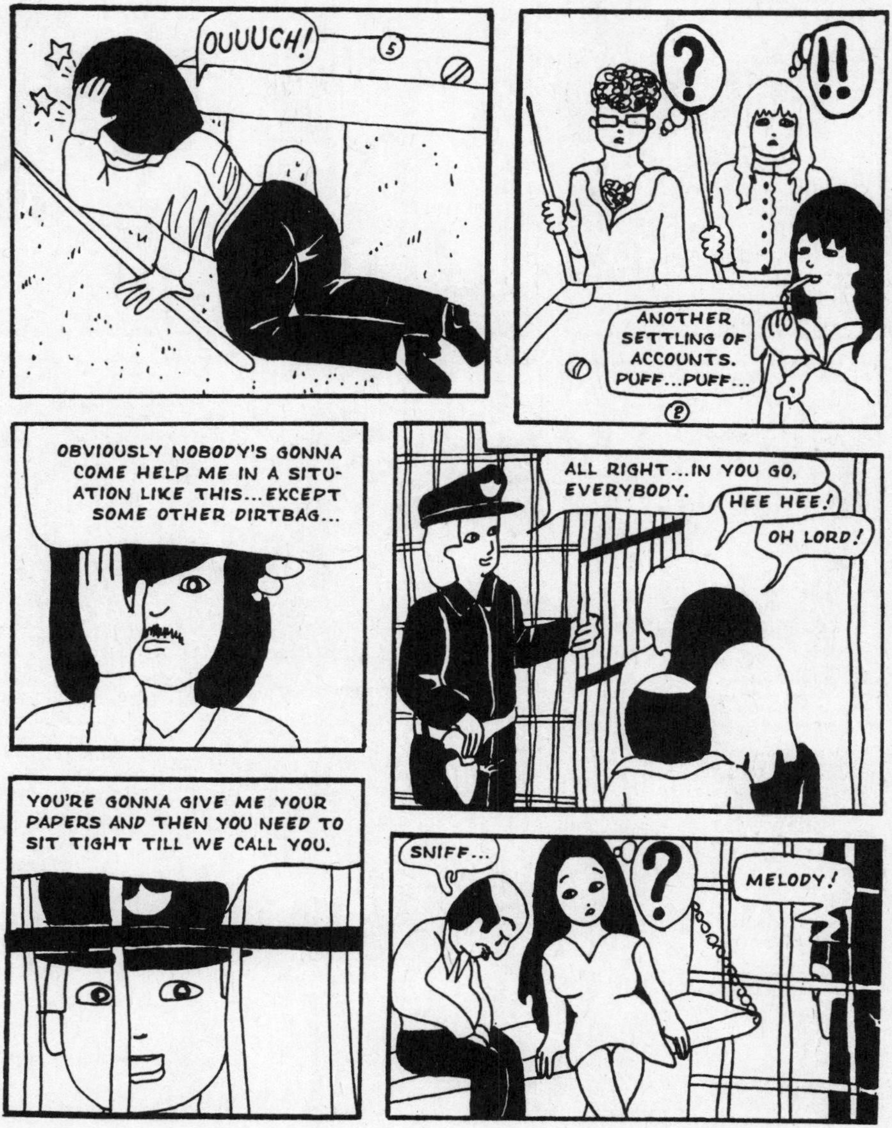

OUUUCH!
?
!!
ANOTHER SETTLING OF ACCOUNTS. PUFF...PUFF...
OBVIOUSLY NOBODY'S GONNA COME HELP ME IN A SITUATION LIKE THIS...EXCEPT SOME OTHER DIRTBAG...
ALL RIGHT...IN YOU GO, EVERYBODY.
HEE HEE!
OH LORD!
YOU'RE GONNA GIVE ME YOUR PAPERS AND THEN YOU NEED TO SIT TIGHT TILL WE CALL YOU.
SNIFF...
?
MELODY!

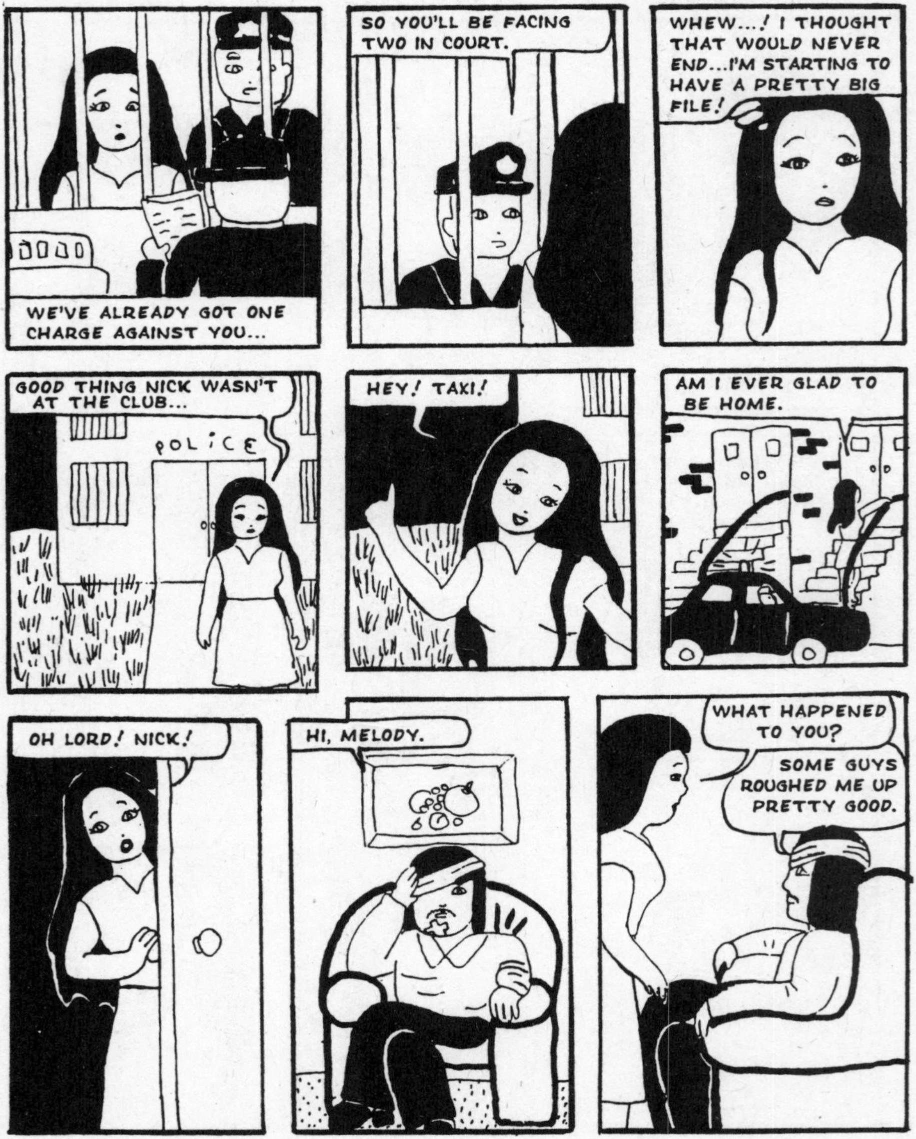
WE'VE ALREADY GOT ONE CHARGE AGAINST YOU...
SO YOU'LL BE FACING TWO IN COURT.
WHEW...! I THOUGHT THAT WOULD NEVER END...I'M STARTING TO HAVE A PRETTY BIG FILE!
GOOD THING NICK WASN'T AT THE CLUB...
POLICE
HEY! TAXI!
AM I EVER GLAD TO BE HOME.
OH LORD! NICK!
HI, MELODY.
WHAT HAPPENED TO YOU?
SOME GUYS ROUGHED ME UP PRETTY GOOD.

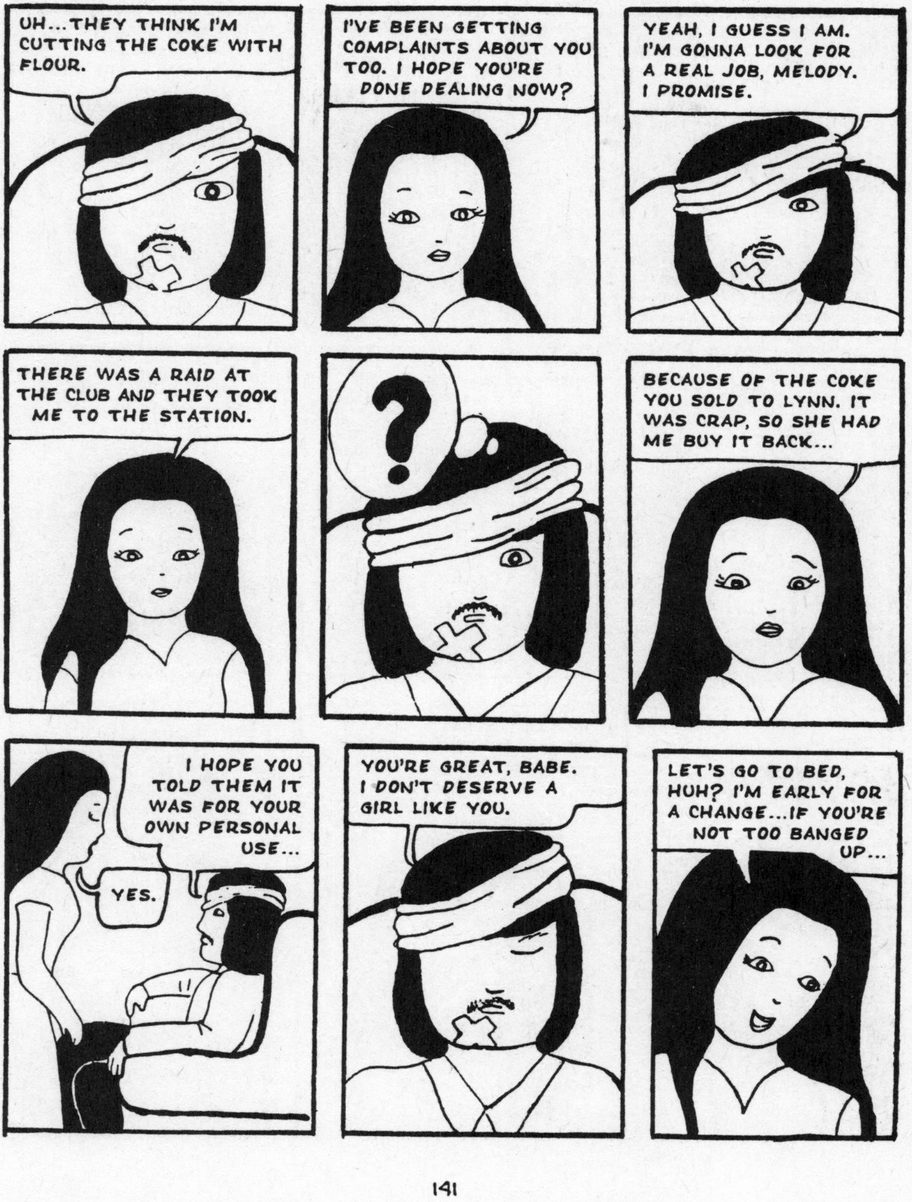
UH...THEY THINK I'M CUTTING THE COKE WITH FLOUR.
I'VE BEEN GETTING COMPLAINTS ABOUT YOU TOO. I HOPE YOU'RE DONE DEALING NOW?
YEAH, I GUESS I AM. I'M GONNA LOOK FOR A REAL JOB, MELODY. I PROMISE.
THERE WAS A RAID AT THE CLUB AND THEY TOOK ME TO THE STATION.
?
BECAUSE OF THE COKE YOU SOLD TO LYNN. IT WAS CRAP, SO SHE HAD ME BUY IT BACK...
I HOPE YOU TOLD THEM IT WAS FOR YOUR OWN PERSONAL USE...
YES.
YOU'RE GREAT, BABE. I DON'T DESERVE A GIRL LIKE YOU.
LET'S GO TO BED, HUH? I'M EARLY FOR A CHANGE...IF YOU'RE NOT TOO BANGED UP...

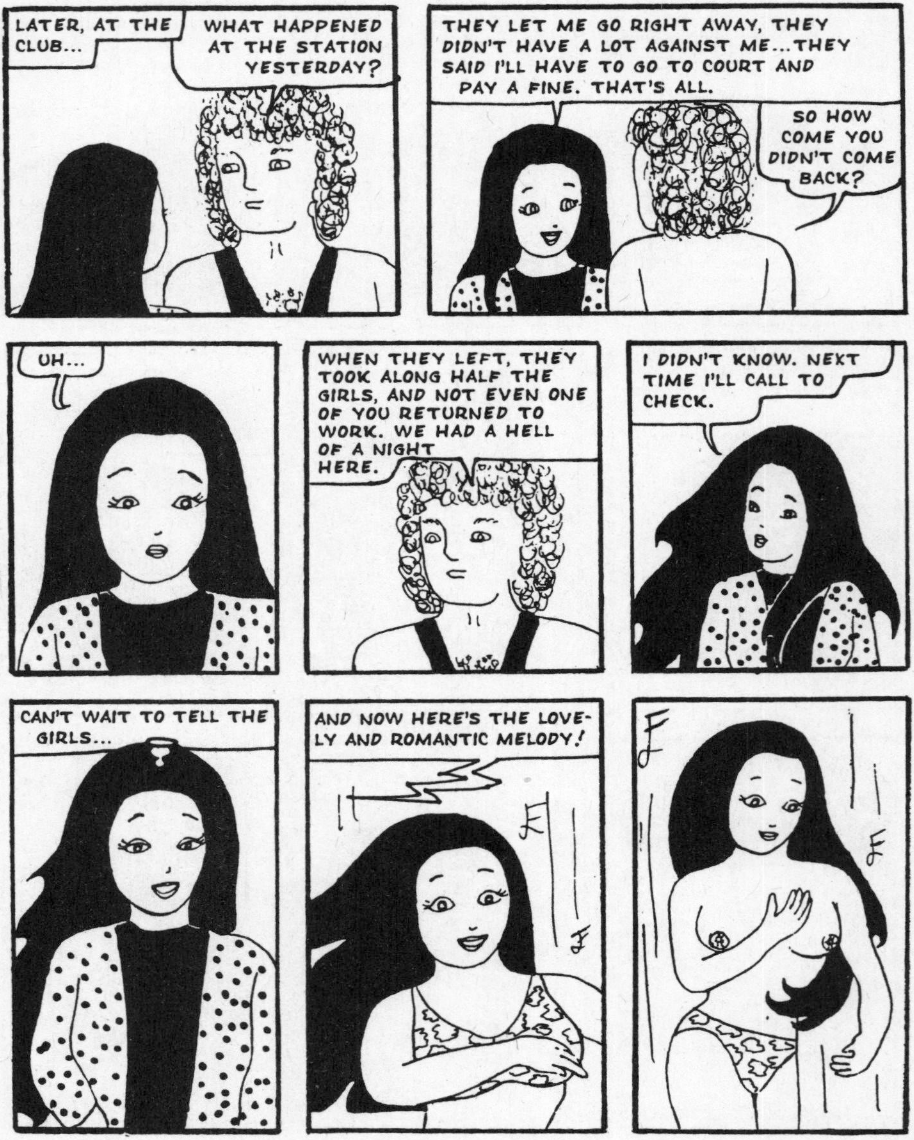

LATER, AT THE CLUB...
WHAT HAPPENED AT THE STATION YESTERDAY?
THEY LET ME GO RIGHT AWAY, THEY DIDN'T HAVE A LOT AGAINST ME...THEY SAID I'LL HAVE TO GO TO COURT AND PAY A FINE. THAT'S ALL.
SO HOW COME YOU DIDN'T COME BACK?
UH...
WHEN THEY LEFT, THEY TOOK ALONG HALF THE GIRLS, AND NOT EVEN ONE OF YOU RETURNED TO WORK. WE HAD A HELL OF A NIGHT HERE.
I DIDN'T KNOW. NEXT TIME I'LL CALL TO CHECK.
CAN'T WAIT TO TELL THE GIRLS...
AND NOW HERE'S THE LOVELY AND ROMANTIC MELODY!

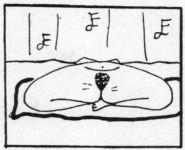

I'M TOO OLD NOW, AND I MISSED OUT WHEN I WAS YOUNG.

HELL, YEAH! SHE'S A REAL LITTLE DEVIL! THAT GIRL COULD GIVE A SAINT A HARD-ON.

HERE'S TO THE YOUTH OF TODAY, BOYS!

THAT WAS GREAT, MISS...IF I WERE YOUNGER, I'D ASK YOU OUT!

YOU'RE SWEET.

I FEEL SORRY FOR SOME OF THESE POOR GUYS, DON'T YOU?

A BIT...BUT AFTER ALL, WE'RE HERE TO GIVE THEM A GOOD TIME!

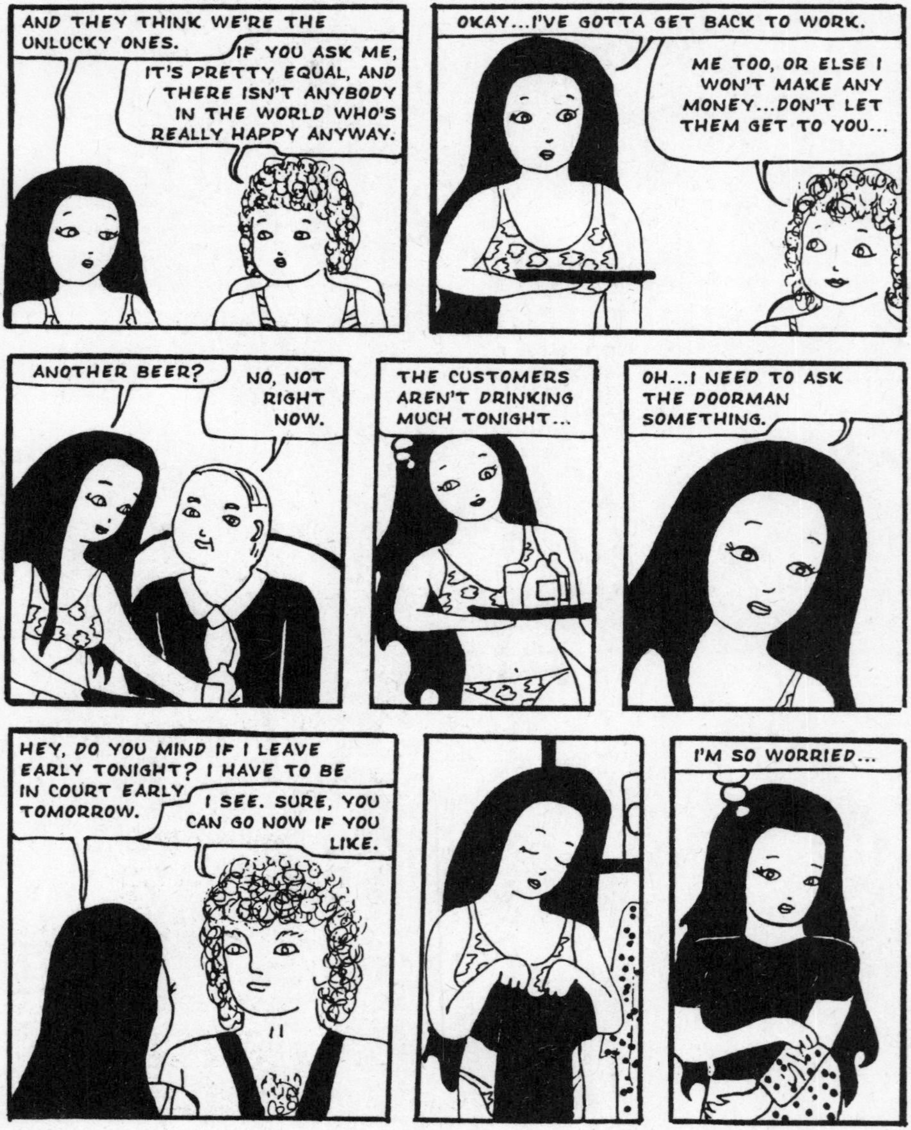
AND THEY THINK WE'RE THE UNLUCKY ONES.
IF YOU ASK ME, IT'S PRETTY EQUAL, AND THERE ISN'T ANYBODY IN THE WORLD WHO'S REALLY HAPPY ANYWAY.
OKAY...I'VE GOTTA GET BACK TO WORK.
ME TOO, OR ELSE I WON'T MAKE ANY MONEY...DON'T LET THEM GET TO YOU...
ANOTHER BEER?
NO, NOT RIGHT NOW.
THE CUSTOMERS AREN'T DRINKING MUCH TONIGHT...
OH...I NEED TO ASK THE DOORMAN SOMETHING.
HEY, DO YOU MIND IF I LEAVE EARLY TONIGHT? I HAVE TO BE IN COURT EARLY TOMORROW.
I SEE. SURE, YOU CAN GO NOW IF YOU LIKE.
I'M SO WORRIED...

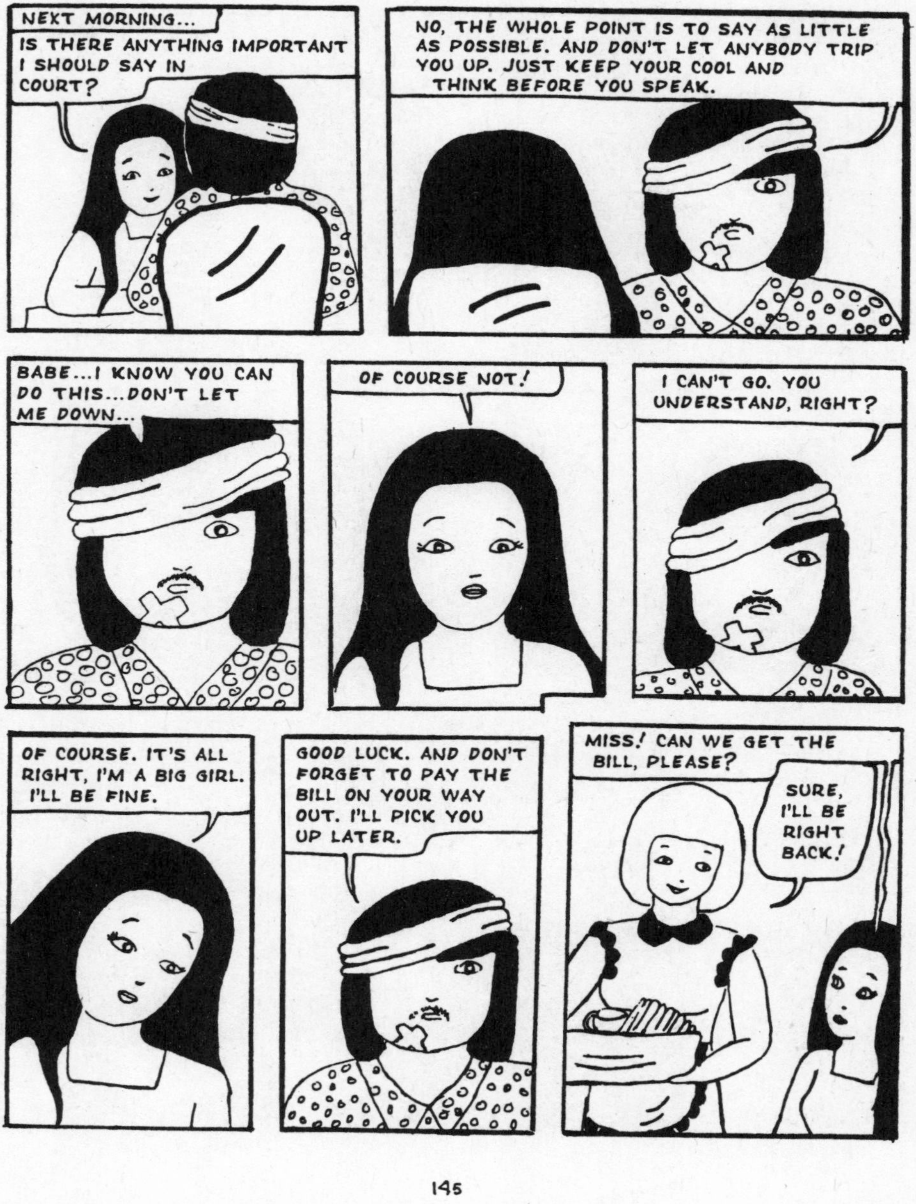
NEXT MORNING...
IS THERE ANYTHING IMPORTANT I SHOULD SAY IN COURT?
NO, THE WHOLE POINT IS TO SAY AS LITTLE AS POSSIBLE. AND DON'T LET ANYBODY TRIP YOU UP. JUST KEEP YOUR COOL AND THINK BEFORE YOU SPEAK.
BABE...I KNOW YOU CAN DO THIS...DON'T LET ME DOWN...
OF COURSE NOT!
I CAN'T GO. YOU UNDERSTAND, RIGHT?
OF COURSE. IT'S ALL RIGHT, I'M A BIG GIRL. I'LL BE FINE.
GOOD LUCK. AND DON'T FORGET TO PAY THE BILL ON YOUR WAY OUT. I'LL PICK YOU UP LATER.
MISS! CAN WE GET THE BILL, PLEASE?
SURE, I'LL BE RIGHT BACK!

AT THE COURTHOUSE...

HELLO! I'M MELODY. I HAVE AN APPOINTMENT WITH THE JUDGE THIS MORNING.

COURTROOM NO. 69. HE'S WAITING FOR YOU.

WHICH WAY?

FIRST DOOR TO THE RIGHT.

69

BLAH BLAH... BLAH BLAH...

ZZZZ

SO, YOUR HONOUR?

HM HM...AH! GUILTY! NEXT.

ALL RIGHT. MISS MELODY, STEP UP, PLEASE.

OH GOD! MY NERVES! I'M SCARED.

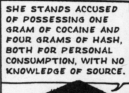

SHE STANDS ACCUSED OF POSSESSING ONE GRAM OF COCAINE AND FOUR GRAMS OF HASH, BOTH FOR PERSONAL CONSUMPTION, WITH NO KNOWLEDGE OF SOURCE.

DO YOU SWEAR TO THE TRUTH OF YOUR STATEMENT?

YES, I DO.

LIAR.

AFTER A VERY LONG HEARING AND COUNTLESS QUESTIONS...

ALL RIGHT...YOU'LL PAY A FINE THIS TIME, BUT WE WON'T BE AS EASY ON YOU IF WE SEE YOU AGAIN. NEXT!

IT'S CRAZY FOR THEM TO MAKE PEOPLE SUFFER LIKE THIS... WE LIVE IN A FREE COUNTRY, AFTER ALL.

I'D LIKE TO PAY RIGHT NOW, IF POSSIBLE.

OF COURSE.

NICK'S GOING TO BE HAPPY...
TOOT! TOOT!
NICK! LOOK OUT!
BANG
BING... BING...
YOU OKAY?
NICK!
BABY! YOU ALL RIGHT?
YES.

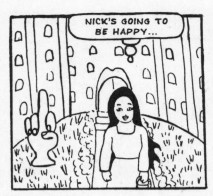

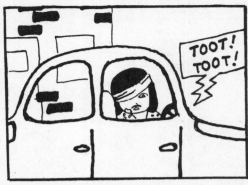

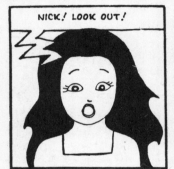

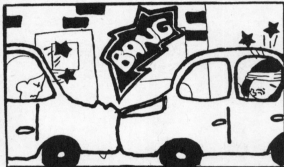

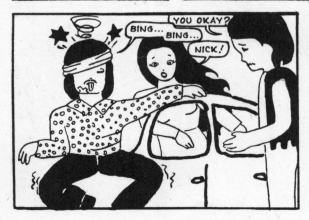

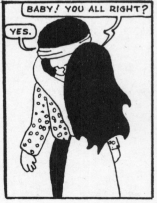

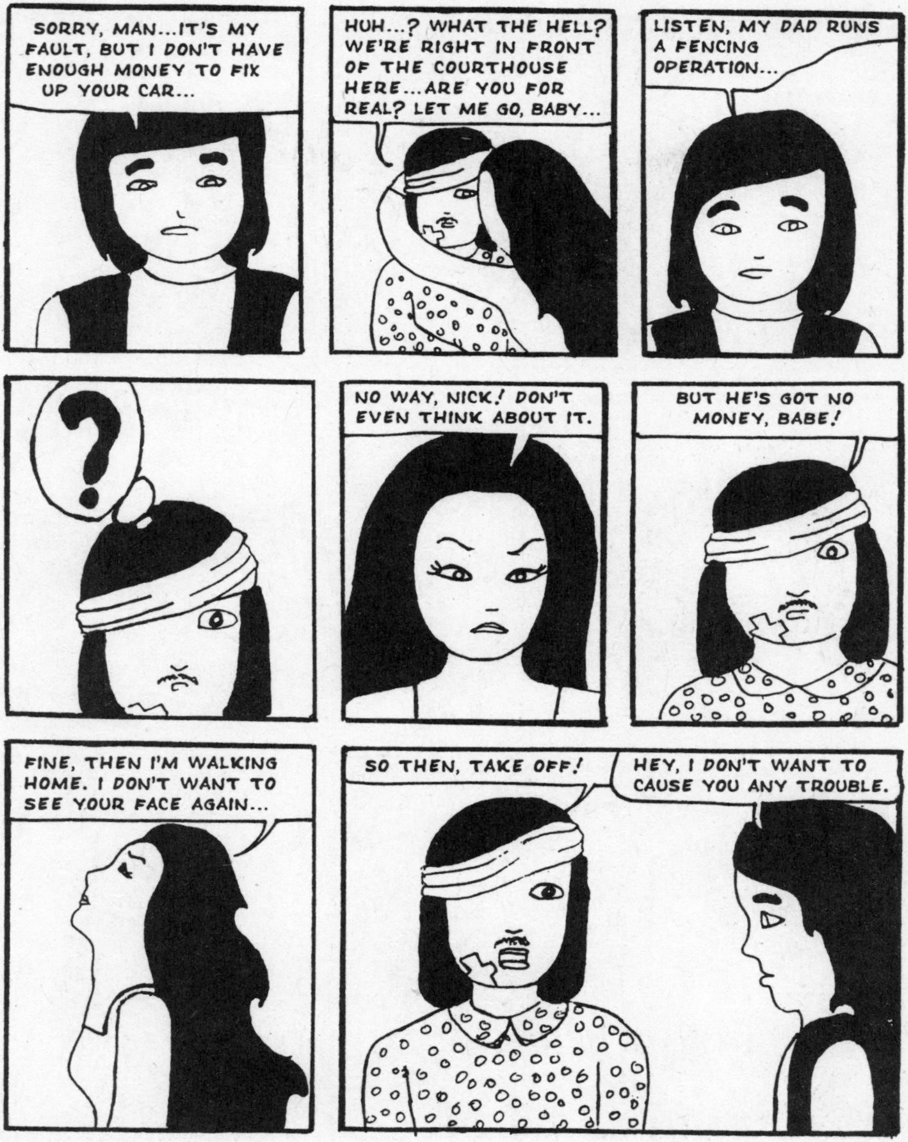
SORRY, MAN...IT'S MY FAULT, BUT I DON'T HAVE ENOUGH MONEY TO FIX UP YOUR CAR...
HUH...? WHAT THE HELL? WE'RE RIGHT IN FRONT OF THE COURTHOUSE HERE...ARE YOU FOR REAL? LET ME GO, BABY...
LISTEN, MY DAD RUNS A FENCING OPERATION...
?
NO WAY, NICK! DON'T EVEN THINK ABOUT IT.
BUT HE'S GOT NO MONEY, BABE!
FINE, THEN I'M WALKING HOME. I DON'T WANT TO SEE YOUR FACE AGAIN...
SO THEN, TAKE OFF!
HEY, I DON'T WANT TO CAUSE YOU ANY TROUBLE.

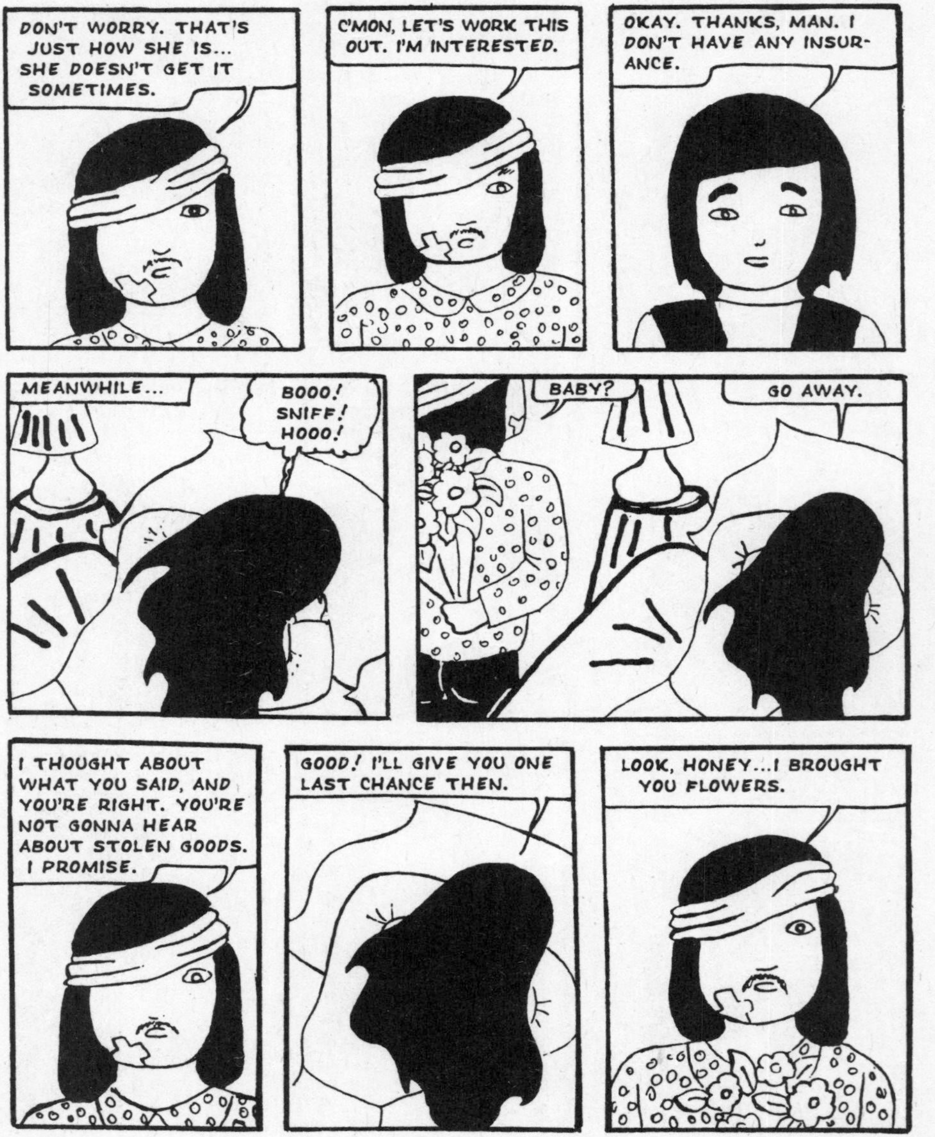
DON'T WORRY. THAT'S JUST HOW SHE IS... SHE DOESN'T GET IT SOMETIMES.
C'MON, LET'S WORK THIS OUT. I'M INTERESTED.
OKAY. THANKS, MAN. I DON'T HAVE ANY INSUR-ANCE.
MEANWHILE...
BOOO! SNIFF! HOOO!
BABY?
GO AWAY.
I THOUGHT ABOUT WHAT YOU SAID, AND YOU'RE RIGHT. YOU'RE NOT GONNA HEAR ABOUT STOLEN GOODS. I PROMISE.
GOOD! I'LL GIVE YOU ONE LAST CHANCE THEN.
LOOK, HONEY...I BROUGHT YOU FLOWERS.

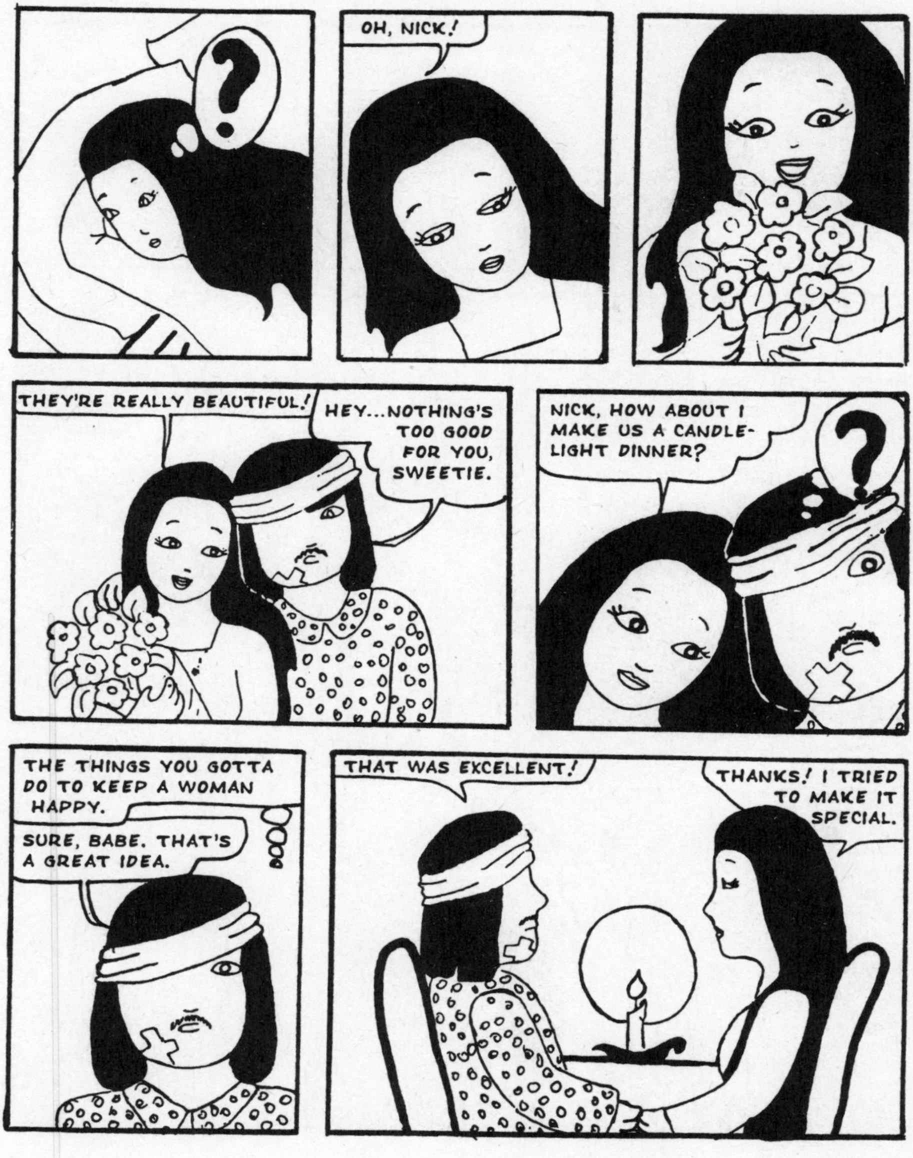
OH, NICK!
THEY'RE REALLY BEAUTIFUL!
HEY...NOTHING'S TOO GOOD FOR YOU, SWEETIE.
NICK, HOW ABOUT I MAKE US A CANDLE-LIGHT DINNER?
THE THINGS YOU GOTTA DO TO KEEP A WOMAN HAPPY.
SURE, BABE. THAT'S A GREAT IDEA.
THAT WAS EXCELLENT!
THANKS! I TRIED TO MAKE IT SPECIAL.

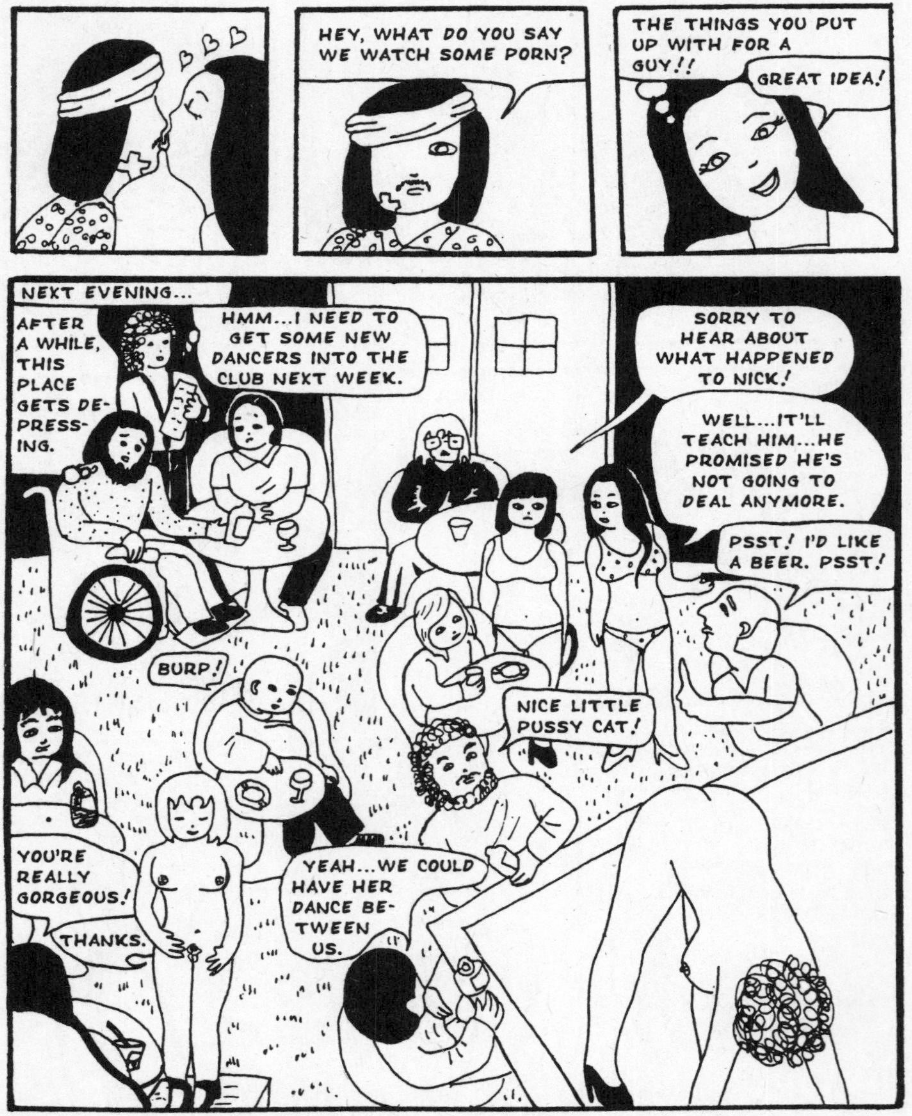
HEY, WHAT DO YOU SAY WE WATCH SOME PORN?
THE THINGS YOU PUT UP WITH FOR A GUY!!
GREAT IDEA!
NEXT EVENING...
AFTER A WHILE, THIS PLACE GETS DE-PRESS-ING.
HMM...I NEED TO GET SOME NEW DANCERS INTO THE CLUB NEXT WEEK.
SORRY TO HEAR ABOUT WHAT HAPPENED TO NICK!
WELL...IT'LL TEACH HIM...HE PROMISED HE'S NOT GOING TO DEAL ANYMORE.
PSST! I'D LIKE A BEER. PSST!
BURP!
NICE LITTLE PUSSY CAT!
YOU'RE REALLY GORGEOUS!
THANKS.
YEAH...WE COULD HAVE HER DANCE BE-TWEEN US.

?
ANOTHER BEER, PLEASE!
TOO LATE, HERE COMES THE END!
DAMN! I WAS JUST GETTING STARTED...

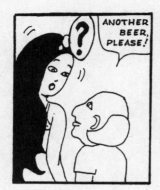

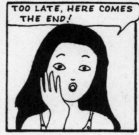

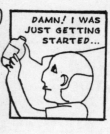

Melody's
Orgy

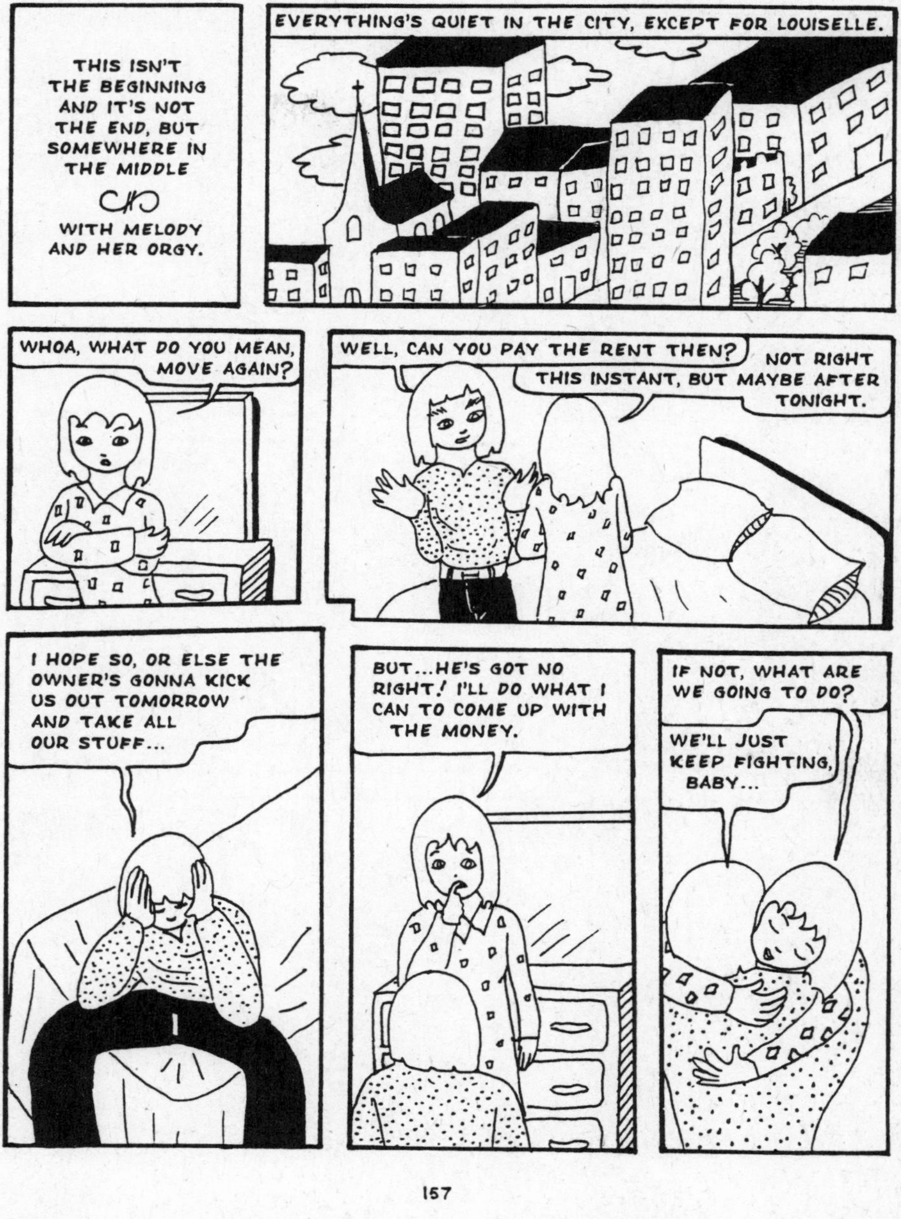
THIS ISN'T THE BEGINNING AND IT'S NOT THE END, BUT SOMEWHERE IN THE MIDDLE
WITH MELODY AND HER ORGY.
EVERYTHING'S QUIET IN THE CITY, EXCEPT FOR LOUISELLE.
WHOA, WHAT DO YOU MEAN, MOVE AGAIN?
WELL, CAN YOU PAY THE RENT THEN?
NOT RIGHT THIS INSTANT, BUT MAYBE AFTER TONIGHT.
I HOPE SO, OR ELSE THE OWNER'S GONNA KICK US OUT TOMORROW AND TAKE ALL OUR STUFF...
BUT...HE'S GOT NO RIGHT! I'LL DO WHAT I CAN TO COME UP WITH THE MONEY.
IF NOT, WHAT ARE WE GOING TO DO?
WE'LL JUST KEEP FIGHTING, BABY...

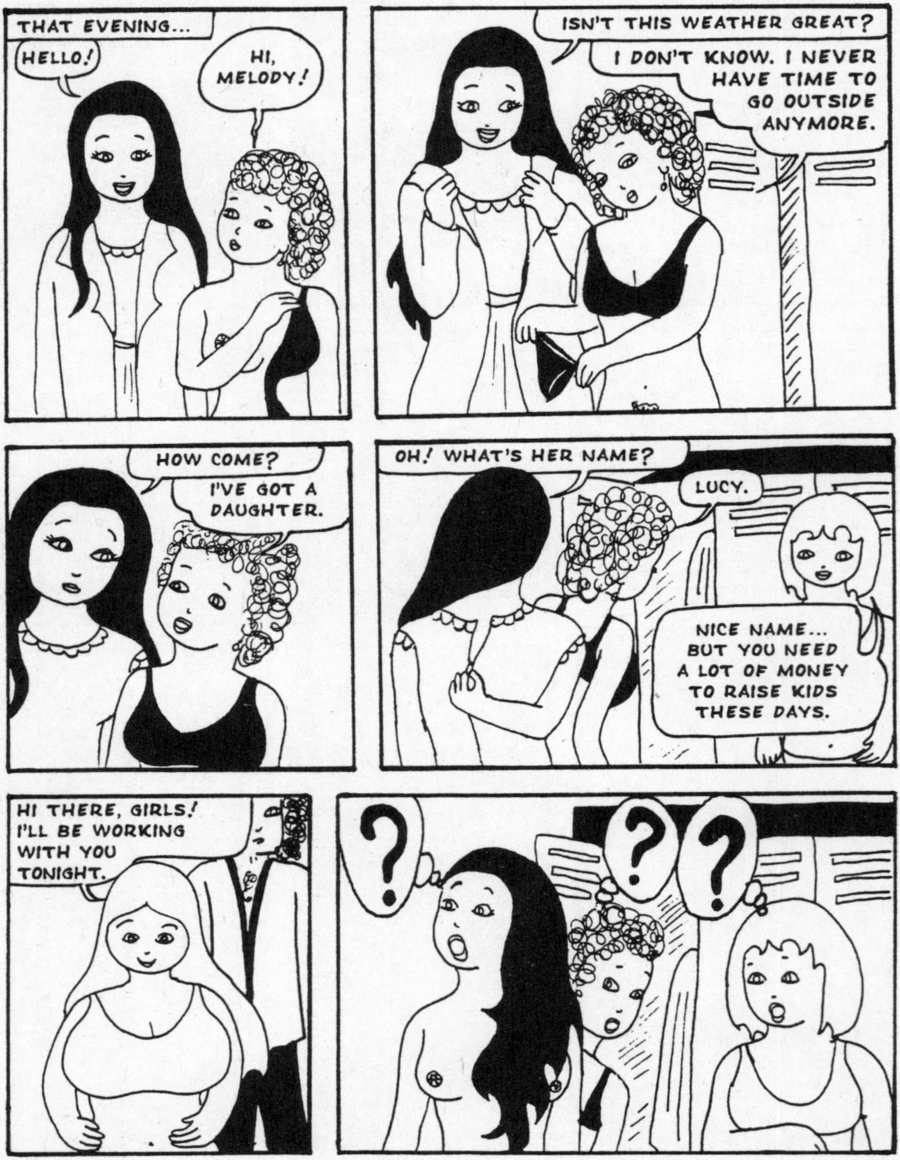
THAT EVENING...
HELLO!
HI, MELODY!
ISN'T THIS WEATHER GREAT?
I DON'T KNOW. I NEVER HAVE TIME TO GO OUTSIDE ANYMORE.
HOW COME?
I'VE GOT A DAUGHTER.
OH! WHAT'S HER NAME?
LUCY.
NICE NAME... BUT YOU NEED A LOT OF MONEY TO RAISE KIDS THESE DAYS.
HI THERE, GIRLS! I'LL BE WORKING WITH YOU TONIGHT.
?
?
?

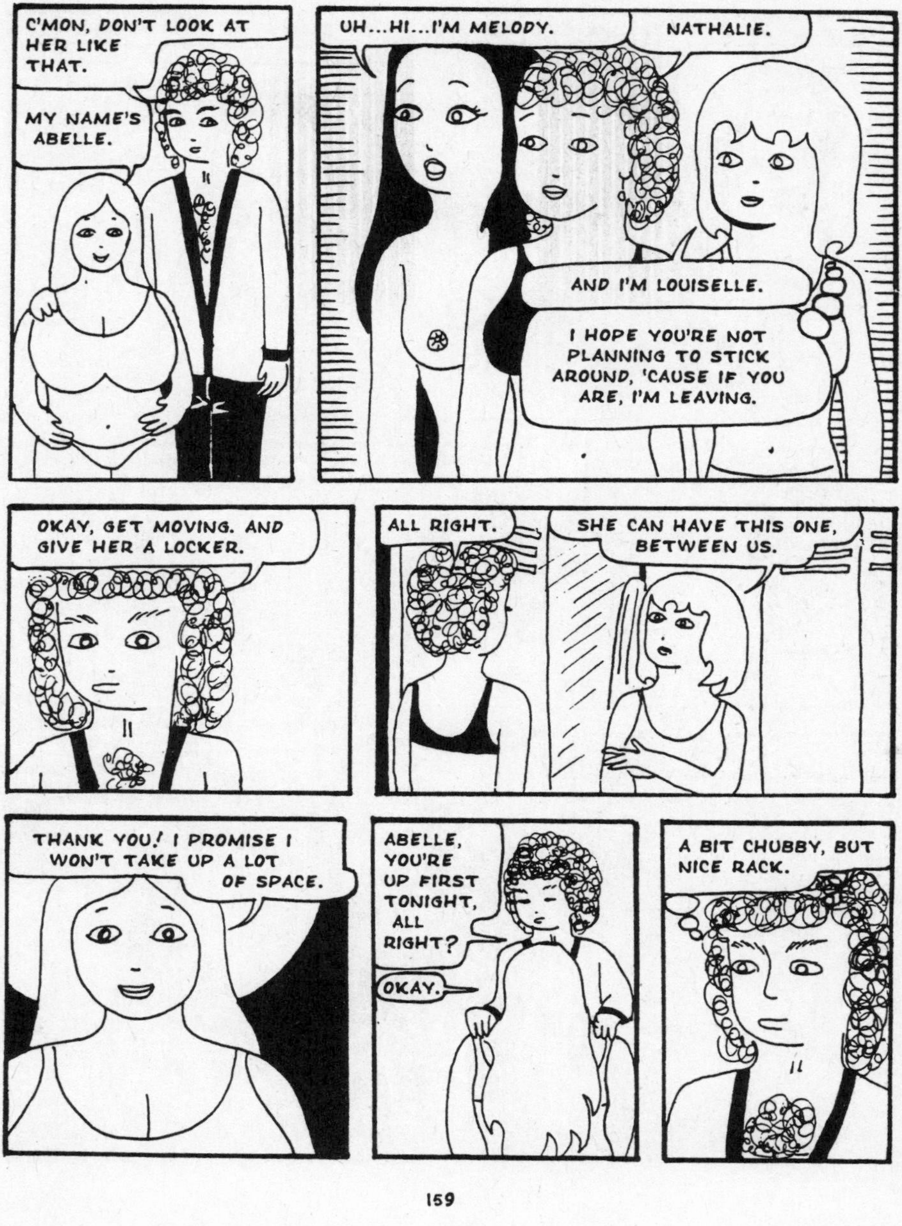
C'MON, DON'T LOOK AT HER LIKE THAT.
MY NAME'S ABELLE.
UH...HI...I'M MELODY.
NATHALIE.
AND I'M LOUISELLE.
I HOPE YOU'RE NOT PLANNING TO STICK AROUND, 'CAUSE IF YOU ARE, I'M LEAVING.
OKAY, GET MOVING. AND GIVE HER A LOCKER.
ALL RIGHT.
SHE CAN HAVE THIS ONE, BETWEEN US.
THANK YOU! I PROMISE I WON'T TAKE UP A LOT OF SPACE.
ABELLE, YOU'RE UP FIRST TONIGHT, ALL RIGHT?
OKAY.
A BIT CHUBBY, BUT NICE RACK.

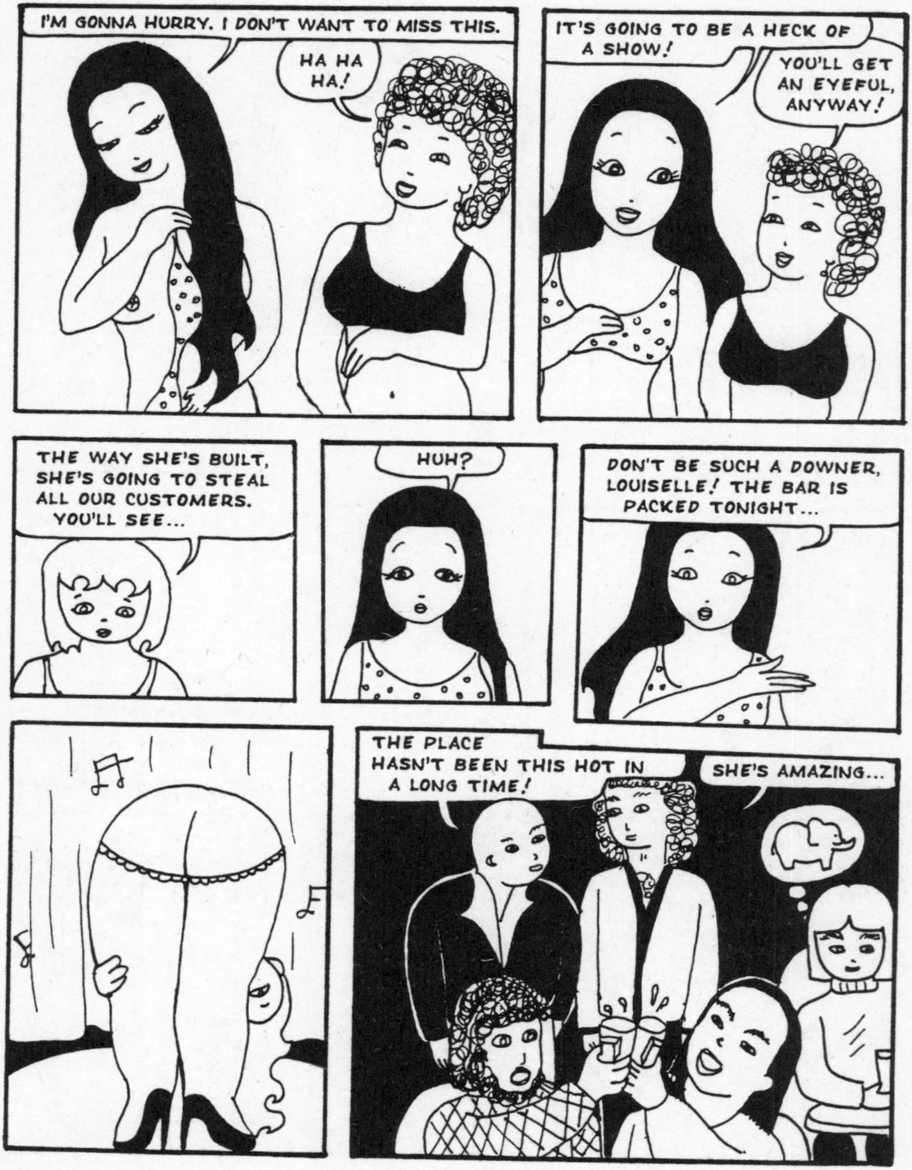
I'M GONNA HURRY. I DON'T WANT TO MISS THIS.
HA HA HA!
IT'S GOING TO BE A HECK OF A SHOW!
YOU'LL GET AN EYEFUL, ANYWAY!
THE WAY SHE'S BUILT, SHE'S GOING TO STEAL ALL OUR CUSTOMERS. YOU'LL SEE...
HUH?
DON'T BE SUCH A DOWNER, LOUISELLE! THE BAR IS PACKED TONIGHT...
THE PLACE HASN'T BEEN THIS HOT IN A LONG TIME!
SHE'S AMAZING...

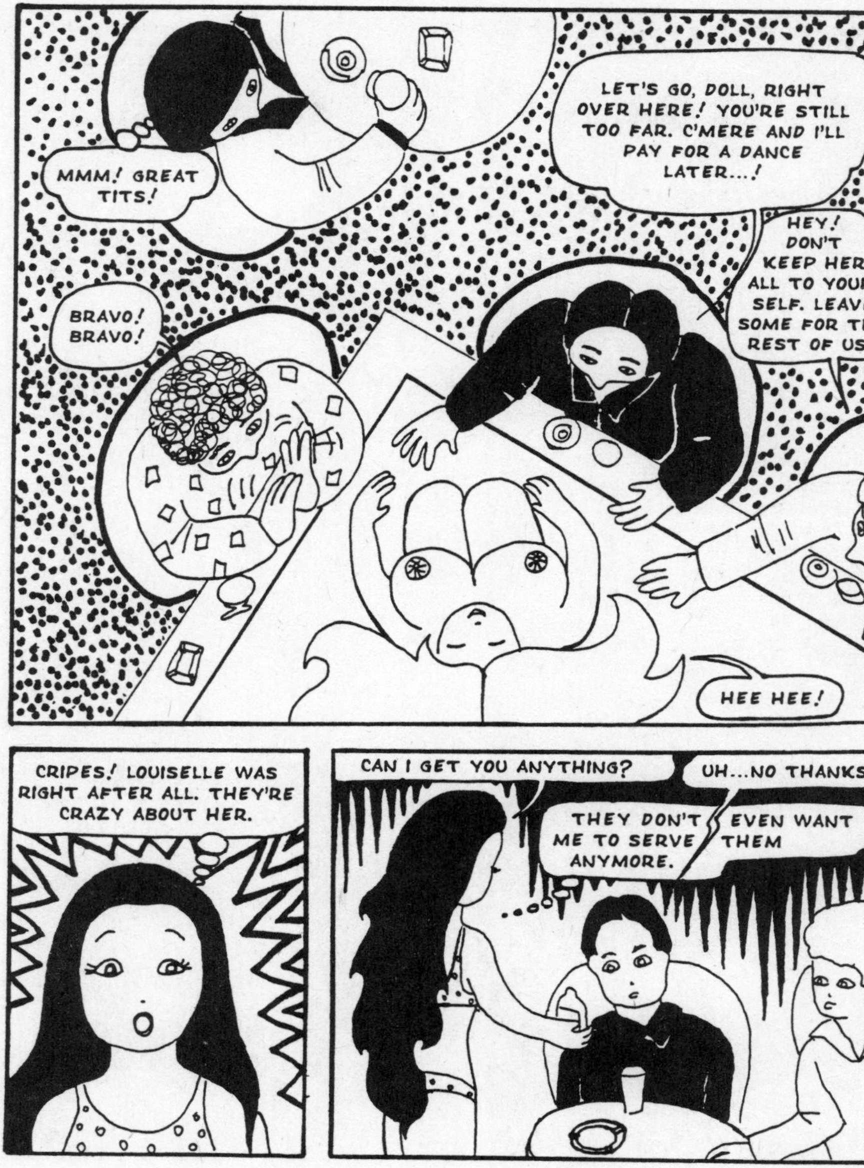

MMM! GREAT TITS!
LET'S GO, DOLL, RIGHT OVER HERE! YOU'RE STILL TOO FAR. C'MERE AND I'LL PAY FOR A DANCE LATER...!
BRAVO! BRAVO!
HEY! DON'T KEEP HER ALL TO YOURSELF. LEAVE SOME FOR THE REST OF US!
HEE HEE!
CRIPES! LOUISELLE WAS RIGHT AFTER ALL. THEY'RE CRAZY ABOUT HER.
CAN I GET YOU ANYTHING?
UH...NO THANKS.
THEY DON'T EVEN WANT ME TO SERVE THEM ANYMORE.

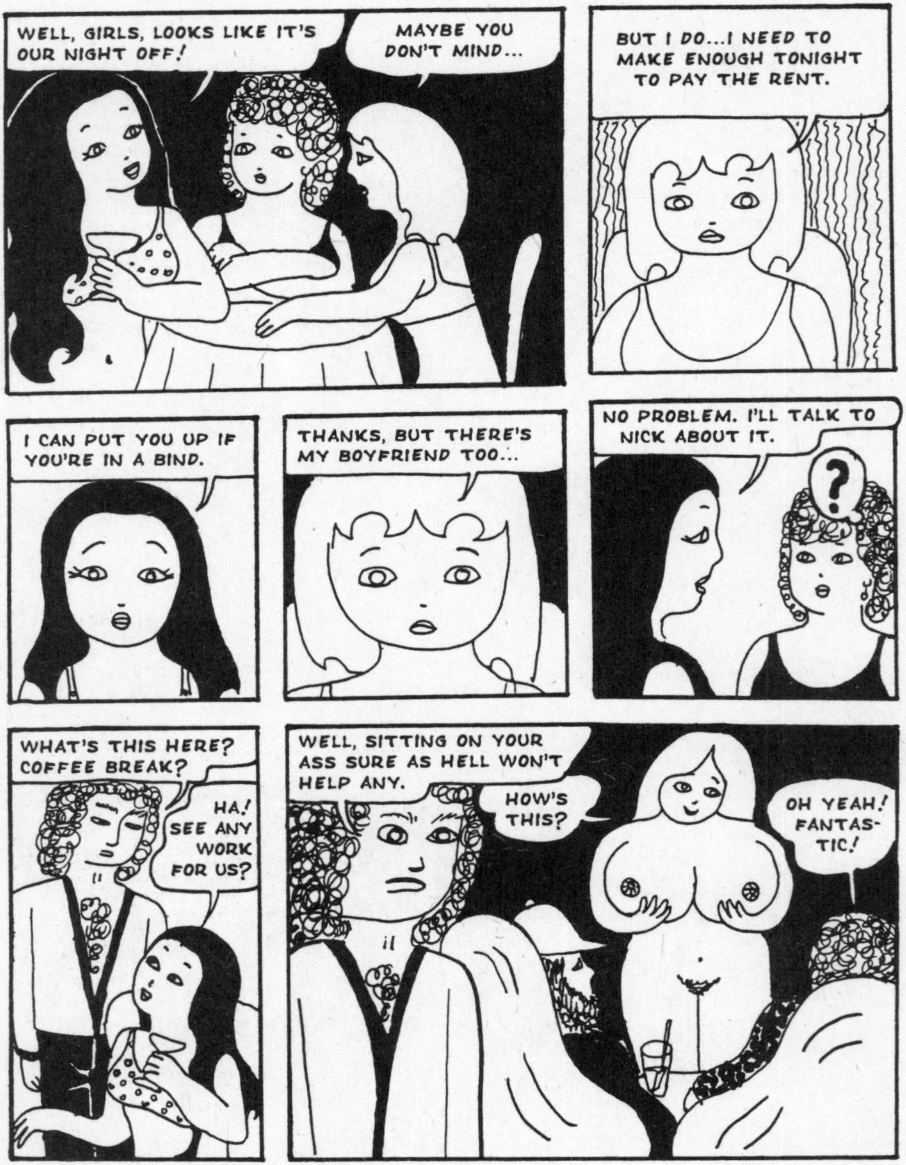
WELL, GIRLS, LOOKS LIKE IT'S OUR NIGHT OFF!
MAYBE YOU DON'T MIND...
BUT I DO...I NEED TO MAKE ENOUGH TONIGHT TO PAY THE RENT.
I CAN PUT YOU UP IF YOU'RE IN A BIND.
THANKS, BUT THERE'S MY BOYFRIEND TOO...
NO PROBLEM. I'LL TALK TO NICK ABOUT IT.
?
WHAT'S THIS HERE? COFFEE BREAK?
HA! SEE ANY WORK FOR US?
WELL, SITTING ON YOUR ASS SURE AS HELL WON'T HELP ANY.
HOW'S THIS?
OH YEAH! FANTAS-TIC!

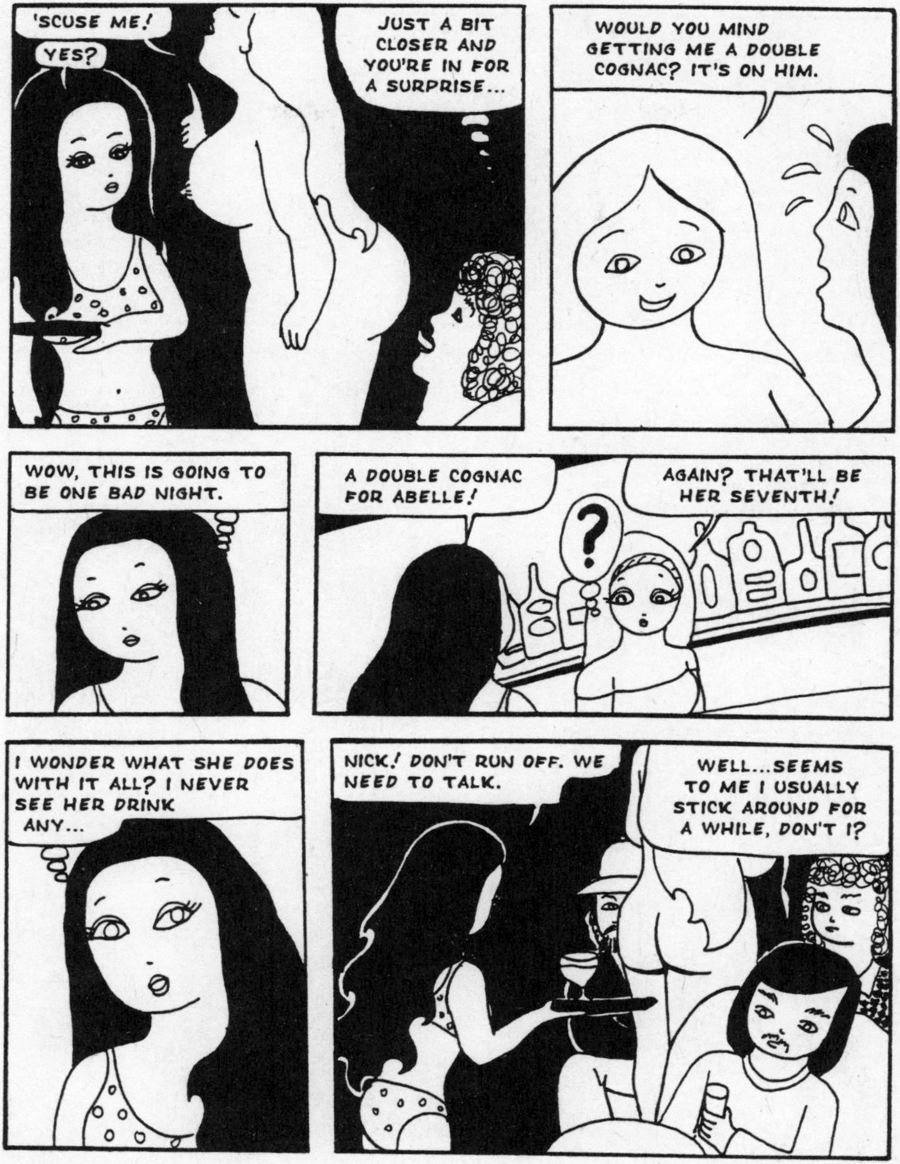
'SCUSE ME!
YES?
JUST A BIT CLOSER AND YOU'RE IN FOR A SURPRISE...
WOULD YOU MIND GETTING ME A DOUBLE COGNAC? IT'S ON HIM.
WOW, THIS IS GOING TO BE ONE BAD NIGHT.
A DOUBLE COGNAC FOR ABELLE!
AGAIN? THAT'LL BE HER SEVENTH!
?
I WONDER WHAT SHE DOES WITH IT ALL? I NEVER SEE HER DRINK ANY...
NICK! DON'T RUN OFF. WE NEED TO TALK.
WELL...SEEMS TO ME I USUALLY STICK AROUND FOR A WHILE, DON'T I?

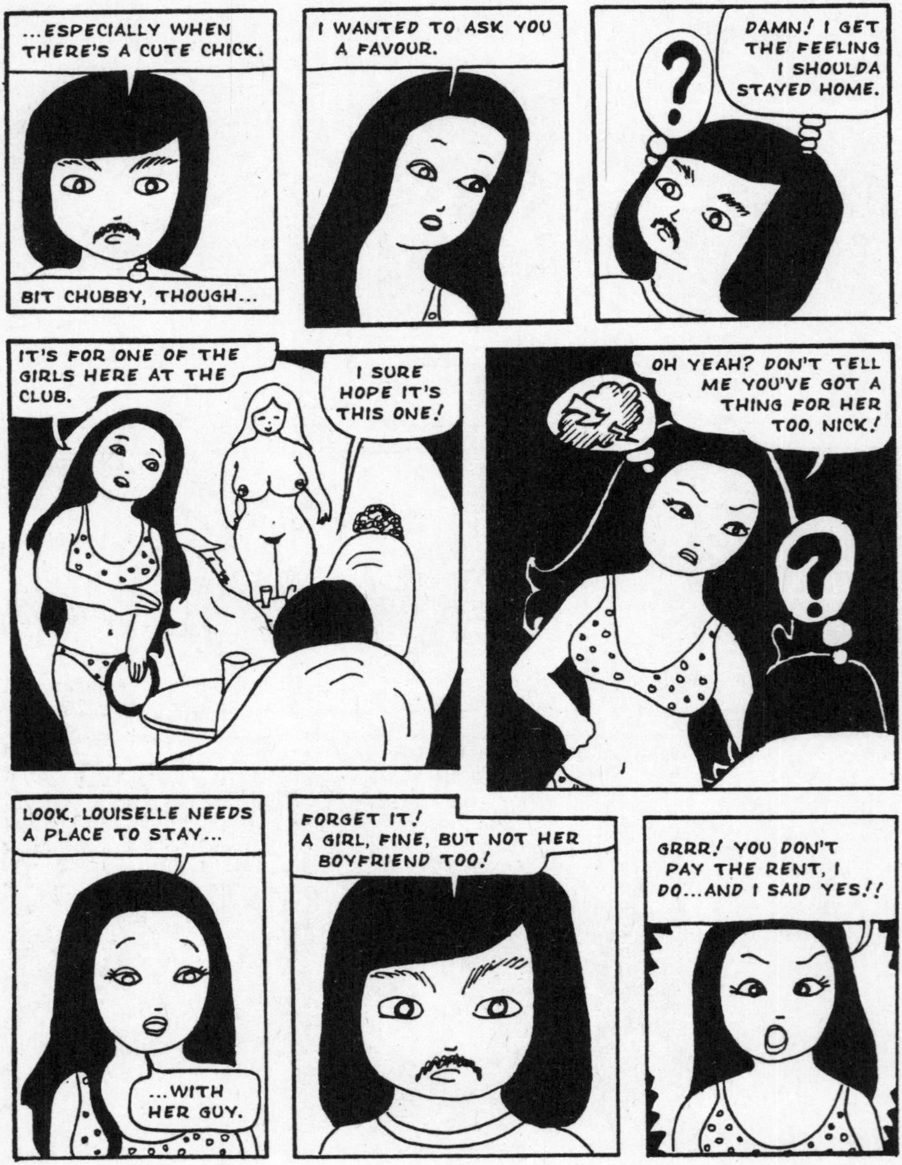
...ESPECIALLY WHEN THERE'S A CUTE CHICK.
BIT CHUBBY, THOUGH...
I WANTED TO ASK YOU A FAVOUR.
DAMN! I GET THE FEELING I SHOULDA STAYED HOME.
IT'S FOR ONE OF THE GIRLS HERE AT THE CLUB.
I SURE HOPE IT'S THIS ONE!
OH YEAH? DON'T TELL ME YOU'VE GOT A THING FOR HER TOO, NICK!
LOOK, LOUISELLE NEEDS A PLACE TO STAY...
...WITH HER GUY.
FORGET IT! A GIRL, FINE, BUT NOT HER BOYFRIEND TOO!
GRRR! YOU DON'T PAY THE RENT, I DO...AND I SAID YES!!

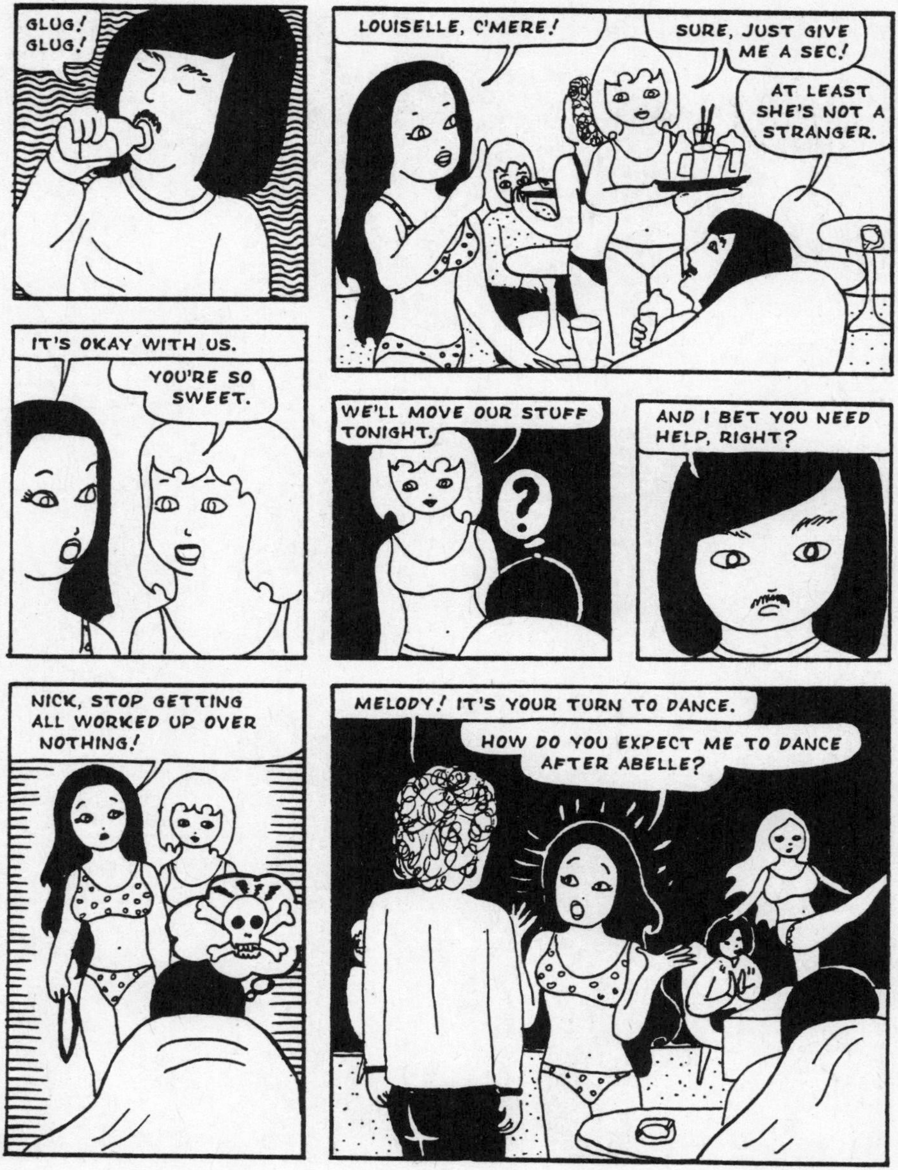
GLUG! GLUG!
LOUISELLE, C'MERE!
SURE, JUST GIVE ME A SEC!
AT LEAST SHE'S NOT A STRANGER.
IT'S OKAY WITH US.
YOU'RE SO SWEET.
WE'LL MOVE OUR STUFF TONIGHT.
?
AND I BET YOU NEED HELP, RIGHT?
NICK, STOP GETTING ALL WORKED UP OVER NOTHING!
MELODY! IT'S YOUR TURN TO DANCE.
HOW DO YOU EXPECT ME TO DANCE AFTER ABELLE?

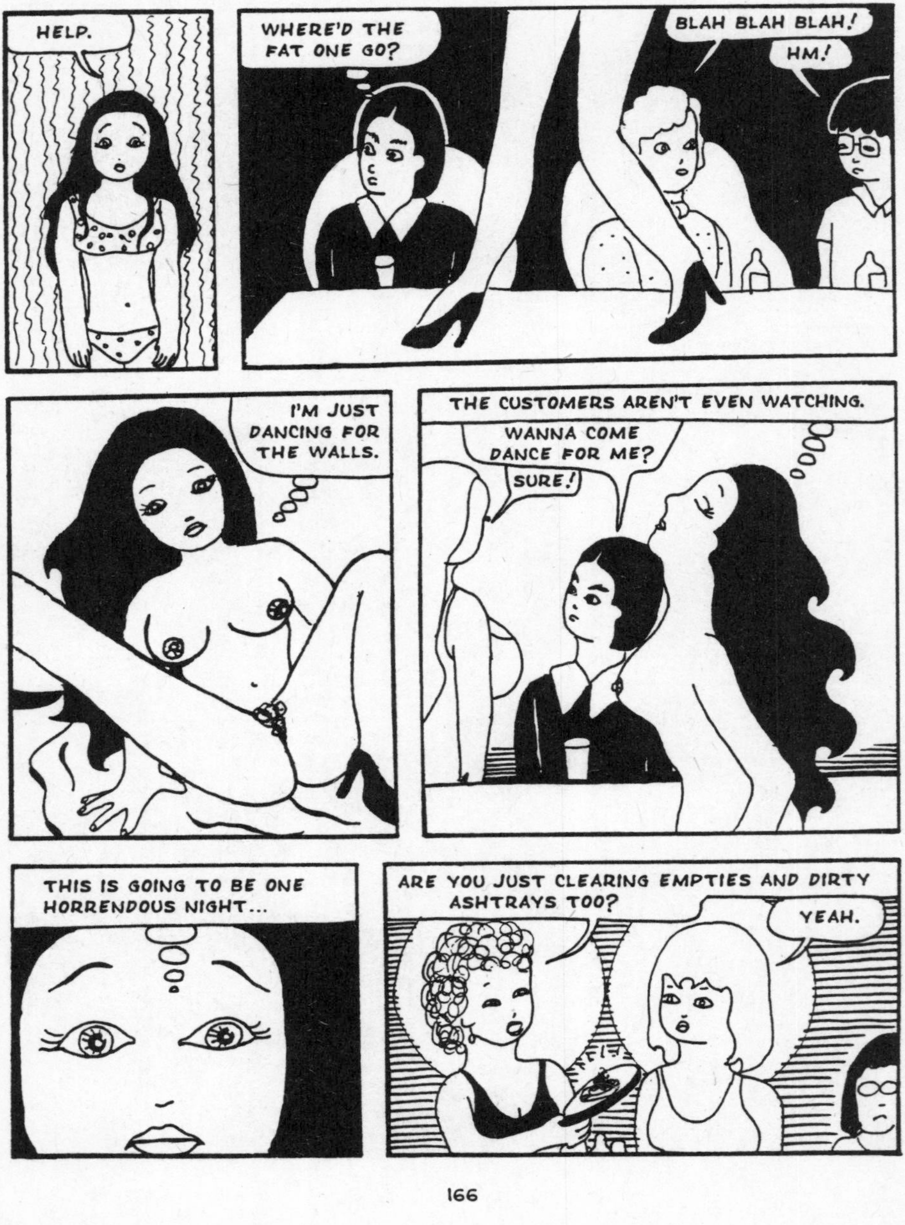
HELP.
WHERE'D THE FAT ONE GO?
BLAH BLAH BLAH!
HM!
I'M JUST DANCING FOR THE WALLS.
THE CUSTOMERS AREN'T EVEN WATCHING.
WANNA COME DANCE FOR ME?
SURE!
THIS IS GOING TO BE ONE HORRENDOUS NIGHT...
ARE YOU JUST CLEARING EMPTIES AND DIRTY ASHTRAYS TOO?
YEAH.

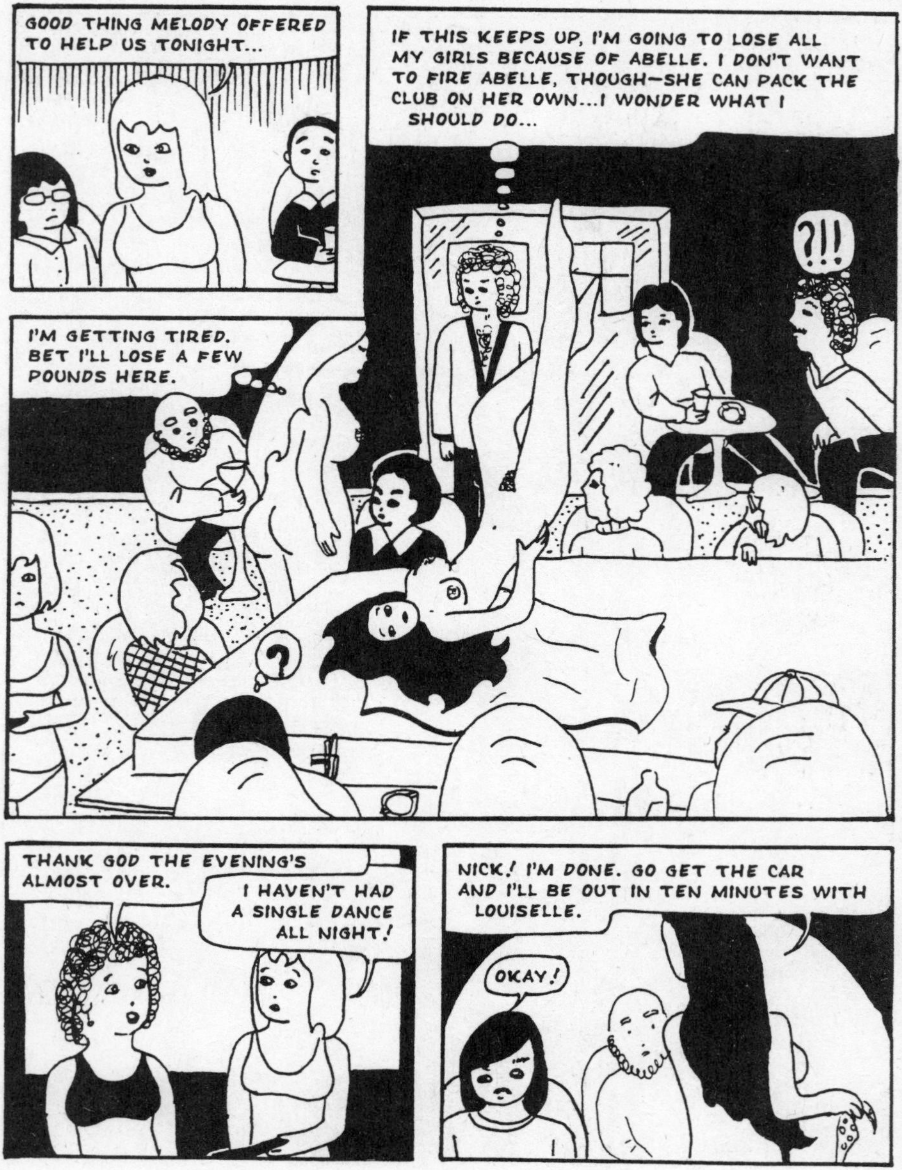
GOOD THING MELODY OFFERED TO HELP US TONIGHT...
IF THIS KEEPS UP, I'M GOING TO LOSE ALL MY GIRLS BECAUSE OF ABELLE. I DON'T WANT TO FIRE ABELLE, THOUGH—SHE CAN PACK THE CLUB ON HER OWN...I WONDER WHAT I SHOULD DO...
?!!
I'M GETTING TIRED. BET I'LL LOSE A FEW POUNDS HERE.
?
THANK GOD THE EVENING'S ALMOST OVER.
I HAVEN'T HAD A SINGLE DANCE ALL NIGHT!
NICK! I'M DONE. GO GET THE CAR AND I'LL BE OUT IN TEN MINUTES WITH LOUISELLE.
OKAY!

CLOSING TIME...
WHAT A NIGHT!
TELL ME ABOUT IT!
AFTER YOU, LADIES...
WHERE TO?
STRAIGHT AS SHE GOES.
THAT'S FUNNY.
HERE.
SOON AFTER...
IT'S REALLY NICE OF YOU TWO TO HELP US OUT.
NO PROBLEM! IT'S THE LEAST WE COULD DO.
THE OWNER IS GONNA BE SURPRISED TO SEE WE'RE GONE.
THIRD FLOOR, FOR CHRISSAKE!

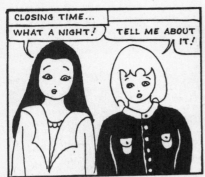

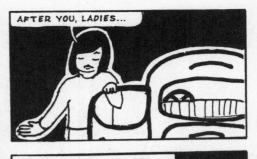

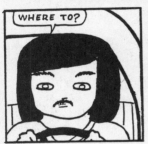

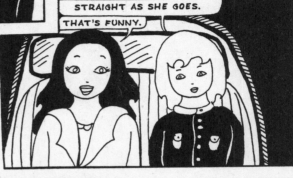

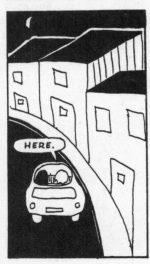

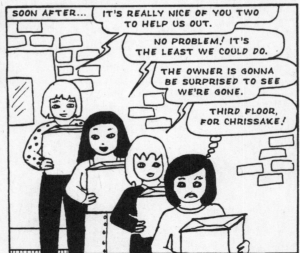

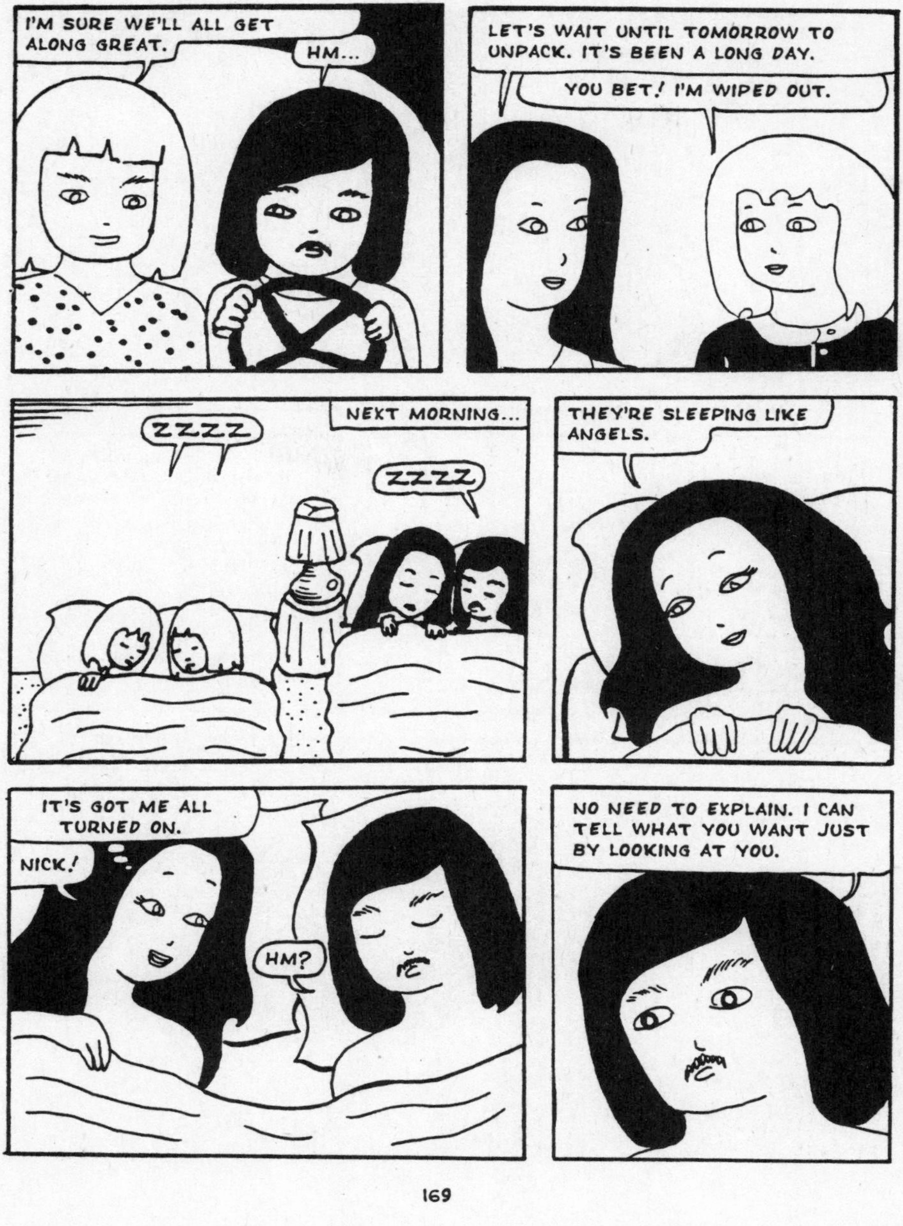
I'M SURE WE'LL ALL GET ALONG GREAT.
HM...
LET'S WAIT UNTIL TOMORROW TO UNPACK. IT'S BEEN A LONG DAY.
YOU BET! I'M WIPED OUT.
NEXT MORNING...
ZZZZ
ZZZZ
THEY'RE SLEEPING LIKE ANGELS.
IT'S GOT ME ALL TURNED ON.
NICK!
HM?
NO NEED TO EXPLAIN. I CAN TELL WHAT YOU WANT JUST BY LOOKING AT YOU.

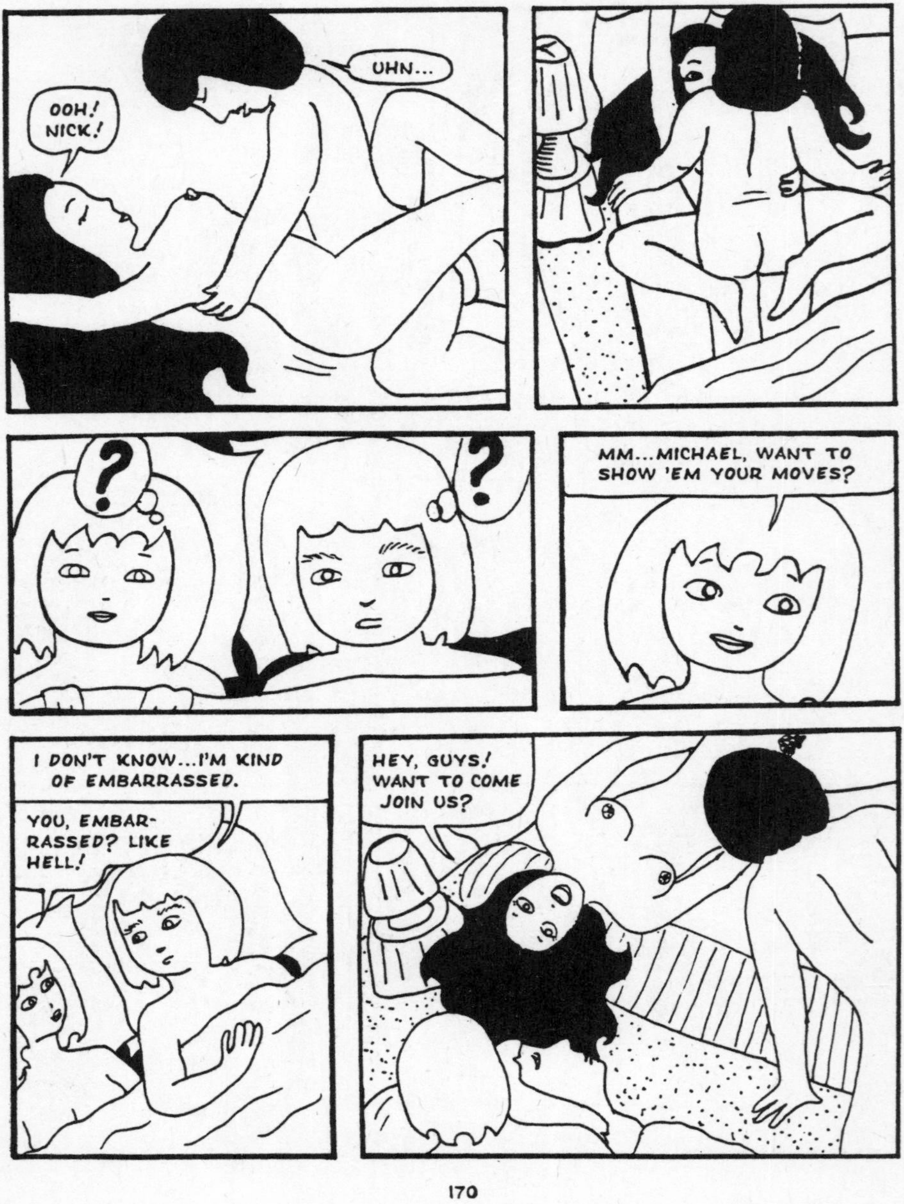
UHN...
OOH! NICK!
MM...MICHAEL, WANT TO SHOW 'EM YOUR MOVES?
I DON'T KNOW...I'M KIND OF EMBARRASSED.
YOU, EMBARRASSED? LIKE HELL!
HEY, GUYS! WANT TO COME JOIN US?

PRETTY WILD! I'VE NEVER DONE THIS BEFORE.
MELODY! I REALLY WANT YOU!
ME TOO, BABY. C'MERE, LET ME KISS YOU.
HEY, WHAT ABOUT ME?
MMM...
HOLY CHRIST!
WELL...MIGHT AS WELL JERK OFF. WOW!

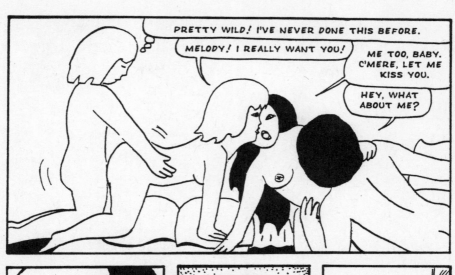

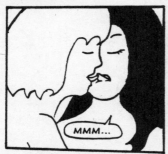

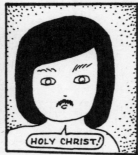

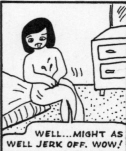

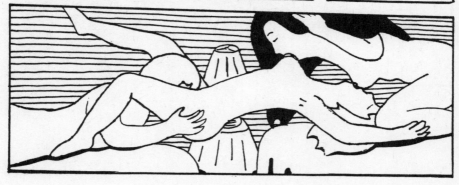

LOUISELLE! COME
HERE. I WANT YOU
CLOSE TO ME.

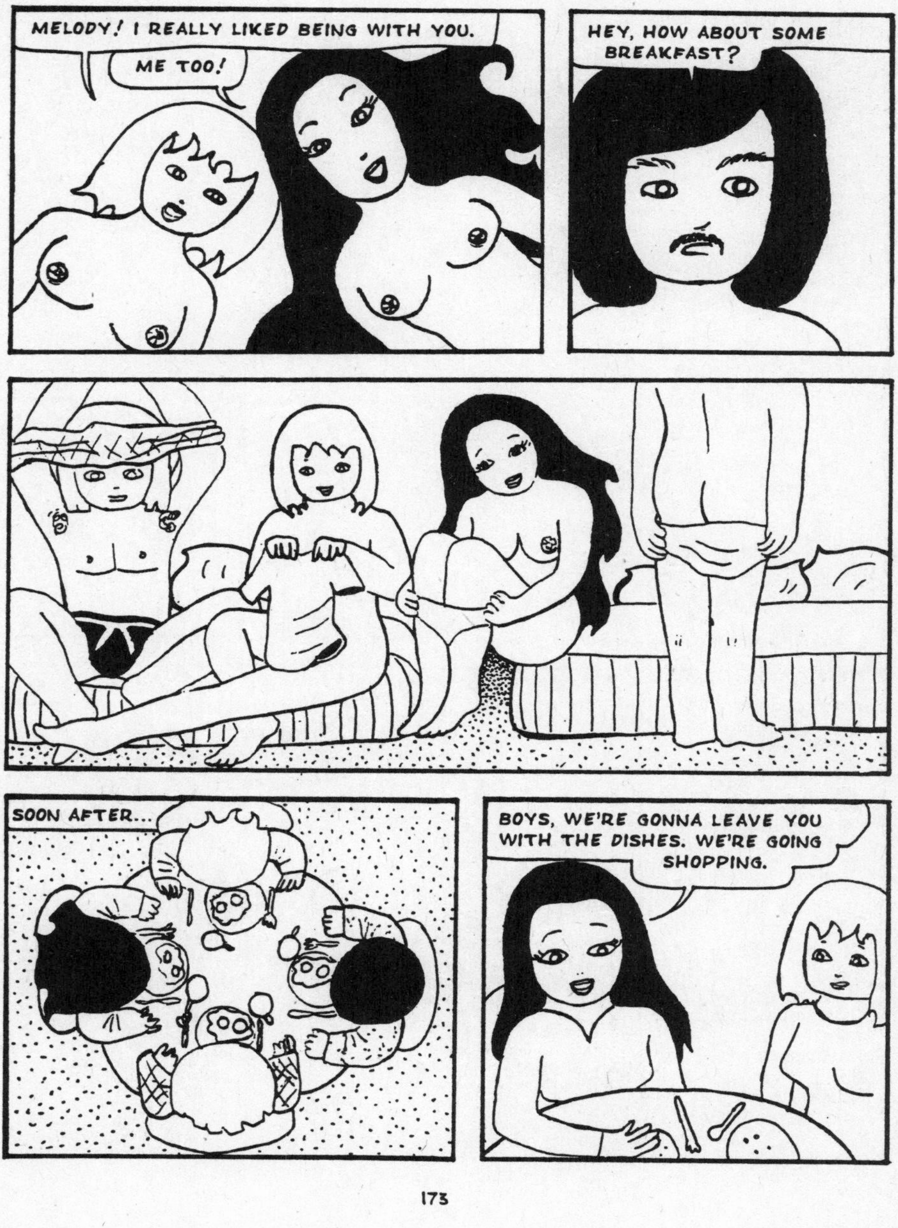
MELODY! I REALLY LIKED BEING WITH YOU.
ME TOO!
HEY, HOW ABOUT SOME BREAKFAST?
SOON AFTER...
BOYS, WE'RE GONNA LEAVE YOU WITH THE DISHES. WE'RE GOING SHOPPING.

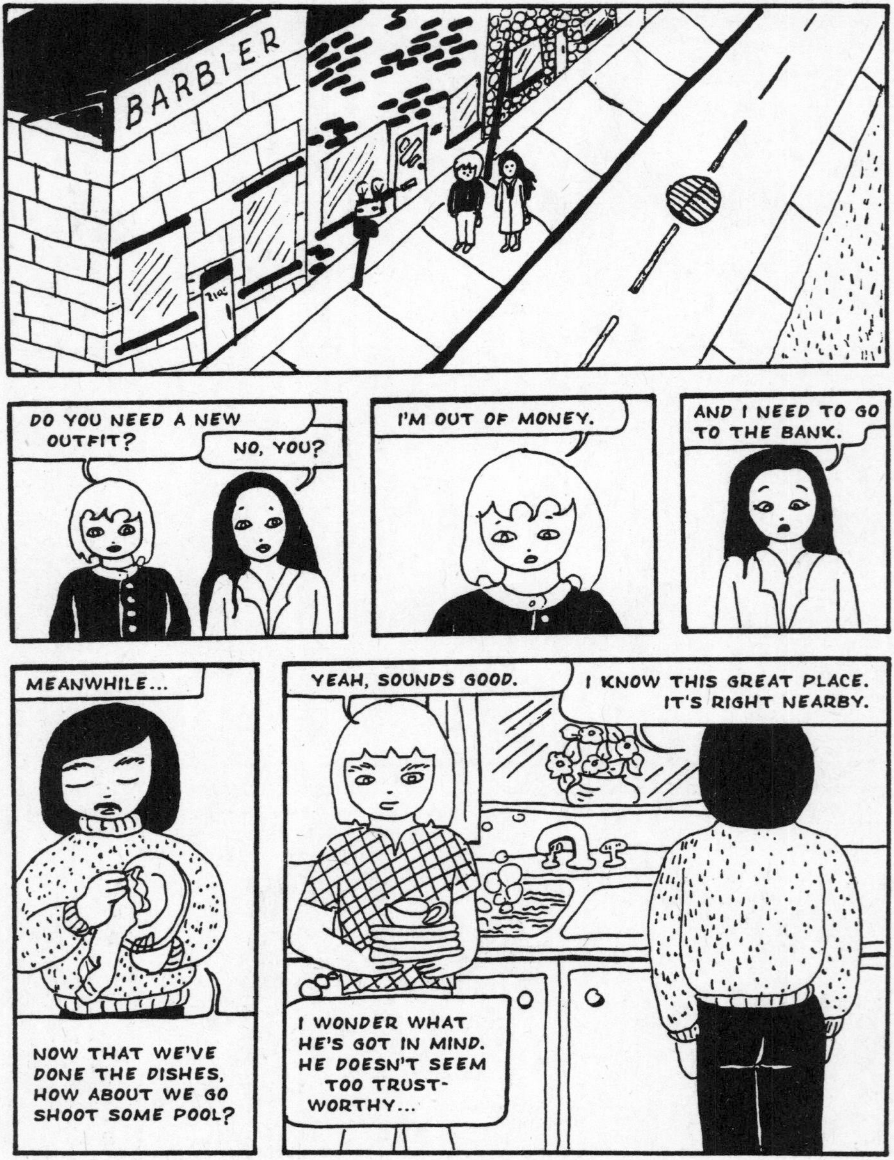
BARBIER
DO YOU NEED A NEW OUTFIT?
NO, YOU?
I'M OUT OF MONEY.
AND I NEED TO GO TO THE BANK.
MEANWHILE...
NOW THAT WE'VE DONE THE DISHES, HOW ABOUT WE GO SHOOT SOME POOL?
YEAH, SOUNDS GOOD.
I KNOW THIS GREAT PLACE. IT'S RIGHT NEARBY.
I WONDER WHAT HE'S GOT IN MIND. HE DOESN'T SEEM TOO TRUST-WORTHY...

THERE, THAT TABLE'S FREE.
HEYA, NICK!
WHAT THE HELL'S HE DOING WITH THAT JERK?
HEY! COME MEET MY FRIEND.
UH, YOU THINK WE CAN TRUST HIM?
WELL, HE'S TOTALLY BROKE.
HM...GOOD PLAYERS HERE.
HEY, MICHAEL, ARE YOU INTERESTED IN EARNING SOME EASY CASH?
?
WELL, I GUESS IT DEPENDS, RIGHT?
COME WITH US. WE'LL LET YOU SEE FOR YOURSELF.

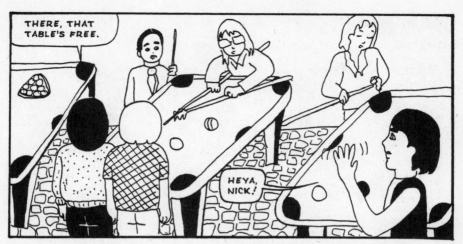

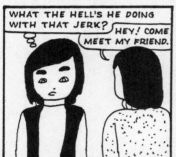

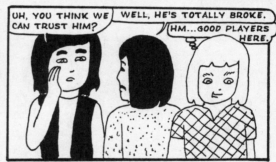

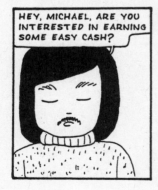

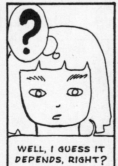

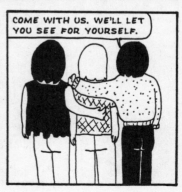

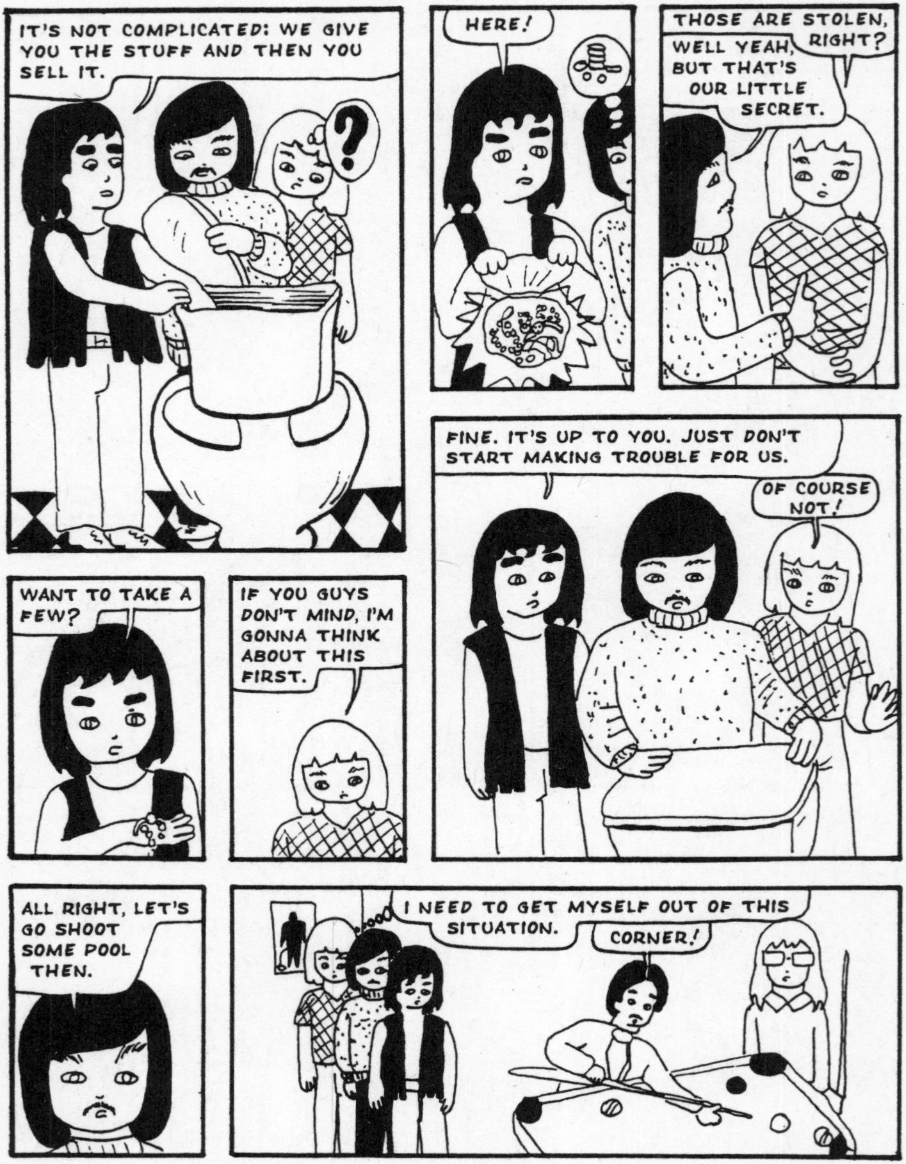
IT'S NOT COMPLICATED: WE GIVE YOU THE STUFF AND THEN YOU SELL IT.
HERE!
THOSE ARE STOLEN, RIGHT?
WELL YEAH, BUT THAT'S OUR LITTLE SECRET.
FINE. IT'S UP TO YOU. JUST DON'T START MAKING TROUBLE FOR US.
OF COURSE NOT!
WANT TO TAKE A FEW?
IF YOU GUYS DON'T MIND, I'M GONNA THINK ABOUT THIS FIRST.
ALL RIGHT, LET'S GO SHOOT SOME POOL THEN.
I NEED TO GET MYSELF OUT OF THIS SITUATION.
CORNER!

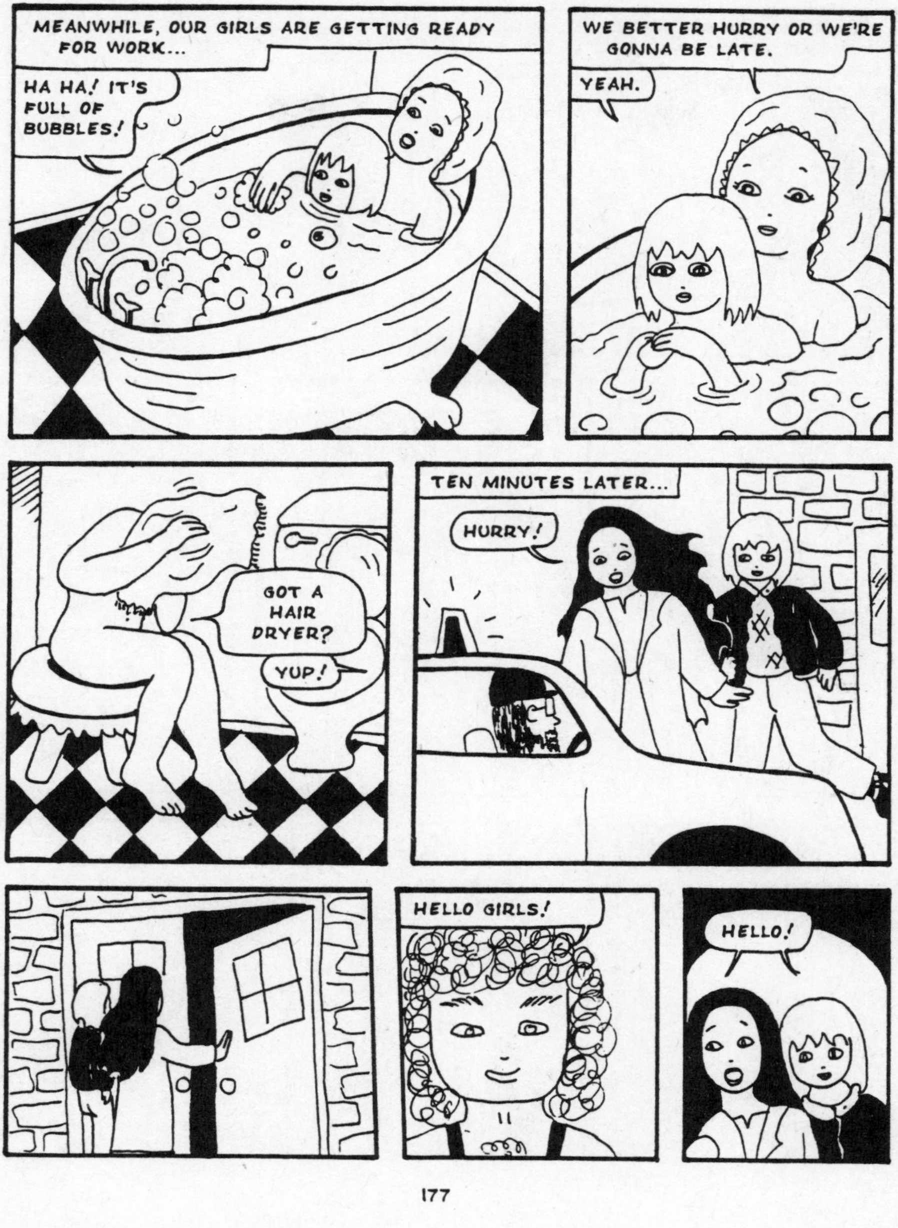
MEANWHILE, OUR GIRLS ARE GETTING READY FOR WORK...
HA HA! IT'S FULL OF BUBBLES!
WE BETTER HURRY OR WE'RE GONNA BE LATE.
YEAH.
GOT A HAIR DRYER?
YUP!
TEN MINUTES LATER...
HURRY!
HELLO GIRLS!
HELLO!

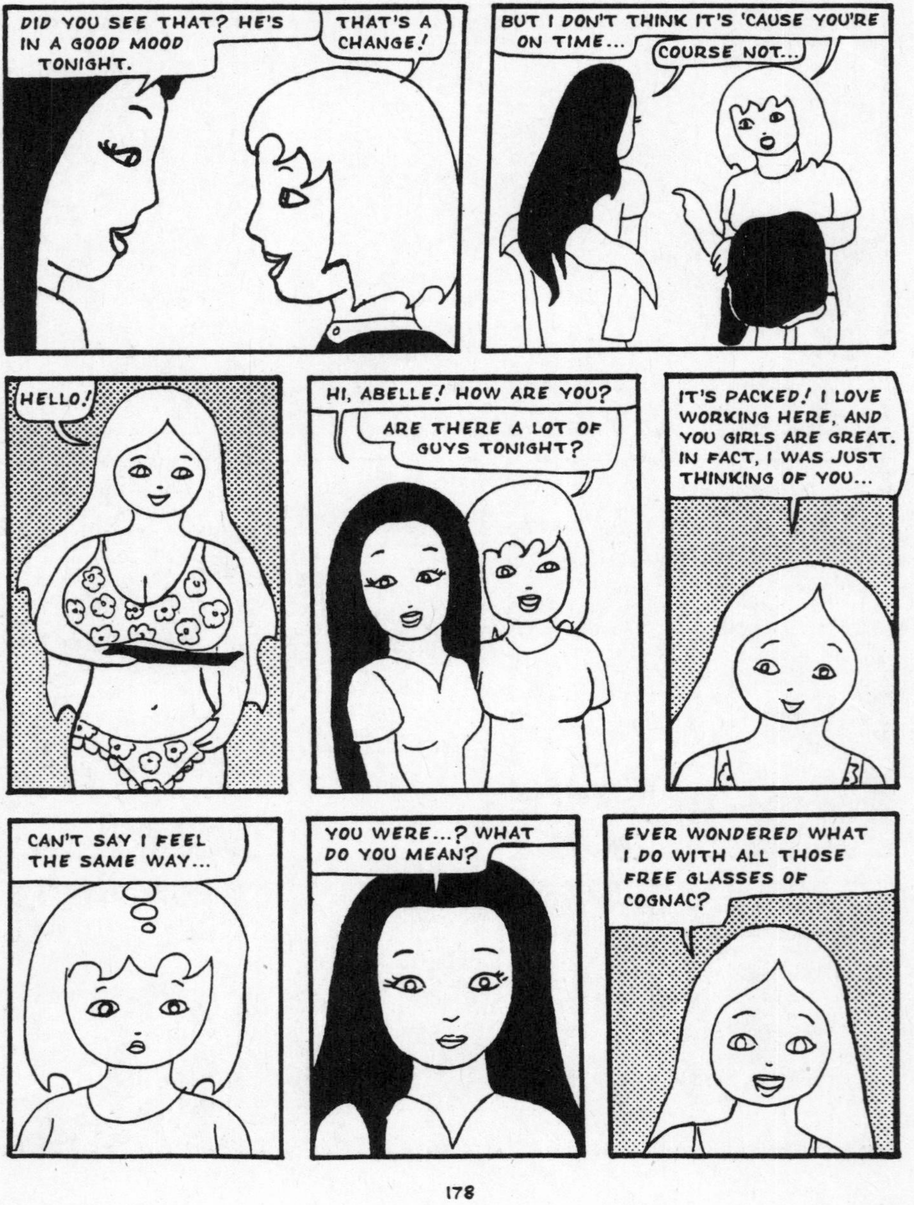
DID YOU SEE THAT? HE'S IN A GOOD MOOD TONIGHT.
THAT'S A CHANGE!
BUT I DON'T THINK IT'S 'CAUSE YOU'RE ON TIME...
COURSE NOT...
HELLO!
HI, ABELLE! HOW ARE YOU?
ARE THERE A LOT OF GUYS TONIGHT?
IT'S PACKED! I LOVE WORKING HERE, AND YOU GIRLS ARE GREAT. IN FACT, I WAS JUST THINKING OF YOU...
CAN'T SAY I FEEL THE SAME WAY...
YOU WERE...? WHAT DO YOU MEAN?
EVER WONDERED WHAT I DO WITH ALL THOSE FREE GLASSES OF COGNAC?

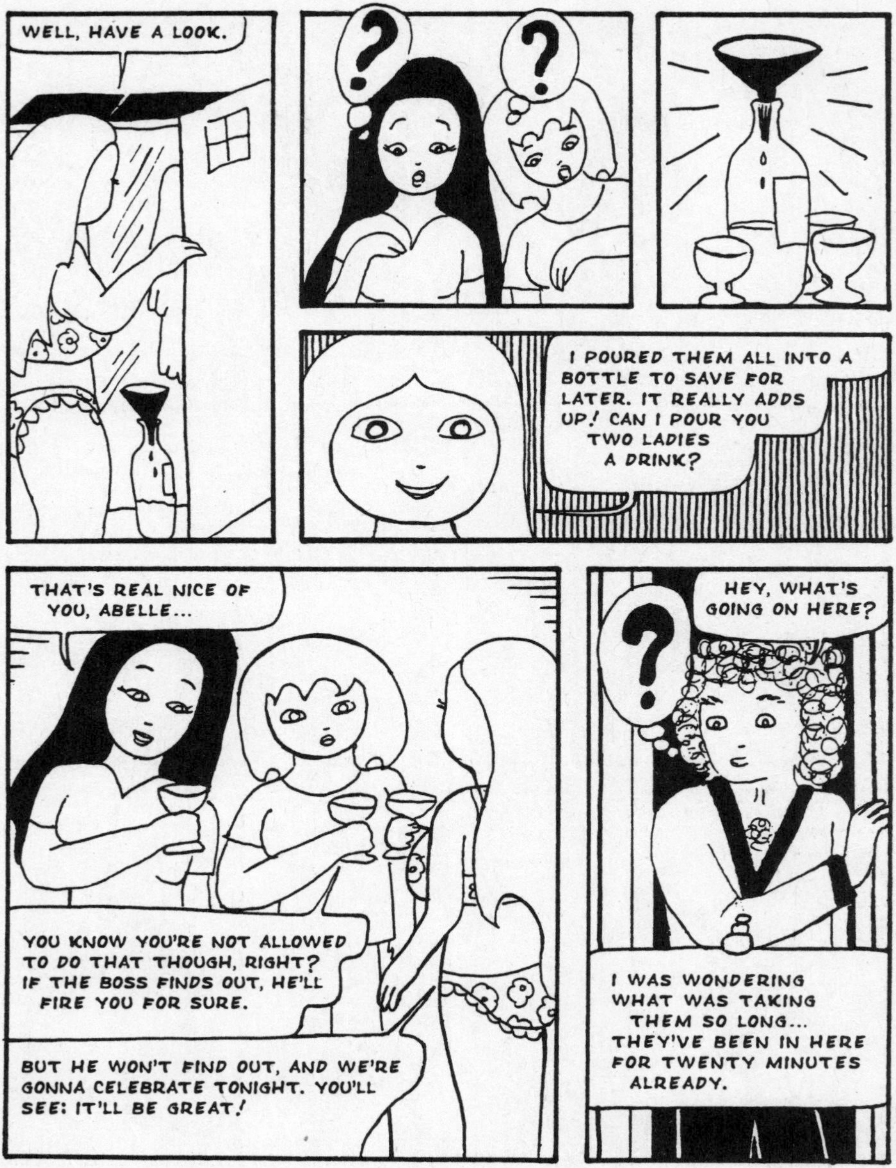
WELL, HAVE A LOOK.
?
?
I POURED THEM ALL INTO A BOTTLE TO SAVE FOR LATER. IT REALLY ADDS UP! CAN I POUR YOU TWO LADIES A DRINK?
THAT'S REAL NICE OF YOU, ABELLE...
YOU KNOW YOU'RE NOT ALLOWED TO DO THAT THOUGH, RIGHT? IF THE BOSS FINDS OUT, HE'LL FIRE YOU FOR SURE.
BUT HE WON'T FIND OUT, AND WE'RE GONNA CELEBRATE TONIGHT. YOU'LL SEE: IT'LL BE GREAT!
HEY, WHAT'S GOING ON HERE?
?
I WAS WONDERING WHAT WAS TAKING THEM SO LONG... THEY'VE BEEN IN HERE FOR TWENTY MINUTES ALREADY.

HEY, NO HARM DONE! WE'RE JUST HAVING A DRINK.
I'M GIVING YOU ALL THREE MINUTES TO GET OUT ON THE FLOOR !!!
YEAH, YEAH. DON'T GET ALL WORKED UP.
C'MON, YOU WERE IN SUCH A GOOD MOOD EARLIER!
IT'S MY FAULT.
YOU GIRLS ARE GONNA MAKE ME CRAZY!
LOOK, I'LL BE DRESSED IN A SECOND.
ME TOO.
THERE! I'M READY.

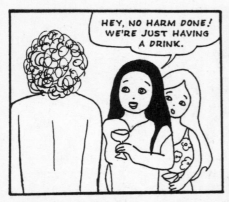

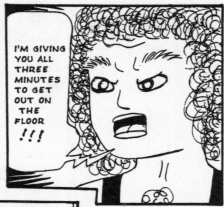

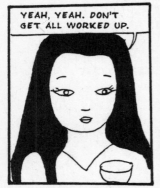

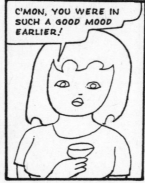

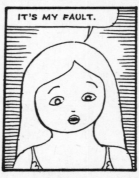

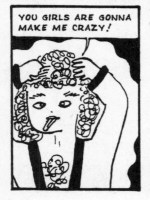

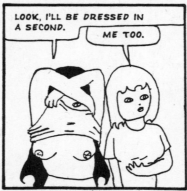

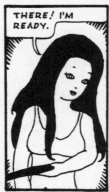

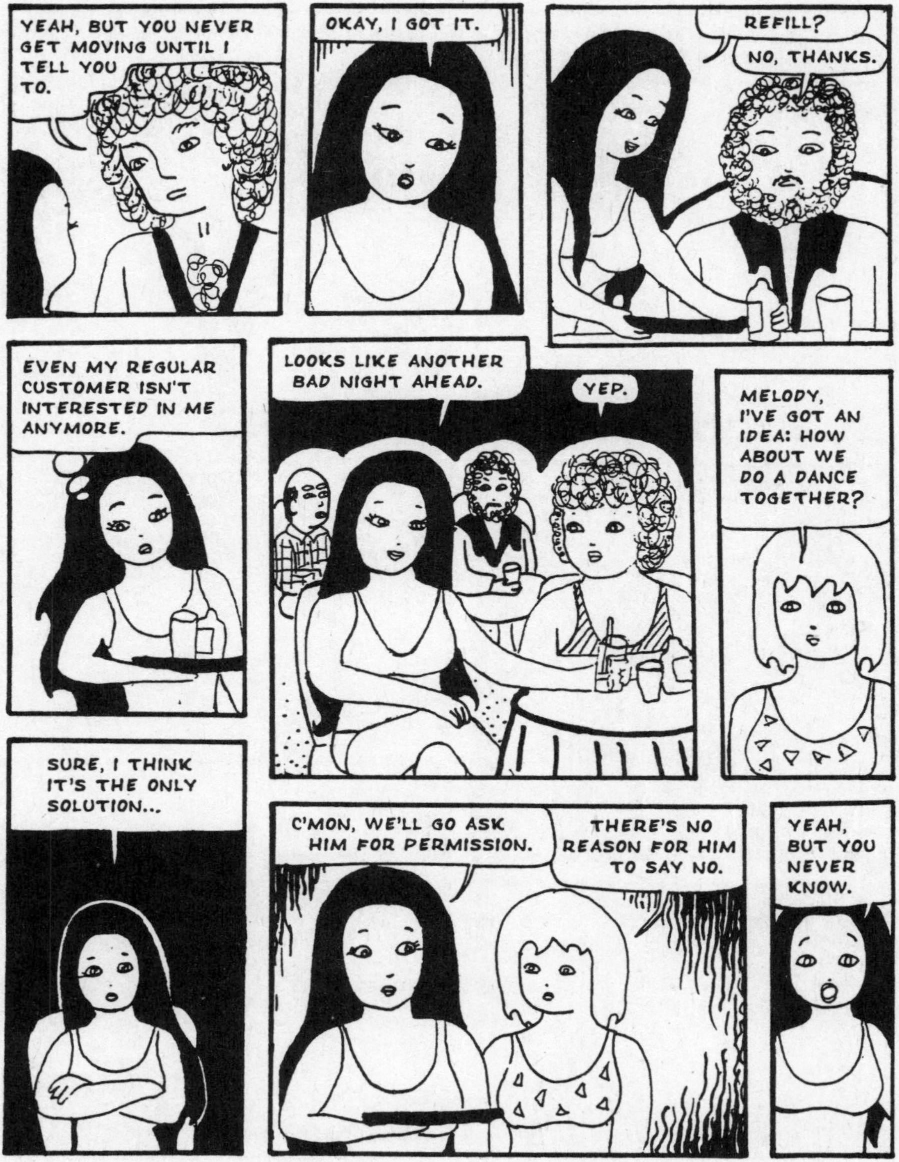
YEAH, BUT YOU NEVER GET MOVING UNTIL I TELL YOU TO.
OKAY, I GOT IT.
REFILL?
NO, THANKS.
EVEN MY REGULAR CUSTOMER ISN'T INTERESTED IN ME ANYMORE.
LOOKS LIKE ANOTHER BAD NIGHT AHEAD.
YEP.
MELODY, I'VE GOT AN IDEA: HOW ABOUT WE DO A DANCE TOGETHER?
SURE, I THINK IT'S THE ONLY SOLUTION...
C'MON, WE'LL GO ASK HIM FOR PERMISSION.
THERE'S NO REASON FOR HIM TO SAY NO.
YEAH, BUT YOU NEVER KNOW.

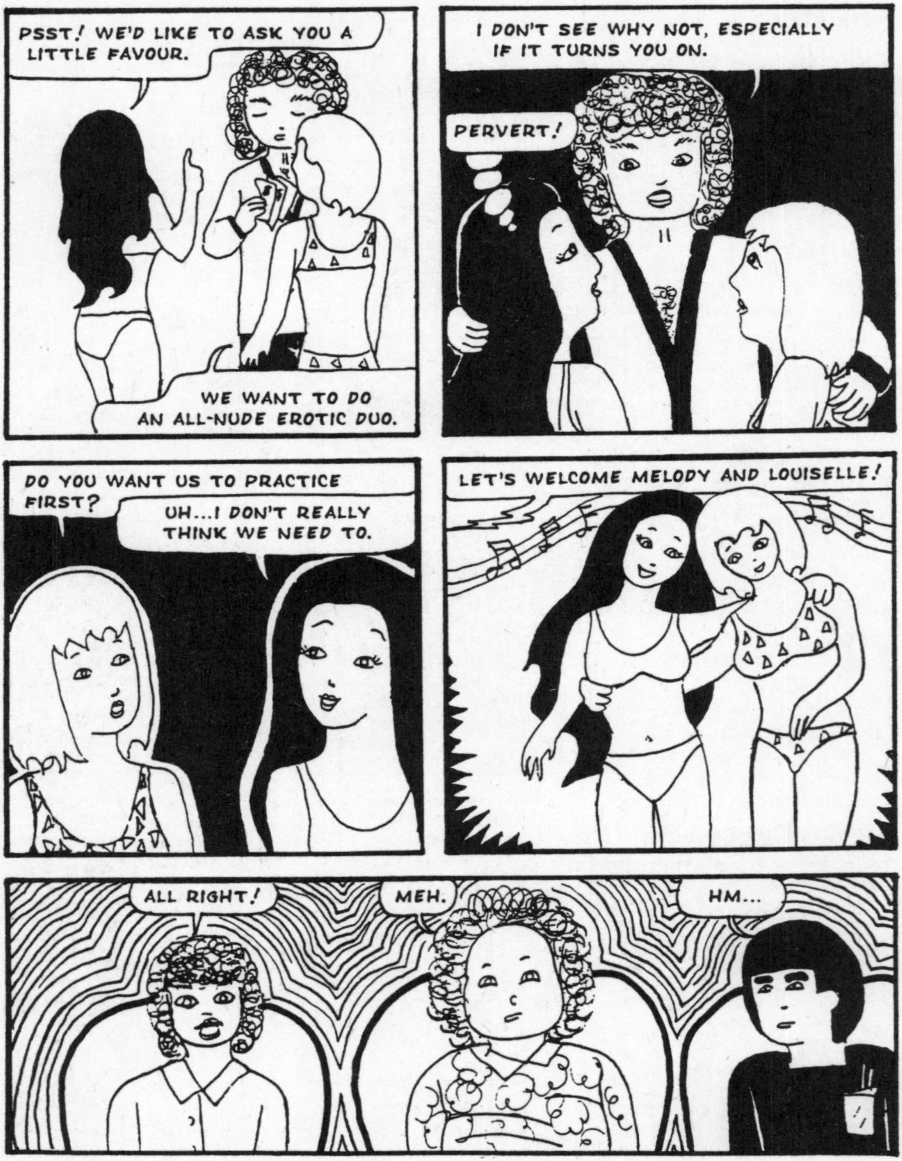
PSST! WE'D LIKE TO ASK YOU A LITTLE FAVOUR.
WE WANT TO DO AN ALL-NUDE EROTIC DUO.
I DON'T SEE WHY NOT, ESPECIALLY IF IT TURNS YOU ON.
PERVERT!
DO YOU WANT US TO PRACTICE FIRST?
UH...I DON'T REALLY THINK WE NEED TO.
LET'S WELCOME MELODY AND LOUISELLE!
ALL RIGHT!
MEH.
HM...

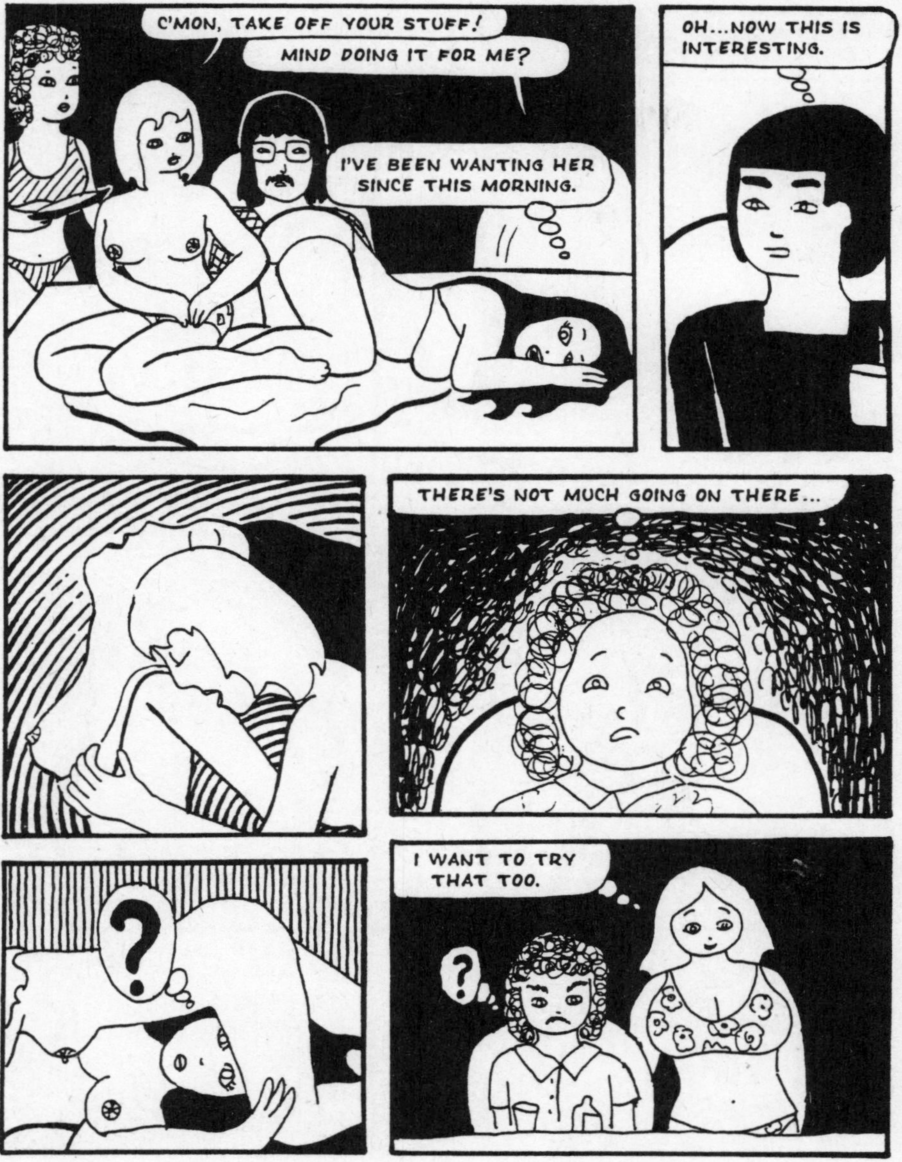
C'MON, TAKE OFF YOUR STUFF!
MIND DOING IT FOR ME?
I'VE BEEN WANTING HER SINCE THIS MORNING.
OH...NOW THIS IS INTERESTING.
THERE'S NOT MUCH GOING ON THERE...
?
I WANT TO TRY THAT TOO.
?

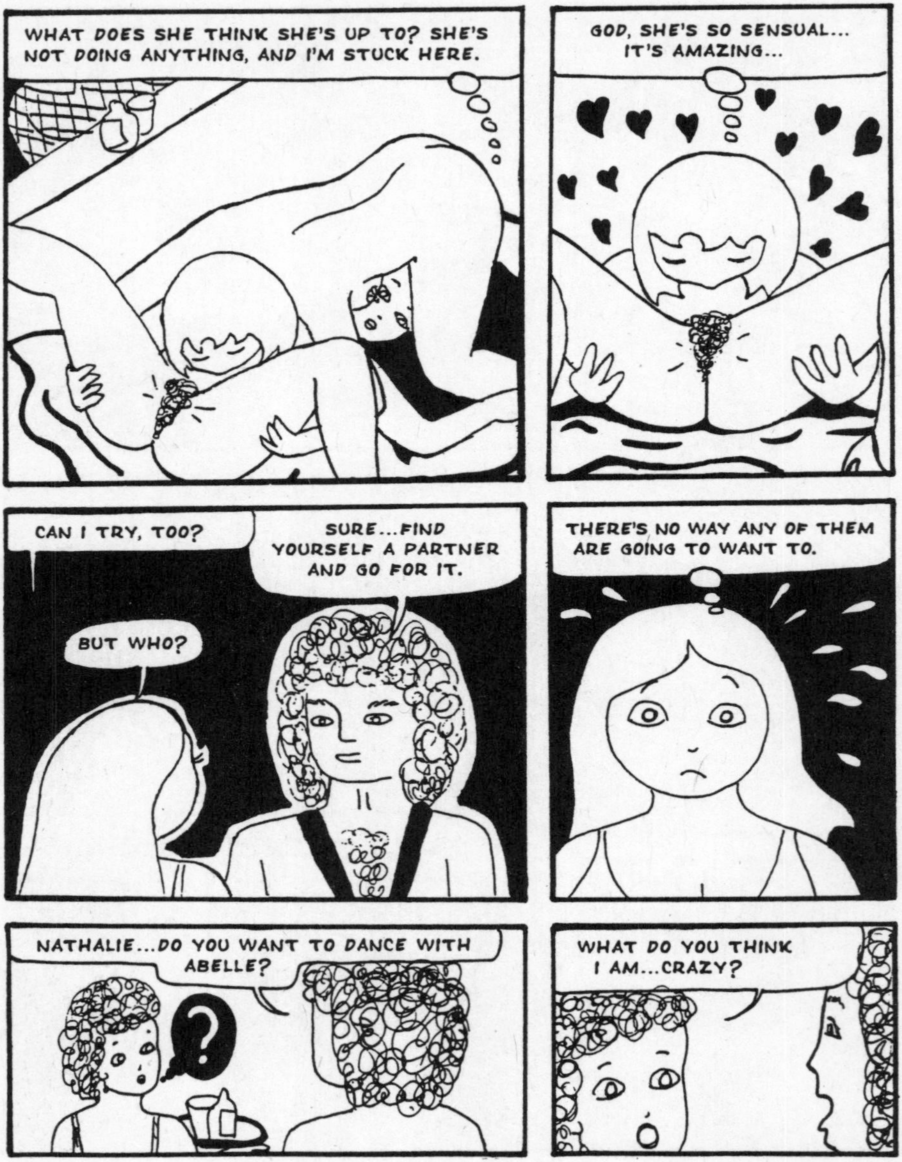
WHAT DOES SHE THINK SHE'S UP TO? SHE'S NOT DOING ANYTHING, AND I'M STUCK HERE.
GOD, SHE'S SO SENSUAL... IT'S AMAZING...
CAN I TRY, TOO?
SURE...FIND YOURSELF A PARTNER AND GO FOR IT.
BUT WHO?
THERE'S NO WAY ANY OF THEM ARE GOING TO WANT TO.
NATHALIE...DO YOU WANT TO DANCE WITH ABELLE?
?
WHAT DO YOU THINK I AM...CRAZY?

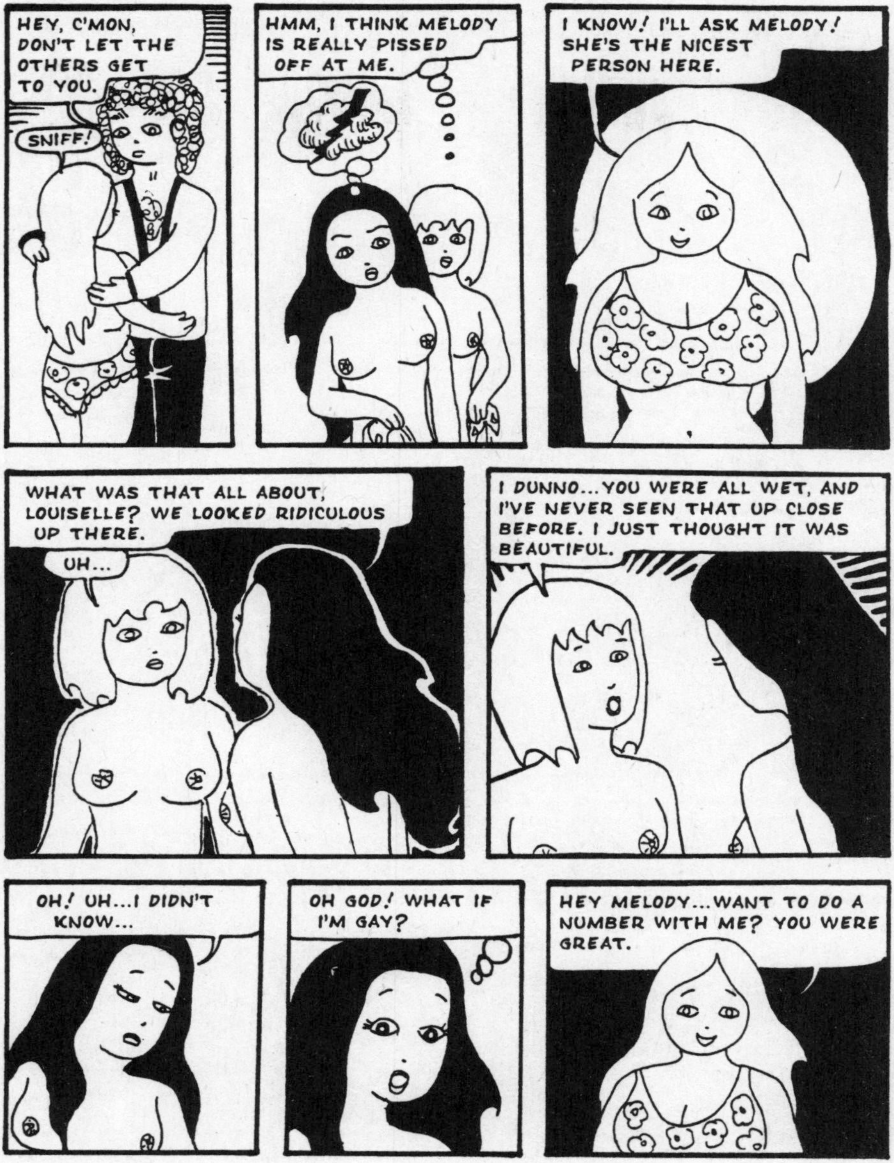
HEY, C'MON, DON'T LET THE OTHERS GET TO YOU.
SNIFF!
HMM, I THINK MELODY IS REALLY PISSED OFF AT ME.
I KNOW! I'LL ASK MELODY! SHE'S THE NICEST PERSON HERE.
WHAT WAS THAT ALL ABOUT, LOUISELLE? WE LOOKED RIDICULOUS UP THERE.
UH...
I DUNNO...YOU WERE ALL WET, AND I'VE NEVER SEEN THAT UP CLOSE BEFORE. I JUST THOUGHT IT WAS BEAUTIFUL.
OH! UH...I DIDN'T KNOW...
OH GOD! WHAT IF I'M GAY?
HEY MELODY...WANT TO DO A NUMBER WITH ME? YOU WERE GREAT.

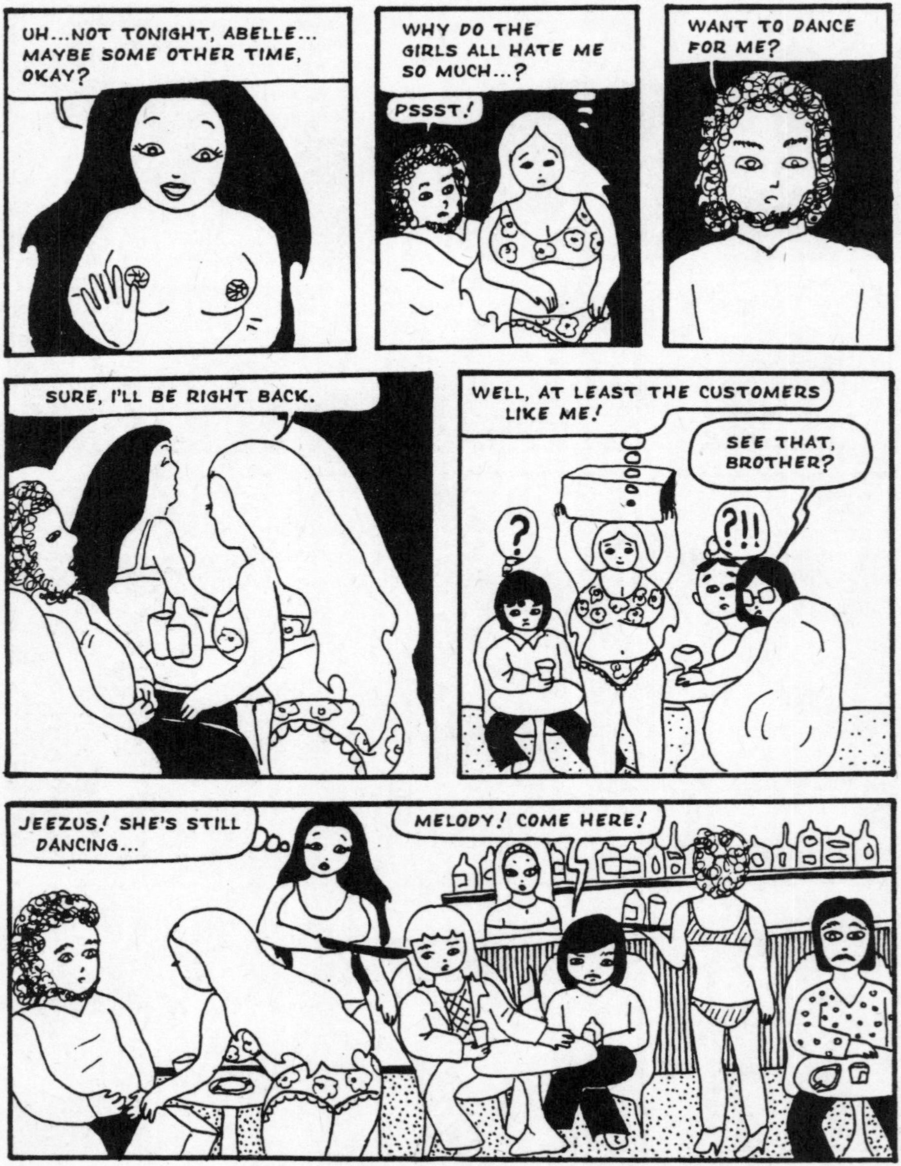
UH...NOT TONIGHT, ABELLE... MAYBE SOME OTHER TIME, OKAY?
WHY DO THE GIRLS ALL HATE ME SO MUCH...?
PSSST!
WANT TO DANCE FOR ME?
SURE, I'LL BE RIGHT BACK.
WELL, AT LEAST THE CUSTOMERS LIKE ME!
?
SEE THAT, BROTHER?
?!!
JEEZUS! SHE'S STILL DANCING...
MELODY! COME HERE!

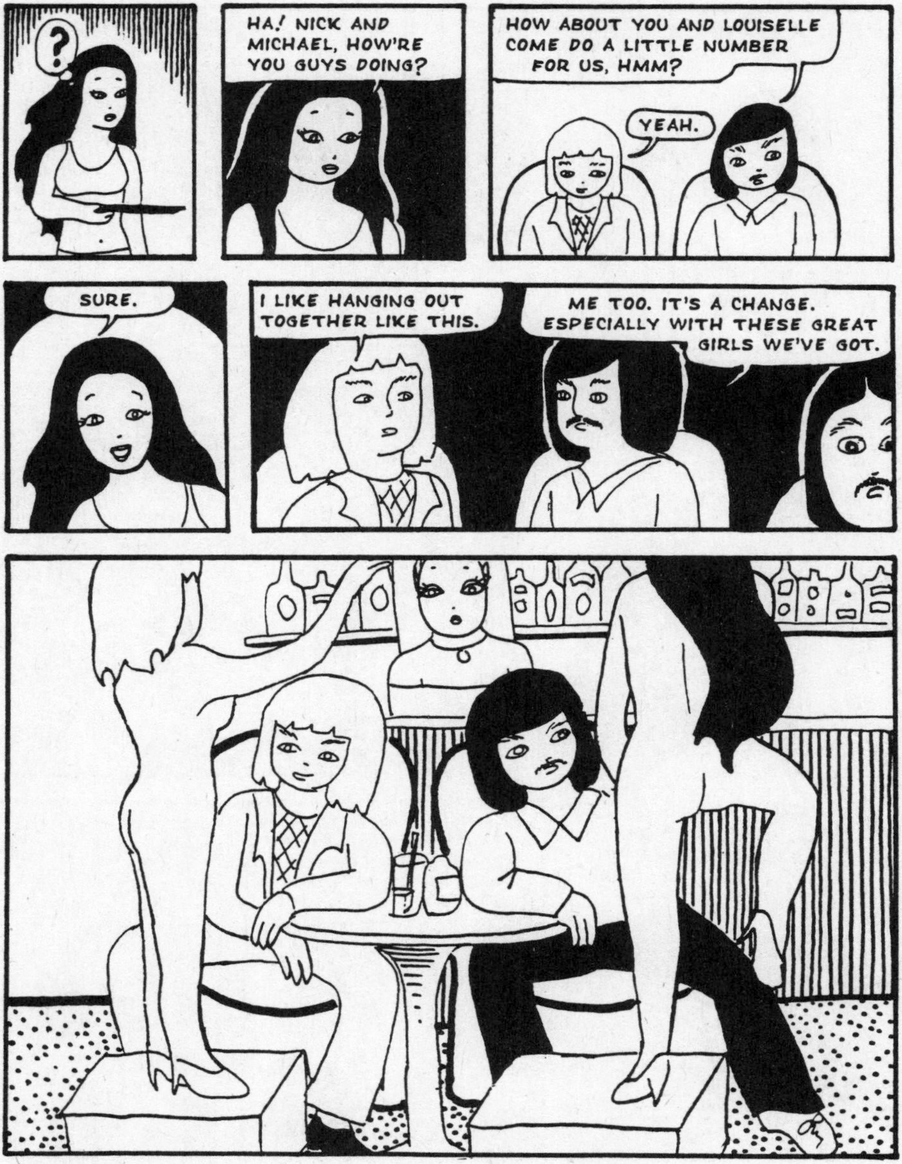
?
HA! NICK AND MICHAEL, HOW'RE YOU GUYS DOING?
HOW ABOUT YOU AND LOUISELLE COME DO A LITTLE NUMBER FOR US, HMM?
YEAH.
SURE.
I LIKE HANGING OUT TOGETHER LIKE THIS.
ME TOO. IT'S A CHANGE. ESPECIALLY WITH THESE GREAT GIRLS WE'VE GOT.

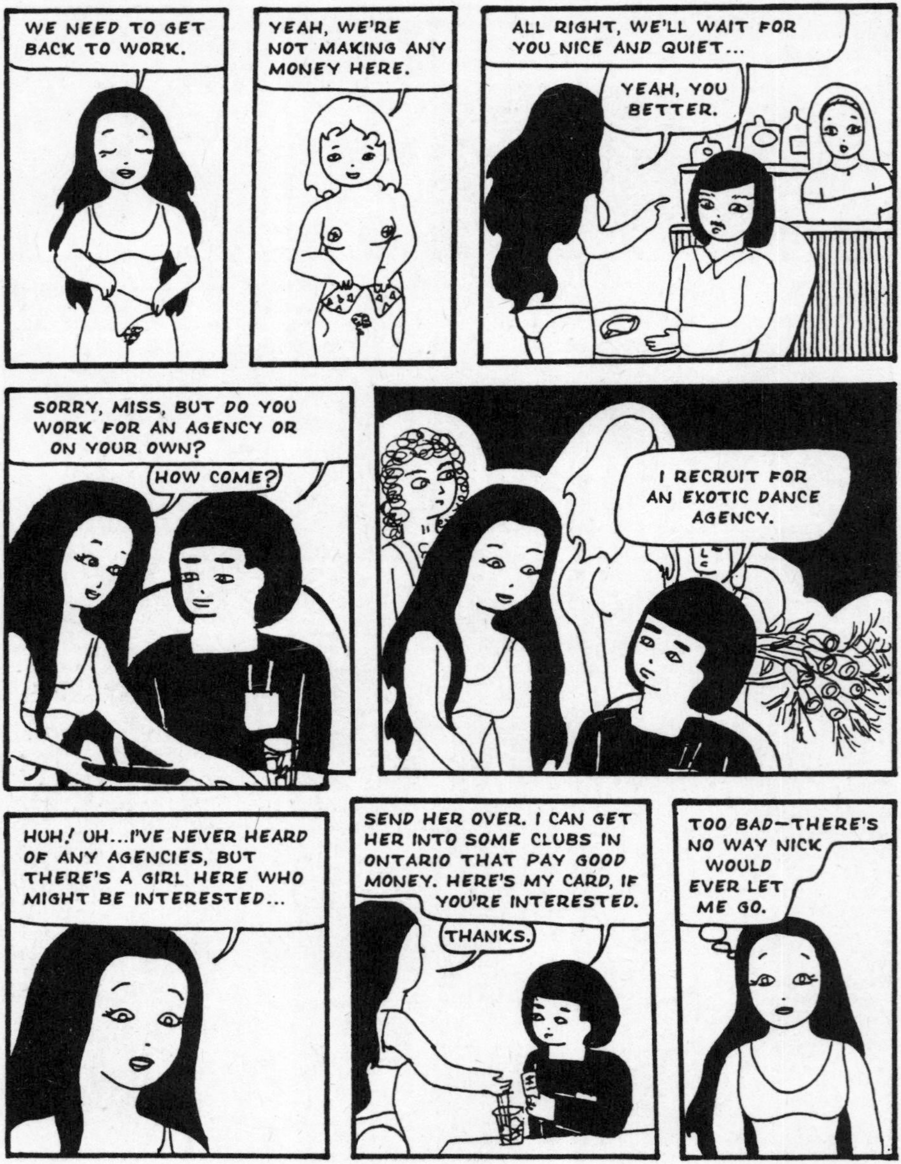
WE NEED TO GET BACK TO WORK.
YEAH, WE'RE NOT MAKING ANY MONEY HERE.
ALL RIGHT, WE'LL WAIT FOR YOU NICE AND QUIET...
YEAH, YOU BETTER.
SORRY, MISS, BUT DO YOU WORK FOR AN AGENCY OR ON YOUR OWN?
HOW COME?
I RECRUIT FOR AN EXOTIC DANCE AGENCY.
HUH! UH...I'VE NEVER HEARD OF ANY AGENCIES, BUT THERE'S A GIRL HERE WHO MIGHT BE INTERESTED...
SEND HER OVER. I CAN GET HER INTO SOME CLUBS IN ONTARIO THAT PAY GOOD MONEY. HERE'S MY CARD, IF YOU'RE INTERESTED.
THANKS.
TOO BAD—THERE'S NO WAY NICK WOULD EVER LET ME GO.

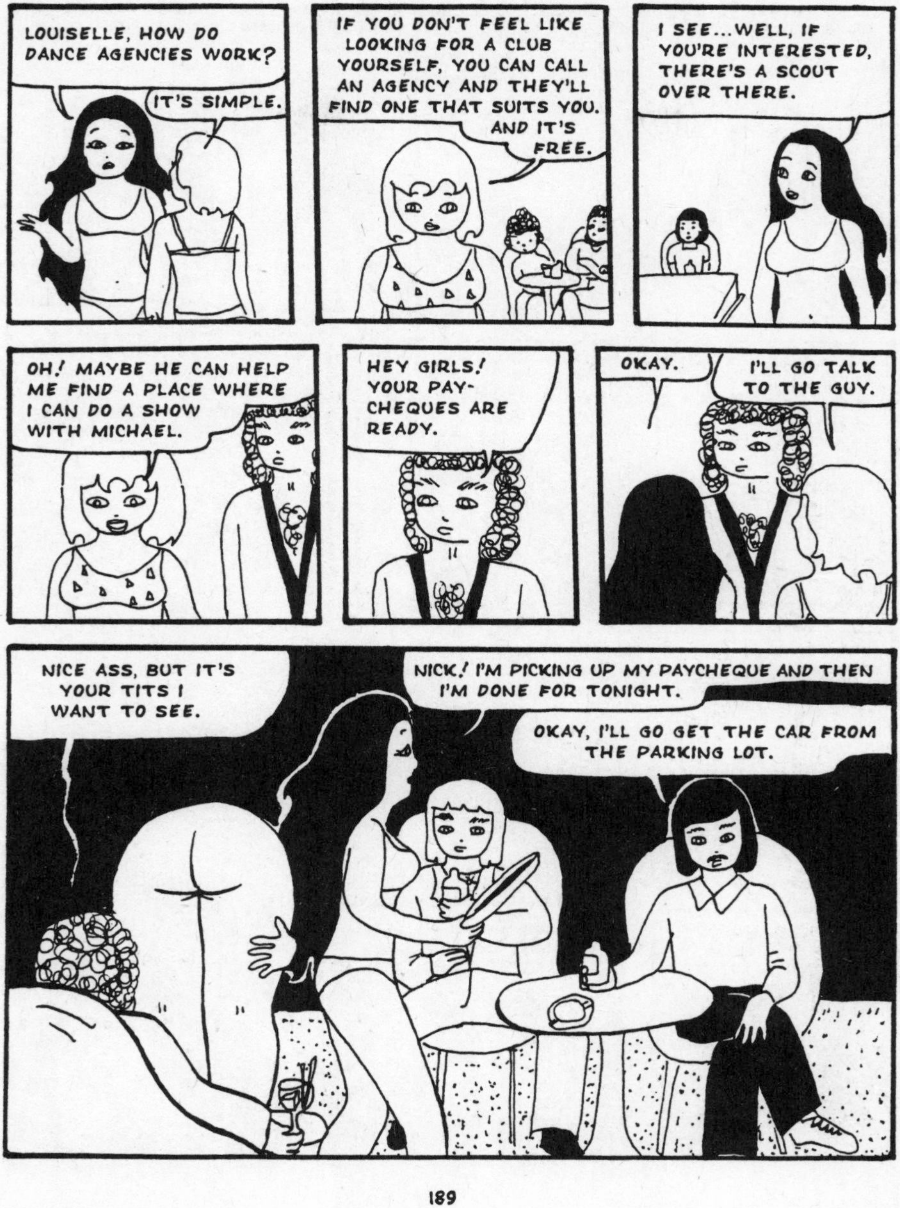
LOUISELLE, HOW DO DANCE AGENCIES WORK?
IT'S SIMPLE.
IF YOU DON'T FEEL LIKE LOOKING FOR A CLUB YOURSELF, YOU CAN CALL AN AGENCY AND THEY'LL FIND ONE THAT SUITS YOU.
AND IT'S FREE.
I SEE...WELL, IF YOU'RE INTERESTED, THERE'S A SCOUT OVER THERE.
OH! MAYBE HE CAN HELP ME FIND A PLACE WHERE I CAN DO A SHOW WITH MICHAEL.
HEY GIRLS! YOUR PAY-CHEQUES ARE READY.
OKAY.
I'LL GO TALK TO THE GUY.
NICE ASS, BUT IT'S YOUR TITS I WANT TO SEE.
NICK! I'M PICKING UP MY PAYCHEQUE AND THEN I'M DONE FOR TONIGHT.
OKAY, I'LL GO GET THE CAR FROM THE PARKING LOT.

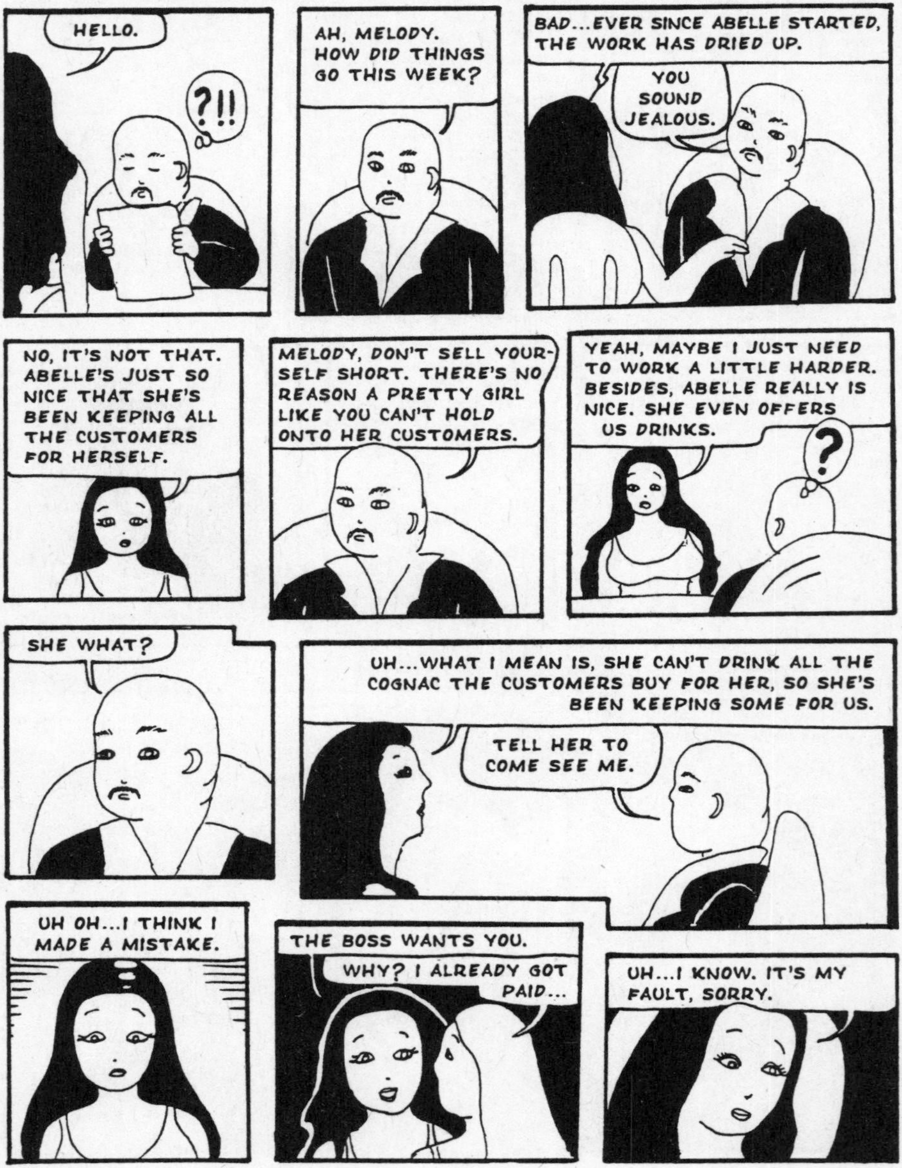
HELLO.
?!!
AH, MELODY.
HOW DID THINGS GO THIS WEEK?
BAD...EVER SINCE ABELLE STARTED, THE WORK HAS DRIED UP.
YOU SOUND JEALOUS.
NO, IT'S NOT THAT. ABELLE'S JUST SO NICE THAT SHE'S BEEN KEEPING ALL THE CUSTOMERS FOR HERSELF.
MELODY, DON'T SELL YOURSELF SHORT. THERE'S NO REASON A PRETTY GIRL LIKE YOU CAN'T HOLD ONTO HER CUSTOMERS.
YEAH, MAYBE I JUST NEED TO WORK A LITTLE HARDER. BESIDES, ABELLE REALLY IS NICE. SHE EVEN OFFERS US DRINKS.
?
SHE WHAT?
UH...WHAT I MEAN IS, SHE CAN'T DRINK ALL THE COGNAC THE CUSTOMERS BUY FOR HER, SO SHE'S BEEN KEEPING SOME FOR US.
TELL HER TO COME SEE ME.
UH OH...I THINK I MADE A MISTAKE.
THE BOSS WANTS YOU.
WHY? I ALREADY GOT PAID...
UH...I KNOW. IT'S MY FAULT, SORRY.

BUT...WHAT'VE I DONE?

SOON AFTER...

BAR

MELODY, WE'RE GOING TO MY AUNT'S TO-MORROW. SHE WANTS TO MEET YOU.

I WONDER WHAT HE'S UP TO NOW?

OH YEAH?

NEXT MORNING...

SHIT. WE OVERSLEPT.

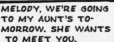

MELODY! WAKE UP...

HM...

SHHHH! TRY TO BE QUIET.

MELODY, I'VE FOUND WORK...I'LL EXPLAIN AT THE RESTAURANT. BUT YOU NEED TO GET DRESSED, WE'RE LATE.

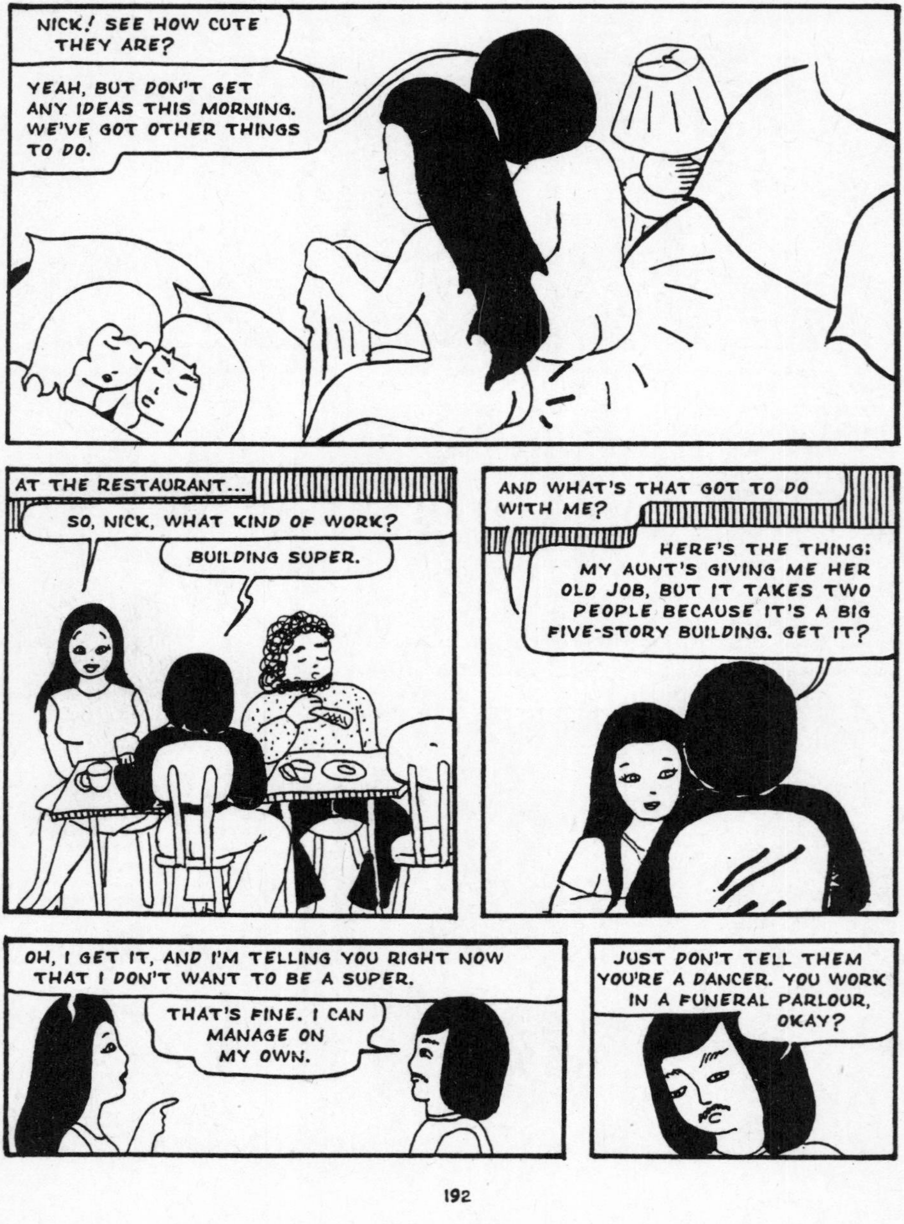
NICK! SEE HOW CUTE THEY ARE?
YEAH, BUT DON'T GET ANY IDEAS THIS MORNING. WE'VE GOT OTHER THINGS TO DO.
AT THE RESTAURANT...
SO, NICK, WHAT KIND OF WORK?
BUILDING SUPER.
AND WHAT'S THAT GOT TO DO WITH ME?
HERE'S THE THING: MY AUNT'S GIVING ME HER OLD JOB, BUT IT TAKES TWO PEOPLE BECAUSE IT'S A BIG FIVE-STORY BUILDING. GET IT?
OH, I GET IT, AND I'M TELLING YOU RIGHT NOW THAT I DON'T WANT TO BE A SUPER.
THAT'S FINE. I CAN MANAGE ON MY OWN.
JUST DON'T TELL THEM YOU'RE A DANCER. YOU WORK IN A FUNERAL PARLOUR, OKAY?

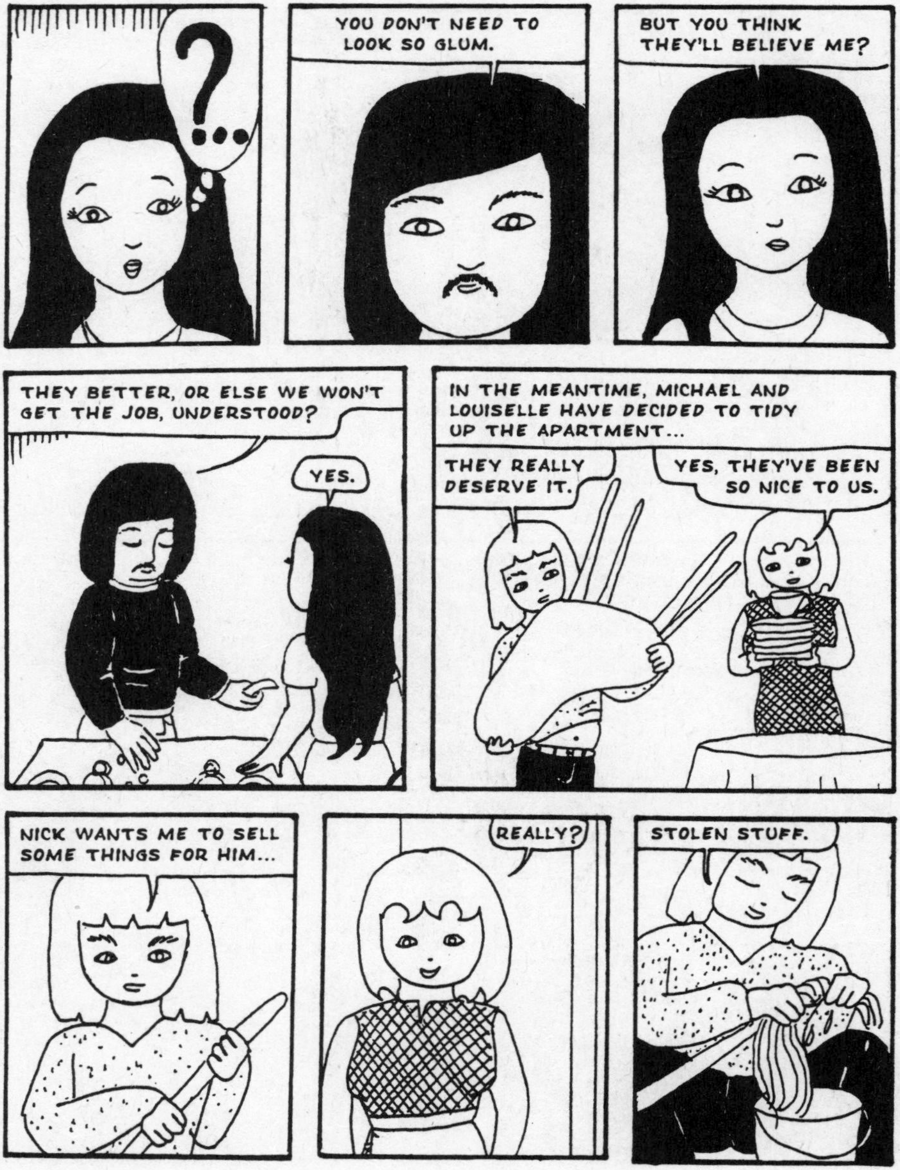
?...
YOU DON'T NEED TO LOOK SO GLUM.
BUT YOU THINK THEY'LL BELIEVE ME?
THEY BETTER, OR ELSE WE WON'T GET THE JOB, UNDERSTOOD?
YES.
IN THE MEANTIME, MICHAEL AND LOUISELLE HAVE DECIDED TO TIDY UP THE APARTMENT...
THEY REALLY DESERVE IT.
YES, THEY'VE BEEN SO NICE TO US.
NICK WANTS ME TO SELL SOME THINGS FOR HIM...
REALLY?
STOLEN STUFF.

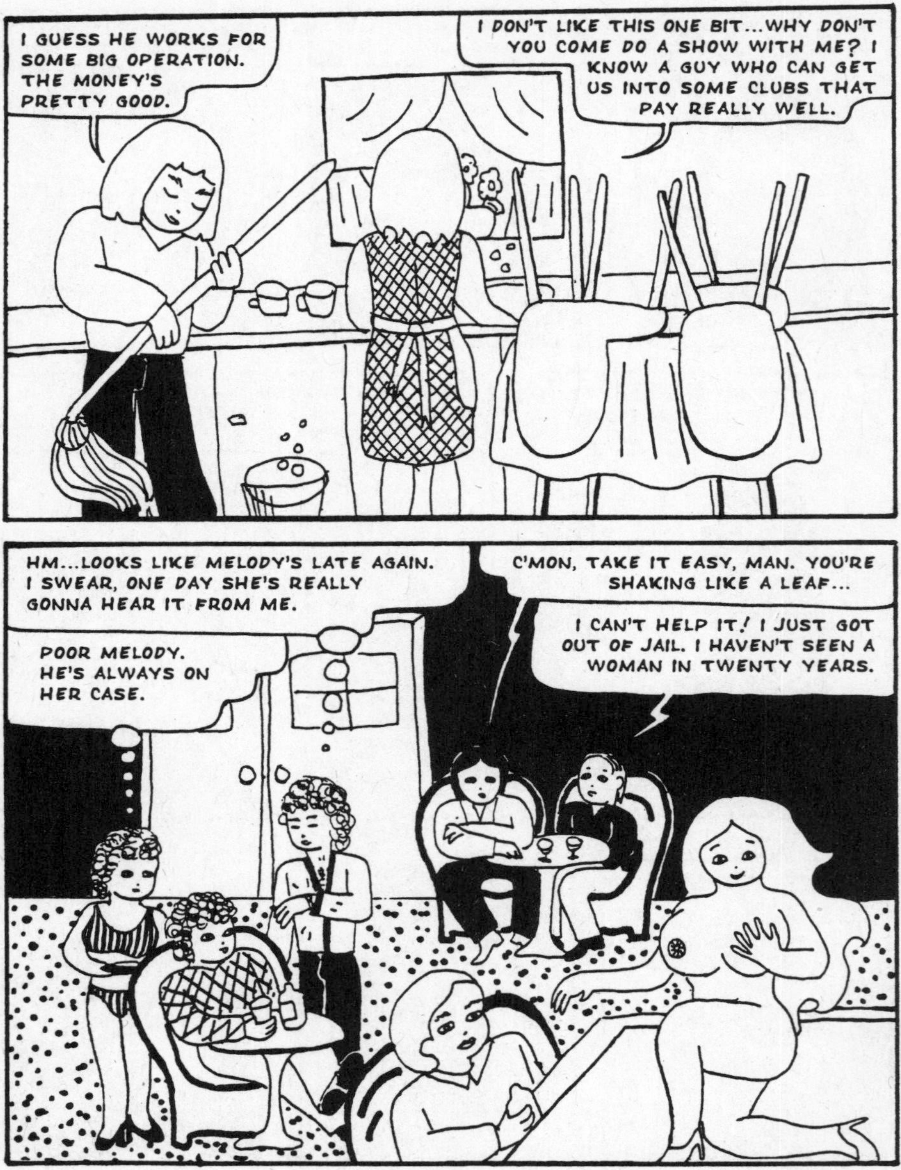
I GUESS HE WORKS FOR SOME BIG OPERATION. THE MONEY'S PRETTY GOOD.
I DON'T LIKE THIS ONE BIT...WHY DON'T YOU COME DO A SHOW WITH ME? I KNOW A GUY WHO CAN GET US INTO SOME CLUBS THAT PAY REALLY WELL.
HM...LOOKS LIKE MELODY'S LATE AGAIN. I SWEAR, ONE DAY SHE'S REALLY GONNA HEAR IT FROM ME.
POOR MELODY. HE'S ALWAYS ON HER CASE.
C'MON, TAKE IT EASY, MAN. YOU'RE SHAKING LIKE A LEAF...
I CAN'T HELP IT! I JUST GOT OUT OF JAIL. I HAVEN'T SEEN A WOMAN IN TWENTY YEARS.

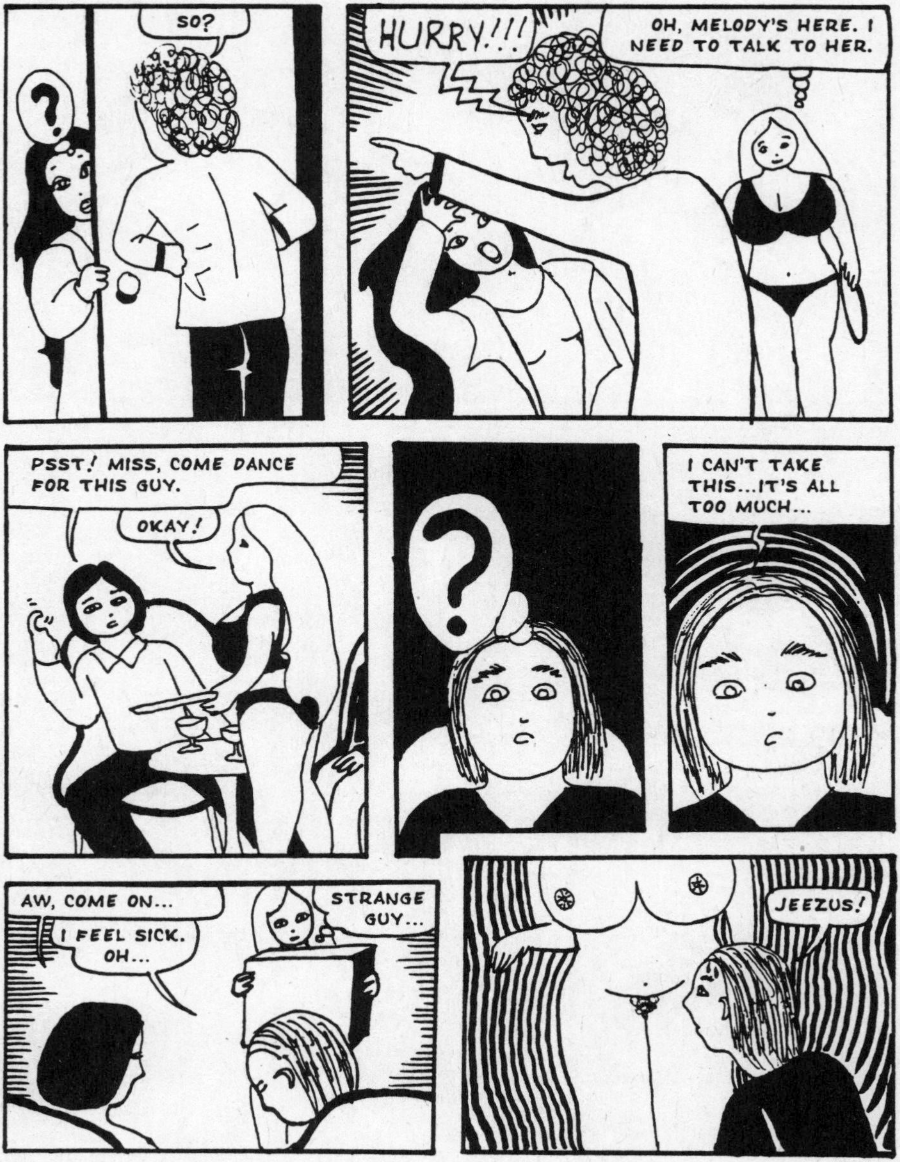
SO?
HURRY!!!
OH, MELODY'S HERE. I NEED TO TALK TO HER.
PSST! MISS, COME DANCE FOR THIS GUY.
OKAY!
I CAN'T TAKE THIS...IT'S ALL TOO MUCH...
AW, COME ON...
I FEEL SICK. OH...
STRANGE GUY...
JEEZUS!

Oooh!

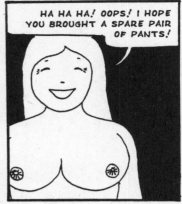

HA HA HA! OOPS! I HOPE YOU BROUGHT A SPARE PAIR OF PANTS!

I'M REALLY SORRY.

WE'RE GOING TO WORK FOR THE AGENCY.

OH, THAT'S GREAT! AND NICK GOT A JOB AS A SUPER THANKS TO HIS AUNT.

WE'RE LEAVING TO-NIGHT. I'VE BROUGHT ALL OUR STUFF ALONG.

MELODY, I WANTED TO TELL YOU THAT THE BOSS WASN'T ANGRY.

OH! I'M GLAD!

HE DOESN'T WANT ME TO BOTTLE THE DRINKS ANYMORE, THAT'S ALL.

HE'S WORRIED THE GIRLS MIGHT TRY TO SELL SOME ON THE SIDE.

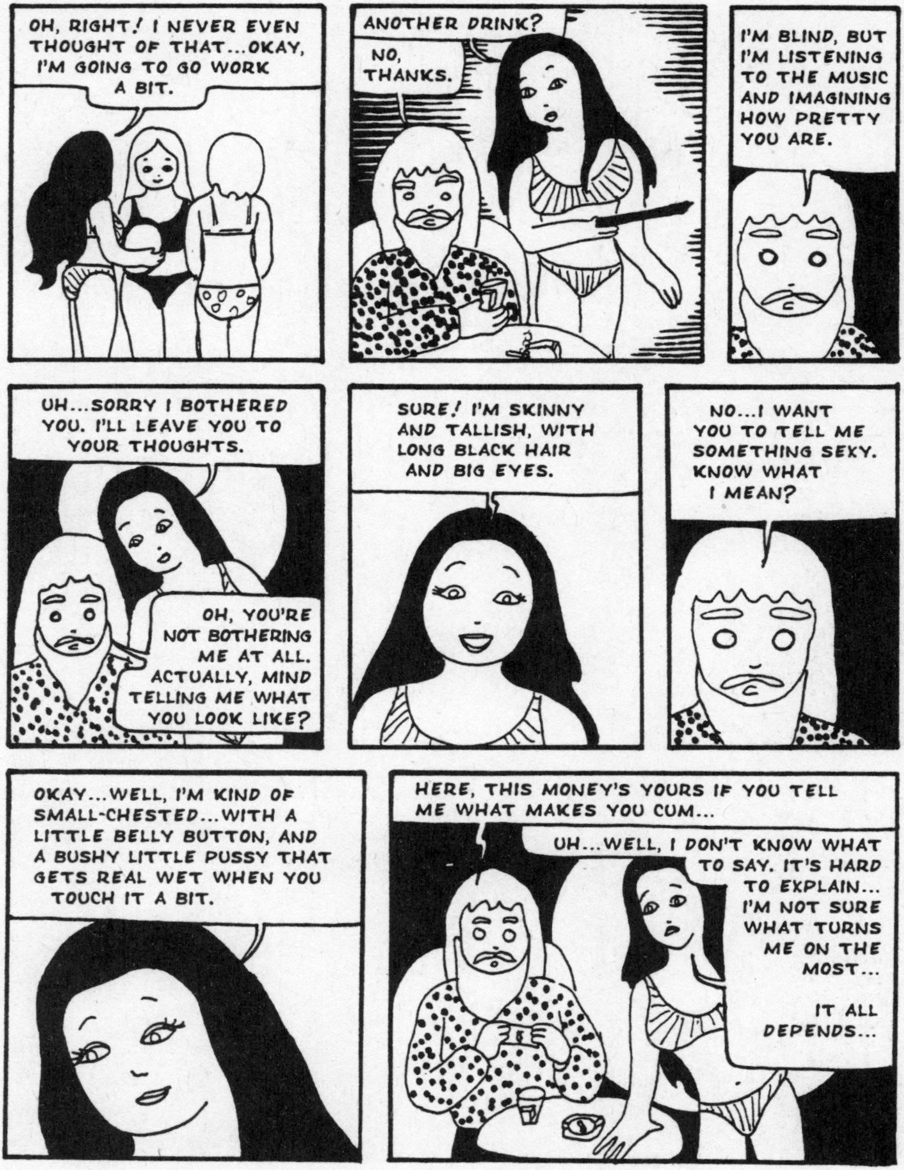
OH, RIGHT! I NEVER EVEN THOUGHT OF THAT...OKAY, I'M GOING TO GO WORK A BIT.
ANOTHER DRINK?
NO, THANKS.
I'M BLIND, BUT I'M LISTENING TO THE MUSIC AND IMAGINING HOW PRETTY YOU ARE.
UH...SORRY I BOTHERED YOU. I'LL LEAVE YOU TO YOUR THOUGHTS.
OH, YOU'RE NOT BOTHERING ME AT ALL. ACTUALLY, MIND TELLING ME WHAT YOU LOOK LIKE?
SURE! I'M SKINNY AND TALLISH, WITH LONG BLACK HAIR AND BIG EYES.
NO...I WANT YOU TO TELL ME SOMETHING SEXY. KNOW WHAT I MEAN?
OKAY...WELL, I'M KIND OF SMALL-CHESTED...WITH A LITTLE BELLY BUTTON, AND A BUSHY LITTLE PUSSY THAT GETS REAL WET WHEN YOU TOUCH IT A BIT.
HERE, THIS MONEY'S YOURS IF YOU TELL ME WHAT MAKES YOU CUM...
UH...WELL, I DON'T KNOW WHAT TO SAY. IT'S HARD TO EXPLAIN... I'M NOT SURE WHAT TURNS ME ON THE MOST...
IT ALL DEPENDS...

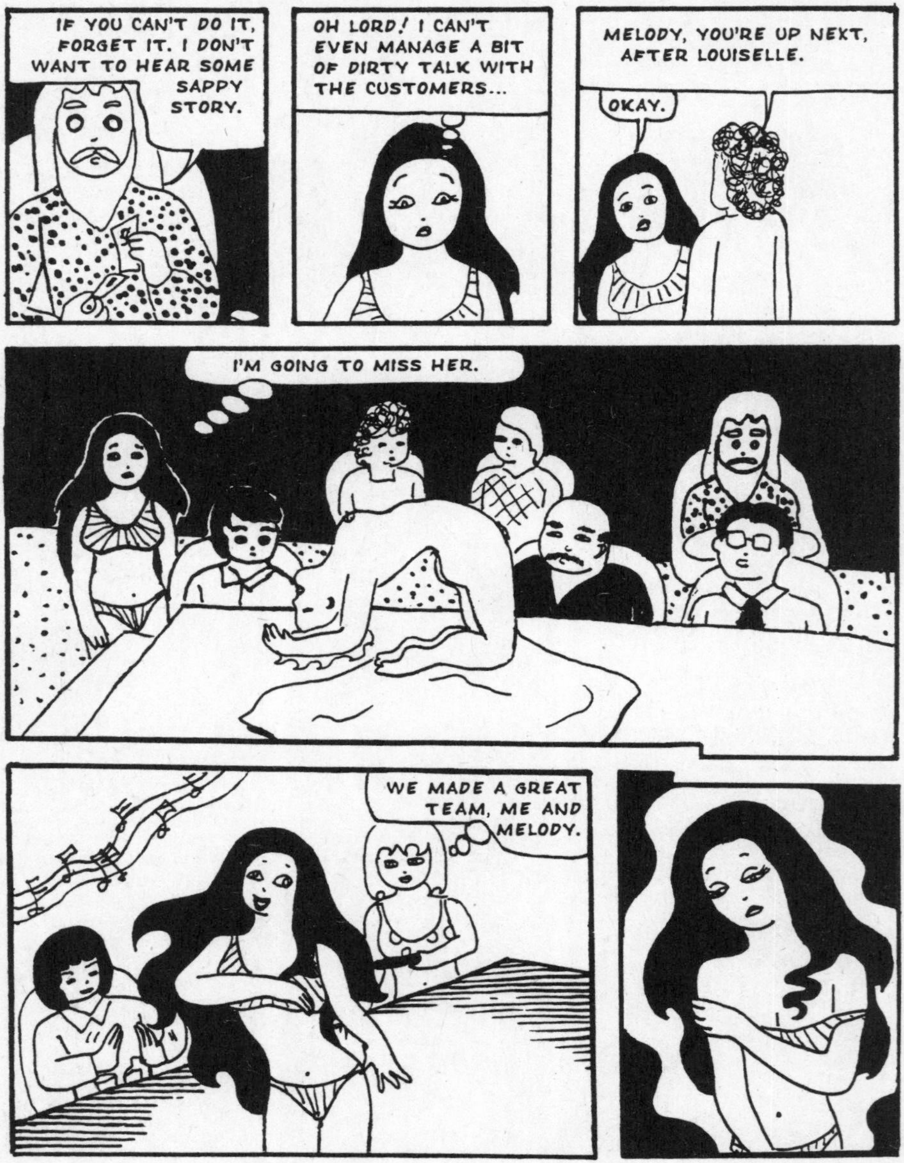

IF YOU CAN'T DO IT, FORGET IT. I DON'T WANT TO HEAR SOME SAPPY STORY.
OH LORD! I CAN'T EVEN MANAGE A BIT OF DIRTY TALK WITH THE CUSTOMERS...
MELODY, YOU'RE UP NEXT, AFTER LOUISELLE.
OKAY.
I'M GOING TO MISS HER.
WE MADE A GREAT TEAM, ME AND MELODY.

IN THE MEANTIME...

WHAT *DO* YOU MEAN, NICK'S GOING TO BE THE NEW SUPER?

WE NEED SOMEONE TO REPLACE US.

HIS WIFE WORKS IN A FUNERAL PARLOUR, SO SHE'S DONE SOME ADMINISTRATION.

IS THAT SO? SHE DID SEEM STRANGE.

MAYBE MY AUNT WILL FINALLY RELAX AND STOP WALKING AROUND IN PYJAMAS ALL DAY.

AND I'LL BE AROUND TO HELP THEM GET STARTED, IN CASE THEY NEED ADVICE.

LISTEN, I LIVED NEXT DOOR TO NICK FOR THIRTEEN YEARS AND THERE'S NO WAY I'D REFER HIM: HE'S A NO-GOOD BUM.

OKAY, GRANDPA, BUT MAYBE HE'S CHANGED.

YVANI, I'VE BEEN AROUND. I KNOW WHAT I'M TALKING ABOUT.

WE'LL SEE WHO'S RIGHT IN THE END I GUESS.

YOU NEED TO LEARN TO GIVE PEOPLE A SECOND CHANCE, ALEX.

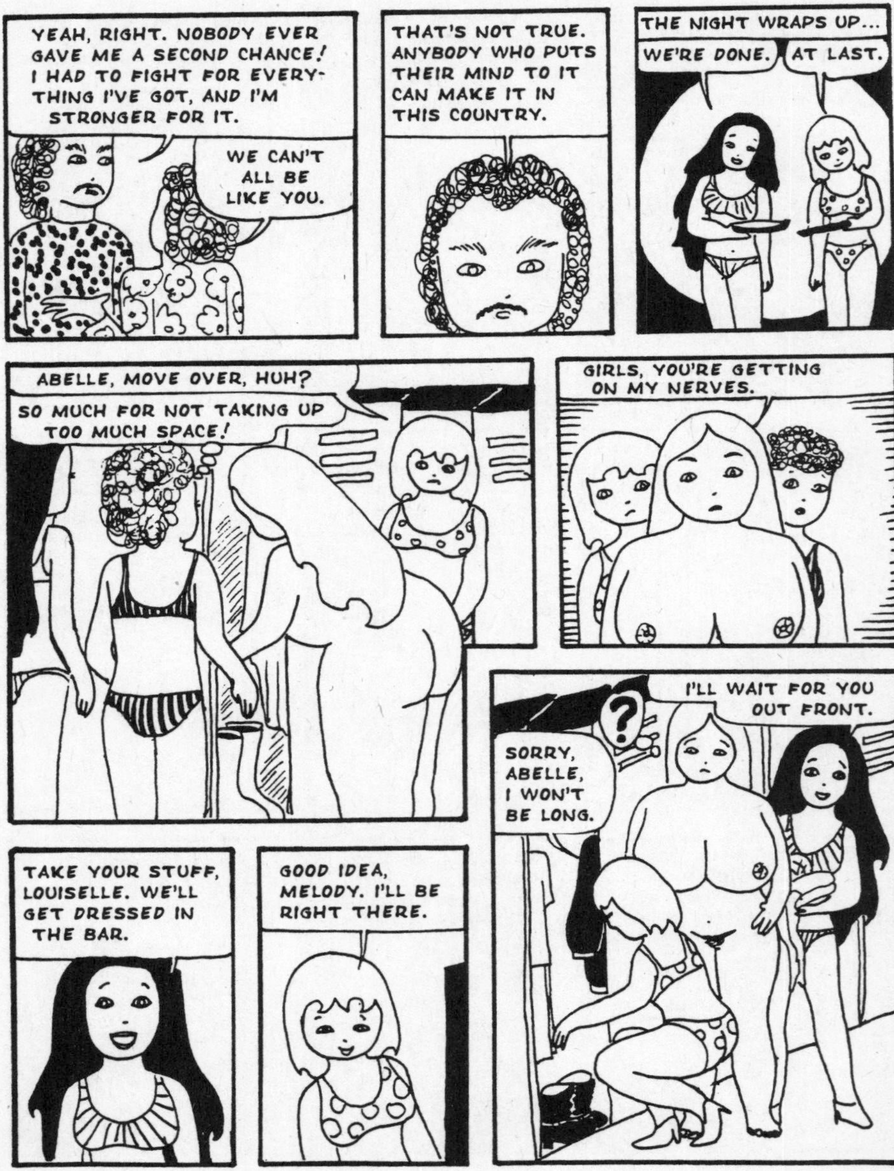
YEAH, RIGHT. NOBODY EVER GAVE ME A SECOND CHANCE! I HAD TO FIGHT FOR EVERY-THING I'VE GOT, AND I'M STRONGER FOR IT.
WE CAN'T ALL BE LIKE YOU.
THAT'S NOT TRUE. ANYBODY WHO PUTS THEIR MIND TO IT CAN MAKE IT IN THIS COUNTRY.
THE NIGHT WRAPS UP...
WE'RE DONE.
AT LAST.
ABELLE, MOVE OVER, HUH?
SO MUCH FOR NOT TAKING UP TOO MUCH SPACE!
GIRLS, YOU'RE GETTING ON MY NERVES.
TAKE YOUR STUFF, LOUISELLE. WE'LL GET DRESSED IN THE BAR.
GOOD IDEA, MELODY. I'LL BE RIGHT THERE.
I'LL WAIT FOR YOU OUT FRONT.
?
SORRY, ABELLE, I WON'T BE LONG.

WHAT'RE YOU GIRLS DOING HERE?
THE DRES-SING ROOM'S TOO CROWDED.
HURRY UP!
YEAH, YEAH... WE'RE DONE!

Melody the Superintendent

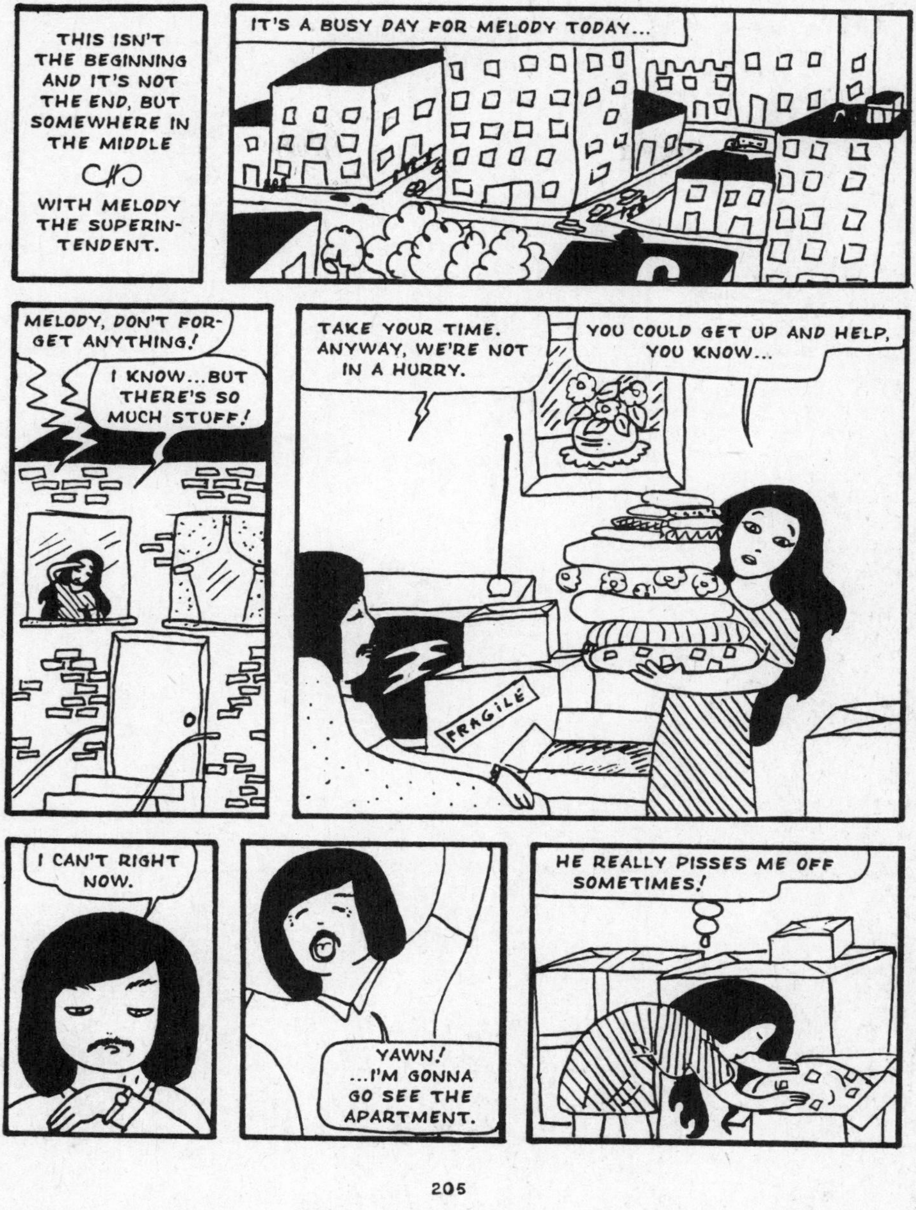
THIS ISN'T THE BEGINNING AND IT'S NOT THE END, BUT SOMEWHERE IN THE MIDDLE
WITH MELODY THE SUPERIN-TENDENT.
IT'S A BUSY DAY FOR MELODY TODAY...
MELODY, DON'T FOR-GET ANYTHING!
I KNOW...BUT THERE'S SO MUCH STUFF!
TAKE YOUR TIME. ANYWAY, WE'RE NOT IN A HURRY.
YOU COULD GET UP AND HELP, YOU KNOW...
FRAGILE
I CAN'T RIGHT NOW.
YAWN! ...I'M GONNA GO SEE THE APARTMENT.
HE REALLY PISSES ME OFF SOMETIMES!

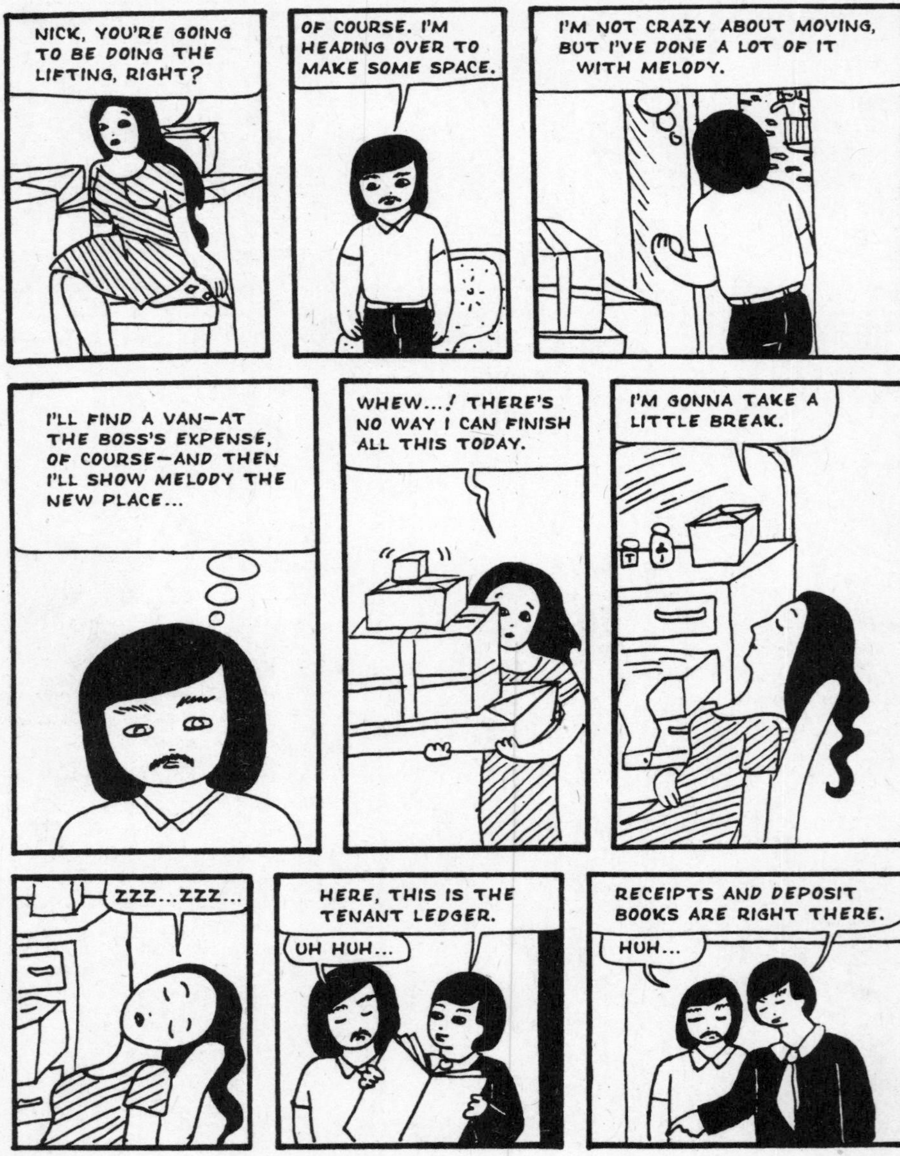
NICK, YOU'RE GOING TO BE DOING THE LIFTING, RIGHT?
OF COURSE. I'M HEADING OVER TO MAKE SOME SPACE.
I'M NOT CRAZY ABOUT MOVING, BUT I'VE DONE A LOT OF IT WITH MELODY.
I'LL FIND A VAN—AT THE BOSS'S EXPENSE, OF COURSE—AND THEN I'LL SHOW MELODY THE NEW PLACE...
WHEW...! THERE'S NO WAY I CAN FINISH ALL THIS TODAY.
I'M GONNA TAKE A LITTLE BREAK.
ZZZ...ZZZ...
HERE, THIS IS THE TENANT LEDGER.
UH HUH...
RECEIPTS AND DEPOSIT BOOKS ARE RIGHT THERE.
HUH...

AND THIS IS THE LIST OF THINGS YOU NEED TO DO.

HUH...

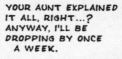

YOUR AUNT EXPLAINED IT ALL, RIGHT...? ANYWAY, I'LL BE DROPPING BY ONCE A WEEK.

OKAY. WELL, IT'S IN YOUR HANDS NOW.

DRING... DRING...

HERE COMES THE INVASION...TIME TO GO!

SO LONG!

SEE YA!

DRING...

ALL RIGHT, WHAT'S GOING ON?

OH, ARE YOU NEW?

HELLO!

DID YOU JUST GET IN?

MY MOM WANTS TO SEE YOU.

HEY, DON'T ALL TALK AT THE SAME TIME!

MY STOVE IS BROKEN.

MY DOOR SQUEAKS.

I'M MISSING A CURTAIN.

THERE'S FUNNY LITTLE BUGS IN THE CUPBOARDS.

?

I SEE...DON'T WORRY, I'LL TAKE CARE OF EVERYTHING ASSOON AS I CAN.

I BETTER GET OUT OF HERE, AND FAST.

OH, AND THE FAUCET IS LEAKING.

OUR TABLE LEG IS BROKEN.

MY NEIGHBOUR HAS CATS...

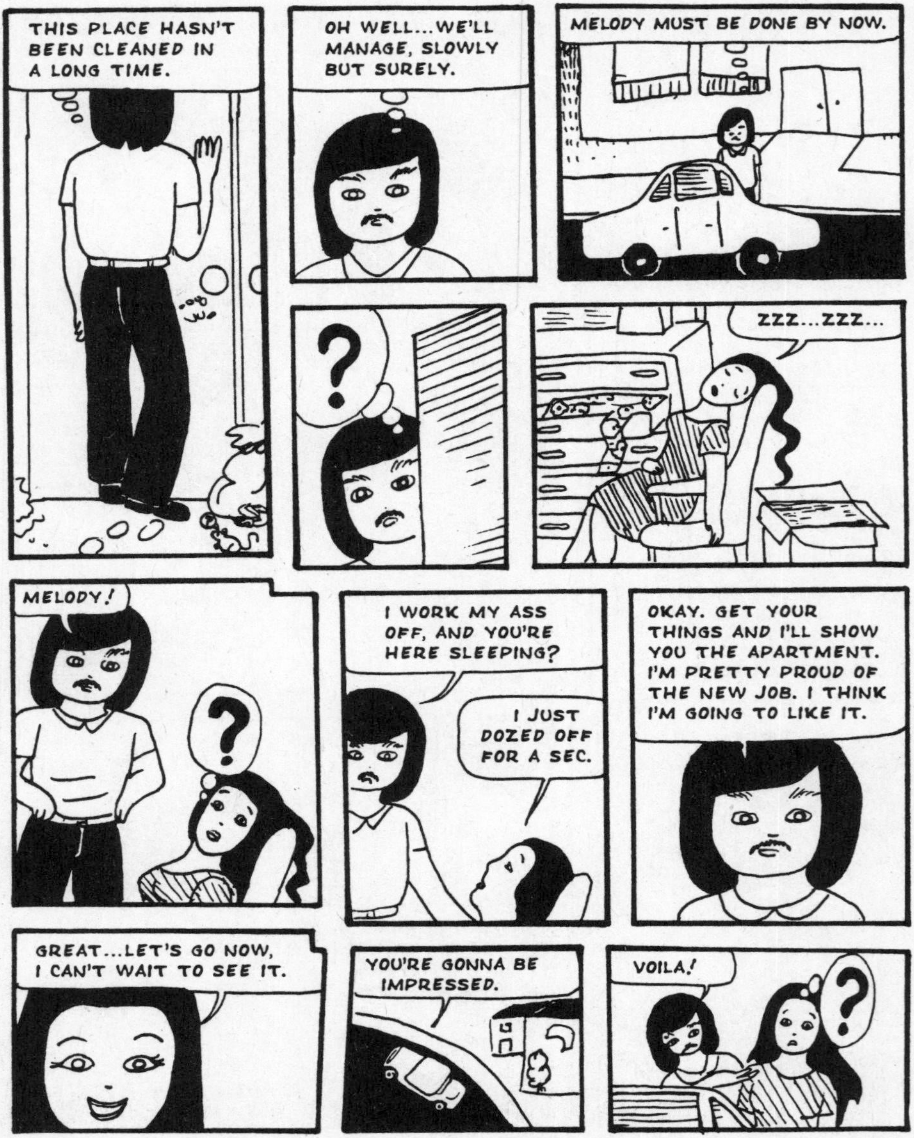
THIS PLACE HASN'T BEEN CLEANED IN A LONG TIME.
OH WELL...WE'LL MANAGE, SLOWLY BUT SURELY.
MELODY MUST BE DONE BY NOW.
?
ZZZ...ZZZ...
MELODY!
?
I WORK MY ASS OFF, AND YOU'RE HERE SLEEPING?
I JUST DOZED OFF FOR A SEC.
OKAY. GET YOUR THINGS AND I'LL SHOW YOU THE APARTMENT. I'M PRETTY PROUD OF THE NEW JOB. I THINK I'M GOING TO LIKE IT.
GREAT...LET'S GO NOW, I CAN'T WAIT TO SEE IT.
YOU'RE GONNA BE IMPRESSED.
VOILA!
?

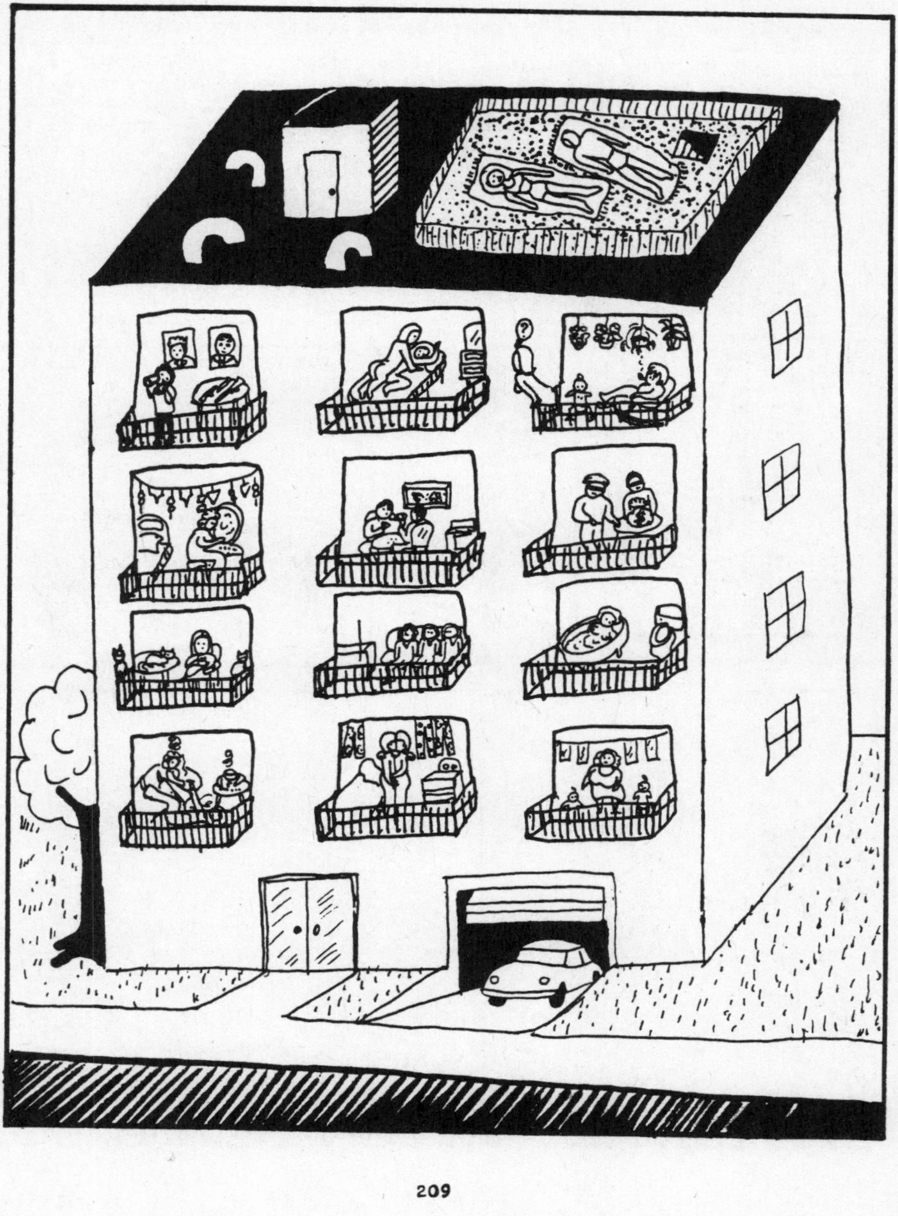
?

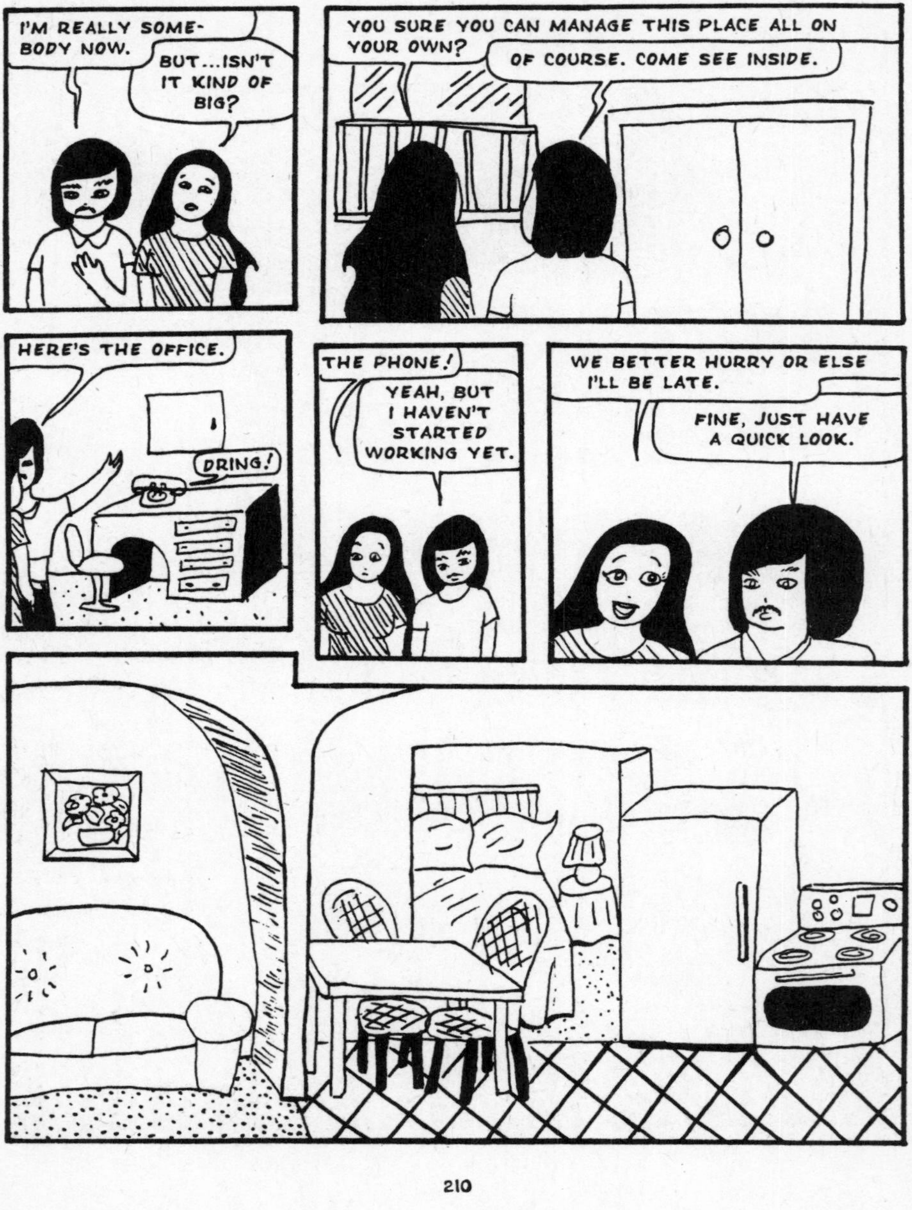

I'M REALLY SOMEBODY NOW.
BUT...ISN'T IT KIND OF BIG?
YOU SURE YOU CAN MANAGE THIS PLACE ALL ON YOUR OWN?
OF COURSE. COME SEE INSIDE.
HERE'S THE OFFICE.
DRING!
THE PHONE!
YEAH, BUT I HAVEN'T STARTED WORKING YET.
WE BETTER HURRY OR ELSE I'LL BE LATE.
FINE, JUST HAVE A QUICK LOOK.

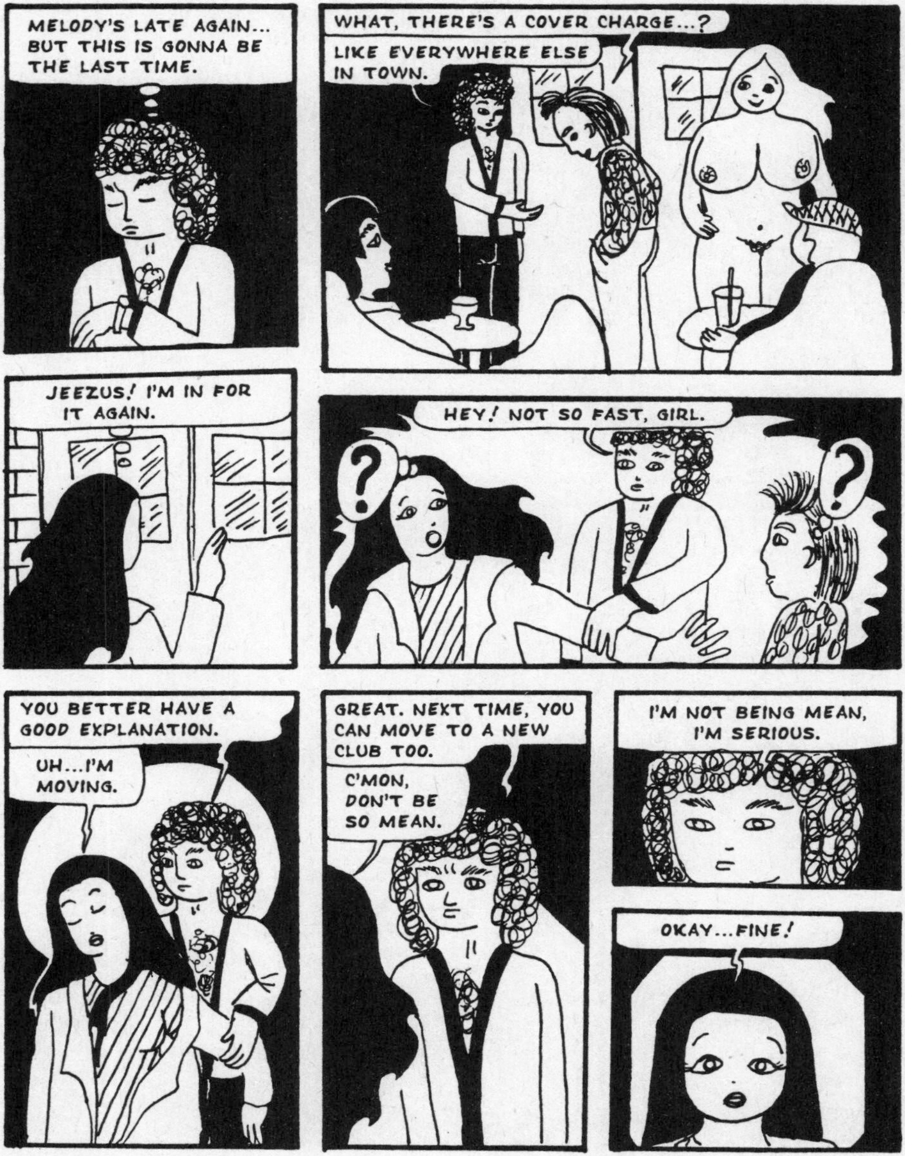
MELODY'S LATE AGAIN... BUT THIS IS GONNA BE THE LAST TIME.
WHAT, THERE'S A COVER CHARGE...?
LIKE EVERYWHERE ELSE IN TOWN.
JEEZUS! I'M IN FOR IT AGAIN.
HEY! NOT SO FAST, GIRL.
?
YOU BETTER HAVE A GOOD EXPLANATION.
UH...I'M MOVING.
GREAT. NEXT TIME, YOU CAN MOVE TO A NEW CLUB TOO.
C'MON, DON'T BE SO MEAN.
I'M NOT BEING MEAN, I'M SERIOUS.
OKAY...FINE!

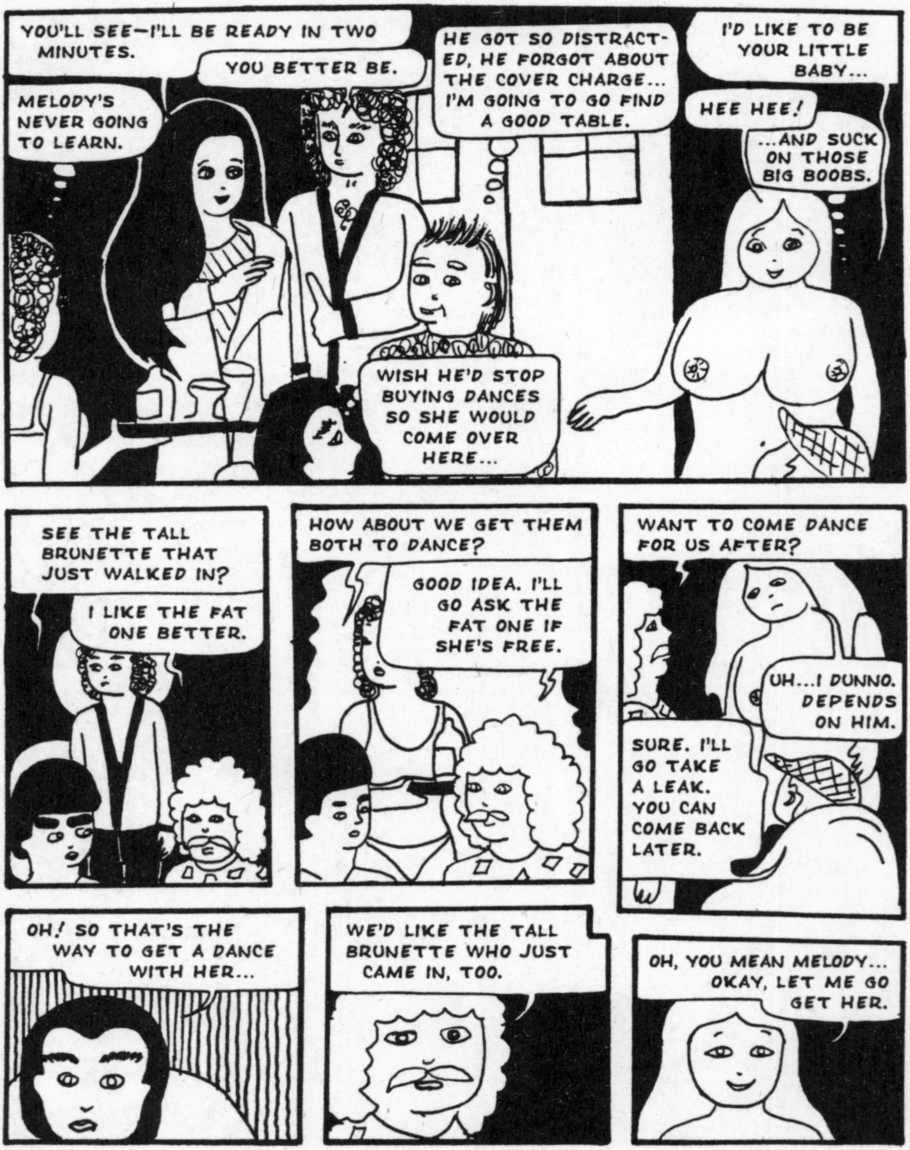
YOU'LL SEE—I'LL BE READY IN TWO MINUTES.
YOU BETTER BE.
MELODY'S NEVER GOING TO LEARN.
HE GOT SO DISTRACTED, HE FORGOT ABOUT THE COVER CHARGE... I'M GOING TO GO FIND A GOOD TABLE.
WISH HE'D STOP BUYING DANCES SO SHE WOULD COME OVER HERE...
I'D LIKE TO BE YOUR LITTLE BABY...
HEE HEE!
...AND SUCK ON THOSE BIG BOOBS.
SEE THE TALL BRUNETTE THAT JUST WALKED IN?
I LIKE THE FAT ONE BETTER.
HOW ABOUT WE GET THEM BOTH TO DANCE?
GOOD IDEA. I'LL GO ASK THE FAT ONE IF SHE'S FREE.
WANT TO COME DANCE FOR US AFTER?
UH...I DUNNO. DEPENDS ON HIM.
SURE. I'LL GO TAKE A LEAK. YOU CAN COME BACK LATER.
OH! SO THAT'S THE WAY TO GET A DANCE WITH HER...
WE'D LIKE THE TALL BRUNETTE WHO JUST CAME IN, TOO.
OH, YOU MEAN MELODY... OKAY, LET ME GO GET HER.

HEY, LOOK! A STRIP CLUB, GUYS!
ALL RIGHT! LET'S GO SEE SOME BITCHES.
YEAH, AND WE'LL MAKE SURE THEY DON'T SCREW US, TOO...HA HA HA!
GOT ANY CHANGE? CHECK YOUR POCKETS.
ONLY THING IN THERE IS HOLES.
HA HA HA!
I'LL HAVE TO KEEP AN EYE ON THEM. THEY LOOK LIKE TROUBLE.
GET A LOAD OF THIS, GUYS!
HA HA HA! SNIFF! SNIFF!
HA HA! FART! FART!
?
?

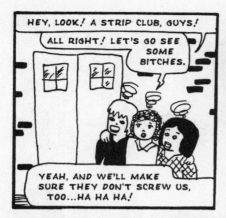

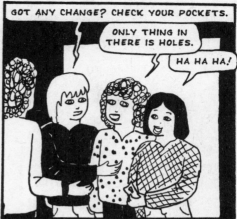

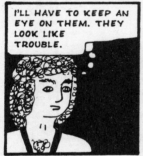

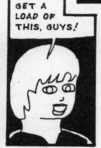

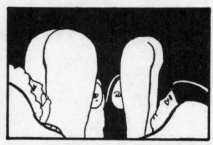

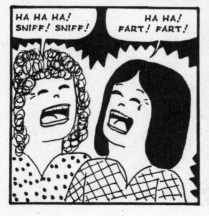

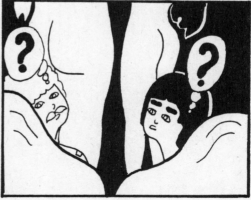

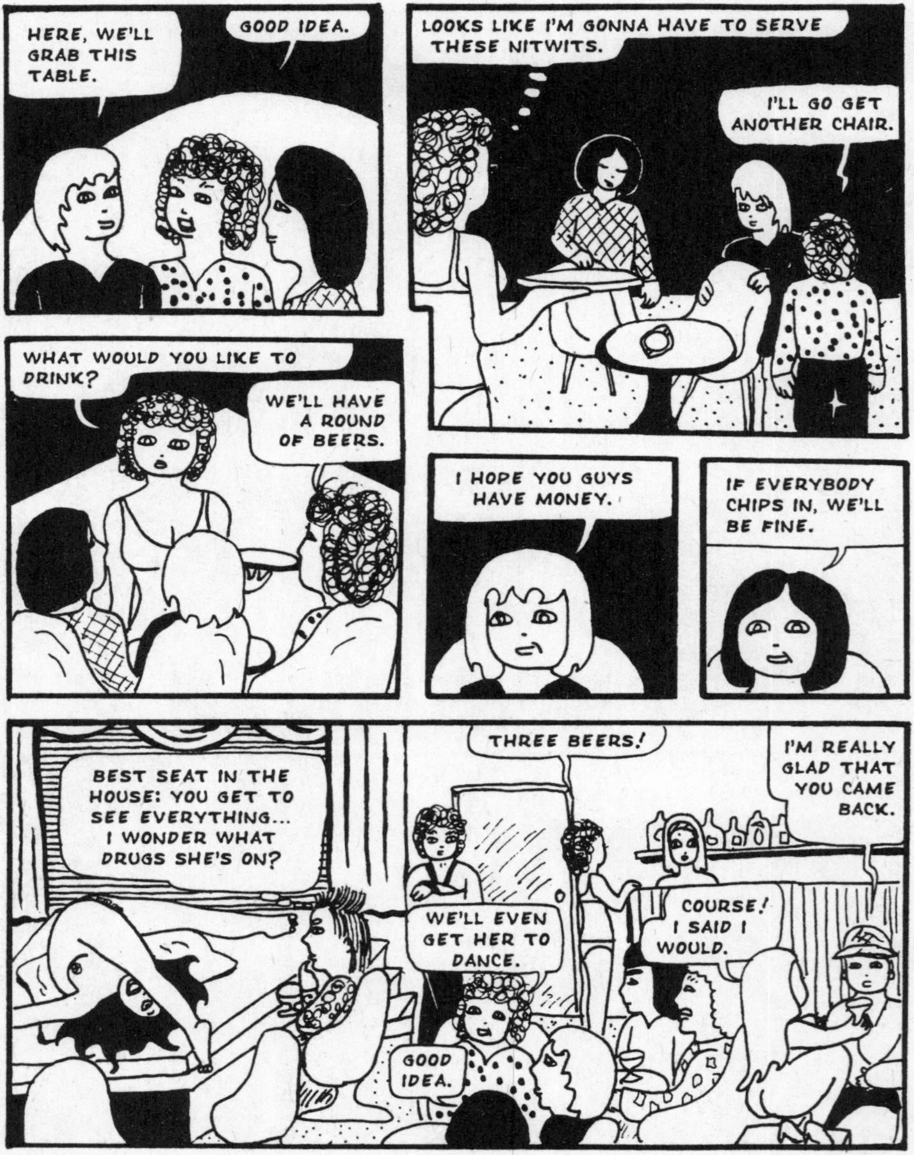
HERE, WE'LL GRAB THIS TABLE.
GOOD IDEA.
LOOKS LIKE I'M GONNA HAVE TO SERVE THESE NITWITS.
I'LL GO GET ANOTHER CHAIR.
WHAT WOULD YOU LIKE TO DRINK?
WE'LL HAVE A ROUND OF BEERS.
I HOPE YOU GUYS HAVE MONEY.
IF EVERYBODY CHIPS IN, WE'LL BE FINE.
BEST SEAT IN THE HOUSE: YOU GET TO SEE EVERYTHING... I WONDER WHAT DRUGS SHE'S ON?
THREE BEERS!
I'M REALLY GLAD THAT YOU CAME BACK.
WE'LL EVEN GET HER TO DANCE.
COURSE! I SAID I WOULD.
GOOD IDEA.

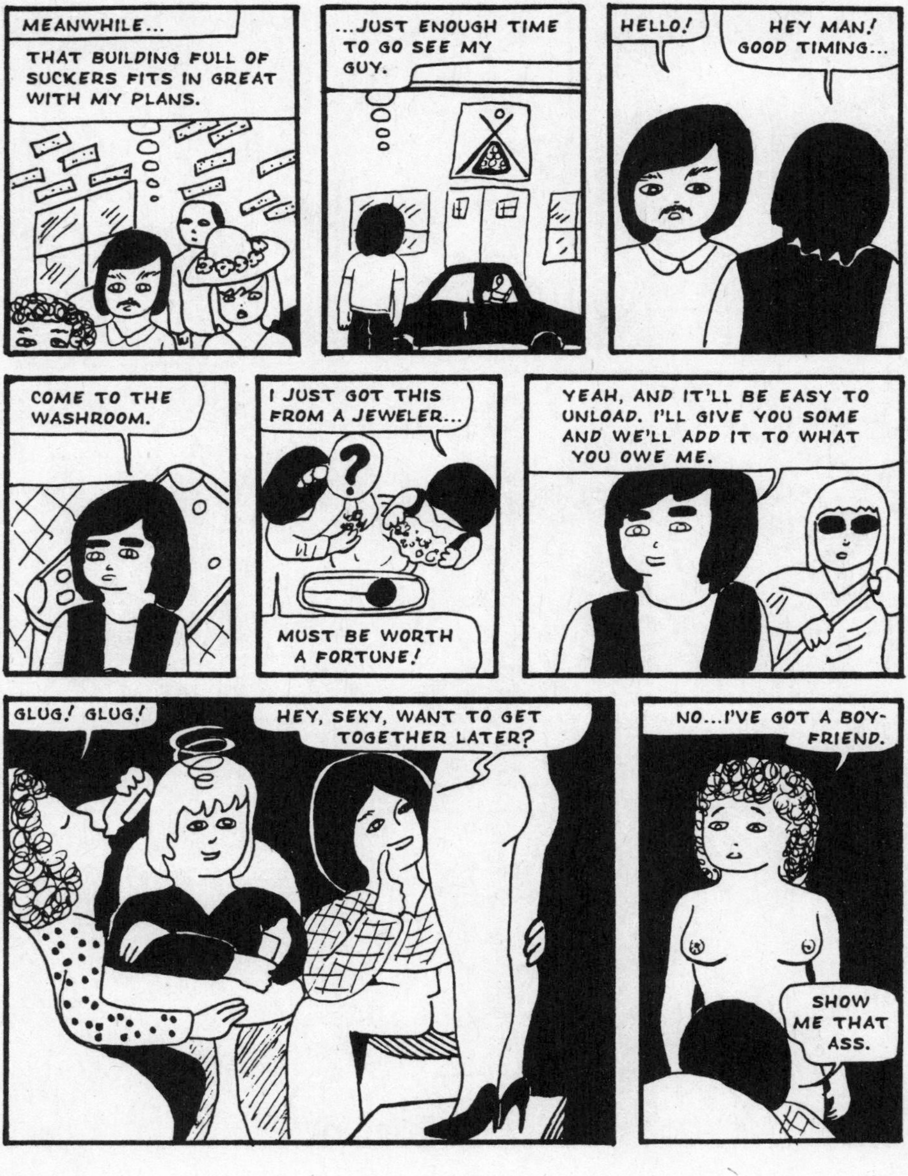
MEANWHILE...
THAT BUILDING FULL OF SUCKERS FITS IN GREAT WITH MY PLANS.
...JUST ENOUGH TIME TO GO SEE MY GUY.
HELLO!
HEY MAN! GOOD TIMING...
COME TO THE WASHROOM.
I JUST GOT THIS FROM A JEWELER...
?
MUST BE WORTH A FORTUNE!
YEAH, AND IT'LL BE EASY TO UNLOAD. I'LL GIVE YOU SOME AND WE'LL ADD IT TO WHAT YOU OWE ME.
GLUG! GLUG!
HEY, SEXY, WANT TO GET TOGETHER LATER?
NO...I'VE GOT A BOY-FRIEND.
SHOW ME THAT ASS.

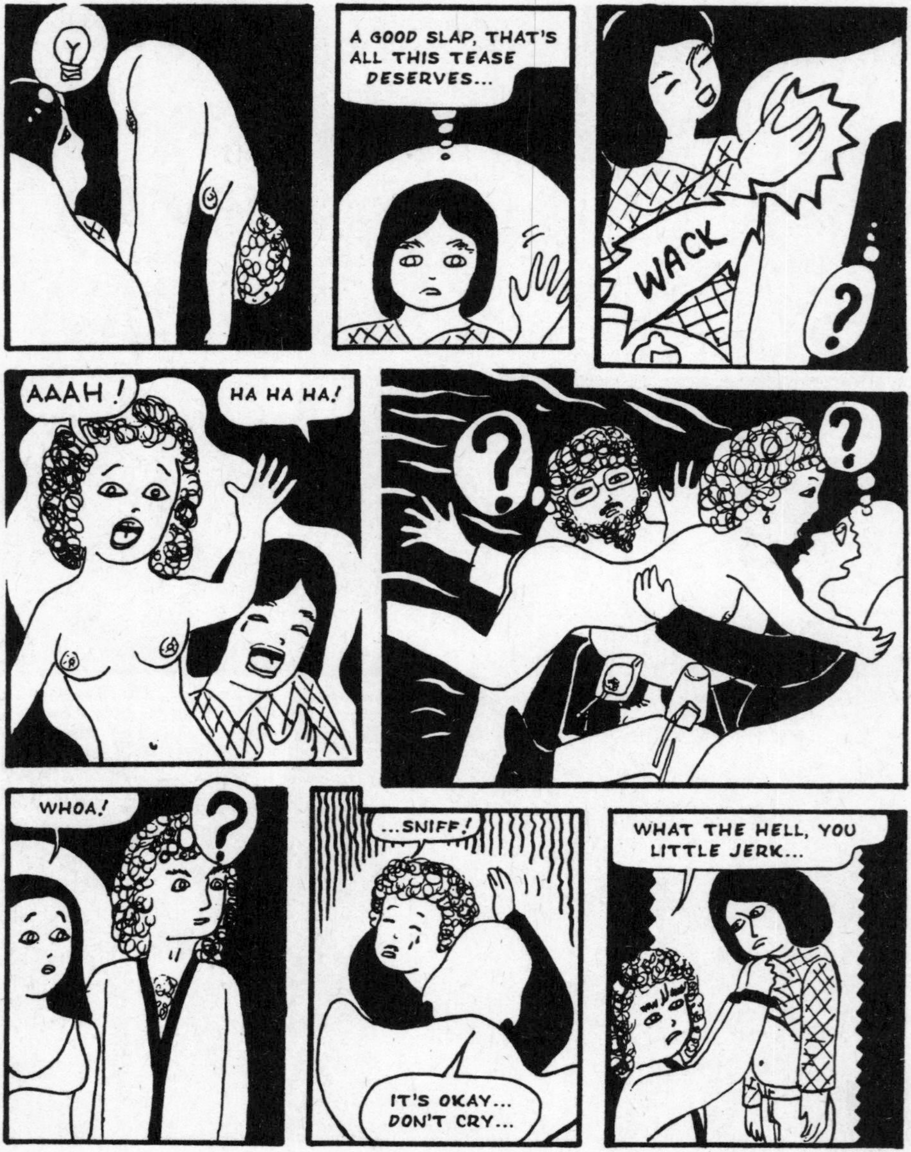
A GOOD SLAP, THAT'S ALL THIS TEASE DESERVES...
WACK
AAAH!
HA HA HA!
WHOA!
...SNIFF!
IT'S OKAY... DON'T CRY...
WHAT THE HELL, YOU LITTLE JERK...

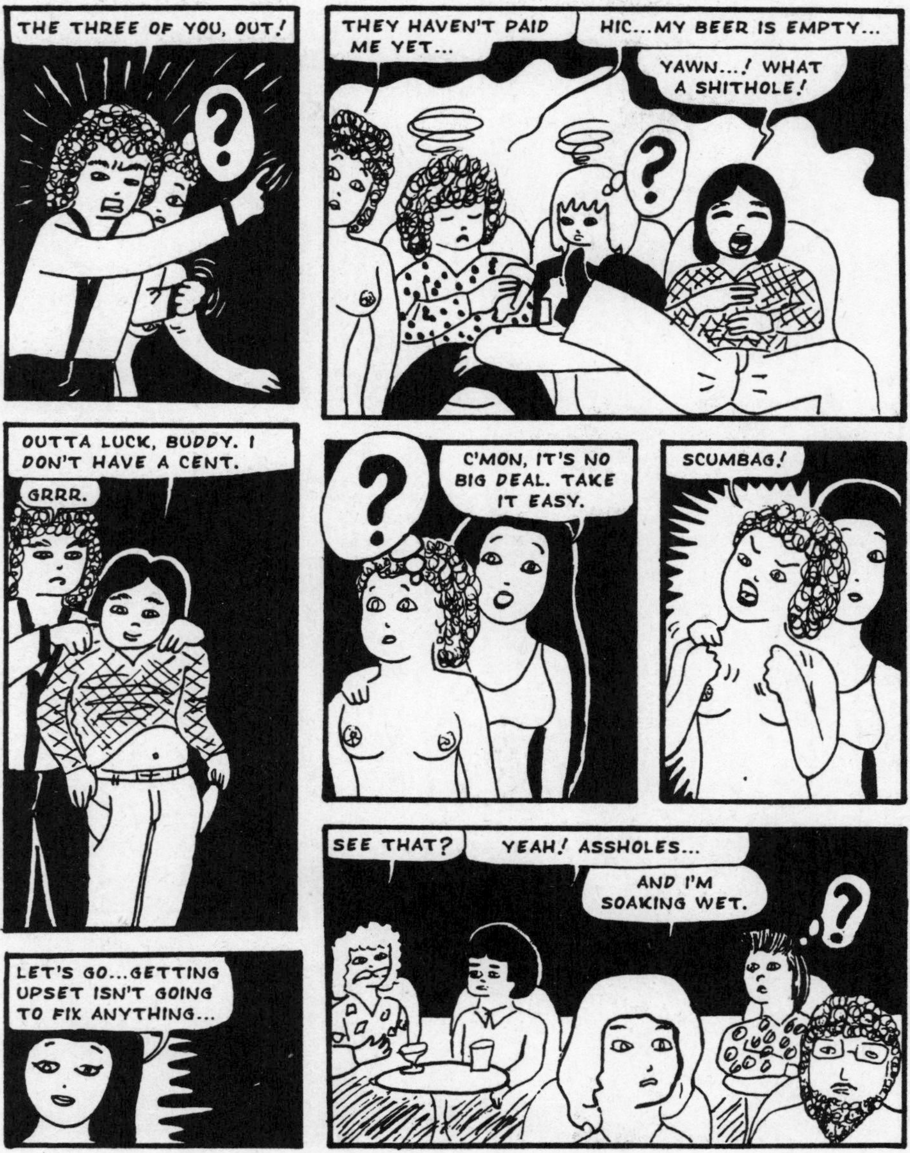
THE THREE OF YOU, OUT!
?
THEY HAVEN'T PAID ME YET...
HIC... MY BEER IS EMPTY...
YAWN...! WHAT A SHITHOLE!
?
OUTTA LUCK, BUDDY. I DON'T HAVE A CENT.
GRRR.
?
C'MON, IT'S NO BIG DEAL. TAKE IT EASY.
SCUMBAG!
LET'S GO... GETTING UPSET ISN'T GOING TO FIX ANYTHING...
SEE THAT?
YEAH! ASSHOLES...
AND I'M SOAKING WET.
?

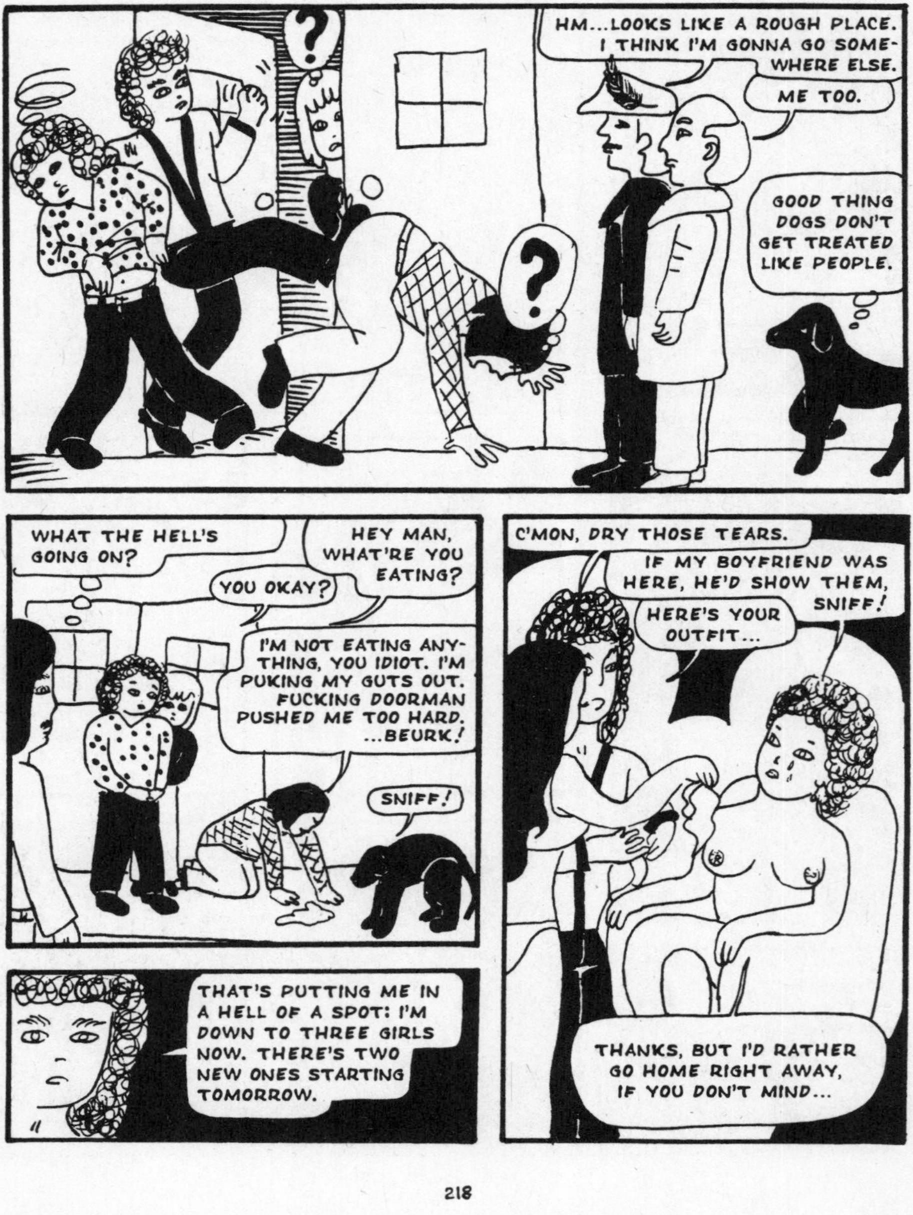
?
?
HM...LOOKS LIKE A ROUGH PLACE. I THINK I'M GONNA GO SOMEWHERE ELSE.
ME TOO.
GOOD THING DOGS DON'T GET TREATED LIKE PEOPLE.
WHAT THE HELL'S GOING ON?
HEY MAN, WHAT'RE YOU EATING?
YOU OKAY?
I'M NOT EATING ANYTHING, YOU IDIOT. I'M PUKING MY GUTS OUT. FUCKING DOORMAN PUSHED ME TOO HARD. ...BEURK!
SNIFF!
THAT'S PUTTING ME IN A HELL OF A SPOT: I'M DOWN TO THREE GIRLS NOW. THERE'S TWO NEW ONES STARTING TOMORROW.
C'MON, DRY THOSE TEARS.
IF MY BOYFRIEND WAS HERE, HE'D SHOW THEM, SNIFF!
HERE'S YOUR OUTFIT...
THANKS, BUT I'D RATHER GO HOME RIGHT AWAY, IF YOU DON'T MIND...

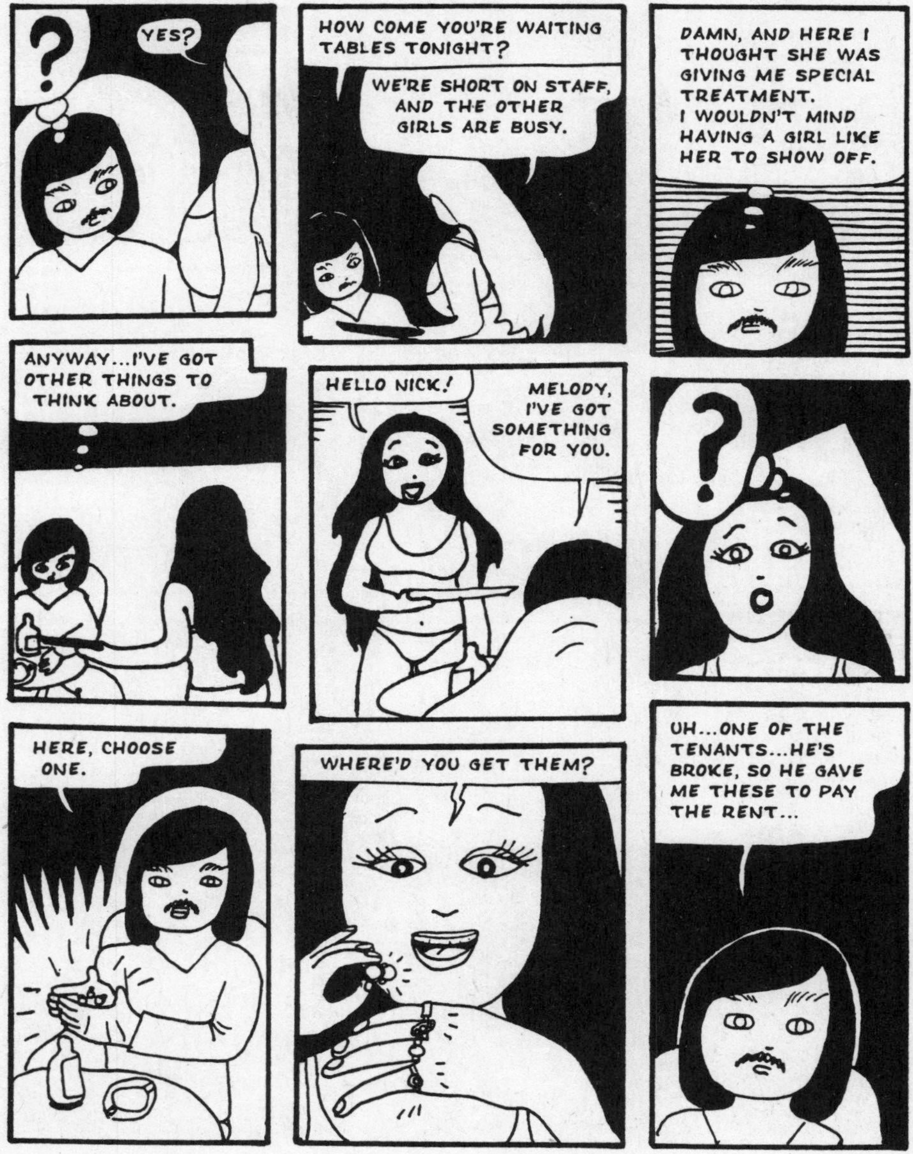
YES?
HOW COME YOU'RE WAITING TABLES TONIGHT?
WE'RE SHORT ON STAFF, AND THE OTHER GIRLS ARE BUSY.
DAMN, AND HERE I THOUGHT SHE WAS GIVING ME SPECIAL TREATMENT.
I WOULDN'T MIND HAVING A GIRL LIKE HER TO SHOW OFF.
ANYWAY...I'VE GOT OTHER THINGS TO THINK ABOUT.
HELLO NICK!
MELODY, I'VE GOT SOMETHING FOR YOU.
HERE, CHOOSE ONE.
WHERE'D YOU GET THEM?
UH...ONE OF THE TENANTS...HE'S BROKE, SO HE GAVE ME THESE TO PAY THE RENT...

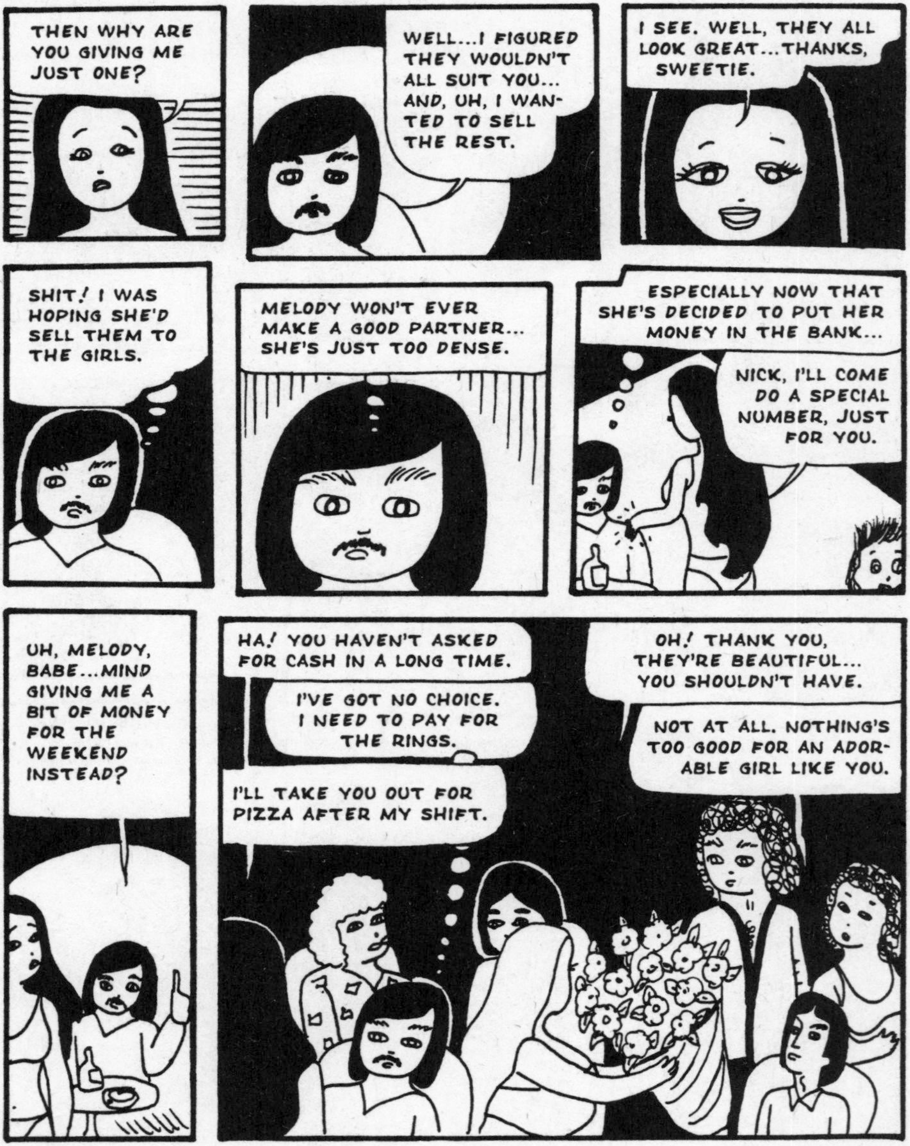
THEN WHY ARE YOU GIVING ME JUST ONE?
WELL...I FIGURED THEY WOULDN'T ALL SUIT YOU... AND, UH, I WANTED TO SELL THE REST.
I SEE. WELL, THEY ALL LOOK GREAT...THANKS, SWEETIE.
SHIT! I WAS HOPING SHE'D SELL THEM TO THE GIRLS.
MELODY WON'T EVER MAKE A GOOD PARTNER... SHE'S JUST TOO DENSE.
ESPECIALLY NOW THAT SHE'S DECIDED TO PUT HER MONEY IN THE BANK...
NICK, I'LL COME DO A SPECIAL NUMBER, JUST FOR YOU.
UH, MELODY, BABE...MIND GIVING ME A BIT OF MONEY FOR THE WEEKEND INSTEAD?
HA! YOU HAVEN'T ASKED FOR CASH IN A LONG TIME.
I'VE GOT NO CHOICE. I NEED TO PAY FOR THE RINGS.
I'LL TAKE YOU OUT FOR PIZZA AFTER MY SHIFT.
OH! THANK YOU, THEY'RE BEAUTIFUL... YOU SHOULDN'T HAVE.
NOT AT ALL. NOTHING'S TOO GOOD FOR AN ADORABLE GIRL LIKE YOU.

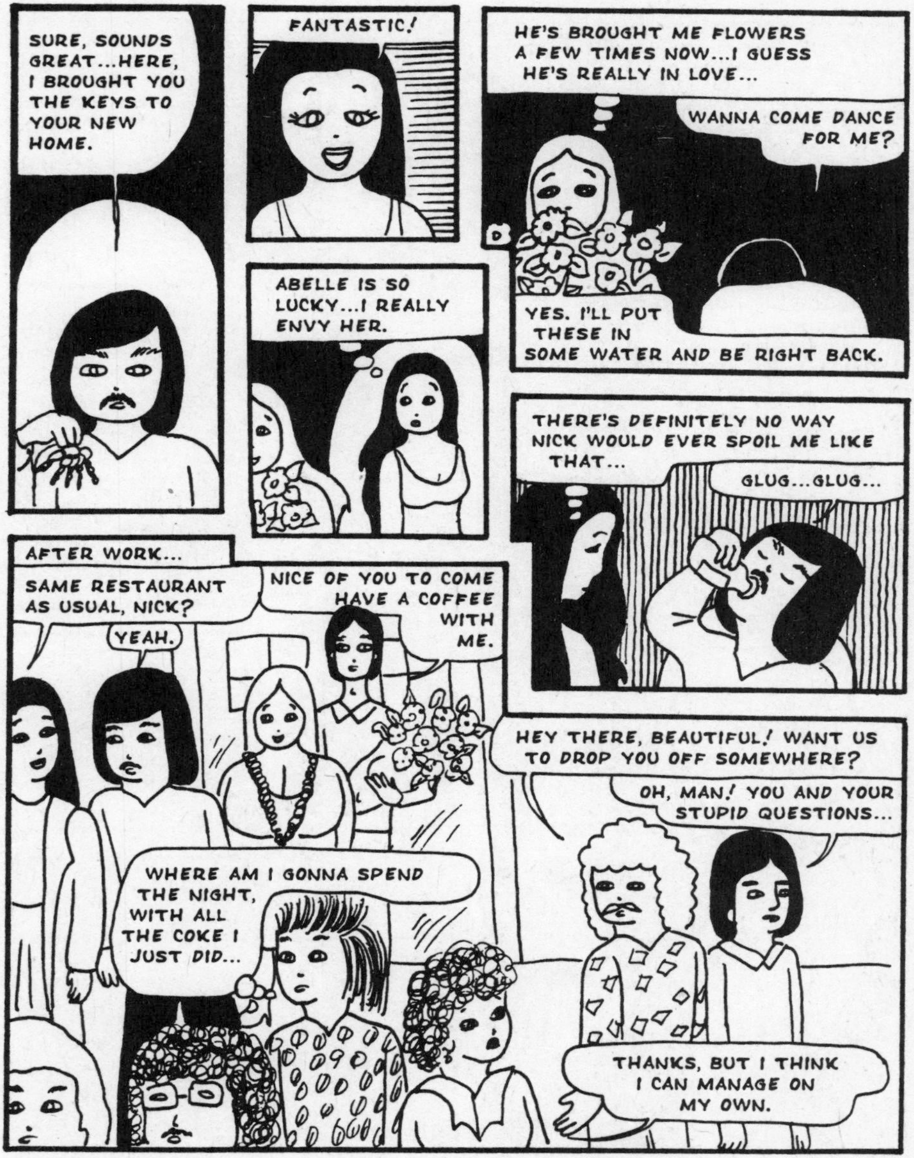
SURE, SOUNDS GREAT...HERE, I BROUGHT YOU THE KEYS TO YOUR NEW HOME.
FANTASTIC!
ABELLE IS SO LUCKY...I REALLY ENVY HER.
HE'S BROUGHT ME FLOWERS A FEW TIMES NOW...I GUESS HE'S REALLY IN LOVE...
WANNA COME DANCE FOR ME?
YES. I'LL PUT THESE IN SOME WATER AND BE RIGHT BACK.
THERE'S DEFINITELY NO WAY NICK WOULD EVER SPOIL ME LIKE THAT...
GLUG...GLUG...
AFTER WORK...
SAME RESTAURANT AS USUAL, NICK?
YEAH.
NICE OF YOU TO COME HAVE A COFFEE WITH ME.
WHERE AM I GONNA SPEND THE NIGHT, WITH ALL THE COKE I JUST DID...
HEY THERE, BEAUTIFUL! WANT US TO DROP YOU OFF SOMEWHERE?
OH, MAN! YOU AND YOUR STUPID QUESTIONS...
THANKS, BUT I THINK I CAN MANAGE ON MY OWN.

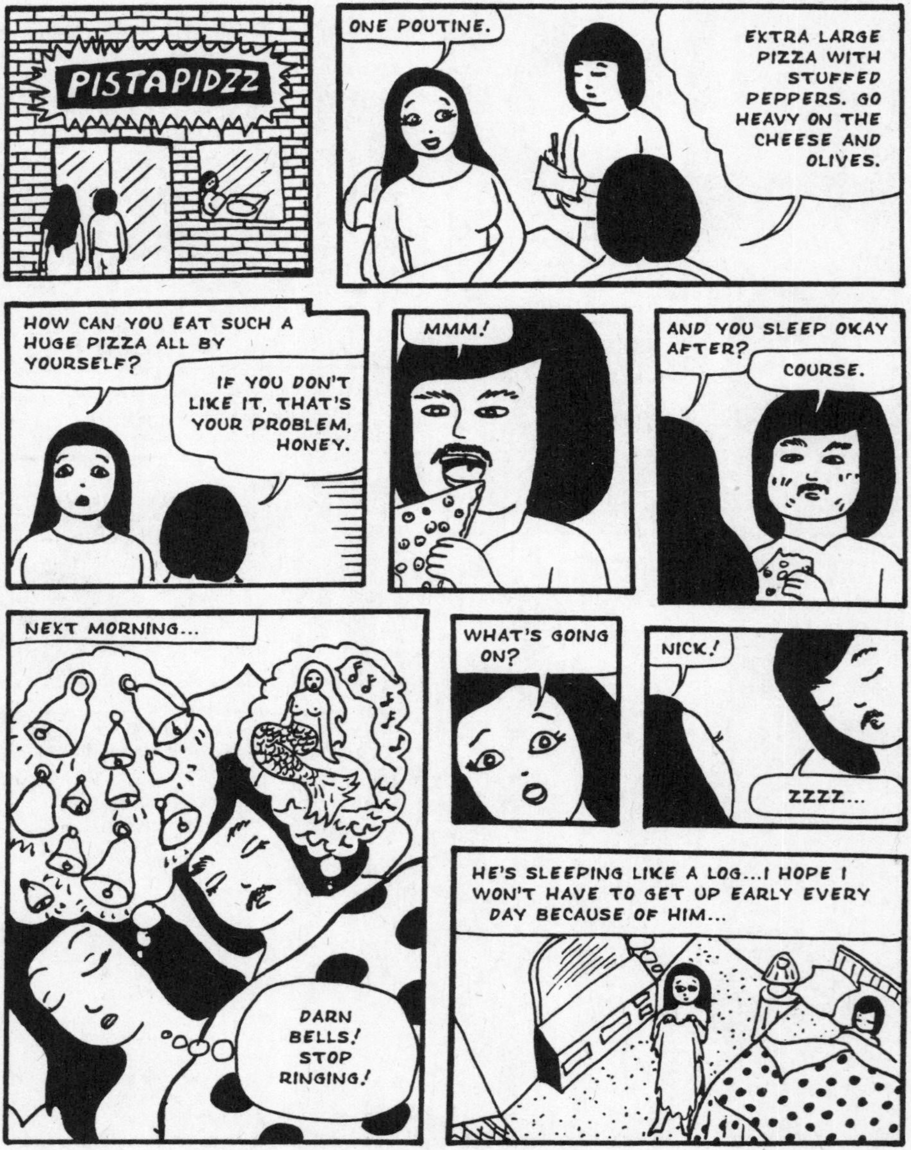
PISTAPIDZZ
ONE POUTINE.
EXTRA LARGE PIZZA WITH STUFFED PEPPERS. GO HEAVY ON THE CHEESE AND OLIVES.
HOW CAN YOU EAT SUCH A HUGE PIZZA ALL BY YOURSELF?
IF YOU DON'T LIKE IT, THAT'S YOUR PROBLEM, HONEY.
MMM!
AND YOU SLEEP OKAY AFTER?
COURSE.
NEXT MORNING...
DARN BELLS! STOP RINGING!
WHAT'S GOING ON?
NICK!
ZZZZ...
HE'S SLEEPING LIKE A LOG...I HOPE I WON'T HAVE TO GET UP EARLY EVERY DAY BECAUSE OF HIM...

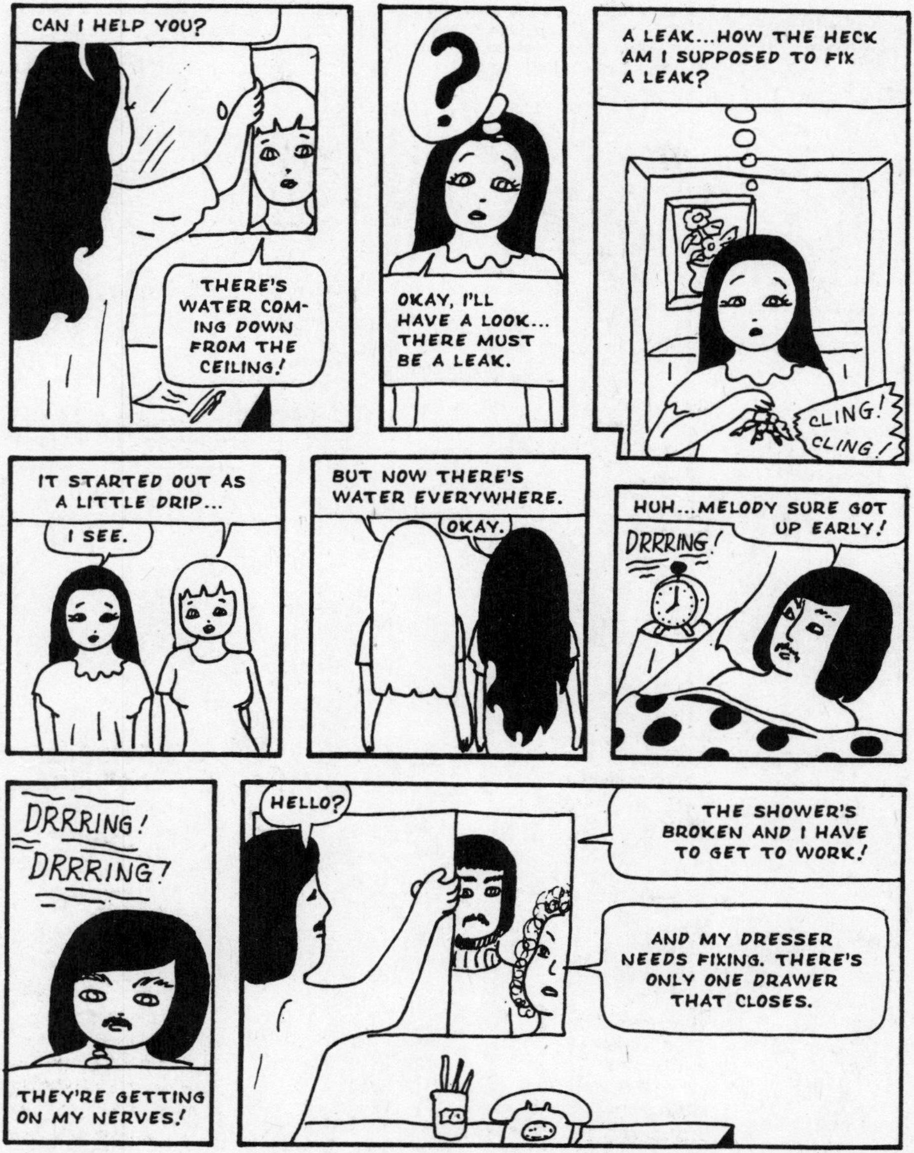

CAN I HELP YOU?
THERE'S WATER COMING DOWN FROM THE CEILING!
?
OKAY, I'LL HAVE A LOOK... THERE MUST BE A LEAK.
A LEAK...HOW THE HECK AM I SUPPOSED TO FIX A LEAK?
CLING! CLING!
IT STARTED OUT AS A LITTLE DRIP...
I SEE.
BUT NOW THERE'S WATER EVERYWHERE.
OKAY.
HUH...MELODY SURE GOT UP EARLY!
DRRRING!
DRRRING!
DRRRING!
THEY'RE GETTING ON MY NERVES!
HELLO?
THE SHOWER'S BROKEN AND I HAVE TO GET TO WORK!
AND MY DRESSER NEEDS FIXING. THERE'S ONLY ONE DRAWER THAT CLOSES.

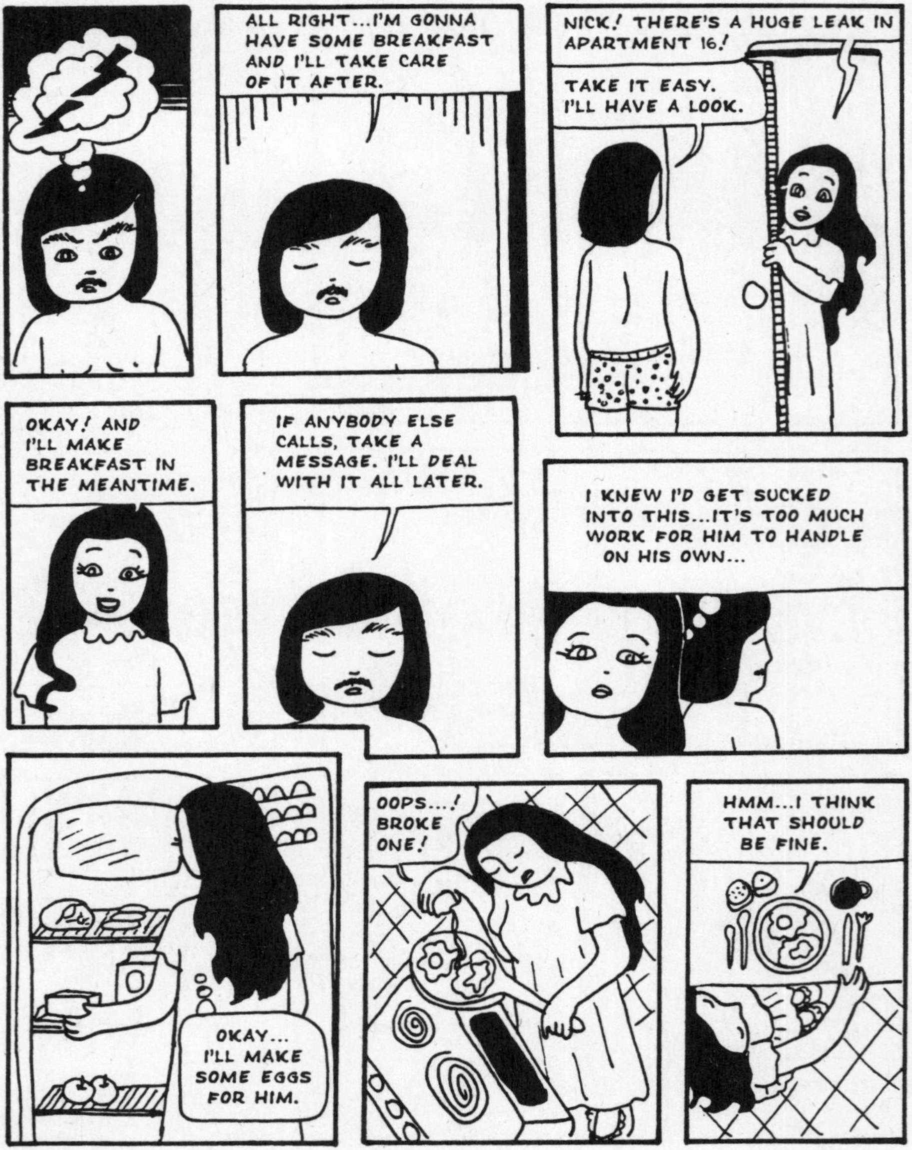
ALL RIGHT...I'M GONNA HAVE SOME BREAKFAST AND I'LL TAKE CARE OF IT AFTER.
NICK! THERE'S A HUGE LEAK IN APARTMENT 16!
TAKE IT EASY. I'LL HAVE A LOOK.
OKAY! AND I'LL MAKE BREAKFAST IN THE MEANTIME.
IF ANYBODY ELSE CALLS, TAKE A MESSAGE. I'LL DEAL WITH IT ALL LATER.
I KNEW I'D GET SUCKED INTO THIS...IT'S TOO MUCH WORK FOR HIM TO HANDLE ON HIS OWN...
OKAY... I'LL MAKE SOME EGGS FOR HIM.
OOPS...! BROKE ONE!
HMM...I THINK THAT SHOULD BE FINE.

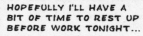

I'M GOING TO GO TAKE A SHOWER.

HOPEFULLY I'LL HAVE A BIT OF TIME TO REST UP BEFORE WORK TONIGHT...

NICK MUST BE DONE EATING BY NOW...

HE'S NOT EVEN BACK YET...!

DRING!
DRING!

OKAY, THAT'S TAKEN CARE OF...I'M STARVING!

YOU BROKE ONE!

MELODY! IT'S COLD!

YOU CAN'T EVEN FRY AN EGG! IN FACT, YOU CAN'T DO ANYTHING RIGHT! I'M GOING OUT FOR BREAKFAST!!!

WHAT'S NEW...?

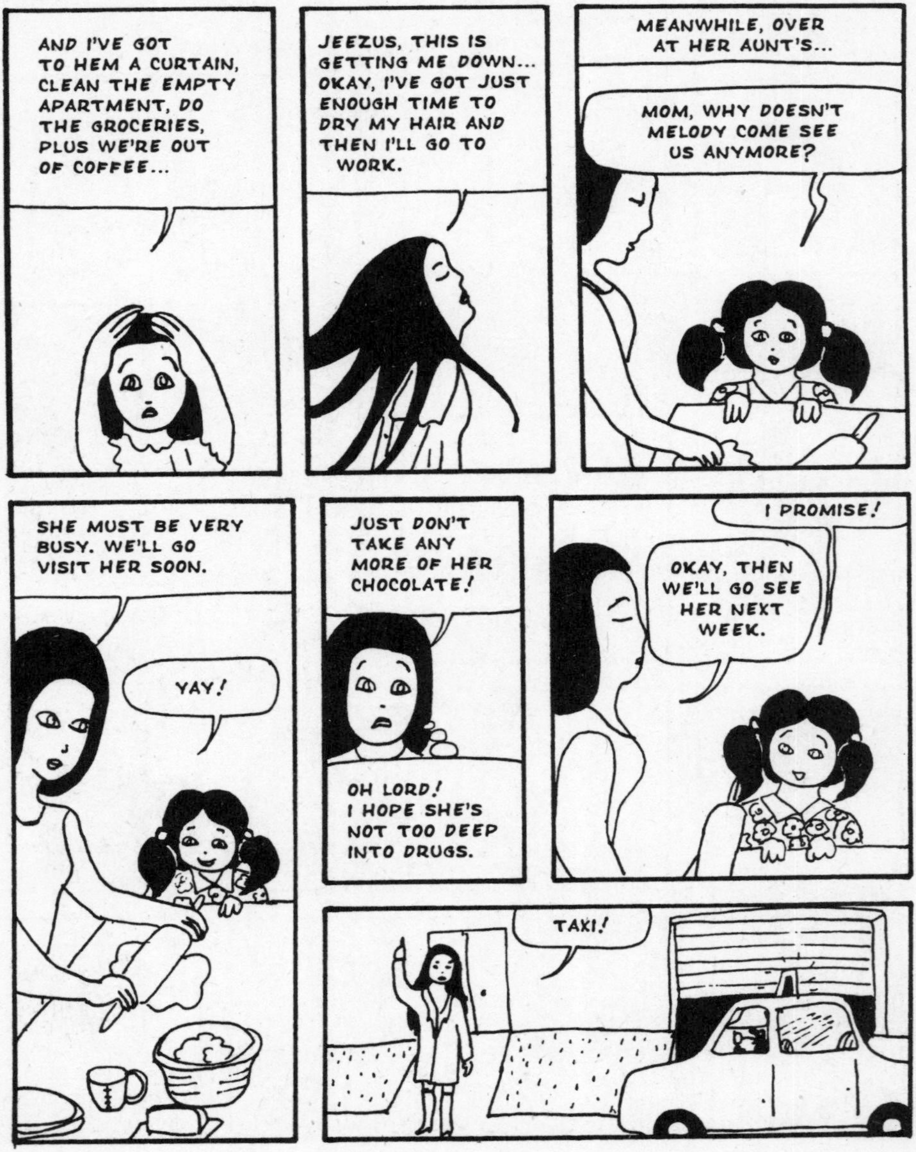
AND I'VE GOT TO HEM A CURTAIN, CLEAN THE EMPTY APARTMENT, DO THE GROCERIES, PLUS WE'RE OUT OF COFFEE...
JEEZUS, THIS IS GETTING ME DOWN... OKAY, I'VE GOT JUST ENOUGH TIME TO DRY MY HAIR AND THEN I'LL GO TO WORK.
MEANWHILE, OVER AT HER AUNT'S...
MOM, WHY DOESN'T MELODY COME SEE US ANYMORE?
SHE MUST BE VERY BUSY. WE'LL GO VISIT HER SOON.
YAY!
JUST DON'T TAKE ANY MORE OF HER CHOCOLATE!
OH LORD! I HOPE SHE'S NOT TOO DEEP INTO DRUGS.
I PROMISE!
OKAY, THEN WE'LL GO SEE HER NEXT WEEK.
TAXI!

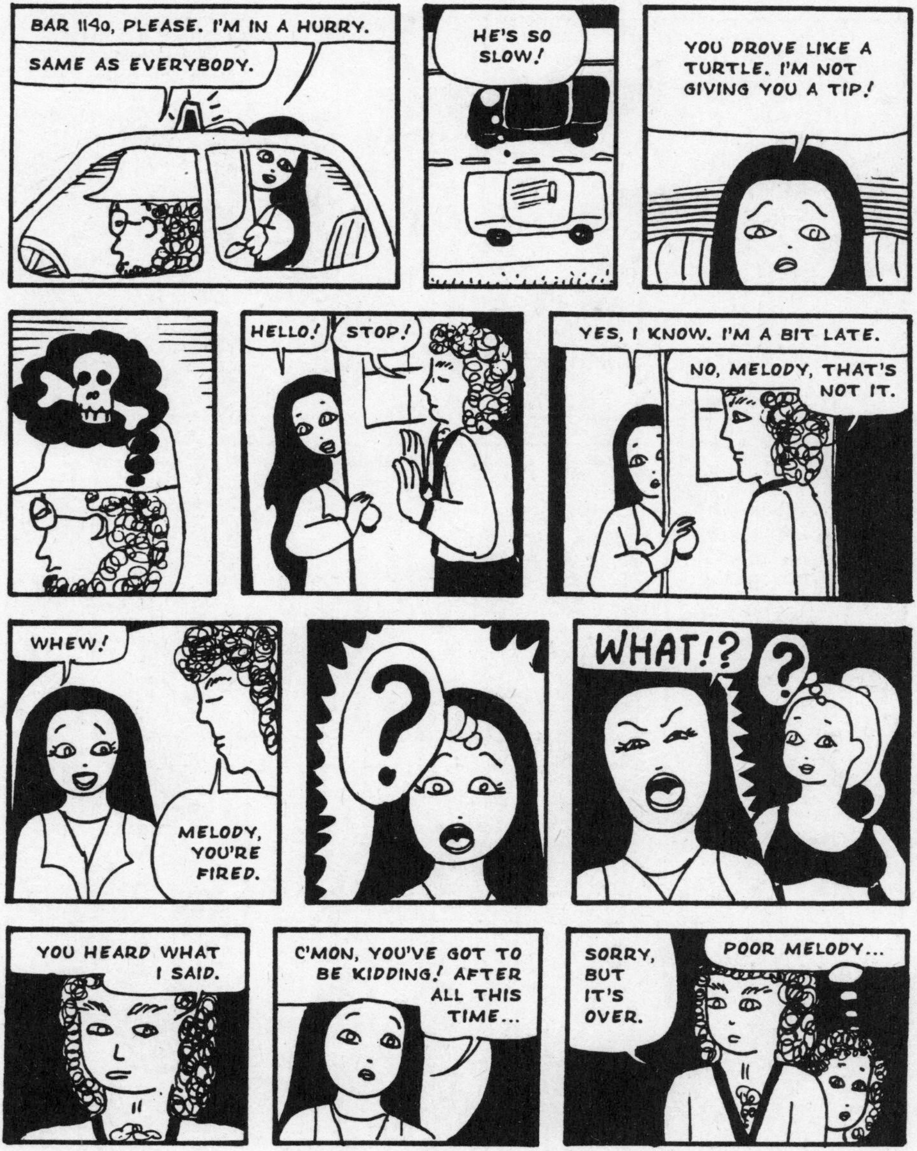
BAR 1140, PLEASE. I'M IN A HURRY.
SAME AS EVERYBODY.
HE'S SO SLOW!
YOU DROVE LIKE A TURTLE. I'M NOT GIVING YOU A TIP!
HELLO!
STOP!
YES, I KNOW. I'M A BIT LATE.
NO, MELODY, THAT'S NOT IT.
WHEW!
MELODY, YOU'RE FIRED.
?
WHAT!?
?
YOU HEARD WHAT I SAID.
C'MON, YOU'VE GOT TO BE KIDDING! AFTER ALL THIS TIME...
SORRY, BUT IT'S OVER.
POOR MELODY...

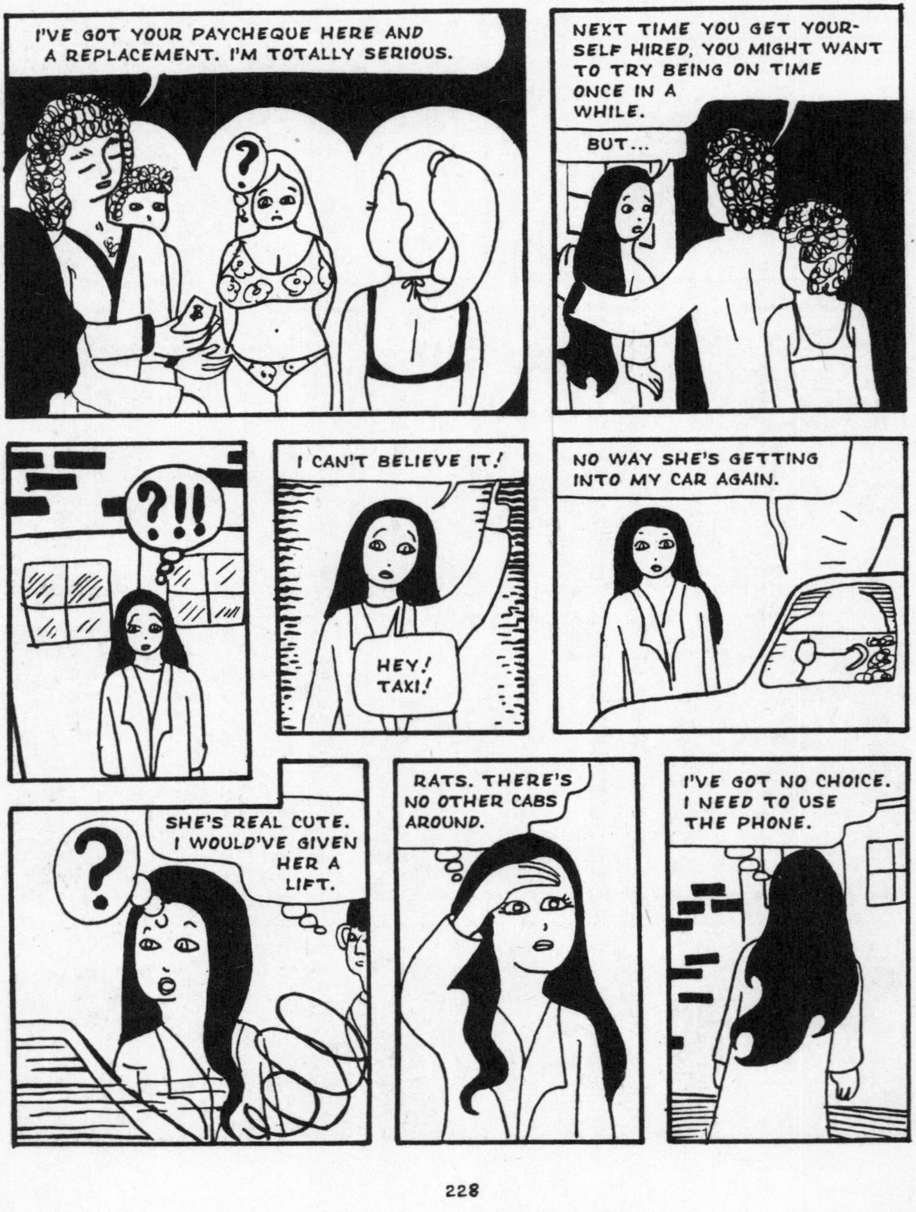
I'VE GOT YOUR PAYCHEQUE HERE AND A REPLACEMENT. I'M TOTALLY SERIOUS.
?
NEXT TIME YOU GET YOURSELF HIRED, YOU MIGHT WANT TO TRY BEING ON TIME ONCE IN A WHILE.
BUT...
?!!
I CAN'T BELIEVE IT!
HEY! TAXI!
NO WAY SHE'S GETTING INTO MY CAR AGAIN.
SHE'S REAL CUTE. I WOULD'VE GIVEN HER A LIFT.
?
RATS. THERE'S NO OTHER CABS AROUND.
I'VE GOT NO CHOICE. I NEED TO USE THE PHONE.

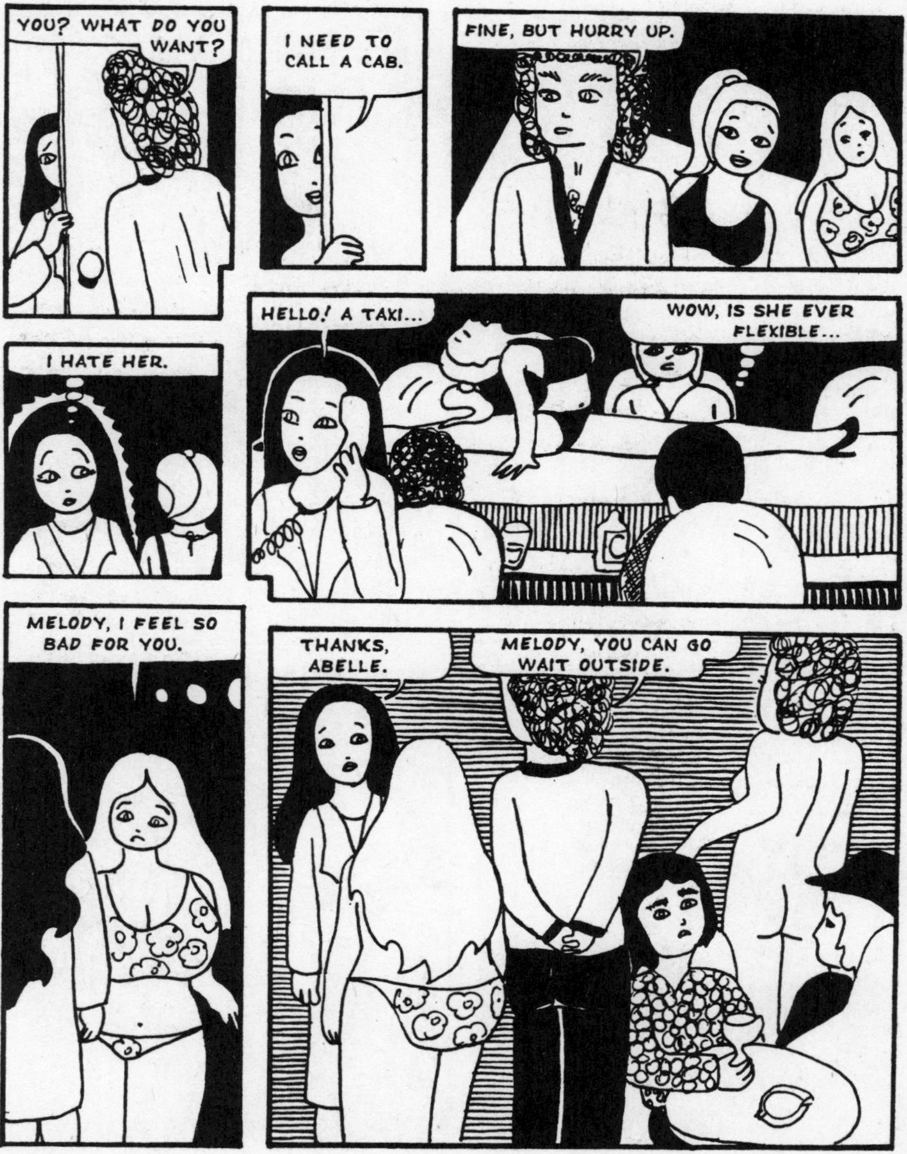
YOU? WHAT DO YOU WANT?
I NEED TO CALL A CAB.
FINE, BUT HURRY UP.
I HATE HER.
HELLO! A TAXI...
WOW, IS SHE EVER FLEXIBLE...
MELODY, I FEEL SO BAD FOR YOU.
THANKS, ABELLE.
MELODY, YOU CAN GO WAIT OUTSIDE.

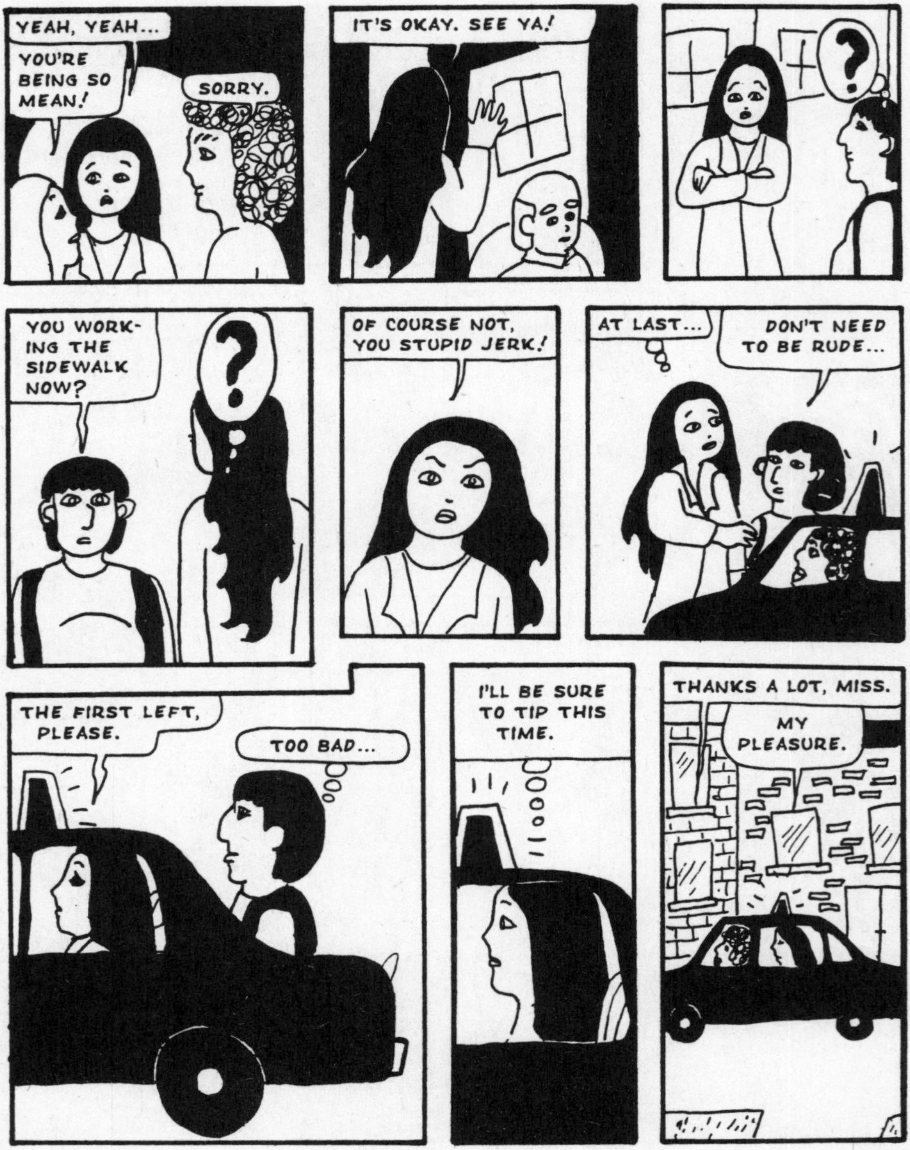
YEAH, YEAH...
YOU'RE BEING SO MEAN!
SORRY.
IT'S OKAY. SEE YA!
?
YOU WORKING THE SIDEWALK NOW?
?
OF COURSE NOT, YOU STUPID JERK!
AT LAST...
DON'T NEED TO BE RUDE...
THE FIRST LEFT, PLEASE.
TOO BAD...
I'LL BE SURE TO TIP THIS TIME.
THANKS A LOT, MISS.
MY PLEASURE.

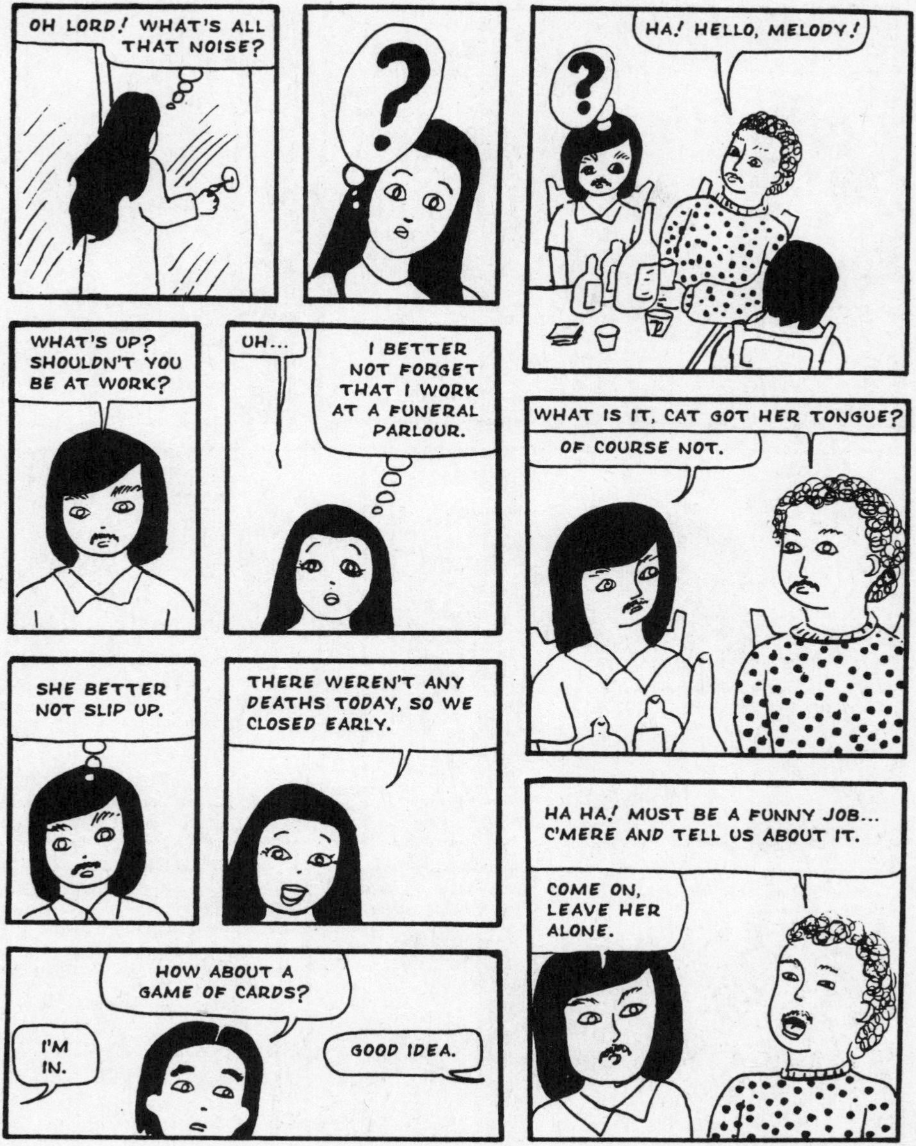
OH LORD! WHAT'S ALL THAT NOISE?
?
?
HA! HELLO, MELODY!
WHAT'S UP? SHOULDN'T YOU BE AT WORK?
UH...
I BETTER NOT FORGET THAT I WORK AT A FUNERAL PARLOUR.
WHAT IS IT, CAT GOT HER TONGUE?
OF COURSE NOT.
SHE BETTER NOT SLIP UP.
THERE WEREN'T ANY DEATHS TODAY, SO WE CLOSED EARLY.
HA HA! MUST BE A FUNNY JOB... C'MERE AND TELL US ABOUT IT.
COME ON, LEAVE HER ALONE.
HOW ABOUT A GAME OF CARDS?
I'M IN.
GOOD IDEA.

IT'S OKAY, I WANT TO PLAY TOO.

NOW YOU'RE TALKIN'!! I LIKE A WOMAN WHO PLAYS CARDS.

I BETTER KEEP AN EYE ON HIM... LOOKS LIKE HE'S TRYING TO MAKE A MOVE ON MELODY...HE'S ALWAYS GOING AFTER OTHER GUYS' GIRL-FRIENDS.

MAYBE MELODY QUIT HER JOB TO HELP ME TAKE CARE OF THIS PLACE...

I'LL TAKE A CARD.

CHECK.

I'LL RAISE.

I BET HE'S BLUFFING.

I'M GONNA RERAISE.

YOU'RE PLAYING LIKE AN IDIOT!

MAYBE HE'S LIKE ME: NO MATTER WHAT I DO, SOMEHOW I ALWAYS PLAY TO LOSE.

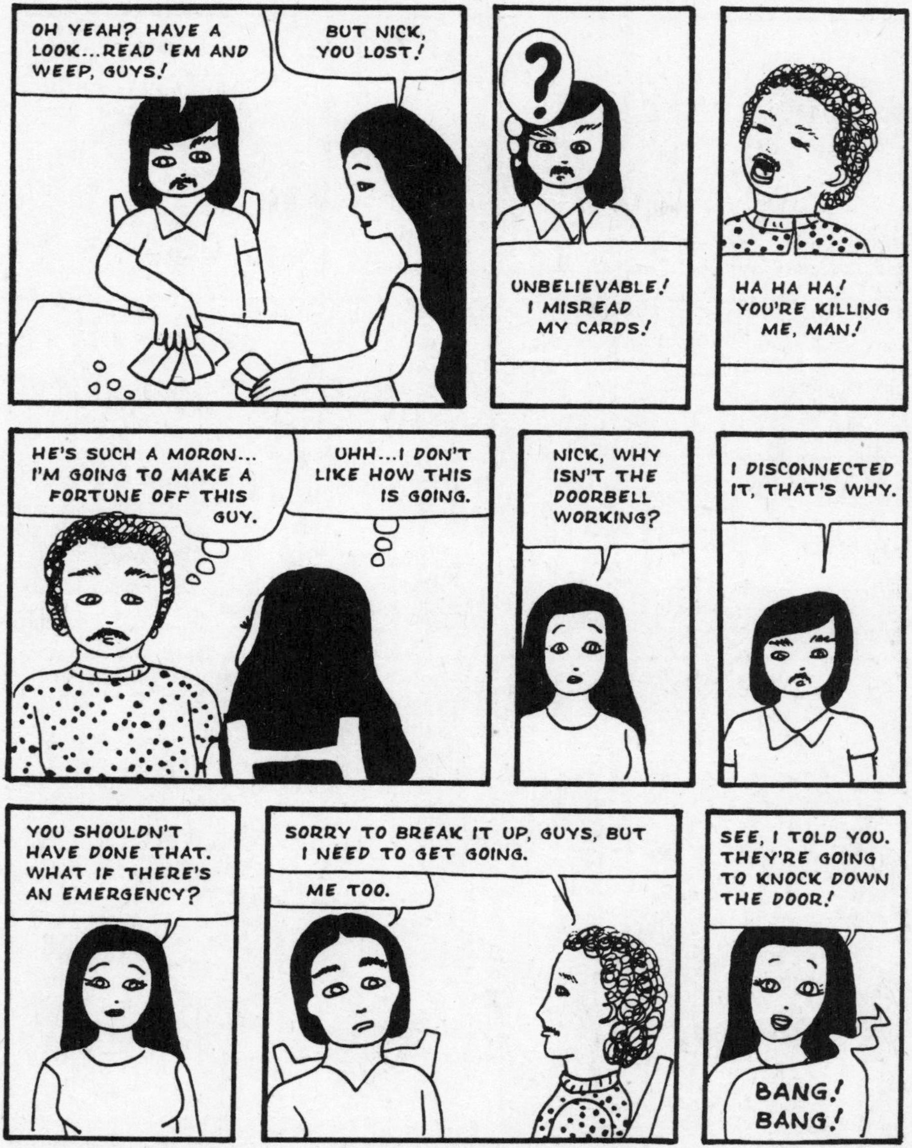
OH YEAH? HAVE A LOOK...READ 'EM AND WEEP, GUYS!
BUT NICK, YOU LOST!
?
UNBELIEVABLE! I MISREAD MY CARDS!
HA HA HA! YOU'RE KILLING ME, MAN!
HE'S SUCH A MORON... I'M GOING TO MAKE A FORTUNE OFF THIS GUY.
UHH...I DON'T LIKE HOW THIS IS GOING.
NICK, WHY ISN'T THE DOORBELL WORKING?
I DISCONNECTED IT, THAT'S WHY.
YOU SHOULDN'T HAVE DONE THAT. WHAT IF THERE'S AN EMERGENCY?
SORRY TO BREAK IT UP, GUYS, BUT I NEED TO GET GOING.
ME TOO.
SEE, I TOLD YOU. THEY'RE GOING TO KNOCK DOWN THE DOOR!
BANG! BANG!

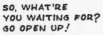

SO, WHAT'RE YOU WAITING FOR? GO OPEN UP!

BANG!

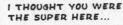

I THOUGHT YOU WERE THE SUPER HERE...

BANG! BANG!

FIRST I'M GONNA SAY GOODBYE TO MY GUESTS, AND THEN I'LL SEE WHAT NEEDS FIXING THIS TIME.

OH DEAR!

THE TWO OF YOU BETTER HAVE A GOOD EXCUSE FOR NOT ANSWERING THE DOOR!

UH... COME IN. NICK IS IN THE KITCHEN...

NICK! SOMEONE'S HERE TO SEE YOU.

IS THERE SOME KIND OF PROBLEM?

THAT'S EXACTLY WHAT I WANTED TO ASK YOU.

UH...SO LONG, GUYS. I NEED TO GO DOWNTOWN.

I'VE GOT TO FIND MYSELF A NEW CLUB.

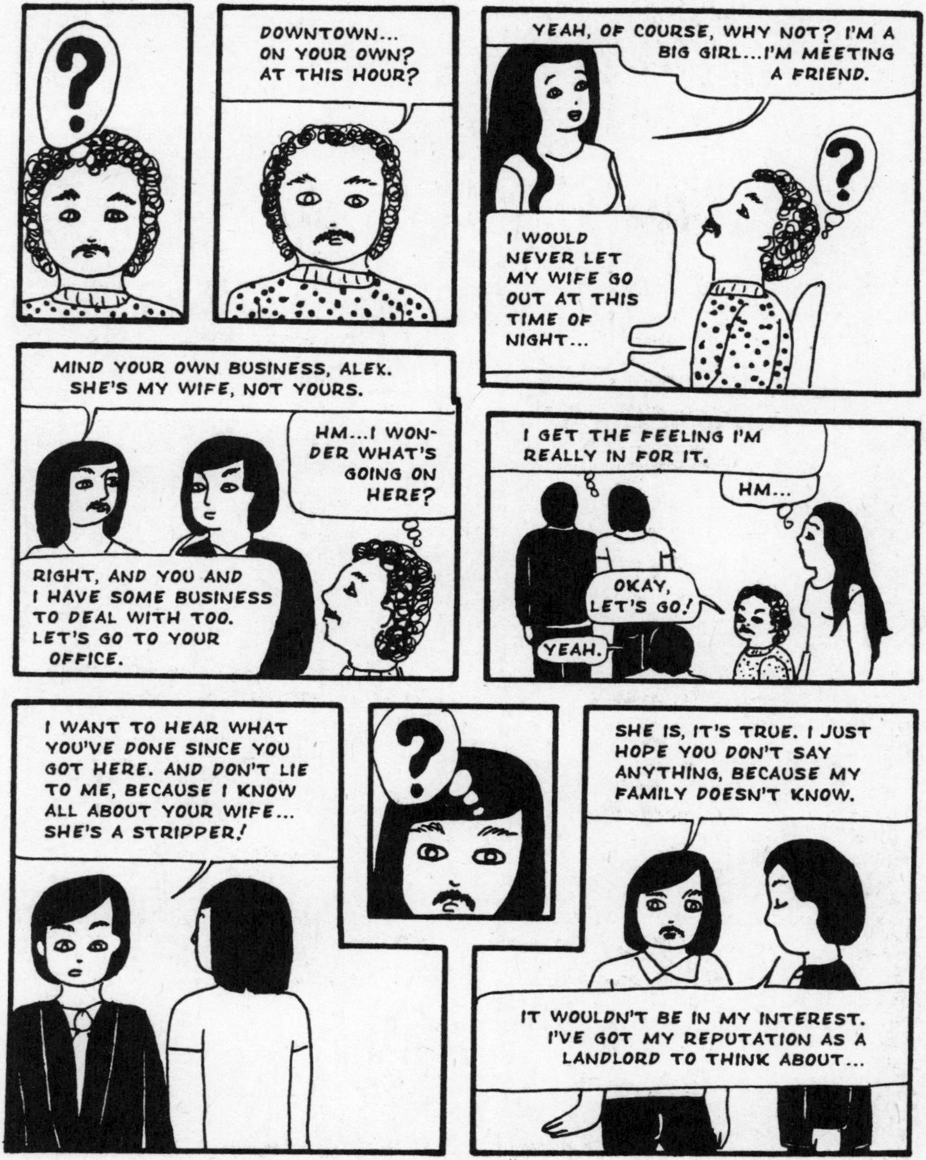
DOWNTOWN... ON YOUR OWN? AT THIS HOUR?
YEAH, OF COURSE, WHY NOT? I'M A BIG GIRL...I'M MEETING A FRIEND.
I WOULD NEVER LET MY WIFE GO OUT AT THIS TIME OF NIGHT...
MIND YOUR OWN BUSINESS, ALEX. SHE'S MY WIFE, NOT YOURS.
HM...I WONDER WHAT'S GOING ON HERE?
RIGHT, AND YOU AND I HAVE SOME BUSINESS TO DEAL WITH TOO. LET'S GO TO YOUR OFFICE.
I GET THE FEELING I'M REALLY IN FOR IT.
HM...
OKAY, LET'S GO!
YEAH.
I WANT TO HEAR WHAT YOU'VE DONE SINCE YOU GOT HERE. AND DON'T LIE TO ME, BECAUSE I KNOW ALL ABOUT YOUR WIFE... SHE'S A STRIPPER!
SHE IS, IT'S TRUE. I JUST HOPE YOU DON'T SAY ANYTHING, BECAUSE MY FAMILY DOESN'T KNOW.
IT WOULDN'T BE IN MY INTEREST. I'VE GOT MY REPUTATION AS A LANDLORD TO THINK ABOUT...

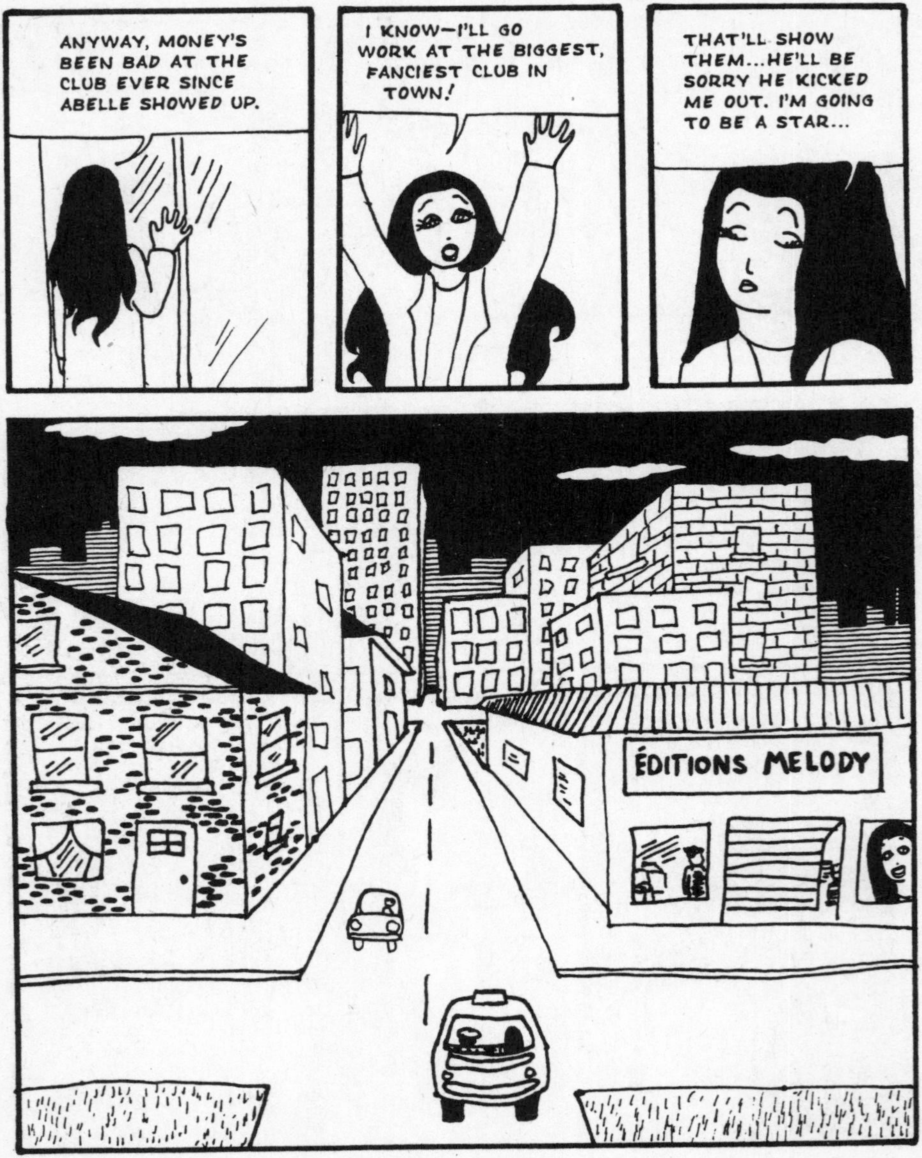
ANYWAY, MONEY'S BEEN BAD AT THE CLUB EVER SINCE ABELLE SHOWED UP.
I KNOW—I'LL GO WORK AT THE BIGGEST, FANCIEST CLUB IN TOWN!
THAT'LL SHOW THEM...HE'LL BE SORRY HE KICKED ME OUT. I'M GOING TO BE A STAR...
ÉDITIONS MELODY

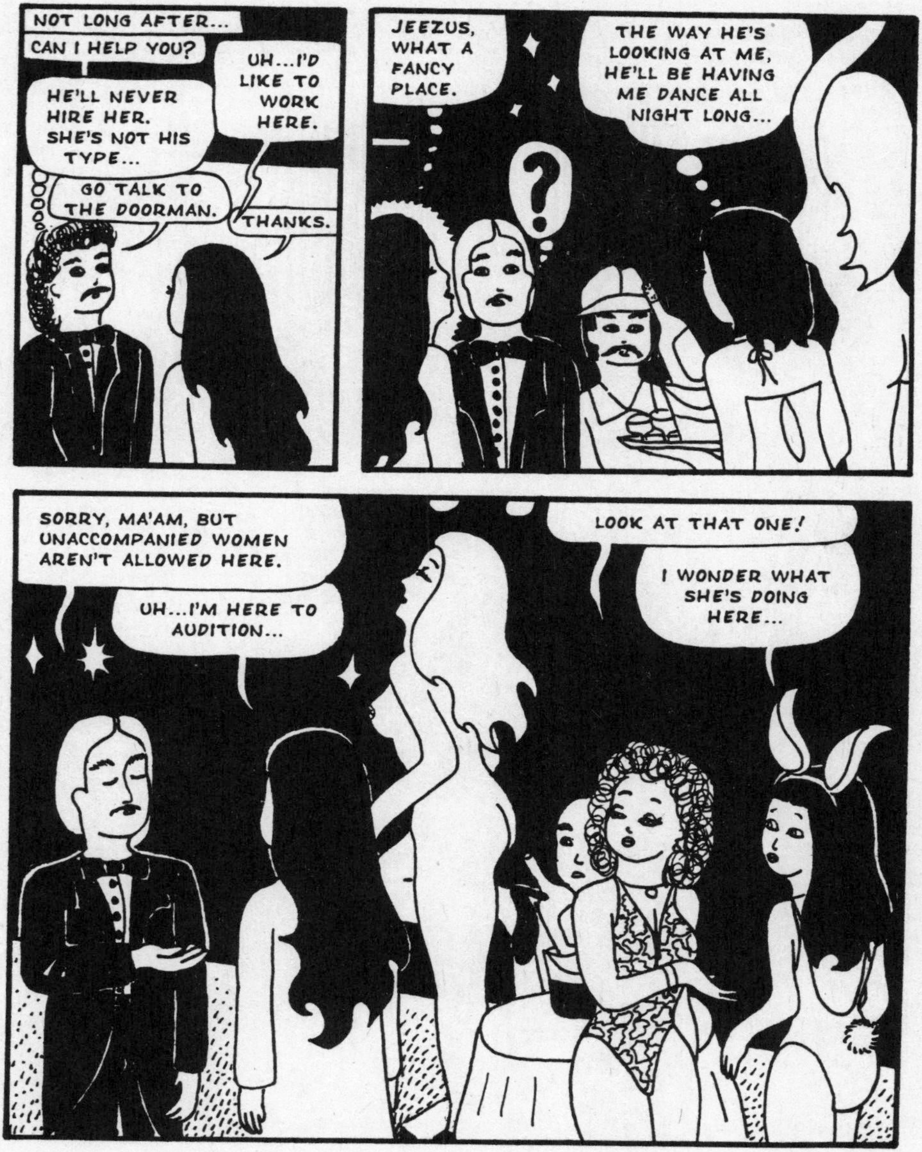
NOT LONG AFTER...
CAN I HELP YOU?
UH...I'D LIKE TO WORK HERE.
HE'LL NEVER HIRE HER. SHE'S NOT HIS TYPE...
GO TALK TO THE DOORMAN.
THANKS.
JEEZUS, WHAT A FANCY PLACE.
THE WAY HE'S LOOKING AT ME, HE'LL BE HAVING ME DANCE ALL NIGHT LONG...
?
SORRY, MA'AM, BUT UNACCOMPANIED WOMEN AREN'T ALLOWED HERE.
UH...I'M HERE TO AUDITION...
LOOK AT THAT ONE!
I WONDER WHAT SHE'S DOING HERE...

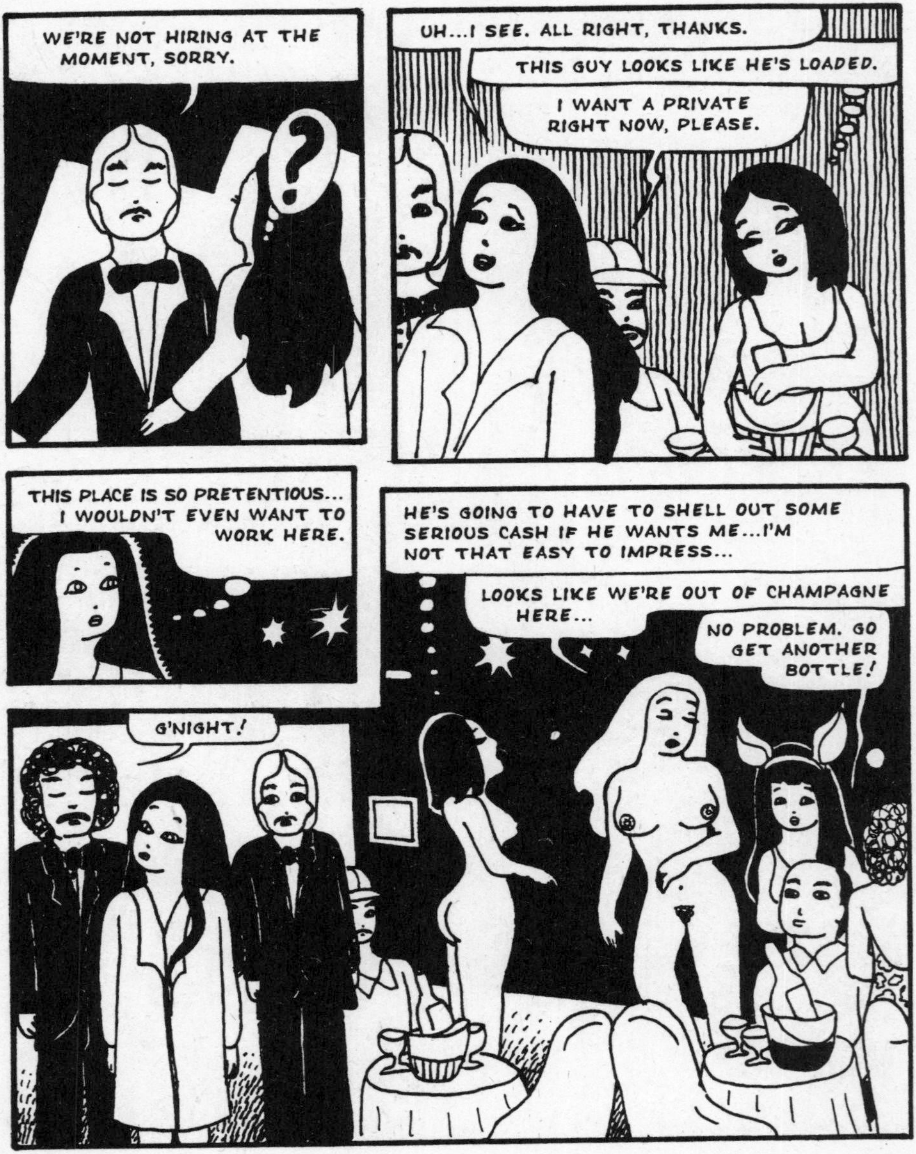
WE'RE NOT HIRING AT THE MOMENT, SORRY.
UH...I SEE. ALL RIGHT, THANKS.
THIS GUY LOOKS LIKE HE'S LOADED.
I WANT A PRIVATE RIGHT NOW, PLEASE.
THIS PLACE IS SO PRETENTIOUS... I WOULDN'T EVEN WANT TO WORK HERE.
HE'S GOING TO HAVE TO SHELL OUT SOME SERIOUS CASH IF HE WANTS ME...I'M NOT THAT EASY TO IMPRESS...
LOOKS LIKE WE'RE OUT OF CHAMPAGNE HERE...
NO PROBLEM. GO GET ANOTHER BOTTLE!
G'NIGHT!

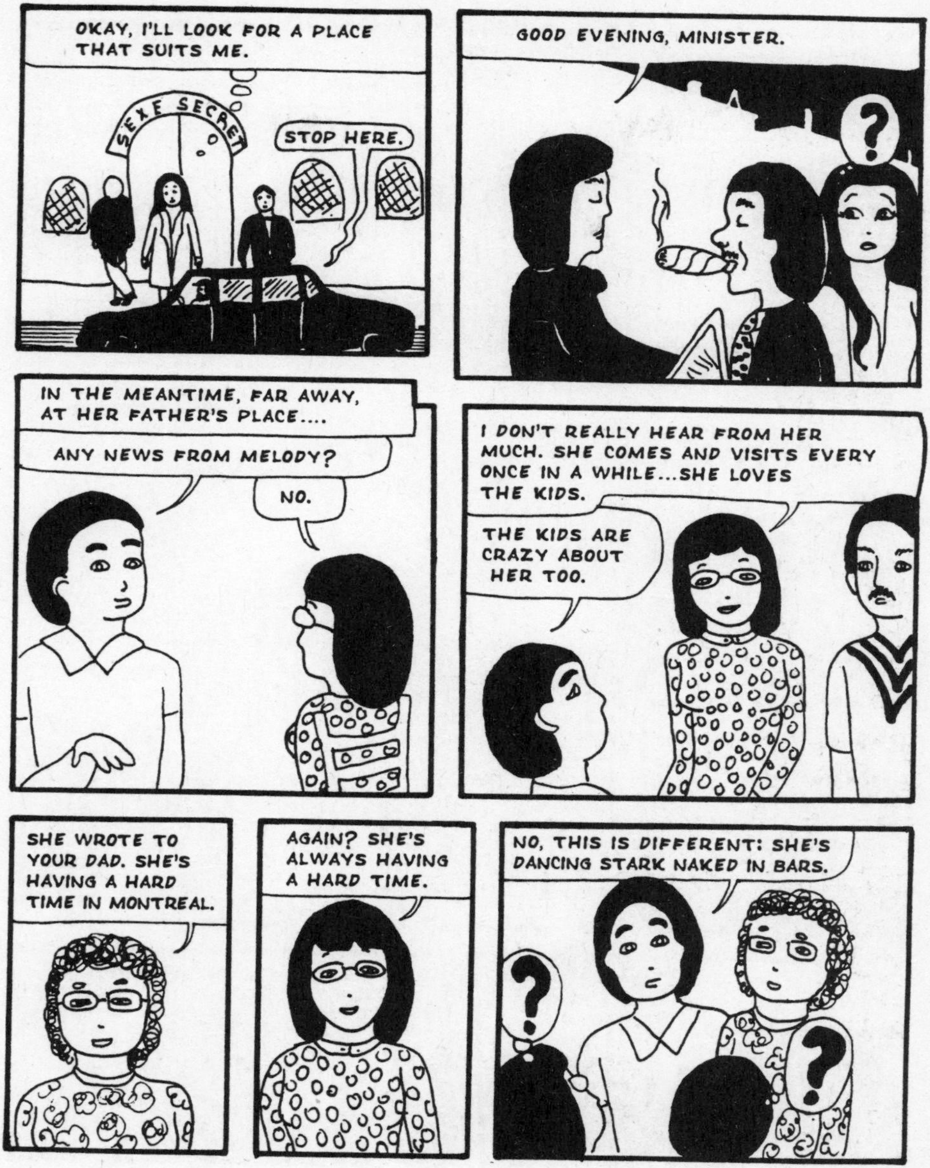
OKAY, I'LL LOOK FOR A PLACE THAT SUITS ME.
SEXE SECRET
STOP HERE.
GOOD EVENING, MINISTER.
?
IN THE MEANTIME, FAR AWAY, AT HER FATHER'S PLACE....
ANY NEWS FROM MELODY?
NO.
I DON'T REALLY HEAR FROM HER MUCH. SHE COMES AND VISITS EVERY ONCE IN A WHILE...SHE LOVES THE KIDS.
THE KIDS ARE CRAZY ABOUT HER TOO.
SHE WROTE TO YOUR DAD. SHE'S HAVING A HARD TIME IN MONTREAL.
AGAIN? SHE'S ALWAYS HAVING A HARD TIME.
NO, THIS IS DIFFERENT: SHE'S DANCING STARK NAKED IN BARS.
?
?

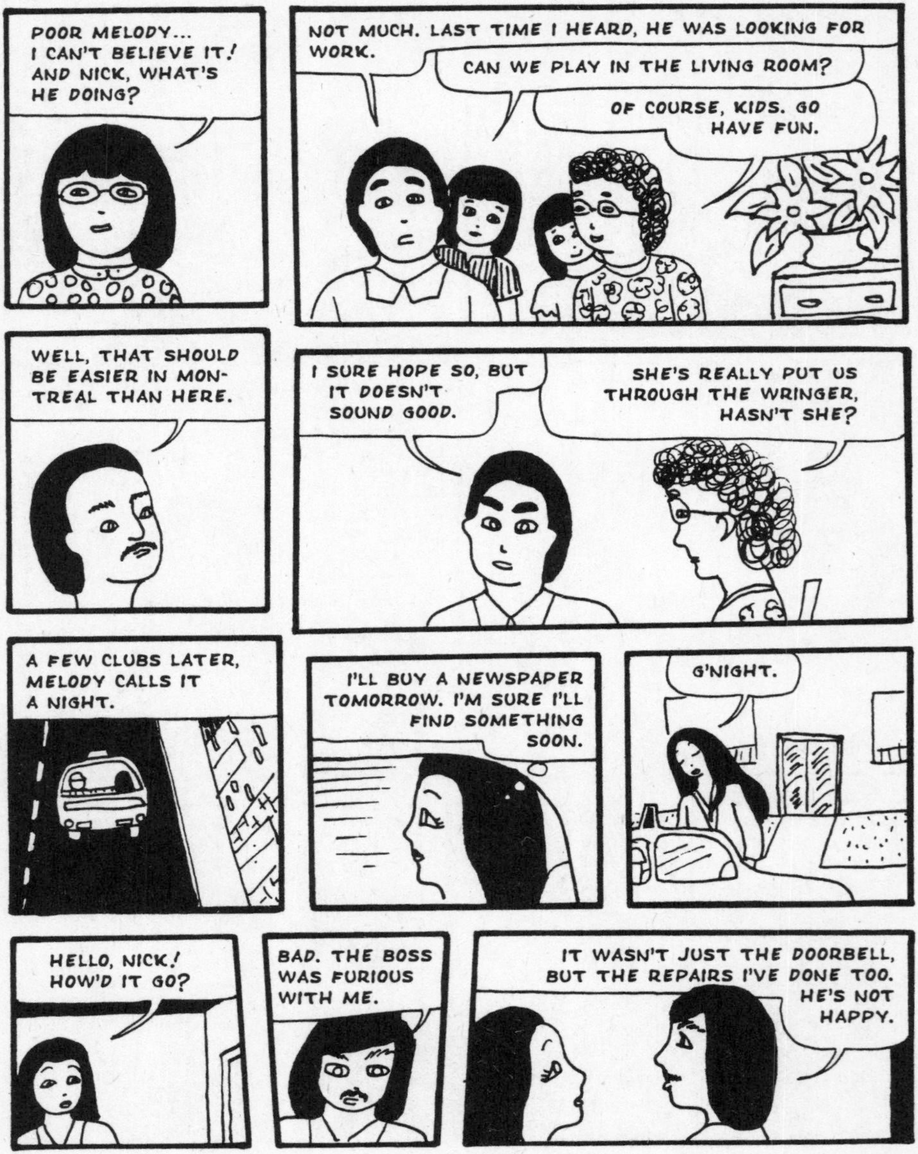
POOR MELODY... I CAN'T BELIEVE IT! AND NICK, WHAT'S HE DOING?
NOT MUCH. LAST TIME I HEARD, HE WAS LOOKING FOR WORK.
CAN WE PLAY IN THE LIVING ROOM?
OF COURSE, KIDS. GO HAVE FUN.
WELL, THAT SHOULD BE EASIER IN MONTREAL THAN HERE.
I SURE HOPE SO, BUT IT DOESN'T SOUND GOOD.
SHE'S REALLY PUT US THROUGH THE WRINGER, HASN'T SHE?
A FEW CLUBS LATER, MELODY CALLS IT A NIGHT.
I'LL BUY A NEWSPAPER TOMORROW. I'M SURE I'LL FIND SOMETHING SOON.
G'NIGHT.
HELLO, NICK! HOW'D IT GO?
BAD. THE BOSS WAS FURIOUS WITH ME.
IT WASN'T JUST THE DOORBELL, BUT THE REPAIRS I'VE DONE TOO. HE'S NOT HAPPY.

LET'S GO TO BED. YOU'LL SEE, THINGS WILL WORK THEM-SELVES OUT.
YOU'RE STILL NEW ON THE JOB... IT'LL GET BETTER. YOU GOT OFF TO A ROUGH START, THAT'S ALL.
YEAH...
I'LL CALL MY AUNT TOMORROW AND ASK HER FOR SOME ADVICE.
GOOD IDEA. AND I NEED TO FIND A JOB.
SO YOU HAD A BAD DAY TOO?
YES.
C'MERE, WE'RE GONNA MAKE EACH OTHER FEEL BETTER.
HEY, GO EASY!
I WANT YOU, BABE.
ME TOO, NICK. JUST LET ME TURN OFF THE LIGHT AND GET INTO BED, OKAY?

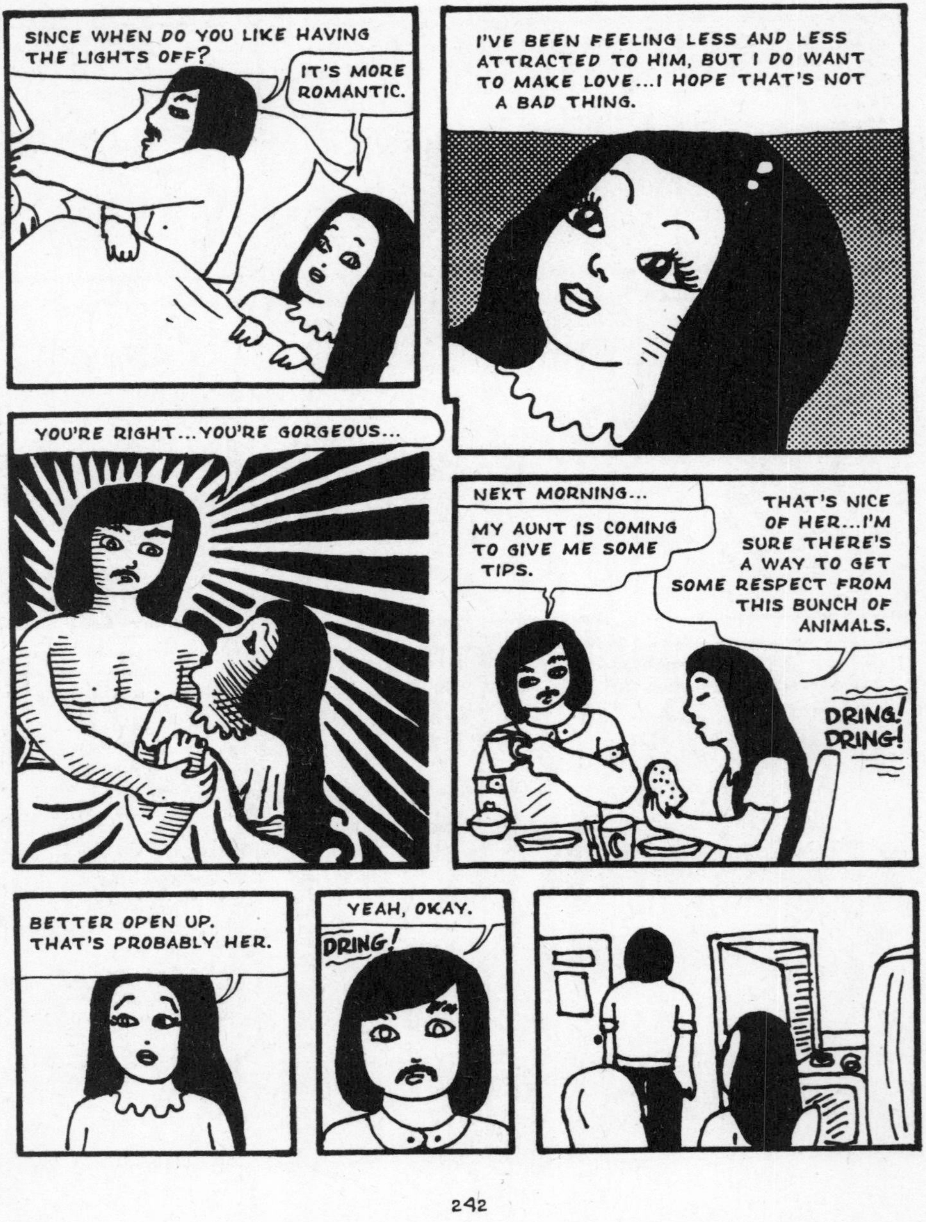
SINCE WHEN DO YOU LIKE HAVING THE LIGHTS OFF?
IT'S MORE ROMANTIC.
I'VE BEEN FEELING LESS AND LESS ATTRACTED TO HIM, BUT I DO WANT TO MAKE LOVE... I HOPE THAT'S NOT A BAD THING.
YOU'RE RIGHT... YOU'RE GORGEOUS...
NEXT MORNING...
MY AUNT IS COMING TO GIVE ME SOME TIPS.
THAT'S NICE OF HER... I'M SURE THERE'S A WAY TO GET SOME RESPECT FROM THIS BUNCH OF ANIMALS.
DRING! DRING!
BETTER OPEN UP. THAT'S PROBABLY HER.
YEAH, OKAY.
DRING!

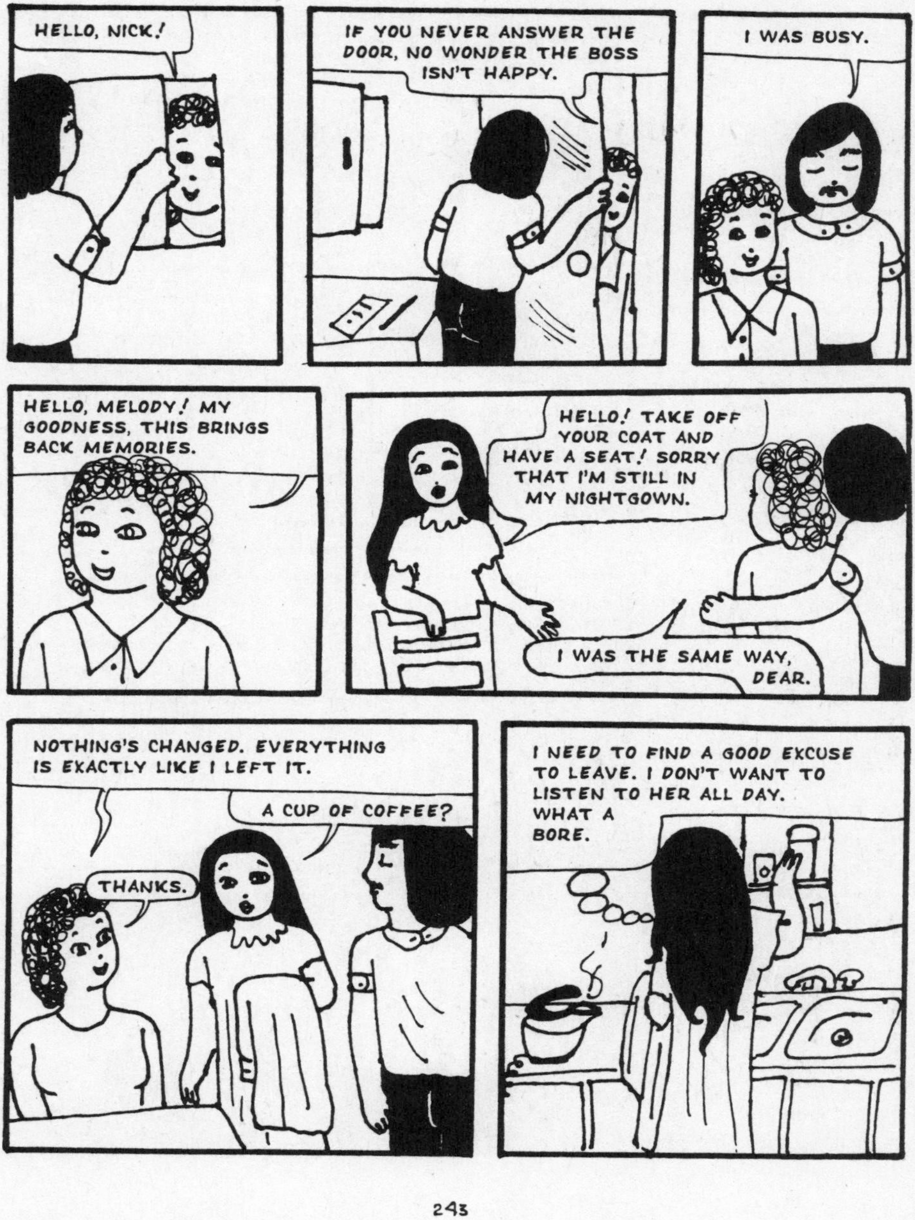
HELLO, NICK!
IF YOU NEVER ANSWER THE DOOR, NO WONDER THE BOSS ISN'T HAPPY.
I WAS BUSY.
HELLO, MELODY! MY GOODNESS, THIS BRINGS BACK MEMORIES.
HELLO! TAKE OFF YOUR COAT AND HAVE A SEAT! SORRY THAT I'M STILL IN MY NIGHTGOWN.
I WAS THE SAME WAY, DEAR.
NOTHING'S CHANGED. EVERYTHING IS EXACTLY LIKE I LEFT IT.
A CUP OF COFFEE?
THANKS.
I NEED TO FIND A GOOD EXCUSE TO LEAVE. I DON'T WANT TO LISTEN TO HER ALL DAY. WHAT A BORE.

GO GET DRESSED, MELODY. YOU'VE GOT ERRANDS TO RUN. I'LL MAKE THE COFFEE.

THANKS.

THAT LITTLE WIFE OF YOURS IS A SWEETHEART... YOU TWO MAKE A REALLY NICE COUPLE.

YEAH, I'M NOT COMPLAINING.

NICK...I'M ON MY WAY. SORRY TO HAVE TO RUN!

OH, NO PROBLEM!

LATER!

SERIOUSLY, I HAVE A HARD TIME PUTTING UP WITH HIS FAMILY...ESPECIALLY SINCE I ALWAYS HAVE TO LIE TO THEM. ANYWAY, I JUST HOPE I FIND SOME WORK TODAY. THAT WOULD MAKE EVERYTHING BETTER.

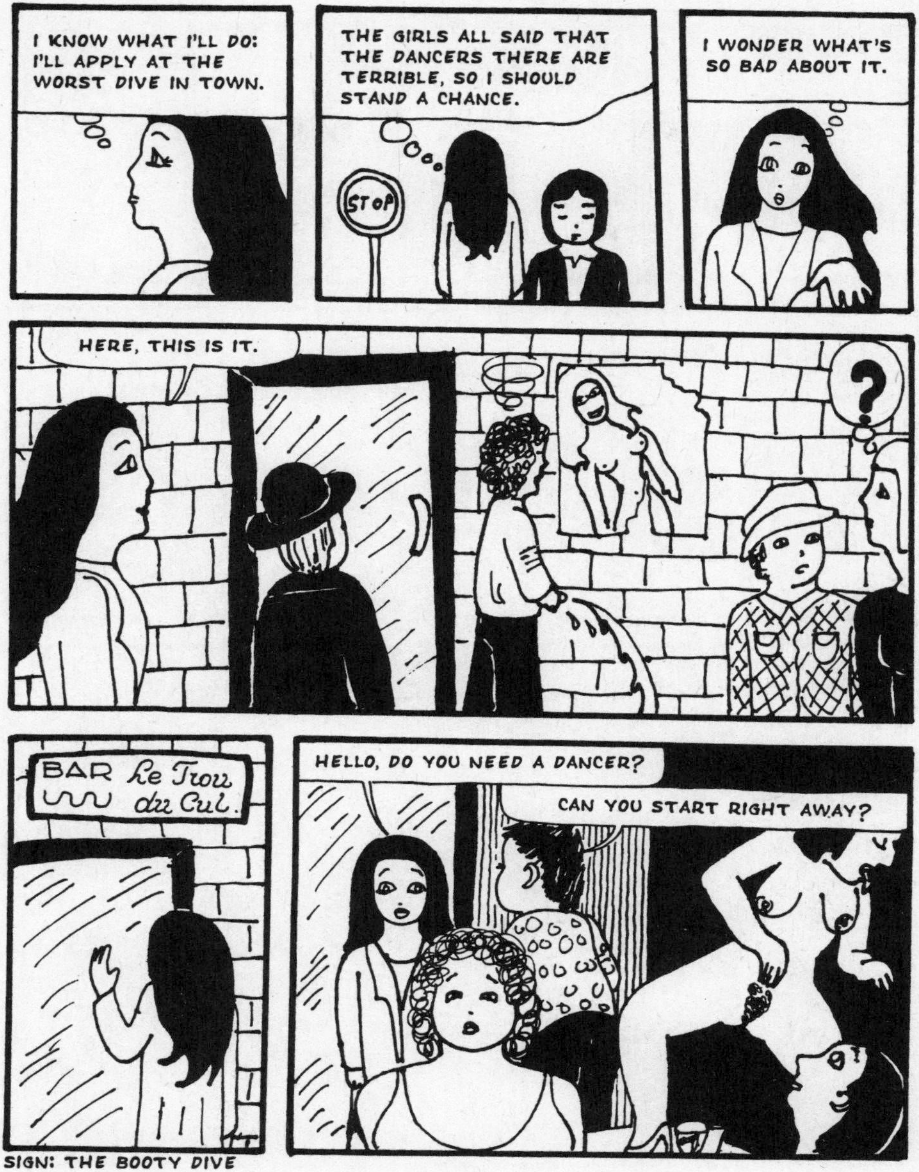
I KNOW WHAT I'LL DO: I'LL APPLY AT THE WORST DIVE IN TOWN.
THE GIRLS ALL SAID THAT THE DANCERS THERE ARE TERRIBLE, SO I SHOULD STAND A CHANCE.
STOP
I WONDER WHAT'S SO BAD ABOUT IT.
HERE, THIS IS IT.
?
BAR Le Trou du Cul.
HELLO, DO YOU NEED A DANCER?
CAN YOU START RIGHT AWAY?

SIGN: THE BOOTY DIVE

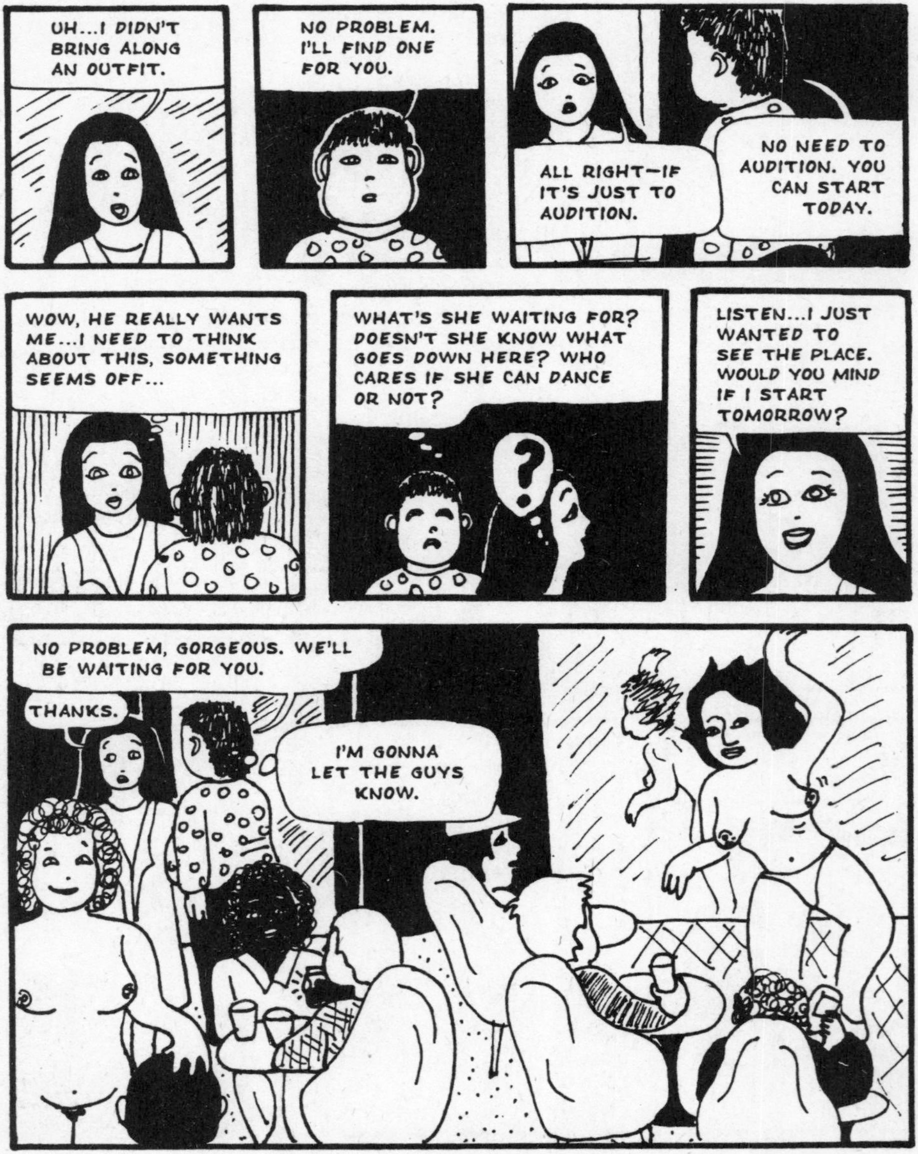
UH...I DIDN'T BRING ALONG AN OUTFIT.
NO PROBLEM. I'LL FIND ONE FOR YOU.
ALL RIGHT—IF IT'S JUST TO AUDITION.
NO NEED TO AUDITION. YOU CAN START TODAY.
WOW, HE REALLY WANTS ME...I NEED TO THINK ABOUT THIS, SOMETHING SEEMS OFF...
WHAT'S SHE WAITING FOR? DOESN'T SHE KNOW WHAT GOES DOWN HERE? WHO CARES IF SHE CAN DANCE OR NOT?
?
LISTEN...I JUST WANTED TO SEE THE PLACE. WOULD YOU MIND IF I START TOMORROW?
NO PROBLEM, GORGEOUS. WE'LL BE WAITING FOR YOU.
THANKS.
I'M GONNA LET THE GUYS KNOW.

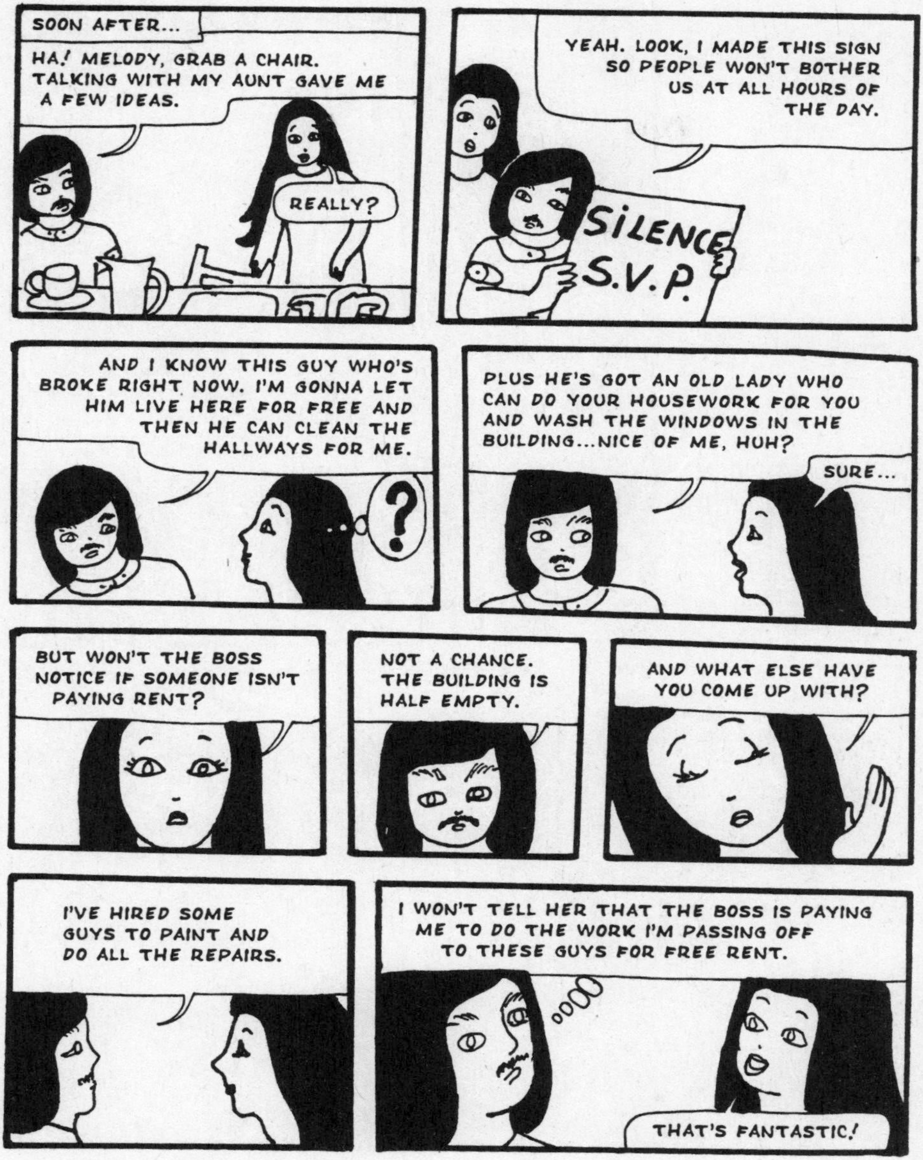
SOON AFTER...
HA! MELODY, GRAB A CHAIR. TALKING WITH MY AUNT GAVE ME A FEW IDEAS.
REALLY?
YEAH. LOOK, I MADE THIS SIGN SO PEOPLE WON'T BOTHER US AT ALL HOURS OF THE DAY.
SILENCE S.V.P.
AND I KNOW THIS GUY WHO'S BROKE RIGHT NOW. I'M GONNA LET HIM LIVE HERE FOR FREE AND THEN HE CAN CLEAN THE HALLWAYS FOR ME.
?
PLUS HE'S GOT AN OLD LADY WHO CAN DO YOUR HOUSEWORK FOR YOU AND WASH THE WINDOWS IN THE BUILDING...NICE OF ME, HUH?
SURE...
BUT WON'T THE BOSS NOTICE IF SOMEONE ISN'T PAYING RENT?
NOT A CHANCE. THE BUILDING IS HALF EMPTY.
AND WHAT ELSE HAVE YOU COME UP WITH?
I'VE HIRED SOME GUYS TO PAINT AND DO ALL THE REPAIRS.
I WON'T TELL HER THAT THE BOSS IS PAYING ME TO DO THE WORK I'M PASSING OFF TO THESE GUYS FOR FREE RENT.
THAT'S FANTASTIC!

AND I'VE FOUND MYSELF A NEW CLUB. I START TOMORROW.

WHERE?

UH...IT'S CALLED THE BOOTY DIVE.

I SEE. YOU'VE DECIDED TO GO FOR THE BIG BUCKS.

WELL, IT'S NONE OF MY BUSINESS... YOU'RE THE ONE WHO'S GOT TO DEAL WITH IT, AFTER ALL.

I HAVE NO IDEA WHAT HE'S TRYING TO TELL ME...

NOW THAT WE WON'T BE WORKING AS HARD, HOW ABOUT WE GO OUT FOR SUPPER?

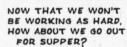

ALL RIGHT.

GONNA HAVE TO EAT WELL TO KEEP UP YOUR STRENGTH.

WE'LL GO HAVE A NICE MEAL AT THE BOILED CRUST... IT'S THE BEST RESTAURANT IN TOWN.

EXCEPT THE LINEUP IS LONG WHEN YOU'RE AT THE END OF IT...

Melody Hits
Bottom

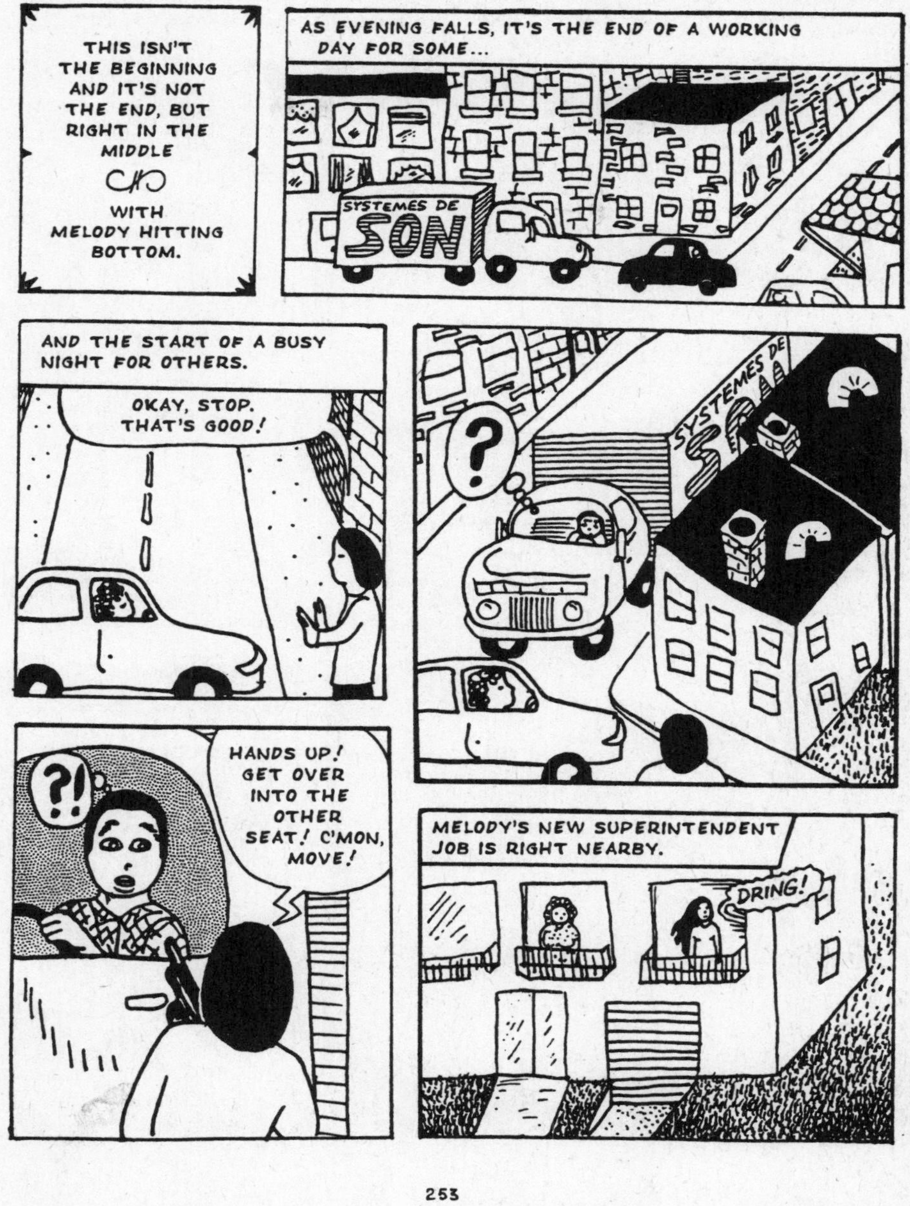
THIS ISN'T THE BEGINNING AND IT'S NOT THE END, BUT RIGHT IN THE MIDDLE
WITH MELODY HITTING BOTTOM.
AS EVENING FALLS, IT'S THE END OF A WORKING DAY FOR SOME...
SYSTEMES DE SON
AND THE START OF A BUSY NIGHT FOR OTHERS.
OKAY, STOP. THAT'S GOOD!
?
SYSTEMES DE
?!
HANDS UP! GET OVER INTO THE OTHER SEAT! C'MON, MOVE!
MELODY'S NEW SUPERINTENDENT JOB IS RIGHT NEARBY.
DRING!

HELLO...? OH, AUNTIE, HI....! YOU'RE COMING TODAY...? THAT'S WONDERFUL!

OKAY...ELIZA AND I'LL BE THERE SOON...

MOM...HEY, MOM!

I WANNA TALK TO MELODY TOO!

GREAT...WE'LL BE WAITING...BYE!

?

THAT'S NOT YOUR AUNT WHO'S COMING, IS IT?

SURE IS!

YOU'RE KIDDING...AFTER EVERYTHING SHE'S DONE... I DON'T KNOW HOW YOU PUT UP WITH HER.

NICK! DRUGS SCARE HER...THAT'S WHY SHE CALLED THE COPS*...SHE WAS JUST TRYING TO PROTECT ME.

NOBODY IN MY FAMILY WOULD EVER MAKE TROUBLE FOR ME...AND THERE'S NO WAY THEY'D TRY TO PUT ME IN JAIL! THEY ACCEPT ME THE WAY I AM.

OH, COME ON, NICK...! THAT'S NOT WHAT SHE WANTED. SHE THOUGHT I WAS IN DANGER...AND I COULD HAVE BEEN, ADMIT IT.

*SEE "MELODY AND THE POLICE."

WHATEVER. I'M NOT WAITING AROUND TO WELCOME HER.

FINE, THEN GO! YOU'LL NEVER UNDER- STAND ANY- BODY WHO'S NOT PART OF YOUR LITTLE WORLD!

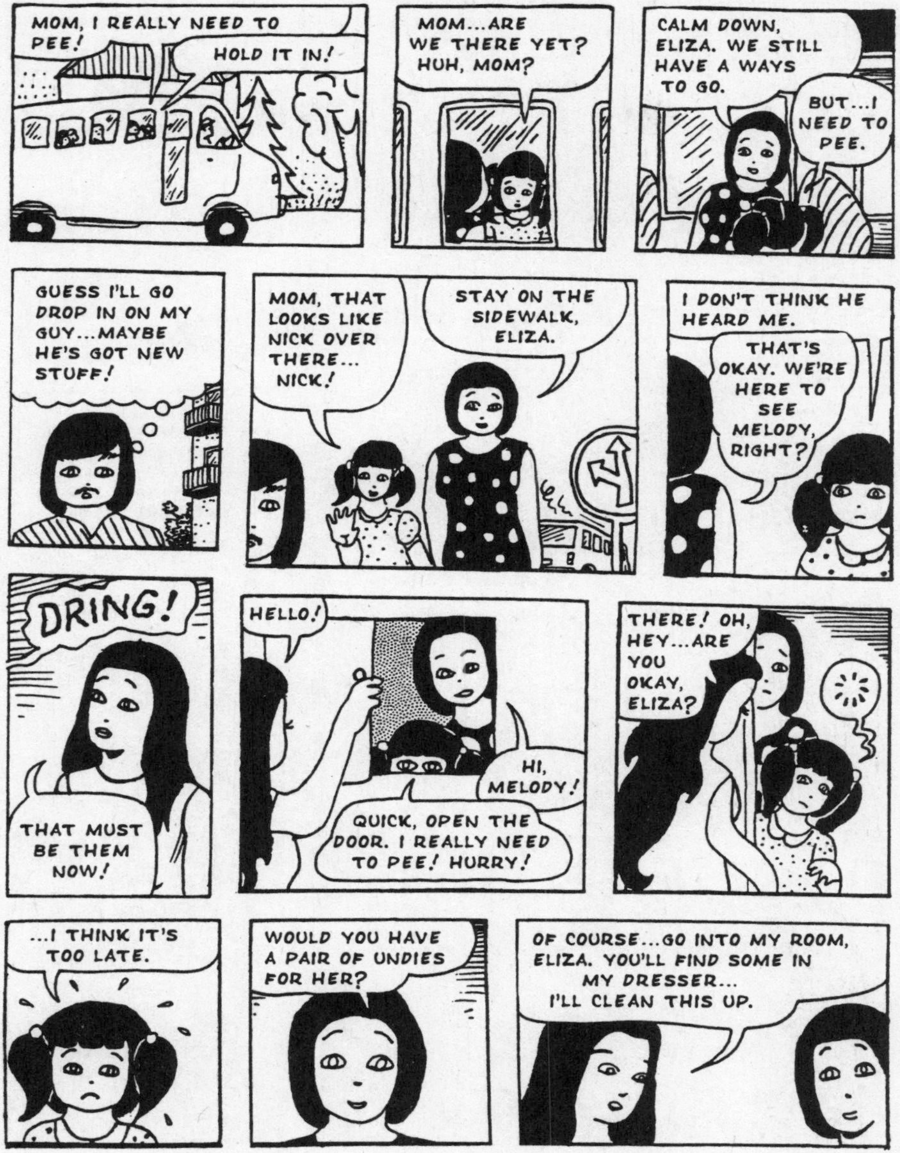

MOM, I REALLY NEED TO PEE!
HOLD IT IN!
MOM...ARE WE THERE YET? HUH, MOM?
CALM DOWN, ELIZA. WE STILL HAVE A WAYS TO GO.
BUT...I NEED TO PEE.
GUESS I'LL GO DROP IN ON MY GUY...MAYBE HE'S GOT NEW STUFF!
MOM, THAT LOOKS LIKE NICK OVER THERE... NICK!
STAY ON THE SIDEWALK, ELIZA.
I DON'T THINK HE HEARD ME.
THAT'S OKAY. WE'RE HERE TO SEE MELODY, RIGHT?
DRING!
THAT MUST BE THEM NOW!
HELLO!
HI, MELODY!
QUICK, OPEN THE DOOR. I REALLY NEED TO PEE! HURRY!
THERE! OH, HEY...ARE YOU OKAY, ELIZA?
...I THINK IT'S TOO LATE.
WOULD YOU HAVE A PAIR OF UNDIES FOR HER?
OF COURSE...GO INTO MY ROOM, ELIZA. YOU'LL FIND SOME IN MY DRESSER... I'LL CLEAN THIS UP.

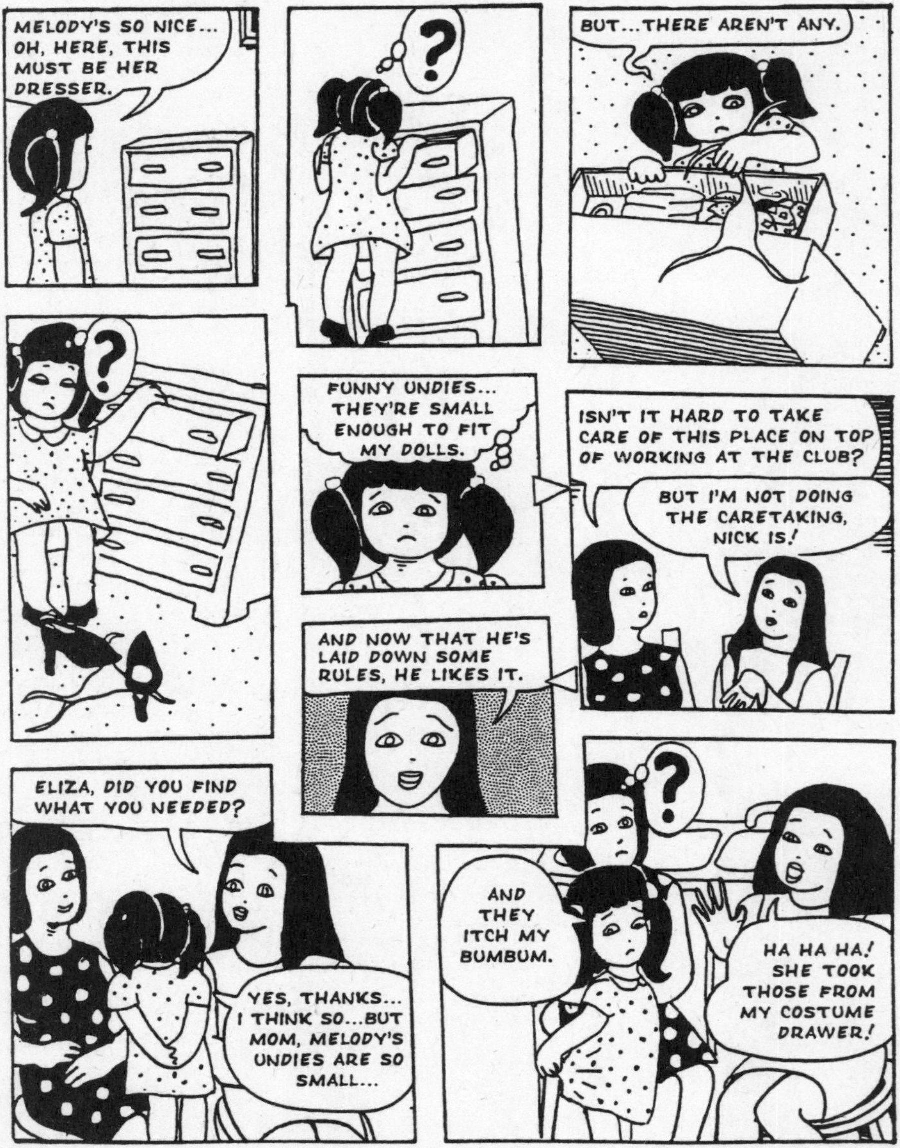
MELODY'S SO NICE... OH, HERE, THIS MUST BE HER DRESSER.
?
BUT...THERE AREN'T ANY.
?
FUNNY UNDIES... THEY'RE SMALL ENOUGH TO FIT MY DOLLS.
ISN'T IT HARD TO TAKE CARE OF THIS PLACE ON TOP OF WORKING AT THE CLUB?
BUT I'M NOT DOING THE CARETAKING, NICK IS!
AND NOW THAT HE'S LAID DOWN SOME RULES, HE LIKES IT.
ELIZA, DID YOU FIND WHAT YOU NEEDED?
YES, THANKS... I THINK SO...BUT MOM, MELODY'S UNDIES ARE SO SMALL...
?
AND THEY ITCH MY BUMBUM.
HA HA HA! SHE TOOK THOSE FROM MY COSTUME DRAWER!

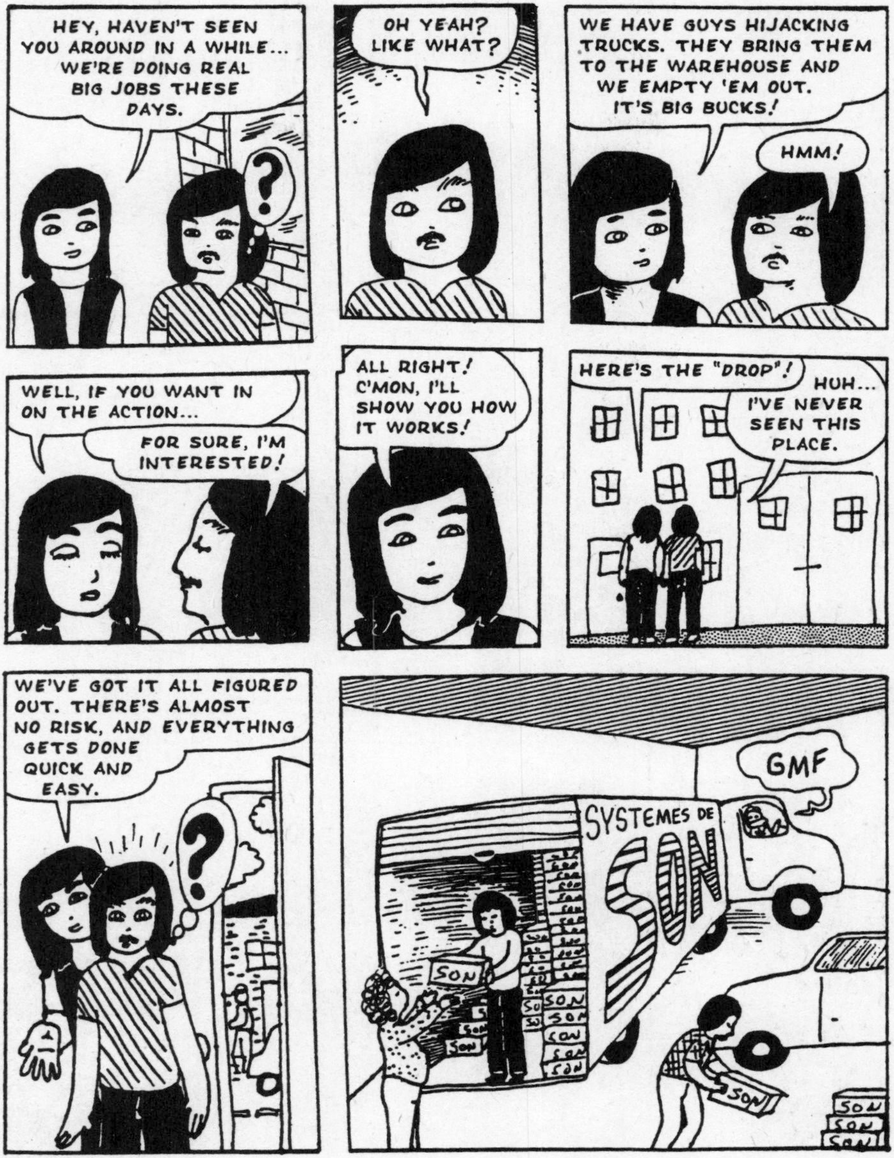
HEY, HAVEN'T SEEN YOU AROUND IN A WHILE... WE'RE DOING REAL BIG JOBS THESE DAYS.
?
OH YEAH? LIKE WHAT?
WE HAVE GUYS HIJACKING TRUCKS. THEY BRING THEM TO THE WAREHOUSE AND WE EMPTY 'EM OUT. IT'S BIG BUCKS!
HMM!
WELL, IF YOU WANT IN ON THE ACTION...
FOR SURE, I'M INTERESTED!
ALL RIGHT! C'MON, I'LL SHOW YOU HOW IT WORKS!
HERE'S THE "DROP"!
HUH... I'VE NEVER SEEN THIS PLACE.
WE'VE GOT IT ALL FIGURED OUT. THERE'S ALMOST NO RISK, AND EVERYTHING GETS DONE QUICK AND EASY.
?
GMF
SYSTEMES DE SON
SON

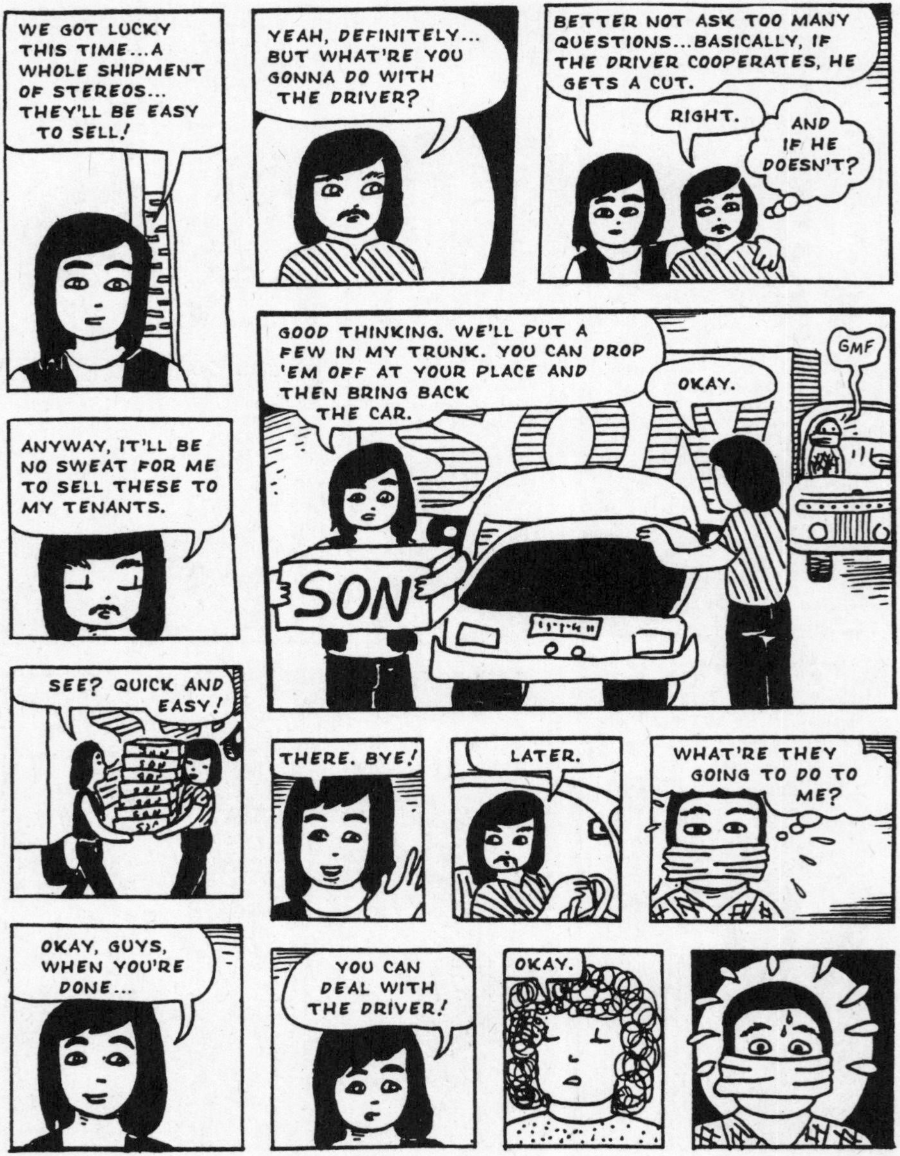

WE GOT LUCKY THIS TIME...A WHOLE SHIPMENT OF STEREOS... THEY'LL BE EASY TO SELL!
YEAH, DEFINITELY... BUT WHAT'RE YOU GONNA DO WITH THE DRIVER?
BETTER NOT ASK TOO MANY QUESTIONS...BASICALLY, IF THE DRIVER COOPERATES, HE GETS A CUT.
RIGHT.
AND IF HE DOESN'T?
ANYWAY, IT'LL BE NO SWEAT FOR ME TO SELL THESE TO MY TENANTS.
GOOD THINKING. WE'LL PUT A FEW IN MY TRUNK. YOU CAN DROP 'EM OFF AT YOUR PLACE AND THEN BRING BACK THE CAR.
OKAY.
GMF
SON
SEE? QUICK AND EASY!
THERE. BYE!
LATER.
WHAT'RE THEY GOING TO DO TO ME?
OKAY, GUYS, WHEN YOU'RE DONE...
YOU CAN DEAL WITH THE DRIVER!
OKAY.

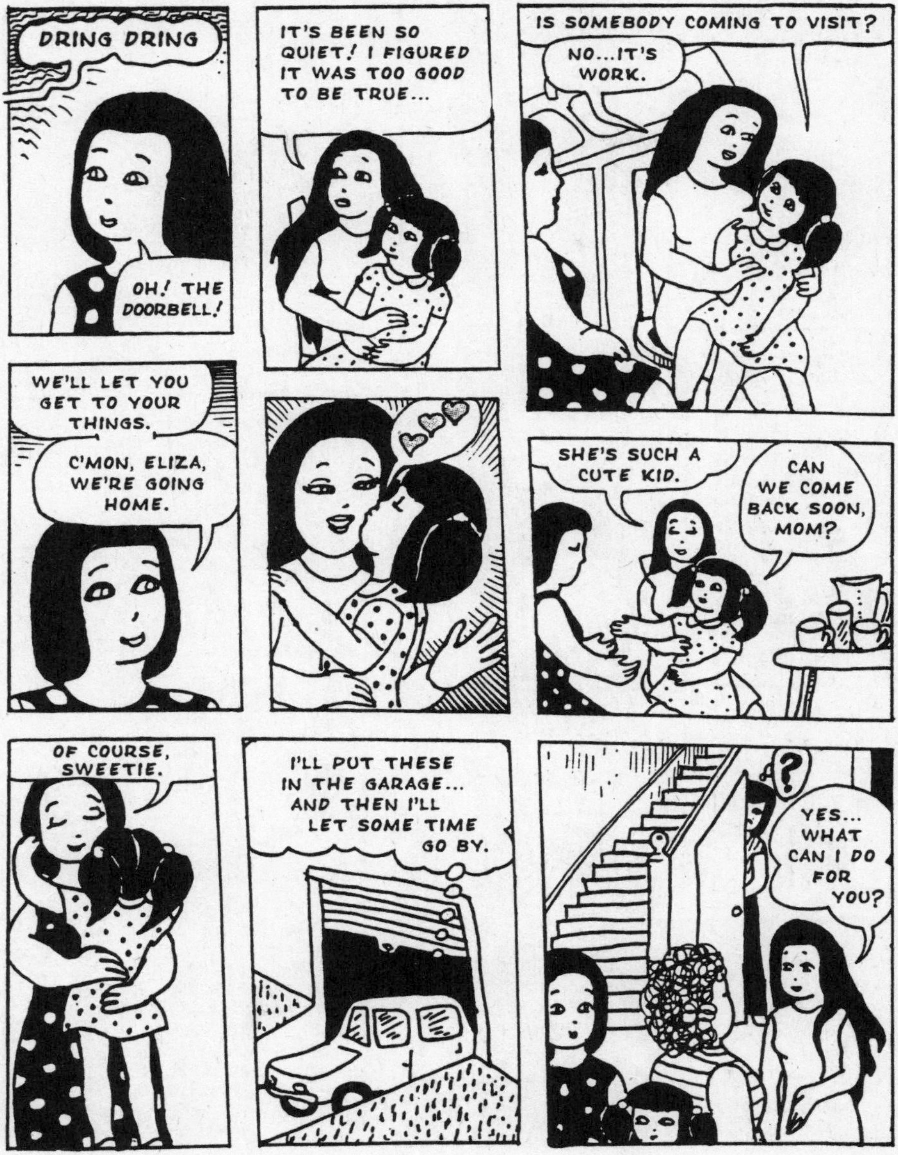
DRING DRING
OH! THE DOORBELL!
IT'S BEEN SO QUIET! I FIGURED IT WAS TOO GOOD TO BE TRUE...
IS SOMEBODY COMING TO VISIT?
NO...IT'S WORK.
WE'LL LET YOU GET TO YOUR THINGS.
C'MON, ELIZA, WE'RE GOING HOME.
SHE'S SUCH A CUTE KID.
CAN WE COME BACK SOON, MOM?
OF COURSE, SWEETIE.
I'LL PUT THESE IN THE GARAGE... AND THEN I'LL LET SOME TIME GO BY.
?
YES... WHAT CAN I DO FOR YOU?

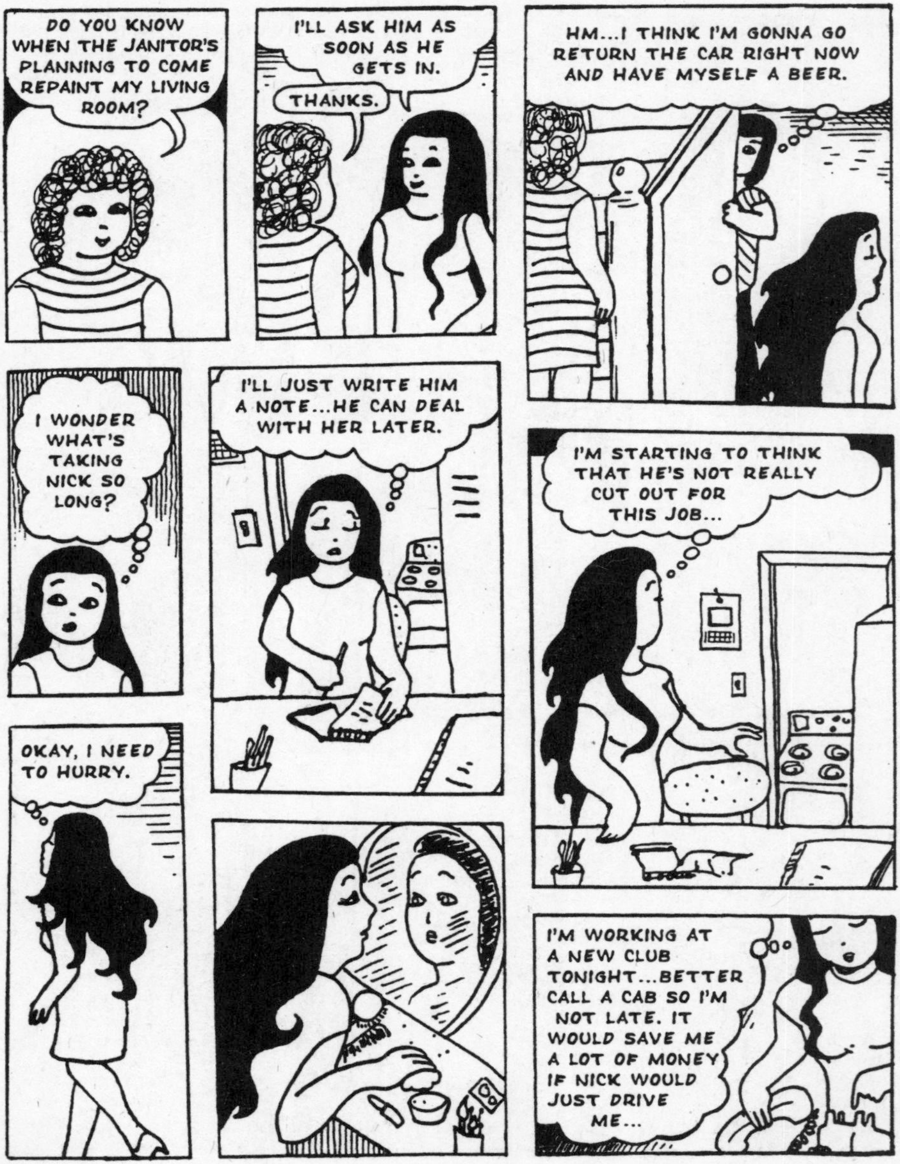
DO YOU KNOW WHEN THE JANITOR'S PLANNING TO COME REPAINT MY LIVING ROOM?
I'LL ASK HIM AS SOON AS HE GETS IN.
THANKS.
HM...I THINK I'M GONNA GO RETURN THE CAR RIGHT NOW AND HAVE MYSELF A BEER.
I WONDER WHAT'S TAKING NICK SO LONG?
I'LL JUST WRITE HIM A NOTE...HE CAN DEAL WITH HER LATER.
I'M STARTING TO THINK THAT HE'S NOT REALLY CUT OUT FOR THIS JOB...
OKAY, I NEED TO HURRY.
I'M WORKING AT A NEW CLUB TONIGHT...BETTER CALL A CAB SO I'M NOT LATE. IT WOULD SAVE ME A LOT OF MONEY IF NICK WOULD JUST DRIVE ME...

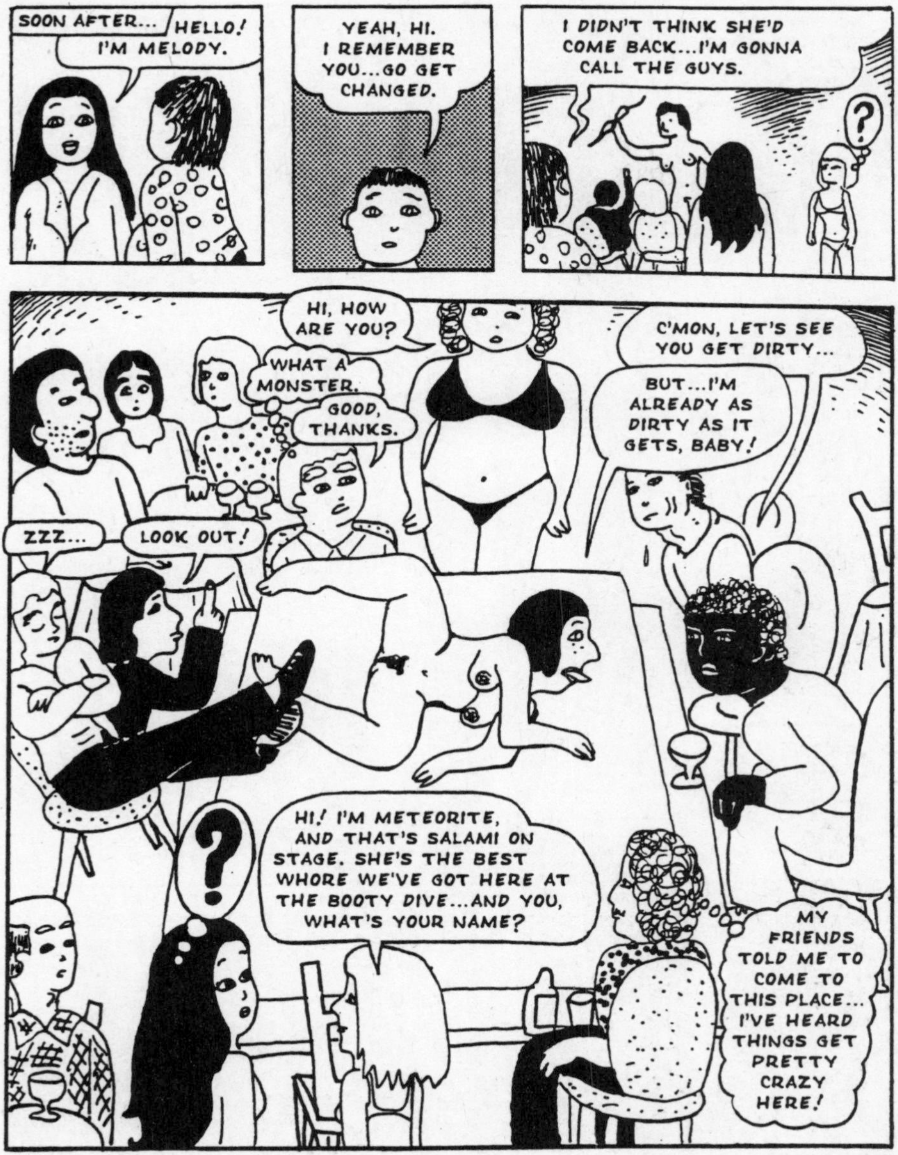
SOON AFTER...
HELLO! I'M MELODY.
YEAH, HI. I REMEMBER YOU...GO GET CHANGED.
I DIDN'T THINK SHE'D COME BACK...I'M GONNA CALL THE GUYS.
?
HI, HOW ARE YOU?
WHAT A MONSTER.
GOOD, THANKS.
C'MON, LET'S SEE YOU GET DIRTY...
BUT...I'M ALREADY AS DIRTY AS IT GETS, BABY!
ZZZ...
LOOK OUT!
?
HI! I'M METEORITE, AND THAT'S SALAMI ON STAGE. SHE'S THE BEST WHORE WE'VE GOT HERE AT THE BOOTY DIVE...AND YOU, WHAT'S YOUR NAME?
MY FRIENDS TOLD ME TO COME TO THIS PLACE... I'VE HEARD THINGS GET PRETTY CRAZY HERE!

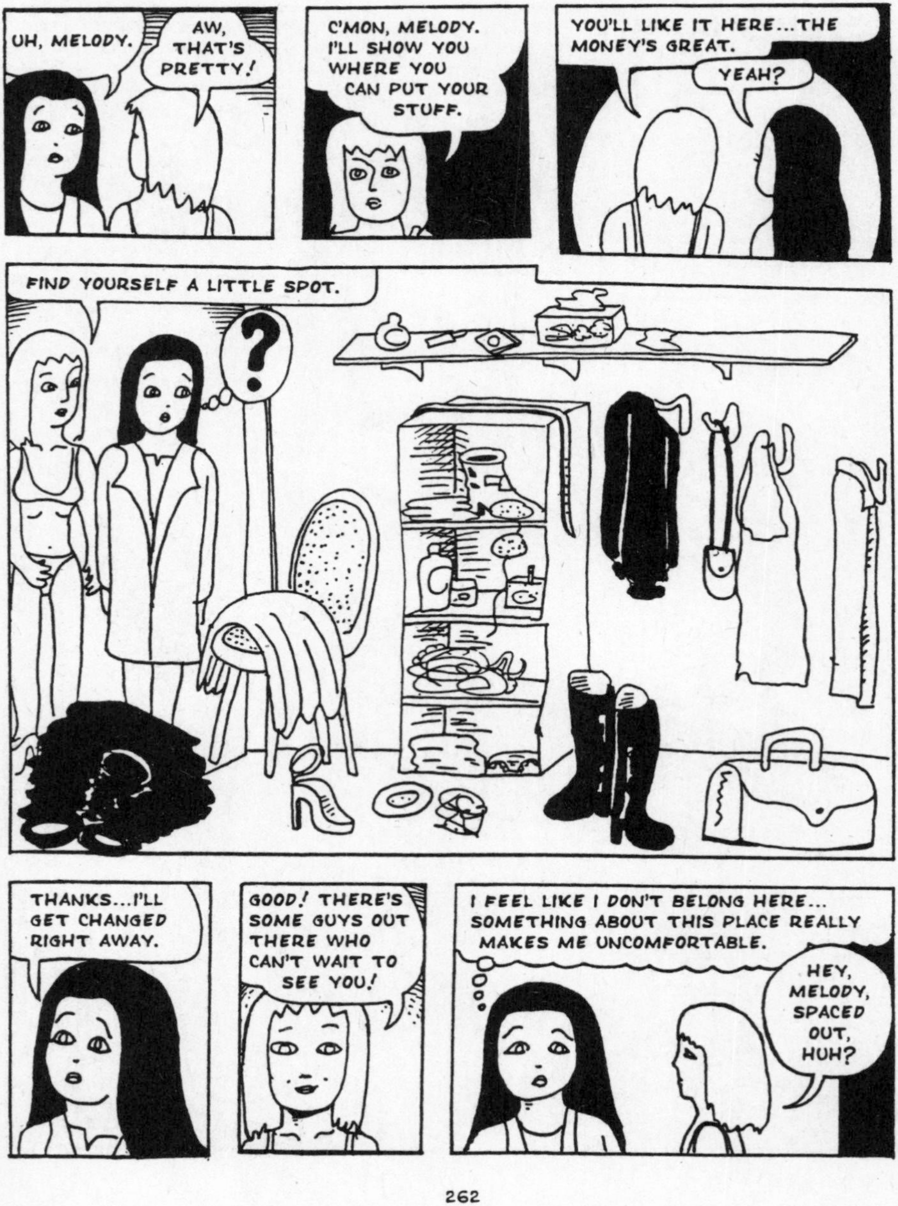
UH, MELODY.
AW, THAT'S PRETTY!
C'MON, MELODY. I'LL SHOW YOU WHERE YOU CAN PUT YOUR STUFF.
YOU'LL LIKE IT HERE...THE MONEY'S GREAT.
YEAH?
FIND YOURSELF A LITTLE SPOT.
?
THANKS...I'LL GET CHANGED RIGHT AWAY.
GOOD! THERE'S SOME GUYS OUT THERE WHO CAN'T WAIT TO SEE YOU!
I FEEL LIKE I DON'T BELONG HERE... SOMETHING ABOUT THIS PLACE REALLY MAKES ME UNCOMFORTABLE.
HEY, MELODY, SPACED OUT, HUH?

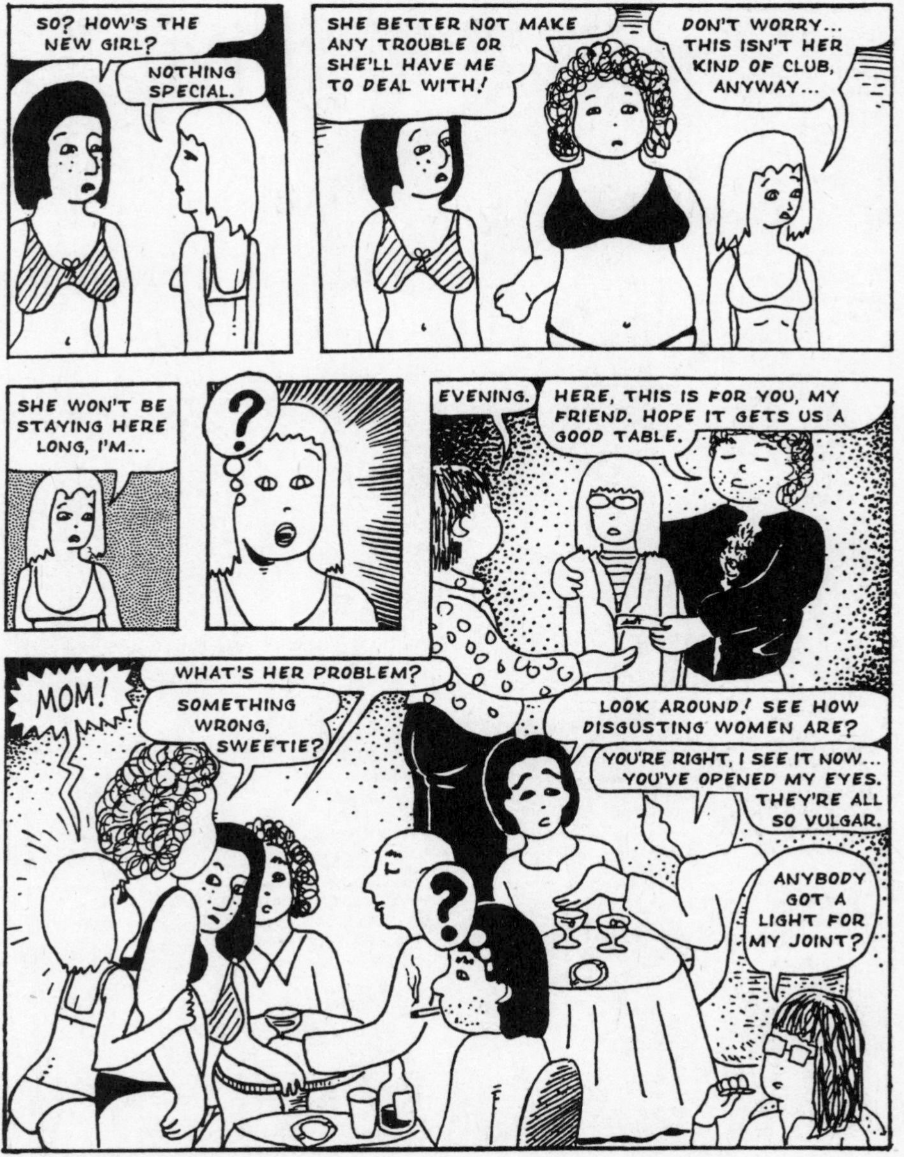
SO? HOW'S THE NEW GIRL?
NOTHING SPECIAL.
SHE BETTER NOT MAKE ANY TROUBLE OR SHE'LL HAVE ME TO DEAL WITH!
DON'T WORRY... THIS ISN'T HER KIND OF CLUB, ANYWAY...
SHE WON'T BE STAYING HERE LONG, I'M...
?
EVENING.
HERE, THIS IS FOR YOU, MY FRIEND. HOPE IT GETS US A GOOD TABLE.
MOM!
WHAT'S HER PROBLEM?
SOMETHING WRONG, SWEETIE?
LOOK AROUND! SEE HOW DISGUSTING WOMEN ARE?
YOU'RE RIGHT, I SEE IT NOW... YOU'VE OPENED MY EYES. THEY'RE ALL SO VULGAR.
?
ANYBODY GOT A LIGHT FOR MY JOINT?

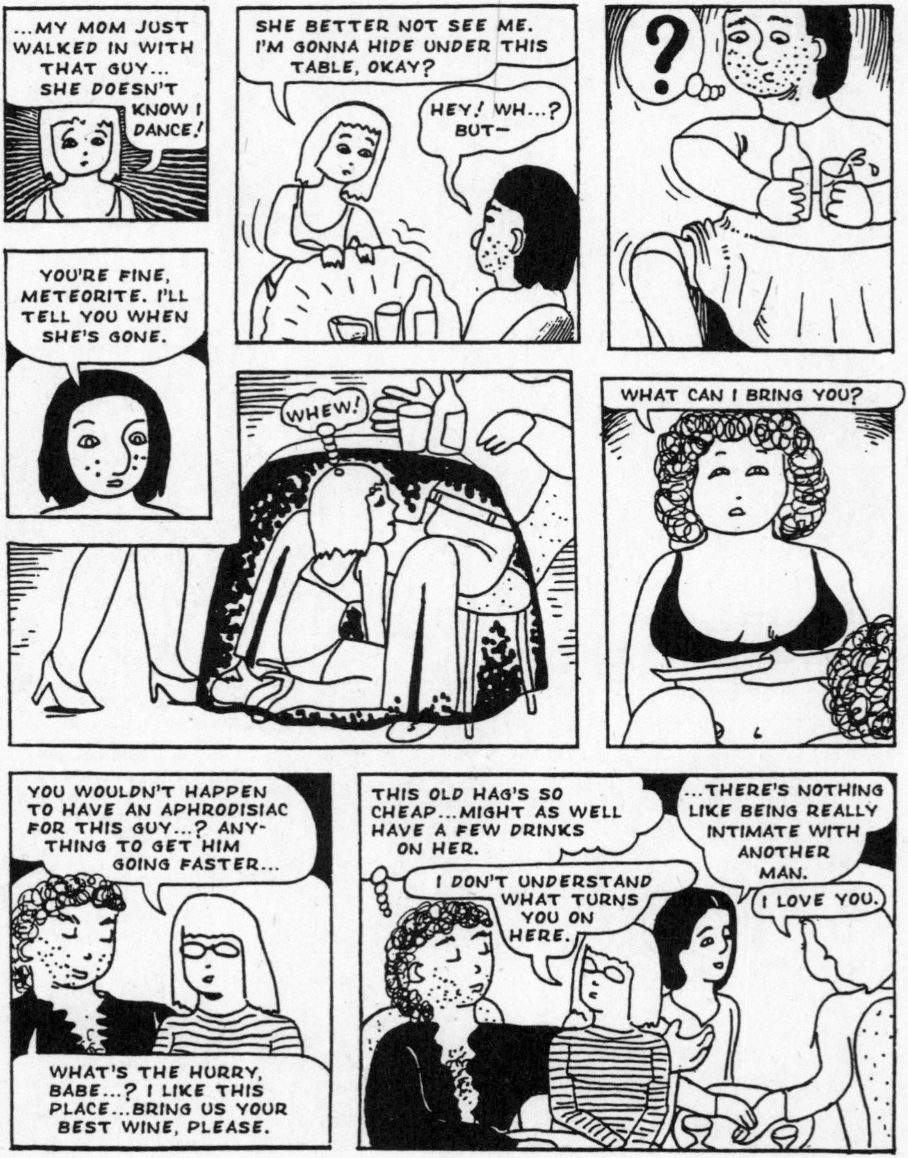
...MY MOM JUST WALKED IN WITH THAT GUY... SHE DOESN'T KNOW I DANCE!
SHE BETTER NOT SEE ME. I'M GONNA HIDE UNDER THIS TABLE, OKAY?
HEY! WH...? BUT–
?
YOU'RE FINE, METEORITE. I'LL TELL YOU WHEN SHE'S GONE.
WHEW!
WHAT CAN I BRING YOU?
YOU WOULDN'T HAPPEN TO HAVE AN APHRODISIAC FOR THIS GUY...? ANYTHING TO GET HIM GOING FASTER...
WHAT'S THE HURRY, BABE...? I LIKE THIS PLACE...BRING US YOUR BEST WINE, PLEASE.
THIS OLD HAG'S SO CHEAP...MIGHT AS WELL HAVE A FEW DRINKS ON HER.
I DON'T UNDERSTAND WHAT TURNS YOU ON HERE.
...THERE'S NOTHING LIKE BEING REALLY INTIMATE WITH ANOTHER MAN.
I LOVE YOU.

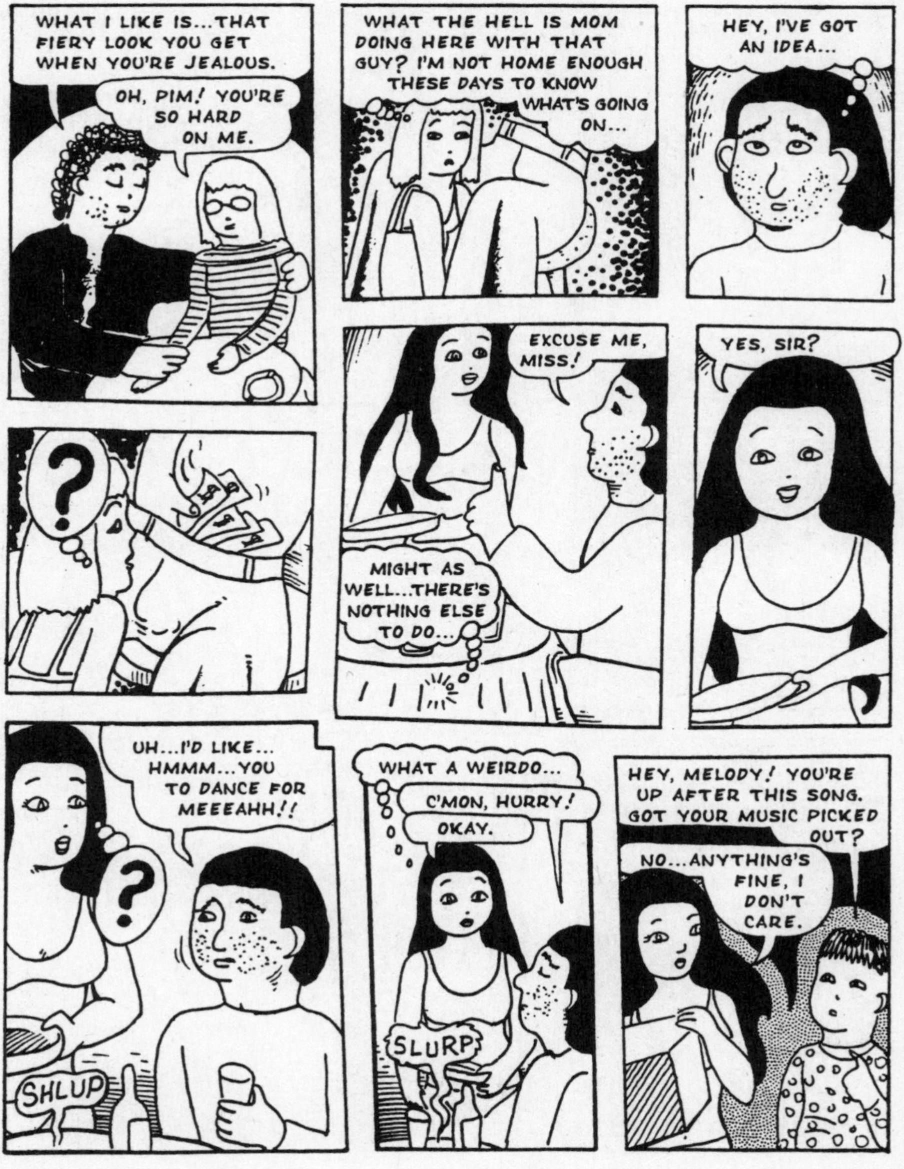
WHAT I LIKE IS...THAT FIERY LOOK YOU GET WHEN YOU'RE JEALOUS.
OH, PIM! YOU'RE SO HARD ON ME.
WHAT THE HELL IS MOM DOING HERE WITH THAT GUY? I'M NOT HOME ENOUGH THESE DAYS TO KNOW WHAT'S GOING ON...
HEY, I'VE GOT AN IDEA...
?
EXCUSE ME, MISS!
MIGHT AS WELL...THERE'S NOTHING ELSE TO DO...
YES, SIR?
UH...I'D LIKE... HMMM...YOU TO DANCE FOR MEEEAHH!!
?
SHLUP
WHAT A WEIRDO...
C'MON, HURRY!
OKAY.
SLURP
HEY, MELODY! YOU'RE UP AFTER THIS SONG. GOT YOUR MUSIC PICKED OUT?
NO...ANYTHING'S FINE, I DON'T CARE.

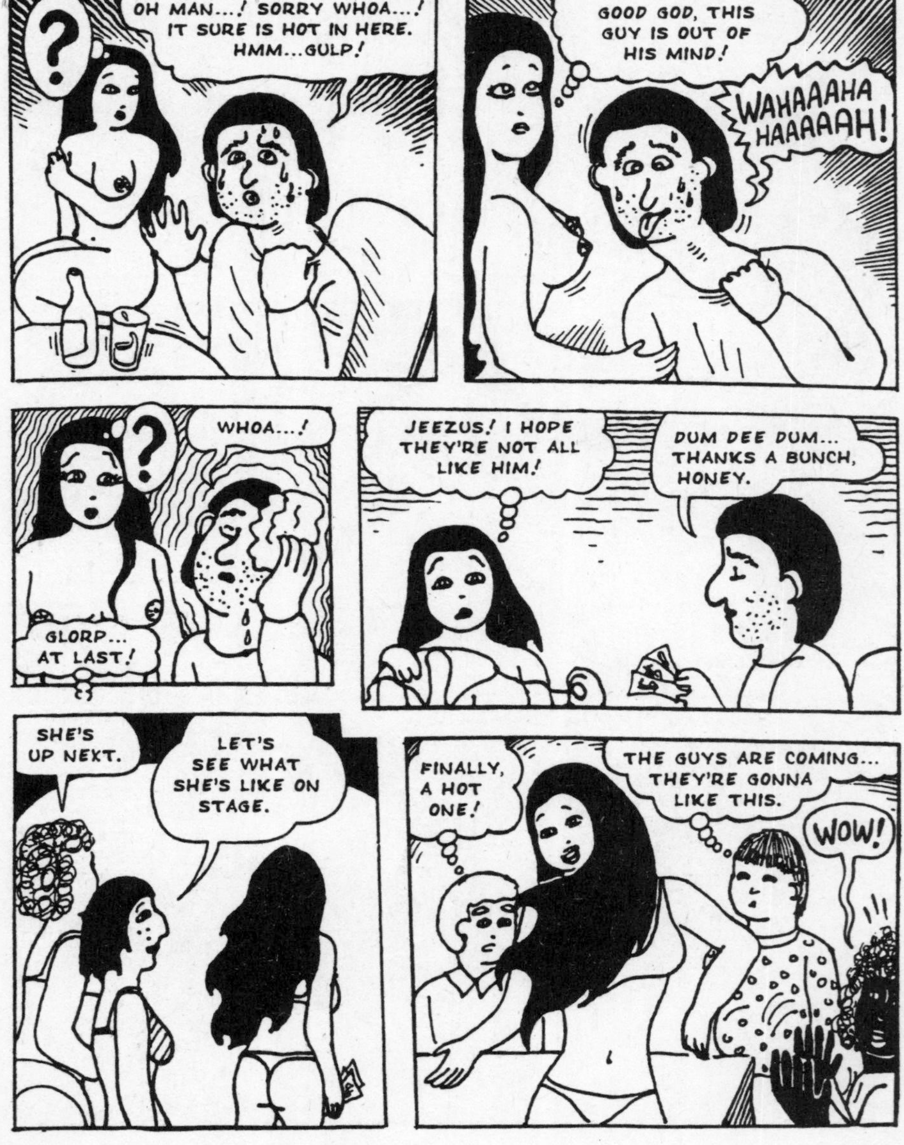
?
OH MAN...! SORRY WHOA...! IT SURE IS HOT IN HERE. HMM...GULP!
GOOD GOD, THIS GUY IS OUT OF HIS MIND!
WAHAAAHA HAAAAAH!
?
WHOA...!
GLORP... AT LAST!
JEEZUS! I HOPE THEY'RE NOT ALL LIKE HIM!
DUM DEE DUM... THANKS A BUNCH, HONEY.
SHE'S UP NEXT.
LET'S SEE WHAT SHE'S LIKE ON STAGE.
FINALLY, A HOT ONE!
THE GUYS ARE COMING... THEY'RE GONNA LIKE THIS.
WOW!

NOW THAT YOU'RE NICE AND TURNED ON, LET'S GO.
ALL RIGHT... HIC... YOU WON'T REGRET IT.
...THE LOVE OF A WOMAN IS NOTHING COMPARED TO BROTHERLY LOVE... AND I LOVE YOU MORE THAN A BROTHER...
METEORITE... YOUR MOM'S GONE. YOU CAN COME OUT.
FINALLY!
THANKS.
GOOD NIGHT, FOLKS.
THE CUSTOMERS LIKE ME, BUT I STILL CAN'T STAND THE ATMOSPHERE HERE... I FEEL SICK TO MY STOMACH...
LOOK AT THAT ASS!
I HOPE THIS ONE PUTS OUT.
I DUNNO, I HAVEN'T TRIED. YOU'RE BETTER AT THAT KIND OF THING.
C'MON, I WANNA SEE YOU GET DIRTY!

BOY, PEOPLE SURE CAN BE CRUDE!
?
?
HAAAh
HAAAh
WHAT'S SHE FREAKING OUT ABOUT?
?
?
?
?
?
?
WHAT'S WRONG?
OH LORD! THERE'S SPIDERS HERE!
HA HA HA! JUST WAIT TILL SHE'S FACE TO FACE WITH MY BIG ANACONDA, YEAH!
I DIDN'T KNOW THAT SPIDERS STAY UP THIS LATE...
MAYBE IT'S A NOCTURNAL SPIDER?

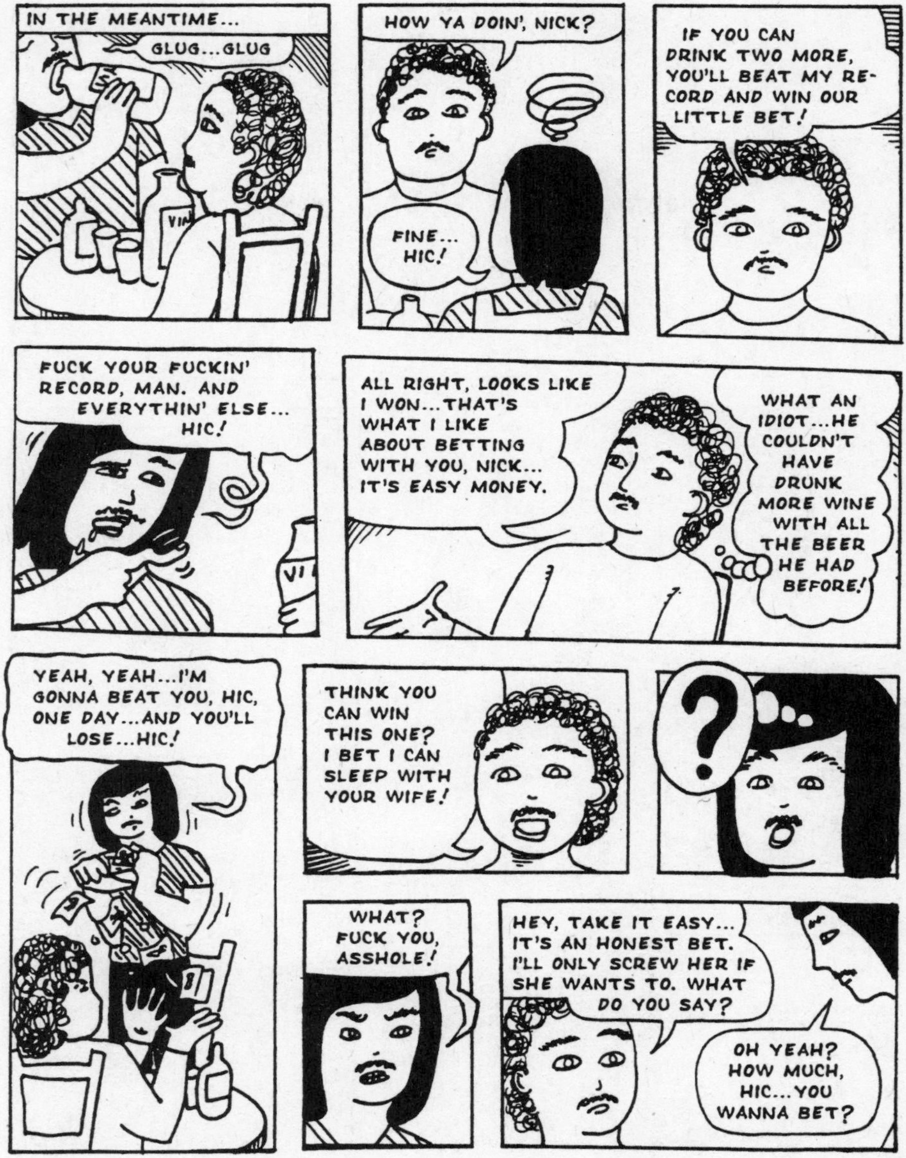
IN THE MEANTIME...
GLUG...GLUG
HOW YA DOIN', NICK?
FINE... HIC!
IF YOU CAN DRINK TWO MORE, YOU'LL BEAT MY RECORD AND WIN OUR LITTLE BET!
FUCK YOUR FUCKIN' RECORD, MAN. AND EVERYTHIN' ELSE... HIC!
ALL RIGHT, LOOKS LIKE I WON...THAT'S WHAT I LIKE ABOUT BETTING WITH YOU, NICK... IT'S EASY MONEY.
WHAT AN IDIOT...HE COULDN'T HAVE DRUNK MORE WINE WITH ALL THE BEER HE HAD BEFORE!
YEAH, YEAH...I'M GONNA BEAT YOU, HIC, ONE DAY...AND YOU'LL LOSE...HIC!
THINK YOU CAN WIN THIS ONE? I BET I CAN SLEEP WITH YOUR WIFE!
?
WHAT? FUCK YOU, ASSHOLE!
HEY, TAKE IT EASY... IT'S AN HONEST BET. I'LL ONLY SCREW HER IF SHE WANTS TO. WHAT DO YOU SAY?
OH YEAH? HOW MUCH, HIC...YOU WANNA BET?

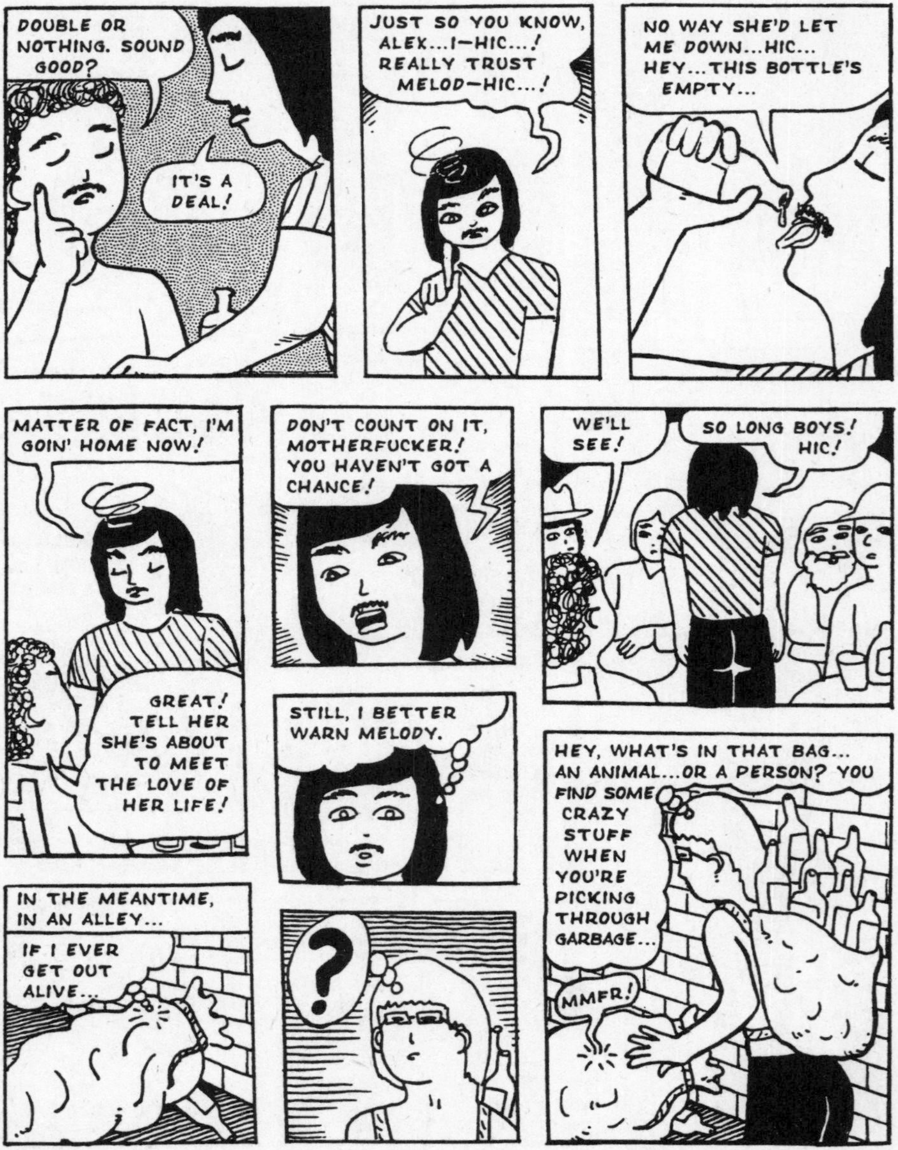
DOUBLE OR NOTHING. SOUND GOOD?
IT'S A DEAL!
JUST SO YOU KNOW, ALEX...I—HIC...! REALLY TRUST MELOD—HIC...!
NO WAY SHE'D LET ME DOWN...HIC... HEY...THIS BOTTLE'S EMPTY...
MATTER OF FACT, I'M GOIN' HOME NOW!
GREAT! TELL HER SHE'S ABOUT TO MEET THE LOVE OF HER LIFE!
DON'T COUNT ON IT, MOTHERFUCKER! YOU HAVEN'T GOT A CHANCE!
STILL, I BETTER WARN MELODY.
WE'LL SEE!
SO LONG BOYS! HIC!
IN THE MEANTIME, IN AN ALLEY...
IF I EVER GET OUT ALIVE...
?
HEY, WHAT'S IN THAT BAG... AN ANIMAL...OR A PERSON? YOU FIND SOME CRAZY STUFF WHEN YOU'RE PICKING THROUGH GARBAGE...
MMFR!

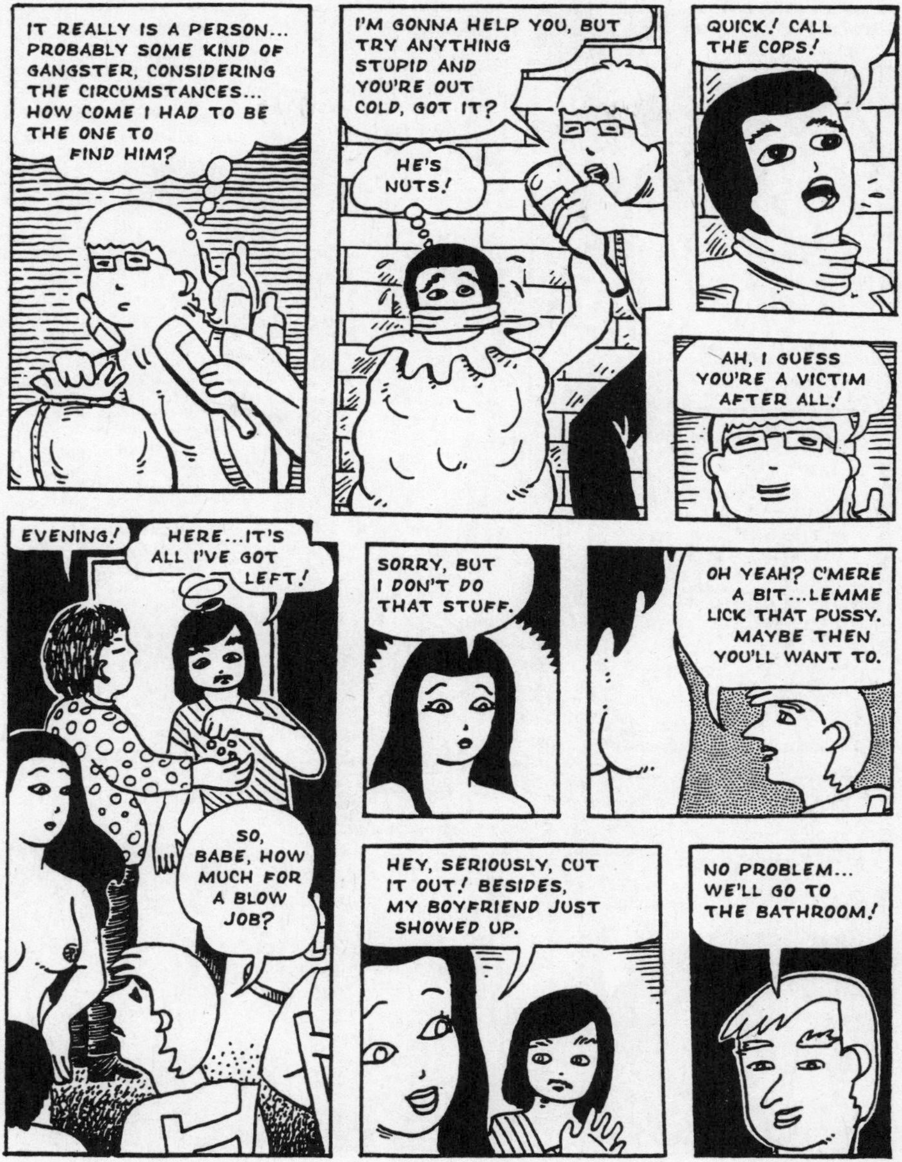
IT REALLY IS A PERSON... PROBABLY SOME KIND OF GANGSTER, CONSIDERING THE CIRCUMSTANCES... HOW COME I HAD TO BE THE ONE TO FIND HIM?
I'M GONNA HELP YOU, BUT TRY ANYTHING STUPID AND YOU'RE OUT COLD, GOT IT?
HE'S NUTS!
QUICK! CALL THE COPS!
AH, I GUESS YOU'RE A VICTIM AFTER ALL!
EVENING!
HERE...IT'S ALL I'VE GOT LEFT!
SO, BABE, HOW MUCH FOR A BLOW JOB?
SORRY, BUT I DON'T DO THAT STUFF.
OH YEAH? C'MERE A BIT...LEMME LICK THAT PUSSY. MAYBE THEN YOU'LL WANT TO.
HEY, SERIOUSLY, CUT IT OUT! BESIDES, MY BOYFRIEND JUST SHOWED UP.
NO PROBLEM... WE'LL GO TO THE BATHROOM!

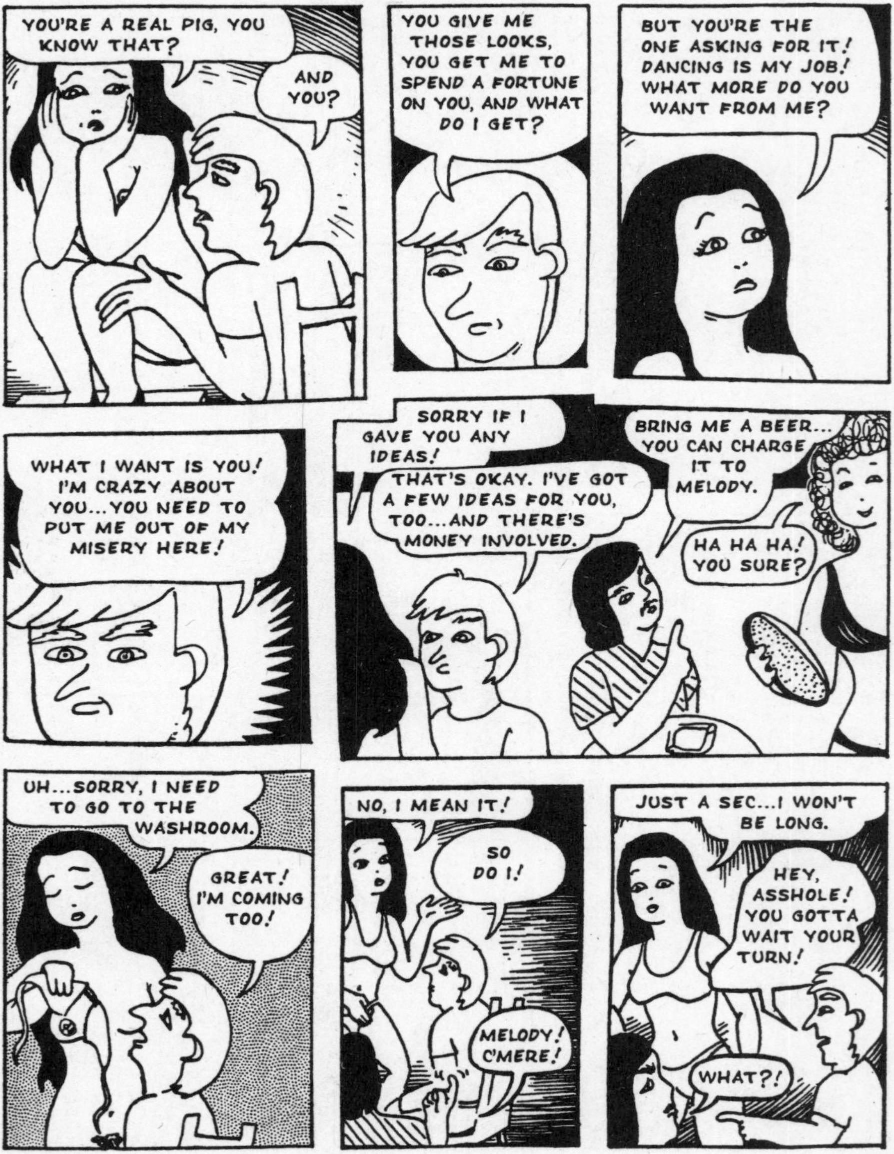
YOU'RE A REAL PIG, YOU KNOW THAT?
AND YOU?
YOU GIVE ME THOSE LOOKS, YOU GET ME TO SPEND A FORTUNE ON YOU, AND WHAT DO I GET?
BUT YOU'RE THE ONE ASKING FOR IT! DANCING IS MY JOB! WHAT MORE DO YOU WANT FROM ME?
WHAT I WANT IS YOU! I'M CRAZY ABOUT YOU...YOU NEED TO PUT ME OUT OF MY MISERY HERE!
SORRY IF I GAVE YOU ANY IDEAS!
THAT'S OKAY. I'VE GOT A FEW IDEAS FOR YOU, TOO...AND THERE'S MONEY INVOLVED.
BRING ME A BEER... YOU CAN CHARGE IT TO MELODY.
HA HA HA! YOU SURE?
UH...SORRY, I NEED TO GO TO THE WASHROOM.
GREAT! I'M COMING TOO!
NO, I MEAN IT!
SO DO I!
MELODY! C'MERE!
JUST A SEC...I WON'T BE LONG.
HEY, ASSHOLE! YOU GOTTA WAIT YOUR TURN!
WHAT?!

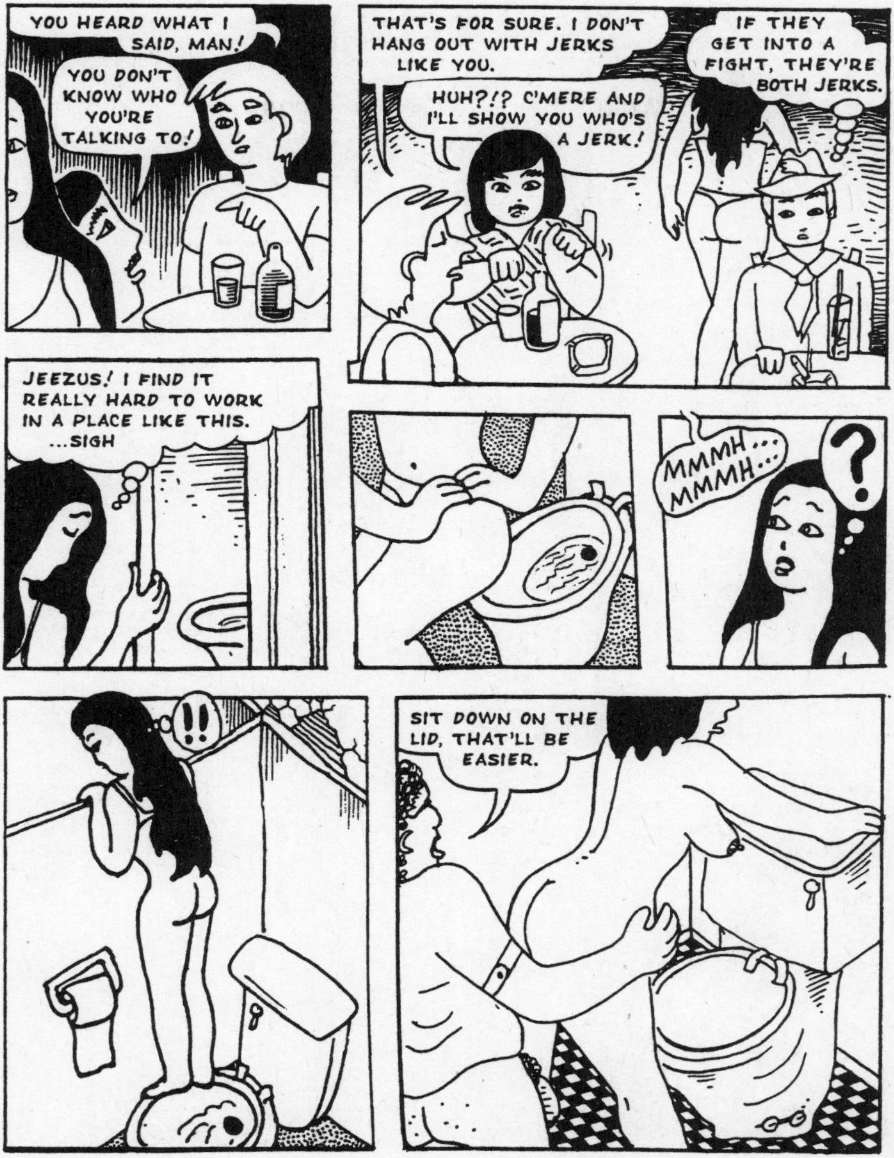
YOU HEARD WHAT I SAID, MAN!
YOU DON'T KNOW WHO YOU'RE TALKING TO!
THAT'S FOR SURE. I DON'T HANG OUT WITH JERKS LIKE YOU.
HUH?!? C'MERE AND I'LL SHOW YOU WHO'S A JERK!
IF THEY GET INTO A FIGHT, THEY'RE BOTH JERKS.
JEEZUS! I FIND IT REALLY HARD TO WORK IN A PLACE LIKE THIS. ...SIGH
MMMH... MMMH...
?
!!
SIT DOWN ON THE LID, THAT'LL BE EASIER.

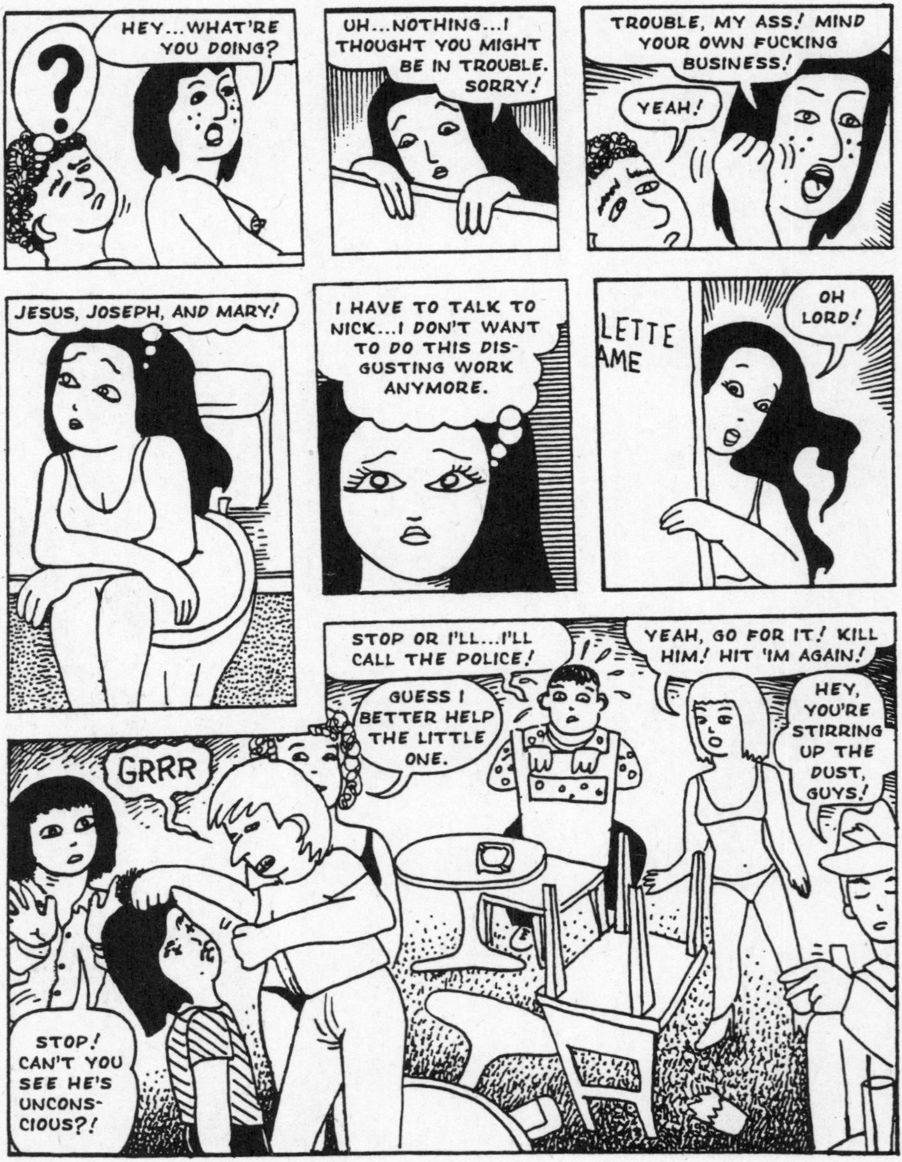
?
HEY...WHAT'RE YOU DOING?
UH...NOTHING...I THOUGHT YOU MIGHT BE IN TROUBLE. SORRY!
TROUBLE, MY ASS! MIND YOUR OWN FUCKING BUSINESS!
YEAH!
JESUS, JOSEPH, AND MARY!
I HAVE TO TALK TO NICK...I DON'T WANT TO DO THIS DISGUSTING WORK ANYMORE.
LETTE
AME
OH LORD!
STOP OR I'LL...I'LL CALL THE POLICE!
YEAH, GO FOR IT! KILL HIM! HIT 'IM AGAIN!
GRRR
GUESS I BETTER HELP THE LITTLE ONE.
HEY, YOU'RE STIRRING UP THE DUST, GUYS!
STOP! CAN'T YOU SEE HE'S UNCONSCIOUS?!

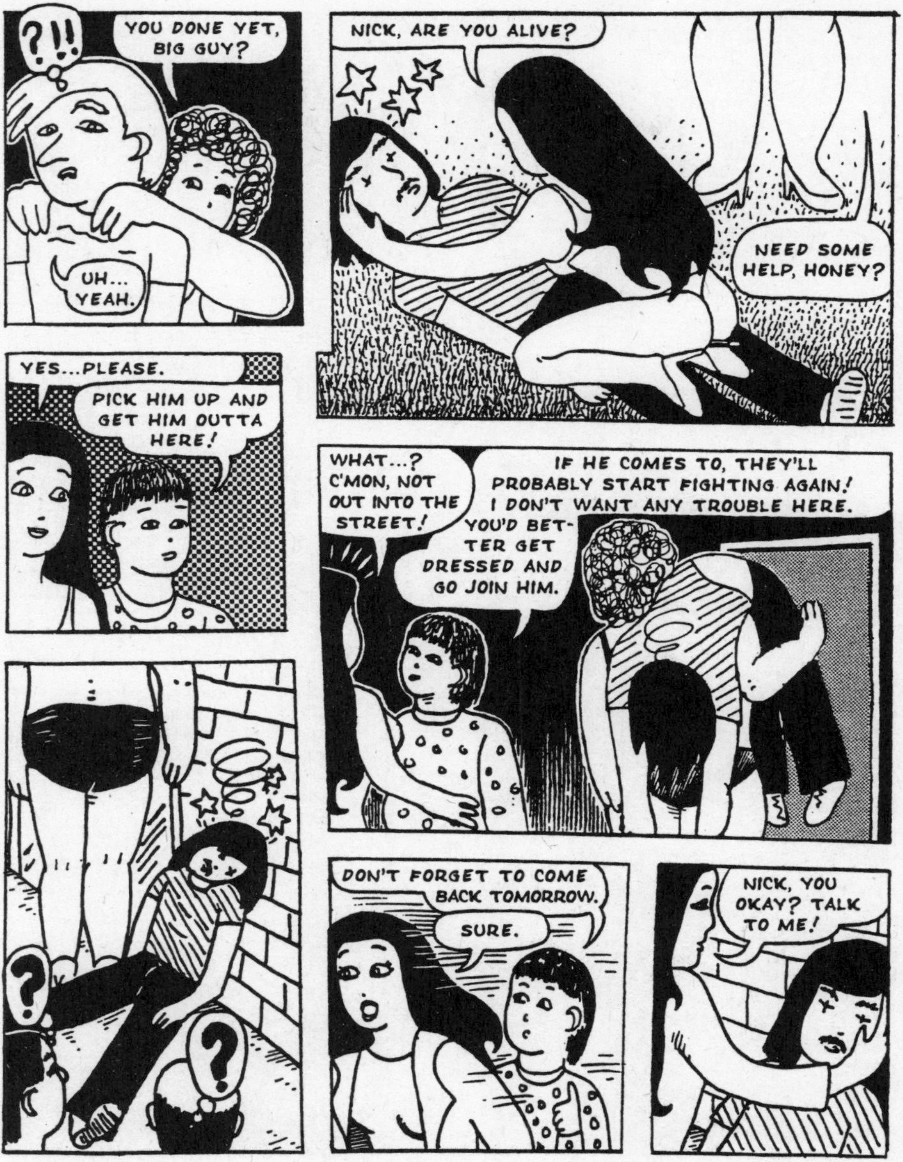
?!!
YOU DONE YET, BIG GUY?
UH... YEAH.
NICK, ARE YOU ALIVE?
NEED SOME HELP, HONEY?
YES...PLEASE.
PICK HIM UP AND GET HIM OUTTA HERE!
WHAT...? C'MON, NOT OUT INTO THE STREET!
IF HE COMES TO, THEY'LL PROBABLY START FIGHTING AGAIN! I DON'T WANT ANY TROUBLE HERE.
YOU'D BETTER GET DRESSED AND GO JOIN HIM.
?
?
DON'T FORGET TO COME BACK TOMORROW.
SURE.
NICK, YOU OKAY? TALK TO ME!

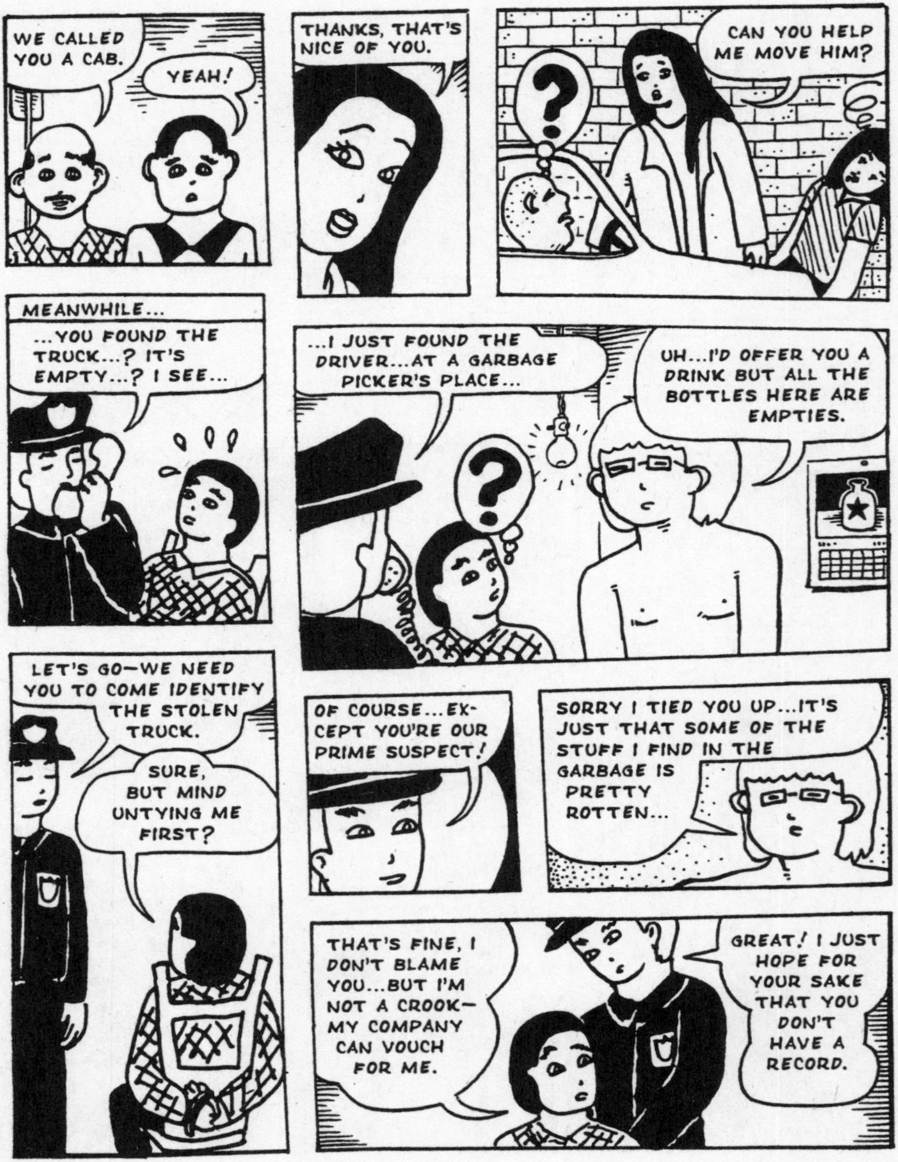
WE CALLED YOU A CAB.
YEAH!
THANKS, THAT'S NICE OF YOU.
CAN YOU HELP ME MOVE HIM?
?
MEANWHILE...
...YOU FOUND THE TRUCK...? IT'S EMPTY...? I SEE...
...I JUST FOUND THE DRIVER...AT A GARBAGE PICKER'S PLACE...
UH...I'D OFFER YOU A DRINK BUT ALL THE BOTTLES HERE ARE EMPTIES.
?
LET'S GO—WE NEED YOU TO COME IDENTIFY THE STOLEN TRUCK.
SURE, BUT MIND UNTYING ME FIRST?
OF COURSE...EX-CEPT YOU'RE OUR PRIME SUSPECT!
SORRY I TIED YOU UP...IT'S JUST THAT SOME OF THE STUFF I FIND IN THE GARBAGE IS PRETTY ROTTEN...
THAT'S FINE, I DON'T BLAME YOU...BUT I'M NOT A CROOK—MY COMPANY CAN VOUCH FOR ME.
GREAT! I JUST HOPE FOR YOUR SAKE THAT YOU DON'T HAVE A RECORD.

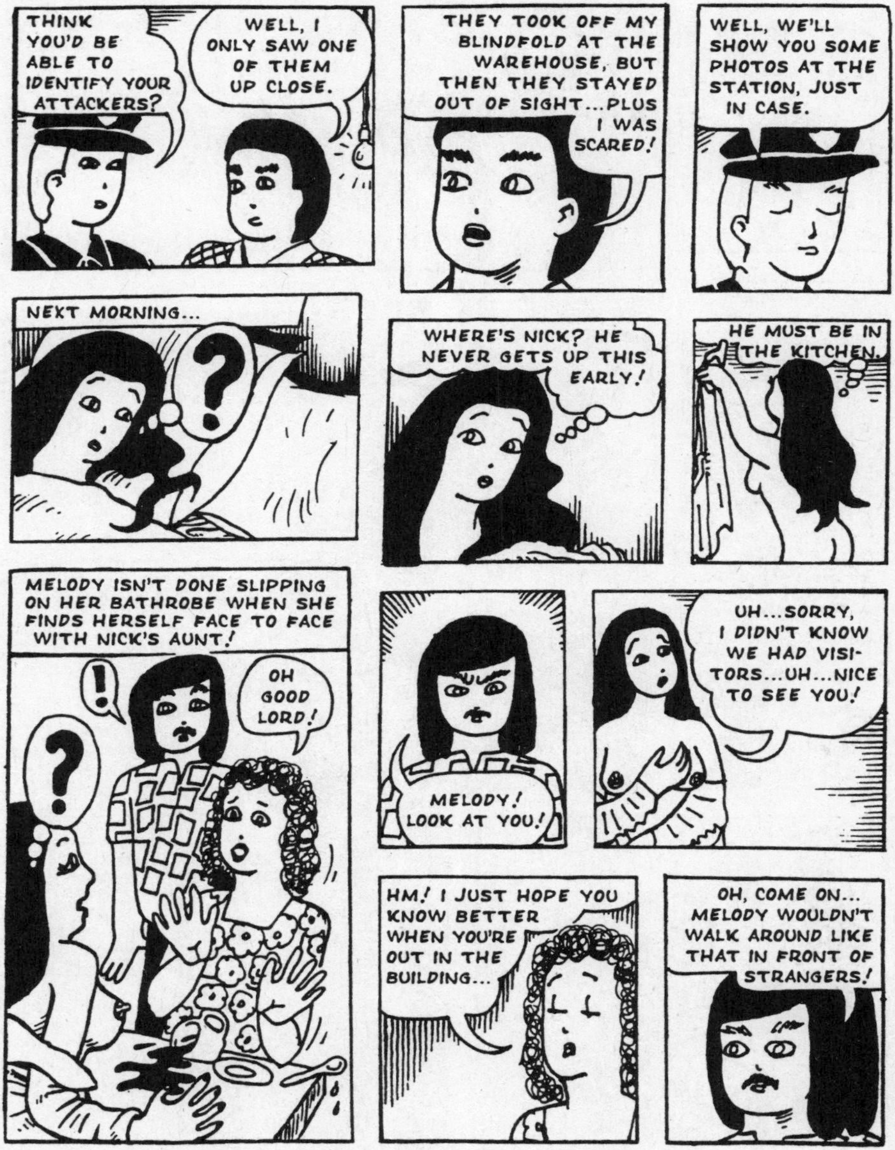
THINK YOU'D BE ABLE TO IDENTIFY YOUR ATTACKERS?
WELL, I ONLY SAW ONE OF THEM UP CLOSE.
THEY TOOK OFF MY BLINDFOLD AT THE WAREHOUSE, BUT THEN THEY STAYED OUT OF SIGHT...PLUS I WAS SCARED!
WELL, WE'LL SHOW YOU SOME PHOTOS AT THE STATION, JUST IN CASE.
NEXT MORNING...
?
WHERE'S NICK? HE NEVER GETS UP THIS EARLY!
HE MUST BE IN THE KITCHEN.
MELODY ISN'T DONE SLIPPING ON HER BATHROBE WHEN SHE FINDS HERSELF FACE TO FACE WITH NICK'S AUNT!
!
OH GOOD LORD!
?
MELODY! LOOK AT YOU!
UH...SORRY, I DIDN'T KNOW WE HAD VISITORS...UH...NICE TO SEE YOU!
HM! I JUST HOPE YOU KNOW BETTER WHEN YOU'RE OUT IN THE BUILDING...
OH, COME ON... MELODY WOULDN'T WALK AROUND LIKE THAT IN FRONT OF STRANGERS!

HOW COME YOU'RE AWAKE THIS EARLY, NICK?

I DON'T KNOW... I SLEPT LIKE A DEAD MAN, BUT I WAS UP WHEN MY AUNT RANG.

I DIDN'T MEAN TO BARGE IN ON YOU...I'M JUST A BIT BORED, NOW THAT I'M NOT WORKING, YOU KNOW.

MELODY, HOW ABOUT YOU GET DRESSED?

UH...YES. YES, OF COURSE!

JEEZUS...I'VE BECOME PRETTY BOLD EVER SINCE I STARTED DANCING...AND I USED TO BE SO QUIET AND SHY. IT'S LIKE I'VE LOST ALL MY MODESTY.

IF I WANTED TO QUIT DANCING, I COULD WORK FULL-TIME AS A SUPER... BUT I DON'T WANT TO...OH LORD!

NICK! MAKE ME ANOTHER CUP OF COFFEE...I NEED IT!

OF COURSE! BUT YOU SHOULDN'T LET YOURSELF GET ALL WORKED UP OVER NOTHING!

POOR HER... IF SHE ONLY KNEW!

THIS CRAZY JOB IS STARTING TO GET TO ME!

MELODY! YOU LIKE PLAYING CARDS, DON'T YOU?

UH...YEAH, SOMETIMES.

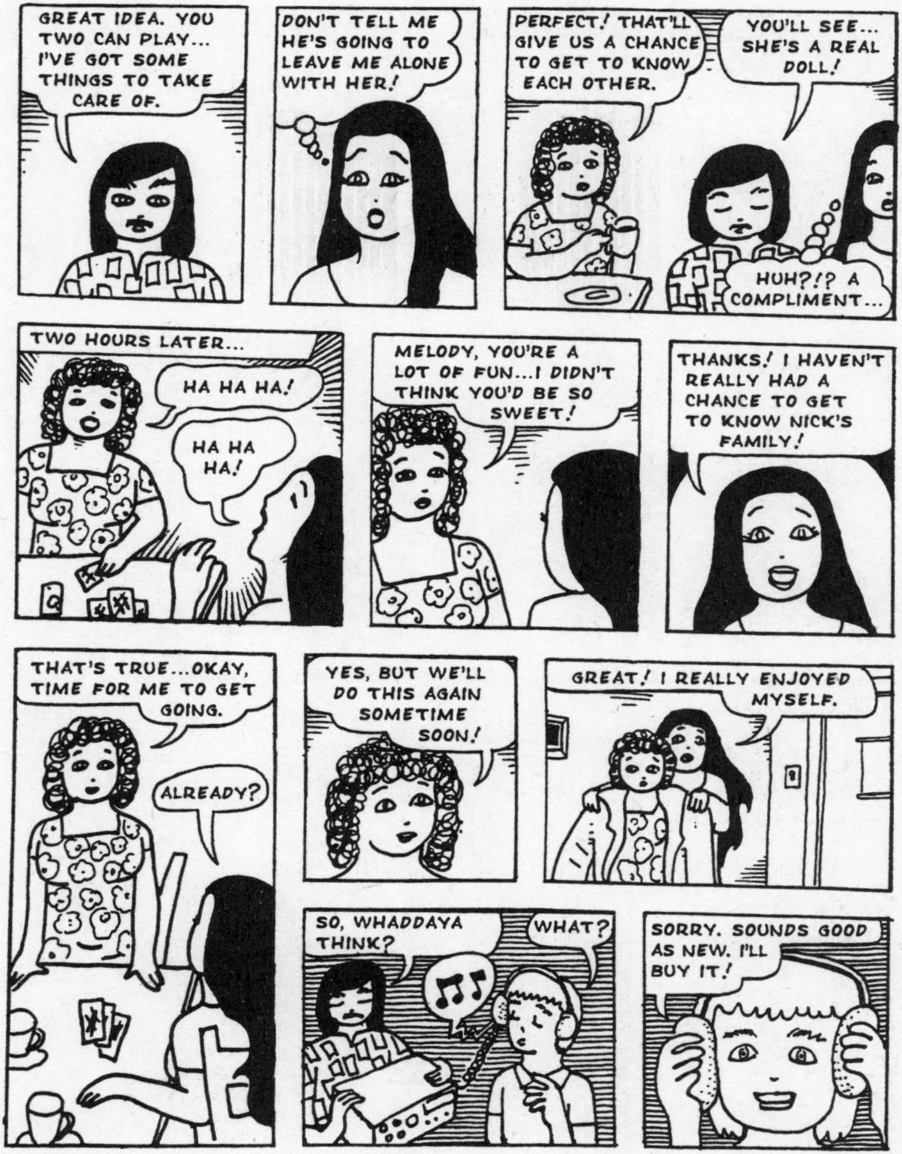
GREAT IDEA. YOU TWO CAN PLAY... I'VE GOT SOME THINGS TO TAKE CARE OF.
DON'T TELL ME HE'S GOING TO LEAVE ME ALONE WITH HER!
PERFECT! THAT'LL GIVE US A CHANCE TO GET TO KNOW EACH OTHER.
YOU'LL SEE... SHE'S A REAL DOLL!
HUH?!? A COMPLIMENT...
TWO HOURS LATER...
HA HA HA!
HA HA HA!
MELODY, YOU'RE A LOT OF FUN...I DIDN'T THINK YOU'D BE SO SWEET!
THANKS! I HAVEN'T REALLY HAD A CHANCE TO GET TO KNOW NICK'S FAMILY!
THAT'S TRUE...OKAY, TIME FOR ME TO GET GOING.
ALREADY?
YES, BUT WE'LL DO THIS AGAIN SOMETIME SOON!
GREAT! I REALLY ENJOYED MYSELF.
SO, WHADDAYA THINK?
WHAT?
SORRY. SOUNDS GOOD AS NEW. I'LL BUY IT!

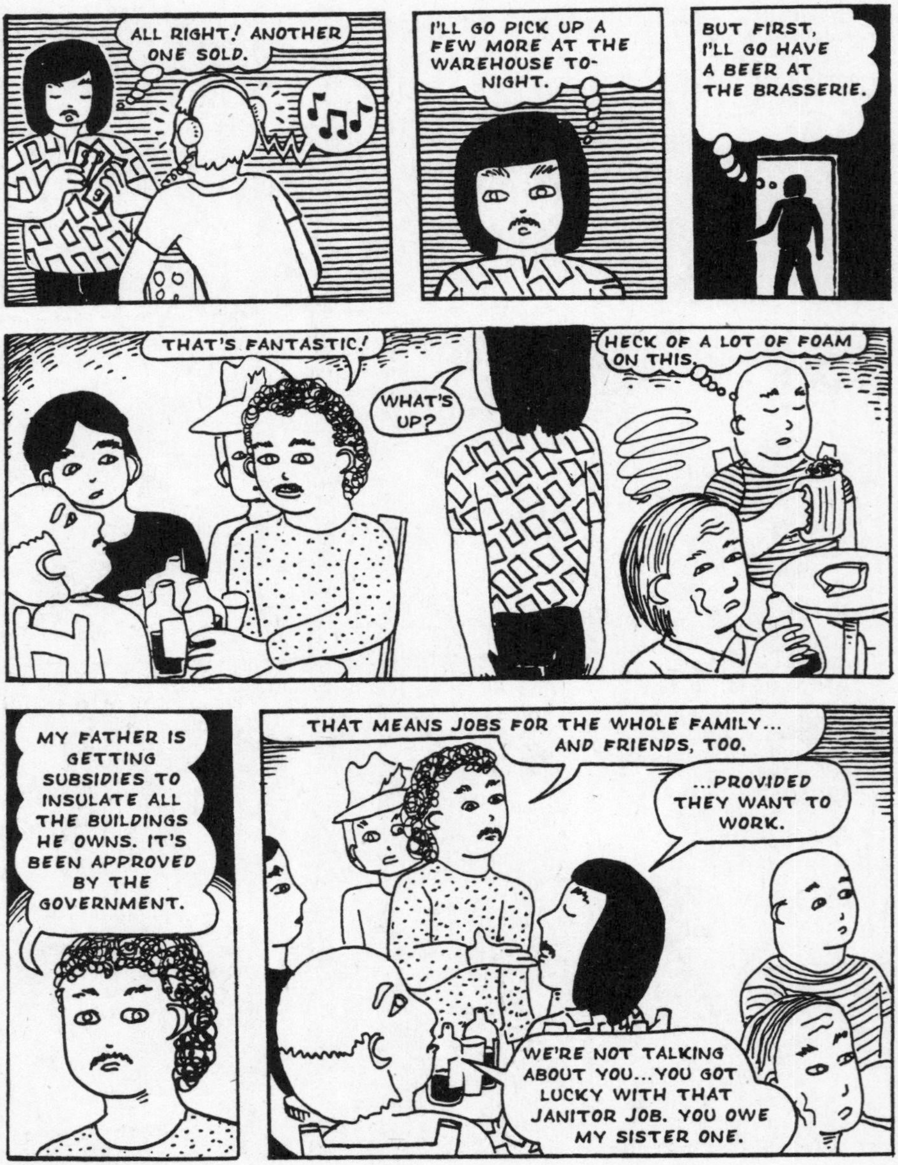
ALL RIGHT! ANOTHER ONE SOLD.
I'LL GO PICK UP A FEW MORE AT THE WAREHOUSE TO-NIGHT.
BUT FIRST, I'LL GO HAVE A BEER AT THE BRASSERIE.
THAT'S FANTASTIC!
WHAT'S UP?
HECK OF A LOT OF FOAM ON THIS.
MY FATHER IS GETTING SUBSIDIES TO INSULATE ALL THE BUILDINGS HE OWNS. IT'S BEEN APPROVED BY THE GOVERNMENT.
THAT MEANS JOBS FOR THE WHOLE FAMILY... AND FRIENDS, TOO.
...PROVIDED THEY WANT TO WORK.
WE'RE NOT TALKING ABOUT YOU...YOU GOT LUCKY WITH THAT JANITOR JOB. YOU OWE MY SISTER ONE.

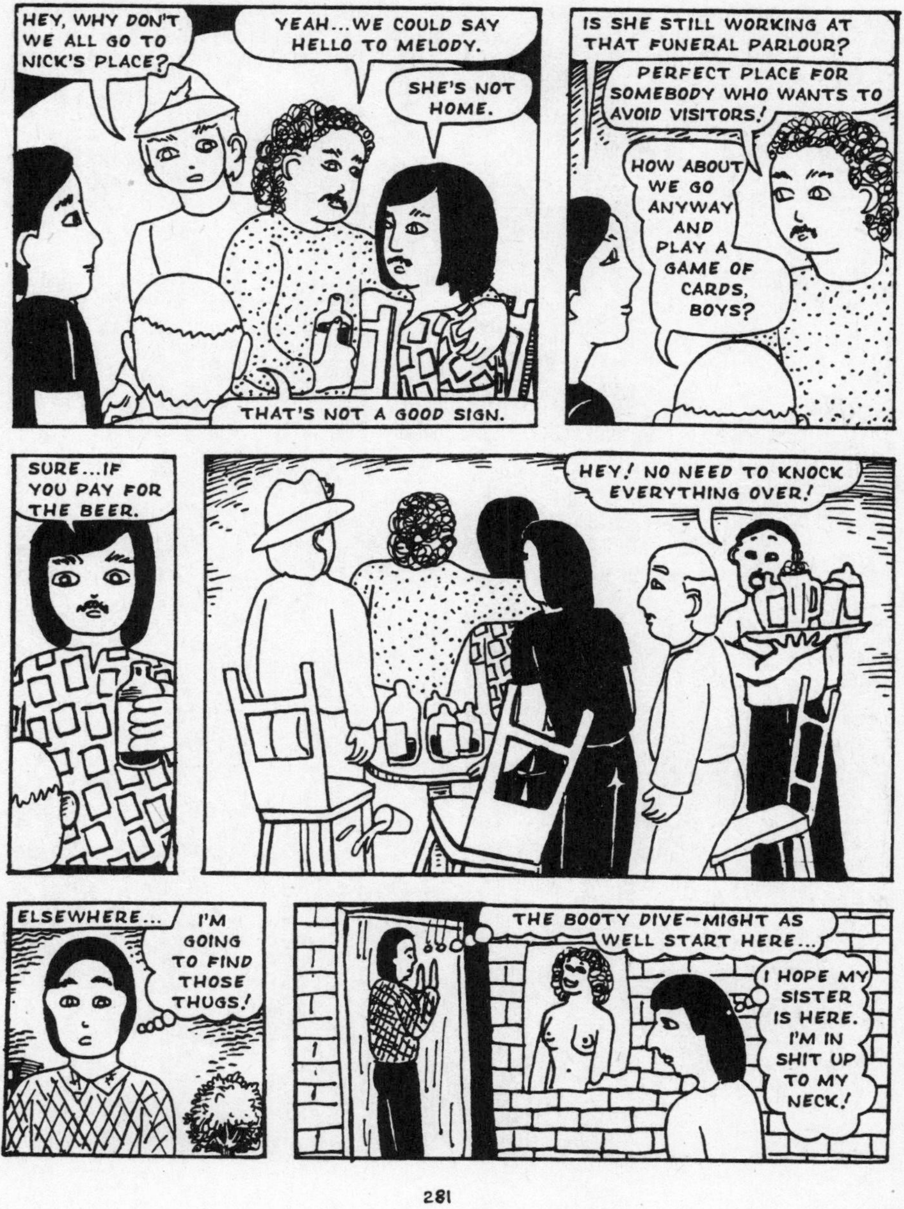
HEY, WHY DON'T WE ALL GO TO NICK'S PLACE?
YEAH...WE COULD SAY HELLO TO MELODY.
SHE'S NOT HOME.
THAT'S NOT A GOOD SIGN.
IS SHE STILL WORKING AT THAT FUNERAL PARLOUR?
PERFECT PLACE FOR SOMEBODY WHO WANTS TO AVOID VISITORS!
HOW ABOUT WE GO ANYWAY AND PLAY A GAME OF CARDS, BOYS?
SURE...IF YOU PAY FOR THE BEER.
HEY! NO NEED TO KNOCK EVERYTHING OVER!
ELSEWHERE...
I'M GOING TO FIND THOSE THUGS!
THE BOOTY DIVE—MIGHT AS WELL START HERE...
I HOPE MY SISTER IS HERE. I'M IN SHIT UP TO MY NECK!

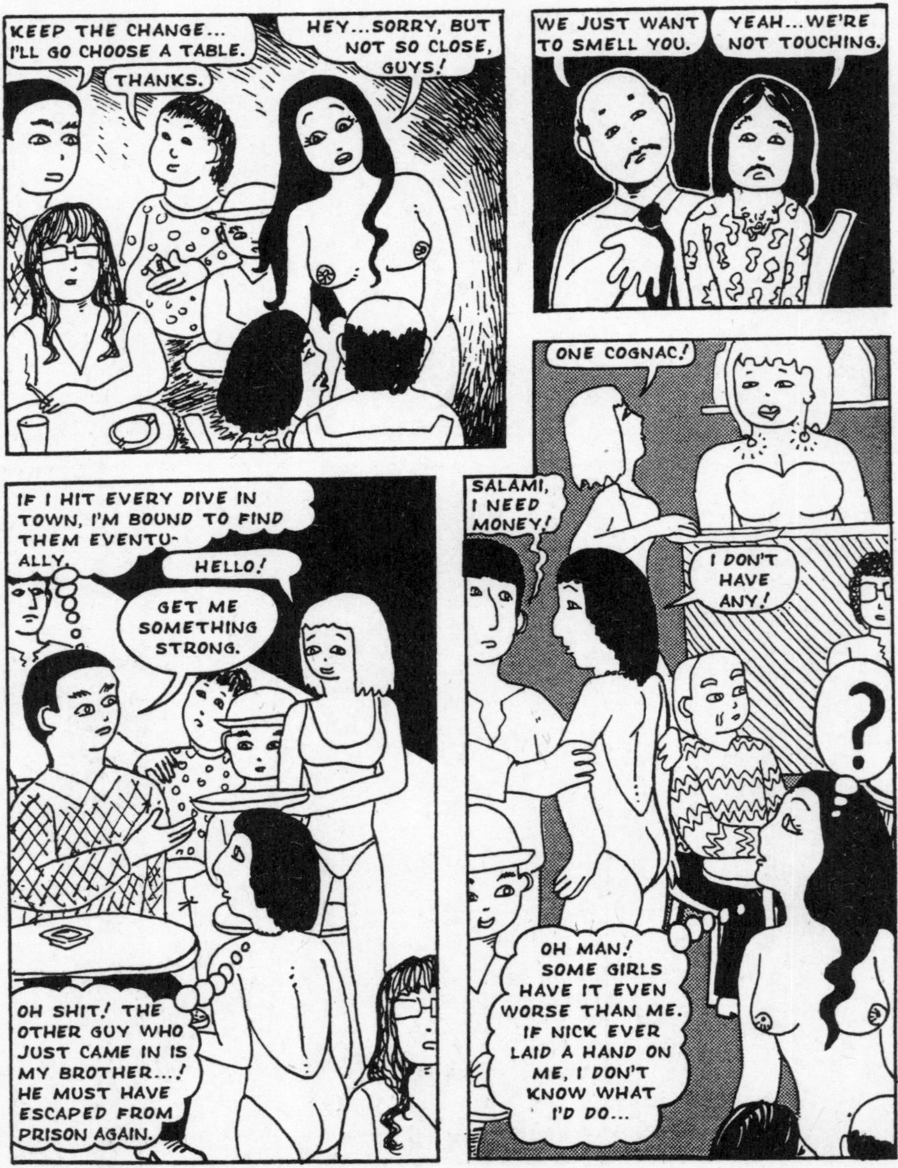
KEEP THE CHANGE... I'LL GO CHOOSE A TABLE.
THANKS.
HEY... SORRY, BUT NOT SO CLOSE, GUYS!
WE JUST WANT TO SMELL YOU.
YEAH... WE'RE NOT TOUCHING.
IF I HIT EVERY DIVE IN TOWN, I'M BOUND TO FIND THEM EVENTU-ALLY.
HELLO!
GET ME SOMETHING STRONG.
OH SHIT! THE OTHER GUY WHO JUST CAME IN IS MY BROTHER...! HE MUST HAVE ESCAPED FROM PRISON AGAIN.
ONE COGNAC!
SALAMI, I NEED MONEY!
I DON'T HAVE ANY!
?
OH MAN! SOME GIRLS HAVE IT EVEN WORSE THAN ME. IF NICK EVER LAID A HAND ON ME, I DON'T KNOW WHAT I'D DO...

HEY, CUTIE... WOULDN'T HAPPEN TO KNOW ANYBODY WHO'S GOT SOME NICE SOUND SYSTEMS TO SELL?
UH, NO.
OKAY, I'VE GOTTA GO NOW. IT'S MY TURN TO BE UP ON STAGE.
PROMISE YOU'LL COME BACK! WE'RE NOT DONE SMELLING YOUR WONDERFUL SCENT...
AT LEAST THERE'S ONE GIRL WHO'S WILLING TO GO ON STAGE WITH-OUT BEING TOLD.
MAYBE THAT'S NOT THE RIGHT APPROACH... DON'T WANT TO SCARE 'EM AWAY.
ANOTHER HOUR TO GO AND I'M DONE...AT LAST!
THE ONLY ONE I'D RECOGNIZE IS THE BIG CURLY-HAIRED GUY WHO STUFFED ME INTO THE BAG...AND HE'S NOT HERE.
?
DON'T MAKE ME BEAT IT OUT OF YOU.
OKAY, HOW MUCH?

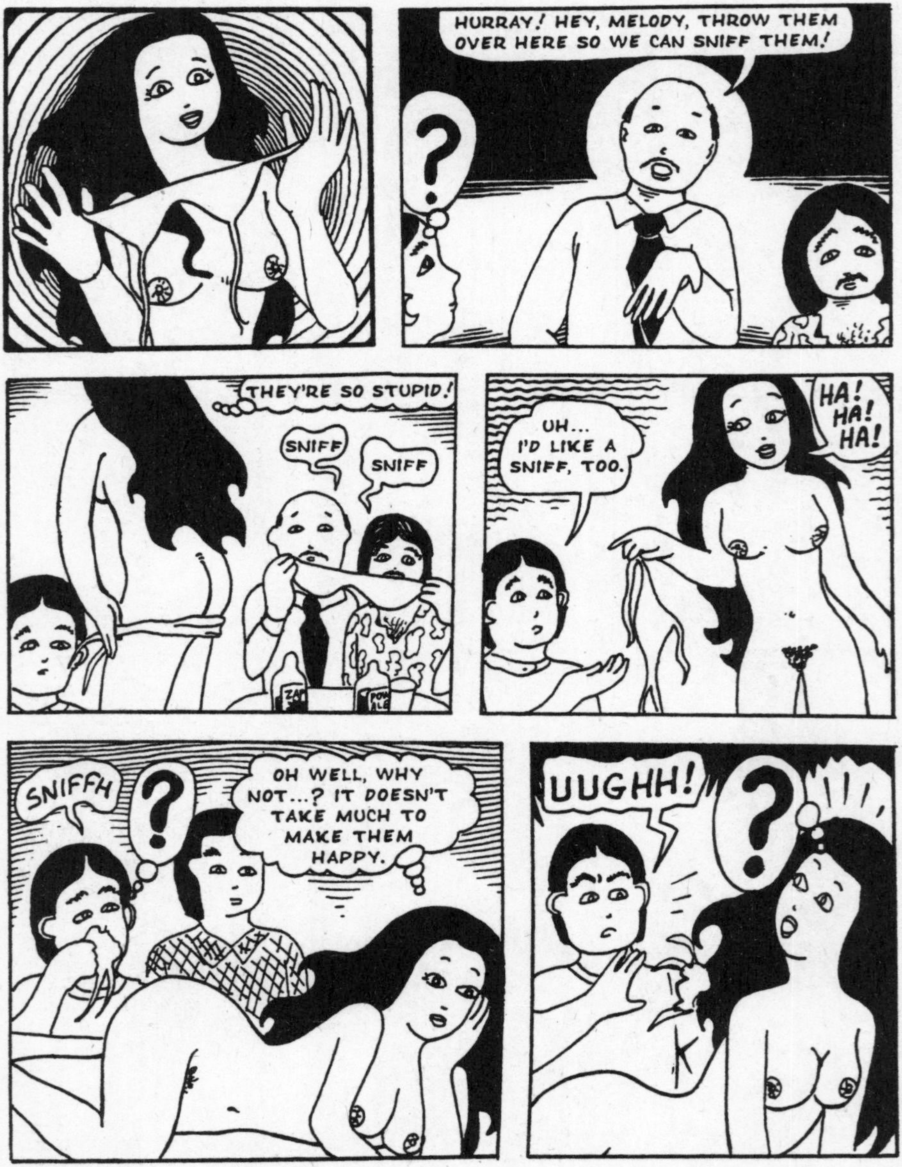
HURRAY! HEY, MELODY, THROW THEM OVER HERE SO WE CAN SNIFF THEM!
?
THEY'RE SO STUPID!
SNIFF
SNIFF
UH... I'D LIKE A SNIFF, TOO.
HA! HA! HA!
SNIFFH
?
OH WELL, WHY NOT...? IT DOESN'T TAKE MUCH TO MAKE THEM HAPPY.
UUGHH!
?

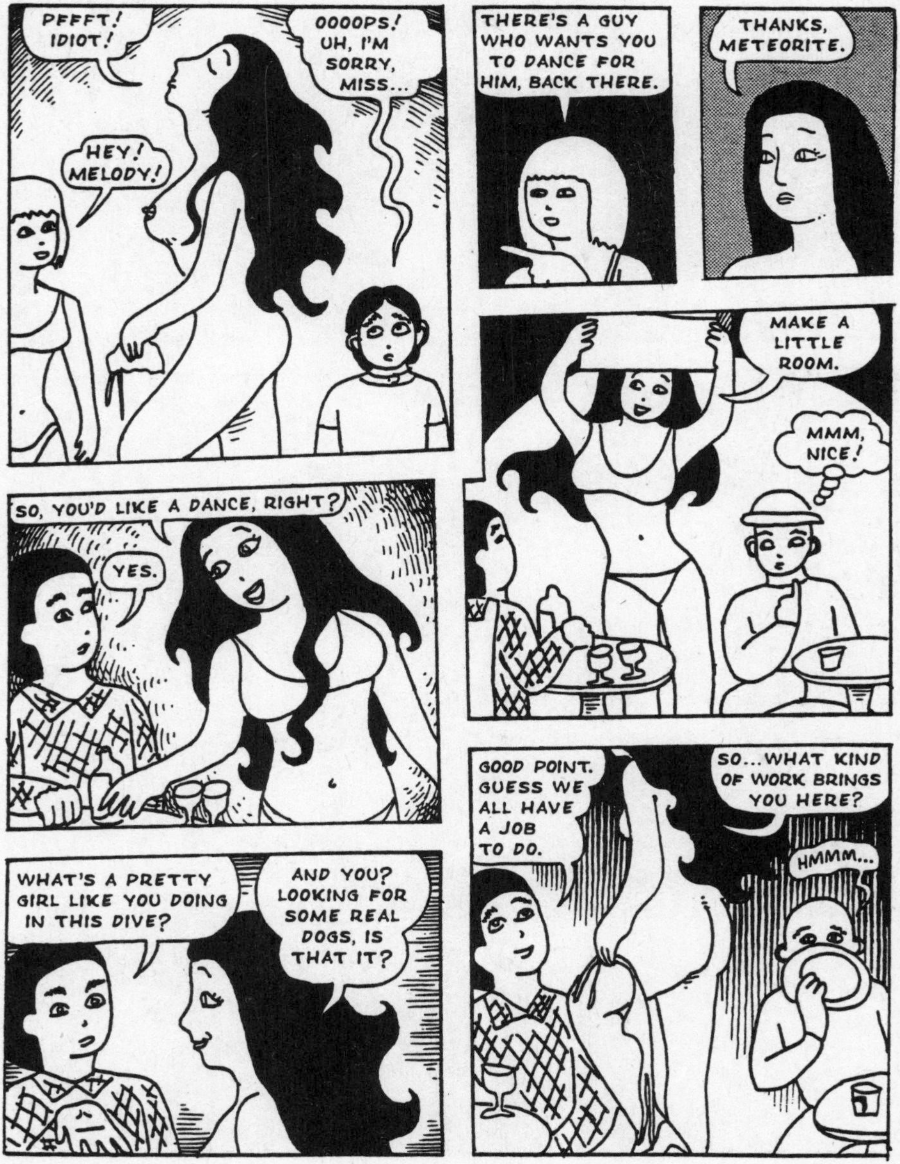
PFFFT! IDIOT!
OOOOPS! UH, I'M SORRY, MISS...
HEY! MELODY!
THERE'S A GUY WHO WANTS YOU TO DANCE FOR HIM, BACK THERE.
THANKS, METEORITE.
SO, YOU'D LIKE A DANCE, RIGHT?
YES.
MAKE A LITTLE ROOM.
MMM, NICE!
WHAT'S A PRETTY GIRL LIKE YOU DOING IN THIS DIVE?
AND YOU? LOOKING FOR SOME REAL DOGS, IS THAT IT?
GOOD POINT. GUESS WE ALL HAVE A JOB TO DO.
SO...WHAT KIND OF WORK BRINGS YOU HERE?
HMMM...

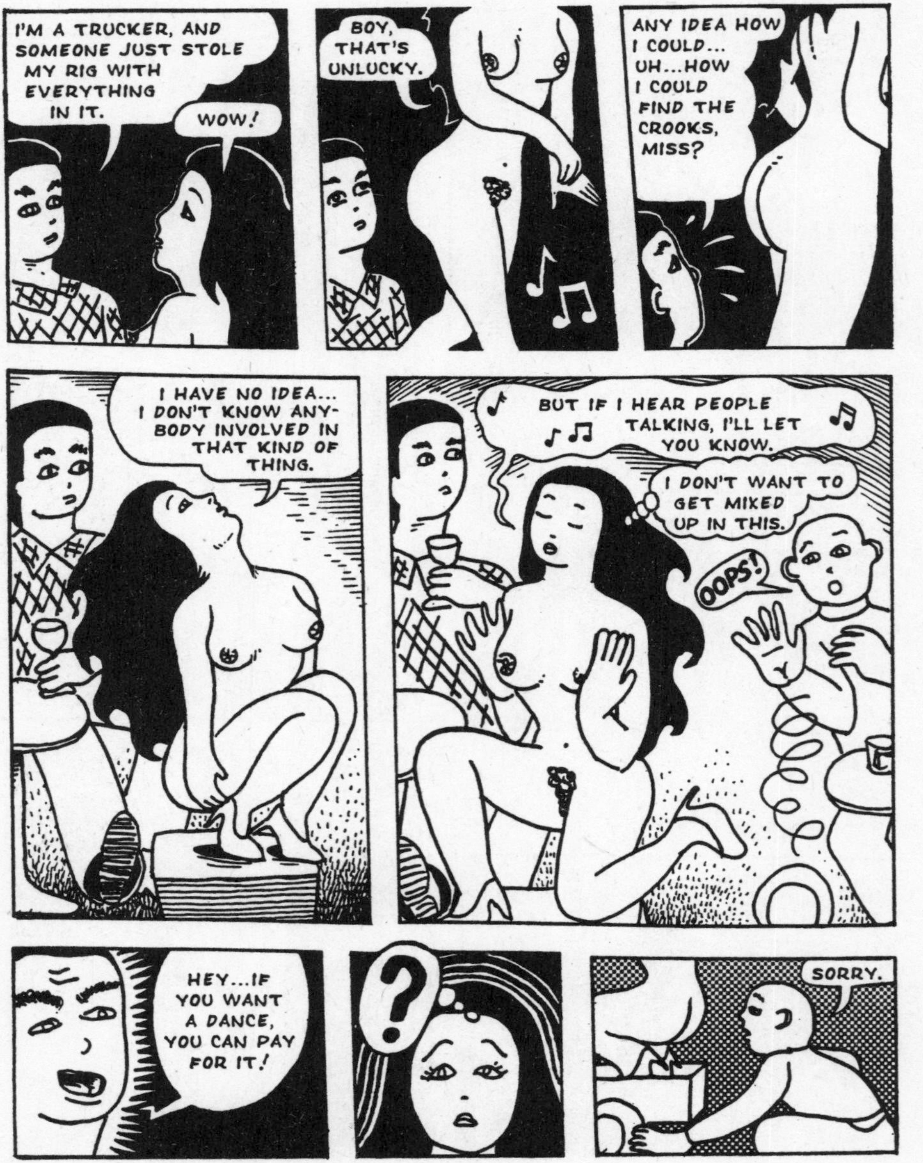
I'M A TRUCKER, AND SOMEONE JUST STOLE MY RIG WITH EVERYTHING IN IT.
WOW!
BOY, THAT'S UNLUCKY.
ANY IDEA HOW I COULD... UH...HOW I COULD FIND THE CROOKS, MISS?
I HAVE NO IDEA... I DON'T KNOW ANY-BODY INVOLVED IN THAT KIND OF THING.
BUT IF I HEAR PEOPLE TALKING, I'LL LET YOU KNOW.
I DON'T WANT TO GET MIXED UP IN THIS.
OOPS!
HEY...IF YOU WANT A DANCE, YOU CAN PAY FOR IT!
?
SORRY.

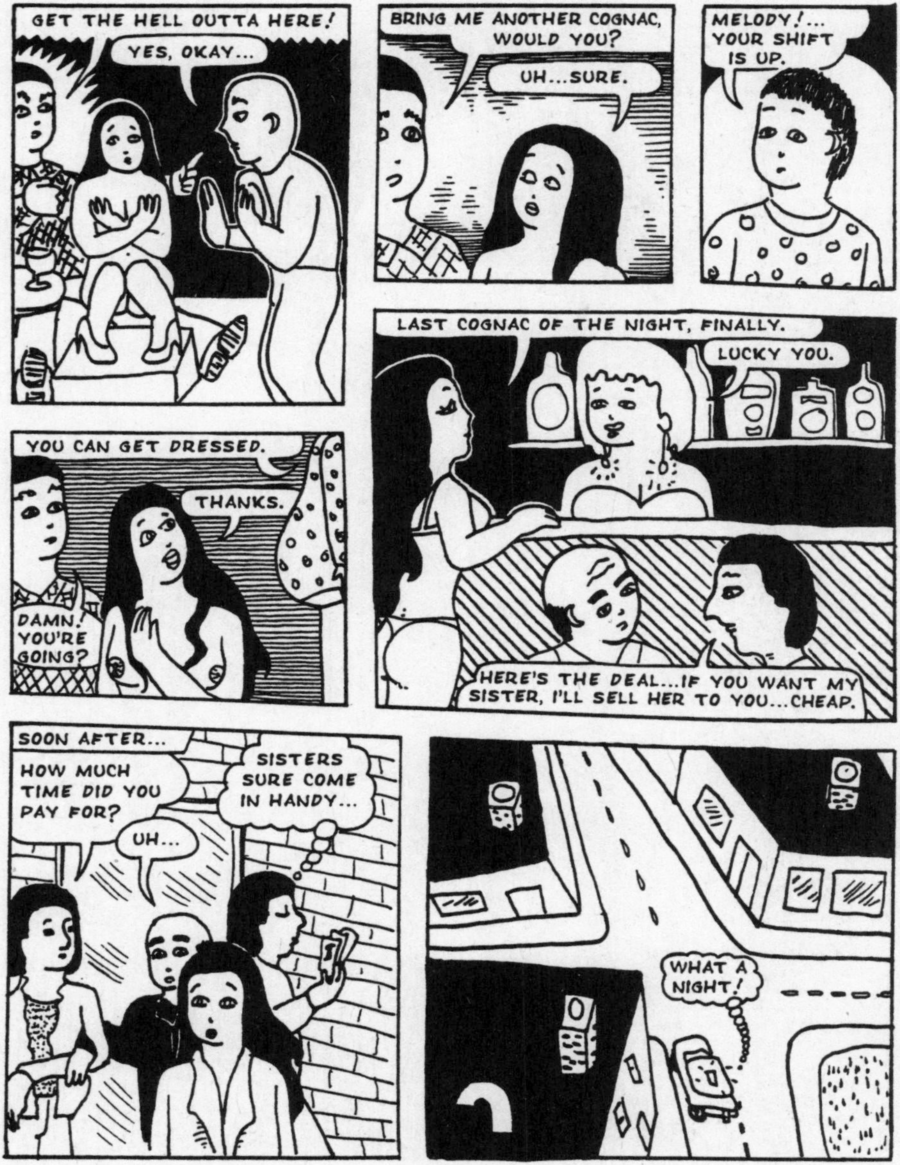
GET THE HELL OUTTA HERE!
YES, OKAY...
BRING ME ANOTHER COGNAC, WOULD YOU?
UH...SURE.
MELODY!... YOUR SHIFT IS UP.
YOU CAN GET DRESSED.
THANKS.
DAMN! YOU'RE GOING?
LAST COGNAC OF THE NIGHT, FINALLY.
LUCKY YOU.
HERE'S THE DEAL...IF YOU WANT MY SISTER, I'LL SELL HER TO YOU...CHEAP.
SOON AFTER...
HOW MUCH TIME DID YOU PAY FOR?
UH...
SISTERS SURE COME IN HANDY...
WHAT A NIGHT!

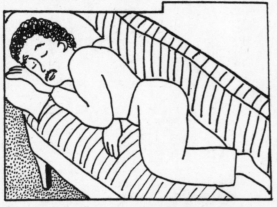

ALEX... WHAT'S UP?

OH! HI THERE, MELODY!

WHERE'S NICK?

NOT A CLUE... THE GUYS WERE HERE AND THEN THEY LEFT. GUESS THEY FORGOT ME.

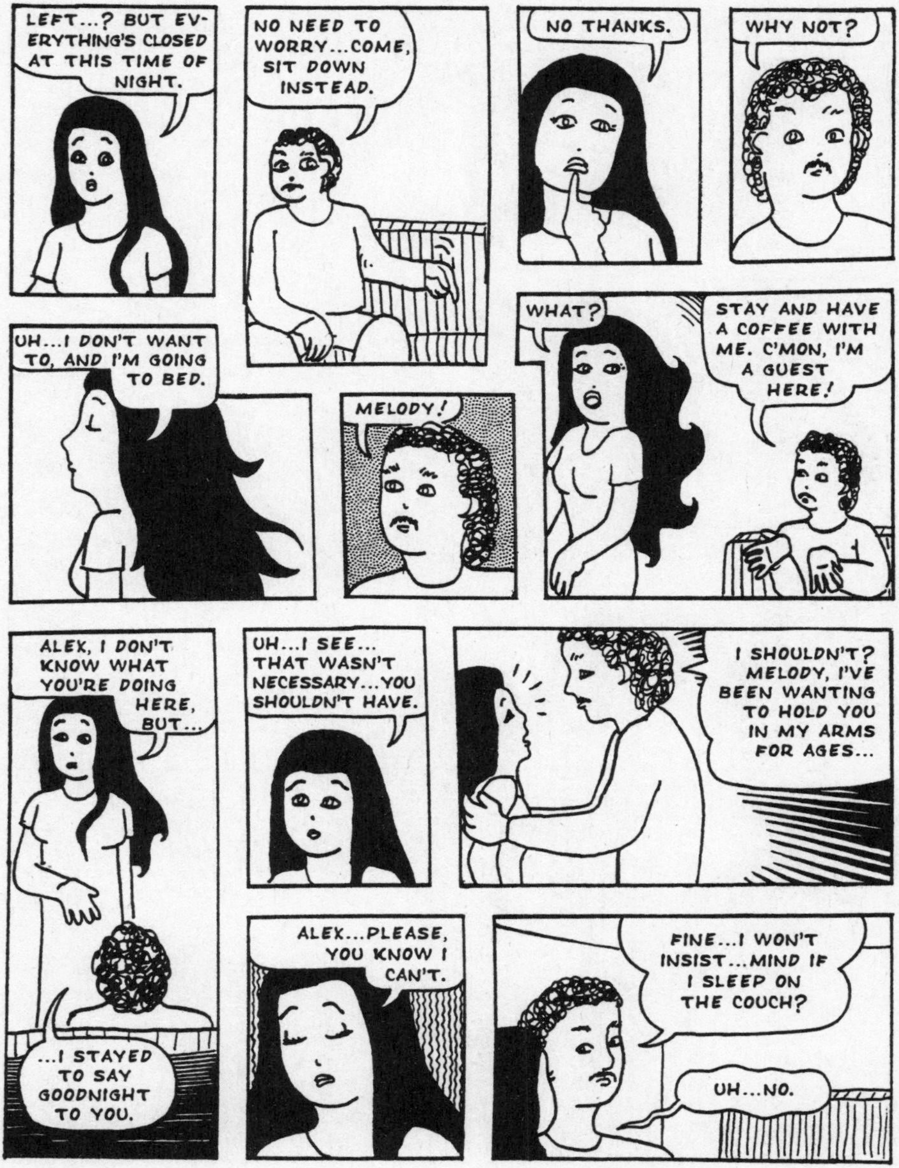
LEFT...? BUT EV-ERYTHING'S CLOSED AT THIS TIME OF NIGHT.
NO NEED TO WORRY...COME, SIT DOWN INSTEAD.
NO THANKS.
WHY NOT?
UH...I DON'T WANT TO, AND I'M GOING TO BED.
MELODY!
WHAT?
STAY AND HAVE A COFFEE WITH ME. C'MON, I'M A GUEST HERE!
ALEX, I DON'T KNOW WHAT YOU'RE DOING HERE, BUT...
...I STAYED TO SAY GOODNIGHT TO YOU.
UH...I SEE... THAT WASN'T NECESSARY...YOU SHOULDN'T HAVE.
I SHOULDN'T? MELODY, I'VE BEEN WANTING TO HOLD YOU IN MY ARMS FOR AGES...
ALEX...PLEASE, YOU KNOW I CAN'T.
FINE...I WON'T INSIST...MIND IF I SLEEP ON THE COUCH?
UH...NO.

GOOD NIGHT!

WHAT'S HE THINKING, COMING HERE TO SLEEP?

ALL I NEED TO DO NOW IS WAIT...SHE'LL BE BACK...

HOW'M I GONNA SLEEP?

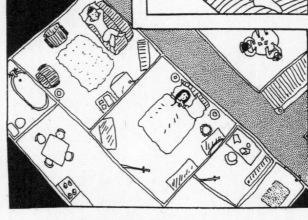

...THIS IS CRAZY.

ALEX, I CAN'T SLEEP BECAUSE OF YOU...

SAME HERE! SO WHY PUSH ME AWAY IF YOU WANT ME TOO?

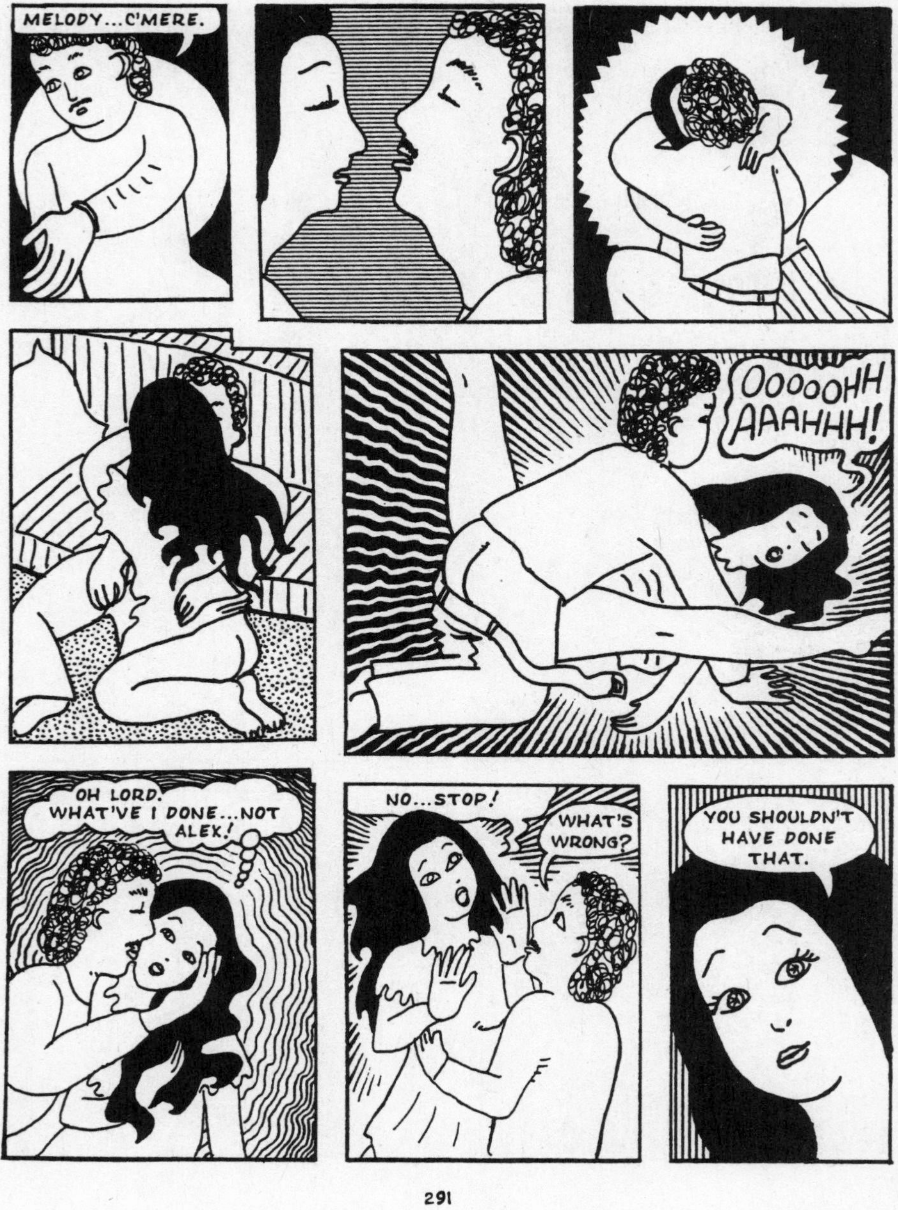
MELODY...C'MERE.
OOOOOHH AAAHHH!
OH LORD. WHAT'VE I DONE...NOT ALEX!
NO...STOP!
WHAT'S WRONG?
YOU SHOULDN'T HAVE DONE THAT.

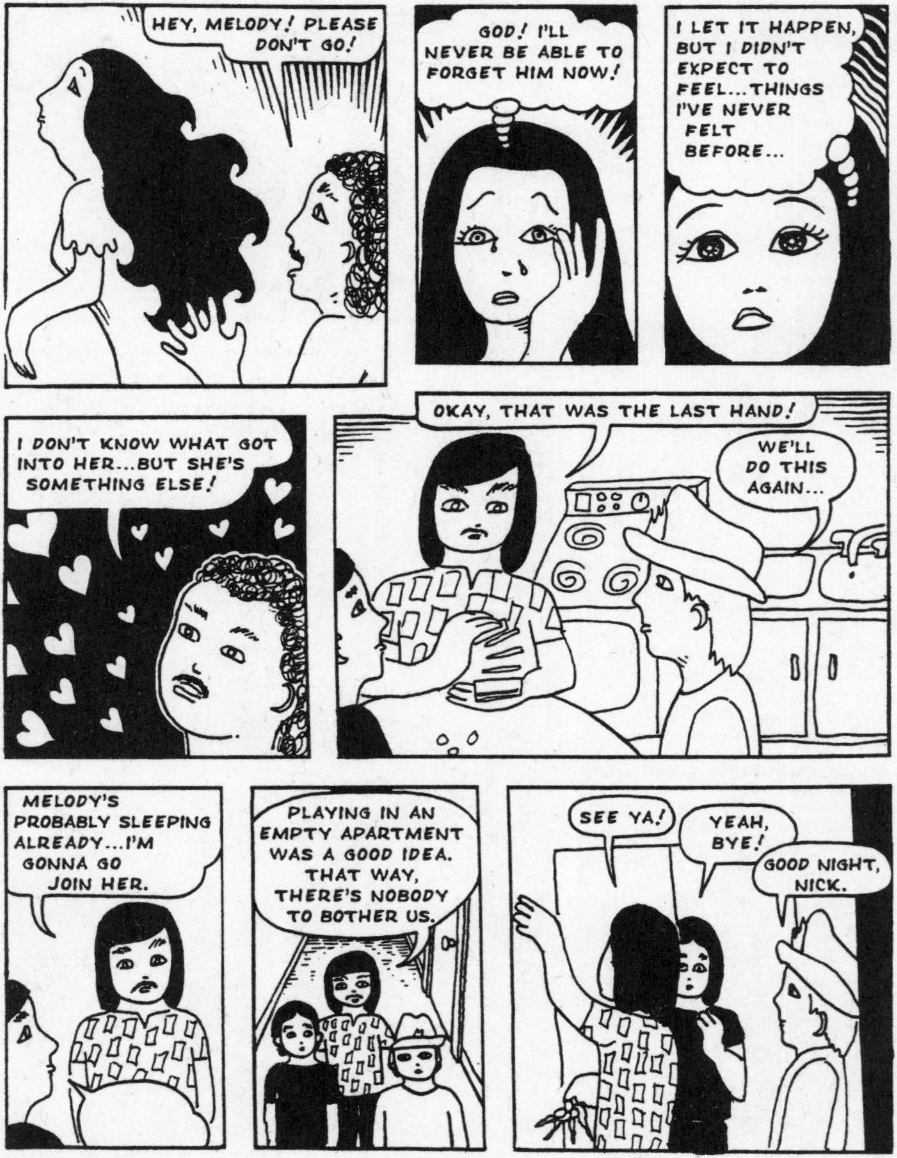
HEY, MELODY! PLEASE DON'T GO!
GOD! I'LL NEVER BE ABLE TO FORGET HIM NOW!
I LET IT HAPPEN, BUT I DIDN'T EXPECT TO FEEL... THINGS I'VE NEVER FELT BEFORE...
I DON'T KNOW WHAT GOT INTO HER...BUT SHE'S SOMETHING ELSE!
OKAY, THAT WAS THE LAST HAND!
WE'LL DO THIS AGAIN...
MELODY'S PROBABLY SLEEPING ALREADY...I'M GONNA GO JOIN HER.
PLAYING IN AN EMPTY APARTMENT WAS A GOOD IDEA. THAT WAY, THERE'S NOBODY TO BOTHER US.
SEE YA!
YEAH, BYE!
GOOD NIGHT, NICK.

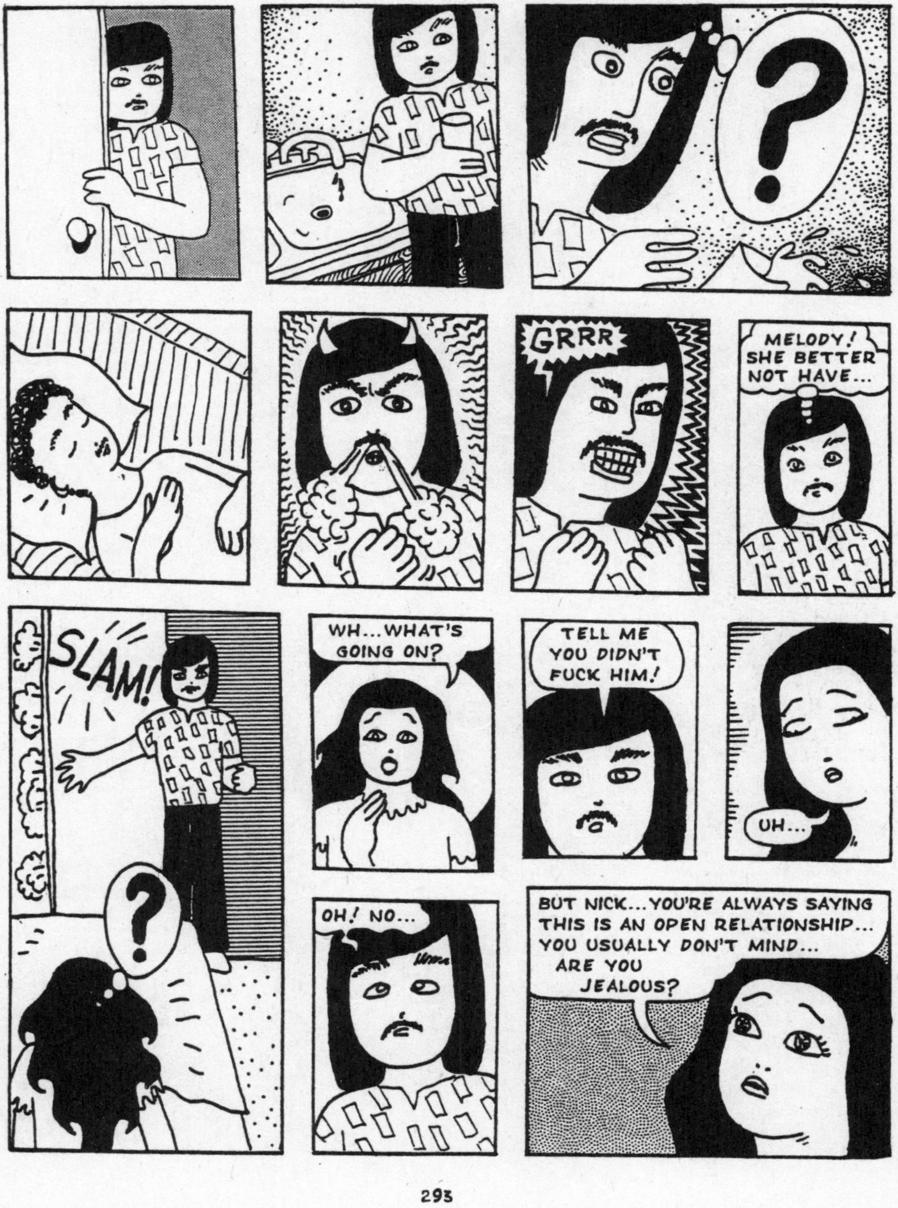
?
GRRR
MELODY! SHE BETTER NOT HAVE...
SLAM!
?
WH...WHAT'S GOING ON?
TELL ME YOU DIDN'T FUCK HIM!
UH...
OH! NO...
BUT NICK...YOU'RE ALWAYS SAYING THIS IS AN OPEN RELATIONSHIP... YOU USUALLY DON'T MIND... ARE YOU JEALOUS?

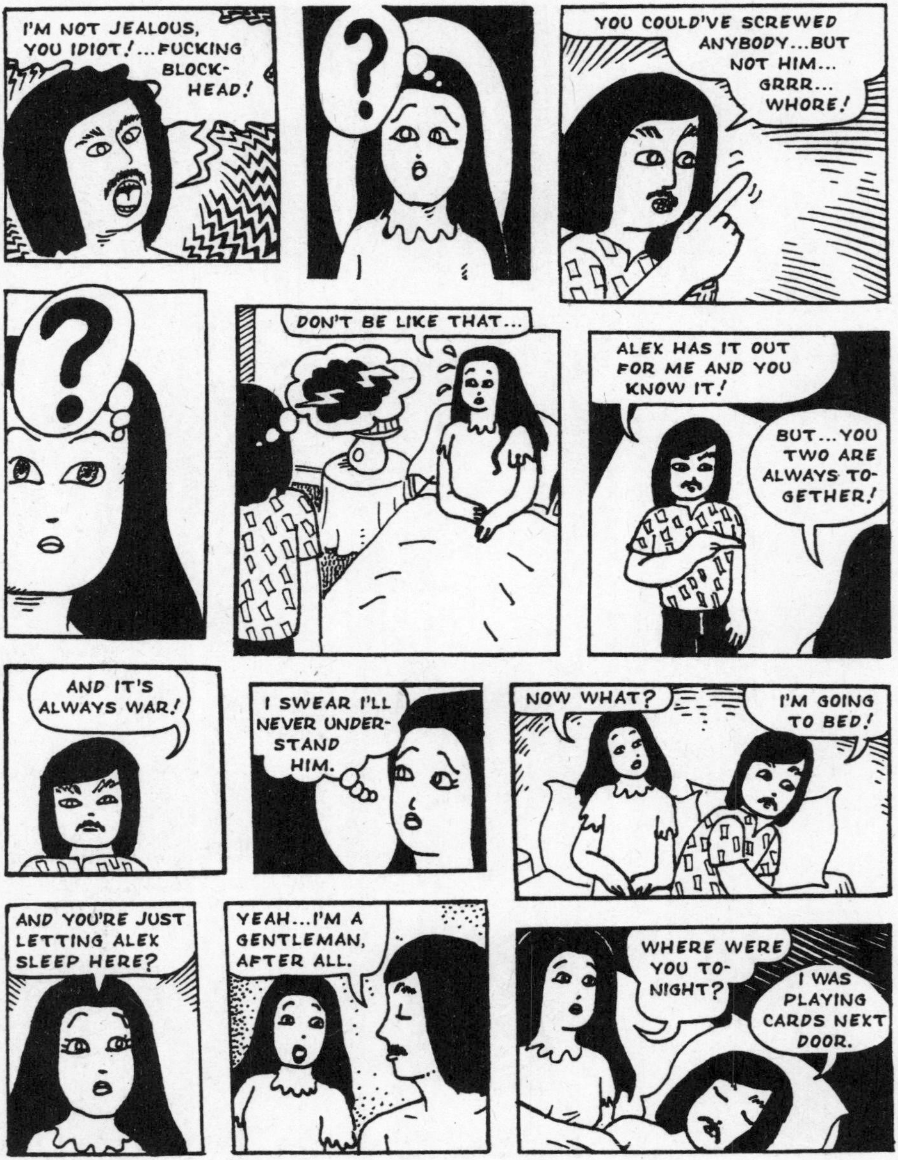
I'M NOT JEALOUS, YOU IDIOT!...FUCKING BLOCK-HEAD!
YOU COULD'VE SCREWED ANYBODY...BUT NOT HIM... GRRR... WHORE!
DON'T BE LIKE THAT...
ALEX HAS IT OUT FOR ME AND YOU KNOW IT!
BUT...YOU TWO ARE ALWAYS TO-GETHER!
AND IT'S ALWAYS WAR!
I SWEAR I'LL NEVER UNDER-STAND HIM.
NOW WHAT?
I'M GOING TO BED!
AND YOU'RE JUST LETTING ALEX SLEEP HERE?
YEAH...I'M A GENTLEMAN, AFTER ALL.
WHERE WERE YOU TO-NIGHT?
I WAS PLAYING CARDS NEXT DOOR.

FUCK! WHAT REALLY GETS TO ME IS THAT I LOST THAT BET WITH ALEX... SHIT!
LISTEN, NICK... YOU SHOULDN'T HAVE LEFT HIM HERE TO BEGIN WITH!
?
I DIDN'T LEAVE HIM HERE... HE DIDN'T FOLLOW US, THAT'S ALL.
MORNING...
THANKS FOR MAKING COFFEE!
YOU CAN MAKE YOUR OWN COFFEE.
GOT UP ON THE WRONG SIDE OF THE BED?
YEAH!
?
COME IN, WHY DON'T YOU?
TOO SHY?
UH... NO.

I WISH I COULD JUST DISAPPEAR INTO THE WALL...
NICK, I'M TAKING THE DAY OFF TODAY. I'M GOING TO GO VISIT MY AUNT.
SURE.
MAYBE THE FRESH AIR'LL DO YOU SOME GOOD.
YEAH, BUT IT WON'T CLEAR HER HEAD.
ESPE-CIALLY IF SHE STARTS THINKING ABOUT ME.
SHE NEEDS TO CLEAR HER LUNGS, NOT HER HEAD!
HE BETTER NOT TRY TO KEEP ON SCORING WITH HER!!!
UH, I THINK I'M STILL TIRED...I'M GOING BACK TO BED.
?
ME TOO!
ASSHOLE!
HAHAHA!

HA HA HA! JUST KIDDING. I'M GONNA GO SLEEP IN MY OWN BED!
EVEN BETTER... HOW ABOUT IN YOUR GRAVE?
BYE, MELODY!
I HOPE THIS ISN'T THE END...

Melody and the Birthday Wish

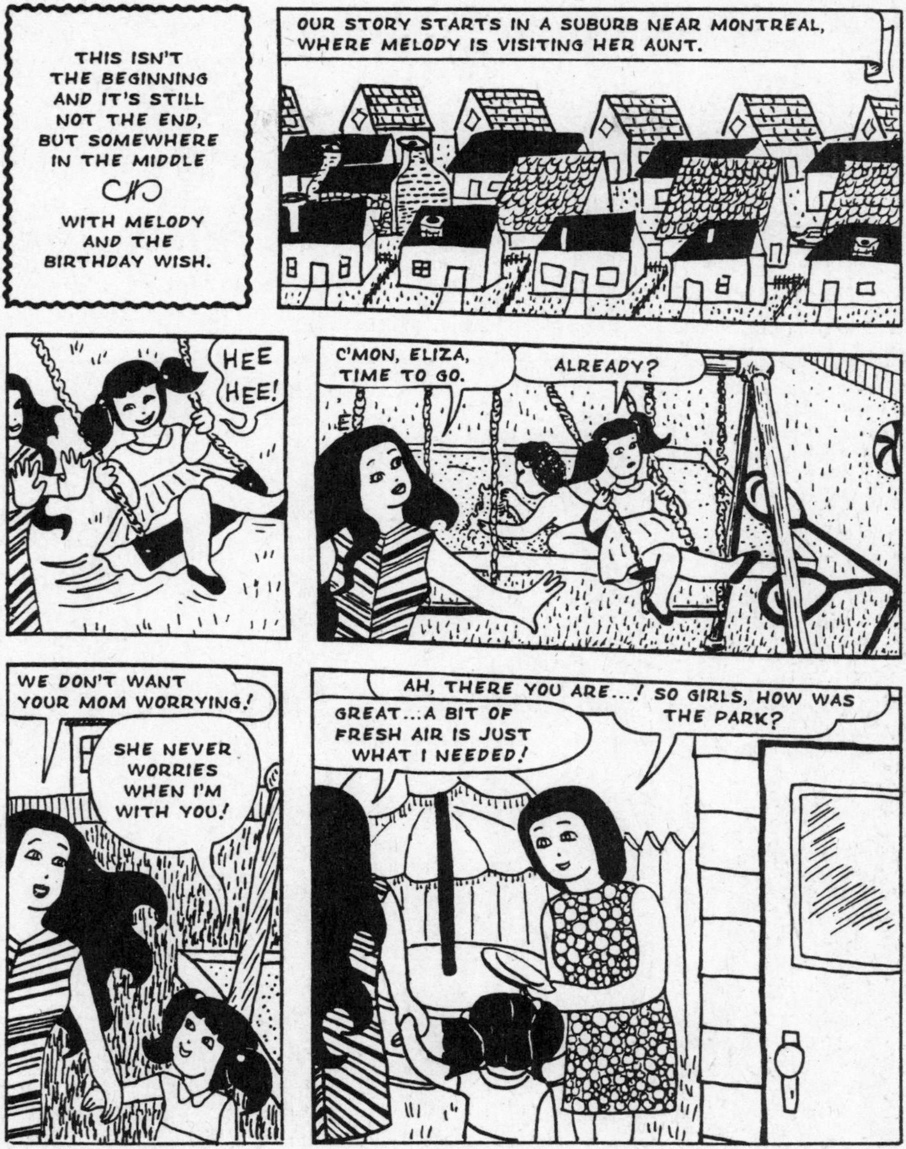
THIS ISN'T THE BEGINNING AND IT'S STILL NOT THE END, BUT SOMEWHERE IN THE MIDDLE
WITH MELODY AND THE BIRTHDAY WISH.
OUR STORY STARTS IN A SUBURB NEAR MONTREAL, WHERE MELODY IS VISITING HER AUNT.
HEE HEE!
C'MON, ELIZA, TIME TO GO.
ALREADY?
WE DON'T WANT YOUR MOM WORRYING!
SHE NEVER WORRIES WHEN I'M WITH YOU!
AH, THERE YOU ARE...!
SO GIRLS, HOW WAS THE PARK?
GREAT...A BIT OF FRESH AIR IS JUST WHAT I NEEDED!

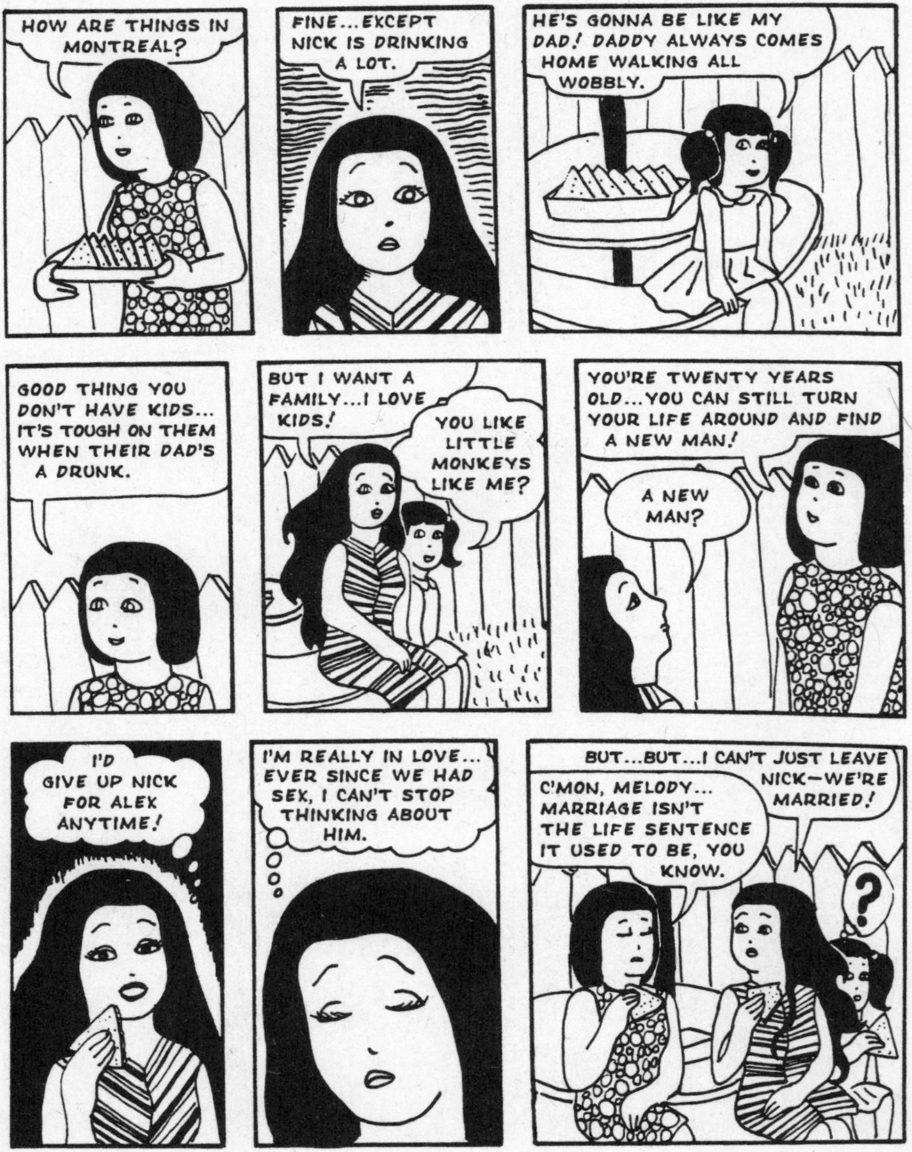
HOW ARE THINGS IN MONTREAL?
FINE...EXCEPT NICK IS DRINKING A LOT.
HE'S GONNA BE LIKE MY DAD! DADDY ALWAYS COMES HOME WALKING ALL WOBBLY.
GOOD THING YOU DON'T HAVE KIDS... IT'S TOUGH ON THEM WHEN THEIR DAD'S A DRUNK.
BUT I WANT A FAMILY...I LOVE KIDS!
YOU LIKE LITTLE MONKEYS LIKE ME?
YOU'RE TWENTY YEARS OLD...YOU CAN STILL TURN YOUR LIFE AROUND AND FIND A NEW MAN!
A NEW MAN?
I'D GIVE UP NICK FOR ALEX ANYTIME!
I'M REALLY IN LOVE... EVER SINCE WE HAD SEX, I CAN'T STOP THINKING ABOUT HIM.
BUT...BUT...I CAN'T JUST LEAVE NICK—WE'RE MARRIED!
C'MON, MELODY... MARRIAGE ISN'T THE LIFE SENTENCE IT USED TO BE, YOU KNOW.
?

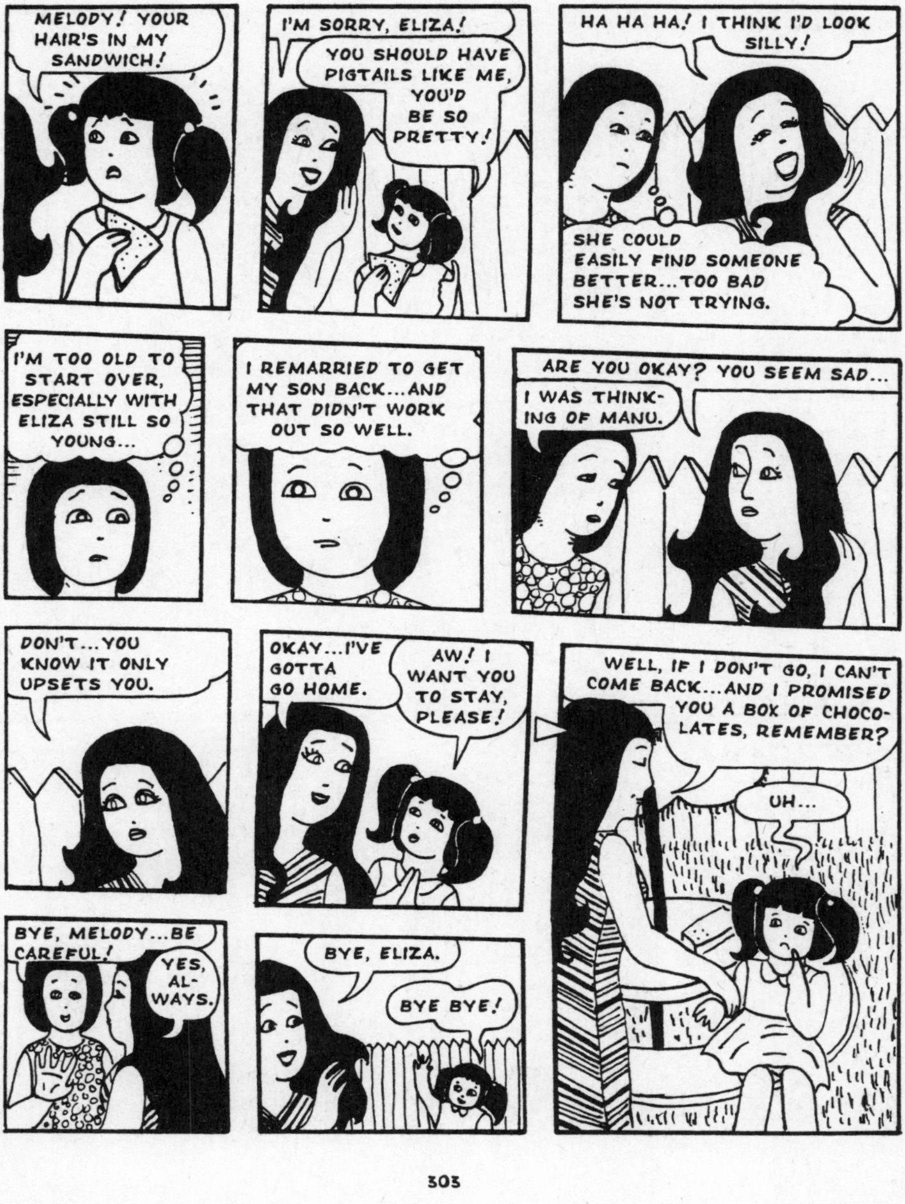
MELODY! YOUR HAIR'S IN MY SANDWICH!
I'M SORRY, ELIZA!
YOU SHOULD HAVE PIGTAILS LIKE ME, YOU'D BE SO PRETTY!
HA HA HA! I THINK I'D LOOK SILLY!
SHE COULD EASILY FIND SOMEONE BETTER...TOO BAD SHE'S NOT TRYING.
I'M TOO OLD TO START OVER, ESPECIALLY WITH ELIZA STILL SO YOUNG...
I REMARRIED TO GET MY SON BACK...AND THAT DIDN'T WORK OUT SO WELL.
ARE YOU OKAY? YOU SEEM SAD...
I WAS THINKING OF MANU.
DON'T...YOU KNOW IT ONLY UPSETS YOU.
OKAY...I'VE GOTTA GO HOME.
AW! I WANT YOU TO STAY, PLEASE!
WELL, IF I DON'T GO, I CAN'T COME BACK...AND I PROMISED YOU A BOX OF CHOCOLATES, REMEMBER?
UH...
BYE, MELODY...BE CAREFUL!
YES, ALWAYS.
BYE, ELIZA.
BYE BYE!

MY POOR AUNT...SHE HASN'T BEEN LUCKY IN LOVE...AND SHE REALLY DOESN'T LIKE NICK VERY MUCH...
IT'S ALWAYS A PARTY WHEN MELODY'S OUT!
BUT SHE DOESN'T KEEP YOU FROM DRINKING, DOES SHE?
NO...BUT DRINKING WITH SOMEONE WHO DOESN'T DRINK...IT'S WORSE THAN DRINKING ALONE.
HELLO!
OH! MELODY!
?
HE LOOKS HAPPY TO SEE HER...TOO HAPPY, IF YOU ASK ME!
DRING
DRING

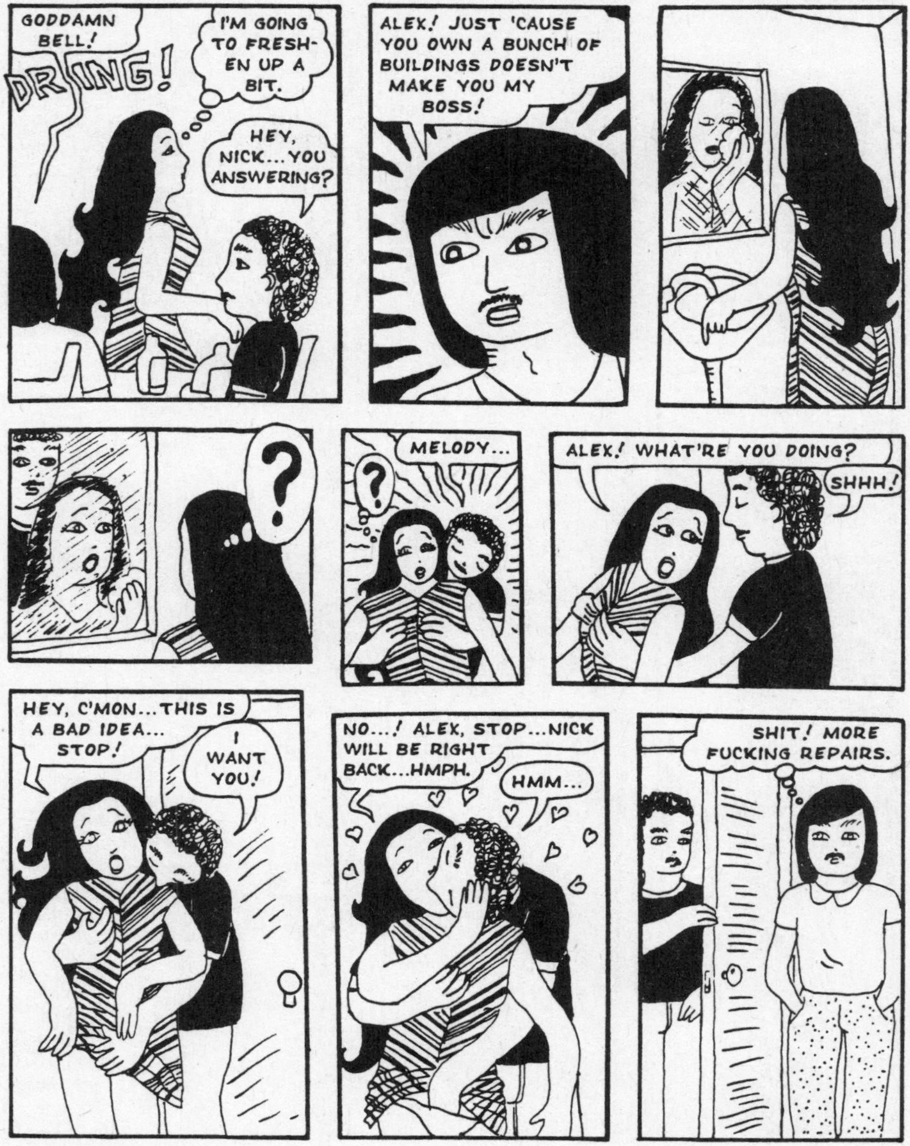
GODDAMN BELL!
DRING!
I'M GOING TO FRESH-EN UP A BIT.
HEY, NICK... YOU ANSWERING?
ALEX! JUST 'CAUSE YOU OWN A BUNCH OF BUILDINGS DOESN'T MAKE YOU MY BOSS!
?
MELODY...
?
ALEX! WHAT'RE YOU DOING?
SHHH!
HEY, C'MON... THIS IS A BAD IDEA... STOP!
I WANT YOU!
NO...! ALEX, STOP... NICK WILL BE RIGHT BACK... HMPH.
HMM...
SHIT! MORE FUCKING REPAIRS.

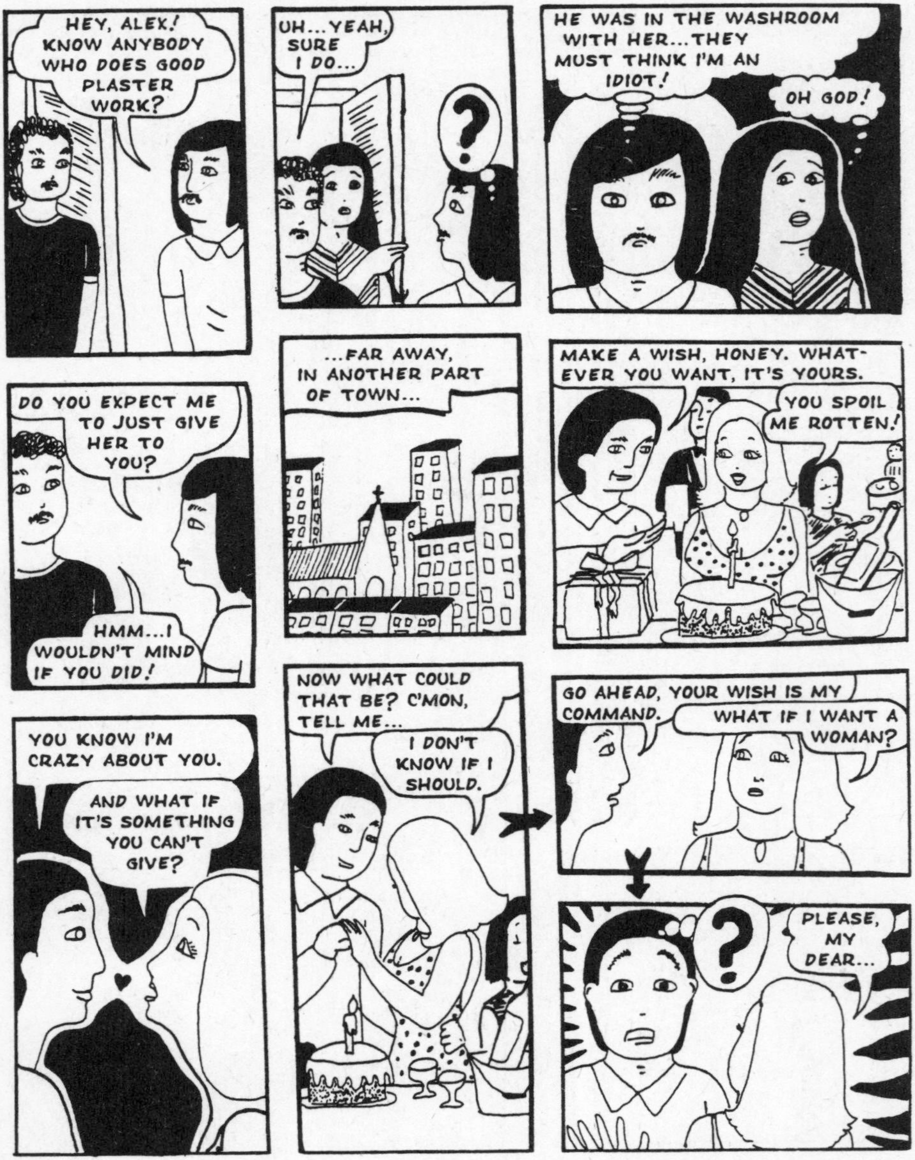
HEY, ALEX! KNOW ANYBODY WHO DOES GOOD PLASTER WORK?
UH...YEAH, SURE I DO...
?
HE WAS IN THE WASHROOM WITH HER...THEY MUST THINK I'M AN IDIOT!
OH GOD!
DO YOU EXPECT ME TO JUST GIVE HER TO YOU?
HMM...I WOULDN'T MIND IF YOU DID!
...FAR AWAY, IN ANOTHER PART OF TOWN...
MAKE A WISH, HONEY. WHATEVER YOU WANT, IT'S YOURS.
YOU SPOIL ME ROTTEN!
YOU KNOW I'M CRAZY ABOUT YOU.
AND WHAT IF IT'S SOMETHING YOU CAN'T GIVE?
NOW WHAT COULD THAT BE? C'MON, TELL ME...
I DON'T KNOW IF I SHOULD.
GO AHEAD, YOUR WISH IS MY COMMAND.
WHAT IF I WANT A WOMAN?
?
PLEASE, MY DEAR...

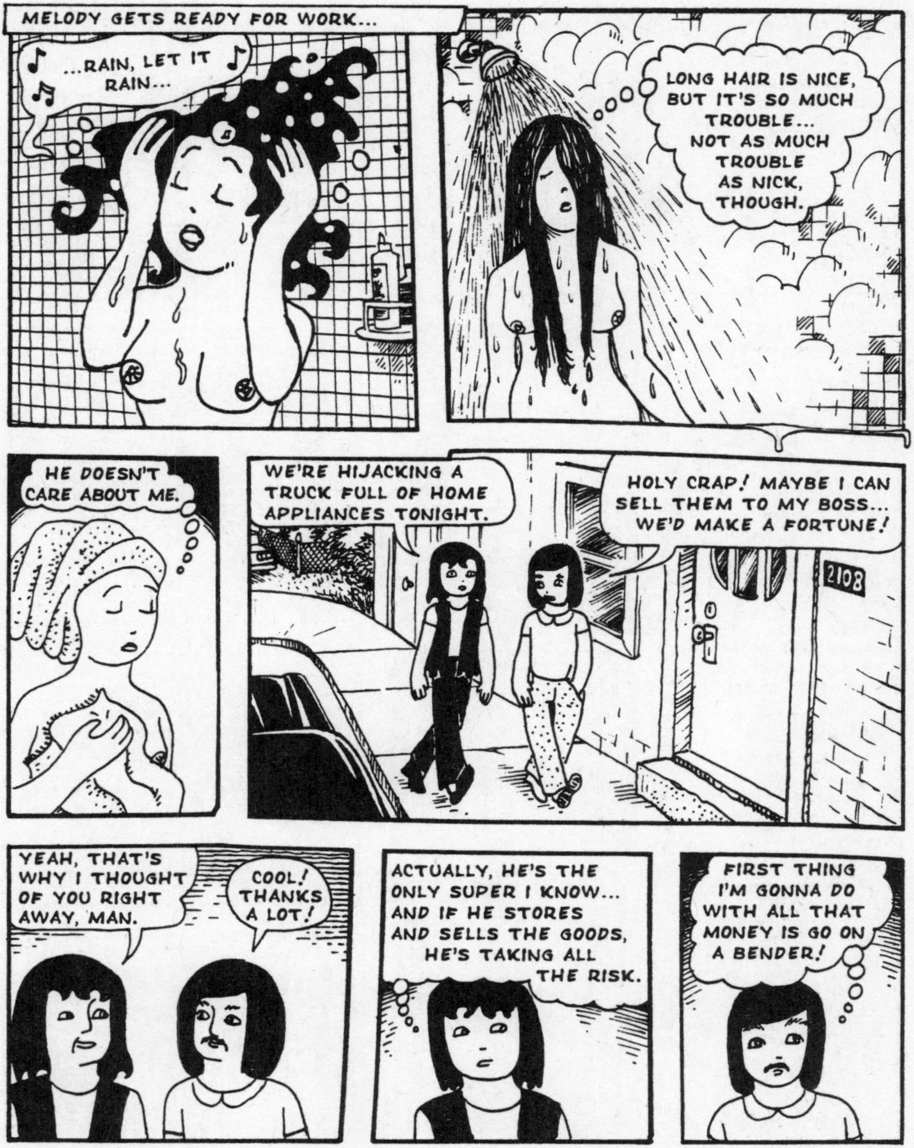
MELODY GETS READY FOR WORK...
...RAIN, LET IT RAIN...
LONG HAIR IS NICE, BUT IT'S SO MUCH TROUBLE... NOT AS MUCH TROUBLE AS NICK, THOUGH.
HE DOESN'T CARE ABOUT ME.
WE'RE HIJACKING A TRUCK FULL OF HOME APPLIANCES TONIGHT.
HOLY CRAP! MAYBE I CAN SELL THEM TO MY BOSS... WE'D MAKE A FORTUNE!
2108
YEAH, THAT'S WHY I THOUGHT OF YOU RIGHT AWAY, MAN.
COOL! THANKS A LOT!
ACTUALLY, HE'S THE ONLY SUPER I KNOW... AND IF HE STORES AND SELLS THE GOODS, HE'S TAKING ALL THE RISK.
FIRST THING I'M GONNA DO WITH ALL THAT MONEY IS GO ON A BENDER!

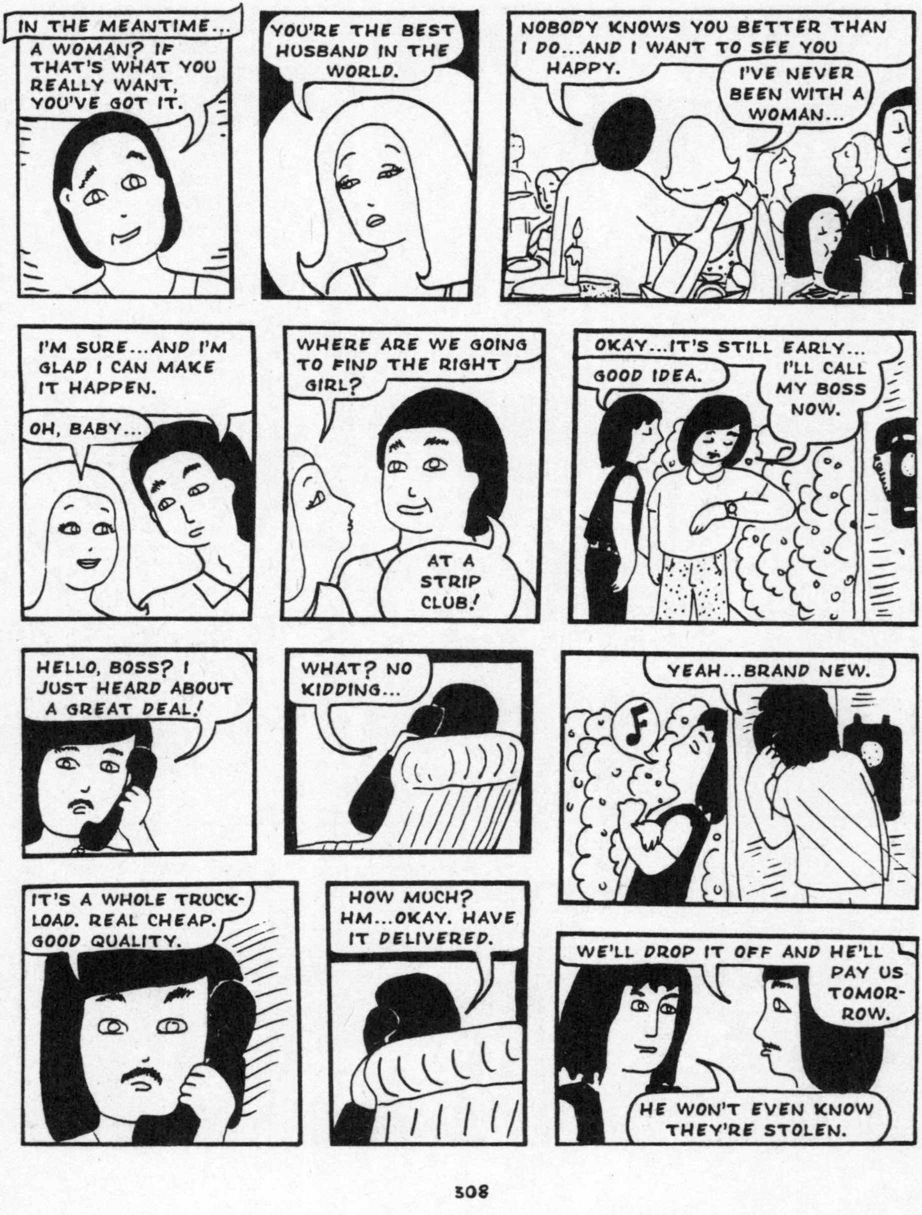
IN THE MEANTIME...
A WOMAN? IF THAT'S WHAT YOU REALLY WANT, YOU'VE GOT IT.
YOU'RE THE BEST HUSBAND IN THE WORLD.
NOBODY KNOWS YOU BETTER THAN I DO...AND I WANT TO SEE YOU HAPPY.
I'VE NEVER BEEN WITH A WOMAN...
I'M SURE...AND I'M GLAD I CAN MAKE IT HAPPEN.
OH, BABY...
WHERE ARE WE GOING TO FIND THE RIGHT GIRL?
AT A STRIP CLUB!
OKAY...IT'S STILL EARLY...
GOOD IDEA.
I'LL CALL MY BOSS NOW.
HELLO, BOSS? I JUST HEARD ABOUT A GREAT DEAL!
WHAT? NO KIDDING...
YEAH...BRAND NEW.
IT'S A WHOLE TRUCK-LOAD. REAL CHEAP. GOOD QUALITY.
HOW MUCH? HM...OKAY. HAVE IT DELIVERED.
WE'LL DROP IT OFF AND HE'LL PAY US TOMOR-ROW.
HE WON'T EVEN KNOW THEY'RE STOLEN.

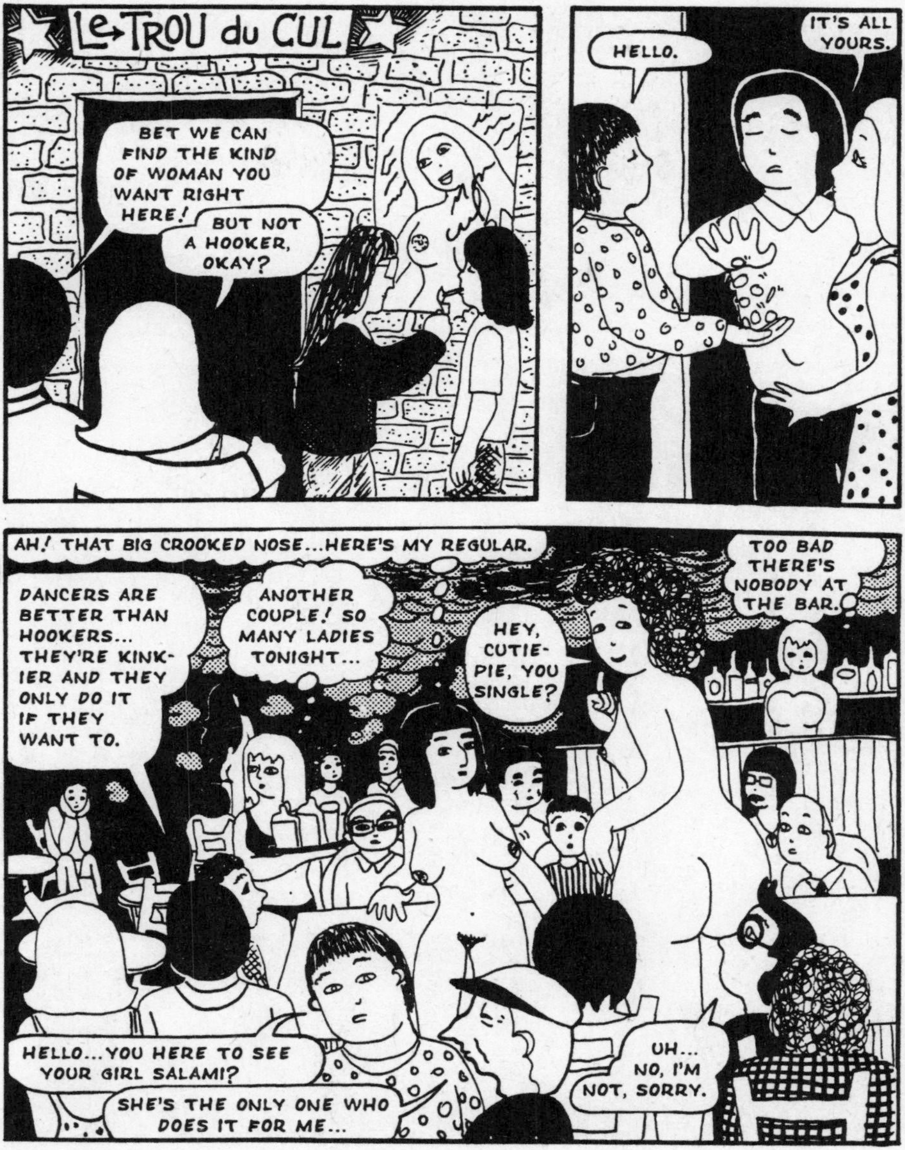
LE TROU du CUL
BET WE CAN FIND THE KIND OF WOMAN YOU WANT RIGHT HERE!
BUT NOT A HOOKER, OKAY?
HELLO.
IT'S ALL YOURS.
AH! THAT BIG CROOKED NOSE... HERE'S MY REGULAR.
DANCERS ARE BETTER THAN HOOKERS... THEY'RE KINKIER AND THEY ONLY DO IT IF THEY WANT TO.
ANOTHER COUPLE! SO MANY LADIES TONIGHT...
HEY, CUTIE-PIE, YOU SINGLE?
TOO BAD THERE'S NOBODY AT THE BAR.
HELLO... YOU HERE TO SEE YOUR GIRL SALAMI?
SHE'S THE ONLY ONE WHO DOES IT FOR ME...
UH... NO, I'M NOT, SORRY.

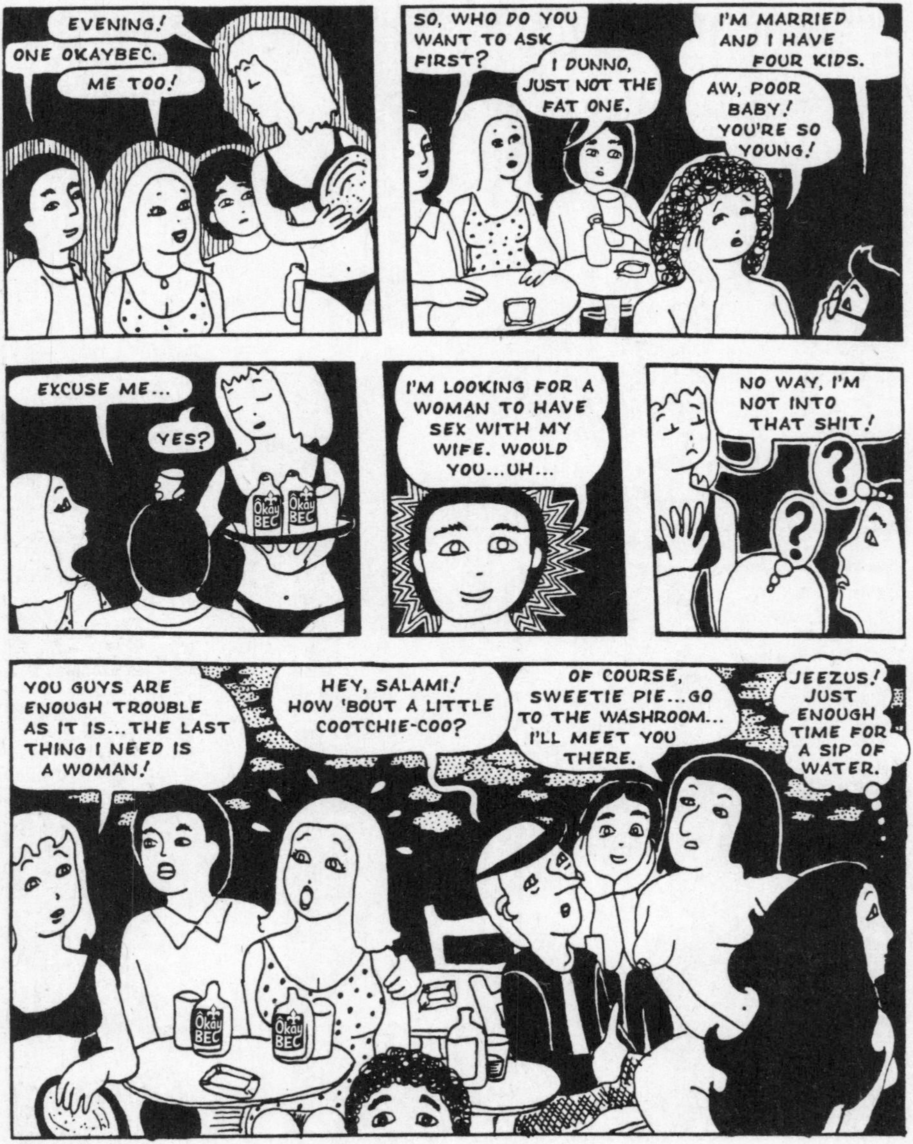
EVENING!
ONE OKAYBEC.
ME TOO!
SO, WHO DO YOU WANT TO ASK FIRST?
I DUNNO, JUST NOT THE FAT ONE.
I'M MARRIED AND I HAVE FOUR KIDS.
AW, POOR BABY! YOU'RE SO YOUNG!
EXCUSE ME...
YES?
ÔKAY BEC
I'M LOOKING FOR A WOMAN TO HAVE SEX WITH MY WIFE. WOULD YOU...UH...
NO WAY, I'M NOT INTO THAT SHIT!
?
?
YOU GUYS ARE ENOUGH TROUBLE AS IT IS...THE LAST THING I NEED IS A WOMAN!
HEY, SALAMI! HOW 'BOUT A LITTLE COOTCHIE-COO?
OF COURSE, SWEETIE PIE...GO TO THE WASHROOM... I'LL MEET YOU THERE.
JEEZUS! JUST ENOUGH TIME FOR A SIP OF WATER.
ÔKAY BEC

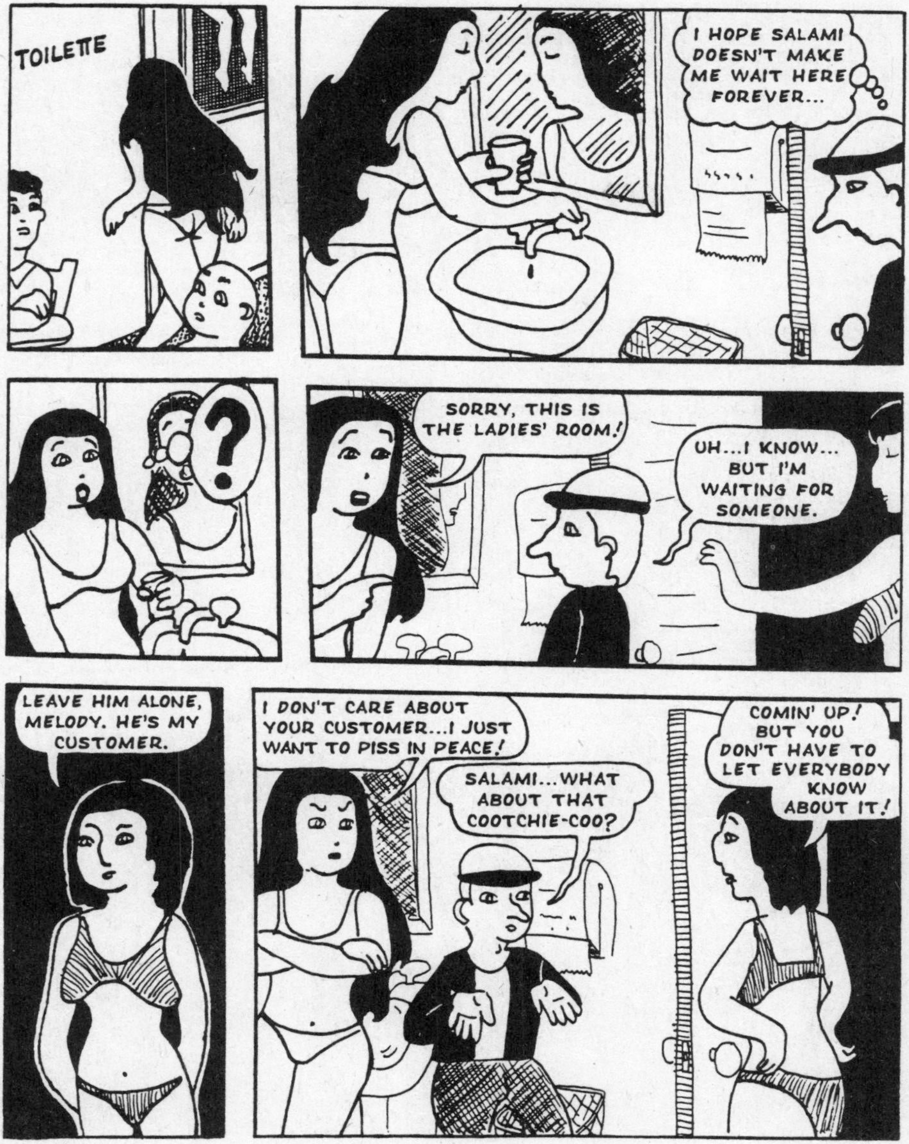
TOILETTE
I HOPE SALAMI DOESN'T MAKE ME WAIT HERE FOREVER...
?
SORRY, THIS IS THE LADIES' ROOM!
UH...I KNOW... BUT I'M WAITING FOR SOMEONE.
LEAVE HIM ALONE, MELODY. HE'S MY CUSTOMER.
I DON'T CARE ABOUT YOUR CUSTOMER...I JUST WANT TO PISS IN PEACE!
SALAMI...WHAT ABOUT THAT COOTCHIE-COO?
COMIN' UP! BUT YOU DON'T HAVE TO LET EVERYBODY KNOW ABOUT IT!

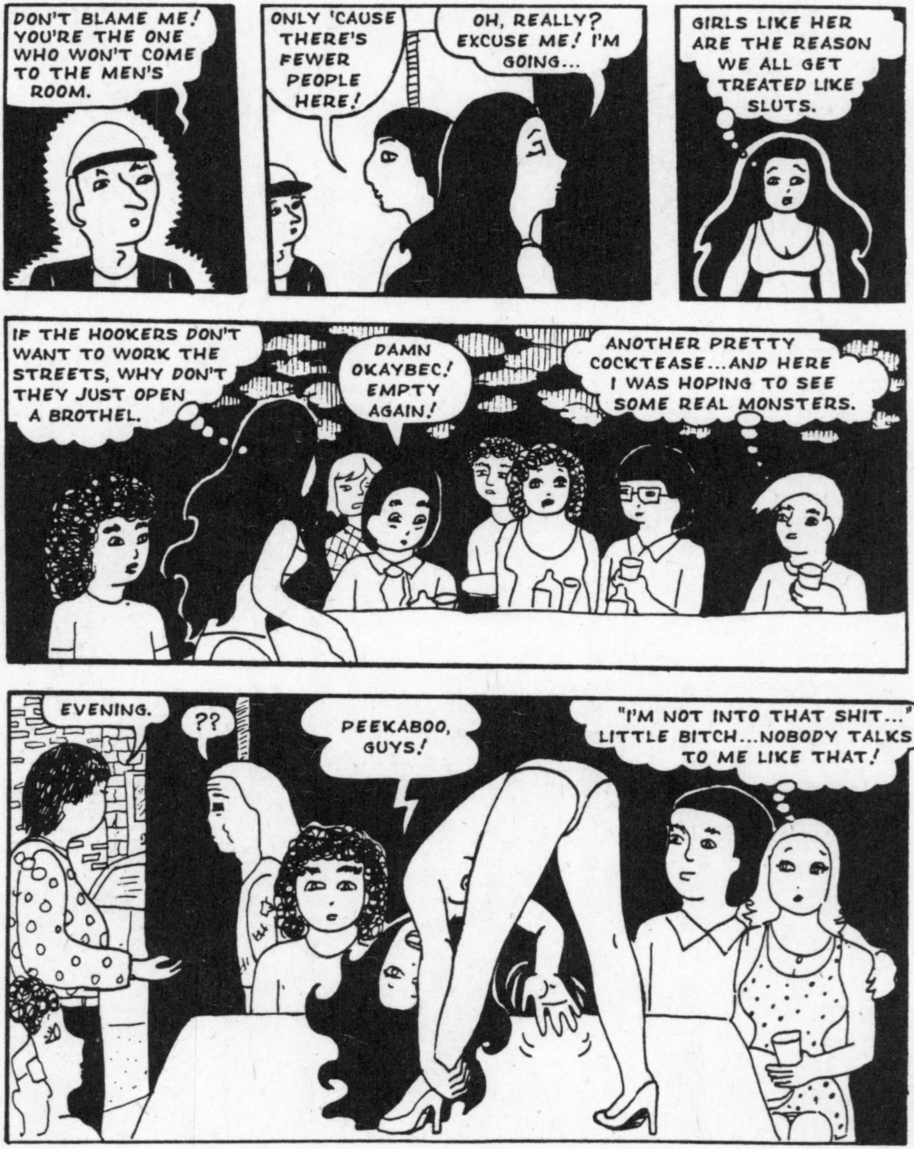
DON'T BLAME ME! YOU'RE THE ONE WHO WON'T COME TO THE MEN'S ROOM.
ONLY 'CAUSE THERE'S FEWER PEOPLE HERE!
OH, REALLY? EXCUSE ME! I'M GOING...
GIRLS LIKE HER ARE THE REASON WE ALL GET TREATED LIKE SLUTS.
IF THE HOOKERS DON'T WANT TO WORK THE STREETS, WHY DON'T THEY JUST OPEN A BROTHEL.
DAMN OKAYBEC! EMPTY AGAIN!
ANOTHER PRETTY COCKTEASE...AND HERE I WAS HOPING TO SEE SOME REAL MONSTERS.
EVENING.
??
PEEKABOO, GUYS!
"I'M NOT INTO THAT SHIT..." LITTLE BITCH...NOBODY TALKS TO ME LIKE THAT!

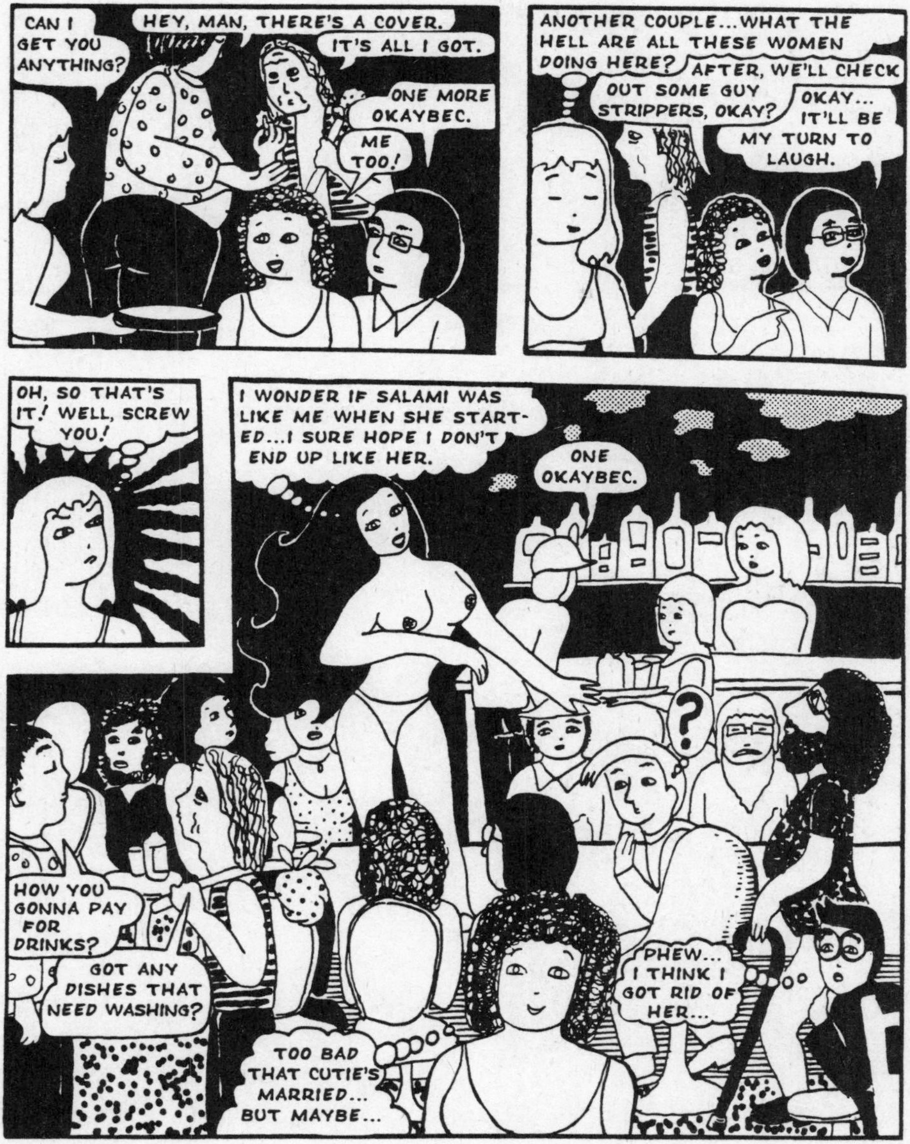
CAN I GET YOU ANYTHING?
HEY, MAN, THERE'S A COVER.
IT'S ALL I GOT.
ONE MORE OKAYBEC.
ME TOO!
ANOTHER COUPLE...WHAT THE HELL ARE ALL THESE WOMEN DOING HERE?
AFTER, WE'LL CHECK OUT SOME GUY STRIPPERS, OKAY?
OKAY... IT'LL BE MY TURN TO LAUGH.
OH, SO THAT'S IT! WELL, SCREW YOU!
I WONDER IF SALAMI WAS LIKE ME WHEN SHE STARTED...I SURE HOPE I DON'T END UP LIKE HER.
ONE OKAYBEC.
?
HOW YOU GONNA PAY FOR DRINKS?
GOT ANY DISHES THAT NEED WASHING?
TOO BAD THAT CUTIE'S MARRIED... BUT MAYBE...
PHEW... I THINK I GOT RID OF HER...

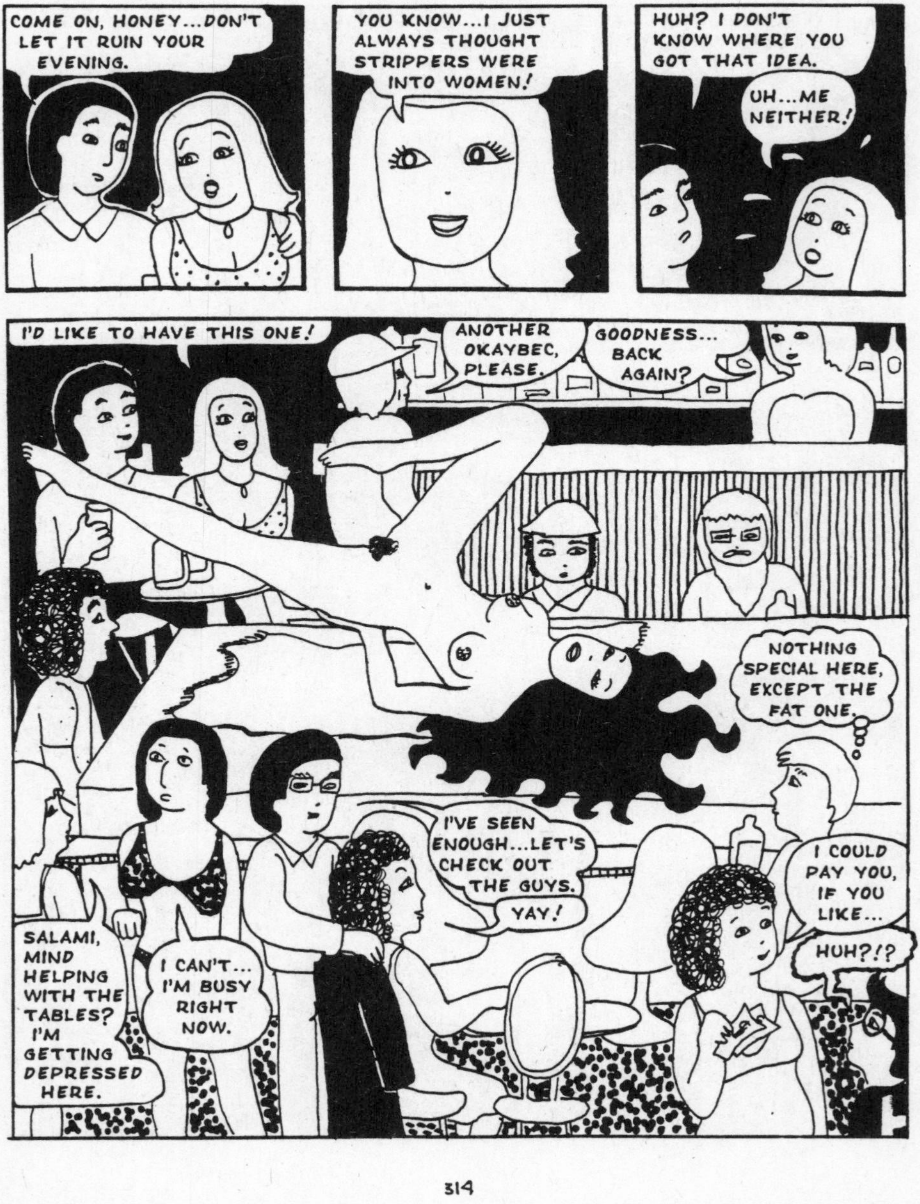
COME ON, HONEY...DON'T LET IT RUIN YOUR EVENING.
YOU KNOW...I JUST ALWAYS THOUGHT STRIPPERS WERE INTO WOMEN!
HUH? I DON'T KNOW WHERE YOU GOT THAT IDEA.
UH...ME NEITHER!
I'D LIKE TO HAVE THIS ONE!
ANOTHER OKAYBEC, PLEASE.
GOODNESS... BACK AGAIN?
NOTHING SPECIAL HERE, EXCEPT THE FAT ONE.
SALAMI, MIND HELPING WITH THE TABLES? I'M GETTING DEPRESSED HERE.
I CAN'T... I'M BUSY RIGHT NOW.
I'VE SEEN ENOUGH...LET'S CHECK OUT THE GUYS.
YAY!
I COULD PAY YOU, IF YOU LIKE...
HUH?!?

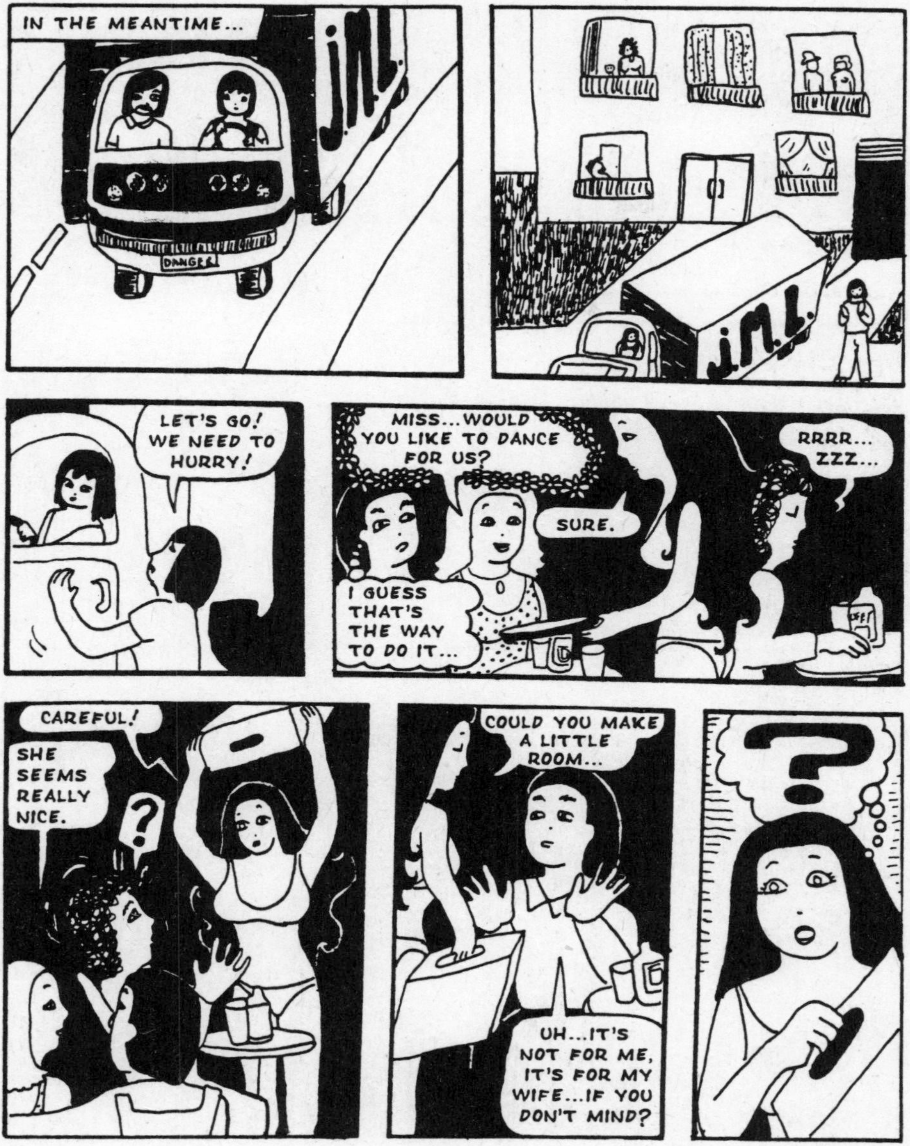
IN THE MEANTIME...
LET'S GO! WE NEED TO HURRY!
MISS...WOULD YOU LIKE TO DANCE FOR US?
SURE.
I GUESS THAT'S THE WAY TO DO IT...
RRRR... ZZZ...
CAREFUL!
SHE SEEMS REALLY NICE.
?
COULD YOU MAKE A LITTLE ROOM...
UH...IT'S NOT FOR ME, IT'S FOR MY WIFE...IF YOU DON'T MIND?
?

UH...NO, I DON'T MIND...
THANKS! IT'S FOR MY BIRTHDAY.
HAPPY BIRTHDAY!
THANKS... THIS WAS MY BIRTHDAY WISH.
I'VE NEVER DANCED FOR A WOMAN BEFORE... IT'S DIFFERENT... MORE SUBTLE SOMEHOW.
HAVE YOU EVER DONE IT WITH A WOMAN?
HM? YES, ONCE.
CAN YOU TELL ME HOW...UH... I MEAN, WHAT'S IT LIKE?
I GUESS IT'S NOT MUCH DIFFERENT FROM DOING IT WITH A GUY...YOU NEED TO LIKE EACH OTHER, THOUGH, AND IT HAS TO COME FROM THE HEART... BUT AS FAR AS PLEASURE GOES, FOR SURE THERE'S SOMETHING MISSING WHEN IT'S TWO GIRLS... BUT IT'S FUN.
WANT TO TRY WITH ME?
WOW, SHE'S FAST!
MAYBE...YOU'RE PRETTY.
TO-NIGHT?

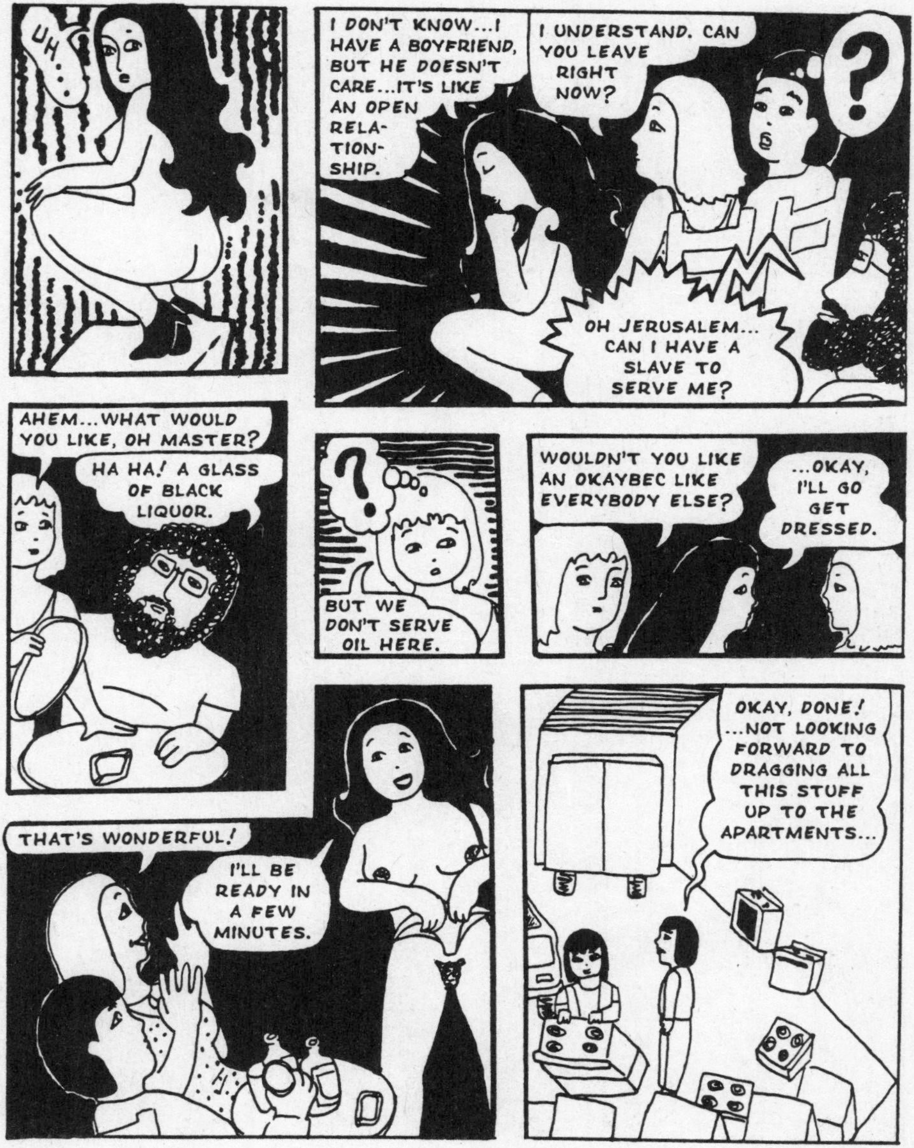
UH...
I DON'T KNOW...I HAVE A BOYFRIEND, BUT HE DOESN'T CARE...IT'S LIKE AN OPEN RELA-TION-SHIP.
I UNDERSTAND. CAN YOU LEAVE RIGHT NOW?
?
OH JERUSALEM... CAN I HAVE A SLAVE TO SERVE ME?
AHEM...WHAT WOULD YOU LIKE, OH MASTER?
HA HA! A GLASS OF BLACK LIQUOR.
?
BUT WE DON'T SERVE OIL HERE.
WOULDN'T YOU LIKE AN OKAYBEC LIKE EVERYBODY ELSE?
...OKAY, I'LL GO GET DRESSED.
THAT'S WONDERFUL!
I'LL BE READY IN A FEW MINUTES.
OKAY, DONE! ...NOT LOOKING FORWARD TO DRAGGING ALL THIS STUFF UP TO THE APARTMENTS...

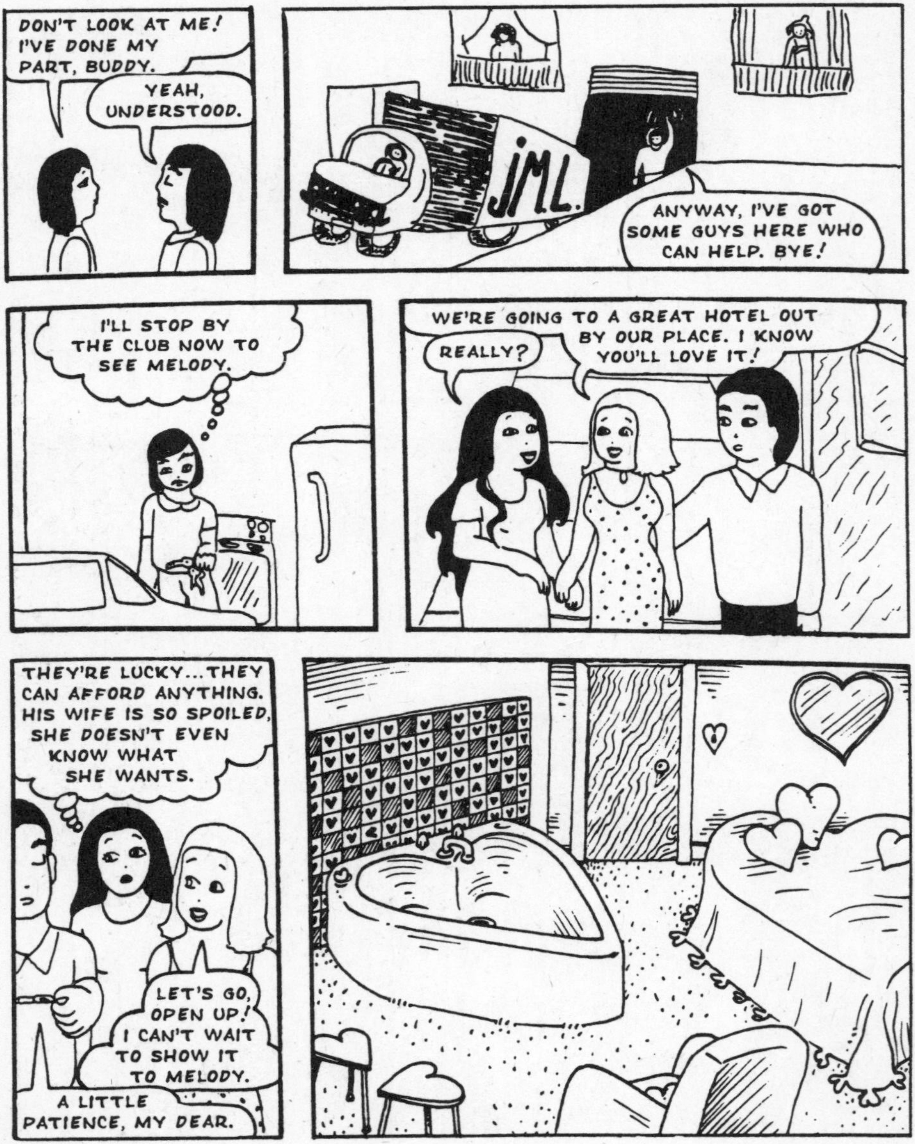
DON'T LOOK AT ME! I'VE DONE MY PART, BUDDY.
YEAH, UNDERSTOOD.
jML.
ANYWAY, I'VE GOT SOME GUYS HERE WHO CAN HELP. BYE!
I'LL STOP BY THE CLUB NOW TO SEE MELODY.
WE'RE GOING TO A GREAT HOTEL OUT BY OUR PLACE. I KNOW YOU'LL LOVE IT!
REALLY?
THEY'RE LUCKY... THEY CAN AFFORD ANYTHING. HIS WIFE IS SO SPOILED, SHE DOESN'T EVEN KNOW WHAT SHE WANTS.
LET'S GO, OPEN UP! I CAN'T WAIT TO SHOW IT TO MELODY.
A LITTLE PATIENCE, MY DEAR.

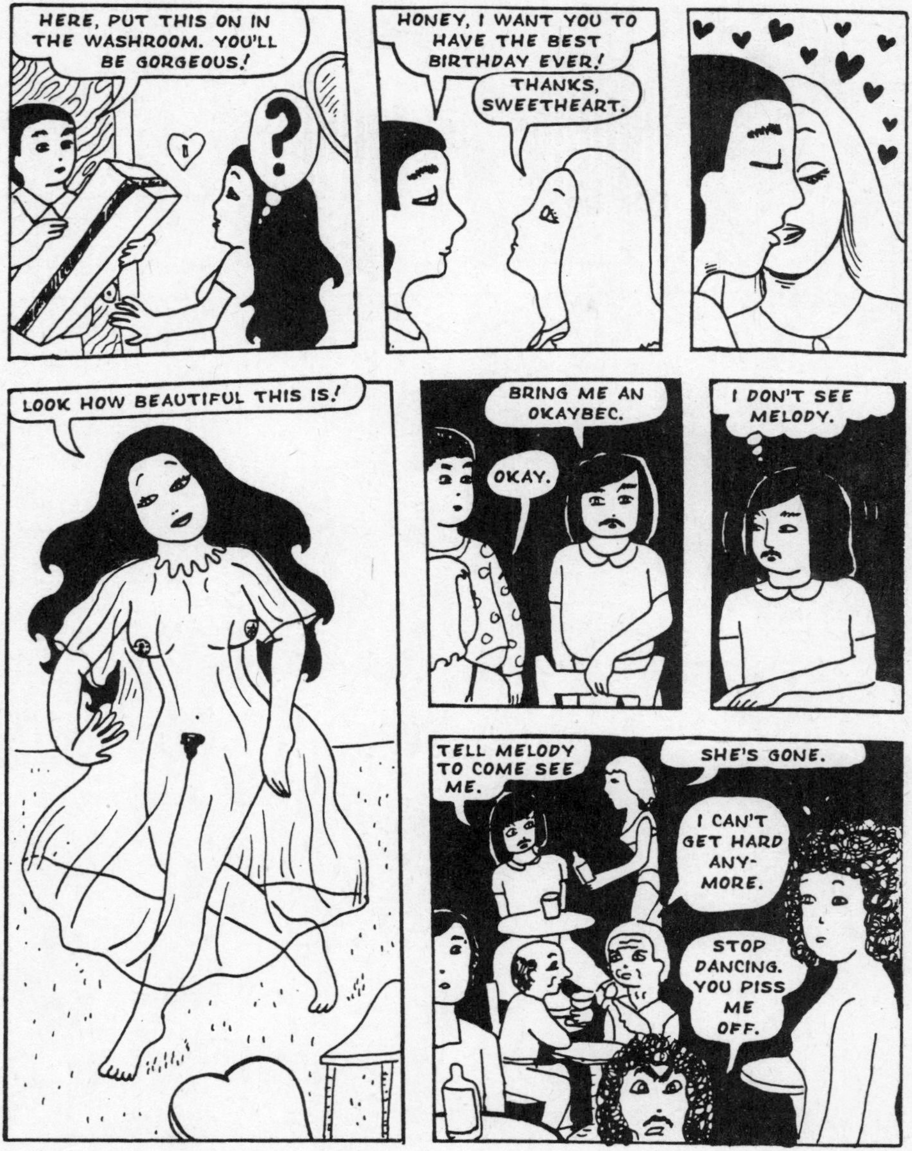
HERE, PUT THIS ON IN THE WASHROOM. YOU'LL BE GORGEOUS!
?
HONEY, I WANT YOU TO HAVE THE BEST BIRTHDAY EVER!
THANKS, SWEETHEART.
LOOK HOW BEAUTIFUL THIS IS!
BRING ME AN OKAYBEC.
OKAY.
I DON'T SEE MELODY.
TELL MELODY TO COME SEE ME.
SHE'S GONE.
I CAN'T GET HARD ANY-MORE.
STOP DANCING. YOU PISS ME OFF.

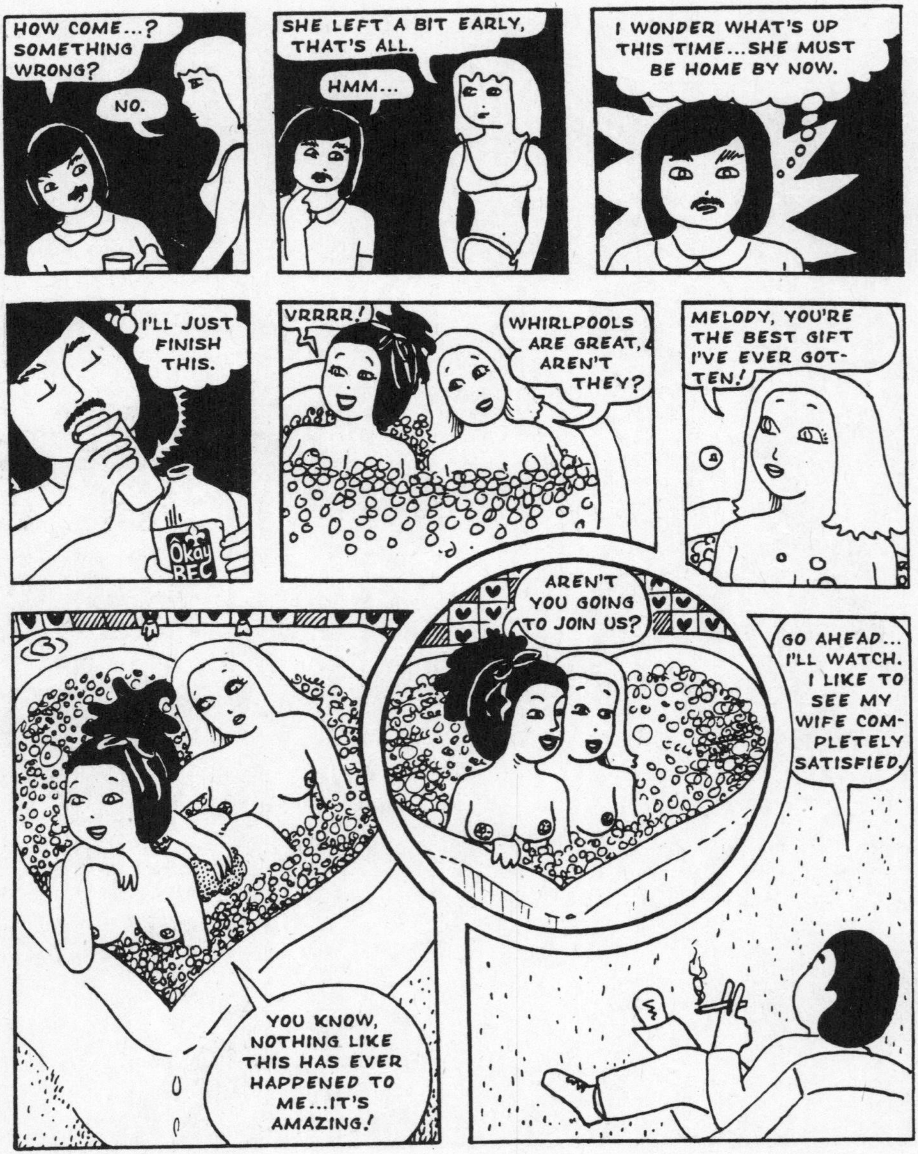
HOW COME...? SOMETHING WRONG?
NO.
SHE LEFT A BIT EARLY, THAT'S ALL.
HMM...
I WONDER WHAT'S UP THIS TIME...SHE MUST BE HOME BY NOW.
I'LL JUST FINISH THIS.
VRRRR!
WHIRLPOOLS ARE GREAT, AREN'T THEY?
MELODY, YOU'RE THE BEST GIFT I'VE EVER GOT-TEN!
YOU KNOW, NOTHING LIKE THIS HAS EVER HAPPENED TO ME...IT'S AMAZING!
AREN'T YOU GOING TO JOIN US?
GO AHEAD... I'LL WATCH. I LIKE TO SEE MY WIFE COM-PLETELY SATISFIED.

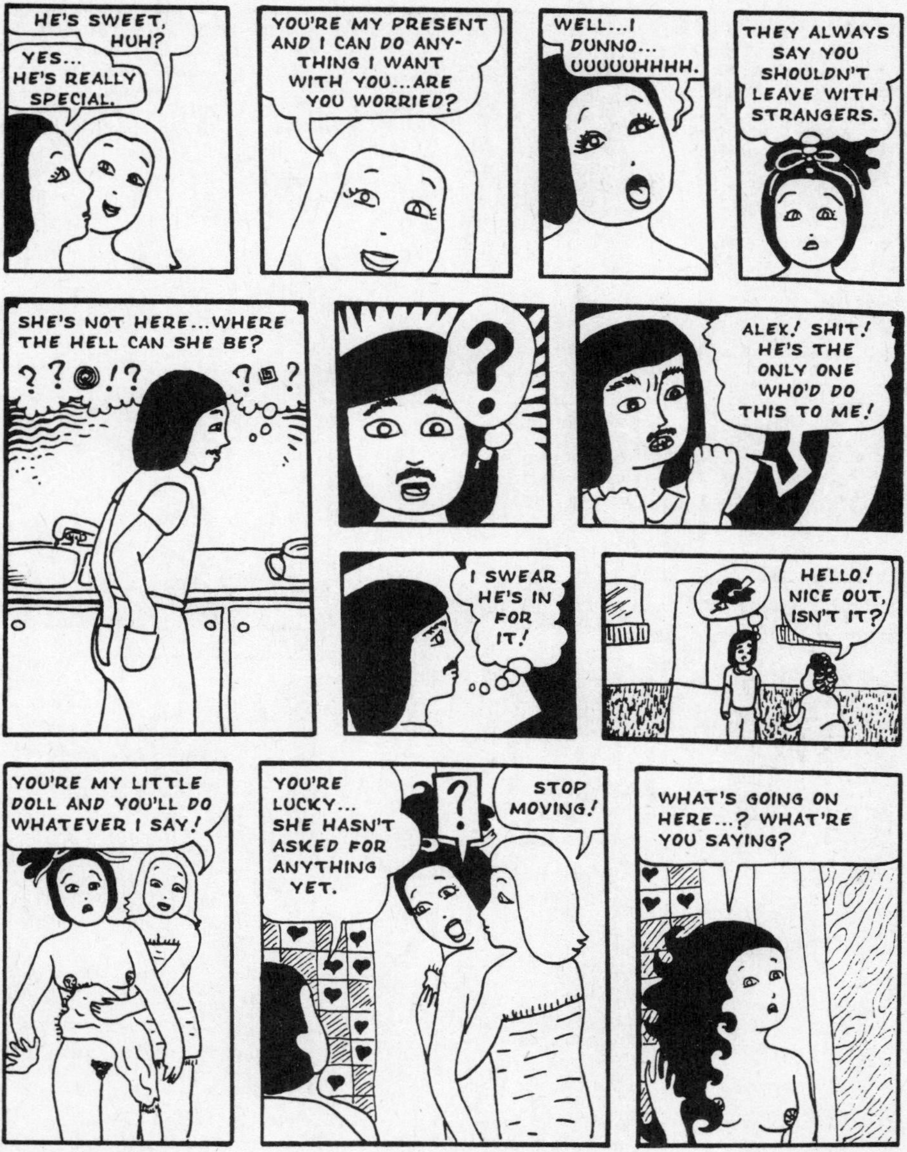
HE'S SWEET, HUH?
YES... HE'S REALLY SPECIAL.
YOU'RE MY PRESENT AND I CAN DO ANYTHING I WANT WITH YOU...ARE YOU WORRIED?
WELL...I DUNNO... UUUUUHHHH.
THEY ALWAYS SAY YOU SHOULDN'T LEAVE WITH STRANGERS.
SHE'S NOT HERE...WHERE THE HELL CAN SHE BE?
??!?
?
ALEX! SHIT! HE'S THE ONLY ONE WHO'D DO THIS TO ME!
I SWEAR HE'S IN FOR IT!
HELLO! NICE OUT, ISN'T IT?
YOU'RE MY LITTLE DOLL AND YOU'LL DO WHATEVER I SAY!
YOU'RE LUCKY... SHE HASN'T ASKED FOR ANYTHING YET.
?
STOP MOVING!
WHAT'S GOING ON HERE...? WHAT'RE YOU SAYING?

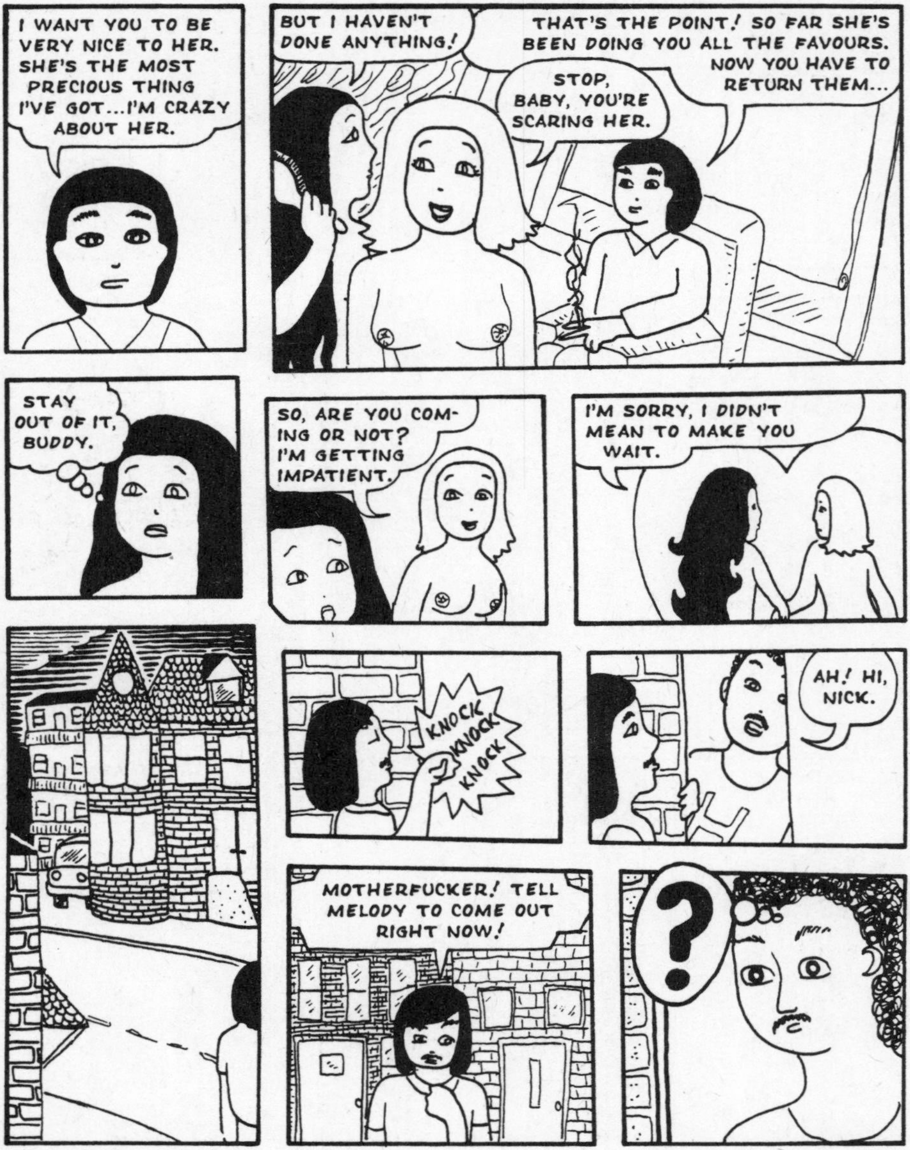
I WANT YOU TO BE VERY NICE TO HER. SHE'S THE MOST PRECIOUS THING I'VE GOT...I'M CRAZY ABOUT HER.
BUT I HAVEN'T DONE ANYTHING!
THAT'S THE POINT! SO FAR SHE'S BEEN DOING YOU ALL THE FAVOURS. NOW YOU HAVE TO RETURN THEM...
STOP, BABY, YOU'RE SCARING HER.
STAY OUT OF IT, BUDDY.
SO, ARE YOU COMING OR NOT? I'M GETTING IMPATIENT.
I'M SORRY, I DIDN'T MEAN TO MAKE YOU WAIT.
KNOCK KNOCK KNOCK
AH! HI, NICK.
MOTHERFUCKER! TELL MELODY TO COME OUT RIGHT NOW!
?

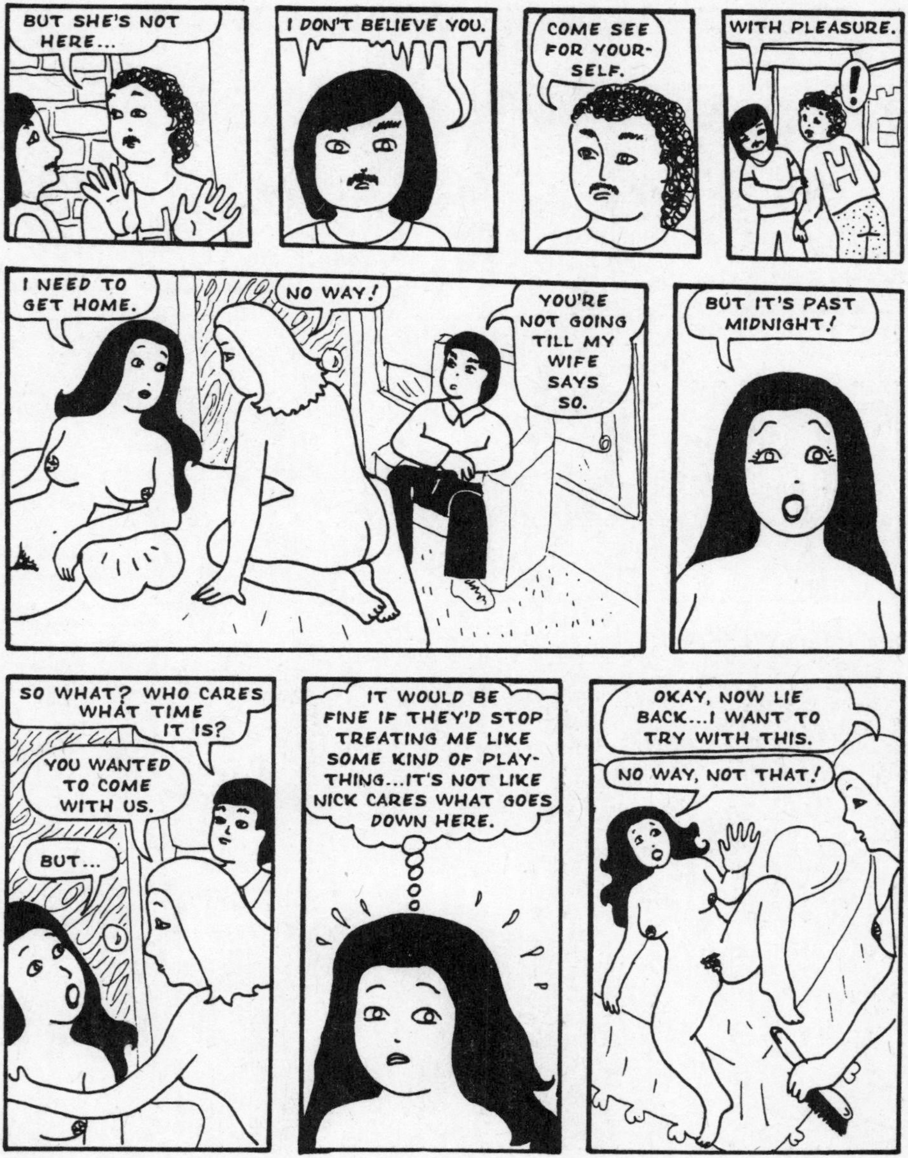
BUT SHE'S NOT HERE...
I DON'T BELIEVE YOU.
COME SEE FOR YOURSELF.
WITH PLEASURE.
!
I NEED TO GET HOME.
NO WAY!
YOU'RE NOT GOING TILL MY WIFE SAYS SO.
BUT IT'S PAST MIDNIGHT!
SO WHAT? WHO CARES WHAT TIME IT IS?
YOU WANTED TO COME WITH US.
BUT...
IT WOULD BE FINE IF THEY'D STOP TREATING ME LIKE SOME KIND OF PLAYTHING...IT'S NOT LIKE NICK CARES WHAT GOES DOWN HERE.
OKAY, NOW LIE BACK...I WANT TO TRY WITH THIS.
NO WAY, NOT THAT!

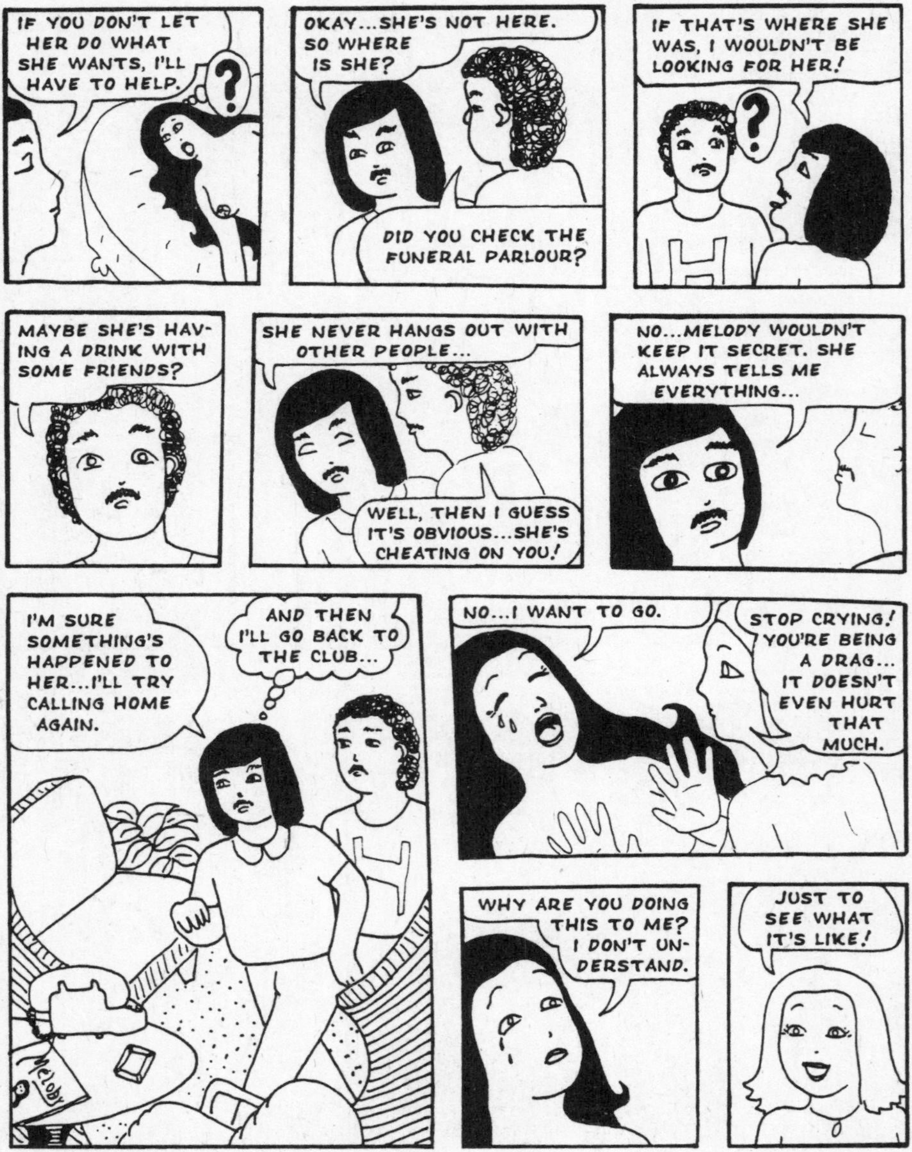
IF YOU DON'T LET HER DO WHAT SHE WANTS, I'LL HAVE TO HELP.
?
OKAY...SHE'S NOT HERE. SO WHERE IS SHE?
DID YOU CHECK THE FUNERAL PARLOUR?
IF THAT'S WHERE SHE WAS, I WOULDN'T BE LOOKING FOR HER!
?
MAYBE SHE'S HAVING A DRINK WITH SOME FRIENDS?
SHE NEVER HANGS OUT WITH OTHER PEOPLE...
WELL, THEN I GUESS IT'S OBVIOUS...SHE'S CHEATING ON YOU!
NO...MELODY WOULDN'T KEEP IT SECRET. SHE ALWAYS TELLS ME EVERYTHING...
I'M SURE SOMETHING'S HAPPENED TO HER...I'LL TRY CALLING HOME AGAIN.
AND THEN I'LL GO BACK TO THE CLUB...
MELODY
NO...I WANT TO GO.
STOP CRYING! YOU'RE BEING A DRAG... IT DOESN'T EVEN HURT THAT MUCH.
WHY ARE YOU DOING THIS TO ME? I DON'T UNDERSTAND.
JUST TO SEE WHAT IT'S LIKE!

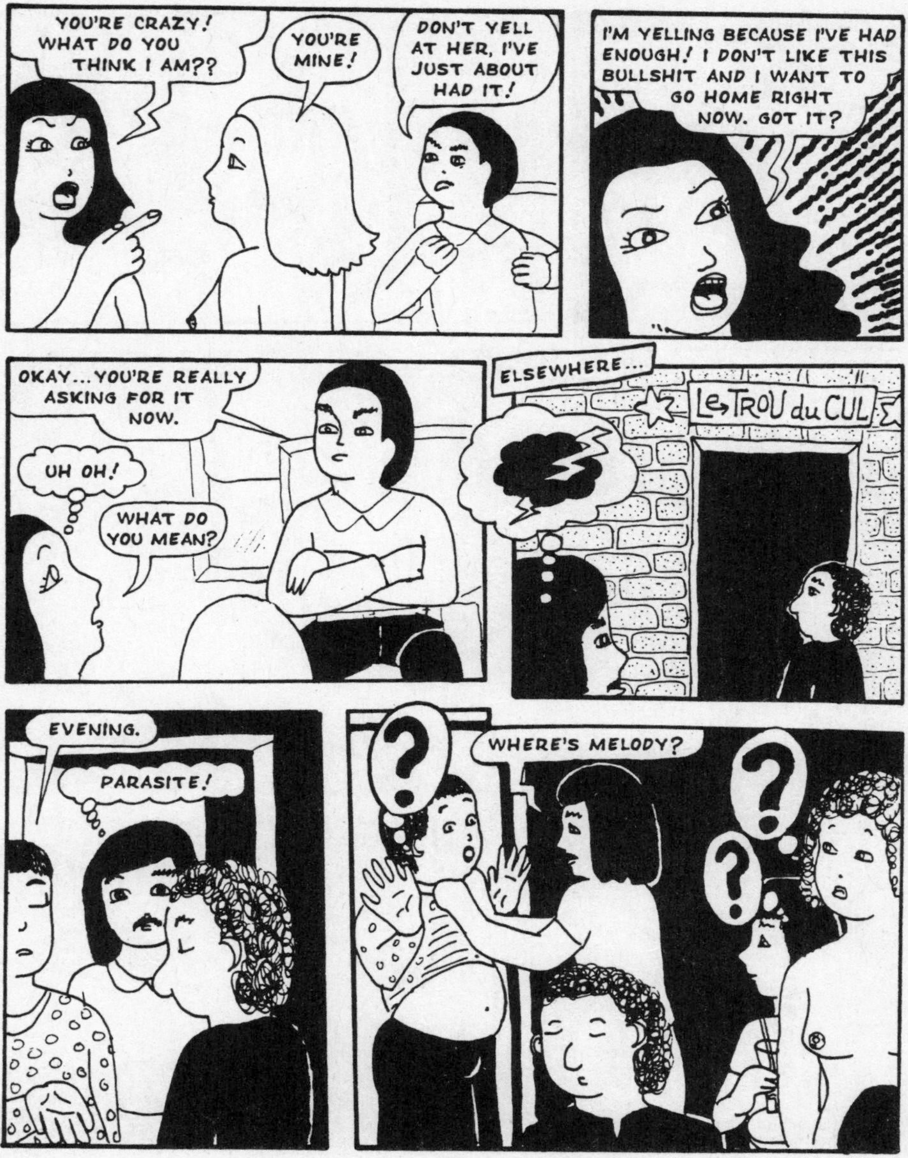

YOU'RE CRAZY! WHAT DO YOU THINK I AM??
YOU'RE MINE!
DON'T YELL AT HER, I'VE JUST ABOUT HAD IT!
I'M YELLING BECAUSE I'VE HAD ENOUGH! I DON'T LIKE THIS BULLSHIT AND I WANT TO GO HOME RIGHT NOW. GOT IT?
OKAY... YOU'RE REALLY ASKING FOR IT NOW.
UH OH!
WHAT DO YOU MEAN?
ELSEWHERE...
Le TROU du CUL
EVENING.
PARASITE!
WHERE'S MELODY?

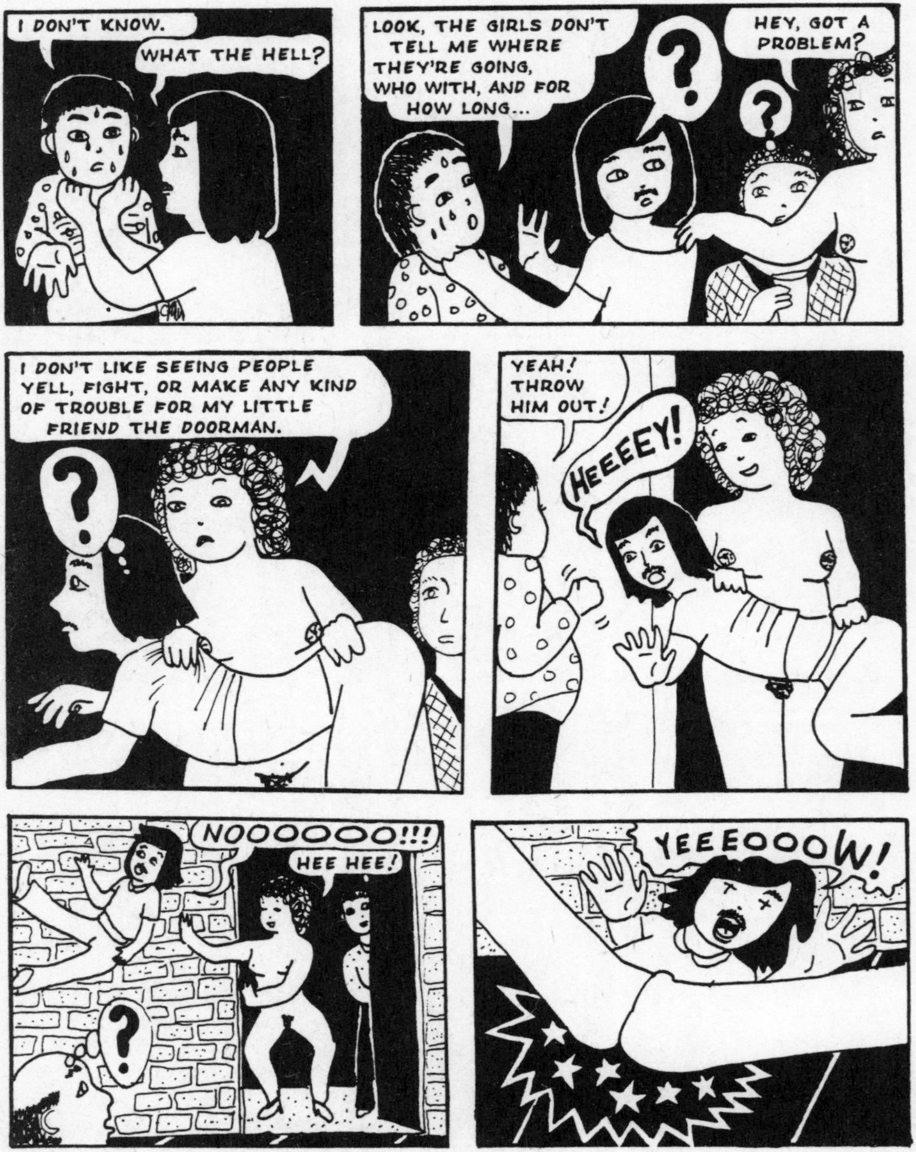
I DON'T KNOW.
WHAT THE HELL?
LOOK, THE GIRLS DON'T TELL ME WHERE THEY'RE GOING, WHO WITH, AND FOR HOW LONG...
?
HEY, GOT A PROBLEM?
?
I DON'T LIKE SEEING PEOPLE YELL, FIGHT, OR MAKE ANY KIND OF TROUBLE FOR MY LITTLE FRIEND THE DOORMAN.
?
YEAH! THROW HIM OUT!
HEEEEY!
NOOOOOO!!!
HEE HEE!
?
YEEEOOOW!

BUNCHA ASSHOLES! YOU'VE LOCKED UP MY GIRLFRIEND! YOU'RE GONNA PAY FOR THIS!
SORRY, YOU'VE GOT IT WRONG.
MELODY ASKED TO LEAVE EARLY...I CAN'T KEEP THE GIRLS FROM HOOKING UP WITH CUSTOMERS— YOU KNOW HOW IT GOES HERE. SO DON'T BLAME IT ON ME.
?
?
MELODY'S TURNING TRICKS... NOW THAT I DON'T BELIEVE.
HEY...CAN YOU SET ME UP WITH HER?
IF SHE WERE AROUND, I WOULDN'T BE HAVING ALL THIS TROUBLE.
MY LITTLE MELODY... INCREDIBLE!
THERE, SHE'S DOING YOU ANOTHER FAVOUR...SHE NEVER GOES DOWN ON ME.
OKAY, FINE! JUST LET GO OF MY HAIR!

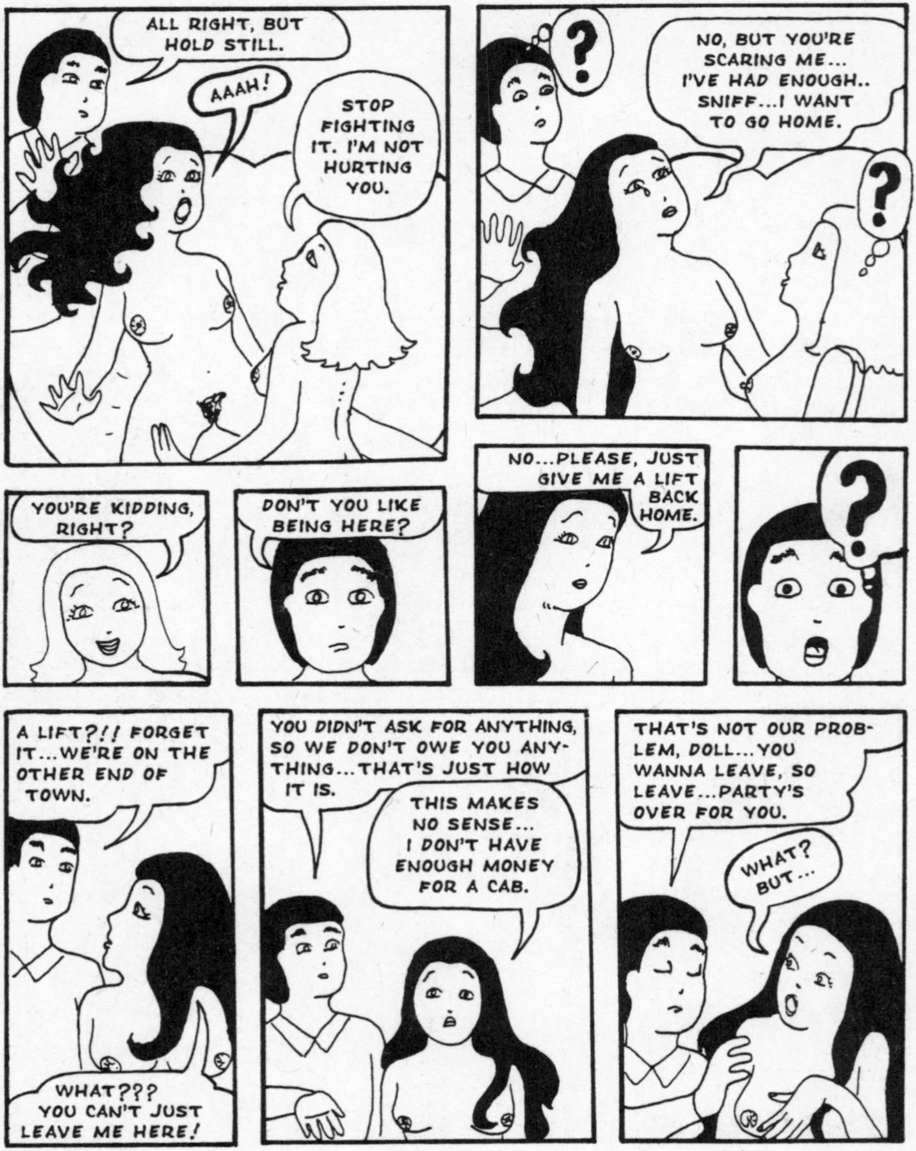

ALL RIGHT, BUT HOLD STILL.
AAAH!
STOP FIGHTING IT. I'M NOT HURTING YOU.
?
NO, BUT YOU'RE SCARING ME... I'VE HAD ENOUGH.. SNIFF...I WANT TO GO HOME.
?
YOU'RE KIDDING, RIGHT?
DON'T YOU LIKE BEING HERE?
NO...PLEASE, JUST GIVE ME A LIFT BACK HOME.
?
A LIFT?!! FORGET IT...WE'RE ON THE OTHER END OF TOWN.
WHAT??? YOU CAN'T JUST LEAVE ME HERE!
YOU DIDN'T ASK FOR ANYTHING, SO WE DON'T OWE YOU ANYTHING...THAT'S JUST HOW IT IS.
THIS MAKES NO SENSE... I DON'T HAVE ENOUGH MONEY FOR A CAB.
THAT'S NOT OUR PROBLEM, DOLL...YOU WANNA LEAVE, SO LEAVE...PARTY'S OVER FOR YOU.
WHAT? BUT...

I BETTER GET OUT OF HERE BEFORE THEY CHANGE THEIR MINDS...
WHERE'S MY DARN DRESS?
BABY...THAT WAS A BEAUTIFUL BIRTHDAY PRESENT. HOW'M I EVER GOING TO THANK YOU?
IF YOU'RE HAPPY, THAT'S ALL THAT MATTERS, HONEY.
BETTER NOT WRECK THE MOMENT FOR THOSE TWO CRAZIES...I'M JUST GONNA SLIP OUT OF HERE.
08
109
WHERE THE HECK AM I?
101
102
SIR! SORRY, BUT WHICH WAY IS MONTREAL?
BUS
OTHER SIDE OF THE BRIDGE!

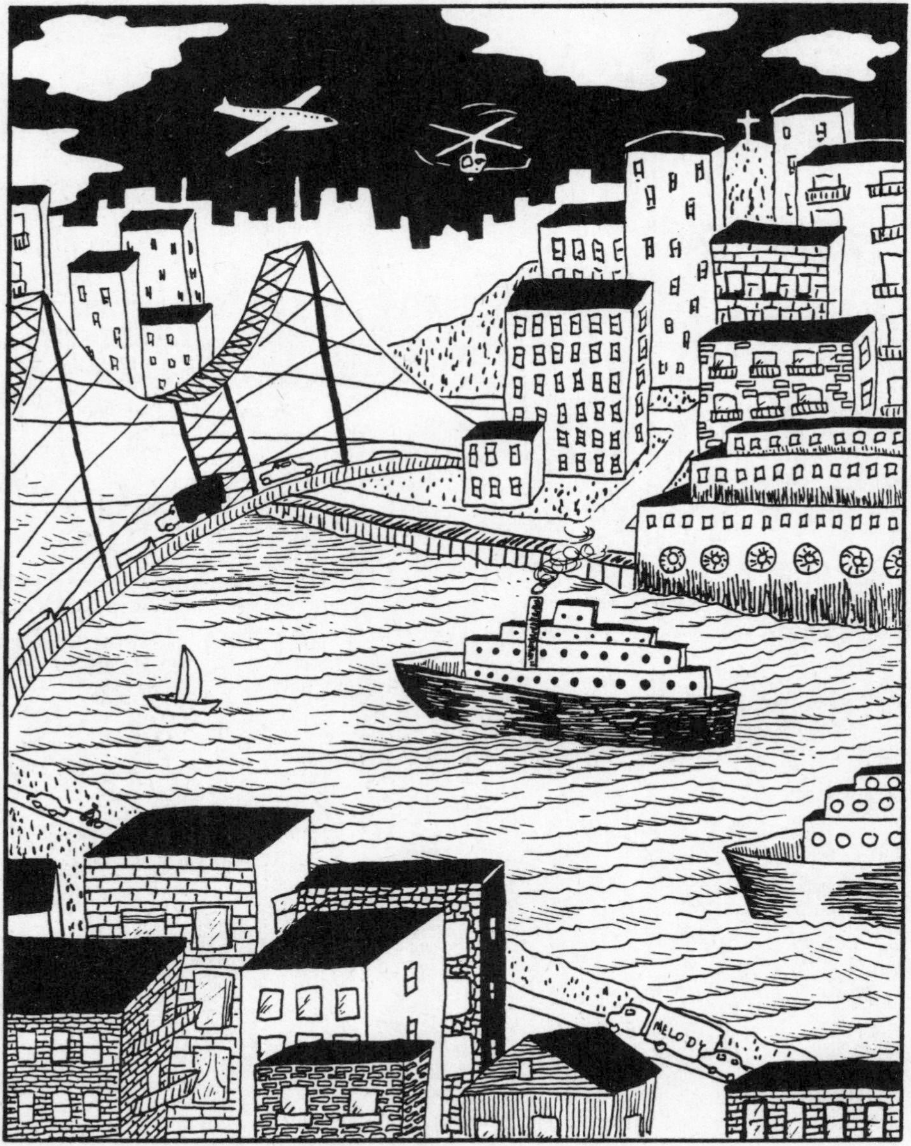
MELODY

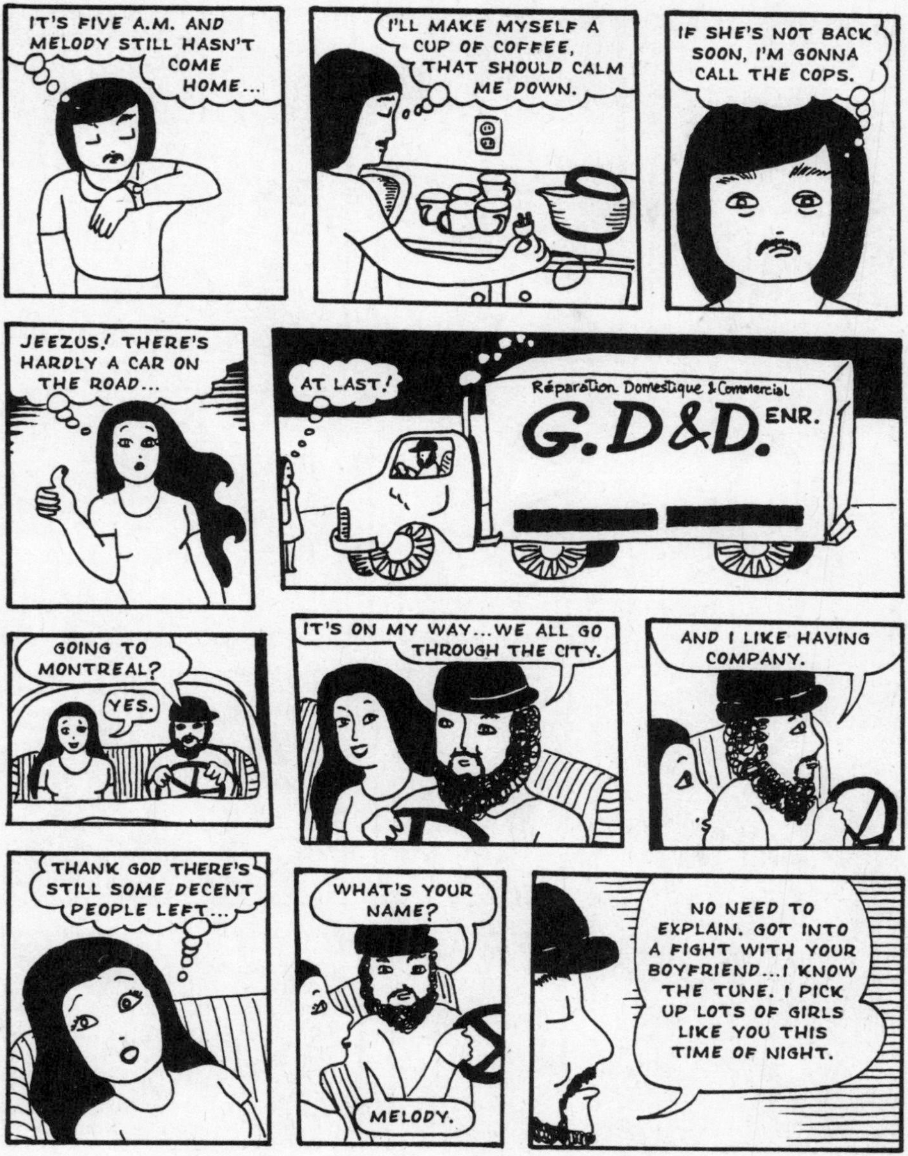
IT'S FIVE A.M. AND MELODY STILL HASN'T COME HOME...
I'LL MAKE MYSELF A CUP OF COFFEE, THAT SHOULD CALM ME DOWN.
IF SHE'S NOT BACK SOON, I'M GONNA CALL THE COPS.
JEEZUS! THERE'S HARDLY A CAR ON THE ROAD...
AT LAST!
Réparation Domestique & Commercial
G.D&D. ENR.
GOING TO MONTREAL?
YES.
IT'S ON MY WAY...WE ALL GO THROUGH THE CITY.
AND I LIKE HAVING COMPANY.
THANK GOD THERE'S STILL SOME DECENT PEOPLE LEFT...
WHAT'S YOUR NAME?
MELODY.
NO NEED TO EXPLAIN. GOT INTO A FIGHT WITH YOUR BOYFRIEND...I KNOW THE TUNE. I PICK UP LOTS OF GIRLS LIKE YOU THIS TIME OF NIGHT.

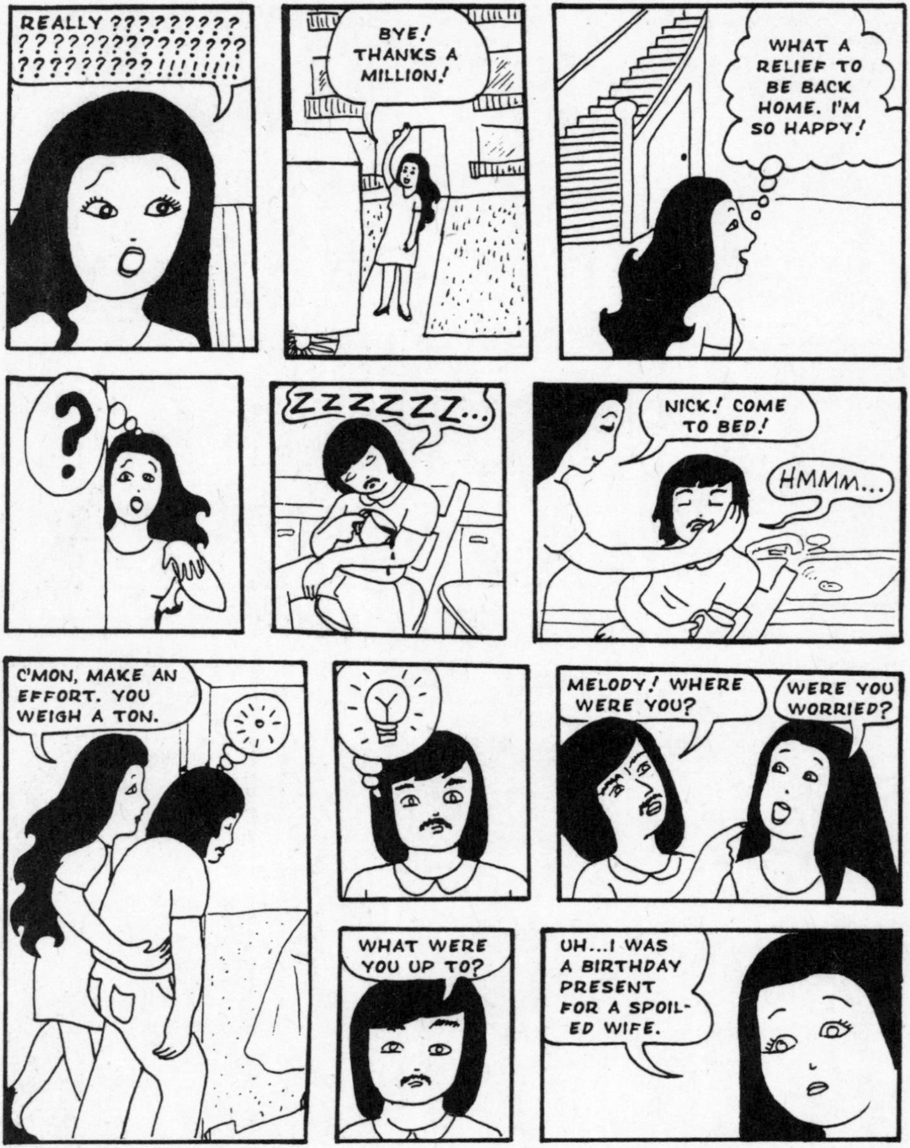
REALLY ????????? ???????????????? ??????????!!!!!!!!
BYE! THANKS A MILLION!
WHAT A RELIEF TO BE BACK HOME. I'M SO HAPPY!
?
ZZZZZZ...
NICK! COME TO BED!
HMMM...
C'MON, MAKE AN EFFORT. YOU WEIGH A TON.
MELODY! WHERE WERE YOU?
WERE YOU WORRIED?
WHAT WERE YOU UP TO?
UH...I WAS A BIRTHDAY PRESENT FOR A SPOIL-ED WIFE.

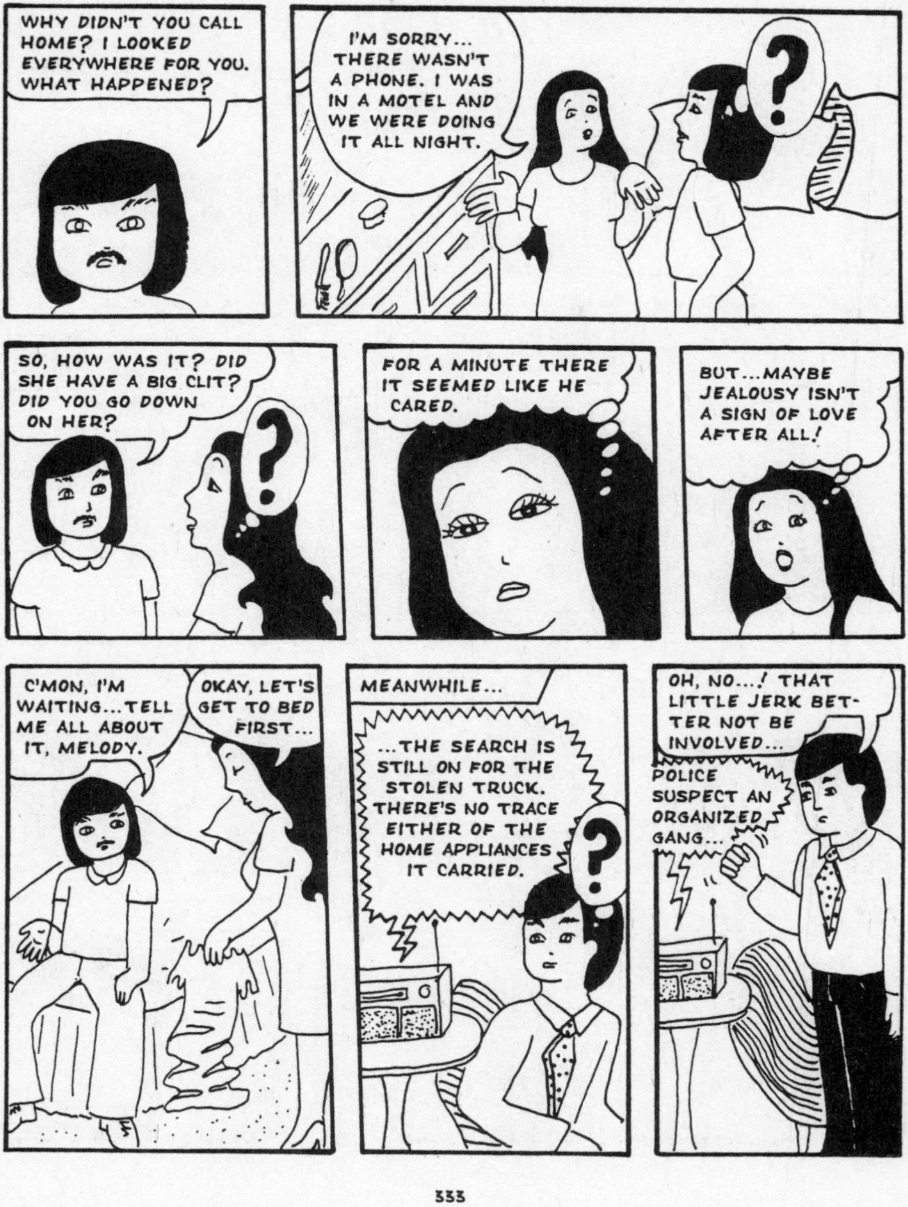
WHY DIDN'T YOU CALL HOME? I LOOKED EVERYWHERE FOR YOU. WHAT HAPPENED?
I'M SORRY... THERE WASN'T A PHONE. I WAS IN A MOTEL AND WE WERE DOING IT ALL NIGHT.
?
SO, HOW WAS IT? DID SHE HAVE A BIG CLIT? DID YOU GO DOWN ON HER?
?
FOR A MINUTE THERE IT SEEMED LIKE HE CARED.
BUT...MAYBE JEALOUSY ISN'T A SIGN OF LOVE AFTER ALL!
C'MON, I'M WAITING...TELL ME ALL ABOUT IT, MELODY.
OKAY, LET'S GET TO BED FIRST...
MEANWHILE...
...THE SEARCH IS STILL ON FOR THE STOLEN TRUCK. THERE'S NO TRACE EITHER OF THE HOME APPLIANCES IT CARRIED.
?
OH, NO...! THAT LITTLE JERK BETTER NOT BE INVOLVED...
POLICE SUSPECT AN ORGANIZED GANG...

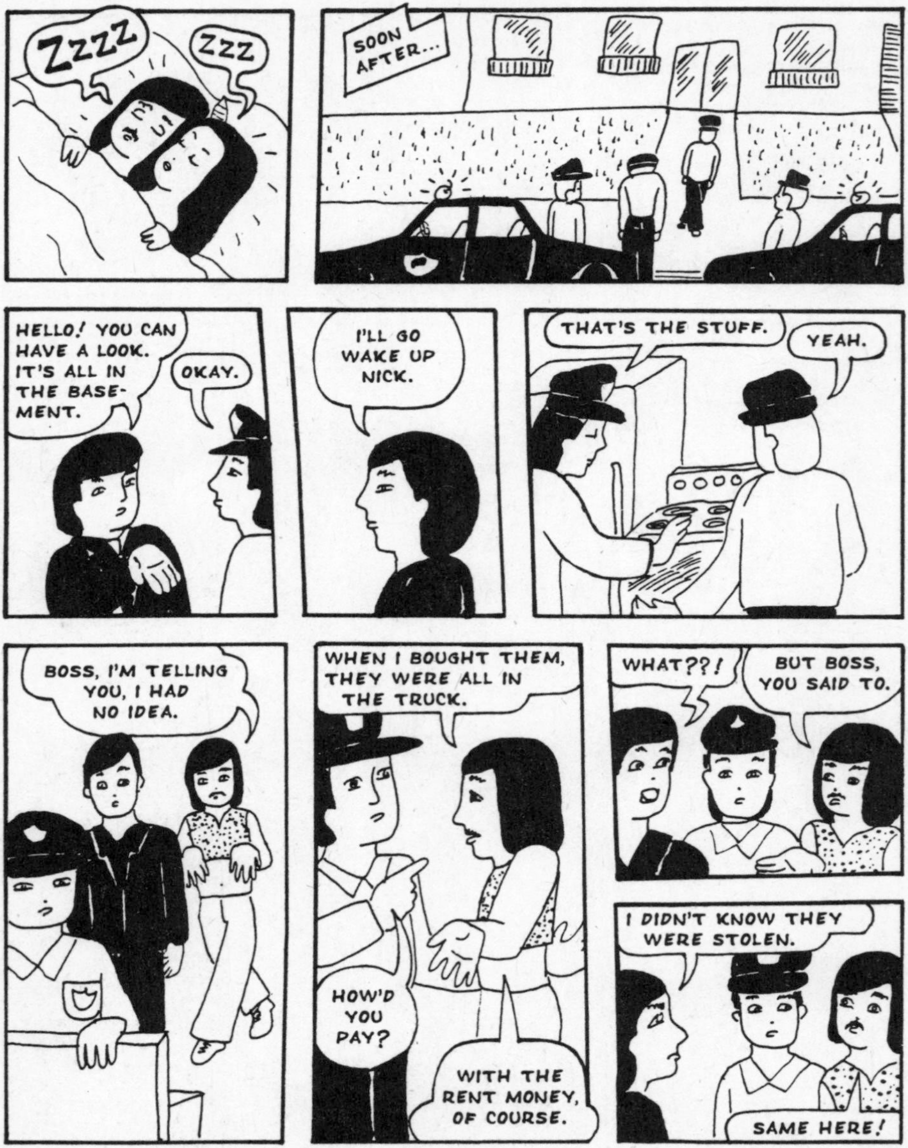
ZZZZ
ZZZ
SOON AFTER...
HELLO! YOU CAN HAVE A LOOK. IT'S ALL IN THE BASEMENT.
OKAY.
I'LL GO WAKE UP NICK.
THAT'S THE STUFF.
YEAH.
BOSS, I'M TELLING YOU, I HAD NO IDEA.
WHEN I BOUGHT THEM, THEY WERE ALL IN THE TRUCK.
HOW'D YOU PAY?
WITH THE RENT MONEY, OF COURSE.
WHAT??!
BUT BOSS, YOU SAID TO.
I DIDN'T KNOW THEY WERE STOLEN.
SAME HERE!

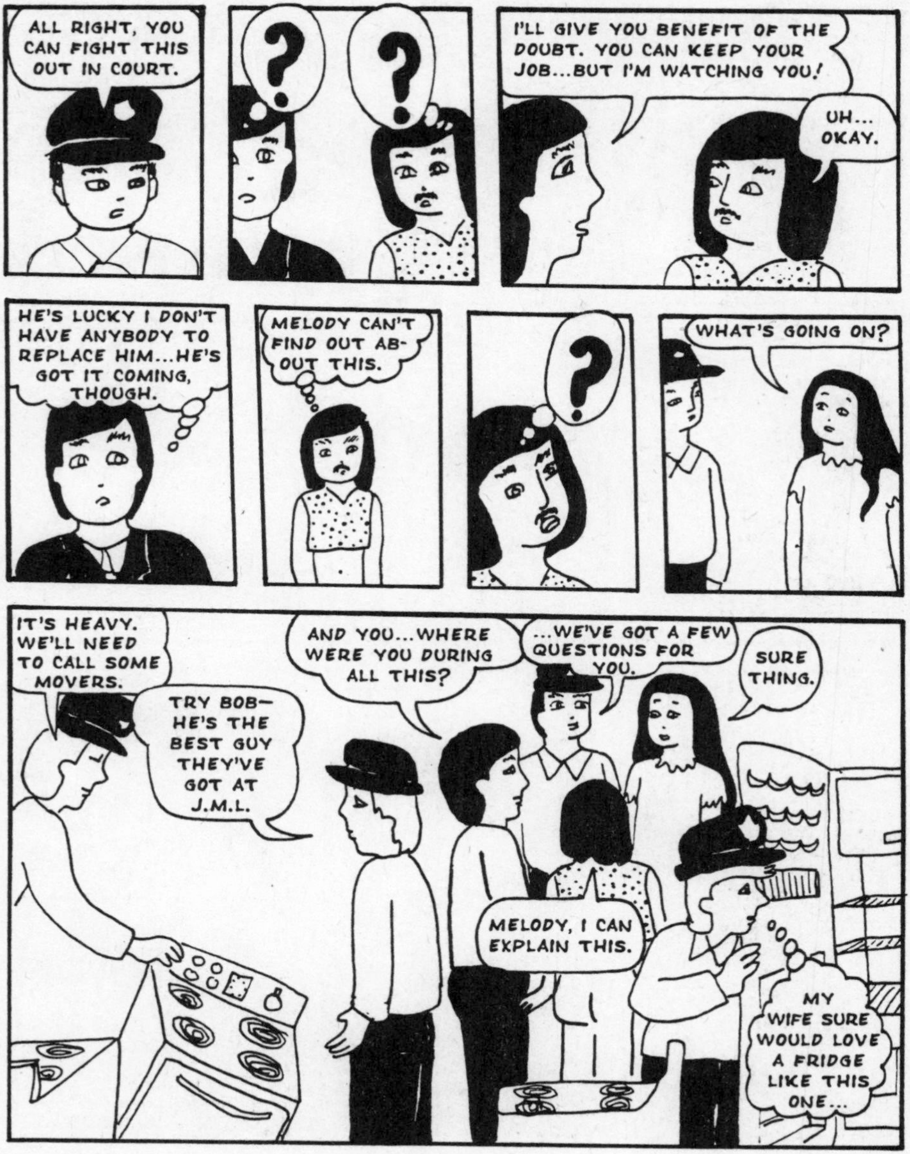
ALL RIGHT, YOU CAN FIGHT THIS OUT IN COURT.
?
?
I'LL GIVE YOU BENEFIT OF THE DOUBT. YOU CAN KEEP YOUR JOB...BUT I'M WATCHING YOU!
UH... OKAY.
HE'S LUCKY I DON'T HAVE ANYBODY TO REPLACE HIM...HE'S GOT IT COMING, THOUGH.
MELODY CAN'T FIND OUT ABOUT THIS.
?
WHAT'S GOING ON?
IT'S HEAVY. WE'LL NEED TO CALL SOME MOVERS.
TRY BOB— HE'S THE BEST GUY THEY'VE GOT AT J.M.L.
AND YOU...WHERE WERE YOU DURING ALL THIS?
...WE'VE GOT A FEW QUESTIONS FOR YOU.
SURE THING.
MELODY, I CAN EXPLAIN THIS.
MY WIFE SURE WOULD LOVE A FRIDGE LIKE THIS ONE...

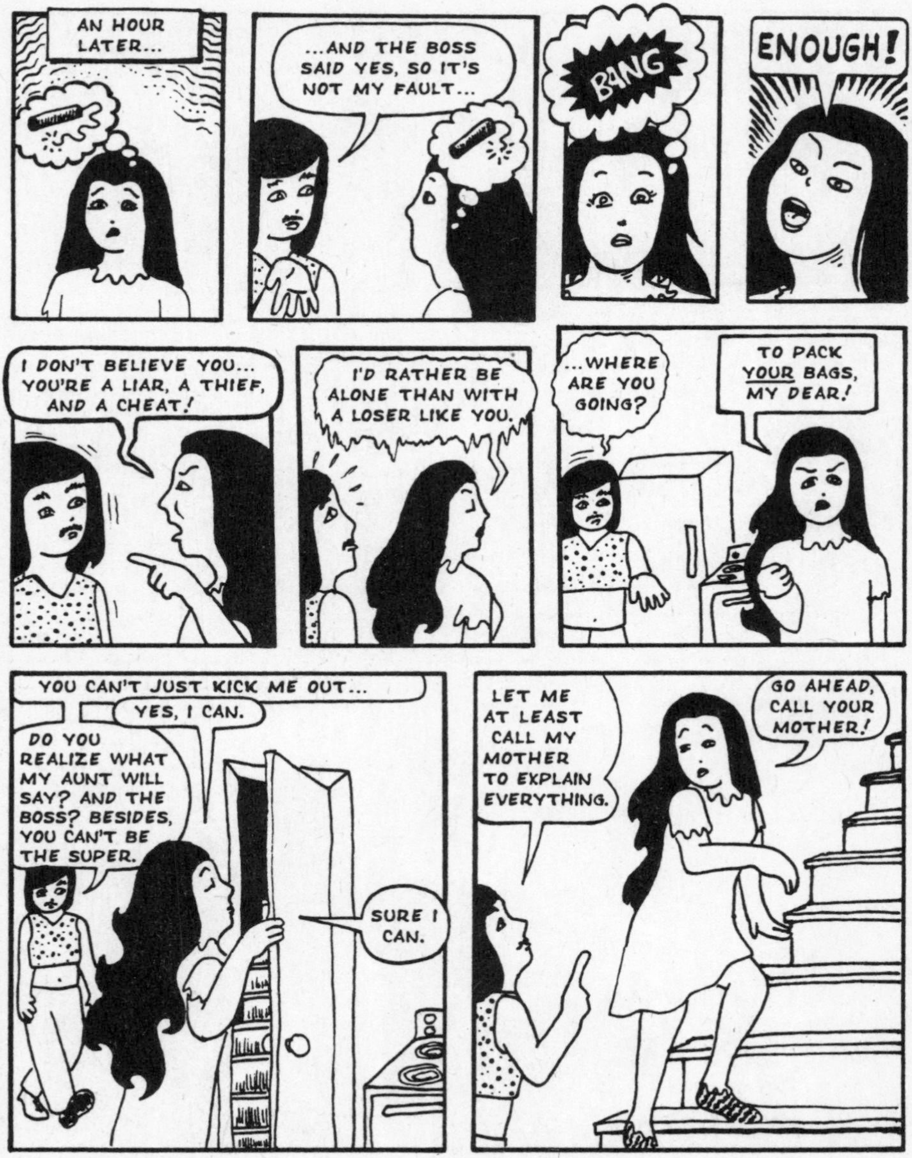

AN HOUR LATER...
...AND THE BOSS SAID YES, SO IT'S NOT MY FAULT...
BANG
ENOUGH!
I DON'T BELIEVE YOU... YOU'RE A LIAR, A THIEF, AND A CHEAT!
I'D RATHER BE ALONE THAN WITH A LOSER LIKE YOU.
...WHERE ARE YOU GOING?
TO PACK YOUR BAGS, MY DEAR!
YOU CAN'T JUST KICK ME OUT...
YES, I CAN.
DO YOU REALIZE WHAT MY AUNT WILL SAY? AND THE BOSS? BESIDES, YOU CAN'T BE THE SUPER.
SURE I CAN.
LET ME AT LEAST CALL MY MOTHER TO EXPLAIN EVERYTHING.
GO AHEAD, CALL YOUR MOTHER!

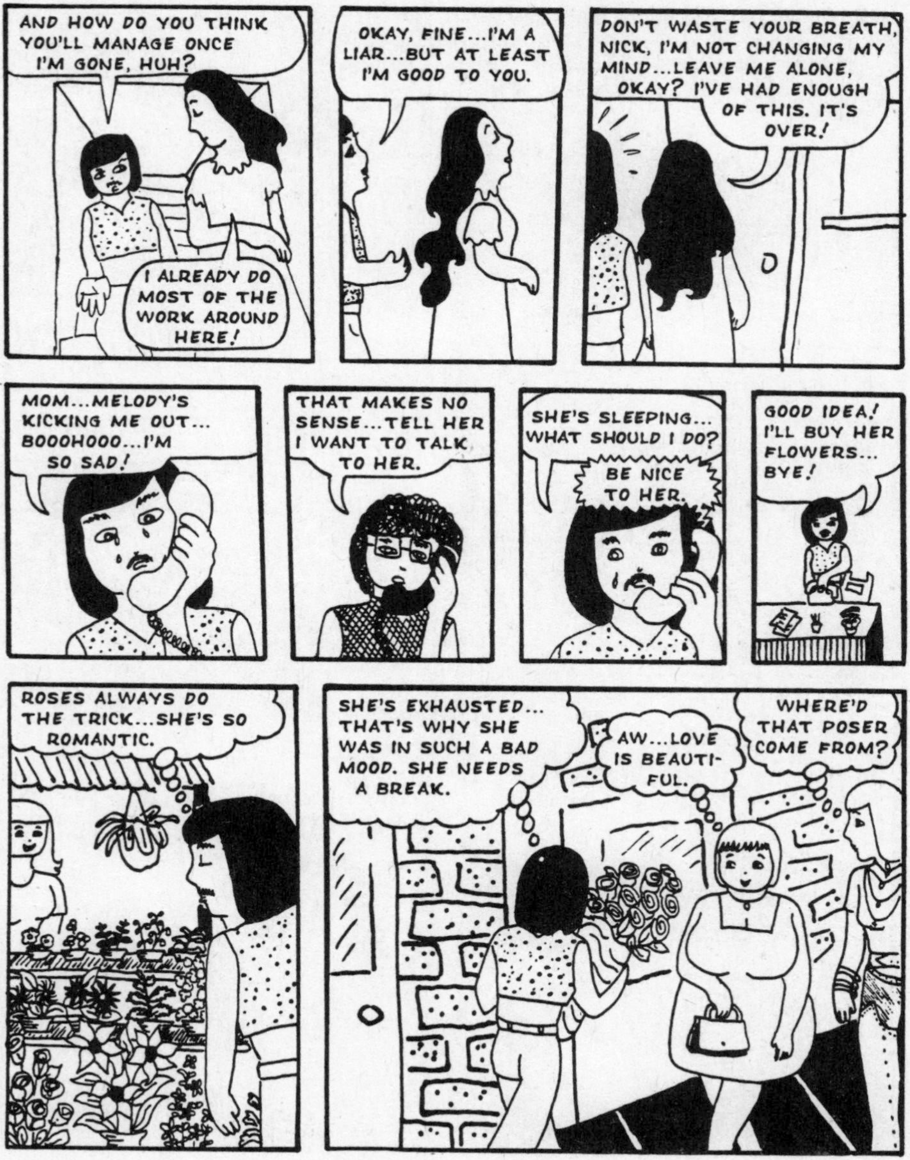
AND HOW DO YOU THINK YOU'LL MANAGE ONCE I'M GONE, HUH?
I ALREADY DO MOST OF THE WORK AROUND HERE!
OKAY, FINE...I'M A LIAR...BUT AT LEAST I'M GOOD TO YOU.
DON'T WASTE YOUR BREATH, NICK, I'M NOT CHANGING MY MIND...LEAVE ME ALONE, OKAY? I'VE HAD ENOUGH OF THIS. IT'S OVER!
MOM...MELODY'S KICKING ME OUT... BOOOHOOO...I'M SO SAD!
THAT MAKES NO SENSE...TELL HER I WANT TO TALK TO HER.
SHE'S SLEEPING... WHAT SHOULD I DO?
BE NICE TO HER.
GOOD IDEA! I'LL BUY HER FLOWERS... BYE!
ROSES ALWAYS DO THE TRICK...SHE'S SO ROMANTIC.
SHE'S EXHAUSTED... THAT'S WHY SHE WAS IN SUCH A BAD MOOD. SHE NEEDS A BREAK.
AW...LOVE IS BEAUTI-FUL.
WHERE'D THAT POSER COME FROM?

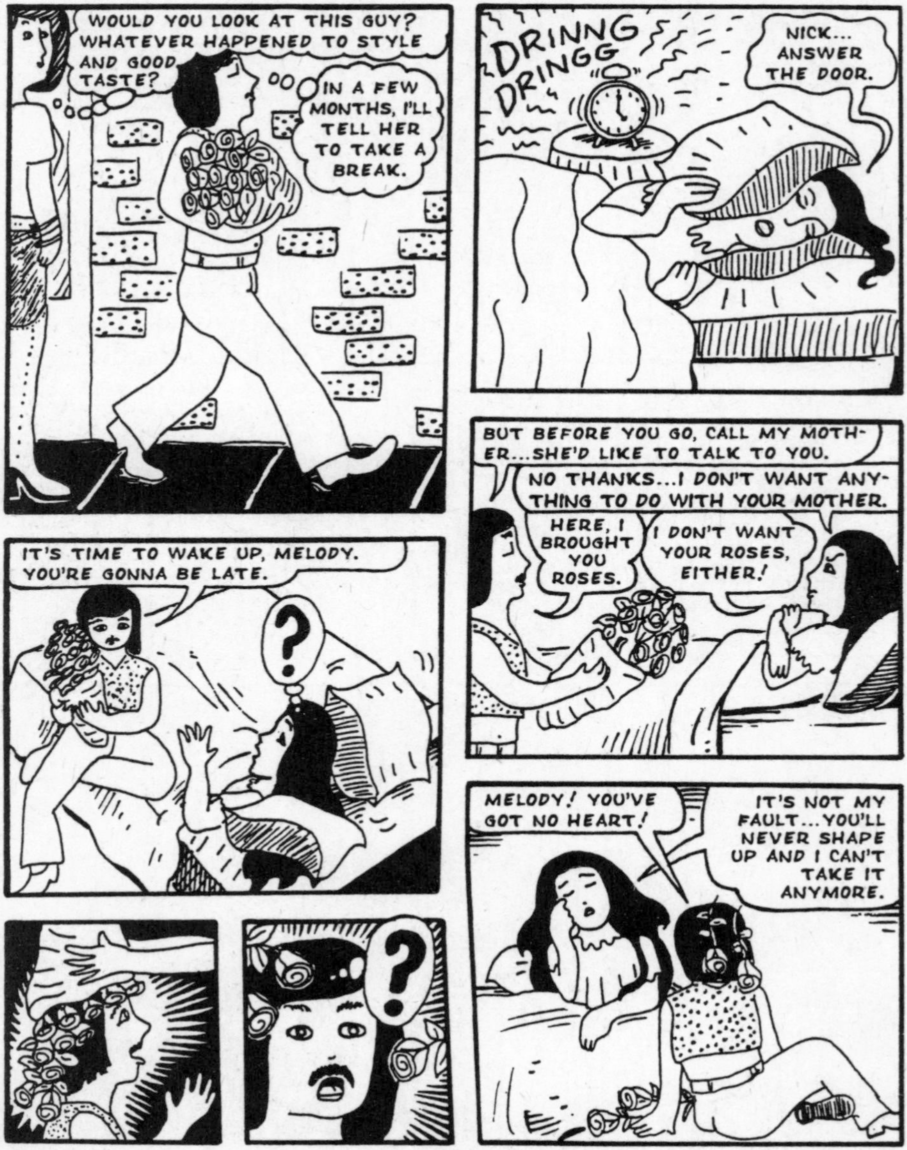
WOULD YOU LOOK AT THIS GUY? WHATEVER HAPPENED TO STYLE AND GOOD TASTE?
IN A FEW MONTHS, I'LL TELL HER TO TAKE A BREAK.
DRINNG DRINGG
NICK... ANSWER THE DOOR.
IT'S TIME TO WAKE UP, MELODY. YOU'RE GONNA BE LATE.
?
BUT BEFORE YOU GO, CALL MY MOTHER...SHE'D LIKE TO TALK TO YOU.
NO THANKS...I DON'T WANT ANYTHING TO DO WITH YOUR MOTHER.
HERE, I BROUGHT YOU ROSES.
I DON'T WANT YOUR ROSES, EITHER!
?
MELODY! YOU'VE GOT NO HEART!
IT'S NOT MY FAULT...YOU'LL NEVER SHAPE UP AND I CAN'T TAKE IT ANYMORE.

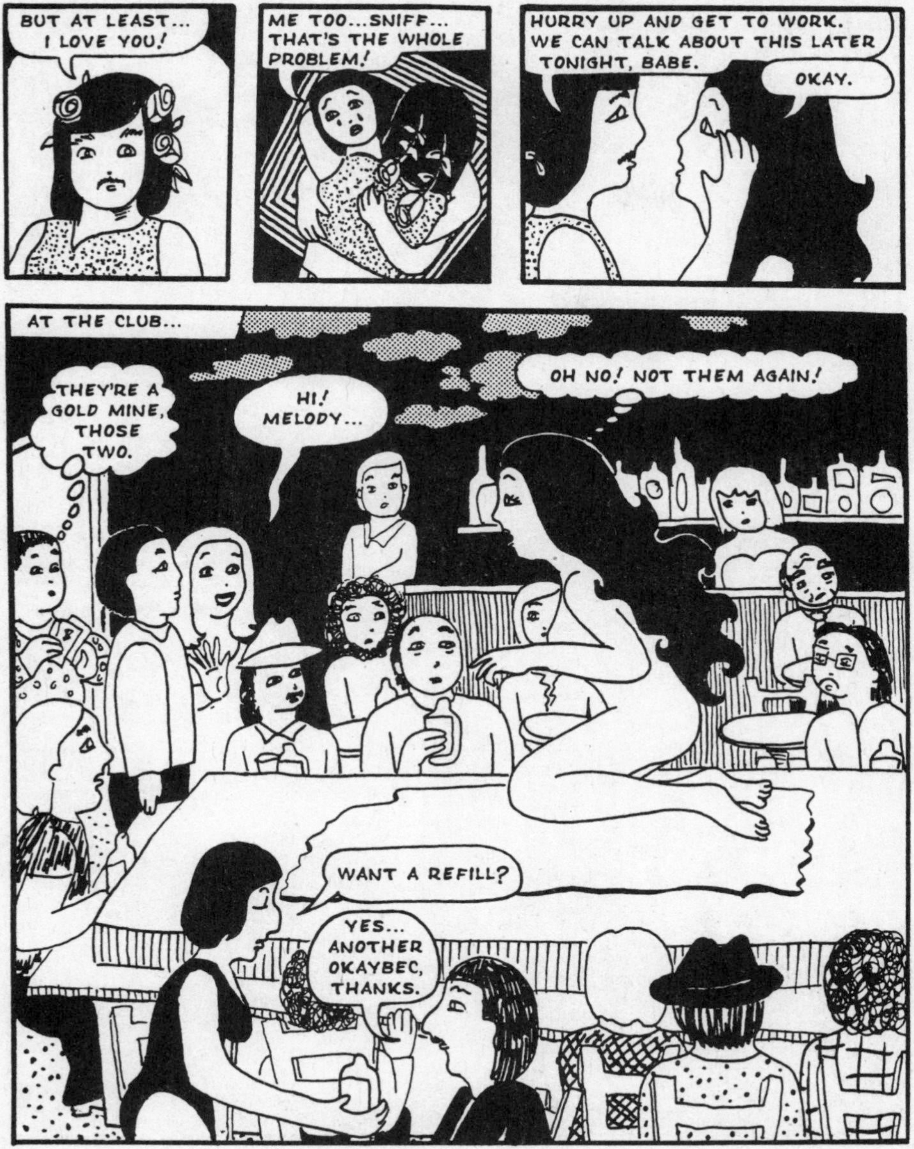
BUT AT LEAST... I LOVE YOU!
ME TOO...SNIFF... THAT'S THE WHOLE PROBLEM!
HURRY UP AND GET TO WORK. WE CAN TALK ABOUT THIS LATER TONIGHT, BABE.
OKAY.
AT THE CLUB...
THEY'RE A GOLD MINE, THOSE TWO.
HI! MELODY...
OH NO! NOT THEM AGAIN!
WANT A REFILL?
YES... ANOTHER OKAYBEC, THANKS.

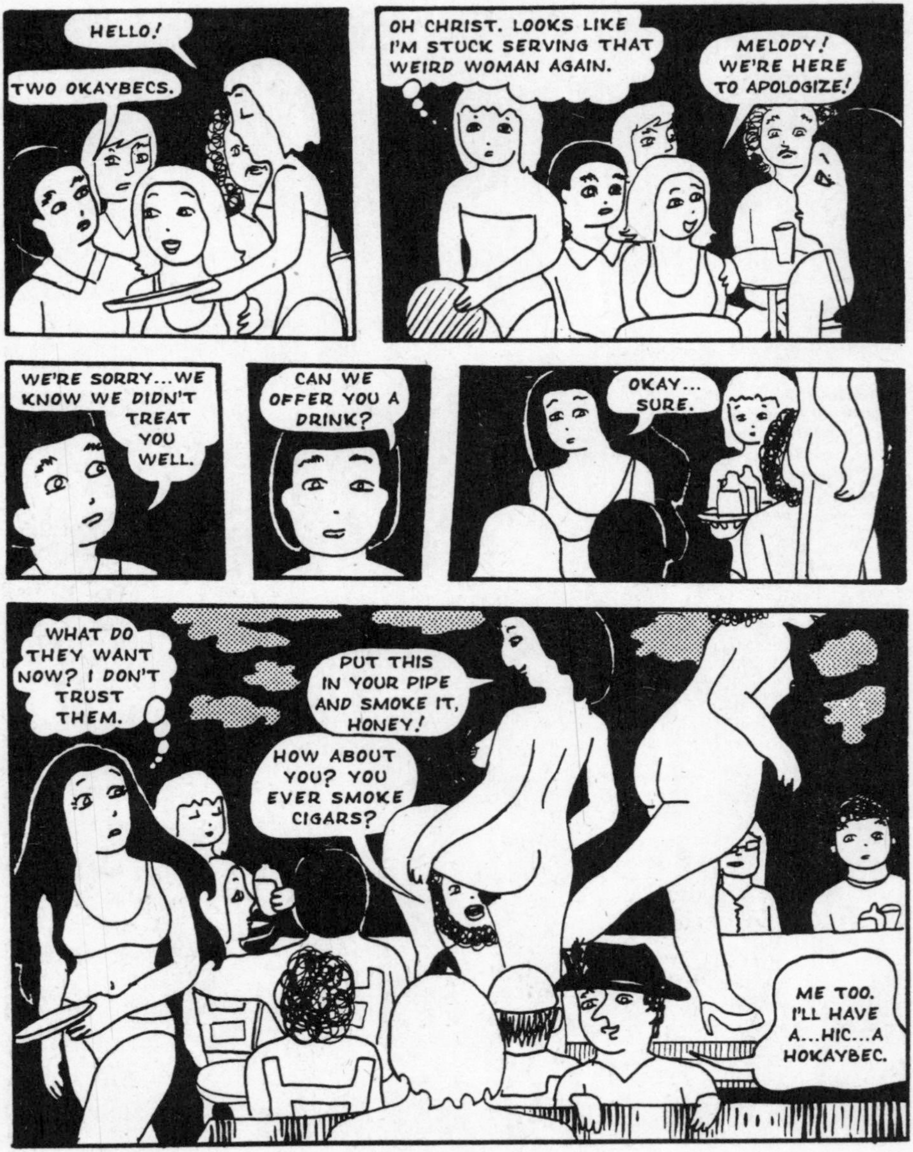

HELLO!
TWO OKAYBECS.
OH CHRIST. LOOKS LIKE I'M STUCK SERVING THAT WEIRD WOMAN AGAIN.
MELODY! WE'RE HERE TO APOLOGIZE!
WE'RE SORRY...WE KNOW WE DIDN'T TREAT YOU WELL.
CAN WE OFFER YOU A DRINK?
OKAY... SURE.
WHAT DO THEY WANT NOW? I DON'T TRUST THEM.
PUT THIS IN YOUR PIPE AND SMOKE IT, HONEY!
HOW ABOUT YOU? YOU EVER SMOKE CIGARS?
ME TOO. I'LL HAVE A...HIC...A HOKAYBEC.

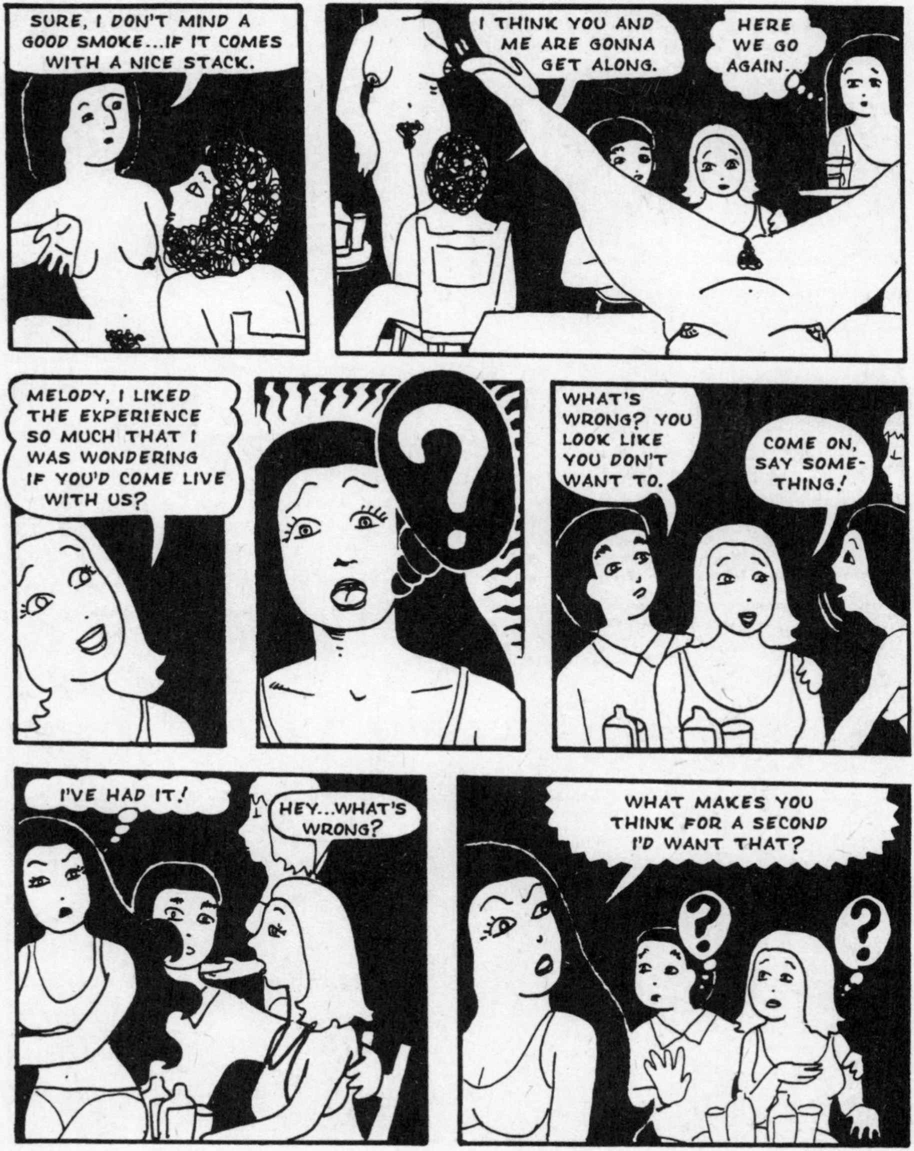
SURE, I DON'T MIND A GOOD SMOKE...IF IT COMES WITH A NICE STACK.
I THINK YOU AND ME ARE GONNA GET ALONG.
HERE WE GO AGAIN...
MELODY, I LIKED THE EXPERIENCE SO MUCH THAT I WAS WONDERING IF YOU'D COME LIVE WITH US?
?
WHAT'S WRONG? YOU LOOK LIKE YOU DON'T WANT TO.
COME ON, SAY SOME-THING!
I'VE HAD IT!
HEY...WHAT'S WRONG?
WHAT MAKES YOU THINK FOR A SECOND I'D WANT THAT?
?
?

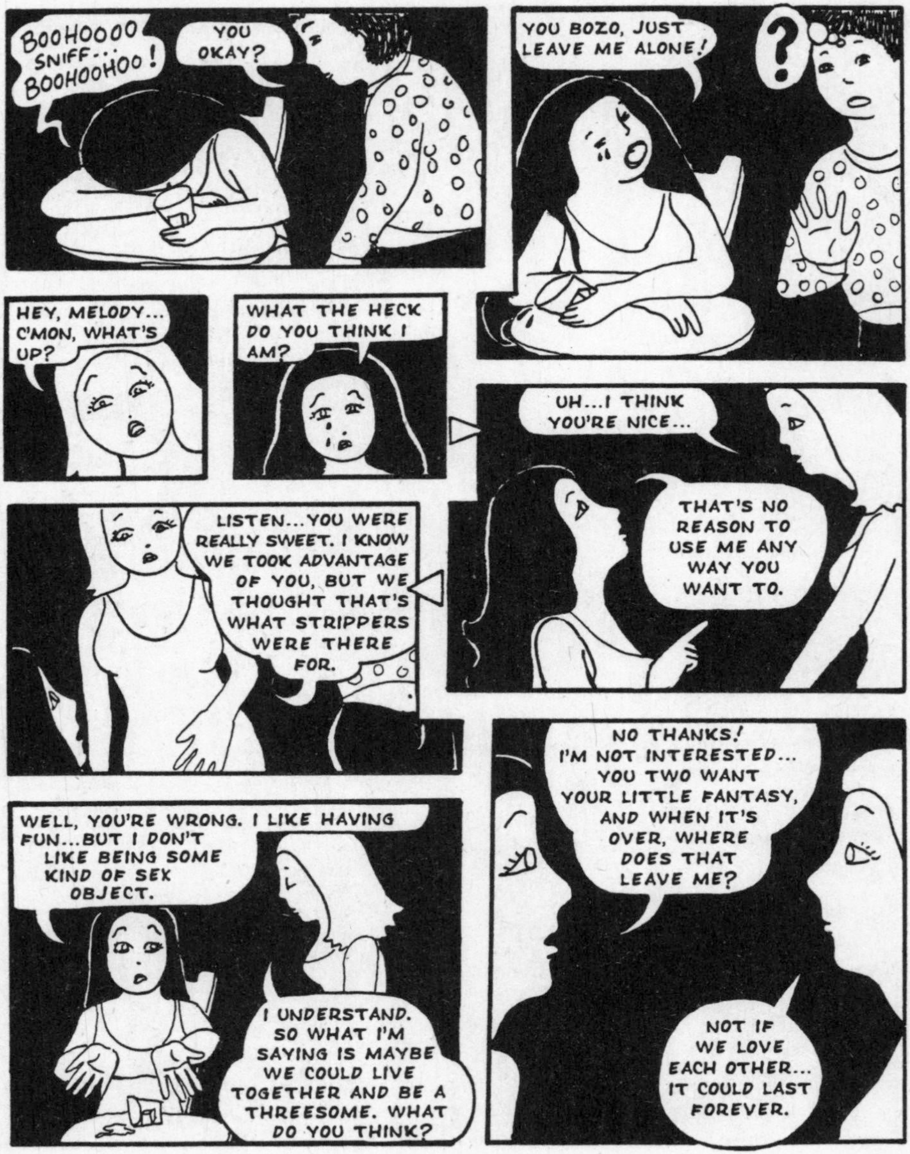
BOOHOOOO SNIFF... BOOHOOHOO!
YOU OKAY?
YOU BOZO, JUST LEAVE ME ALONE!
?
HEY, MELODY... C'MON, WHAT'S UP?
WHAT THE HECK DO YOU THINK I AM?
UH...I THINK YOU'RE NICE...
THAT'S NO REASON TO USE ME ANY WAY YOU WANT TO.
LISTEN...YOU WERE REALLY SWEET. I KNOW WE TOOK ADVANTAGE OF YOU, BUT WE THOUGHT THAT'S WHAT STRIPPERS WERE THERE FOR.
WELL, YOU'RE WRONG. I LIKE HAVING FUN...BUT I DON'T LIKE BEING SOME KIND OF SEX OBJECT.
I UNDERSTAND. SO WHAT I'M SAYING IS MAYBE WE COULD LIVE TOGETHER AND BE A THREESOME. WHAT DO YOU THINK?
NO THANKS! I'M NOT INTERESTED... YOU TWO WANT YOUR LITTLE FANTASY, AND WHEN IT'S OVER, WHERE DOES THAT LEAVE ME?
NOT IF WE LOVE EACH OTHER... IT COULD LAST FOREVER.

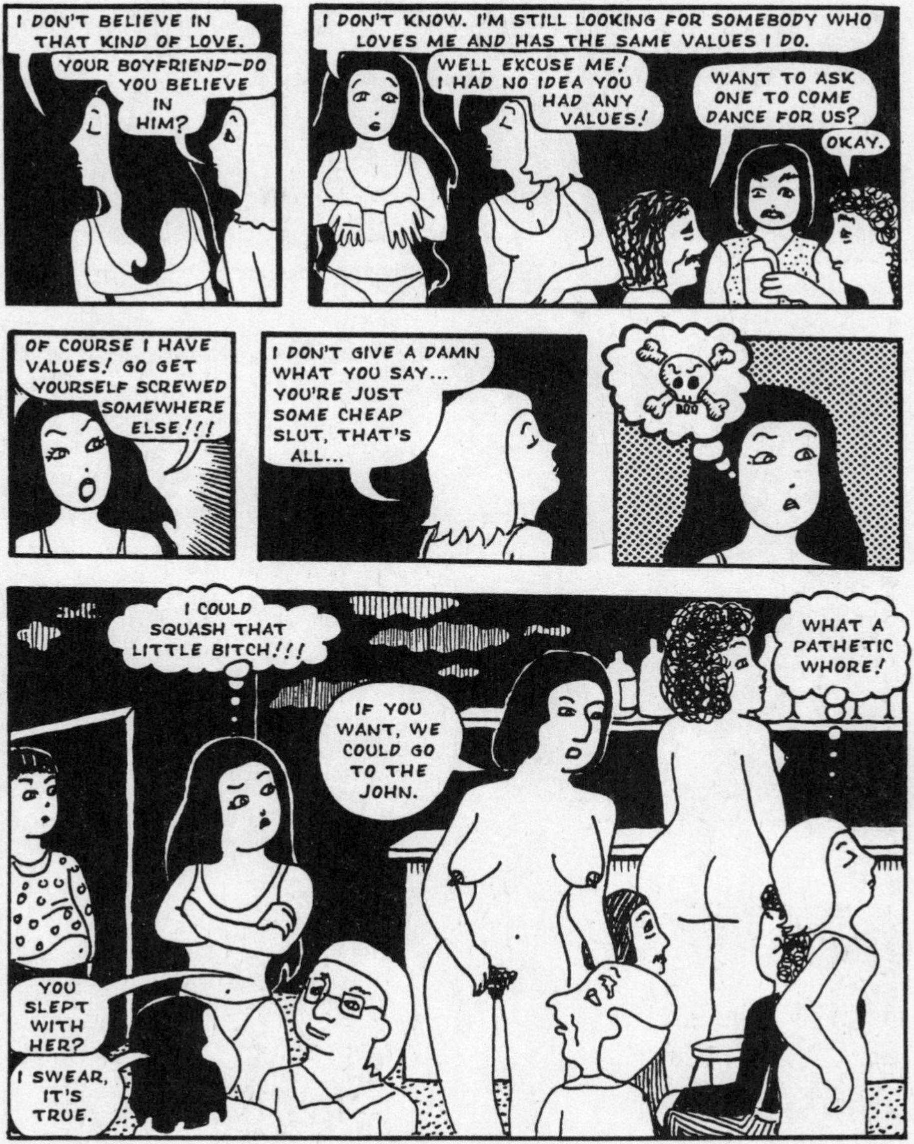
I DON'T BELIEVE IN THAT KIND OF LOVE.
YOUR BOYFRIEND—DO YOU BELIEVE IN HIM?
I DON'T KNOW. I'M STILL LOOKING FOR SOMEBODY WHO LOVES ME AND HAS THE SAME VALUES I DO.
WELL EXCUSE ME! I HAD NO IDEA YOU HAD ANY VALUES!
WANT TO ASK ONE TO COME DANCE FOR US?
OKAY.
OF COURSE I HAVE VALUES! GO GET YOURSELF SCREWED SOMEWHERE ELSE!!!
I DON'T GIVE A DAMN WHAT YOU SAY... YOU'RE JUST SOME CHEAP SLUT, THAT'S ALL...
I COULD SQUASH THAT LITTLE BITCH!!!
IF YOU WANT, WE COULD GO TO THE JOHN.
WHAT A PATHETIC WHORE!
YOU SLEPT WITH HER?
I SWEAR, IT'S TRUE.

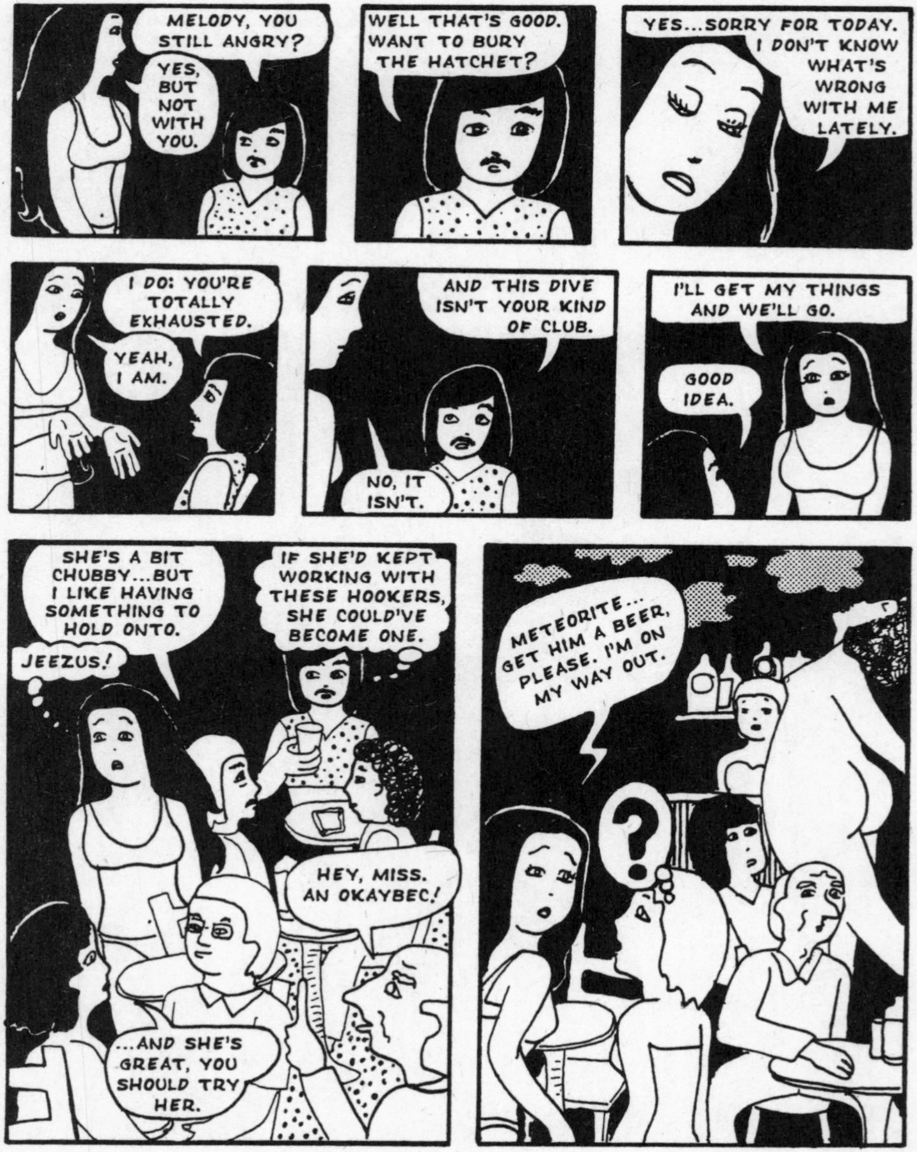
MELODY, YOU STILL ANGRY?
YES, BUT NOT WITH YOU.
WELL THAT'S GOOD. WANT TO BURY THE HATCHET?
YES...SORRY FOR TODAY. I DON'T KNOW WHAT'S WRONG WITH ME LATELY.
I DO: YOU'RE TOTALLY EXHAUSTED.
YEAH, I AM.
AND THIS DIVE ISN'T YOUR KIND OF CLUB.
NO, IT ISN'T.
I'LL GET MY THINGS AND WE'LL GO.
GOOD IDEA.
SHE'S A BIT CHUBBY...BUT I LIKE HAVING SOMETHING TO HOLD ONTO.
JEEZUS!
IF SHE'D KEPT WORKING WITH THESE HOOKERS, SHE COULD'VE BECOME ONE.
HEY, MISS. AN OKAYBEC!
...AND SHE'S GREAT, YOU SHOULD TRY HER.
METEORITE... GET HIM A BEER, PLEASE. I'M ON MY WAY OUT.
?

YOU'RE WHAT?
THIS ISN'T THE RIGHT PLACE FOR ME...I'M LEAVING.
YOU WON'T BE WORKING HERE ANYMORE?
NO...THIS IS THE END FOR ME. BYE!

High Culture and Good Manners Be Damned
Afterword by BERNARD JOUBERT

Narrating one's life by way of comics was still a scarce undertaking in the mid-1980s when Sylvie Rancourt first imagined *Melody*. In the United States, Justin Green had pioneered the genre in 1972 with his *Binky Brown Meets the Holy Virgin Mary* and Art Spiegelman's masterpiece, *Maus*, was under way. But Rancourt ignored the existence of these underground iconoclasts. Her knowledge of comic art was limited to *Tintin* and popular small formats such as Quebec translations of *Archie* comics and French versions of sexy Italian fumetti bearing titles such as *Maghella*, *Jacula*, and *Lucifera*. She recognized comics as a form of expression but had no knowledge of tools, technique, or history. And that is part of the charm of the pages in this book, its author's ingenuous approach.

The nation's elites would likely have preferred that the pioneer of Canadian autobiographical *bandes dessinées* belong to an honourable profession. High culture and good manners be damned, Rancourt works as a nude dancer in strip clubs and her first readers are the patrons of these establishments. In mid-March 1985, having produced (as an emotional release) the first three chapters of the present volume, based on events that had occurred five years earlier, she published the first as a photocopied zine measuring six and a half by eight and a half inches, its five hundred copies quickly reprinted. Inside, she has changed the names of all persons involved but signed the work with her own, real name. Sales occurred from table to table and reactions were encouraging. After publishing a second issue, similarly well received, Rancourt paid a visit to Quebec's largest magazine distributor. The businessman refused to handle her publication unless it were printed in professional fashion. He probably never expected to see the young lady again but she returned with five thousand copies of the first issue, magazine sized and offset printed with a colour cover. And so in early June 1985, throughout Quebec, *Mélody à ses débuts* could be found on magazine racks. To keep costs down, the printer had advised a manual colour separation be prepared for the cover. Upon launching her first zine, Rancourt had met a cartoonist with experience, Jacques Boivin. She put him in charge of drawing the cover and preparing colour separations for the first two issues of her *Melody* magazine. Jean-Pierre Thibodeau handled the lettering, with Boivin succeeding him after the fifth issue.

Six issues thus appeared, at a steady clip, with newsstand returns gradually encumbering the author/publisher's apartment. Floors began to creak with ominous chatter, keeping the young woman awake at night. The completed seventh issue was never published for newsstand distribution but later produced in *Archives Mélody 1 à 7*, a thick hardcover printed at about 250 copies in 1989. To this editorial adventure must be added a first translation into English of *Mélody à ses débuts* in mini-comic format, at a little over a hundred copies. Jacques Boivin was responsible for this adaptation, seeking to make Rancourt's work known elsewhere among critics and publishers. An initiative rewarded with success. In *Weirdo*, Aline Kominsky-Crumb was enthusiastic: "Strong, straightforward story...My kinda book!!" On the British side, critic Paul Gravett explicated in *Escape*: "Neither titillating nor sordid but astonishingly honest and human." While among publishers, the mini-comic was noticed by Denis Kitchen, one of the historic producers of underground comix. Kitchen was already publishing *Omaha the Cat Dancer* by Reed Waller and Kate Worley so one may suppose that on the subject of dancing in bars, that might suffice. But *Omaha* is a fictional soap opera featuring furry characters. *Melody* deals in reality.

Kitchen wished for the series to be more elaborate for US publication — that the storyline be better developed in order to provide greater insight into character motivation and that more background be added with Boivin in charge of the art, based on thumbnails drafted by Rancourt. She reacted to these editorial requests by transforming the 315 pages of her first seven comics into over a thousand pages of new and revised scripts, including some 250 pages of prelude to her first night on stage. This second undertaking, which lasted ten comic books from 1988 to 1995, does not repeat the book you are presently reading but precedes it. Beginning in Rancourt's native Abitibi in 1979, it portrays Nick and Melody's life in northwestern Quebec, establishing an atmosphere of sexual freedom that scandalizes the local villagers, until the couple moves to Montreal. Nick is already a footdragger with no visible ambition other than drinking and partying with friends. Melody raises chickens. And it becomes evident that even when pictured in greater detail,

Rancourt's memories retain a surprisingly undramatic flavour. At no time does she appear to confess her more difficult days in order to attract pity. She assumes responsibility for her life.

An eleventh episode was later published by Fantagraphics in 2001 (*Melody on Stage*), wherein several panels are recognizable from the early pages of *Mélody à ses débuts*, transposed during Rancourt's rewrite. A twelfth episode remains unfinished. To this body of 315 magazine pages and 289 comic-book pages must be added *Bébé Mélody*, sixty-five pages drawn by Rancourt and published by Boivin in 1996, retelling the early childhood of our heroine (from birth to age three) and an eight-page story, "How I Met Nick," as a bonus to a Kitchen Sink volume (*The Orgies of Abitibi*) in which, again without pathos, Rancourt narrates and illustrates how, at their first meeting, Nick drugged her so that he and his brother might sleep with her. Other stories and illustrations appeared here and there, such as the mini-comic *Club Mélody*, relating exchanges in a notary's office about the opening of a strip club under that name. A bar that in fact did operate in Montreal, from 1990 to 1992.

The critical and public reaction to the *Melody* saga was positive, even though the first detailed assessment of the qualities of Rancourt's work did not appear until after her self-published magazine had disappeared from Quebec newsstands. Its author was no minor figure, however, but Europe's esteemed critic, Thierry Groensteen, in an issue of *Les Cahiers de la bande dessinée* focusing on autobiographical comics, wherein the Quebec creator found herself sandwiched between articles on Crumb, Spiegelman, Moebius, and Nakazawa (no. 73, Jan–Feb 1987). Noting that Rancourt's childish artwork is "in no way clumsy, since it never creates confusion for the reader," Groensteen affirmed that "in addition to being an unprecedented editorial experience," her *Melody* was "a little jewel of raw art." In Quebec's intellectual daily, *Le Devoir*, Pierre Lefebvre in 1992 recalled his astonishment over Rancourt's first comics and praised their freshness and singularity as well as "the shock produced by the contrast between the artwork's innocence and the storyline's gravity." *Melody* made her entry into the Larousse dictionary of comics in 1998, updated by author Patrick Gaumer for subsequent editions in 2004 and 2010.

Nevertheless, the subject matter, sexual representations, and the fact that Rancourt did not engage in a denunciation of her wayward life also provoked outrage. In 1986, *Le Journal de Montréal*, with the largest circulation among French newspapers in America, published this personal response by

Solange Harvey in her column, following a mailing by Rancourt: "I respect you as a person and acknowledge the duties of your work. However, I see no utility whatsoever in your turning it into a pornographic publication. That's unfortunate for you. Don't count on any free publicity. You've fallen into mediocrity and facility." In 1996, at the main cultural center and library in La Sarre, Abitibi, as tenth anniversary celebrations began, administrator Pauline Vallée gathered Rancourt's books from her table in the authors' room and asked her to leave the premises. And even among folks with the best of intentions, one could read that "these strips, at times bordering on pornography and poor taste, would be devoid of interest were they not so candid and naive" (Quebec correspondent Jacques Samson in *Les Cahiers de la bande dessinée* no. 72). Or again, the warning in the first Kitchen Sink comic that "this comic book series does not seek to glamorize nude dancing" and "should not be seen as an endorsement of the lifestyles described." For my part, I maintain that the sex scenes are among the beautiful aspects of *Melody* (talking heads only would have been a shame) and this also applies to Boivin's renderings. Whenever I begin reading a book, running into moral warnings from the editor's desk always irritates me, especially when one of the strengths of a work is to refrain from passing moral judgment. Catechism has other venues.

A more welcome warning concerning the contents of this book would be to forget that *Melody* is now part of the history of comics, perhaps even one of its classics. To travel back in time, to recreate context. To imagine oneself in Jacques Boivin's situation as he gazed with perplexity at an advertisement on the door of a striptease bar, announcing therein would soon be sold a comic book by the author herself. And much like the fact that a comic strip printed in a daily paper or a ten-cent pulp comic book do not produce the same experience as their current fancy reprints, bear in mind that these memoirs appeared alongside ads to go see "Melody" perform at the Bar des Miracles and that in editorials graced with her photo, she sought to coax her co-workers into forming an *Association des danseuses nues du Québec*.

Today, Sylvie Rancourt is no longer a dancer. She has raised five children and creates paintings in which her alter ego often appears.

BERNARD JOUBERT *is France's foremost expert on censorship. He is the author of the 1280–page* Dictionnaire des livres et journaux interdits *(Cercle de la Librairie, 2007, 2nd ed. 2011) and other books and essays, many on the subject of comics and erotica.*

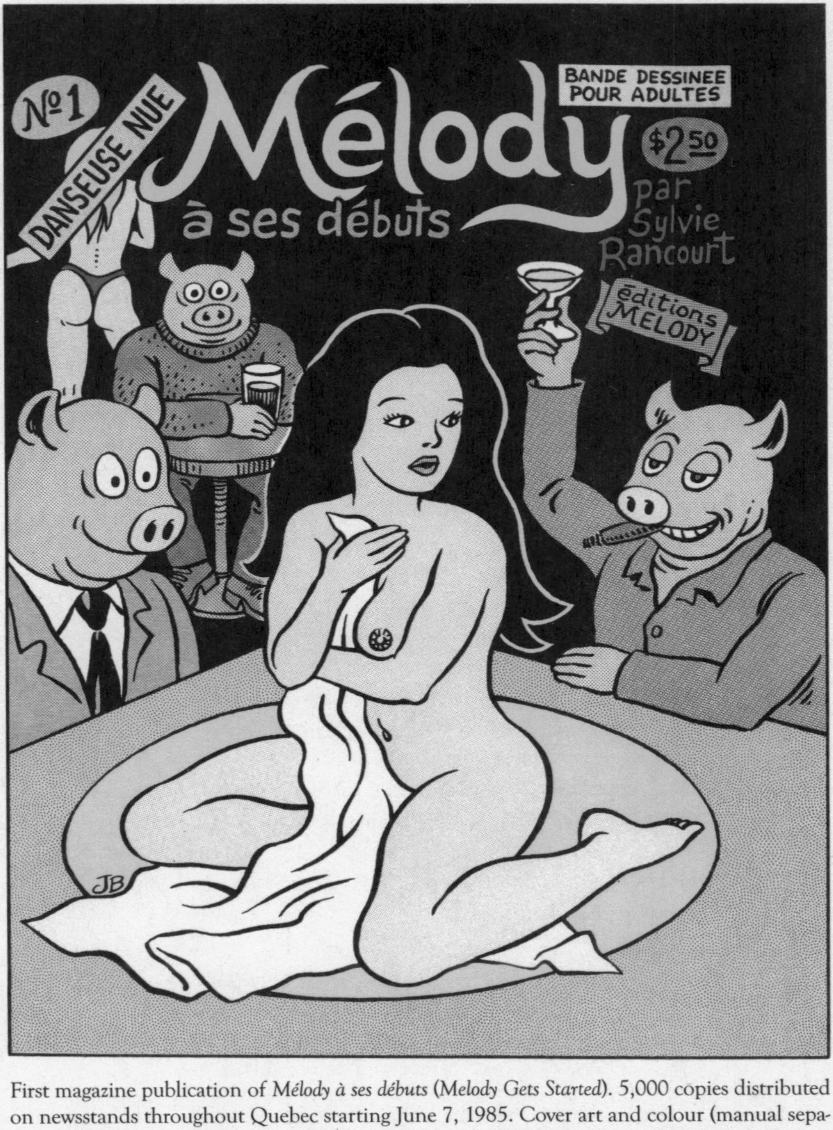

Nº1
DANSEUSE NUE
Mélody
à ses débuts
BANDE DESSINEE POUR ADULTES
$2.50
par Sylvie Rancourt
éditions MELODY
JB

First magazine publication of *Mélody à ses débuts* (*Melody Gets Started*). 5,000 copies distributed on newsstands throughout Quebec starting June 7, 1985. Cover art and colour (manual separation) by Jacques Boivin. Second highest initial newsstand sales of all six distributed issues.

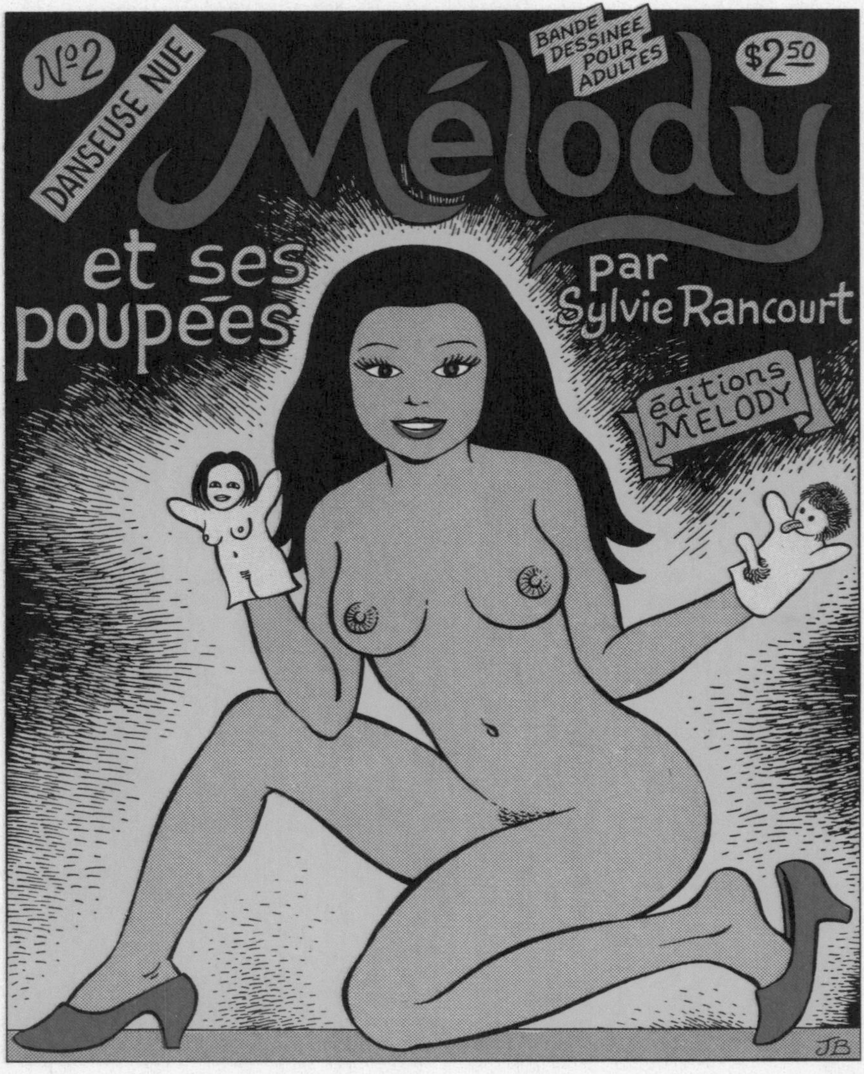
Nº2
DANSEUSE NUE
BANDE DESSINEE POUR ADULTES
$2.50
Mélody
et ses poupées
par Sylvie Rancourt
éditions MELODY
JB

First magazine publication of *Mélody et ses poupées* (*Melody and Her Dolls*). 5,000 copies distributed on Quebec newsstands starting in August 1985. Cover art and manual colour separation by Jacques Boivin. Face retouched (mouth and eyes) by Sylvie Rancourt. Highest initial newsstand sales (1,230 copies) of all six distributed issues.

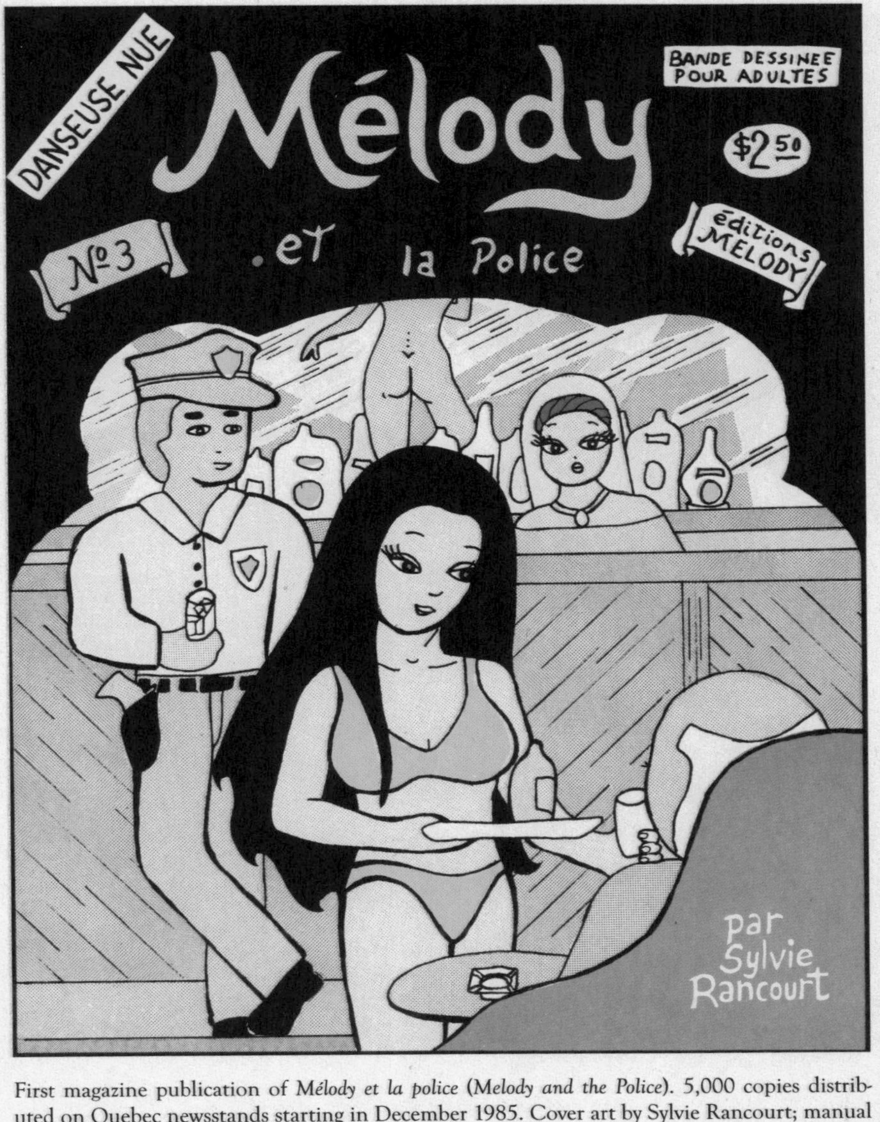
DANSEUSE NUE
Mélody
BANDE DESSINEE POUR ADULTES
$2 50
Nº3
.et la Police
éditions MELODY
par Sylvie Rancourt

First magazine publication of *Mélody et la police* (*Melody and the Police*). 5,000 copies distributed on Quebec newsstands starting in December 1985. Cover art by Sylvie Rancourt; manual colour separation by her brother Samuel. Newsstand returns for first three issues were later redistributed in packs.

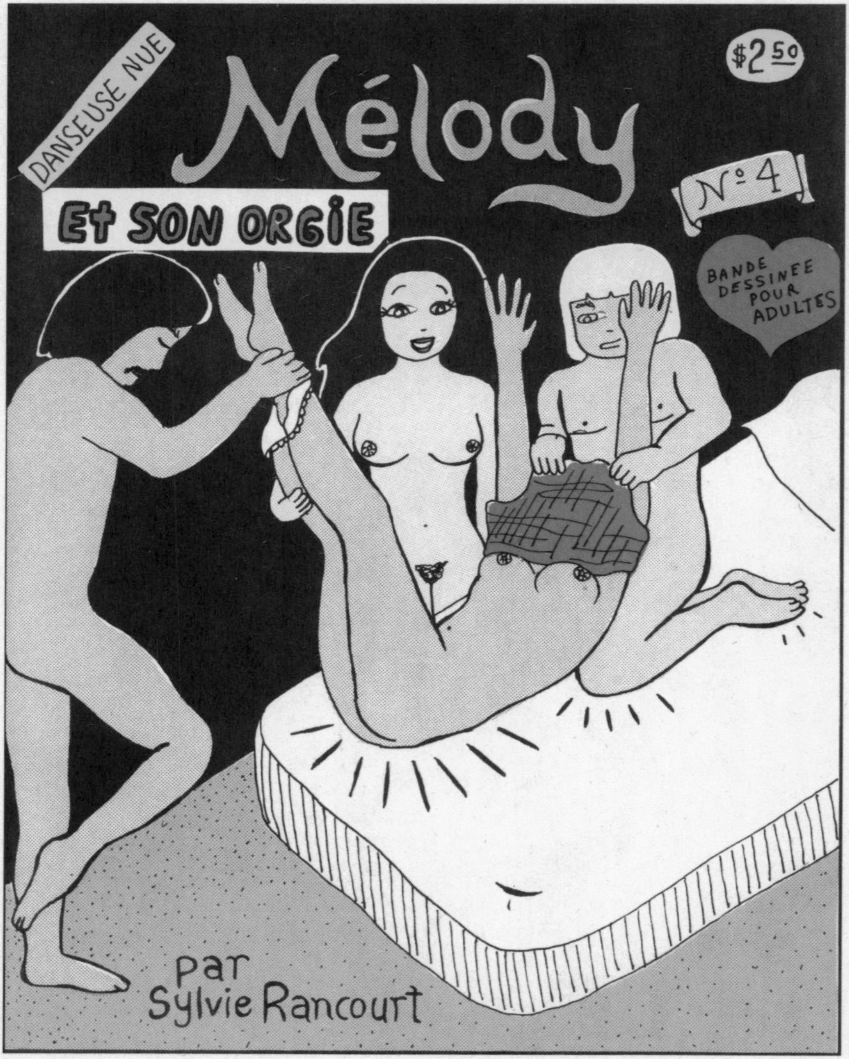
DANSEUSE NUE
Mélody
$2.50
Nº 4
Et SON ORGiE
BANDE DESSINEE POUR ADULTES
par
Sylvie Rancourt

First magazine publication of *Mélody et son orgie* (*Melody's Orgy*). 5,000 copies distributed on Quebec newsstands starting in February 1986. Cover art by Sylvie Rancourt; manual colour separation by her brother Samuel. Newsstand returns from first six issues continued to be sold individually by Sylvie Rancourt in Montreal strip clubs until the early 1990s.

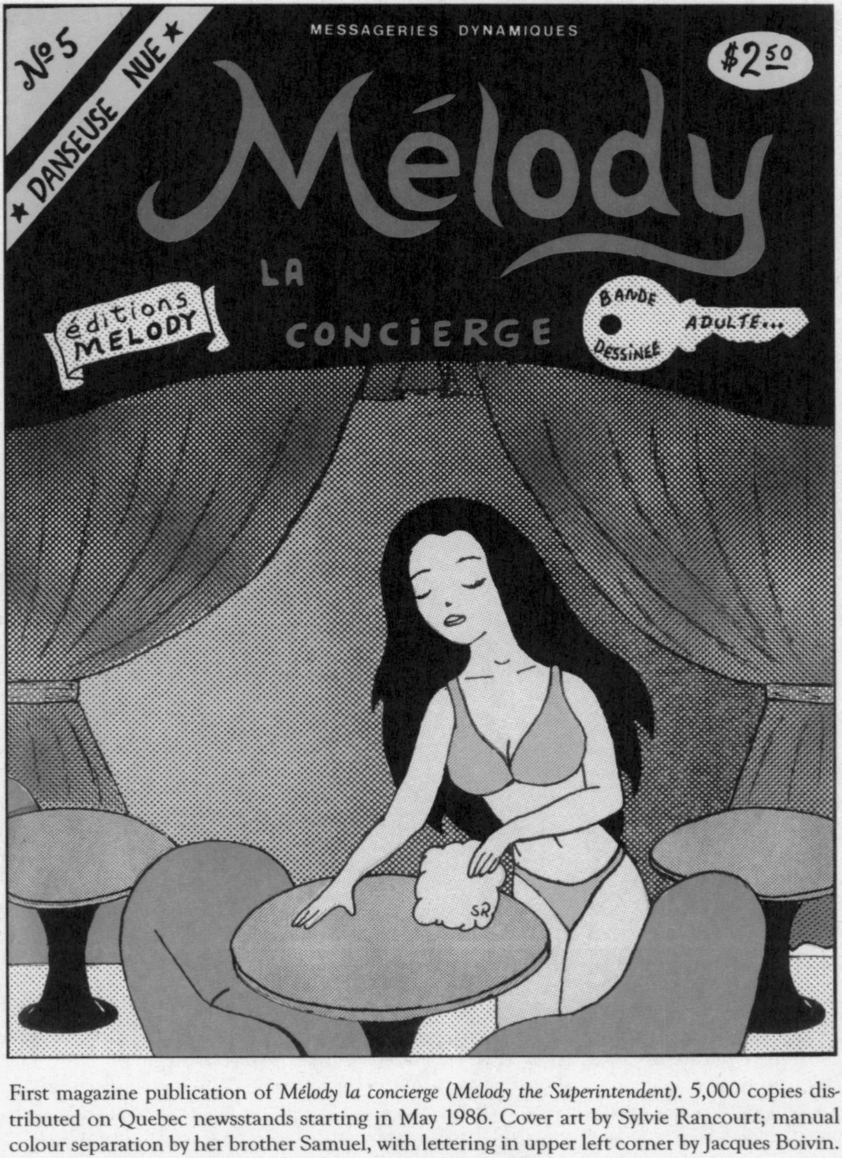
MESSAGERIES DYNAMIQUES
№ 5
★ DANSEUSE NUE ★
$2.50
Mélody
LA
CONCiERGE
éditions
MELODY
BANDE
DESSINÉE
ADULTE...
SR

First magazine publication of *Mélody la concierge* (*Melody the Superintendent*). 5,000 copies distributed on Quebec newsstands starting in May 1986. Cover art by Sylvie Rancourt; manual colour separation by her brother Samuel, with lettering in upper left corner by Jacques Boivin. "Messageries Dynamiques" above title refers to a change in distributors.

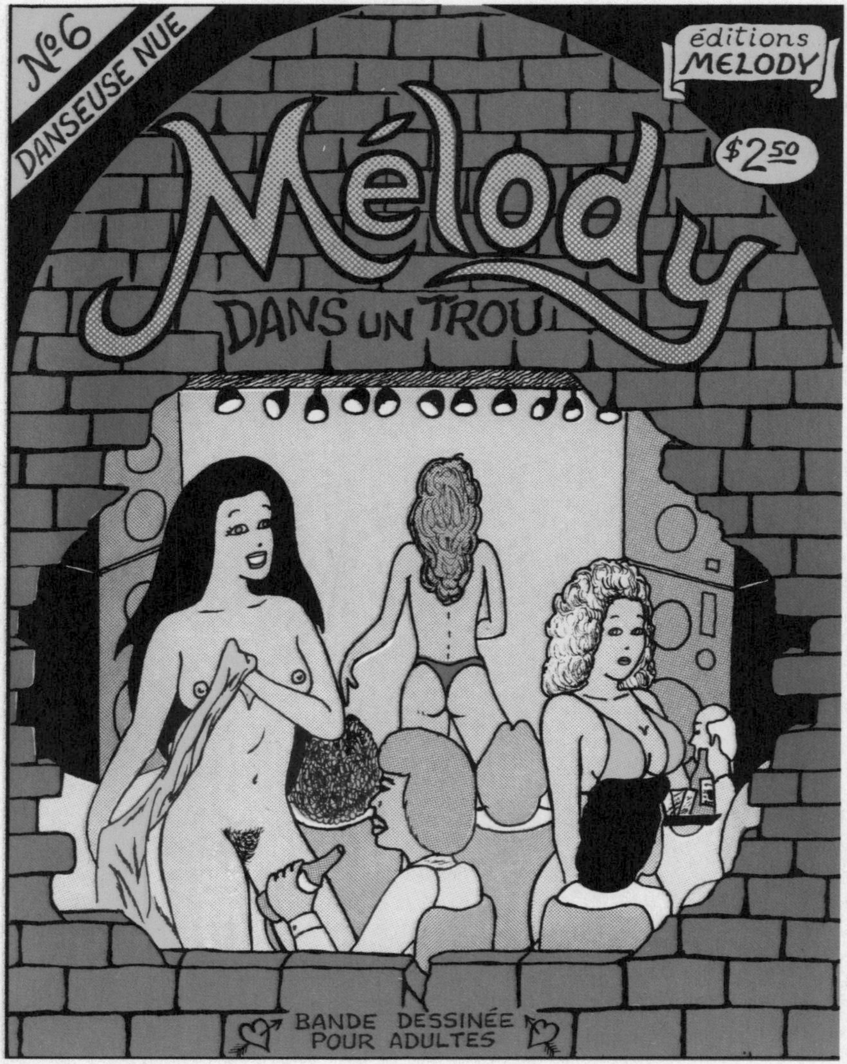

No 6
DANSEUSE NUE
éditions MELODY
$2.50
Mélody
DANS UN TROU
BANDE DESSINÉE
POUR ADULTES

First magazine publication of *Mélody dans un trou* (*Melody Hits Bottom*). 5,000 copies distributed on Quebec newsstands starting in July 1986. Cover art and manual colour separation by Samuel Rancourt, with lettering by Jacques Boivin. Some magazine sales were also carried out by mail order.

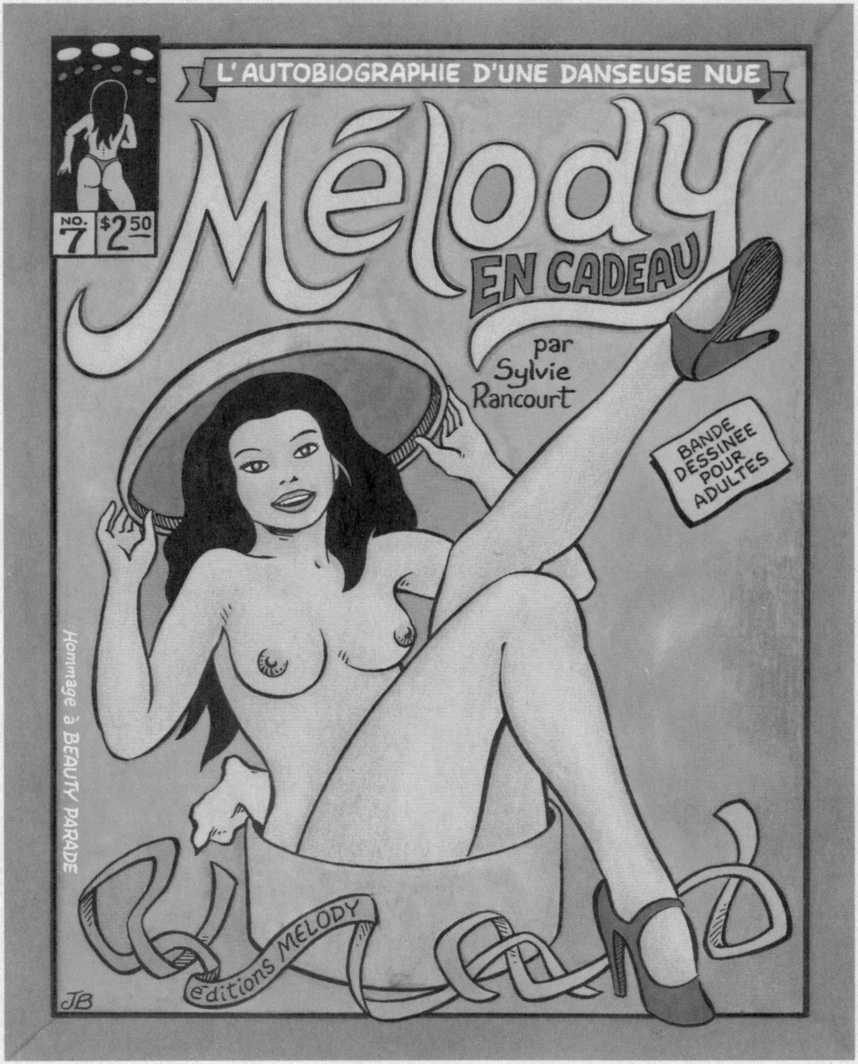
L'AUTOBIOGRAPHIE D'UNE DANSEUSE NUE
NO. 7
$2.50
Mélody
EN CADEAU
par Sylvie Rancourt
BANDE DESSINEE POUR ADULTES
Hommage à BEAUTY PARADE
éditions MELODY
JB

Planned magazine publication of *Mélody en cadeau* (*Melody and the Birthday Wish*). Issue completed in September 1986 but never published due to strange frightening noises at night (read all about it in the text pieces). Inspired from a 1946 Peter Driben painting for *Beauty Parade*. Cover art and colour rough by Jacques Boivin.

drawnandquarterly.com

First paperback edition: June 2015. 10 9 8 7 6 5 4 3 2 1. Printed in Canada.

Library and Archives Canada Cataloguing in Publication: Rancourt, Sylvie [Mélody. English]. *Melody: Story of a nude dancer*/Sylvie Rancourt; Helge Dascher, translator. Translation of: *Mélody*. ISBN 978-1-77046-200-7 (pbk.) 1. Rancourt, Sylvie — Comic books, strips, etc. 2. Stripteasers — Québec (Province) — Montréal — Comic books, strips, etc. I. Dascher, Helge, 1965-, translator II. Title. III. Title: *Mélody*. English. PN6734.M4613R36 2015 741.5'971 C2014-907019-5

Published in the United States by Drawn & Quarterly, a client publisher of Farrar, Straus & Giroux. Orders: 888.330.8477.
Published in Canada by Drawn & Quarterly, a client publisher of Raincoast Books. Orders: 800.663.5714.
Published in the United Kingdom by Drawn & Quarterly, a client publisher of Publishers Group UK. Orders: info@pguk.co.uk.

Drawn & Quarterly acknowledges the financial support of the Government of Canada through the Canada Book Fund, the Canada Council for the Arts, and the National Translation Program for Book Publishing, an initiative of the Roadmap for Canada's Official Languages 2013–2018: Education, Immigration, Communities, for our translation activities.

Nous reconnaissons l'aide financière du gouvernement du Québec par l'entremise de la Société de développement des entreprises culturelles (SODEC) pour nos activités d'édition.
Gouvernement du Québec — Programme de crédit d'impôt pour l'édition de livres — Gestion SODEC.

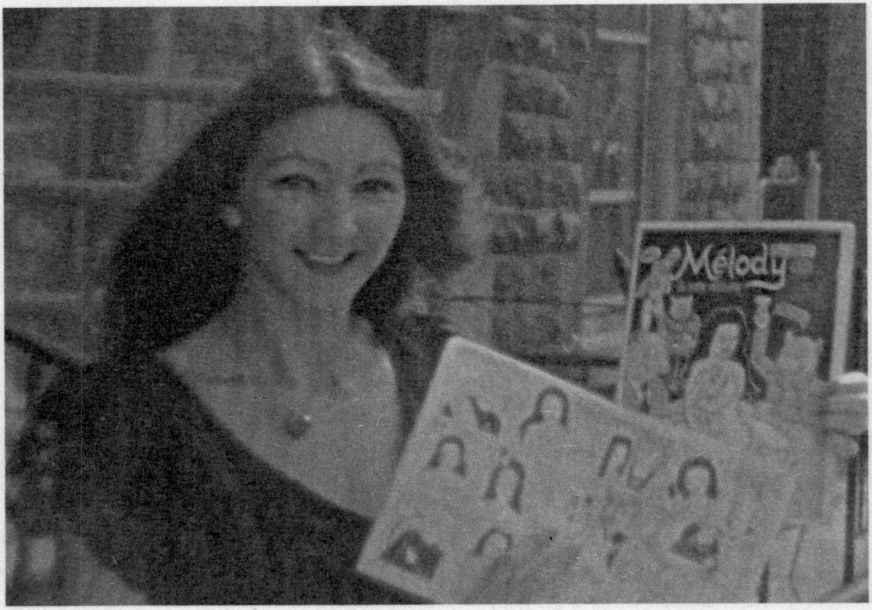
Mélody

Sylvie Rancourt was born in 1959 in northwestern Quebec and moved to Montreal in the early 1980s, where she began performing as a nude dancer and recounting her experiences in comics form. In the 1990s, Rancourt collaborated with Jacques Boivin who translated and illustrated her stories for the English-language market, selling over 125,000 copies. A compilation of early *Melody* comics was recently published in France by Ego Comme X and nominated for the Prix du Patrimoine at the 2014 Angoulême Comics Festival. Sylvie lives on a farm in Abitibi, a region of Quebec, with her second husband and five kids. She danced for ten years – first using her real name, then switching to her stage name "Barby," and eventually settling on "Mélody." The photo above was taken on the streets of Montreal in the summer of 1985, shortly after the publication of *Melody and Her Dolls*.